Visual Perception from a Computer Graphics Perspective

Visual Perception from a Computer Graphics Perspective

William B. Thompson
Roland W. Fleming
Sarah H. Creem-Regehr
Jeanine K. Stefanucci

CRC Press
Taylor & Francis Group
Boca Raton London New York

CRC Press is an imprint of the
Taylor & Francis Group, an **informa** business

AN A K PETERS BOOK

Cover images © Arvo; originally published in Fleming, R. W., Dror, R. O., & Adelson, E. H. (2003). Real-world illumination and the perception of surface reflectance properties. *Journal of Vision*, 3(5):347-368.

CRC Press
2385 NW Executive Center Drive, Suite 320, Boca Raton FL 33431

and by CRC Press
4 Park Square, Milton Park, Abingdon, Oxon, OX14 4RN

CRC Press is an imprint of Taylor & Francis Group, LLC

© 2011 Taylor & Francis Group, LLC

First issued in paperback 2020

Library of Congress Cataloging-in-Publication Data

Visual perception from a computer graphics perspective / William B. Thompson ... [et al.].
  p. cm.
  Includes bibliographical references and index.
  ISBN 978-1-56881-465-0 (hardback)
   1. Visual perception. 2. Vision. 3. Computer graphics--Design. I. Thompson, William B., 1948-

BF241.V5674 2011
152.14--dc22
                                                      2010049713

ISBN-13: 978-1-56881-465-0 (hbk)
ISBN-13: 978-0-367-65928-8 (pbk)

Visit the Taylor & Francis Web site at
http://www.taylorandfrancis.com

and the CRC Press Web site at
http://www.crcpress.com

Contents

Preface

Computer graphics produces images intended to be seen by people, yet relatively few practitioners in the field know much about the specifics of human vision. This book provides an introduction to human visual perception intended for those studying or working in the fields of computer graphics and visualization. The goal is to provide an understanding of human vision with a breadth and depth relevant to both the current state of the art in graphics and visualization and to future developments in those fields. More generally, the material presented is useful for those studying cognitive science, since it covers several topics that are not commonly included in standard perception references while offering a comprehensive overview of visual perception as a whole. Visual neuroscientists will find that the emphasis on visual performance complements studies of biological mechanisms. Finally, much of the material is relevant in motivating methods used in computer vision and image analysis. The book can be used as a text for courses at the graduate or advanced undergraduate level, as an overview of perception for those active as researchers or developers in computer graphics or related fields, and as a reference for students and researchers in vision science.

There are many excellent textbooks providing an introduction to visual perception. This book differs from those texts in several important ways:

- the book ties together image generation and the resulting perceptual phenomena, rather than having a focus only on the visual system itself;

- topics are included that are seldom, if ever, part of introductory perception texts, including the perception of material properties, illumination, the perception of pictorial space, perception and action, and spatial cognition; and

- the emphasis is on visual performance, with coverage of biological mechanisms in specific situations to aid in the understanding of issues of practical importance.

The writing of this book was inspired by William Thompson's chapter, "Visual Perception," appearing in the second edition of Peter Shirley's *Fundamentals of Computer Graphics* (2005). Some text from that chapter has found its way into the book. Further inspiration came from an ACM/SIGGRAPH meeting on Perceptually Adaptive Graphics, held at Snowbird, Utah, in May of 2001; the ACM Transactions on Applied Perception (`http://tap.acm.org`); and the annual ACM Symposia on Applied Perception in Graphics and Visualization (`http://www.apgv.org`).

About the Cover

These photos were taken at MIT by Meredith Talusen for some projects on reflectance estimation by Ron Dror, Alan Willsky, Ted Adelson and Roland Fleming. The images show two spheres with different reflectance properties: one is almost perfectly mirrored, the other has a more pearlescent appearance. Ron Dror created the database that includes these images so that he could build and test a computer vision algorithm for recognizing materials under unknown illumination conditions. This is a task that humans find effortless, even though the image of a given material can change dramatically depending on the context. It may not be immediately obvious, but the two images on the top (spheres with different reflectance properties) are actually more similar to one another—on a pixel-by-pixel basis—than the first and third images (spheres with the same reflectance properties). This is one example of the difficulties faced by the human visual system when reconstructing the world from the retinal images.

Online Resources

The web site for this book is `http://vpfacgp.cs.utah.edu/`. The site contains errata and a variety of useful information about visual perception likely to be of interest to readers.

Acknowledgments

The writing of a book such as this is a major undertaking, which would be difficult or impossible without the help and feedback we have received from many people. These include: Jonathan Bakdash, Adam Bargteil, Irving Biederman, Alex Bigelow, Bobby Bodenhiemer, Margarita Bratkova, Clifton Brooks, Joshua Bross, Susie Carlisle, Anthony Cummings, Sarah Cutler, Laura Dahl, Alexei Efros, Marc Ellens, Lisa Ferrara, Sergei Gepshtein, Michael Geuss, Jessica Hodgins, Mustafa Hussain, Ian Jensen, Alex Johnstone, David Kemker, Jasen Kennington, Dan Kersten, Ian King, James King, Rebecca Koslover, John Kowalski, Heidi Kramer, Vaidyanathan Krishnamoorthy, Brad Loos, Rachel McDonnell, James O'Brien, Andrei Ostanin, David Pilibosian, Dennis Proffitt, Kristina Rand, Brandon Rees, Erik Reinhard, Robert Shakespeare, Ari Shapiro, Lavanya Sharan, Peter Shirley, Jordan Squire, Maureen Stone, David Strayer, Margaret Tarampi, Jason Williams, and Tina Ziemek.

Special thanks go to Alice Peters for her continued support throughout this project. It was a privilege to work with such a knowledgeable and skilled publisher. Thanks also go to the staff at A K Peters and Taylor & Francis, who provided us with fantastic support throughout the project.

I

Introduction

1

Overview

The ultimate purpose of computer graphics is to produce images for people to view. Thus, the success of a computer graphics system depends on how well it conveys relevant information to a human observer. The intrinsic complexity of the physical world and the limitations of display devices make it impossible to present a viewer with the identical patterns of light that would occur when looking at a natural environment. When the goal of a computer graphics system is physical realism, the best we can hope for is that the system be *perceptually effective*; that is, displayed images should "look" as intended. For applications ranging from scientific and information visualization to technical illustration, highlighting relevant information is far more important than visual realism per se. In such systems, perceptual effectiveness becomes an explicit requirement.

One approach to improving the perceptual effectiveness of computer graphics is to adapt the tools and techniques for conveying visual information used by artists and illustrators. A second approach builds directly on knowledge of the human vision system by using perceptual effectiveness as an optimization criterion in the design of computer graphics systems. These two approaches are not completely distinct. Indeed, one of the first systematic examinations of visual perception is found in the notebooks of Leonardo da Vinci.

This book provides an introduction to what is known about visual perception in people, with an emphasis on aspects of human vision that are most relevant to computer graphics. The human visual system is extremely complex in both its operation and its architecture. A book such as this can, at best, provide a summary of key points, and it is important to avoid overgeneralizing from what is presented here. It is also important to note that despite over 150 years of intensive research, our knowledge of many aspects of vision is still very limited and imperfect.

Not covered in this book is any discussion of major challenges that exist when designing and conducting perception research in a manner that is simultaneously informative and methodologically sound. Cunningham and Wallraven (2011) provide an introduction to experimental design particularly appropriate for a computer graphics audience.

1.1   Organization of the Book

Deciding on an organizational structure for a book such as this is a major challenge. This overview chapter is followed by Part II, "Building Blocks," which covers aspects of visual processing that are closely associated with the patterns of light falling on the retina. These aspects are often categorized as *early vision*, meaning that they are the first steps in the visual process, extracting simple features from optical patterns for use in subsequent, more complex analysis. Included in this part of the book are chapters on visual sensitivity to brightness and contrast, contours, color, motion in the image plane, and stereo and accommodation.

Part III, entitled "Surfaces and Movement," focuses on how the visual system is able to estimate properties of the physical environment in which it is situated. We start with a discussion of perspective, which is the basis for much of what the visual system is able to determine about the geometry of the viewed environment, and follow this with chapters on visual texture; illumination, shading and shadows; perception of material properties; and motion in three dimensions. Part III ends with a chapter on the special circumstances surrounding the perception of pictures of the environment, rather than perception of the environment itself.

We have categorized the final set of chapters in the book as "Perception of Higher Level Entities." It includes topics at the interface between visual processing and the remainder of cognition and action. Individual chapters cover spatial orientation and spatial cognition, perception and action, object and scene recognition, and visual attention and search. Event recognition has been split into two chapters, one covering events involving inanimate objects, and the other covering events associated with biological motion.

We have attempted to choose topics and focus the discussion on issues motivated by a need to understand those aspects of perception relevant to computer graphics, without letting the minutia of computer graphics clutter the key perceptual concepts. Much of the material in Parts III and IV of the book does not appear in standard perception references, but it is included here because of its relevance to computer graphics and related application areas, such as visualization. Many vision scientists may find this material interesting as well.

Every chapter includes a section called "Issues Specific to Computer Graphics," which starts with an icon relating computer graphics to visual perception using the categorization shown in Figures 1.1 and 1.4. These sections are intended to draw attention to aspects of visual perception that are directly relevant to computer graphics practitioners but are often not understood or are misunderstood in that community.

Every chapter ends with a section called "Suggestions for Further Reading." These suggestions include a mix of key references and less encyclopedic, but more accessible, sources of information about issues raised in the chapter. References cited within the chapters themselves are collected at the end of the book.

1.2   Computer Graphics

The purpose of computer graphics is to generate one or more images based on descriptions of a scene. These scene descriptions (*models*) can correspond to an existing portion of the physical world, as in flight and driving simulators; hypothesized physical worlds, as in architectural simulations; or fantasized virtual worlds, as in computer games. The images produced may be approximations to photographs of a physical reality corresponding to the scene description, or they might be more-stylized depictions of the scene.

A wide variety of approaches have been used to represent scene descriptions. Most involve some way to specify objects, locations, illumination, and events relevant to the appearance of the scene. Objects are physical entities, with properties involving shape and materials. Locations specify the position of objects and viewpoint in the scene. Illumination describes the characteristics of light sources that affect the appearance of the scene. Events describe changes over time in locations and, perhaps, other temporal changes in object properties.

While there are many different formalisms for scene models, almost all graphics systems, prior to image generation, convert these descriptions into lower levels of representation involving geometry, materials, lighting, and viewpoint. Figure 1.1 outlines how these lower level entities are utilized to create images. The *geometry* of interest is almost always related to surfaces, though a few systems allow representation of subsurface scattering and light passing through semitransparent volumes. For computational simplicity, geometry is typically represented as a mesh of triangles in some appropriate geometric coordinate system. The key aspect of *material* properties that must be represented is how light interacts with the surface. This involves some approximate specification of how the intensity and spectral distribution of light emanating from the surface in a particular direction

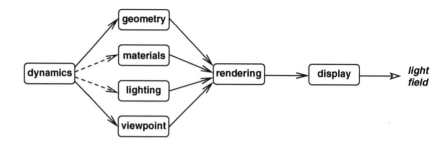

Figure 1.1
Computer graphics images are created from specifications of geometry, materials, lighting, viewpoint, and scene dynamics, using a rendering process usually intended to approximate the physics of real-world image formation.

is related to the intensity and spectral distribution of light falling on the surface from all possible incident directions. *Lighting* must be specified in terms of the location, extent, intensity, and chromaticity of light sources. The *viewpoint* indicates the position and viewing direction within the modeled scene. A model of scene *dynamics* appropriately modifies the representations of geometry and viewpoint (and much less commonly, materials and lighting) to account for temporal changes in the modeled scene.

The representations of geometry, materials, lighting, and viewpoint are combined by a *rendering* algorithm to produce a representation of the patterns of light intensity visible from the specified viewpoint based on a particular model of image projection. Most often, the projection model is the same perspective projection that occurs in conventional cameras, though sometimes orthographic projections are used and (very) occasionally other projective mappings are employed. Most rendering algorithms are approximations to simulations of the actual image formation process that strike a balance between accuracy and computational tractability. Finally, an actual distribution of light energy (a *light field*) is produced by a *display* device, which can be emissive, as in a monitor or projector, or reflective, as in a printed image.

Though huge progress has been made in computer graphics, major challenges remain in all aspects of the process. Modeling real-world geometry often requires sophisticated measurement systems and tools for converting measurements into appropriate representations in a manner that can deal with the large amount of data involved, measurement noise, and the range of scales over which visually relevant geometric properties exist. Creating models of artist- or designer-specified geometry requires user interface tools that allow natural manipulations of complex shapes. Creating effective models of animated characters is particularly difficult for both approaches

involving measurement of actual actors and approaches using artist specifications. While some materials can be characterized by relatively simple
appearance models, many naturally occurring and man-made materials reflect light in a very complex manner that is difficult to approximate in ways
useful for rendering. The specification of illumination in graphical simulations ranges from crude and simplistic specifications, to approaches that
describe natural and artificial light sources with near-complete photometric
accuracy, to lighting design in which each source is chosen, adjusted, and
placed by hand into a model. Lighting design represents a major portion
of the workload in creating a computer-graphics-generated film. Viewpoint
and other aspects of dynamics can be specified by an artist or designer,
controlled interactively by the user, or driven by a physical simulation.

A 100 watt lightbulb outputs on the order of 10^{20} photons/second
(Shirley et al., 2009). The photon flux relevant to the appearance of most
scenes rendered using computer graphics is orders of magnitude larger.
Some photons are absorbed by the first surface they hit. Many others are
reflected, only to hit other surfaces. The light field ultimately imaged onto
the retina is strongly affected by these interactions, which produce a complex pattern of light, shadow, and interreflections. A completely accurate
computational simulation is clearly impossible. As a result, all rendering
algorithms involve trade-offs and approximations to allow completion in
a reasonable amount of time. Still, the computational power devoted to
interactive graphics on some desktop systems can far exceed that of the
main processor.

1.3   Vision Science

> *Vision is a* process *that produces from images of the external world
> a description that is useful to the viewer and not cluttered with irrel-
> evant information.*
> — Marr and Nishihara (1978)

> *[O]ur perceptions are comprised of descriptions of the world, not of
> the energy patterns directly available to our senses. A central puzzle
> in vision is how the brain infers properties of the world from the
> sensory data.*
> —David Knill

These two quotes capture both the essence of vision and the reason it
is such a complex and difficult-to-comprehend phenomenon. The physics
of light and the way in which patterns of light in the world are imaged
by optical systems such as the eye are well understood, though extremely
complicated. Beyond the physics, however, is the enormous gap between
the patterns of light imaged on the retina and the behaviors of the seeing

Light:
- travels far
- travels fast
- travels in straight lines
- interacts with stuff
- bounces off things
- is produced in nature
- has lots of energy
—Steven Shafer

Figure 1.2

The nature of light makes vision a powerful sense.

organism, which relies on vision for its operation. The input to the visual process is a spatial/spectral/temporal distribution of light energy. This distribution is dependent on the physical structure of the world, but the effects of geometry, materials, illumination, and viewpoint are so conflated in the imaged view of the world that it is impossible to disentangle these world properties from the resulting image alone. The output of the visual process is information useful for cognition and action. Not only is this far removed from simple distributions of light, but psychologists are still arguing over what information is actually used to think about and act on the world.

Vision is generally agreed to be the most powerful of the senses in humans. Vision produces more useful information about the world than does hearing, touch, smell, or taste. This is a direct consequence of the physics of light (Figure 1.2). Illumination is pervasive, especially during the day but also at night due to moonlight, starlight, and artificial sources. Surfaces reflect a substantial portion of incident illumination and do so in ways that are idiosyncratic to particular materials and that are dependent on the shape of the surface. The fact that light (mostly) travels in straight lines through the air allows vision to acquire information from distant locations.

The study of vision has a long and rich history. Much of what we know about the eye traces back to the work of philosophers and physicists in the 1600s. Starting in the mid-1800s, there was an explosion of work by perceptual psychologists exploring the phenomenology of vision and proposing models of how vision might work. The mid-1900s saw the start of modern neuroscience, which investigates both the fine-scale workings of individual neurons and the large-scale architectural organization of the brain and nervous system. A substantial portion of neuroscience research has focused on vision. More recently, computer science has contributed to the understanding of visual perception by providing tools for precisely describing hypothesized models of visual computations and by allowing empirical examination of computer vision programs. The term *vision science* was coined to re-

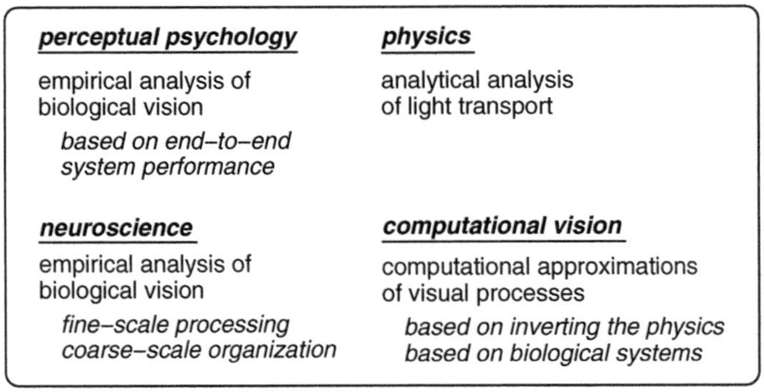

perceptual psychology	physics
empirical analysis of biological vision	analytical analysis of light transport
based on end–to–end system performance	
neuroscience	computational vision
empirical analysis of biological vision	computational approximations of visual processes
fine–scale processing coarse–scale organization	*based on inverting the physics based on biological systems*

Figure 1.3

Understanding vision requires drawing on tools from multiple disciplines.

fer to the multidisciplinary study of visual perception involving perceptual psychology, neuroscience, and computational analysis (Figure 1.3).

Increasingly, the hypothesized workings of vision systems are described using *information-processing models*, which characterize vision as involving a collection of well-defined representations of information, connected by a set of well-defined processes for converting descriptions of information in one set of representations to descriptions in another set of representations. This places an emphasis on *how* vision occurs, not just on the phenomenal characteristics of visual perception. Correctly constructed, information-processing models can be precise and unambiguous, and can be empirically validated using computer simulations.

The most common information processing approach to vision science views the purpose of vision as producing useful descriptions of the world from imaged patterns of light reaching the viewer, though there is substantial debate about the nature of these descriptions in terms of both content and representation. Often, vision is presumed to yield information about aspects of objects, locations, and events in the world, constructed by first inferring properties of geometry, viewpoint, and materials of the scene under view. In practice, it makes little sense to think of these descriptions of objects, locations, and events in isolation. Rather, vision is better understood in the context of the motoric and cognitive functions that it serves.

Figure 1.4 illustrates one way in which the processes involved in visual perception can be usefully organized. Vision starts with *light fields*, which are directional and temporal distributions of light in space. *Sensory* processes in the eye focus portions of the light field onto an image sensor (the *retina*), measure these light levels, and encode this information in a manner that is efficient for transmission to the brain and appropriate for additional processing. Inferences are made about the *geometry* and *materials* of sur-

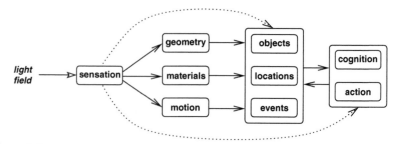

Figure 1.4

Vision produces descriptions of the world from imaged patterns of light reaching the viewer.

faces in the world, and the *motion* of objects and the viewpoint. These in turn are used to infer descriptions of visible *objects*, *locations*, and *events*. These entities are contained within a single box in Figure 1.4, since vision does not seem to treat them as completely separate and distinct. The end product of the process is information relevant to *cognition*, the conscious awareness of the world surrounding the viewer; and *action*, involving motor control to interact with that world. These are also represented inside a single box in the figure, with the degree to which the two are separate and independent a matter of current debate. Cognition and action can also influence the interpretation of objects, locations, and events through a variety of top-down mechanisms. As indicated by the dotted arrows in Figure 1.4, some models of visual perception assert more direct connections between sensed patterns of light and descriptions of objects, locations, and events or direct connections between sensed patterns of light and some aspects of cognition and action. Additional top-down interactions, beyond those shown here, are also likely involved in vision.

While this book concentrates on those aspects of Figure 1.4 that relate directly to *visual perception*, it is important to note that other sensory modalities play a critical role in perception as well. *Audition* not only tells us about the identity of sound sources in the world, but also provides information about where they are located and the general nature of the environmental space in which we are situated. *Tactile* (also called *haptic*) perception, based on the sense of touch, is critical for the control of many actions and also provides us with information about surface geometry and materials. *Olfactory* cues, based on the sense of smell, can provide information for the identification of objects and events and can also help provide information about the immediate environmental space we occupy. Taken together, vision, audition, haptics, and olfaction are sometimes referred to as *allothetic* sensory modalities, since they relate to information external to the body. *Ideothetic* sensory modalities, which relate to information internal to the body, also play a critical role in perception. *Proprioception* is information about relative position of neighboring parts of the body. In the perception literature, proprioception is sometimes divided into *efference*, which refers to the motor control signals sent out to the motor system; and *afference*, which refers to feedback from the joints and muscles. The *vestibular* system measures translational and rotational accelerations, thus providing information relevant to perceiving motion through the world. The ways in which these multiple sources of information are integrated by the perceptual system is still an area of active research.

One source of confusion that may occur in relating the computer-graphics-image-generation process to the human-vision-image-interpretation process is that while terms such as geometry, materials, viewpoint, objects, locations, and events are used in both contexts, the meaning is not always the same. Since computer graphics systems are artifacts, these entities have clear and precise meanings in that context. On the other hand, we can only imperfectly infer what a visual system is able to determine about these properties of the world.

1.4   The Process of Vision

Barrow and Tenenbaum (1981) and Marr (1982) articulated a view of the nature of the visual process that has remained dominant for 30 years. In this view, determining *surface layout*—the location and orientation of visible surfaces in the environment—is thought to be a key step in human vision. Their approach is sometimes called *inverse optics* to emphasize that it presumes that the visual system is acting to computationally invert the image formation process in order to determine the geometry, materials, and lighting in the world that produced a particular pattern of light on the retina. Psychologists use the term *distal stimulus* to refer to the physical world under observation and *proximal stimulus* to refer to the retinal image.[1] Using this terminology, inverse optics involves the generation of a description of aspects of the distal stimulus given the proximal stimulus. Visual perception is said to be *veridical* when the description that is produced accurately reflects the real world.

1.4.1   Visual Determination of Surface Properties

Most discussions of how the vision system extracts information about surface layout from the patterns of light it receives divide the problem into a set of *visual cues*, with each cue describing a particular visual pattern

---

[1]In computer vision, the term *scene* is often used to refer to the external world, while the term *image* is used to refer to the projection of the scene onto a sensing plane.

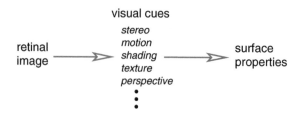

Figure 1.5

Multiple visual cues, combined with assumptions about likely properties of the real world, can be used to estimate shape properties such as surface orientation.

that can be used to infer properties of surface layout or other aspects of the environment (Figure 1.5). In order for a cue to be useful, it has to vary systematically with some environmental property. Visual cues for spatial layout are typically grouped into four categories: *ocularmotor cues* involve information about the position and focus of the eyes; *disparity* cues involve information extracted from viewing the same surface point with two eyes, beyond that available just from the positioning of the eyes; *motion* cues provide information about the world that arises from either the movement of the observer or the movement of objects; *pictorial cues* are static, monocular information resulting from the projection process that transforms three-dimensional surface shapes onto a two-dimensional pattern of light that falls on the retina.

Three hundred years ago, Berkeley (1709) argued:

> It is, I think, agreed by all that distance, of itself and immediately, cannot be seen. For distance being a line directed end-wise to the eye, it projects only one point in the fund of the eye, which point remains invariably the same, whether the distance be longer or shorter.

Figure 1.6 illustrates the point that Berkeley was making. Given only the visual information from one eye, there is no way to distinguish the distance from the viewer of points lying along a single line of sight. More generally, an infinite family of three-dimensional surfaces can project to identical retinal locations (Figure 1.7). This ambiguity represents a serious

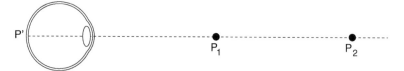

Figure 1.6

Both the points P_1 and P_2 project to the same retinal location P'.

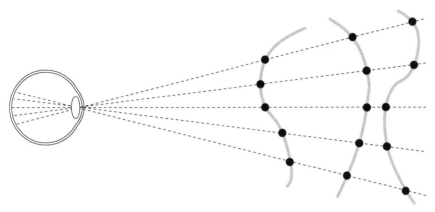

Figure 1.7
Surfaces with distinctly different shapes and distances from the viewer can project onto the same retinal image.

challenge for theories that presume that the visual system is able to invert the image-formation process to accurately determine the structure of the world under view. The problem extends beyond spatial layout, since multiple properties of the visible environment are confounded in the patterns of light imaged on the retina. For example, brightness is a function of both illumination and reflectance, and can depend on environmental properties across large regions of space. Because of this, it is often said that the problem of determining distal properties of the world from proximal stimuli is *underconstrained*, meaning that the proximal stimuli alone are not sufficient to solve for a unique specification of the distal stimuli that generated them.

Because of the ambiguous nature of visual information, the visual system likely interprets visual cues within the context of some sort of probabilistic assumptions about the nature of the natural environment. Some assumptions refer to specific cues, such as interpreting shading by assuming that the direction of illumination is most often from above. Other assumptions apply to the geometry of objects and viewing conditions in the real world, such as the fact that surfaces are typically piecewise smooth.

Further complicating our understanding of how information about surface layout is visually determined is the lack of agreement among vision scientists on the nature of how descriptions of surface shape are represented in the visual system. Marr (1982) argued for a single mental representation of surface shape, which he called the $2\frac{1}{2}$-*D sketch*. The $2\frac{1}{2}$-D sketch was presumed to be a viewer-centered representation of the depth and orientation of points on visible surfaces. Geometry can also be represented in many other ways ways, including the position of points on the surface in 3-space, local curvatures, surface positions relative to some intrinsic axis structure, and many more. It is not yet clear if there is a single, monolithic representation of a given object's shape in the brain, or rather multiple and at least partially redundant representations, supporting different classes of tasks.

Much less is known about the processes used by the visual system to infer information about material properties. Inverse optics, in which geometry, illumination, and reflectance are decoupled, cannot work effectively when one or more of these environmental properties get overly complex, as is almost always the case in the real world. Furthermore, there is evidence of substantial interaction between the perception of three-dimensional surface shape and surface material properties, with each affecting the other. The performance characteristics of materials perception in human vision and the underlying mechanisms involved remain areas of active research.

1.4.2   Visual Determination of Movement

Most theories of visual motion perception presume that the first step involves estimating the two-dimensional motion of the projected image of the world, called *optic flow* (or sometimes *optical flow*) (J. J. Gibson, 1950a). Optic flow can be and probably is used directly to determine many properties relating viewer and environment. These include heading, time-to-collision with obstacles, ordinal and relative distance to surfaces, and many more. Optic flow cannot determine speed, however. To see this, note that the time-varying image from a viewpoint moving through an environment at a given speed remains unchanged if the speed of movement and the size of the environment both double. Researchers disagree on the degree to which motion perception draws on nonmotion cues for surface layout, distance, and speed.

1.4.3   Visual Determination of Higher-Level Properties

Even less consensus exists on the nature of the visual processes that ultimately lead to the perception of objects, locations, and events, and support spatial cognition and action. These processes are often referred to as mid-level or higher-level vision, as they involve the organization of visual elements in a scene with influences from attention, memory, and the goals of the observer. Particularly important are the processes of visual attention, which allow for selection of information through eye movements, binding of features, and detection of events. A classic distinction in higher-level vision is between processing information related to *what* something is, as in object recognition, and processing information related to *where* objects are spatially located or *how* one might interact with them. This broad categorization of two streams of processing follows neuroanatomically defined pathways in the brain and is useful, although it is also clear that both object and spatial information are represented in both pathways from early on in visual processing. Important to defining these processes are concepts of frames of reference—the spatial framework in which information is represented—and the information gained from an active observer within the environment.

The control and data flow in the models of visual perception discussed above are *bottom-up*. The retinal image is processed to extract simple features, which in subsequent processing steps are refined and combined to produce increasingly richer and more-useful representations of the environment under view. Information can flow *top-down* as well. Conscious attentional decisions can affect the processing that occurs in visual search. Context and expectations affect object recognition. Parts of visual processing seem to occur in a mixed bottom-up/top-down manner, with rapid bottom-up processing generating hypotheses about the environment under view that are then refined and validated by focused, top-down processing.

1.4.4   Cue Integration and Probabilistic Models of Perception

The nature or the information about the environment provided by different visual cues often overlaps. Information about a particular aspect of the environment from multiple cues is typically consistent, since the cues will be covarying with the same environmental properties. Conflicts can arise due to the fact that cues are only an estimate of the distal stimulus and can be in error because of incomplete information, incorrect assumptions about the likely nature of the environment, and other factors. The visual system needs to resolve these conflicts in order to arrive at an interpretation of the external world. There is an extensive literature on the *cue integration* needed to deal with conflicting visual information. Empirical evidence exists for qualitatively different strategies, including cue dominance, in which perception is based on only one source of information when multiple sources conflict; a weighted average of information; and cue-specific mechanisms for resolving differences between specific cues.

Probabilistic models of cue integration and subsequent perceptual inferences allow a more principled explanation of the workings of the visual system when faced with conflicting or incomplete information (Kersten, Mamassian, & Yuille, 2004; Mamassian, Landy, & Maloney, 2002; Yuille & Bülthoff, 1996). In these models, perception is based on the proximal stimuli, distributions of the proximal stimuli as a function of distal stimuli in the natural world, distributions of the distal stimuli in the natural world, and the consequences of different percepts (Figure 1.8). There is an obvious advantage to basing a perceptual judgment about the world on the

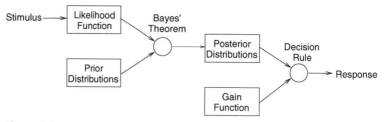

Figure 1.8

The basic steps involved in probabilistic inference for perception (Mamassian et al., 2002). (From Rao, Rajesh P.N., Bruno A. Olshausen, & Michael S. Lewicki, eds., *Probabilistic Models of the Brain: Perception and Neural Function*, Figure 1.6; © 2002 Massachusetts Institute of Technology, by permission of The MIT Press.)

configuration of the world most likely to generate the viewed patterns of light. From an optimal decision standpoint, it is critical to also consider the likelihoods of different potential configurations of the world. An effective perceptual system should not come to a conclusion about the world unlikely to occur in practice unless the perceptual information supporting that conclusion is strong. Optimal decisions need to be based not only on maximizing the likelihood of being correct about the interpretation, but also on the consequences of being wrong. Faced with two possible decisions of near equal likelihood, the best choice will be the alternative with the least cost if the decision is in error.

Proponents of using probabilistic models as a tool to understand visual perception argue that they can provide a unifying framework within which to describe and analyze the disparate aspects of the perceptual system. Most of these models are couched in the notation of *Bayes' theorem* (Bayes, 1763):

$$p(S|I) = \frac{p(I|S)p(S)}{p(I)} , \qquad (1.1)$$

where S is a property of the environment, I is the visual image, $p(I|S)$ is the probability distribution function indicating the likelihood that a given image arose from a given environment, $p(S)$ is the *a priori* probability (often called the *prior* in Bayesian models of perception) of a particular property of the environment occurring in the real world, and $p(I)$ is the overall probability distribution of images occurring in the natural world (Yuille & Bülthoff, 1996). Bayesian models of visual perception presume that the goal of perception is to determine the most likely description of the world S, given one or more views of the world I. In addition to allowing analysis using the formal tools of probability theory, Bayes models decompose the problem of perception based on the nature of the world and of image formation, rather than just on the basis of different processes thought to make up vision. The variable $p(I)$ reflects the fact that most natural images have a well-defined statistical structure. It also allows for the explicit consideration of the distortions and noise associated with the sensory processes involved in vision. The variable $p(S)$ is important because intelligent decisions about what is seen in the environment cannot be made without a sense of what is likely to be seen in the environment. The variable $p(I|S)$ represents a statistical formulation of the image formation process, whether physically manifested in the real world or simulated with computer graphics.

1.4.5   Frames of Reference and Measurement Scales

Descriptions of the location and orientation of points on a visible surface must be done within the context of a particular frame of reference that specifies the origin, orientation, and scaling of the coordinate system used in representing the geometric information. The human vision system uses multiple frames of reference, partly because of the different sorts of information available from different visual cues, and partly because of the different purposes to which the information is put (Klatzky, 1998). *Egocentric* representations are defined with respect to the viewer's body. They can be subdivided into coordinate systems fixed to the eyes, head, or body. *Allocentric* representations, also called *exocentric* representations, are defined with respect to something external to the viewer. Allocentric frames of reference can be local to some configuration of objects in the environment or can be globally defined in terms of distinctive locations, gravity, or geographic properties.

The distance from the viewer to a particular visible location in the environment, expressed in an egocentric representation, is often referred to as *depth* in the perception literature. Surface orientation can be represented in either egocentric or allocentric coordinates. In egocentric representations of orientation, the term *slant* is used to refer to the angle between the line of sight to the point and the surface normal at the point, while the term *tilt* refers to the orientation of the projection of the surface normal onto a plane perpendicular to the line of sight.

Distance and orientation can be expressed in a variety of *measurement scales*. *Absolute* descriptions are specified using a standard that is not part of the sensed information itself. These can be culturally defined standards (e.g., meters) or standards relative to the viewer's body (e.g., eye height, the width of one's shoulders, etc.). *Relative* descriptions relate one perceived geometric property to another (e.g., point **a** is twice as far away as point **b**). *Ordinal* descriptions are a special case of relative measure in which the sign,

Cue	a	r	o	Requirements for absolute depth
Accommodation	x	x	x	very limited range
Binocular convergence	x	x	x	limited range
Binocular disparity	-	x	x	limited range
Linear perspective, height in picture, horizon ratio	x	x	x	requires viewpoint height
Familiar size	x	x	x	
Relative size	-	x	x	subject to errors
Aerial perspective	-	x	x	adaptation to local conditions
Absolute motion parallax	?	x	x	requires viewpoint velocity
Relative motion parallax	-	-	x	
Texture gradients	-	x	-	
Shading	-	x	-	
Occlusion	-	-	x	

Figure 1.9

Common visual cues for absolute (a), relative (r), and ordinal (o) depth.

but not the magnitude, of the relations is all that is represented. Figure 1.9 provides a list of the most commonly considered visual cues, along with a characterization of the sorts of information they can potentially provide. (See also Cutting & Vishton, 1995.)

1.4.6   Adaptation

A general phenomenon in perception across all sensory systems is *adaptation* to constant stimulation. Take for example, the experience of stepping into a bath of hot water. At first it feels hot, but you will quickly adapt after a few seconds and no longer notice the hot temperature. *Sensory adaptation* is a reduction in response caused by previous or constant stimulation. On a neurophysiological level, it can be understood as selective activation of specific neurons tuned to a stimulus feature which then leads to a reduction in firing rate of those neurons for a period of time after adaptation. The resulting perceptual experience is an *aftereffect*, the perception of an "opposite" feature. For example, viewing the downward motion of water in a waterfall for about 15 seconds will then lead the viewer to perceive the stationary rocks around the waterfall as moving upward, in the opposite direction of movement. This effect is known as the *waterfall illusion*. Sensory adaptation effects are short-lived.

Perceptual adaptation also results in a change in perception, but one that occurs at a higher level because of discrepancies between different sensory modalities. Aftereffects due to perceptual adaptation are longer lasting compared to sensory-adaptation aftereffects. An example of perceptual adaptation is the change in perceptual-motor behavior seen from viewing and acting on the world through prisms. Reaching to an object while wearing prisms that shift the visual world will at first show errors in reaching location, but, given feedback, adaptation will occur and accuracy of reaching will improve over time. When the prisms are taken off, reaching errors will occur in the opposite direction, confirming the perceptual adaptation mechanism. (See Chapter 13.)

1.5   Useful Generalizations about Perception

Across a wide range of cues, the visual system is more sensitive to spatial and temporal changes in a sensory property than to the property itself. This effect occurs with visual sensitivity to brightness, color, and many sources of information about spatial layout. It serves to introduce gain control into the visual process, expanding the dynamic range under which vision can operate and adding a degree of invariance to effects such as changes in average illumination. It also leads to redundancy-reducing reencodings of sensory signals, thereby supporting increased bandwidth as information flows throughout the visual system.

The invariance of visual perception to changes in brightness and color of illumination are examples of *perceptual constancy*. In another example of constancy, perception of size and shape is often largely unaffected by changes in viewpoint and other aspects of viewing conditions. Perceptual constancy is closely tied to the idea that the aim of the perceptual system is to veridically recover properties of the distal stimulus (i.e., properties of the world under view). Often, the perception of distal properties dominates, with little or no awareness of proximal properties such as projected size, though under some circumstances it is possible to consciously switch between the two (Carlson, 1960; Gilinsky, 1955).

A number of commonalities found across a range of perceptual phenomenon have been elevated to the status of *perceptual laws*. One example is *Weber's law*, which states that there is a constant ratio between the *just noticeable differences* (jnd) in a stimulus and the magnitude of the stimulus:

$$\frac{\Delta I}{I} = k_1 \,, \tag{1.2}$$

where I is the magnitude of the stimulus, ΔI is the magnitude of the just noticeable difference, and k_1 is a constant particular to the stimulus. Weber's law was postulated in 1846 and still remains a useful characterization of many perceptual effects. *Fechner's law*, proposed in 1860, generalized Weber's law in a way that allowed for the description of the strength of any sensory experience, not solely jnd's:

$$S = k_2 \log(I) \,, \tag{1.3}$$

where S is the perceptual strength of the sensory experience, I is the physical magnitude of the corresponding stimulus, and k_2 is a scaling constant specific to the stimulus. Current practice is to model the association between perceived and actual strength of a stimulus using a power function (*Stevens' law*):

$$S = k_3 I^b ,\qquad(1.4)$$

where S and I are as before, k_3 is another scaling constant, and b is an exponent specific to the stimulus. For a large number of perceptual quantities involving vision, $b < 1$. Note that in the first two characterizations of the perceptual strength of a stimulus and in Stevens' law, when $b < 1$, changes in the stimulus when it has a small average magnitude create larger perceptual effects than do the same physical changes in the stimulus when it has a larger magnitude.

The "laws" described above are not physical constraints on how perception operates. Rather, they are generalizations about how the perceptual system responds to particular physical stimuli. In the field of perceptual psychology, the quantitative study of the relationships between physical stimuli and their perceptual effects is called *psychophysics*. While psychophysical laws are empirically derived observations rather than mechanistic accounts, the fact that so many perceptual effects are well modeled by simple power functions is striking and may provide insights into the mechanisms involved.

1.6 Issues Specific to Computer Graphics

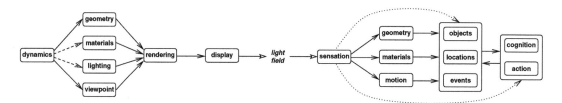

Figures 1.6 and 1.7 highlight the fact that perspective projection removes explicit information about distance and scale from a single, static view of the world. For a stationary observer looking at the world with one eye, were all entities in the world to magically double in size, the nature of the projection function involved in image formation is such that the distribution of light falling on the observer's retina would be unchanged. This is why geometric specifications of geometry in low-level graphics APIs are dimensionless: the actual units do not matter because scaling does not matter. Double all the values relating to position and distance in a

geometric model, including those specifying the location of the viewpoint, and the rendered image remains unchanged.

Computational practicalities make it impossible for computer graphics to accurately simulate the image formation process, particularly for effects involving small-scale geometry, materials, and lighting. As a result, the underconstrained nature of inverse optics is an even greater problem for computer graphics imagery than for the real world, since the computer graphics imagery is not physically correct and is often subject to reduced information due to display limitations. Perceptual judgments based on viewing computer graphics imagery are likely to be less certain and subjected to a variety of biases compared to perception of a corresponding physical world. This has significant impacts when computer graphics is used in applications such as vehicle simulators, where accurate spatial judgments are critical.

In the real world, perceptual cues usually indicate consistent information about the visible environment, since their values covary with the same physical world. This is not true in computer graphics, where image properties affecting one cue may result from aspects of models and rendering distinct from those leading to image properties affecting a different cue. As a result, not only is the information from individual cues likely to be different when viewing computer graphics imagery than when viewing the real world, but cue conflicts are much more likely to occur. This will further degrade the veridicality of perceptual judgments when viewing computer graphics.

Display effects further degrade perception of computer graphics relative to real-world perception, beyond the effects of lack of realism in graphical images themselves. Viewing conditions, the lack of depth information from stereo and motion parallax, and the fact that both the display surface and the environment in which the display is placed are visible all can significantly alter perception. Virtual reality displays attempt to alleviate these problems with visual immersion, which hides from view all but the display surface, stereo, and head tracking for motion parallax.

While many aspects of perception make the information conveyed by viewing graphical renderings less effective than that obtained by viewing the physical world, perceptual constancy aids perception of computer graphics and other graphical material presented on image displays. With very few exceptions, graphical displays cannot match the dynamic range, absolute brightness, resolution, or temporal dynamics of patterns of light in the real world. Constancy makes this less noticeable, particularly for brightness and color. Size constancy allows us to watch a television across the room and not have people appear to be the size of hamsters. Shape constancy allows us to sit toward one side of a movie theater and not have everything on the screen look warped.

1.7   Suggestions for Further Reading

A good overview of computer graphics that is not cluttered with the details of computer graphics programming interfaces:

> Shirley, P., and Marschner, S., Ashikhmin, M., Gleicher, M., Hoffman, N., Johnson, G., et al. (2009). *Fundamentals of computer graphics* (3rd ed.). Natick, MA: A K Peters.

A good introduction to experimental design:

> Cunningham, D. W., & Wallraven, C. (2011). *Experimental design: From psychophysics to user studies.* Natick, MA: A K Peters/CRC Press.

Two popular textbooks used in undergraduate psychology courses on sensation and perception. Both books cover senses other than vision:

> Goldstein, E. B. (2009). *Sensation and perception* (8th ed.). Belmont, CA: Wadsworth.

> Wolfe, J. M., Kluender, K. R., Levi, D. M., Bartoshuk, L. M., Herz, R. S., Klatzky, R. L., et al. (2008). *Sensation & perception* (2nd ed.). Sunderland, MA: Sinauer.

An undergraduate-level text focusing solely on vision:

> Snowden, R., Thompson, P., & Troscianko, T. (2006). *Basic vision: An introduction to visual perception.* Oxford, UK: Oxford University Press.

A graduate-level text and excellent reference, specific to vision:

> Palmer, S. E. (1999). *Vision science—photons to phenomenology,* Cambridge, MA: MIT Press.

An accessible, insightful, and entertaining overview of visual perception:

> Gregory, R. L. (1997). *Eye and brain: The psychology of seeing* (5th ed.). Princeton, NJ: Princeton University Press.

An excellent collection of original research articles of both historic and contemporary significance:

> Yantis, S. (Ed.). (2001). *Visual perception: Essential readings.* Philadelphia, PA: Psychology Press.

The classic reference on the information processing approach to understanding vision:

> Marr, D. (1982). *Vision.* San Francisco: W. H. Freeman.

An overview of visual perception, combined with examples from art:

> Livingston, M. (2002). *Vision and art: The biology of seeing.* New York: Harry N. Abrams.

Several articles and short courses that provide overviews of current uses of knowledge about visual perception in computer graphics (note that many of the topics covered in this book have not yet found their way into the design of computer graphics algorithms, systems, and displays):

Bartz, D., Cunningham, D., Fischer, J., & Wallraven, C. (2008). The role of perception for computer graphics. In *Proceedings Eurographics (State-of-the-Art Reports)* (pp. 65–86). Aire-la-Ville, Switzerland: Eurographics Association.

Ferwerda, J. A. (2008). Psychophysics 101: How to run perception experiments in computer graphics. In *ACM SIGGRAPH course notes* (pp. 87:1–87:60).

O'Sullivan, C., Howlett, S., Morvan, Y., McDonnell, R., & O'Conor, K. (2004). Perceptually adaptive graphics. In *Proceedings Eurographics (State-of-the-Art Reports)*. Aire-la-Ville, Switzerland: Eurographics Association.

II

Building Blocks

2

Visual Sensitivity

[T]he encoded image is a very partial representation of the light that arrives at the eye: there is only a narrow region of high visual acuity in the fovea; the dynamic range of the sensors is very small; and the representation of wavelength is very coarse. You would never buy a camera with such poor optics and coarse spatial sampling.

—Wandell (1995)

Vision systems create descriptions of the visual environment based on properties of the incident light. As a result, it is important to understand what properties of incident light the human vision system can actually detect. Two significant challenges must be overcome by the visual system as it senses and encodes image intensity for further processing. The first is the range of signals that need to be accommodated. Light useful for human functioning in the natural world varies in intensity by about 12–14 orders of magnitude, while fine-scale detail and temporal changes must be recorded over a wide field of view and long intervals of time. The second challenge is to represent this information so that it can be efficiently transmitted and transformed in perceptually useful ways as it is processed by the visual system. The human retina has roughly a hundred times more photoreceptors than optic nerve fibers, meaning that substantial processing and image compression is occurring in the eye before the visual signal ever reaches the brain. Part of understanding visual perception is knowing what information is preserved in this signal and what is not.

One critical observation about the human vision system is that it is primarily sensitive to *patterns* of light rather than the absolute magnitude of light energy. The eye does not operate as a photometer. Instead, it detects spatial, temporal, and spectral patterns in the light imaged on the retina, and information about these patterns of light form the basis for all of visual perception. There is a clear ecological utility to the vision system's sensitivity to variations in light over space and time. Being able to accurately sense changes in the environment is crucial to our survival.[1] A system that measures changes in light energy rather than the magnitude of the energy itself also makes engineering sense because it makes it easier to detect patterns of light over large ranges in light intensity.

This chapter outlines the limits of sensitivity of the human visual system in terms of fine-scale detail, contrast, and dynamic range. Spectral sensitivity is covered in Chapter 4, while temporal sensitivity is addressed in Chapter 5. It is important to note that visual sensitivity is affected by spatial and temporal contexts in multiple and complex ways—ways that can only briefly be covered in a chapter such as this.

2.1   The Human Eye

Figure 2.1

The structure of the human eye.

In human vision, the eyes optically image views of the world, sense the resulting patterns of light, and encode these as neural firing patterns for processing by the rest of the visual system. As a result, the nature of the eye has a profound effect on the nature of the whole of visual processing and, in particular, the sensitivity of the visual system to the patterns of light that it encounters. The human eye is quite complex (Figure 2.1), consisting of a focusable lens, an adjustable lens aperture (the *iris* and *pupil*), a photodetector mosaic (the retina), fluids filling the eye and providing mechanical support (the *aqueous humor* and *vitreous humor*), and sophisticated neural circuitry for processing the sensed information and communicating it to the visual cortex via the optic nerve. Many references on visual perception provide information on the anatomy of the eye and its relationship to vision (e.g., Gregory, 1997; Palmer, 1999). In this chapter, we will concentrate primarily on the overall system performance of the eye and the resulting implications for visual sensitivity.

There is enormous variation between species in eye anatomy. Humans have two eyes, arrayed horizontally on the front of the head, relatively close together. The eyes are movable and, under some circumstances, can move quite quickly. Movement of the two eyes is coupled, so that both point

---

[1]It is sometimes said that the primary goals of vision are to support eating, avoid being eaten, reproduce, and avoid catastrophe while moving. Thinking about vision as a goal-directed activity is often useful but needs to be done at a more detailed level.

Figure 2.2
The size of proximal visual stimuli (i.e., the retinal size of visible entities) is almost always specified in terms of *visual angle*.

in approximately the same direction at all times. Each eye in the human visual system has a field of view of approximately 160° horizontal by 135° vertical. With binocular viewing, there is only partial overlap between the fields of view of the two eyes. This results in a wider overall field of view (approximately 200° horizontal by 135° vertical), with the region of overlap being approximately 120° horizontal by 135° vertical.

Each of these properties has significant consequences for the performance of human vision. Movable eyes with a wide field of view, mounted in a movable head, allow the ability to visually perceive much of the surrounding environment but require complex attentional and visual search mechanisms (see Chapter 16). Eye movement is also important in determining the relative motion between the view and locations in the environment. The wide field of view makes it easier to extract information about self-motion information (see Chapter 11) as well as shape and distance properties related to geometric perspective (see Chapter 7). The overlap in the visual field of the two eyes allows for depth perception using binocular stereo (see Chapter 6), while the close spacing of the eyes makes this work best for locations near the viewer. The fact that the visual fields only partially overlap represents a compromise between wide field of view stereo and even wider monocular viewing of the world.

2.2   Terminology and Units

In discussions of visual sensitivity, the size of viewed entities is almost always expressed in terms of visual angle, not linear extent (see Figure 2.2). The reason for this is that what matters for detectability is size of the projected entity on the retina, not the size of the entity itself in the world. Retinal extent is a function of both the physical extent of the entity in the direction perpendicular to the line of sight and the distance from the eye to the entity. For reference, the sun and moon subtend visual angles of about 0.5°, and, held at arm's length, your thumbnail, thumb joint, and fist subtend angles of 1.5°, 2.0°, and 8–10°, respectively (Wandell, 1995).

Quantifying what is informally thought of as "brightness" is more complicated due to the intrinsic nature of radiant energy and the added complexity of needing to account for the limited spectral response of the visual system. *Radiometric* properties characterize electromagnetic radiation in general. *Photometric* properties are specialized to human vision and involve weighting radiometric properties by the visual system's luminance response curve (see Chapter 4). Thus, signals with the same radiometric intensity and different wavelengths generally have different luminances, due to differences in the eye's sensitivity to these different signals. We will deal here only with photometric properties.

The brightness of a light source is characterized in terms of *lumens* (lm), which is a measure of the power emitted by the light source weighted by the visual spectral sensitivity response function. A 60-watt incandescent light bulb emits on the order of 700 lm; a 23-watt compact fluorescent lamp emits 1500–1600 lm; and a conventional candle emits a bit more than 10 lm. The energy radiated by a light source is directional and often nonuniformly distributed in direction. The *candela* (cd) is the unit of spectral sensitivity light power in a particular direction. It has its roots in the light output of a standard candle of prescribed design and composition, used to define the now obsolete unit of *candlepower*. The brightness of a surface is characterized in terms of the directional light power emitted per unit area, using the units cd/m^2. Figure 2.9 in Section 2.5 relates surface brightness to a range of illumination conditions. While surface brightness characterized in terms of cd/m^2 is dependent on viewing angle, the measure is often used without specifying a direction, implicitly assuming that either the viewing direction is perpendicular to the surface or the surface is radiating energy uniformly in direction.

2.3   Acuity

The ability of the visual system to detect fine-scale patterns is referred to as *visual acuity* or *spatial resolution*. In bright light, the human visual system is capable of distinguishing gratings consisting of high-contrast, parallel light and dark bars as fine as 50–60 cycles/degree, where a "cycle" consists of an adjacent pair of light and dark bars. Phrased in a different manner, the human visual system is able to distinguish as separate entities two structures separated by about an arc minute of visual angle. At luminance levels below about 100 cd/m^2, acuity decreases with decreasing luminance. In moonlight, the highest detectable high-contrast spatial frequency drops to 20–30 cycles/degree. Under starlight, acuity is limited to a maximum of about 10 cycles/degree. In addition to average light level, acuity is substantially affected by contrast and the nature of the pattern under view.

The limits on acuity in the vision system are due to two separate effects. The first is optical limitations of the eye. The second is the nature of the photodetectors in the retina in terms of their ability to spatially localize and discriminate contrast boundaries.

Optical blur in the human eye comes largely from aperture diffraction at the pupil and misfocusing of the image on the retina (Campbell & Green, 1965; Campbell & Gubisch, 1966; Wandell, 1995). Empirical measurements show blur to be close to the diffraction limit for small pupil size. Blur increases with pupil size, even though diffraction scattering decreases, presumably because of decreased depth of field and lens imperfections away from the optical center. The effect is to decrease acuity at lower light levels, due to increased pupil size, beyond the effects of lowered sensitivity in the photoreceptors themselves.

The second limitation on acuity comes from how patterns of light intensity are measured by the retina. The retina is made up of a mosaic of two classes of cells, *cones* and *rods*, each of which operate as light sampling devices. The cones come in three subtypes, as discussed in Chapter 4. While cones are most often discussed in the context of color vision, they serve an important role in measuring brightness patterns as well. The rods operate effectively only in low light conditions. For light levels at or above normal indoor lighting, the rods reach saturation and only the cones are involved in vision.

With normal or corrected-to-normal vision, we usually have the subjective experience of being able to see relatively fine detail wherever we look. This is an illusion, however. Only a small portion of the visual field of each eye is actually sensitive to fine detail. To see this, hold a piece of paper covered with normal-sized text at arm's length, as shown in Figure 2.3. Cover one eye with the hand not holding the paper. While staring at your thumb and not moving your eye, note that the text immediately above your thumb is readable while the text to either side is not. High-acuity vision is limited to a visual angle about twice as large as your thumb held at arm's length. We do not normally notice this because the eyes usually move frequently, allowing different regions of the visual field to be viewed at high resolution. The visual system then integrates this information over time to produce the subjective experience of the whole visual field being seen at high resolution.

Figure 2.4 shows the variable packing density of cones and rods in the human retina. The cones, which are responsible for vision under normal lighting, are packed most closely at the *fovea* of the retina, with the peak cone density being about $1.6 \times 10^5/\text{mm}^2$. When the eye is fixated at a particular point in the environment, the image of that point falls on the fovea. The higher packing density of cones at the fovea results in a higher spatial sampling frequency of the imaged light and hence greater detail in

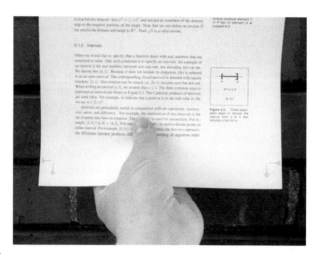

Figure 2.3

If you hold a page of text at arm's length and stare at your thumb, only the text near your thumb will be readable.

the sampled pattern. Depending on the exact definition of fovea that is used, foveal vision encompasses 1°–5.2° of visual angle (Wandell, 1995).

Because the retinal photomosaic consists of discrete, spatially localized rods and cones, digital sampling theory applies to the nature of the responses that are generated. Under some circumstances, aliasing is visually apparent due to undersampling of high-frequency patterns. However, the optical properties of the eye and the way in which rods and cones are distributed across the retina almost always either avoid or mask perceptual patterns associated with aliasing.

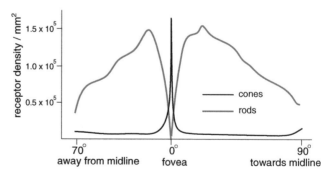

Figure 2.4

Density of rods and cone in the human retina (after Osterberg, 1935).

While a version of Figure 2.4 appears in most introductory texts on human visual perception, it provides only a partial explanation for the neurophysiological limitations on visual acuity. The output of individual rods and cones are pooled in various ways by neural interconnects in the eye before the information is shipped along the optic nerve to the visual cortex. All of the cells in the optic nerve and many of the cells in the visual cortex have an associated retinal *receptive field*. Patterns of light within the receptive field are combined in various ways to produce a single output (the *firing rate*) for the cell. Patterns of light hitting the retina outside of a cell's receptive field have no effect on the firing rate of that cell. This pooling filters the signal provided by the pattern of incident light in ways that have important impacts on the patterns of light that are detectable. In particular, the farther away from the fovea, the larger the area over which brightness is averaged. As a consequence, spatial acuity drops sharply away from the fovea.

Most figures showing rod and cone packing density indicate the location of the retinal *blind spot*, where the nerve bundle carrying optical information from the eye to the brain passes through the retina and there is no sensitivity to light. By and large, the only practical impact of the blind spot on real-world perception is its use as an illusion in introductory perception texts, since normal eye movements otherwise compensate for the temporary loss of information.

While the term *acuity* is most often used to refer to limits in the ability to resolve variability in fine-scale patterns, it can also refer to limits in the ability to resolve fine-scale differences in position. *Vernier acuity* is one form of this positional discrimination. Figure 2.5 provides an example of a test of vernier acuity, in which the task is to determine if a target line appears to the left or right of a reference location. A surprising aspect of human performance on vernier acuity tasks and similar discriminations of two-dimensional spatial position is that positional offsets on the order of five arcseconds are detectable (Westheimer & McKee, 1977). This is roughly

Figure 2.5

Examples of two vernier acuity tasks from Westheimer and McKee (1977). Participants were shown a single pattern and were asked to determine if a target line appears to the left or right of a reference location.

ten times finer than the smallest separation of adjacent parallel lines that can be resolved by the human visual system. Even more striking, this is about a fifth the width of a single cone cell. The extremely fine offsets perceptible in vernier acuity and similar tasks have led to these being called examples of *hyperacuity* (Westheimer, 2009). Importantly, vernier acuity involves the detection of small positional offsets between patterns that are themselves of sufficient retinal extent to be detectable on their own. The actual implementation in the visual system involves comparisons of the outputs from neighboring photoreceptors.

2.4 Contrast

2.4.1 Contrast Sensitivity

Spatial variability in a visual pattern can only be perceived if there is sufficient *contrast* in the pattern. Characterizing the contrast sensitivity of the visual system is complicated by the fact that multiple quantitative measures of contrast are in use. These measures are almost always expressed in dimensionless units, making it difficult or impossible to compare contrasts expressed in two different ways. Furthermore, the measures typically apply only to one sort of pattern. *Michelson contrast* is often used as a measure of contrast in periodic patterns, and is sometimes used as a measure of edge contrast:

$$C_m = \frac{L_{\max} - L_{\min}}{L_{\max} + L_{\min}} , \tag{2.1}$$

where $L_{\max}$ and $L_{\min}$ are the maximum and minimum luminance values. The value of Michelson contrast can range from 0.0, indicating no contrast, to a maximum value of 1.0. Michelson contrast is uninformative when $L_{\min} = 0$, regardless of the value of $L_{\max}$. While this exact situation is physically impossible, Michelson contrast has problems characterizing contrast when part of the pattern is extremely dark.

Weber contrast is typically used to characterize the luminance difference between a single target and a homogeneous background:

$$C_w = \frac{\Delta L}{L} , \tag{2.2}$$

where L is the background luminance and ΔL is the change in luminance between background and target. The value of C_w ranges from 0.0 to arbitrarily large, if ΔL is expressed as an absolute value.

Contrast in video displays is typically quantified as a *contrast ratio*:

$$C_r = \frac{L_{\max}}{L_{\min}} , \tag{2.3}$$

where L_{max} is the brightest value that the display is capable of displaying and L_{min} is what the display produces for "black." Contrast ratios range from 1.0 (no contrast) to arbitrarily large values. One common measure of average contrast in a photograph is the standard deviation of brightness values, where brightness is prenormalized into the range [0.0–1.0]. Variabilities in how L_{max} and L_{min} are measured, together with the sensitivity of C_r to L_{min}, suggest caution in using contrast ratio as a criteria for comparing two different displays, particularly if they use different technologies. For example, it is not easy to judge whether a given checkerboard pattern is higher or lower when displayed on two different devices or when compared with a photograph. Evidently, there is more to the perception of contrast than any single, simple image measurement can capture.

None of these contrast measures account for the complexity of natural scenes. To do so, local spatial frequency measures are likely to be needed (Peli, 1990), but such measures are not in common usage.

As shown in Figure 2.6, there is an interaction between contrast and acuity in human vision. In the figure, the scale of the pattern decreases

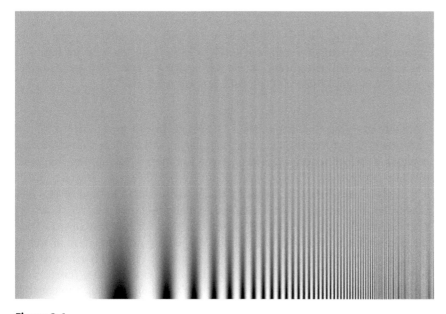

Figure 2.6

The contrast between stripes increases in a constant manner from top to bottom, yet the threshold of visibility varies with frequency. (© Izumi Ohzawa. This illustration was originally due to F.W. Campbell and J.G. Robson, 1968. See also Pelli, 1987.)

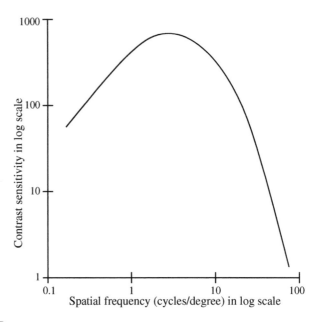

Figure 2.7

Contrast sensitivity, based on Michelson contrast, as a function of spatial frequency (after Campbell & Robson, 1968). The vertical axis is the reciprocal of
the Michelson contrast at which a sine wave grating is just discriminable from a
constant luminance pattern of the same average brightness.

from left to right while the contrast increases from top to bottom. If you
view the figure at a normal viewing distance, it will be clear that the lowest
contrast at which a pattern is visible is a function of the spatial frequency
of the pattern.

Contrast sensitivity is typically specified as the reciprocal of the contrast ratio at which a target is just barely detectable. Figure 2.7 shows the
contrast sensitivity, based on Michelson contrast, for sine wave grating patterns viewed in moderately bright light (500 cd/m^2) as a function of spatial
frequency (Campbell & Robson, 1968). (The just detectable contrast as a
function of spatial frequency is called the *contrast sensitivity function*, or
CSF.) The grating is visible when the contrast is higher (i.e., the contrast
sensitivity is numerically lower) than the line shown in the figure. The
sharp drop-off to the right is due to the acuity limits of the visual system.
No grating finer than about 50–60 cycles/degree will be visible, regardless
of its contrast. The drop-off to the left is an indication of the visual system's relative insensitivity to slowly varying luminance patterns. Contrast
sensitivity peaks at about 2 cycles/degree, at which point the visual system

can detect sinusoidal grating patterns with a peak-to-peak brightness variability on the order of 0.5% of the average brightness. At this luminance level, over most of the spatial frequency range in which sinusoidal grating patterns are visible, detection is possible at contrast levels of about 1% or lower of the average brightness.

At low light levels, contrast sensitivity increases with average luminance. Contrast sensitivity as a function of spatial frequency also changes, with increasing brightness increasing the spatial frequency at which maximum contrast sensitivity occurs and increasing the drop-off in low-frequency sensitivity. At luminance levels above about $100 \, \text{cd/m}^2$, contrast sensitivity is independent of average brightness and so follows Weber's law (Van Nes & Bouman, 1967). There is disagreement as to whether or not other contrast related perceptual effects such as masking (see Section 2.4.2) follow Weber's law (Legge, 1980). The complex manner in which brightness affects contrast-related perceptual effects suggests that care be taken in presuming a general applicability of Weber's law to response characteristics. It is also important to note that the nature of contrast sensitivity functions relating to threshold effects may not carry over to suprathreshold phenomenon. For example, contrast matching when the target contrast is well above the detection threshold does not seem to be dependent on spatial frequency (Georgeson & Sullivan, 1975).

2.4.2 Masking and Facilitation

When two different patterns are combined, visual *masking* or *facilitation* often affects the discriminability of the combined pattern from its constituents. The normal formulation for this effect is to examine a combined pattern C, which is the sum of a signal S and a mask M:

$$C = S + M \, . \tag{2.4}$$

Masking occurs when C cannot be discriminated from M, even when both S and M are clearly visible on their own. In effect, the mask M hides the signal S. By contrast, with facilitation, C is discriminable from M even when S is not visible on its own. Adding the mask M to the signal S exposes aspects of S that were not visible in isolation. Masking is most effective when there is substantial overlap in the spatial frequency distributions of the signal and mask, with the effects of masking substantially diminished when the dominant spatial frequencies differ by a factor of three or more. Orientational alignment is also important to masking for patterns with anisotropic spatial frequency distributions, with the effects of masking dissipating at about 40°.

Figure 2.8 shows an example of masking. In the figure, a signal pattern is combined with three different masks. The first mask has a spatial fre-

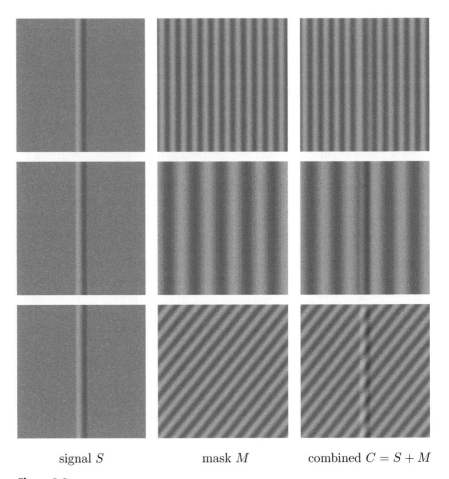

signal S mask M combined $C = S + M$

Figure 2.8

Three identical signal patterns (left column) have added to them three different mask images (middle column) to produce three different combined images (right column, with value rescaled to match signal and masks). The signal is almost completely masked in the top combined image, but clearly visible in the second and third combined images. (After Wandell, 1995.)

quency 20% higher than the signal. When combined with the signal, the signal pattern nearly disappears. The second mask has a spatial frequency 50% lower than the signal. The third mask has a spatial frequency the same as the first, but is oriented 40° off the signal orientation. For the second and third mask pattern, the signal pattern is clearly apparent in the combined image.

In some cases, changes in the amount of contrast in a masking pattern can switch its effect on a particular signal pattern between masking and facilitation. At least for sine wave grating patterns with the same orientation and similar frequencies, a low-contrast masking pattern facilitates discrimination while a higher-contrast pattern causes normal masking, with discrimination being inhibited (Legge & Foley, 1980).

2.5 Dynamic Range

The human visual system is able to operate over a range of light intensities spanning about 14 orders of magnitude (Figure 2.9). Under the right conditions, we can see at least some structure at illumination levels far below starlight on a moonless night. We can also see at light levels well above those resulting from sunlight reflected off of a piece of white paper. However, at any one point in time, the visual system is only able to detect variations in light intensity over a much smaller range, roughly 3 orders of magnitude or perhaps a bit more in brightness variability (Fairchild, 2005; Kunkel & Reinhard, 2010). As the average brightness to which the visual system is exposed changes over time, the range of discriminable brightnesses changes in a corresponding manner. This effect is most obvious if we move rapidly from a brightly lit outdoor area to a very dark room. At first, we are able to see little. After a while, however, details in the room start to become apparent.

Four classes of mechanisms combine to give the human visual system this enormous range of brightness sensitivity. First, the pupil of the eye serves as a variable aperture, dynamically adapting to current light levels. However, the pupil can only vary the amount of light entering the eye by a factor of about 16—far too little to account for more than a small portion of the entire visual dynamic range. The second class of mechanisms is due to the biochemical processes in the photoreceptors that sense light

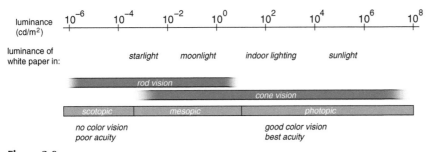

Figure 2.9

Dynamic range in the human visual system.

and generate appropriate neural signals. The nature of this process is such that sensitivity decreases as light intensity increases. The third class of mechanisms aiding the adaptability of the visual system to different brightness levels is the neural circuitry that extracts contours and similar features from the patterns of light on the retina while remaining largely insensitive to average brightness and low spatial frequencies. Finally, the rods and cones are specialized to cover different brightness ranges.

The cones provide visual information over most of what we consider normal lighting conditions, ranging from bright sunlight to dim indoor lighting. The rods are only effective at very low light levels. *Photopic* vision involves bright light in which only the cones are effective. *Scotopic* vision involves dim light in which only the rods are effective. There is a range of intensities within which both cones and rods are sensitive to changes in light, which is referred to as *mesopic* conditions.

As shown in Figure 2.4, the packing density of rods drops to zero at the center of the fovea, significantly reducing acuity in scotopic vision. Because of this, we are unable to see fine detail at illumination levels below partial moonlight. Away from the fovea, the rod density first increases and then decreases. As a result, sensitivity to low light patterns is increased when looking (slightly) away from them. This can be demonstrated by observing a night sky on a moonless night, well away from any city lights. Some stars will be so dim that they will be visible if you look at a point in the sky slightly to the side of the star, but they will disappear if you look directly at them. This occurs because when you look directly at these features, the image of the features falls only on the cones in the retina, which are not

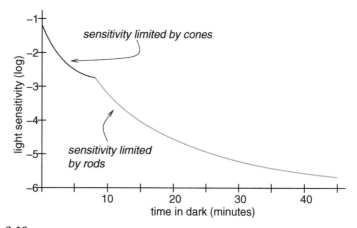

Figure 2.10

Dark adaptation over time (after Auerbach & Wald, 1954, and Gregory, 1997).

sufficiently light sensitive to detect the feature. Looking slightly to the side causes the image to fall on the more light-sensitive rods.

Dark adaptation due to physiological changes in the eye occurs over a substantial period of time. It takes several minutes for significant dark adaptation to occur and 40 minutes or so for complete dark adaptation. Cones and rods adapt at different rates (Auerbach & Wald, 1954). Cones adapt quickly, reaching maximum sensitivity in ten minutes or less. Rod dark adaptation is slower, continuing for 40 minutes or so. Once fully dark adapted, rods are so light sensitive that they generate responses when absorbing a single photon of light (Baylor, 1987; Hecht, Shlaer, & Pirenne, 1942), though overall system sensitivity is less because of transmission losses elsewhere. One consequence of the different adaptation times for cones and rods is that the curve describing overall brightness sensitivity as a function of time in the dark has a two-stage shape, as shown in Figure 2.10. If we move back into the bright light after a period of dark adaptation, vision is not only difficult; it can also actually be painful. *Light adaptation* is required before it is again possible to see clearly. Light adaptation occurs much more quickly than dark adaptation, typically requiring less than a minute.

2.6   Issues Specific to Computer Graphics

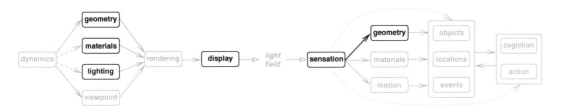

2.6.1   Photometry

Perhaps the situation in which computer graphics practitioners most often encounter photometric units is the characterization of display brightness. The light output of video projectors is described in terms of lumens, using a standard measurement procedure established by the American National Standards Institute (ANSI). The brightness of screen-based displays is now almost always given in cd/m^2. The difference in units precludes direct comparisons between the brightness of a projector and a monitor, which makes sense because the brightness of a projected image is a function both of the brightness of the projector and the area over which the image is projected.

Very few computer graphics rendering systems support photometrically accurate image generation. The ability to describe light sources in physically correct ways is often missing. Color management is often absent, thus precluding correct handling of spectral sensitivity. The interaction of light intensity and reflectivity is typically done in a non-linear manner (see Section 4.3.4 in Chapter 4), further distorting photometric calibration. One of the few exceptions is the Radiance system (Larson & Shakespeare, 2004).

2.6.2   Acuity and Contrast

A high-quality computer monitor typically has a dot pitch (spacing between pixels) on the order of 0.25 mm. Viewed from a distance of 70 cm, the finest detail that can be displayed is about 25 cycles/degree, or about twice as coarse as the finest detail resolvable by the human visual system. A 147 cm (diagonal) 1080p, high-definition television (HDTV) video display has a dot pitch of 0.67 mm. When viewed from a distance of 3 m, this yields a finest displayable detail of 40 cycles/degree, a bit below the visual system's maximum resolution limit. For the less fortunate who must make do with smaller-sized HDTV video displays, at a viewing distance of 3 m the display will be able to present any resolvable grating pattern. Note that these are theoretical acuity limits for the displays themselves, and don't take into consideration bandwidth limitations of the video source.

The degree to which video display devices are matched to the contrast sensitivity of the human visual system is strongly affected by the ways in which brightness values are encoded in the signal sent to the display and in the display itself. The most common image-encoding systems use 8-bit unsigned integer values. This provides 256 distinct achromatic (neutral) brightness levels. While it is an oversimplification to say that perception of contrast follows Weber's law, it is definitely the case that the visual system is more sensitive to fine differences in brightness at lower levels of average brightness than at higher levels. If the image encoding is linear in brightness, then the brightness difference between two numerically adjacent encoded values will not correlate closely with contrast sensitivity over the full range of brightness values. For example, if brightness is encoded linearly and an encoded value of 0 corresponds to no luminance, the contrast between levels 75 and 76 is about 1.3% of average brightness, which is clearly visible, while the contrast between levels 179 and 180 is about 0.5% of average brightness, which is likely not visible.

Most image representations now use some version of *gamma encoding* (also called *gamma compression*) to nonlinearly encode brightness into pixel values in a manner that more effectively matches the encoding to human contrast sensitivity.[2] In its simplest form, gamma encoding involves rescaling brightness values l to be in the range $[0.0–1.0]$, and then applying a power function to the resulting l_S to get a similarly scaled encoded value e_S:

$$e_S = l_S^{1/\gamma} .$$ (2.5)

For many versions of gamma encoding, γ is set to 2.2. (It was 1.8 in earlier versions of Mac OS.) The final pixel value is produced by rescaling e_S over the appropriate range and quantizing to integer values. For an 8-bit grayscale image using gamma encoding with $\gamma = 2.2$ and 0 corresponding to pure black, the Weber contrast of adjacent gray levels is below 0.5% for all pixel values greater or equal to 91. No real images come close to containing values that are truly black, and if the intensity of the darkest actual value (the *black point*) is taken into account in the gamma encoding, the Weber contrast of adjacent pixel values can be kept near or below the detectable threshold over more of the 0–255 range, though gamma encoding using a simple power function has intrinsic problems for numerically small values. (See Chapter 4 for more on gamma encoding.)

To correctly present image intensities, display systems need to invert gamma encoding with a corresponding *gamma decoding* (or *gamma expansion*) process. In non-CRT displays, this requires an explicit transformation from encoded value to displayed brightness. Often, gamma decoding is not an exact inverse of gamma encoding. This is sometimes done intentionally, since a side effect can be to increase contrast, and higher contrast is subjectively preferred by many viewers in many situations. The term *gamma correction* is frequently used to refer to some or all of the gamma encoding/decoding processes. This causes much confusion, since, with the near demise of CRT displays, nothing is being "corrected"; furthermore, the term is used inconsistently, sometimes referring to encoding, sometimes to decoding, and sometimes to both.

2.6.3   Visual Differences and Masking

The development of new image compression techniques requires measures of the perceptual effects of different algorithms and different parameter settings. Likewise, perceptually adaptive rendering systems, which gain efficiency by focusing computational resources on aspects of the process that most affect the final appearance of generated images, need a metric for determining whether the efficiencies come at a cost of degraded appearance.

---

[2]The original motivation for gamma encoding had more to do with the nonlinearities of CRT displays. This is no longer an issue, since the relationship between encoded image values and displayed brightness is completely controllable in LCD and similar sorts of displays.

If two different compression methods produce visually indistinguishable results, the one with the least computational cost is the best. If computation can be saved in rendering without changing appearance, it is likely to be beneficial. The most straightforward metric for these purposes is one that measures some aspect of pixel differences. However, simple signal processing metrics such as mean square error correlate poorly with a subjective sense of image similarity (Eskicioglu & Fisher, 1995). As a result, more-sophisticated ways of evaluating perceptual similarity are required.

The visible difference predictor (VDP) (Daly, 1993) and related techniques (e.g., Chalmers, McNamara, Daly, Myszkowski, & Troscianko, 2000; Myszkowski, 1998) use models of human sensitivity to brightness, spatial frequency, and contrast sensitivity, along with information about visual masking effects, to make such predictions. These methods compare two images by independently normalizing them to correct for viewing conditions, the nonlinear response of the visual system to brightness, and contrast sensitivity. Masking is then accounted for by a process that considers spatial frequency and orientation in both images. Rather than giving an aggregate evaluation of overall discriminability, these techniques operate locally, providing an indication of regions in an image pair likely to appear different from one another. Thus, efforts at improving image quality should be focused on regions of the image or on aspects of the compression or rendering process where they are likely to be most effective.

One argument against the VDP approach is that because it is based on threshold visual distinctiveness, it is too conservative. Often, visual differences can be tolerated as long as the *functional equivalence* between actual and ideal images is maintained (Ferwerda, 2003). The presumption is that it is more important to estimate differences that affect the visual information of relevance to the viewer than to treat all appearance differences equally (Ramanarayanan, Ferwerda, Walter, & Bala, 2007; Z. Wang, Bovik, Sheikh, & Simoncelli, 2004). A more general limitation of using measures of image similarity between pairs of images to evaluate image quality is that we often don't have a usable standard to compare to. For these situations, a more general measure of perceptual effectiveness will be required, though little research has yet been directed at this problem.

As described in Section 2.4.2, masking is said to occur when a pattern C is perceptually indistinguishable from another pattern M, where $C = S + M$ and S is visible on its own. Image rendering, encoding, and compression can produce artifacts that have the potential to be visually distracting. Examples of these artifacts are faceting due to too-coarsely-meshed shaded surfaces, the banding that occurs due to underquantized brightness values, and the 8×8 block patterns that can occur in overcompressed JPEG and MPEG images. Artifacts also occur due to the rendering simplifications associated with limited computational resources, including

inaccurate illumination, geometric simplification, and a host of other effects. In the expression above, M can be taken to be the ideal image, S
the artifacts, and C the actual displayed image. The artifacts can be ignored if the ideal image is such that it masks the artifacts. This leads to
two approaches to utilizing perceptual masking in computer graphics: One
option is to use texture maps containing appropriate spatial frequencies to
hide what would otherwise be distracting artifacts with similar spatial frequency distributions (Ferwerda, Shirley, Pattanaik, & Greenberg, 1997). A
second approach is to use only enough rendering resources to make the generated image visually indistinguishable from the maximum achievable quality (Bartz, Cunningham, Fischer, & Wallraven, 2008; O'Sullivan, Howlett,
Morvan, McDonnell, & O'Conor, 2004). Masking can also be used in the
three-dimensional domain (e.g., to hide watermarks in geometry) (Lavoué,
2009).

2.6.4 Dynamic Range

The maximum brightness obtainable with a good-quality LCD computer
monitor or HDTV system is about 400 cd/m^2, which is equivalent to viewing under bright interior lighting. Some plasma displays are capable of
brightness levels of 1,400 cd/m^2. LCD monitors with adaptive LED back-
lighting have the potential to achieve maximum light levels approaching
10^4 cd/m^2, which is approaching natural outdoor illumination, but as of
this writing such systems are not commercially available. The minimal
displayable brightness of computer monitors and home television systems
is limited in practice by ambient illumination and the reflectivity of the
screen. This makes it difficult to realistically simulate night scenes, and
also makes the contrast ratio numbers that peddlers of consumer electronics like to quote near meaningless. The display precision of essentially all
computer monitors is 8 bits/color, though a (very) few 10- and 12-bit monitors are coming on the market. A number of HDTV systems have a display
precision of 10 bits/color. The range of brightnesses that can be achieved
with print media is far more restrictive, with optimal maximum contrast
ratios on the order of 100:1 and actual contrast ratios typically much less.

Substantial interest has been developing in creating and displaying *high
dynamic range* (HDR) imagery in the photographic and computer graphics
communities (Reinhard, Ward, Pattanaik, & Debevec, 2006). Cameras can
realistically capture about three orders of magnitude of brightness variability in a single exposure. As long as nothing is moving in the scene, multiple
exposures using different exposure settings can be combined to create a
single image covering a far greater range of brightnesses (Debevec & Malik, 1997; Mann & Picard, 1995). The Radiance image-generation system
(Larson & Shakespeare, 2004) supports high dynamic range, photometri-

cally accurate computer graphics rendering. HDR processing requires a
representation with both high dynamic range and substantial precision.
Also desirable is an API to the representation for which pixel values are
multiplicatively related to brightness to avoid distortions due to gamma encoding. Four image file formats in relatively common usage support this:
Radiance HDR (in two version, RGBE and XYZE), TIFF floating point
(with three versions, involving 32-bit, 24-bit, or 16-bit pixel values), TIFF
LogLuv, and EXR.

2.6.5   Tone Mapping

As mentioned in Section 2.6.4, conventional display and print media can
present only a limited range of brightnesses. As a result, a variety of *tone
mapping* techniques have been developed for converting a high dynamic
range image into a form that can be displayed on such limited dynamic
range devices and media (Reinhard et al., 2006). A similar problem has
been faced by painters since at least the Renaissance. Roughly speaking,
the options for dealing with this problem computationally are to allow the
darkest and lightest areas of the image to be clamped to the extremes
allowed by the display device, to rescale the dynamic range to match that
of the display device, or to apply some sort of more complex manipulation
that causes the appearance of a higher dynamic range than is actually
present in the display.

Displaying an HDR image by clamping the brightest and darkest regions eliminates visible patterns in what are often important regions of
the depicted scene. Compressing the dynamic range by doing a simple,
space-invariant remapping of brightness values leads to images that look
subjectively unnatural. *Global* approaches determine a mapping from initial HDR image values to appropriately chosen *low dynamic range* (LDR)
values, without regard to location in the image or surrounding pixel values. Some of these methods perform quite well, as long as the dynamic
range of the input is not too great. Greater compression of dynamic range
is possible using a combination of brightness rescaling and some form of
space-variant processing. Stockham (1972) described a digital filtering approach, which suppressed slow variations in brightness while preserving
high-contrast boundaries. This is effective because the visual system is
much less sensitive to gradual changes in brightness than it is to sharp
boundaries. Reducing these slow variations in brightness allows the contrast of the sharp boundaries to be preserved while remapping the absolute
brightnesses on either side of the boundaries to be within the displayable
range. Many more-recent techniques accomplish a similar transformation,
though with fewer artifacts and/or an ability to deal with greater dynamic
ranges.

Human vision under conditions of dark illumination produces effects such as glare and loss of acuity that are not captured in tone mapping operations. Only a limited amount of work has been done in computer graphics simulating these effects in rendered images designed to be viewed under more-normal viewing conditions (Ferwerda, Pattanaik, Shirley, & Greenberg, 1996; Larson, Rushmeier, & Piatko, 1997; Spencer, Shirley, Zimmerman, & Greenberg, 1995), though there is a well-established technique in film referred to as *day for night* (or *American night*), in which underexposure and a blue filter are combined with daylight illumination to produce a (poor) simulation of the appearance of a night scene. Simulating scotopic or mesopic vision under photopic conditions is particularly challenging because, for most people, the loss of acuity in scotopic or mesopic vision is not accompanied by a strong sense of blur (Haro, Bertalmío, & Caselles, 2006; W. B. Thompson, Shirley, & Ferwerda, 2002).

2.7 Suggestions for Further Reading

Good overviews of the physiology of the eye as it relates to visual perception:

> Gregory, R. L. (1997). *Eye and brain: The psychology of seeing* (5 ed.). Princeton, NJ: Princeton University Press.

> Palmer, S. E. (1999). *Vision science—photons to phenomenology.* Cambridge, MA: MIT Press.

Overviews of photometry with a computer graphics emphasis: in:

> Shirley, P., Marschner, S., Ashikhmin, M., Gleicher, M., Hoffman, N., Johnson, G., et al. (2009). *Fundamentals of computer graphics* (3rd ed.). Natick, MA: A K Peters.

> Reinhard, E., Khan, E. A., Akyüz, A. O. & Johnson, G. M. (2008). *Color Imaging: Fundamentals and Applications* Wellesley, MA: A K Peters.

A comprehensive coverage of the sensitivity of the eye to light intensity:

> Hood, D. C., & Finkelstein, M. A. (1986). Sensitivity to light. In K. R. Boff, I. Kaufman, & J. P. Thomas (Eds.), *Handbook of perception and human performance: Vol. 1. Sensory processes and perception* (chap. 5). New York: Wiley.

Similarly comprehensive coverage of the sensitivity of the eye to contrast:

> Olzak, L. A., & Thomas, J. P. (1986). Seeing spatial patterns. In K. R. Boff, I. Kaufman, & J. P. Thomas (Eds.), *Handbook of perception and human performance: Vol. 1. Sensory processes and perception* (chap. 7). New York: Wiley

An overview of many techniques involving perceptually adaptive computer graphics:

Bartz, D., Cunningham, D., Fischer, J., & Wallraven, C. (2008). The role of perception for computer graphics. In *Proceedings Eurographics (State-of-the-Art Reports)* (pp. 65–86). Aire-la-Ville, Switzerland: Eurographics Association.

Comprehensive coverage of high dynamic range images, including tone mapping:

Reinhard, E., Ward, G., Pattanaik, S., & Debevec, P. (2006). *High dynamic range imaging*. San Francisco, CA: Morgan Kaufmann.

3

2D Image Features

One of the critical events in modern visual neuroscience was the discovery by Hubel and Wiesel (1959, 1968) of cells in the mammalian visual cortex that responded to specific patterns of light falling on the retina. These patterns included oriented contours of sharp changes in brightness, lines of both dark-on-light and light-on-dark polarity, and line endpoints. The visual system implements this detection process by a multistage process. At each stage neural signals, each associated with a specific limited region of the retina (a receptive field, as described in Chapter 2), are combined to produce a set of output signals. The actual mechanisms are complicated and vary in important ways over different portions of the eye and brain. Common to most of the process is that receptive fields consist of *excitatory* regions, in which retinal stimulation increases output, and *inhibitory* regions, in which retinal stimulation attenuates the effects of the excitatory regions. The effect is well approximated by linear signal processing that combines blurring and differentiation, though some aspects of neural processing are clearly nonlinear, and responses to temporal changes are also pervasive.

Marr (1982), building on this work and other studies, proposed a model of visual perception in which a critical step was the reencoding of the retinal image into what he called the *primal sketch*, which was a representation of contours in the retinal image along with information about the local two-dimensional geometry of those contours. Marr hypothesized that the primal sketch contained information sufficient to infer shape information about surfaces (which he referred to as the $2\frac{1}{2}$-D sketch) and three-dimensional objects in the environment. In some of the earliest work in what is now called *computer vision*, Roberts (1965) constructed a system for analyzing images of simple polyhedral objects that had as its first step the extraction of contours based on an analysis of the spatial variability of brightness.[1]

Most modern theories of vision presume that contours of discontinuities in the retinal image are most often due to scene properties relevant to perception, and that the detection of discontinuities in the retinal image is a critical first step in perception. The visual system must then go beyond detecting these discontinuities by interpreting them to determine the particular scene structure that led to their generation. There is substantial evidence that the visual system is also sensitive to regular periodic patterns of light distributed over regions in the retinal image. These *spatial frequency features* seem to play a very different role in visual perception than do contours. Also central to most theories of vision is the existence of processes that *group* these contours, and perhaps other simple features of the retinal image, into more-complex entities, from which information can be inferred about the scene generating the retinal image. This chapter provides an overview of the phenomenology of contour extraction, spatial frequency features, and grouping. More on these topics can be found in almost any introductory text on visual perception. A brief discussion is also included of the implications of this phenomenology for computer graphics.

3.1   Contour Detection and Appearance

[E]xperience building vision systems suggests that interesting things often happen at an edge in an image and it is worth knowing where edges are.

—Forsyth and Ponce (2003)

Forsyth and Ponce were talking about computer vision systems, but their comment applies equally to biological vision. Most discussions of the neuroscience of early vision, and the approach taken in most computer vision systems, emphasize the importance of finding localized, spatially abrupt changes in image brightness—possibly in addition to other sensed image properties. This serves two related purposes: Because such discontinuities often arise from scene structure that is relevant to the goals of visual perception, interpretation of the retinal image is aided by detecting the boundaries and passing on an explicit encoding of these boundaries to subsequent processing steps. Additionally, reencoding the retinal image in terms of explicit contours also creates a more compact encoding, allowing efficiencies in the implementation of the visual system as a whole.

---

[1]In this same work, Roberts describes the first algorithm for hidden line elimination in wireframe rendering and the first use of homogeneous coordinates for perspective computations in computer graphics. He went on to play a central role in the development of the ARPAnet, which was the predecessor of the Internet.

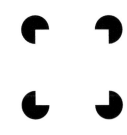

Figure 3.1

The lighter-colored central region is seen as distinct from the darker-colored background, even though there is no sharp discontinuity in brightness on the right side of the central region.

Figure 3.2

A white square with distinct boundaries is seen in the center of the figure, even though no intensity discontinuities are present along much of where the contour is seen.

Under many circumstances, the human visual system is quite sensitive to brightness discontinuities, as discussed in Chapter 2. Mathematically, these *edges* can be characterized as local maxima in the directional first spatial derivative of image intensity (e.g., Canny, 1986) or, almost equivalently, as zero crossings in the Laplacian of image intensity (Marr & Hildreth, 1980). The visual system can also detect spatial discontinuities in other properties, including color, texture, orientation, motion, and stereo disparity. Spatial localization of discontinuities in these nonbrightness image properties is less precise than for brightness discontinuities.

Often more important to visual perception than the detection of edges in isolation is that the visual system is sensitive to the organization of discontinuities in sensed image properties, not just their contrast. Figures 3.1 and 3.2 provide two examples of images where parts of a perceived boundary enclosing a region of the image have little or no local contrast. In Figure 3.1, the right side of the lighter-colored central region merges smoothly and with very little local contrast variability into the background. While the exact location of the right edge of the central region is indistinct, there is a clear sense of the shape of the region and the fact that it is separate from the darker background on all sides. In Figure 3.2, a continuous closed contour is seen around a central region, even though no image contrast is present along much of the apparent contour. The central region appears as a white square set off from the background, even though the background is of an equivalent white. Both of these examples illustrate the perceptual

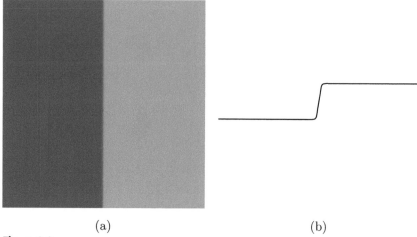

(a)   (b)

Figure 3.3

An example of Mach banding. (a) Two regions of uniform brightness, separated by a uniform gradient. Most viewers will see a dark band to the left of the gradient and a light band to the right of the gradient, with the strength of the effect a function of viewing distance. (b) The brightness profile of (a), showing that no such bands occur in the actual image.

system favoring what Marr (1982) calls the *continuity of discontinuities* usually present in the world.

Figure 3.3 provides an additional example of the complexities associated with the perception of image discontinuities. The visual system is much more sensitive to localized, sharp changes in image properties than it is to more gradual changes. Sometimes, this has the paradoxical effect of causing brightness changes to be seen where none exist. Figure 3.3 is an example of *Mach banding*. The brightness profile of this figure, shown in Figure 3.3(b), is one of two constant brightness regions, separated by a smooth gradient in brightness. While the pattern is non-decreasing in brightness from left to right, brightness does not *look* to be increasing monotonically (Figure 3.3(a)). Rather, there is an apparent dark band to the left of the transition and an apparent light band to the right of the transition. The likely cause of this effect is processing in the visual system that applies what is in essence a high emphasis filter to the retinal image, resulting in overshoot to either side of the actual transition.

Figure 3.4, known as the Craik-O'Brien-Cornsweet illusion (Cornsweet, 1970; Craik, 1996; O'Brien, 1958), is a much more striking example. Here, the presence of an edge causes two regions of identical image intensity to look like they have distinctly different brightness. Figure 3.5 shows

Figure 3.4

The Craik-O'Brien-Cornsweet illusion. See what happens when you cover the vertical line at the center of the figure with one finger.

the brightness profile of the image in Figure 3.4. To convince yourself that in fact the only variability in brightness is near the vertical edge, cover the edge with your finger or a pen. To either side, you will see two uniform brightness patches, each with the same brightness. More can be found about the difference between actual and apparent brightness in Chapter 10. The Craik-O'Brien-Cornsweet illusion can be created not only by brightness variability, but also by appropriate variability in color, stereo disparity, motion, and likely other image properties as well. There has been a fair amount of discussion regarding what causes the effect and what role the effect plays in perception, but as yet there is no consensus on either.

Figure 3.5

The brightness profile along a horizontal line of Figure 3.4.

3.2   Interpretation of Contours

Many different aspects of a scene can lead to discontinuities in brightness, color, texture, or motion in a retinal image. Surface markings, with their associated discontinuities in reflectance, almost always project in such a way as to generate discontinuities in retinal image intensity. Sharp orientation discontinuities in a surface also often lead to image discontinuities, due to changes in the relative orientation between surface and illumination and surface and viewing angle (see Chapter 9). Likewise, shadows and caustics almost always are associated with significant changes in image brightness, though not always sharp discontinuities. (An *optical caustic* is a highlight

(a)   (b)

Figure 3.6

(a) An image of a scene containing discontinuities in brightness due to reflectance, orientation, occlusion, and shadows. (b) A sketch of the brightness discontinuities in (a).

caused by light reflected from or refracted through a curved surface and projected onto another surface.) Occlusion, in which one surface partially hides another, also often produces brightness discontinuities, since different surfaces with different surface and illumination properties are visible to either side of the projection of the silhouette boundary of the occluding surface. Occlusion boundaries also generate discontinuities in optical flow and stereo disparity.

Figure 3.6(a) shows an image with all of these scene properties except a caustic. Figure 3.6(b) illustrates the location of brightness discontinuities in Figure 3.6(a). Critical to note, however, is that brightness discontinuities are not a sufficient basis on their own for perception. The visual system seems to be able to differentiate between the different causes of the sorts of discontinuities shown in Figure 3.6(b) in ways that are important to inferring the scene properties associated with the image shown in Figure 3.6(a). Furthermore, key physical boundaries may be visible despite not having sufficient contrast in the image to cause an edge response such as shown in Figure 3.6(b).

The relationship between discontinuities in image properties and occlusion boundaries is both complex and particularly important to perception. Contours of discontinuities generated by occlusion have an asymmetric interpretation. One side of the contour corresponds to the occlud*ed* surface. The other side of the contour corresponds to the occlud*ing* surface, which

along the line of sight corresponding to the contour is in front of the occluded surface and usually partially hides that surface. In most cases, the
occluded surface continues out of sight behind the occluding surface. As
a result, image contours arising from occlusion provide shape information
about the occluding surface but not the occluded surface.

3.2.1 The Importance of Junctions

In some cases, the two-dimensional pattern of contours in the retinal image directly provides evidence for the scene geometry that generated the
contours. This is particularly true for polyhedral objects made up of flat
surfaces. The line drawing shown in Figure 3.7(a) provides an example,
though this phenomenon applies to intensity images as well as long as the
significant contours are easily visible. Under a simplifying set of assumptions about possible geometry and lighting, it turns out that only a limited
number of qualitatively different corner configurations in the image are possible (Clowes, 1971; Guzman, 1968; Huffman, 1971). Figure 3.7(b) shows
the possible cases when only contours associated with occlusion and orientation discontinuities are present, and all of the corners have exactly three
surfaces coming together at a point. T-junctions are particularly important,
since in this simplified condition the top of the T is necessarily an occlusion
boundary, with the occluding surface opposite the base of the T. Even in
less restrictive situations, T-junctions are a strong indicator of occlusion.

Contour junctions are locally ambiguous with respect to the scene properties with which they are associated. Waltz (1975) proposed a method
by which this ambiguity could be resolved for contours such as shown
in Figure 3.7(a). For contours arising from orientation discontinuities
or occlusion, there are 108 combinatorially possible ways in which to as-
sign possible contour interpretations to the four junction types shown in

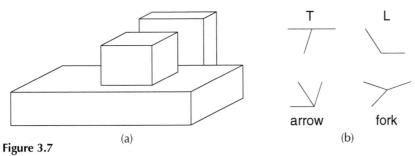

(a)

Figure 3.7
(a) Junctions provide information about occlusion and the convexity or concavity
of corners. (b) Common junction types for planar surface objects.

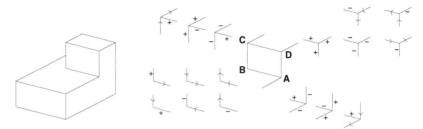

Figure 3.8

On the left is a line drawing of a polyhedral object. A section of this drawing is shown on the right, along with the possible labeling for each line segment of each corner. A + indicates a convex orientation discontinuity, a − indicates a concave orientation discontinuity, and an arrow indicates an occlusion boundary, with the occluding surface to the right. (After Winston, 1992.)

Figure 3.7(b). Under the same set of simplifying assumptions described immediately above, however, only 18 of these possibilities can occur in the real world. Furthermore, under these same set of assumptions, a contour connecting two junctions will have the same interpretation along its entire length. Waltz's method starts by assigning to junctions all contour interpretations possible in the real world (see Figure 3.8) and then eliminating cases in which a contour has different interpretations at its two ends. In most cases, this ultimately leads to a unique interpretation.

The approach to contour interpretation described in Waltz (1975) becomes more difficult when contours arise from illumination, more-complex geometry, and surface markings. Curved surfaces represent a particular challenge (Malik, 1987). Nevertheless, it is clear that the visual system is effective at interpreting the three-dimensional shape of objects in scenes that lead to images of the sort shown in Figure 3.7(a). While the mechanisms are unlikely to be exactly those described by Waltz, the perception of both impossible figures and reversing figures provides evidence for the importance of junction types and contour interpretation.

Figure 3.9(a) shows the Penrose triangle, a well-known example of an *impossible figure*. Cover up any of the three corners of the figure with your hand, and the remainder of the line drawing conveys a clear sense of a three-dimensional shape. When all three corners are visible, the whole of the object can no longer be seen as a real shape. One common account for this is that it is not possible to interpret the contours making up the three T-junctions in a manner consistent with the rest of the shape (Figure 3.9(b)). Figure 3.10(a) shows the Schroeder stairs, a well-known example of a *reversing figure*, which can be seen as one of two possible three-dimensional shapes, each a depth reversal of the other. Most viewers of reversing fig-

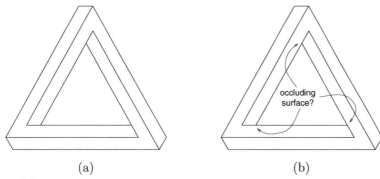

Figure 3.9

(a) An "impossible" figure: the Penrose triangle. (b) The three T-junctions in the figure indicate an incompatible set of occluding surfaces.

ures find one interpretation easier to see than the other. In the case of the Schroeder stairs, the favored percept is usually of stairs going up and to the left. To switch to the alternate view, try staring at one of the Y-junctions at the upper right of the drawing (Figure 3.10(b)). Attending to Y-junctions tends to make them appear convex. Once this happens, the scene geometry associated with the junctions propagates along the contours, changing the appearance of the whole figure.

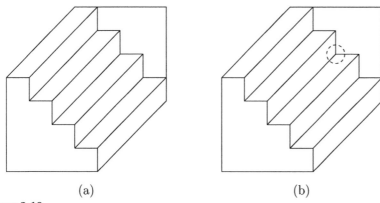

Figure 3.10

(a) A "reversing" figure: the Schroeder stairs. The stairs can be seen as viewed from the top and going up and to the left, or as viewed from the bottom and going down and to the right. (b) It is easiest to see the second interpretation if you focus attention on one of the Y-junctions at the upper right.

(a)   (b)

Figure 3.11

(a) The squared-off inside ends of the bars produce a strong subjective contour effect. (b) Little or no subjective contour is apparent when the bars end in a pointed shape. (After Kennedy, 1988.)

3.2.2 Subjective Contours and Visual Completion

Figure 3.2 is one example of a *subjective contour* (also called an *illusory contour*), which is a boundary perceived in the absence of discontinuities in image brightness or other image properties (Kanizsa, 1976). The existence of subjective contours shows that contour perception is dependent on much more than simple local edge detection in the retinal image. In particular, the perception of subjective contours seems tightly bound to the interpretation of two-dimensional patterns in the retinal image as having arisen from occlusion in the scene. Figure 3.11 provides an example. In Figure 3.11(a), the squared-off ends of the bars suggest that the bars might be occluded by some surface. The inside ends of the bars are close enough together and appropriately aligned so that the visual system can construct a closed contour through all of these suggestions of occlusion. The result is not only that a contour is apparent, but also that it is interpreted as having arisen from a white disk positioned in the scene in front of the bars. In Figure 3.11(b), the inside ends of the bars no longer are consistent with the bars being occluded by a circular disk, and the appearance of a subjective contour is much diminished (Kennedy, 1988). Finally, note that if you view Figure 3.11(a) from sufficiently far away, a subjective contour connects the outside ends of the bars as if they are behind a hole cut in the page. Presumably, this has to do with the visual angle between the bar endings being reduced sufficiently to allow the visual system to construct a contour connecting them.

Subjective contours are seen in the absence of any corresponding image structure. A related effect occurs for surfaces, in which portions of a surface are perceived even though they are not visible in the retinal image. This

Figure 3.12

Visual completion: the left disk appears to be continuing behind the rectangle, while the right disk appears in front of the rectangle, which is seen to continue behind the right disk.

is called *visual completion*, or sometimes *amodal completion*. Figure 3.12 shows an example. The disk on the left of the rectangle appears to be continuing behind the rectangle, while the rectangle itself appears to be continuing behind the right disk. The paired T-junctions at the left and right sides of the gray rectangle provide strong indications of occlusion, with the rectangle being the occluding surface relative to the left disk and the occluded surface relative to the right disk. Multiple factors influence the actual shape that is seen when visual completion occurs. Of the possible shapes consistent with the alignment of local occlusion features, the visual system seems to favor those that are geometrically least complex. Shape familiarity also plays a role, and there is some evidence that identifiable shapes are preferred when they are consistent with the surrounding context (Palmer, 1999).

3.3   Spatial Frequency Features

Contours are not the only potential source of useful information available from the retinal image. *Spatial frequencies* can be used to characterize an image in terms of its periodic structure over the whole or portions of the image. This is done in many image processing and image coding applications. Most common is to use *Fourier analysis*, which decomposes the brightness distribution in an image into a sum of two-dimensional sine wave patterns of particular frequencies, phases, orientations, and amplitudes. Figure 3.13 shows two patterns, each consisting of a single spatial frequency. Figure 3.13(a) consists of a relatively high-frequency pattern, oriented vertically. Figure 3.13(b) shows a lower-frequency pattern, oriented 60° from the vertical. The human visual system appears to have specialized mechanisms for decomposing retinal images in this manner (C. Blakemore & Campbell, 1969).

 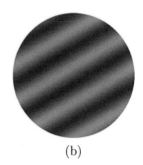

(a)   (b)

Figure 3.13

Two spatial sine wave gratings, with different frequency and orientation: (a) vertically oriented high frequencies, (b) diagonally oriented lower frequencies.

A large number of different *sine wave gratings* (such as shown in Figure 3.13), with different amplitudes, wavelengths, and orientations, must be combined to represent all but the simplest of images. The distribution of amplitudes of these sine wave patterns as a function of frequency, referred to as the *amplitude spectrum*, can provide information useful in inferring properties of the world under view. If substantial fine detail is present, the amplitudes of higher-frequency components will increase relative to the amplitudes of those same components for images with less fine detail. Contours in images of manmade scenes tend to be oriented vertically and horizontally. As a result, Fourier decompositions of such images show larger magnitudes for high-frequency components oriented vertically and horizontally than for high-frequency components at other orientations.

The visual system utilizes information about spatial frequency distributions in the retinal image to make holistic interpretations of image content, to isolate the scale at which image content occurs, and to form the basis of scale-invariant image features. Figure 3.14 illustrates this with an example of a spatial frequency decomposition of a natural image. The low frequency content of the image provides information about the major units in the scene and the overall perspective organization. Mid-frequency content shows the general shape of objects in the scene. High-frequency content isolates fine detail. Chapter 15 provides additional information about the use of spatial frequency features in visual perception.

On average across views of the world, the magnitude of the frequency spectrum falls off approximately as $1/f$, where f is the frequency (Burton & Moorhead, 1987; Field, 1987).[2] This is only an approximation, how-

---

[2]One potential source of confusion is that this relationship is often described in terms of the *power spectrum* of the distribution, which is the square of the amplitude. On average, the power spectrum falls off approximately as $1/f^2$.

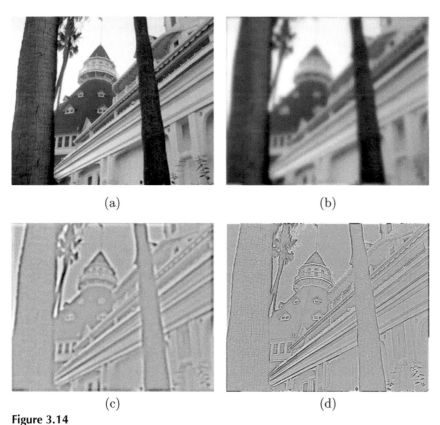

(a)   (b)

(c)   (d)

Figure 3.14
Different spatial frequency bands convey different information about a scene:
(a) original image, (b) low-frequency content, (c) mid-frequency content,
(d) high-frequency content.

ever. Anisotropic variation with orientation is common (Baddeley, 1997;
Torralba & Oliva, 2003), and substantial deviations from the overall $1/f$
dropoff occur for individual, naturally occurring images (Langer, 2000).
In many situations, the spatial frequency statistics of views of the world
are nonstationary, meaning that they change over the extent of the retinal
image. This is due in large part to our existence in a terrestrial world,
and the effect is particularly strong for views of scenes encompassing a
large area due to the likelihood of the viewer looking at a receding ground
plane from a location near the ground (Torralba and Oliva). A number
of models of scene and object recognition have been proposed that combine information about spatial frequency distributions over the whole of
the view and over local regions of the view (see Chapter 15). Finally, while

we started this chapter with the assertion that the cells identified by Hubel and Wiesel (1959, 1968) might form the mechanism for extracting image contours, they are also mathematically sufficient to measure local spatial frequency properties.

3.4   Grouping

It should be clear from Section 3.1 that an important aspect of visual perception is the organization of image features into contours and groupings of contours in ways that are likely to reflect the organization of the scene that generated the image. Many other features are also perceptually grouped. Figure 3.15 shows two examples. In Figure 3.15(a), we see four horizontal rows, each made up of a collection of squares of the same brightness. In Figure 3.15(b), we see three vertical columns, each made up of a collection of squares of different brightness. Phenomena such as shown in Figure 3.15 played a critical role in the development of Gestalt psychology during the early 20th century. A central tenet of Gestalt psychology is that "the whole is different from the sum of its parts."

3.4.1   Perceptual Aggregation and Segregation of Image Entities

The Gestaltists articulated a set of principles describing how the nature of features of individual entities lead to the perception of certain sets of entities as a single grouping, referred to as the *Gestalt laws* of perceptual organization. These principles specified the properties that could lead

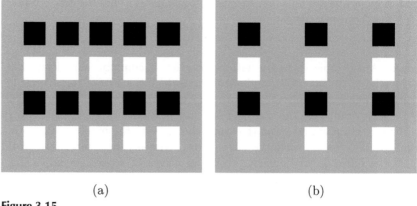

(a)   (b)

Figure 3.15

(a) Individual blocks are perceptually organized into four horizontal rows.
(b) Individual blocks are perceptually organized into three vertical columns.

Term	Definition
Proximity	Entities close together are grouped
Color	Entities of similar brightness and color are grouped
Size	Entities of similar size are grouped
Orientation	Elongated entities with similar orientation are grouped
Symmetry	Curved lines with reflective symmetry are grouped
Parallelism	Curved offset lines with similar shape are grouped
Good continuity	Grouping of line segments favors smoothness
Closure	Entities are grouped if they complete a pattern
Common fate	Entities moving in the same direction are grouped

Table 3.1
Common principles of Gestalt grouping.

to the perception of a whole, along with an attempt to describe the perceptual effects of what happens when multiple grouping properties are in conflict. Table 3.1 summarizes many of these principles. In Figure 3.15(a), the pattern is organized into rows of squares of similar brightness. In Figure 3.15(b), the proximity of blocks dominates over brightness, leading to the perception of three vertical columns.

The visual system not only groups smaller image structures into larger perceptual units, but it also sometimes decomposes image structures into a set of smaller constituent components. Figure 3.16(a) is easily seen as three compact bloblike shapes, one on top of the other. While some might see Figure 3.16(a) as a snowman shape, the phenomenon does not depend on familiarity. Rather, this parsing process favors breaking up patterns at

(a)   (b)

Figure 3.16
(a) Concavities in the silhouette perceptually divide the figure into three parts. (b) The figure perceptually organizes into a series of "humps," separated as shown by the dashed lines. If the figure is viewed upside down, the dashed lines seem centered on the individual parts of the figure. (Figure 3.16(b) after D. D. Hoffman & Richards, 1984.)

points of concavity. D. D. Hoffman and Richards (1984) proposed a model for decomposing shapes into parts that applies both to silhouette boundaries and to patterns interpretable as three-dimensional surfaces, dividing the main shape into parts at negative minima of the principal curvatures, along their associated lines of curvature. In Figure 3.16(b), this division occurs at the troughs in the sinusoidal surface, as marked by the dashed lines. Turn the figure over and the dashed lines will no longer seem to coincide with the natural partitioning of the shape, and instead will be at the center of a set of constituent ridges. (Turning the figure over changes how the parts are perceived because the visual system has a preference for seeing surfaces as if they were being viewed from above.)

3.4.2   The Role of Phenomenological Similarity in Grouping

Most theories of grouping presume that grouping occurs early in the processing of visual information; that it is based primarily on two-dimensional aspects of the projected retinal image; and that it is a prerequisite for other, more-complex aspects of the perception of spatial organization. There is evidence, however, that grouping can be based on phenomenological similarity rather than image similarity. Rock and Brosgole (1964) arranged a rectangular array of lights such that the vertical spacing of lights was closer than the horizontal spacing. When viewed in a dark room, the closer dots grouped, forming the appearance of vertical columns (Figure 3.17(a)). Rotating the array around one vertical edge produced a projected image in which the horizontal spacing was now less than the vertical spacing (Figure 3.17(b)). When viewed with one eye, the pattern now organized

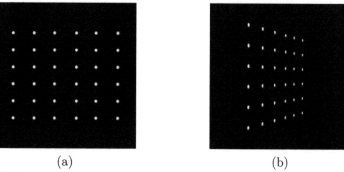

(a)   (b)

Figure 3.17

(a) Rectangular pattern of lights, as in Rock and Brosgole (1964), with horizontal spacing greater than vertical spacing. (b) Monocular view of the same pattern of lights, oriented at 60° to the line of sight, with foreshortening now making the apparent horizontal spacing less than the vertical spacing.

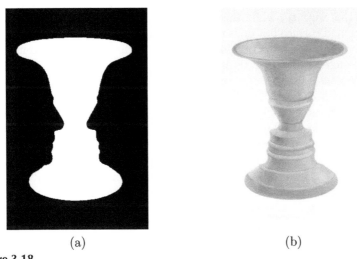

(a)   (b)

Figure 3.18

(a) The Rubin's vase. (b) Under some circumstances, a solid object can be perceived as background, thus causing the actual background to appear as a foreground object. (From `http://www.wikipedia.org/`).

into horizontal rows as expected. However, with binocular viewing vertical columns were still seen, suggesting that when available, the grouping involved three-dimensional proximity. Rock, Nijhawan, Palmer, and Tudor (1992) showed that phenomenological similarity was also involved in grouping based on intensity. The apparent brightness of patterns suggestive of shadowing or transparency is often closer to what it would be if the surface was not shadowed or viewed through another surface than it is to the actual image brightness itself (see Chapter 10). The experiments presented in Rock et al. (1992) support grouping based on perceived brightness of surfaces, not image brightness. The fact that phenomenological similarity appears to play a significant role in groupings presents serious challenges for theories of grouping, since evidence exists for both two-dimensional, image-based grouping affecting perception of surface shape and material properties, and perception of surface shape and material properties affecting grouping.

3.4.3 Figure/Ground Organization

Figure/ground segregation is a special form of grouping that is pervasive in visual perception (E. Rubin, 2001). It is closely related to the asymmetric interpretation of occluding contours, in which one side of the contour is associated with an occluding surface and provides shape information about that surface, while the other side of the contour is associated with an occluded surface but does not indicate anything about the shape of that surface. Figure/ground organization is most often demonstrated using ambiguous figures, of which the *Rubin's vase* (Figure 3.18) is undoubtedly the most famous. The Rubin's vase is usually presented as a black-and-white image, as in Figure 3.18(a). This can be seen either as a white vase-like object in front of a black background that continues behind the vase, or as two faces in profile, looking at one another. Only one or the other percept is possible at a time: it is not possible to simultaneously "see" a vase and two faces. As an indication of the power of figure/ground segregation in perception, Figure 3.18(b) shows that this perceptual instability exists even when there are strong geometric and shading cues favoring the interpretation of the image as a vase and no pictorial support for faces seen in profile other than the silhouette boundary itself.

E. Rubin (2001) highlights the important differences in the perception of figure and ground. Portions of the scene seen as figure are perceived as having a "thing character," while background is perceived as having a "substance character." Figure regions are seen as closer than ground. The contour separating figure and ground contributes to the sense of shape of the figure but not the ground. Perhaps most important for perception as a whole, E. Rubin asserts, is that "in relation to the ground, the figure is more impressive and more dominant. Everything about the figure is remembered better, and the figure brings forth more associations than the ground."

3.5   Issues Specific to Computer Graphics

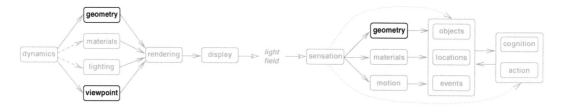

The geometric and photometric simplifications that occur in modeling and rendering can produce perceptual contours in the resulting image where none should exist, or can change the apparent shape of contours. Sometimes contours that should be visible are not. In one important case, the effect of contours on the perception of the brightness of surfaces to either side can be exploited to increase the effective dynamic range of displayed images.

3.5.1   Extraneous Contours and Corners, Indistinct Contours

Almost always, surfaces in computer graphics systems are represented as a mesh of flat, typically triangular, surface patches. Because the time and space complexity of rendering is directly related to the number of such triangles that are potentially visible, it is desirable from a performance perspective to favor models with a smaller number of larger facets. This can raise severe perceptual problems, however. At occlusion boundaries, the use of larger facets to model what should be a smooth surface will lead to a polyline silhouette boundary with noticeable corners. Careful mesh simplification, sensitive to the curvature of the resulting geometry, can help to minimize this effect (Rossignac & Borrel, 1993; Schroeder, Zarge, & Lorensen, 1992). The boundaries between adjacent surface patches are often locations of orientation discontinuity, so a mesh representation that is too coarse can generate distracting shading boundaries between facets. An approach that chooses the level of detail of a meshed representation of surface geometry based on the sensitivity of the visual system to the resulting brightness discontinuities can reduce or eliminate this problem (N. Williams, Luebke, Cohen, Kelley, & Schubert, 2003).

Under some circumstances, perceptual boundaries can appear in what should be smoothly shaded surfaces regardless of how the underlying geometry is represented. Under some circumstances, as discussed in Chapter 2, differences of a single gray level in an 8-bit display are noticeable. As a result, a smoothly shaded surface can break up perceptually into a series of identical brightness patches. The Mach banding effect exacerbates the problem by making the contrast across the patch boundaries appear even larger than the photometry would predict. Paradoxically, smooth surfaces that take on this banded appearance can be made to look smoother by the addition of appropriate *masking noise* (Ferwerda et al., 1997).

While the issues associated with mesh level of detail and brightness quantization have been studied extensively, another problem arising from simplification in geometry, lighting, and materials modeling has received little attention. Taken together, geometry with large flat faces, lighting models based on point sources and no interreflection, and stereotypical surface reflectance models often result in rendered images with much less richness in brightness variability than the real world. Not only does this affect perception of surface materials (see Chapter 10), but it can also reduce the contrast between foreground objects and background surfaces.

Indistinct contours can also arise in visualization applications if too much dependence is made on color. Discontinuities in color are much less visually distinct than discontinuities in brightness, and are difficult to see at all if brightness is exactly matched. Given the variablity in how colors appear on a display device, it is easy to create color-based visualizations that look good in one display environment yet become incomprehensible in another.

3.5.2   Grouping

The visual information on which grouping is based can be distorted by rendering and image display. This has the potential to affect whether groupings appear at all, and can change the components of the scene that are perceptually grouped when multiple grouping cues are involved. Grouping based on detailed shape properties or phenomenological similarity is particularly problematic due to the increased ambiguity of visual information in computer graphics compared to the real world.

Perceptual grouping can play an important role in human-computer interaction (HCI) design and visualization (Rosenholtz, Twarog, Schinkel-Bielefeld, & Wattenberg, 2009). Grouping has the potential to expose information important to the user. Unintentional groupings have the potential to confuse users, making patterns appear in the displayed images that don't correspond to the underlying data. Exploiting grouping for these properties of perceptual grouping in HCI and visualization applications requires an understanding of the grouping cues involved, along with an appreciation of how these cues can be distorted in the image rendering and display processes.

3.5.3   Spatial Frequency Features and Natural Image Statistics

Except for the case of texture synthesis (see Chapter 8), there has been little work in computer graphics exploiting what is known about visual perception relating to spatial frequency features and natural image statistics. No systematic studies have yet been done of the spatial frequency distributions of a large ensemble of rendered images, but it is reasonable to suppose that the nature of the image generation process in computer graphics is sufficiently dissimilar from that in the real world as to result in substantial differences. As a result, it might be possible to modify the statistics of renderings to make the image appear more realistic. A number of other suggestions have been made to utilize an understanding of the perceptual consequences of spatial frequency distributions in the generation of graphical images (Pouli, Cunningham, & Reinhard, 2010; Reinhard, Shirley, Ashikhmin, & Troscianko, 2004), but much remains to be investigated about this problem.

3.6   Suggestions for Further Reading

Almost any introductory text on visual perception covers low-level vision relating to contour extraction, though the discussion is normally weighted toward the neuroscience. Grouping and figure/ground organization are also included in most such texts. One good source for all of these:

> Palmer, S. E. (1999). *Vision science—photons to phenomenology*. Cambridge, MA: MIT Press.

A large volume of work in computer vision addresses many of the issues described in this chapter. A sampling of historical and more contemporary examples:

> Barrow, H. G., & Tenenbaum, J. M. (1981). Computational vision. *Proceedings of the IEEE, 69*(5), 572–595.

> Marr, D. (1982). *Vision*. San Francisco, CA: W. H. Freeman.

> Forsyth, D. A., & Ponce, J. (2003). *Computer vision: A modern approach*. Upper Saddle River, NJ: Prentice Hall.

A good overview of spatial frequency features from a perceptual perspective:

> Torralba, A., & Oliva, A. (2003). Statistics of natural image categories. *Network: Computation in Neural Systems, 14*(3), 391–412.

4

Color

The history of the investigation of colour vision is remarkable for its acrimony.

—Gregory (1997)

The controversies that Gregory is referring to started early in the 19th century and continued into the mid-20th century. These battles are now largely over, since modern neuroscience and increasingly sophisticated psychophysics have resolved most of the issues over which there was such dispute. Still, color is significantly misunderstood by many students and practitioners of computer graphics. Ask the average person involved in computer graphics to define *color* and you will likely get one or both of two common answers: "color is RGB" or "color refers to the wavelength of light." While there is a sliver of validity in both answers, neither captures what is central to the concept of color.

Part of the confusion comes about because the term *color* is used in three different and quite distinct contexts. Sometimes the meaning is related to the spectral distribution of light, though most perceptual psychologists and color scientists avoid this usage. In vision science, the term is almost always reserved for descriptions of the perceptual response to such spectral distributions. Finally, the term can also refer to methods of encoding images for display or processing. This chapter provides an overview of key concepts associated with all these forms of "color," but it is important to note that *color science*, which involves issues associated with the perception and reproduction of color, is hugely complex and difficult to understand at even a high level.

Most humans have a pervasive sense of color when they view the world. Color-sensitive vision is widespread in other species as well, ranging from primates to insects and crustaceans (Kelber, Vorobyev, & Osorio, 2003). This suggests that color plays an important role in visual perception, though the nature of color vision varies widely between species and the evolutionary history of color sensitivity (and the rest of vision) is quite complex (Goldsmith, 1990).

This chapter starts by overviewing the physics of light as it relates to the perception of color and describing the way in which the visual system senses color-dependent information in light imaged on the retina. This is followed by a discussion of the phenomenology of color perception, which is very different than what might be expected from the nature of the spectral distributions associated with color in the physical world. The chapter concludes with coverage of how color can be represented for display purposes, and issues of significant importance to computer graphics, printing, and much of digital media.

4.1 Measuring the Spectral Distribution of Light

In 1666, Isaac Newton used prisms to show that apparently white sunlight could be decomposed into a *spectrum* of colors and that these colors could be recombined to produce light that appeared white (Newton, 1704). We now know that light energy is made up of a collection of photons, each with a particular wavelength. Light, however, is rarely characterizable by a single wavelength. Rather, in almost all circumstances relevant to vision, light consists of a sufficiently large number of photons of a sufficiently large number of different wavelengths that it can be best characterized by statistical properties of the ensemble of photons. The multiple colors seen when sunlight is passed through a prism occur because sunlight contains photons with wavelengths spanning the range detectable by the human visual system. The *spectral distribution* of light is a measure of the average energy of the light at each wavelength. For natural illumination, the spectral distribution of light reflected off of surfaces varies significantly depending on the surface material. The nature of this spectral distribution can therefore provide visual information for the nature of surfaces in the environment.

4.1.1 Visual Sensitivity to Spectral Distributions

Humans are sensitive to light with wavelengths from about 370 nm to about 730 nm (see Color Plate I). This is a very small part of the full electromagnetic spectrum, which ranges from low-frequency radio waves having a wavelength of a meter or more to high-energy gamma rays with a wavelength on the order of a picometer. The range of visible wavelengths, called the *visible spectrum*, roughly corresponds to one of the intervals in the overall electromagnetic spectrum where there is a peak in radiation penetrating the earth's atmosphere, thus providing natural illumination at terrestrial levels. Nonhuman animals with color vision are often sensitive to somewhat different wavelengths. For example, reptiles can sense radiation in the near-infrared region of the E/M spectrum, allowing them to "see" warm-blooded animals even when no external source of illumination is present. The visual sensitivity of many insects and birds extends into the near-ultraviolet.

The manner in which the human visual system measures properties of the spectral distribution of light was first systematically examined in 1801 and remained extremely controversial for 150 years. Signal processing theory tells us that we can accurately measure a spectral distribution by using a collection of photodetectors, each narrowly tuned to a small range of wavelengths and spaced in wavelength sensitivity in a manner dependent on the nature of the variability of the distribution as a function of wavelength. Higher variability requires more photodetectors, more closely spaced in wavelength, while fewer and more broadly tuned photodetectors are sufficient to measure distributions with less variability. In principle, the variability of visual spectra is (almost) arbitrary, meaning that in principle a (near) infinite number of narrowly tuned photodetectors would be required to accurately measure all such spectra. In practice, somewhere between 20 and 70 different wavelength-tuned photodetectors is sufficient to record spectral distributions for most purposes in which the actual distribution is needed (Wandell, 1995). Biological vision systems have far fewer distinct types of wavelength-tuned photodetectors, which has a profound effect on what we see as color in the world around us.

4.1.2   Trichromatic Color Vision

In the fovea, photoreceptors are densely packed. This allows for sensitive measurements of the spatial distribution of light falling on that part of the retina. A consequence of this is that distinctly different spatial distributions usually look distinctly different. (Simultaneous contrast can produce some notable exceptions.) The same is not true of color perception. Many quite different spectral distributions of light can produce a sense of any specific visual color. Correspondingly, the sense that a surface is a specific color provides little direct information about the spectral distribution of light coming from the surface. For example, a spectral distribution consisting of a combination of light at wavelengths of 610 nm and 540 nm, with appropriately chosen relative strengths, will look indistinguishable from light at the single wavelength of 575 nm. Perceptually indistinguishable colors with different spectral compositions are referred to as *metamers*. If we see the color "yellow," we have no way of knowing if it was generated by one or the other of these distributions or an infinite family of other spectral distributions. This sense of color is a purely perceptual quality, not a physical property.

In the early 1800s, Thomas Young showed that shining three colored lights on a white surface could produce an appearance indistinguishable from any pure-spectral (single wavelength) visible color, as long as the three lights were widely separated in the visual spectrum and adjusted appropriately in relative intensity. The specific nature of the lights was not critical, but the effect could not be achieved with only two lights, however chosen. From this, Young hypothesized that the human eye had only three types of spectrally tuned color receptors, corresponding to the three "principal colours" red, yellow, and blue. Somewhat later, he revised the colors to red, green, and violet. Young's ideas were expanded upon by James Clerk Maxwell and Hermann von Helmholtz, and are now known as the *Young-Helmholtz trichromatic theory*. Substantial argument followed about the number and nature of the principal colors involved in human color vision. (See Gregory, 1997, for a brief historical account).

The color matching effects demonstrated by Young, and continued by many other researchers, provided evidence that there were three degrees of freedom in how the retina senses spectral distributions. However, this does not prove that only three types of sensors are involved, and it provides little information about the specific spectral responses of the sensor types. Physiological studies ultimately determined that there in fact were just three types of retinal photoreceptors involved in color vision, collectively referred to as cones. (See also Chapter 2.) An additional type of photoreceptor in the retina, the rods, is effective in low-light situations. On their own, rods provide no information about the spectral distribution of light falling upon them.

While humans with normal color vision are *trichromats*, with three distinct classes of spectrally sensitive photoreceptors, this is not the norm with all species able to distinguish colors (Goldsmith, 1990; E. Thompson, Palacios, & Varela, 2002). Some primates and most nonprimate mammals are *dichromats*. A few species are *tetrachromats* or *pentachromats*. One species of shrimp has at least ten distinct types of spectrally sensitive photoreceptors (Cronin & Marshall, 1989).

It turns out to be extremely difficult to determine the actual spectral responses of the three different types of cones (Baylor, 1987; Schnapf, Kraft, & Baylor, 1987; Stockman, MacLeod, & Johnson, 1993). Psychophysical measurements cannot easily distinguish between nondegenerate linear transformations of response functions. Performing such tests on individuals with certain types of color blindness helps but is still subject to problems. Physiological probes of cone sensitivity require the rare situation in which an intact human retina is removed for medical reasons, and much of the knowledge of the physiology of the human retina as it relates to spectral sensitivity has been inferred from primate studies. An additional complication comes from the fact that psychophysics measures the response of the whole eye, including the optical effects of the cornea and lens, while physiological measurements do not.

While there are minor differences in the cone spectral sensitivities that have been reported in the literature, all are close to what is shown in Figure 4.1. The three curves in the figure have been independently normalized to a peak response of 1.0. The three types of cones are referred to as *S-cones*, *M-cones*, and *L-cones* to suggest a response sensitivity in the short-wavelength, medium-wavelength, and long-wavelength portions of the visible spectrum. S-cones are fairly narrowly tuned, with a peak at 440 nm. The M- and L-cones are more broadly tuned and have substantial overlap in their spectral sensitives. M-cones respond to wavelengths in the middle (greenish) region of the visible spectrum and are maximally sensitive to light with a wavelength of 530 nm. L-cones respond to somewhat longer wavelengths, covering the green and red portions of the visible spectrum, and reach peak sensitivity at 560 nm.

It should be clear from Figure 4.1 that labeling the three cone types as *red*, *green*, and *blue* is misleading, particularly for the M- and L-cones. The implications of the spatial layout of cones on the retina is also not captured by the naive view of cones as RGB sensors, coequal except for their frequency tuning. The distribution of L-, M-, and S-cones follows a ratio of roughly 10:5:1 (De Valois & De Valois, 1993). S-cones are likely completely absent from the central fovea. Wandell (1995) speculates that the coarse spacing of S-cones is related to blurring of short wavelengths due to chromatic abberations in the eye and the resulting decrease in need for high-resolution spatial sensing of these frequencies. Correspondingly, fine spatial detail is sensed using only the M- and L-cones.

Figure 4.2 shows the spectral-sensitivity tuning of rod cells in the retina. The rods are more broadly tuned than any individual cone type, though with a shift toward blue relative to the whole of the visual spectrum. While rod response varies as a function of the spectral distribution of the light incident upon the rod, there is only one type of rod, and so there is no rod-only mechanism for distinguishing between changes in spectral distribution and changes in overall intensity of light. Likewise, the outputs from a single cone type are insufficient to determine properties of the spectral distribution of light falling on the retina, since intensity and spectral sensitivity are confounded. Only by considering ratios between the outputs of two or more of the S-, M-, and L-cone types is it possible to factor out spectral effects from intensity.

Figures 4.1 and 4.2 indicate the responses of the three cone types and the response of rods to light of a particular spectral wavelength. Cone and rod spectral responses are well modeled as linear systems. As a result, the response R of a particular class of retinal photoreceptors with a sensitivity

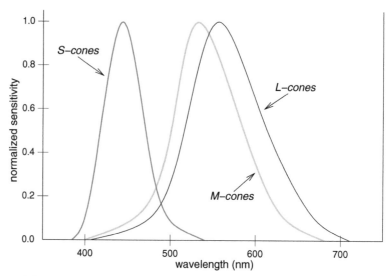

Figure 4.1

Approximate spectral sensitivity of the *short, medium,* and *long* cones. Values are normalized to the peak response of each cone type, so comparisons of the absolute responses for different types is not shown.

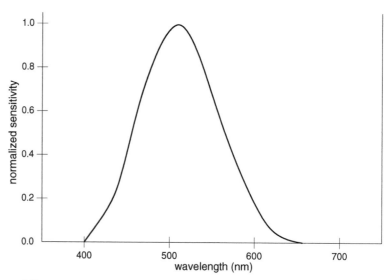

Figure 4.2

Approximate spectral sensitivity of the rods in the human retina. Values are normalized relative to peak response.

response $S(\omega)$ to a spectral distribution $D(\omega)$ is given by

$$R = \int_\lambda S(\lambda) \cdot D(\lambda) \, d\lambda \, . \tag{4.1}$$

The linearity of the spectral responses of cones also explains the phenomenon of being able to construct most visible colors by combining three lights of fixed spectral distribution but adjustable intensity, and the related concept of metamers. Let $T(\omega)$ be the spectral distribution of a target light to be matched by three *primary* lights having spectral distributions $P_1(\omega)$, $P_2(\omega)$, and $P_3(\omega)$. Let $R_{T,\text{type}}$ be the total response of a particular class of cones (type = S, M, or L) to the target illumination distribution, and $R_{Pn,\text{type}}$ be the total response of a particular cone type to distributions associated with the three primaries ($Pn = P_1$, P_2, or P_3). Let w_1, w_2, and w_3 be relative weightings of the three primaries, obtained by adjusting their brightness in proportion to the weights.

For photopic viewing conditions, only the cones provide information relevant to the apparent color of incident light. As a result, the target will appear to be the same color as the weighted combination of primary lights if

$$\begin{aligned}
R_{T,\text{S}} &= w_1 \cdot R_{P_1,\text{S}} + w_2 \cdot R_{P_2,\text{S}} + w_3 \cdot R_{P_3,\text{S}} \, , \\
R_{T,\text{M}} &= w_1 \cdot R_{P_1,\text{M}} + w_2 \cdot R_{P_2,\text{M}} + w_3 \cdot R_{P_3,\text{M}} \, , \\
R_{T,\text{L}} &= w_1 \cdot R_{P_1,\text{L}} + w_2 \cdot R_{P_2,\text{L}} + w_3 \cdot R_{P_3,\text{L}} \, .
\end{aligned} \tag{4.2}$$

This linear system of equations can be expressed in matrix form:

$$\begin{bmatrix} R_{T,\text{S}} \\ R_{T,\text{L}} \\ R_{T,\text{M}} \end{bmatrix} = \begin{bmatrix} R_{P_1,\text{S}} & R_{P_2,\text{S}} & R_{P_3,\text{S}} \\ R_{P_1,\text{M}} & R_{P_2,\text{M}} & R_{P_3,\text{M}} \\ R_{P_1,\text{L}} & R_{P_2,\text{L}} & R_{P_3,\text{L}} \end{bmatrix} \begin{bmatrix} w_1 \\ w_2 \\ w_3 \end{bmatrix} \, . \tag{4.3}$$

This leads directly to a solution for the weighting coefficients of the three primary lights:

$$\begin{bmatrix} w_1 \\ w_2 \\ w_3 \end{bmatrix} = \begin{bmatrix} R_{P_1,\text{S}} & R_{P_2,\text{S}} & R_{P_3,\text{S}} \\ R_{P_1,\text{M}} & R_{P_2,\text{M}} & R_{P_3,\text{M}} \\ R_{P_1,\text{L}} & R_{P_2,\text{L}} & R_{P_3,\text{L}} \end{bmatrix}^{-1} \begin{bmatrix} R_{T,\text{S}} \\ R_{T,\text{L}} \\ R_{T,\text{M}} \end{bmatrix} \, . \tag{4.4}$$

In practice, this inverse will usually exist when $P_1(\omega)$, $P_2(\omega)$, and $P_3(\omega)$ are well separated from one another.

Figure 4.3 illustrates this effect. Two spectra are shown. One corresponds to light reflected off of butter. The other spectral distribution is what would be required to reproduce the color of the butter using a LCD monitor with fluorescent backlight. (The exact spectral distribution of light reflected by butter will depend on the spectral distribution of the illuminating light, while the matching LCD monitor spectral distribution

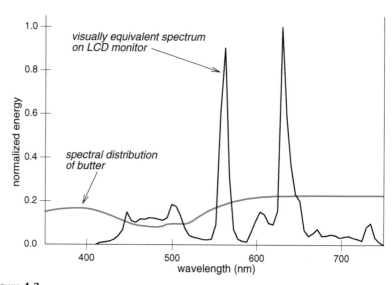

Figure 4.3

The spectral distribution of daylight reflected off of butter and a visually equivalent spectral distibution produced on an LCD monitor

will depend both on this and on the specifics of the monitor.) These two very different spectra produce the same perceived color, since they result in the same S-, M-, and L-cone responses.

The lack of sensitivity of rods to red light can be used to speed dark adaptation in situations where it may be necessary to move rapidly between photopic/mesopic and scotopic conditions. An individual in a room lit only with red light of the appropriate brightness can see with relatively high acuity, yet will be able to quickly switch to lower light levels since the rods will not have been saturated by the bright light and so won't require the normal ten minutes or so to recover sensitivity (see Chapter 2).

Another wavelength-related consequence of the spectral sensitivity of rods occurs when red and blue surfaces are viewed under varying light levels in or near the mesopic range. As light levels decrease and the rods contribute increasingly to the perception of brightness, the red surface can switch from seeming brighter than the blue to appearing darker than the blue, an effect known as the *Purkinje shift* (Minnaert, 1954).

4.2   The Perception of Color

The existence of three classes of spectrally tuned photoreceptors in the human eye and the tuning curves of those receptors (Figure 4.1) explains the range of wavelengths that can be sensed, the ability to discriminate between different spectral distributions, and the limitations of that discrimination ability as described in the trichromatic theory of color vision. The nature of the retinal photoreceptors tells us almost nothing, however, about the phenomenology of color vision. In particular, we have no direct awareness of the responses of the S-, M-, and L-cones. Two classes of reencodings of the retinal photoreceptor signals have been proposed to better explain the perception of uniform patterns of colored light. Opponent process models account for both neural processing in the retina and certain phenomenological effects associated with different colors. Descriptions of colors in terms of hue, value, and chroma or similar terms attempt to account for the separate dimensions by which colors are naturally characterized. Critical aspects of color perception can only be understood by considering the response of the visual system to complex spatial patterns with varying brightness and spectral distributions, as is the norm in the real world. Most important among these is color constancy, which allows the visual system to estimate reflectance properties of surfaces under varying illumination conditions.

4.2.1   Opponent Process Model of Color Vision

One of the strongest arguments against the Young-Helmholtz trichromatic theory was Hering's (1874/1964) observations about the opponent nature of color perception. Some color combinations provoke a sense of two colors mixed together: orange has a red-yellow appearance, while cyan has a blue-green appearance. Other color mixtures are not easily seen as color combinations. No color looks red-green or blue-yellow. Hering hypothesized that the visual system encoded color not in terms of the three primaries—red, green, and blue—but instead in terms of three opponent values: red-green, blue-yellow, and black-white. Each of these values represented relative amounts of the two endpoints in the original stimuli.

Additional evidence for the opponent process model of color perception came from afterimage effects. Staring at a patch of red for 30–60 seconds and then looking at a white surface produces a green afterimage, while staring at a green patch and then looking at a white surface produces a red afterimage. Staring at a blue patch leads to a yellow afterimage; staring at a yellow patch leads to a blue afterimage. Staring at black or white surfaces also produces a complementary after-image, but the subjective sensation is a bit different than for colors. Yet more evidence for the presence of an opponent color encoding in the human visual system comes from certain types of color blindness.

The conflict between trichromatic and opponent process models for how spectral distributions are sensed in the human visual system was finally resolved by *multi-stage* models of color perception (De Valois & De Valois,

1993; Hurvich & Jameson, 1957). Substantial physiological evidence is now available that the outputs of S-, M-, and L-cones are recombined into an opponent encoding rather like the red/green, blue/yellow, white/black model of Hering. Much of this is done in the retina itself, based on sums and differences of various combinations of cone outputs. In addition to explaining a number of phenomenological effects involving color perception, this reencoding of the color information has the effect of explicitly representing brightness independently of color. Many aspects of visual perception, particularly those involving stereo and motion, depend primarily on this brightness signal. Finally, multi-stage processing of the color signals might serve to decorrelate the outputs of the M- and L-cones, which are quite similar to one another due to the broad overlap of the M- and L- response curves (Wandell, 1995). Such a decorrelation would lead to a much more efficient transmission of information along the optic nerve.

4.2.2   Hue, Value, and Chroma

The conscious awareness of a color is often described by three separate and largely independent properties. One of these characterizes the color relative to the appearance of the color spectrum (Color Plate I), ranging from dark violet to dark red. This corresponds most closely to the informal sense of the word *color*. A second characterizes the color in terms of its apparent brightness. The third characterizes the color in terms of its saturation, referring to the purity or vividness of the color. Colors can range from totally unsaturated gray to partially saturated pastels to fully saturated "pure" colors.

Munsell (1905) formalized these concepts, using the terms *hue, value,* and *chroma*:

> Hue is the quality by which we distinguish one color from another, as a red from a yellow, a green, a blue, or a purple.... Value is the quality by which we distinguish a light color from a dark one.... Chroma is the quality by which we distinguish a strong color from a weak one.

Refinements of the Munsell system resulted in a characterization of colors as points in a cylindrical coordinate system, as shown in Color Plate II. In contrast to spectral values represented in a linear wavelength (or frequency) scale, the Munsell system specifies hue in terms of an angular coordinate system. Five principal colors (red, yellow, green, blue, and purple) and five intermediate colors (yellow-red, green-yellow, blue-green, purple-blue, and red-purple) were laid out over this angular range. This reflects the fact that the extremes of the visible spectrum are actually similar in appearance, something that would not be predicted if color perception were thought of only in terms of the responses of the S-, M-, and L-cones. (See Color Plate III, where for most people the red patch will seem closer in color to the violet patch than to the green patch, even though red and violet are at near opposite ends of the visible spectrum.) Opponent process characterizations of color naturally match the circular nature of hue representations, with opponent colors located opposite one another. Chroma is specified as a radial distance out from the axis of the cylinder, with the axis itself corresponding to a shade of gray. Finally, value varies along the axis of the cylinder and ranged from black to white. Munsell assigned a numeric scale to each of these dimensions, so that a specific color could be described in terms of three such numbers. Along each dimension, an attempt was made to make the representation perceptually uniform, meaning that the magnitude of the numeric difference between the characterizations of two colors should be an indication of how dissimilar they looked in that property.

4.2.3   Color Constancy

There is a linear relationship between the intensity of light L reaching the eye from a particular surface point in the world, the intensity of light I illuminating that surface point, and the reflectivity R of the surface at the point being observed:

$$L = \alpha I \cdot R \,, \tag{4.5}$$

where α is dependent on the relationship between the surface geometry, the pattern of incident illumination, and the viewing direction. While the eye is only able to directly measure L, human vision is much better at estimating R than L. To see this, view Figure 4.4 in bright direct light. Use your hand to shadow one of the patterns, leaving the other directly illuminated. While the light reflected off of the two patterns will be significantly different, the apparent brightness of the two center squares will seem nearly the same. This phenomenon is referred to as *lightness constancy*, and is further discussed in Chapter 10.

A similar conflation of illumination and reflectance properties occurs with color. In most circumstances, the spectral distribution of light reaching the eye is the product of the spectral distribution of the illumination and the spectral properties of surface reflection associated with the direction of incident illumination and viewing direction. As with brightness, however, we mostly see the effects of the surface, not of the illumination. For an example of this *color constancy*, look at a piece of white paper under a variety of illumination sources: outdoors at various times of day, under both direct sunlight and in the shade, and indoors, under both incandescent and fluorescent artificial lighting. The paper will look "white" in all cases, even though there will be substantial variations in the spectral

Figure 4.4

Lightness constancy. While viewing the figures in bright direct light, shadow one of the patterns with your hand and notice that the apparent brightness of the two center squares remains nearly the same.

distribution sensed by the eye, due to the variations in spectral distribution of the light sources. While color constancy is not perfect, the color of viewed surfaces will look nearly the same across a broad range of naturally occurring illuminations.

Figure 4.5 illustrates the problem that must be solved by the visual system in order to achieve color constancy. On the left, solar illumination with a particular spectral distribution (top) reflects off of a surface with reflectivity characterized by a different spectral distribution (bottom), resulting in a pattern of light images on the retina with a spectral distribution (middle) that is a weighted product of the solar and surface distributions. On the right is the same situation, except now indoor incandescent lighting is involved, with a very different spectral distribution than solar illumination. Though the surface-reflection properties are the same, the spectral distribution of light reaching the eye is quite different. Color constancy requires estimation of the spectral properties of the surface (or at least a tri-stimulus characterization of those properties), given the outputs of the L-, M-, and S-cones as they respond to the incident light.

One of the most important processes in human color constancy is adaptation. There are several different types of adaptation. These range from simple local photoreceptor adaptation, which leads to color afterimages with prolonged viewing, to more complex gain control processes such as von Kries adaptation, which adjusts the response of the whole visual field. Put simply, these processes adjust the visual system's white balance to

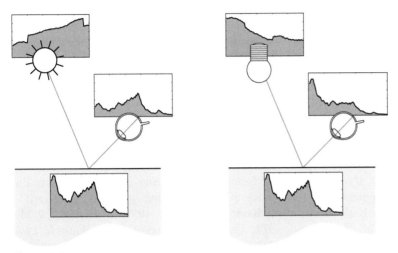

Figure 4.5
Color constancy requires estimation of the spectral properties of a reflective surface, given a spectral distribution of light seen by the eye that is also affected by the spectral properties of the illumination.

reduce the effects of the illuminant spectrum, much like automatic white balancing in a camera.

Lightness and color constancy are compelling examples of the fact that the visual system does not operate as a photometer, with perception based directly on accurate, quantitative measurements of incident light. Rather, the visual system makes sophisticated inferences about the nature of the world under view, with little direct correlation between these percepts and the low-level stimuli from which they are generated. In the case of color, E. H. Land (1959a) asserts: "In images neither the wave-length of the stimulus nor the energy at each wave-length determines the color." E. H. Land and others (e.g., D. B. Judd, 1940; Kraft & Brainard, 1999) argue that the apparent color of a visible location in the environment depends in critical ways on the surrounding visual context, and cannot be determined based only on the spectral distribution of light imaged from the location itself.

E. H. Land (1959a, 1959b, 1959c) describes an effect that is both unexpected and compelling in its demonstration of the difference between the appearance of a single spectral distribution seen in isolation and the appearance of the same spectral distribution seen within the spatial context of other spectral distributions. E. H. Land constructed a camera that could produce two black-and-white photographic transparencies of the same scene, one shot through a green filter and the other shot through a red filter. If the two transparencies were then projected with appropriate registration onto a white surface, with the transparency originally taken through the red filter projected through a red filter but the transparency originally taken through the green filter projected with no added color, a scene with nearly the full range of colors appears. Take away the spatial modulation provided by the two black-and-white transparencies, and the red and white lights mix to form a uniform pink. The trichromatic theory of color vision not withstanding, many naturally appearing color images can be produced with only two primary colors!

Substantial theoretical and empirical work has been directed at attempting to understand the mechanisms underlying lightness and color constancy, though we are far from a complete and general understanding of the phenomenon. (For a sampling of existing work, see Cataliotti & Gilchrist, 1995; Horn, 1974; Kraft & Brainard, 1999; E. H. Land & McCann, 1971; E. H. Land, 1977; Maloney & Wandell, 1986; Wallach, 1948; Webster & Mollon, 1995; plus Section 3.3 in Palmer, 1999.) Almost all of these approaches either directly or indirectly presume that the spatial variability of illumination over most of the image is small compared with the spatial variability of reflectance. This leads to a presumption that sharp changes in brightness or color are likely due to sharp changes in reflectance, and furthermore that the ratio of brightnesses across the change is related to the ratio of reflectances. Some models go further by proposing mechanisms by which spatial discontinuities in brightness might be segregated based on whether they are due to changes in illumination, reflectance, or geometry. Brightness and color adaptation also likely play a role. The restricted nature of naturally occurring illumination and reflectances might also be exploited in a variety of ways.

4.2.4 Categorical Perception of Colors

None of the aspects of color perception discussed above account for the fact that we see a small number of distinct colors when looking at a continuous spectrum of visible light (Color Plate I) or in a naturally occurring rainbow. For most people, the visible spectrum appears to be divided into four to six distinct colors: red, yellow, green, and blue, plus perhaps light blue and purple. Considering nonmonochromatic colors as well, which vary more in saturation than the pure spectral colors, there are only eleven basic color terms commonly used in English: *red, green, blue, yellow, black, white, gray, orange, purple, brown,* and *pink*, though there is a much larger set of terms used to describe variations of these colors. The partitioning of the intrinsically continuous space of spectral distributions into a relatively small set of perceptual categories associated with well-defined linguistic terms seems to be a basic property of perception, not just a cultural artifact (Berlin & Kay, 1969; Uchikawa & Boyntona, 1987), though aspects of language and learning may be involved (Özgen & Davies, 2002). People vary in their ability to discriminate spectral colors with similar hues as a function of wavelength (W. D. Wright & Pitt, 1934), and this might offer a partial explanation of the banding seen when viewing the visible spectrum. Gregory (1997) argues that peaks in hue sensitivity occur in those portions of the visible spectrum where there are substantial slope differences in the spectral responses L-, M-, and S-cones, resulting in large differences in the relative outputs of the L-, M-, and S-cones as a function of small spectral variations.

4.3   Issues Specific to Computer Graphics

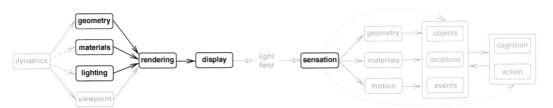

Constructing an image display that could accurately generate the full range of naturally occurring spectral distributions over the range of wavelengths covering the visible spectrum would be extremely difficult. Making a display in which these spectral distributions varied over the spatial extent of an image would be even more challenging. Fortunately, the low dimensionality of human color discrimination allows for a much simpler solution to the problem of displaying correctly appearing colors. The trichromatic nature of human vision and the phenomenon of metamers mean that naturally appearing colors can be produced by combining three *primary colors*, appropriately weighted in intensity.[1] These primaries need not correspond to the spectral sensitivity curves of the S-, M-, and L-cones, nor need they be a single spectral frequency, but they do need to be distinct from each other and collectively spread out over the visible spectrum.

Almost all color monitors and similar image displays use three primary colors, consisting of a distinct red, a distinct green, and a distinct blue. This leads to the ubiquitous *red-green-blue* (*RGB*) description of color. There are at least three significant problems with the RGB color representation. The first is that different display devices have different spectral distributions for their red, green, and blue primaries. The physics associated with generating primary colors varies substantially between LCD, DLP, plasma, LED, CRT, OLED, and other technologies. As a result, the

---

[1]It is a good thing that there is little practical need for image displays intended to be viewed by a mantis shrimp (Cronin & Marshall, 1989).

spectral distribution of a primary in one technology may be quite different from the spectral distribution in another primary, even if both primaries have the same name (red, green, or blue). Thus, standardization is required in defining the meaning of an RGB encoding of color, along with a way of converting this specification to the appropriate primary weightings for a specific display device. The second problem involves print media, where a spectral distribution is produced by subtracting part of the incident illumination using inks, rather than adding together different-colored primaries. The primaries most often used to specify color in printing are quite different from the RGB representation. Finally, the RGB encoding is a poor choice for evaluating many of the perceptual phenomena described earlier in this chapter.

4.3.1   Standardizing the Representation of Color

Since 1913, the Commission Internationale de l'Eclairage (CIE) has been the dominant international standards organization responsible for formalizing specifications for colorimetry. In 1924, the CIE published data defining a *photopic luminous efficiency function*, $V(\lambda)$, which specified perceived brightness as a function of wavelength. While this 1924 luminosity function is deficient in a number of ways (and the CIE issued a revised standard $V_M(\lambda)$ in 1988), the 1924 standard is the one employed in the most common color specification in use today. In 1951, the CIE added a *scotopic luminous efficiency function*, $V'(\lambda)$, specifying perceived brightness as a function of wavelength under conditions in which only the retinal rods are active. Figure 4.6 shows plots of both $V(\lambda)$ and $V'(\lambda)$. Note that the plots (and the standards themselves) are normalized, and so the magnitudes of the two curves cannot be directly compared. Qualitative comparisons are possible, however, and the figure clearly shows the decreased sensitivity to longer wavelengths of scotopic vision compared to photopic vision.

The CIE specifies colors in terms of *color spaces*, each with its own set of *color primaries*. The color primaries are described in terms of spectral sensitivity distributions, as in Equation (4.1). They can be thought of as the P_n's in Equations (4.2)–(4.4), though they don't need to correspond to physically achievable spectral distributions. Color spaces are vector spaces, with as many dimensions as color primaries. An arbitrary spectral distribution is mapped onto a point in this space defined by values of Equation (4.1) computed for each axis. Thus, each axis of the color space indicates the amount (brightness) of the corresponding primary that needs to be combined to generate a color perceptually indistinguishable from the original color.

The CIE color spaces were derived from data obtained using *color matching experiments*. These involved projecting a set of target lights and

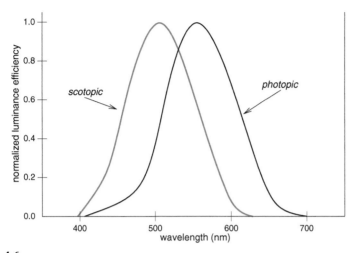

Figure 4.6

CIE normalized luminance response curves for scotopic (low light) and photopic (normal light) viewing.

the combination of three primary lights side by side onto a white screen. Observers adjusted the brightness of the primary lights until the combination appeared the same as the target. This was done for target lights spanning the range of the visible spectrum. Data from multiple observers were combined into a characterization of a *standard observer*. Finally linear transformation techniques similar to that shown in Equations (4.2)–(4.4) were used to remap the empirically derived sensitivity curves onto an alternate set of primary spectral sensitivities, as required by the objectives of the particular standard. (See Wyszecki & Stiles, 1982, for more on the process.)

The CIE RGB color space, published in 1931, combined color matching data from two different sets of primaries to create sensitivity curves for primaries with narrow band spectra at 435.8 nm (blue), 546.1 nm (green), and 700 nm (red). The corresponding response curves $\bar{b}(\lambda)$, $\bar{g}(\lambda)$, and $\bar{r}(\lambda)$ are shown in Figure 4.7. The negative lobe in the $\bar{r}(\lambda)$ function means that the *color gamut* (the range of displayable colors) would be significantly limited in any actual display that used these primaries, since for a portion of the spectral range, "negative light" would be required. Gamut limitations would also occur in any numeric RGB encoding based on these primaries, unless negative values were supported. (In the empirical color matching experiments, the linearity of color sensitivity allows negative light to be simulated by adding positive light with the same spectral distribution to the target.)

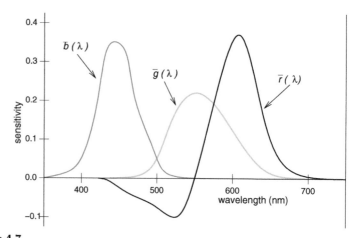

Figure 4.7
Spectral sensitivity for the CIE $\bar{b}(\lambda)$, $\bar{g}(\lambda)$, and $\bar{r}(\lambda)$ primaries. (Note that this is *not* the spectral distribution of the primaries themselves!)

The CIE followed up its specification of the RGB color space with the definition of a new color space it called XYZ. The new space was specified such that one of the dimensions, Y, corresponded to the photopic luminous efficiency function $V(\lambda)$, and that Y plus the other two dimensions X and Z

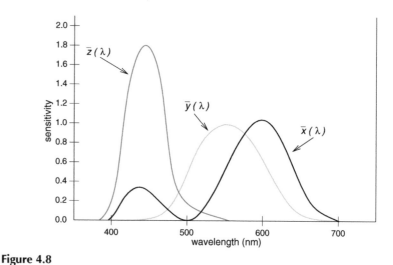

Figure 4.8
Spectral sensitivity of the CIE $\bar{x}(\lambda)$, $\bar{y}(\lambda)$, and $\bar{z}(\lambda)$ primaries. (As with Figure 4.7, this is *not* the spectral distribution of the primaries.)

would be positively valued for the full range of spectral colors. The three resulting sensitivity curves, $\bar{x}(\lambda)$ for X, $\bar{y}(\lambda)$ for Y, and $\bar{z}(\lambda)$ for Z, are shown in Figure 4.8. It is important to emphasize that these sensitivity curves are used to specify perceptual colors and are not intended to be the actual primaries used in an image display. (More on this can be found in Section 4.3.3.)

The color matching experiments on which the 1931 CIE XYZ specification was based involved test and matching patterns that together fell within a 2° field of view (about the angle subtended by a person's thumb joint, held at arm's length). A supplemental standard was published by the CIE in 1964, based on color matching data over a 10° field of view. While the CIE recommends use of the 1964 color matching functions for patterns larger than 4° of visual angle, it is the 1931 CIE XYZ standard that is in more common usage.

For many purposes, values in the CIE XYZ color space are restated in an xyY formalism, where

$$x = \frac{X}{X+Y+Z} \; , \quad y = \frac{Y}{X+Y+Z} \; , \quad z = \frac{Y}{X+Y+Z} = 1 - x - y \; . \quad (4.6)$$

CIE xyY uses the two normalized chromaticity values x and y and the luminance value Y which specifies absolute brightness. It is equivalent in representational power to the CIE XYZ space, since

$$X = \frac{Y}{y}x \; , \quad Z = \frac{Y}{y}(1 - x - y) \; . \quad (4.7)$$

CIE xyY has the advantage of decoupling chromaticity from brightness, with xy representing apparent color independent of absolute brightness. Color Plate IV shows a plot of x and y in the CIE xyY color space, with the pure spectral colors appearing along the outer curved boundary.

4.3.2 Subtractive Color Representations

So far, the descriptions of the trichromatic theory of color perception, color matching, and the CIE color spaces have all presumed that a wide range of perceptible colors can be created by adding together a small set of primary colors, appropriately modulated in brightness. This is exactly what is done in video monitors and projectors. The physics of light is quite different for print media and paintings. In these cases, portions of the ambient illumination are reflected off the surface containing the image, while the remainder of the incident light is absorbed. The balance between reflected and absorbed light is wavelength dependent. Since reflective surfaces are taking away a portion of the light incident upon them, rather than generating light of their own, the effect is often referred to as *subtractive color*.

The most common ink combination used in color printing is cyan, magenta, yellow, and black. As a result, image values intended for printing are typically represented using a four-dimensional CMYK color space, with each dimension representing the amount of one of the ink colors. As with additive color displays such as monitors, the spectral profile of inks even with the same name is highly variable, and so device-dependent processing must be done for specific printers (see Section 4.3.3). The gamut of colors perceptually achievable with CMYK inks is different than what is achievable with monitors and other additive color displays. Accurate transformations of values between well-specified RGB and CMYK color spaces are straightforward for values within the gamut of both, but a workflow that mixes the two can result in restrictions on the range of colors ultimately produced. In addition, using computer displays to do photo editing of images ultimately intended for print is complicated by the difficulty of displaying colors on a monitor that look the same as they will on the printed page.

4.3.3   Color Management

Until fairly recently, the RGB encodings of image values likely to be encountered by those working in computer graphics and related fields rarely conformed to explicit standards. The numeric values in an encoding were often device-specific, either resulting from a particular image-acquisition device or tailored to a particular display device. Values might or might not have been gamma encoded. If gamma compression was done, it might have been an artifact of the image acquisition device or done by an explicit transform, but in either case there was rarely an indication in the file encoding of the exponent used. The result was that there was much ambiguity in what was actually meant by an RGB pixel value.

The CIE RGB color space standard provides a precise mechanism for encoding perceptually relevant information about spectral distributions, at least within the limitations of the color matching experiments used to create the relevant sensitivity profiles, but it is ineffective as an image representation involving limited precision pixels because of its uneven ability to cover the gamut of a conventional image display. CIE XYZ also has a gamut problem, in that much of the representable color space is not physically realizable, resulting in inefficient use of precision in pixel encodings. (CIE XYZ encoding is used for some limited purposes, including the API for the LogLuv high dynamic range image file format (Larson, 1998)). Furthermore, none of the CIE specifications deal with gamma compression.

Modern *color management systems* remove the ambiguity in pixel encoding while also standardizing the appearance of displayed images across different display devices. There are three components to a color management system. A *color profile* specifies the properties of a pixel representation in terms of the spectral sensitivity associated with each primary, any nonlinear transformations between intensity and encoded value that might be present, and several other factors. The color profile is attached as meta data to images stored in files. A device-dependent *input transform* takes input acquisition values and converts them to the standard representation specified in a predetermined color profile. A device-dependent *output transform* converts values in an image representation to the values needed by the output device in order to achieve the desired effect indicated in the color profile.

The International Color Consortium (ICC) has developed the color profile system in most common use today. ICC profiles provide for a gamma expansion transformation, mapping encoded pixel values into a linear space. The mapping can be described in a piecewise fashion over the range of encoded values to avoid the problems that occur when a simple power function is applied to numerically small values. The profile also provides a linear transformation matrix that can convert linearized pixel values to the CIE XYZ color space. As a result, the information in a color profile is sufficient to convert pixel values to and from a precisely and unambiguously defined standard. A color management system then must use properties of input and output devices to transform input values to conform to a chosen profile and transform values with an associated profile into whatever is needed by an output device. Note that while the color properties of the primaries are specified relative to the CIE XYZ color space, the transformation between device and represented values can be done in one step, rather than first transforming to XYZ space and then transforming to the target space.

To simplify color management, most consumer digital imaging is now done using a single color profile, called the *sRGB* standard. Whatever their internal workings, scanners and cameras output image files with values conforming to the sRGB standard. Likewise, display devices operate as intended when fed values conforming to sRGB, regardless of what is done internal to the device. sRGB is the preferred standard for images on the World Wide Web, since many web browsers ignore color profile information even if available. One problem with the sRGB profile is that it has a relatively limited gamut. Professional digital imaging often uses the Adobe RGB profile, or one of several other wide gamut profiles. These provide the ability to represent a wider range of colors, which is particularly important when a single representation is being used for both image displays and print media.

4.3.4   Color Management and Rendering

Color management plays a critical role in computer graphics rendering and other digital image generation systems. Any image pipeline using RGB pixel values should be constructed with a clear understanding of what the R, G, and B actually mean. Images input into such a system should use color management to make sure that values used internally conform to the desired standard. Images output by such a system should have attached color profiles making clear how the R, G, and B values are to be interpreted. The most straightforward approach is to use the same interpretation of primaries throughout the image generation workflow process. If the chosen specification is sRGB, however, consideration needs to be given to whether or not the limited gamut will cause problems. A few systems emphasizing the generation of photometrically accurate imagery avoid this problem by using the CIE XYZ representation directly.

The nonlinear mapping from intensity to encoded values used in limited precision image representations (gamma encoding) is a particular concern for rendering. Many computer graphics and image processing operations associated with generating and manipulating image values assume that the values are linear in intensity. Almost no images encoded with 8-bits per color actually are linear in intensity. Thus, using such images as texture maps without first linearizing their values will lead to unintended consequences. Unfortunately, this introduces a new problem. The primary reason for gamma encoding in the first place is to better utilize the available precision in low-bit-count representations. Linearizing the values means that effective precision is reduced. The solution is wider pixel representations in the rendering pipeline, but this is not always practical. Correct use of color management is becoming common in the games and film industries, and software rendering is now often done with 16 bits/color, which largely eliminates artifacts due to limited precisions.

4.3.5 Perceptual Color Representations

Color matching experiments are sufficient to determine when two spectral distributions will appear to be the same color when viewed under identical conditions, but they are not sufficient to determine what that color will look like. While the CIE XYZ color space was derived from color matching results, and values in the CIE XYZ color space and the various color managed RGB spaces derived from it do provide some intuitive sense of the color represented (see Color Plate IV), they don't provide a formal specification of the appearance of the color. Two approaches have been taken to designing alternative color spaces that are more useful for determining the appearance of colors. One approach emphasizes quantifying perceptual differences between different colors; the other remaps color specification into a representation with separate indications of brightness, hue, and saturation.

The XYZ and RGB color spaces are vector spaces, with well-defined Euclidean distances,

$$D_{i,j} = \sqrt{(C_{1,i} - C_{1,j})^2 + (C_{2,i} - C_{2,j})^2 + (C_{3,i} - C_{3,j})^2} \,, \qquad (4.8)$$

where $D_{i,j}$ is the distance in the color space between colors i and j, $C_{k,i}$ is the color space value of color i along dimension k of the color space, and $C_{k,j}$ is the color space value of color j along dimension k of the space. However, these distances do not correspond closely to perceived differences in color appearance. In response, the CIE created two new color spaces, both derived from the XYZ color space, along with an indication of what XYZ value is seen as "white." The CIE L*a*b* and CIE L*u*v* spaces are different in how they are computed from CIE XYZ values, but both attempt to make the color space *perceptually uniform*. In such color spaces, distance as defined in Equation (4.8) correlates with perceived difference in color, at least for colors that are fairly similar to one another. Reinhard, Khan, Akyüz, and Johnson (2008) provide specifications for the CIE L*a*b* and L*u*v* spaces, along with a number of other efforts at creating perceptually uniform color spaces.

Choosing between the CIE L*a*b* and CIE L*u*v* color spaces is largely a matter of practice, with CIE L*a*b* used more for video displays and CIE L*u*v* used more in printing and materials (Reinhard et al., 2008). Usage of perceptually uniform color spaces in computer graphics is relatively rare. CIE L*u*v* has been used in a radiosity algorithm (S. Gibson & Hubbold, 1997) and is the internal representation used in the TIFF LogLuv file format (Larson, 1998). CIE L*a*b* has been used in an algorithm for converting color images to grayscale in a way that preserves significant color boundaries (A. A. Gooch, Olsen, Tumblin, & Gooch, 2005).

Perceptually uniform color spaces still do not necessarily provide an intuitive sense of how a color appears. One way to get closer to a representation conforming to our conscious awareness of the nature of color is to use the Munsell hue, value, chroma representation (Section 4.2.2). Newhall, Nickerson, and Judd (1943) provide a tabular mapping between the Munsell encoding and CIE xyY, assuming that the surfaces described in the Munsell system are viewed under a particular illumination. (These values are reprinted in Wyszecki & Stiles, 1982.) A variety of transformations from RGB encodings to encodings of hue, saturation, and brightness have been suggested (Reinhard et al., 2008; Smith, 1978). All of these share common problems, in that they don't have a clear perceptual basis and are not well defined due to their lack of a precisely defined RGB basis. They have been little used in computer graphics, but are often used in color selection applications because they provide a more in-

tuitive way to describe and manipulate colors than does an RGB encoding
(Ware, 2000).

4.4   Suggestions for Further Reading

An overview of color perception is part of any text covering vision. Two good
sources for a more comprehensive description of color perception:

> Wandell, B. A. (1995). *Foundations of vision.* Sunderland, MA: Sinauer.

> Palmer, S. E. (1999). *Vision science—photons to phenomenology.* Cam-
> bridge, MA: MIT Press.

For reprints of many of the classic papers in color perception:

> Byrne, A., & Hilbert, D. R. (Eds.). (1997). *Readings on Color: Vol. 2. The
> science of color.* Cambridge, MA: MIT Press.

Two good references on color science:

> Wyszecki, G., & Stiles, W. S. (1982). *Color science: Concepts and methods,
> quantitative data and formulae* (2nd ed.). New York: John Wiley & Sons.

> Fairchild, M. D. (2005). *Color appearance models* (2nd ed.). Hoboken, NJ:
> Wiley.

Coverage of color from an engineering and applications perspective:

> Reinhard, E., Khan, E. A., Akyüz, A. O., & Johnson, G. M. (2008). *Color
> imaging: Fundamentals and applications.* Wellesley, MA: A K Peters.

> Stone, M. C. (2003). *A field guide to digital color.* Natick, MA: A K Peters.

5

2D Motion

Detection of movement is essential for survival of all but the very simplest creatures. Moving objects are likely to be dangerous prey, or potential food, or a mate. They generally demand action of some kind, while stationary objects may be ignored with safety.

—Gregory (1997)

When reading about visual perception and looking at static figures on a printed page, it is easy to forget that motion is ubiquitous in our visual experience. The patterns of light that fall on the retina are constantly changing due to eye and body motion and the movement of objects in the world. These changing patterns represent a rich source of information about the world, and so it is not surprising that visual motion is a dominant perceptual cue. Visual motion is computationally informative, providing substantial amounts of information about the external environment and usually providing this information with less ambiguity than other cues. It is perceptually salient, often predominating over other sources of visual information, and a key property in controlling attention. It is neurologically pervasive, with a large portion of cells in the mammalian visual cortex sensitive to motion.

Visual motion arises from relative movement between the eye and distinctive visible structures in the environment. This movement can come about because of eye, head, or body motion; movement through the environment; or movement of objects in the environment. In common with much of the rest of vision, motion perception involves the extraction of information from the projection of light coming from the environment and the use of this information to infer properties of the environment and the relationship between the viewer and that environment. This chapter covers how the visual system processes the changing two-dimensional patterns of light that result from image projection over time. A subsequent chapter covers how properties of visual motion can lead to descriptions of the external environment and of movement relative to that environment and entities within it.

5.1   Sensing Visual Motion

Relative motion between the eye and visible surfaces in the three-dimensional environment produces changes in the associated two-dimensional retinal image. The detectability of motion in a particular pattern of light falling on the retina is a complex function of speed, direction, pattern size, and contrast. The issue is further complicated because simultaneous contrast effects occur for motion perception in a manner similar to that observed in brightness perception, with the apparent two-dimensional motion of a region affected by contrasting optic flow in surrounding regions. In the extreme case of a single small pattern moving against a contrasting, homogenous background, perceivable motion requires a rate of motion corresponding to $0.2°$–$0.3°$/second of visual angle (Palmer, 1999). Motion of the same pattern moving against a textured pattern is detectable at about a tenth of this speed. Spatial and temporal changes interact, with motion affecting the the detectability of visual patterns as a function of spatial frequency (D. H. Kelly, 1979; Gepshtein & Kubovy, 2007).

Two very different sensory processes are involved in the perception of visual motion. One detects changes in the retinal image; the other utilizes information about the position and rate of rotation of the eyes. Gregory (1997) calls these the *image-retina* and *eye-head systems*. To see how these two interact—and to get an appreciation for the complexities associated with integrating these two sources of information—try the following two exercises. First, look at your surroundings moving your eyes slowly left and right. The world appears stable and unmoving, despite the fact that substantial image motion is occurring on the retina. Now, hold out your index finger at arm's length and move it slowly left and right while holding your head stationary and moving your eyes to keep focused on your finger. (You will find this much easier to do if you close one eye, for reasons having to do with the limited range of depths that can simultaneously be processed by the stereo system.) Your finger will clearly be seen as moving, despite the fact that the projection of your finger remains essentially stationary on the retina. Taken together, these two simple demonstrations show that the perception of what is moving relative to the viewer is neither a simple function of eye motion in isolation nor a simple function of retinal image motion in isolation.

5.2   Image Changes Seen as Motion

The time-varying retinal image can be characterized by specifying the way in which patterns of light move on the image. A useful way to do this is to define a two-dimensional vector field over the image that corresponds to the projection of three-dimensional relative movement vectors for each visible point in the environment (J. J. Gibson, 1950a). The most common term for this two-dimensional vector field is *optic flow*, though some authors use the term *motion field* instead, using *optic flow* to refer to apparent (as opposed to actual) image velocities. While optic flow is normally treated as an image property, it is sometimes specified in terms of a rotationally stabilized coordinate system, which J. J. Gibson (1950b) called the *optic array*. In this formulation, optic flow is a function of both the changing retinal image and eye motions.

Image motion involves changes occurring over both time and space. To avoid the complexities of nonplanar projection in the eye, we will adopt the common simplification of treating the projection as planar, even though it is not. The time-varying retinal image can be characterized as a function of three variables, two of which specify a geometric location in the projected image, and the third of which specifies time (Adelson & Bergen, 1985; Bolles, Baker, & Marimont, 1987). Figure 5.1 shows an example, taken from a video sequence of a person walking from right to left in front of a stationary camera. The dimension marked t in the figure specifies time, while the dimensions marked x and y specify an image location at a particular point in time. Figure 5.1(a) shows frames from the image sequence. Figure 5.1(b) shows the sequence as a dense space-time volume. Figure 5.1(c) shows the space-time volume with a portion removed. A is the lower half of the initial frame of the sequence, B shows the evolution of the middle line of the sequence over the first half of the sequence, C is the upper half of the frame halfway through the sequence, and D shows the evolution of the top line of the images over the second half of the sequence. Figure 5.1(d) shows the space-time sequence with all of the top half removed except for the final frame. In Figures 5.1(c) and 5.1(d), the space-time streaks parallel to the time axis t in B arise from portions of the background that are stationary in the image because of the stationary camera. The diagonal streaks in B are associated with the body of the walker as he moves from right to left. Figure 5.2 shows the space-time volume resulting from a similar scene in which the camera is panning from left to right as the person walks. Now, in surface B, the person appears as a streak oriented parallel to the time axis for part of the sequence, with background structure appearing as diagonal streaks.

A variety of models have been proposed by vision scientists for how the visual system uses space-time filtering to detect moving brightness patterns

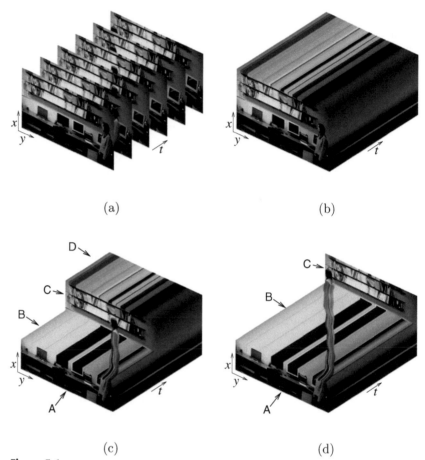

(a)   (b)

(c)   (d)

Figure 5.1

Characterizing image motion in terms of image location and time. (a) Frames
from an image sequence of a person moving from right to left in front of a stationary camera, stacked in temporal order from front to back. (b) The frames in (a),
represented as a space-time volume. (c) The space-time volume with A showing
the lower half of the initial frame of the sequence, B showing the evolution of
the middle line of the sequence over the first half of the sequence, C showing the
upper half of the sequence frame halfway through, and D showing the evolution
of the top line of the sequence over the second half of the sequence. (d) Similar
to (c), except that B shows the evolution of the middle line of the sequence over
the whole of the sequence and C shows the upper half of the last frame of the
sequence.

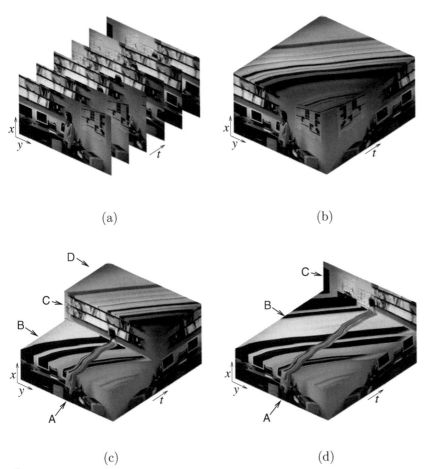

(a)   (b)

(c)   (d)

Figure 5.2

The same illustration as shown in Figure 5.1, except that the video sequence
involves the camera panning from right to left, following the person who is walking. (a) Frames from the image sequence stacked in temporal order from front to
back. (b) The frames in (a), represented as a space-time volume. (c) The space-
time volume with A showing the lower half of the initial frame of the sequence, B
showing the evolution of the middle line of the sequence over the first half of the
sequence, C showing the upper half of the sequence frame halfway through, and
D showing the evolution of the top line of the sequence over the second half of
the sequence. (d) Similar to (c), except that B shows the evolution of the middle
line of the sequence over the whole of the sequence and C shows the upper half
of the last frame of the sequence.

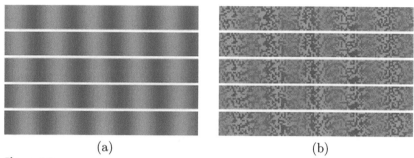

(a)   (b)

Figure 5.3

Each strip is a frame in a motion sequence. (a) First-order motion, in which a pattern of contrast edges moves left to right. (b) Second-order motion, in which the pattern is stationary, but bands of higher and lower pattern contrast move left to right. Both generate a sense of visual motion. (After Z.-L. Lu & Sperling, 2001.)

in the retinal image (e.g., Adelson & Bergen, 1985; Fleet & Jepson, 1990; Reichardt, 1961; Watson & Ahumada, 1985). Space-time filtering can be thought of as characterizing Figures 5.1 and 5.2 in terms of the distribution of streaks of particular spatial extent (size) and orientation with respect to the time axis (magnitude and direction of optic flow). Computer vision researchers have addressed the same problem using methods directly relating spatial and temporal image gradients (e.g., Fennema & Thompson, 1979; Horn & Schunck, 1981). While these various models differ substantially in the details of the computation involved, all analyze the time varying image in essentially the same manner (Adelson & Bergen, 1986; van Santen & Sperling, 1985).

The visual system is also sensitive to motion of patterns not easily described as moving brightness patterns (Cavanagh, 1992; Z.-L. Lu & Sperling, 1996, 2001). For example, motion is clearly seen if the contrast of a static textured pattern is modified by a variable modulation function which itself is moving. Figure 5.3 provides an illustration of this class of stimuli. Figure 5.3(a) shows a pattern characterized by moving contrast boundaries. Such patterns produce the distinctive linear structure in the three-dimensional space-time volume as used in Figures 5.1 and 5.2. Figure 5.3(b), shows a stationary texture, with the contrast of the texture varying in a sinusoidal pattern that drifts right from frame to frame. Even though there are no moving contrast boundaries in Figure 5.3(b), visual motion is still apparent in the animation. In this case, however, there is no longer a distinctive signature in the space-time volume characterizing the time-varying image.

These so-called *second-order motion* patterns (also called *non-Fourier motion*) can also be generated by variations in contrast, flicker patterns,

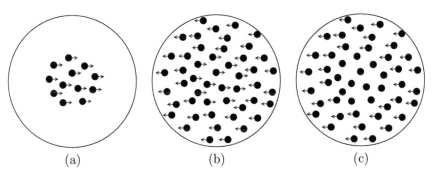

(a)   (b)   (c)

Figure 5.4

Motion contrast. (a) A textured pattern moves across an untextured background.
(b) A textured pattern moves in a contrasting direction to a moving textured
background. (c) Background motion can induce a sense of motion in the opposite
direction of a surrounded, stationary textured pattern. The arrows in the figure
illustrate dot speed, but do not appear in the moving image.

and several other display effects. While the pure second-order displays used
in perception experiments do not seem to correspond to naturally occurring
patterns, similar effects occur in the real world due to both transparency
and occlusion (Fleet & Langley, 1994; Hegdé, Albright, & Stoner, 2004).
This is significant, given the important role visual motion plays in recognizing and interpreting occlusion boundaries.

The perception of visual motion depends not only on localized changes
in the retinal image but also on the surrounding context. Motion of a
small texture patch will be easier to detect and appear to move faster if
the patch is surrounded by a texture moving in a contrasting direction
(Figure 5.4(b)) than if it appears in isolation (Figure 5.4(a)). The effect is
sufficiently powerful that surrounding a small stationary texture patch with
moving texture will often produce the perception that the central patch is
moving in the direction opposite the surrounding texture, an effect known
at *induced motion* (Figure 5.4(c)). A related phenomenon is shown in
Figure 5.5, where two small entities in an image, here marked A and B, are
moving to the right at the same speed and are surrounded by a moving
texture pattern with the property that the image plane motion increases
from left to right. Perceptually, A will be seen as moving faster than B
(Loomis & Nakayama, 1973). This is because the perceived speed of A is
increased because it is surrounded by a region of slower velocity, while the
perceived speed of B is decreased because it is surrounded by a region of
faster velocity.

This is the same *simultaneous contrast* effect that occurs for brightness,
color, and a host of other perceptual stimuli. As with these other visual

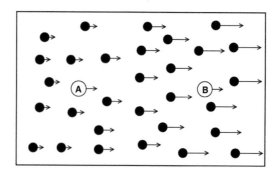

Figure 5.5

Two objects in the image (marked A and B) are moving at the same speed to the right, as indicated by the arrows. They appear against a background of moving dots, where the speed of the background dots slowly increases from left to right. The arrows in the figure illustrate dot speed, but do not appear in the moving image.

properties, the perceptual system is more sensitive to changes in a property rather than the absolute magnitude of the property itself. Changes in a wide variety of image properties can provide information about the scene under view. They are also more easily sensed than absolute magnitudes, which require a zero reference and proper scaling, both of which are particularly difficult for visual motion. In terms of sensing retinal motion, utilizing local spatial changes in motion avoids many of the complications of needing to compensate for eye rotations (Nakayama & Loomis, 1974;

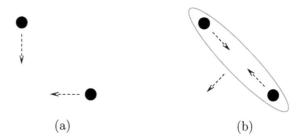

(a)   (b)

Figure 5.6

(a) Two dots move in orthogonal directions. (b) The dots are perceived as moving toward one another along a diagonal, with the two dots forming a configuration seen as moving along the opposite diagonal.

Reiger & Lawton, 1985). Finally, the ability to detect spatially changing optic flow facilitates the detection of discontinuities in retinal motion,
which are necessarily due to significant geometric features of the scene (see
Chapter 11).

A more complex example of the effects of context occurs when the visual
system perceives the separate movement of different entities as part of a
single moving configuration. Figure 5.6 illustrates a situation in which two
moving dots are present, one moving from top to bottom along the left
edge of the image, the other moving from right to left along the bottom
of the image. When viewed, the dominant percept is of two dots moving
toward one another along a diagonal (Johansson, 1950). Separately, there
is a sense of the two dots forming a single configuration moving in the
orthogonal direction (though, in the original experiment, about a third of
the participants needed to be appropriately prompted before they saw this
configurational motion).

Motion perception is sensitive to sensory adaptation, as described in
Section 1.4.6. Figure 5.7 illustrates the waterfall illusion, one of the best-
known sensory aftereffects (Addams, 1834). In the waterfall illusion, staring at a continuously moving pattern for a period of time and then transferring the view to a nearby stationary surface causes that surface to appear
to be moving in the opposite direction. This is likely due to the way in
which motion signals are encoded in the perceptual system.

(a)   (b)

Figure 5.7

The waterfall illusion. (a) Staring at a continuously moving pattern produces
sensory adaptation. (b) One manifestation of this adaptation occurs if fixation
is moved to a nearby stationary surface, which will seem to move in the opposite
direction, due to a sensory aftereffect.

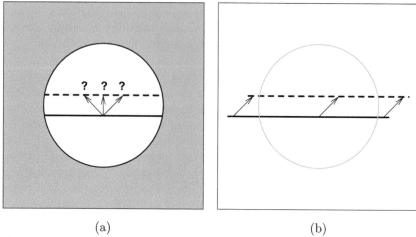

(a)   (b)

Figure 5.8

The aperture problem. (a) If a straight line or edge moves in such a way that its endpoints are hidden, the visual information is not sufficient to determine the actual motion of the line. (b) The two-dimensional image motion of a line is unambiguous if there are visible endpoints, corners, or other distinctive markings on the line.

5.3   Local Ambiguity

The motion of straight lines and edges is ambiguous if no endpoints or corners are visible, a phenomenon referred to as the *aperture problem*. The aperture problem arises because the component of motion parallel to the line or edge does not produce any visual changes. Figure 5.8 illustrates the problem. In Figure 5.8(a), a horizontal line moves upward, with its endpoints occluded by an aperture. In this situation, there is no way to visually determine how much the line is moving side to side. In Figure 5.8(b), the occluding aperture has been removed and the endpoints of the line now provide unambiguous visual information for the two-dimensional motion of the line.

In practice, situations such as in Figure 5.8(a) almost never occur, except for intentional illusions, such as rotating barber poles. However, the initial processing used by the visual system to estimate retinal image motion operates over local regions, effectively imposing an aperture on the sensed brightness patterns. The geometry of the real world is such that under most circumstances, optic flow varies slowly over much of the field of view. The visual system exploits this property by combining ambiguous information about the movement of multiple nearby small edge segments into a single estimate of two-dimensional movement, assuming that all or most of the edge elements have similar image motion.

Normal flow is defined as that component of optic flow parallel to the image gradient. (For contours, this is essentially the same as the optic flow projected onto the normal vector of the contour.) For straight contours, it is, in principle, possible to determine the normal flow, $\vec{f}_n$, but no local computation can recover the full optic flow $\vec{f}$. Even when the contour is curved, local computations will, in general, recover $\vec{f}_n$ more accurately than $\vec{f}$. Given a value for normal flow at a point, it is possible to determine the family of optic flow values at that point, all of which would project to the same normal flow value,

$$\vec{f}_n \cdot \vec{f} = \left(|\vec{f}_n|\right)^2 . \qquad (5.1)$$

This is shown graphically for two different edge segments in Figures 5.9(a), 5.9(b), and 5.9(c). Given the normal flow $\vec{f}_{n1}, \ldots, \vec{f}_{nk}$ at two or more edge elements having differing orientations, if all edge elements have the same optic flow $\vec{f}$ (i.e., the same two-dimensional image motion), then that flow can be found by solving the system of equations

$$\vec{f}_{n1} \cdot \vec{f} = \left(|\vec{f}_{n1}|\right)^2$$

$$\vdots \qquad\qquad (5.2)$$

$$\vec{f}_{nk} \cdot \vec{f} = \left(|\vec{f}_{nk}|\right)^2 .$$

Figure 5.9(d) graphically illustrates how the constraints on optic flow arising from two different edge segments can be intersected to determine the unique value of optic flow common to both elements. Note that this flow value is *not* just the average of the two normal flows.

Optic flow discontinuities at occlusion boundaries present difficulties for the formulation shown in Equation (5.2), since in this situation there may be distinctly different flow values on either side of the boundary that should not be combined into a single estimate. Transparency presents a similar difficulty, since two independently moving surfaces might both be visible along a single line of sight. Little is known about how the visual system avoids this problem. Part of the solution may come from the fact that the visual system selectively combines normal flow values from multiple edge elements, favoring combinations of edges with similar contrast and spatial frequency (Adelson & Movshon, 1982).

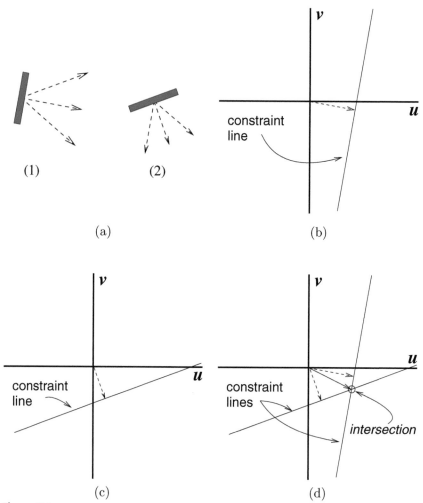

Figure 5.9

Resolving the ambiguity of local optic flow. (a) The dashed arrows indicate some of the optic flows that are possible for two moving edge elements with particular orientations and normal flows. (b) The possible optic flow values for edge element (1) can be plotted as a constraint line in (u, v) optic flow space. (c) The same plot for edge element (2). (d) The intersection of the two constraint lines is the only optic flow value simultaneously consistent with both edge motions.

5.4 Apparent Motion

Discontinuous motion—in which a series of static images is presented for a discrete interval in time, and the sequence of images contains patterns that move by discrete intervals in space—can, under some circumstances, appear nearly indistinguishable from continuous motion. The effect is called *apparent motion* to highlight that the appearance of continuous motion is an illusion. Toys exploiting the apparent motion phenomenon, including the phenakistiscope, the zoetrope, and the praxinoscope (Dulac & Gaudreault, 2005) date back to the nineteenth century, and the effect was known much earlier than that. Animated computer graphics, film,[1] and video would not be possible without this important perceptual phenomena.

The formal study of the perception of apparent motion started not with sequentially presented pictures as in the zoetrope, but rather with simple flashing lights. In 1873, Sigmund Exner experimented with two alternating, spark-generated lights, offset in space in an otherwise dark room. For some combinations of alternating frequency and distance between the flashes, a single spot of light was seen to move back and forth between the two spark generator locations. Apparent motion studies using similar sorts of time-varying visual patterns continue to this day, though the display technology has changed dramatically in the interval.

Early studies involving alternating flashing lights distinguished between four qualitatively distinct perceptual categories. For a fixed distance between the lights, a slow alternation rate (typically on the order of 1–2 cycles per second or less) results in the lights appearing to alternate with no motion between them. Speeding up the alternation rate produces a strong sense of a light moving back and forth between the two locations, with the light clearly apparent as it moves across the interval. This is referred to as *beta apparent motion*. At somewhat faster intervals, there is still a sense of motion between the two light locations, but, paradoxically, the moving light is no longer seen as translating across the interval. This is referred to as *phi apparent motion*. While not typically included in the categorization of apparent motion phenomenon, at yet faster alternation rates the sense of motion goes away and both lights appear to be rapidly flickering. Finally, even faster alternation rates (≥ 60 Hz) cause both lights to appear to be on constantly. This is called *flicker fusion*.

Apparent motion, when looking at alternating flashing lights or other simple patterns alternating in location, can occur even when the two locations are substantially displaced from one another in terms of visual angle. The same turns out not to be true for apparent motion of more-complex

---

[1] We will use the term *film* to mean what is also called motion pictures, movies, or cinema.

textured patterns. Braddick (1974) explored the perception of motion using what are now called *random dot kinematograms*. Two images were alternately displayed. Each consisted of a regularly arrayed and tightly packed set of small squares, with each square equally likely to be black or white. The second image was produced from the first by displaying a rectangular portion of the first image. At the leading edge of the rectangle, the covered-up dots were discarded and replaced by dots in the displaced pattern. At the trailing edge, new dots were added at random. Such a pattern can produce a strong sense of a moving rectangle, even though the borders of the rectangle are not apparent in either of the images when viewed in isolation. Importantly, the perception of apparent motion when viewing these random dot patterns started to degrade when the rectangle was displaced by 5 arc minutes of visual angle, and disappeared completely when the displacement exceeded about 20 arc minutes of visual angle. In contrast, perception of apparent motion based on alternating lights sometimes can occur over displacements as large as several degrees (Kolers, 1972).

Braddick (1974) argued that the differences between the characteristics of flashing-light displays and of random dot displays necessary to generate a sense of visual motion are evidence of the existence of separate *short-range* and *long-range* motion-perception processes in the visual system. In addition to requiring smaller displacements, Braddick provided evidence that short-range apparent motion perception is distinguished from long-range apparent motion perception by requiring more rapid temporal frequencies and by an insensitivity to motion when one pattern is presented only to the left eye and the other pattern is presented only to the right eye. Ramachandran and Gregory (1978) showed that the textured patterns used to generate short-range apparent motion required contrast in brightness, not just in color, and concluded that "colour and motion are handled separately by the human visual system and that colour provides only a weak 'cue,' at best, to movement perception." While the short-range/long-range distinction is widely accepted, some have argued that the difference is a consequence of differing stimuli rather than differing perceptual processes (e.g., Cavanagh & Mather, 1989). Nevertheless, there is substantial evidence that the human visual system is sensitive to distinctly different patterns of temporal change, consistent with multiple, distinct perceptual processes (Z.-L. Lu & Sperling, 2001).

Most accounts of the perception of motion in film and video directly or indirectly refer to the classic literature on apparent motion, almost all of which was based on experiments involving alternating presentations of a single pair of patterns. Sometimes, it is specifically asserted that motion pictures are seen to be moving because they fall into the range of beta apparent motion. One consequence of this particular claim, rarely if ever stated, is the prediction that the appearance of motion in motion pictures

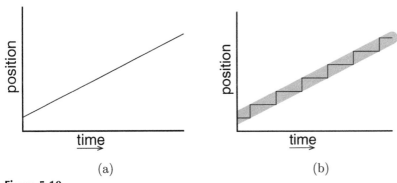

Figure 5.10

(a) Continuous motion of a point over time in one dimension. (b) Discontinuous motion of the same point over time, as it would appear in a motion picture or video. Under some circumstances, it is difficult for the visual system to distinguish between these two situations.

and video will degrade as the frame rate increases and the type of apparent motion moves from beta to phi. This appears not to be the case in practice.

In reality, of course, motion pictures and video are nothing like alternating-image apparent motion stimuli. Rather, they consist of a sequence of still images in which complex patterns of light move in a spatially and temporally coherent manner. In alternating pattern displays, the direction of motion reverses with each presentation frame. In motion pictures and video, pattern movement on the image plane almost always continues in the same general direction with the same general speed for multiple frames. This continuity of positional change can substantially improve the subjective sense of real movement (Sperling, 1976).

Figure 5.10 provides a simplified, one-dimensional illustration of motion perception based on the viewing of a sequence of still images depicting continuous motion. Figure 5.10(a) shows the image plane position over time of a point moving with constant velocity. Figure 5.10(b) is the equivalent image position over time that would occur while viewing a motion picture or video of the moving point. Under the right circumstances, the two displays will have the same appearance. When this happens, the visual system, in effect, perceives the average motion in Figure 5.10(b), ignoring the jerky change in actual point position.

A signal processing analysis provides insight into why the situation presented in Figure 5.10(b) is sometimes nearly indistinguishable from that shown in Figure 5.10(a). This analysis starts with the presumption that the visual information for motion is contained in the spatial and temporal variability of image intensity in the space-time volume shown in Figures 5.1

and 5.2. As with any physically realizable measurement device, there are limits to the rates of spatial and temporal change that can be detected by the visual system (see Chapter 2). While the specifics are beyond the scope of this book, the sensitivity of the visual system to motion-induced visual change can be characterized in terms of spatial and temporal frequencies, with spatial frequency distributions indicating changes in brightness over the retinal image at some particular point in time, and temporal frequency distributions indicating changes in brightness over the retinal image at some particular retinal location.

The sensitivity limits of the visual system depend on a complex interaction between contrast, spatial and temporal frequency, and a variety of other factors. In general terms, however, neither spatial variability finer than about 50 cycles/degree or temporal variability faster than about 60 Hz can be seen by the human visual system. Furthermore, the upper limits of detectable spatial and temporal frequency are roughly independent of one another (Robson, 1966). Watson, Ahumada, and Farrell (1986) define a *window of visibility* arising from these limits, conjecturing that "two [visual motion] stimuli will appear identical if their [space-time frequency] spectra, after passing through the window of visibility, are identical."

One potential source of confusion associated with the window of visibility is that it is defined in terms of spatial and temporal frequencies, not speed of motion. Spatial frequency distributions characterize the nature of change over the image at a single point in time. Temporal frequency distributions characterize the nature of change over time at fixed locations in the image. Spatial frequency, temporal frequency, and speed of image motion are related. For a fixed spatial frequency, increasing speed leads to increasing temporal frequency. For a fixed speed, increasing temporal frequency results from increased spatial frequency.

Watson et al. (1986) provide a formal analysis of when continuous motion and a stroboscopically presented equivalent will appear to be the same. Informally, converting the continuous motion to a set of still images presented over discrete intervals in time adds additional high frequencies to the space-time frequency spectrum of the continuous motion. If most of this added energy falls outside of the window of visibility, the two motions will appear essentially the same. There are two ways in which visible space-time high frequencies added by converting continuous motion to stroboscopic motion can be moved out of the window of visibility. One option is to increase the frame rate of the stroboscopic motion, which increases the extraneous high-frequency information. If the frame rate is sufficiently rapid, these frequencies will fall outside the window of visibility. The second possibility is to apply a low-pass temporal filter to the displayed image (i.e., add *motion blur*), which will also reduce the spatial frequencies in the direction of moving contours. Motion picture and video cameras do this automatically, as a direct consequence of their need to integrate light over a period of time in order to determine the brightness distribution for each frame.

5.5   Eye Movements

As indicated in Section 5.1, the visual system needs information about both the motion of patterns of light on the retina and the motion of the eye itself in order to determine the movement of entities in the environment relative to the viewer. Eye rotations serve multiple purposes and are controlled by multiple distinct mechanisms. Only some of these types of eye movements are directly related to the perception of visual motion on the retina. Additional information about the roles eye motion plays in visual perception can be found in Chapters 11 and 16.

Smooth-pursuit eye movements are continuous rotations of the eye, with a maximum velocity no more than about $100°$/second, that serve to keep the projection of an entity of interest (object, location, etc.) on or near the fovea. Most obviously, this means that the visual system has access to detailed information about such an entity over time, even when movement between the entity and viewer is occurring. In addition, the movement of the eye needed to keep the location of interest centered on the fovea provides an indication of the angular velocity of movement relative to the viewer's head. This source of motion information is distinctly different from that provided by retinal image motion, yet both contribute to the perception of movement relative to the viewer. The ways in which these sources of information are integrated to form a single percept of speed and direction seem to depend on many factors, including velocity, the size of the tracked entity, and perhaps whether the movement is seen as due to object or observer motion (Krukowski, Pirog, Beutter, Brooks, & Stone, 2003; Royden, Crowell, & Banks, 1994; Turano & Heidenreich, 1999).

A second class of eye motions serves to compensate for head rotations so that the eyes tend to remain pointed in the same direction with respect to the environment even when the head is turned. Two very different mechanisms are involved, though the functions are similar. Vestibular eye movements are driven by signals originating in the inner ear. When a rotational acceleration in one direction is detected, the *vestibular-ocular reflex* causes the eyes to rotate in the opposite direction (Skavenski, Hansen, Steinman, & Winterson, 1979; Viirre, Tweed, Milner, & Vilis, 1986). Vestibular influences on eye motion also can occur during translational movements (Angelaki, 2004). The *optokinetic reflex* performs a similar visual stabilization function, but based on large area retinal motion rather than inertial effects (Schweigart, Mergner, Evdokimidis, Morand, & Becker, 1997).

The remaining types of eye motion serve functions not directly related to motion perception. *Saccades* focus areas of interest in the environment on the fovea. Saccades occur very quickly. The time from a triggering stimulus to the completion of the eye movement is 150–200 ms. Most of this time is spent in the vision system planning the saccade. The actual motion takes 20 ms or so, on average. The eyes are moving very quickly during a saccade, with the maximum rotational velocity often exceeding 500°/second. Between saccades, the eyes point toward an area of interest (*fixate*), taking 250–300 ms or so to acquire fine-detail visual information. Contrast sensitivity is reduced during saccades, particularly for low spatial frequencies. This serves to reduce retinal motion signals that might otherwise be confusing since saccades are not associated with tracking a single object or location, but rather are very rapid eye movements from one location to another. The visual system integrates the mosaic of small patches of high-resolution imagery arising from multiple fixations to form an overall subjective sense of fine detail over a wide field of view, though the exact mechanism by which this is done is not well understood.

Vergence movements point the two eyes at the same location in the environment. Vergence is an integral part of stereo vision, important both for aligning the two retinal images sufficiently so that disparity can be determined and for scaling depth from stereo in order to determine absolute distance. More on this topic is included in Chapter 6.

Finally, when stimulated by constant brightness illumination, the photoreceptors in the eye quickly fatigue and cease to generate a meaningful output. Except in very contrived situations, we do not notice this even if we concentrate on fixing our gaze on a stationary pattern. The reason is that the eye continuously makes small, involuntary tremors, called *physiological nystagmus*, which cause sufficient changes in luminance over the retina to keep the photoreceptors functioning effectively.

5.6 Issues Specific to Computer Graphics

The perceptual phenomena of apparent motion is central to perceiving natural-appearing motion in real-time computer graphics, film, and video. The nature of apparent motion and the situations under which apparent and real motion appear to be similar presented serious challenges to the development of motion picture technology. The rate at which film can be moved through a motion picture camera and projector is limited by the need to physically move it into place, hold a frame stationary for the duration of the exposure or presentation, and then move the next frame into place. Projection needs to be blanked using a shutter whenever the film is being moved to avoid motion blur inconsistent with the motion intended to be perceived. Economic considerations also entered into the choice of frame rate, particularly in the early days of film, since the faster the frame rate the more expense was involved for the film stock. Silent film cameras and projectors were hand operated, with camera speeds ranging between about 15 and 25 frames per second. Projection speeds were rarely matched to camera speeds, and might even be intentionally varied for different showings of the same film (Card, 1955). The frame rates used for silent films were sufficiently slow to produce noticeable motion artifacts and flicker.

Driven largely by the advent of *talkies* (sound film), frame rates were standardized at 24 frames per second. Standardization was necessary, since to facilitate synchronization the audio was encoded on the same film stock as the imagery, and variable projection speed would not only change the speed of visible motion but would also change the pitch of the sound. At 24 frames per second, the blanking between frame produces noticeable flicker. A clever solution to this problem reduces the perception of flicker without the need to increase the 24-frames-per-second rate at which individual images are shown. For each frame of the film, a shutter in the projector blanks the projected image two, or sometimes three, times. This results in images being projected at a rate of 48 Hz or 72 Hz, near or above the flicker-fusion rate, though distinctive images are only changing at a rate of 24 Hz.

Analog broadcast television faced a different set of challenges when standards were being set. In this case, maximum frame rates were limited by bandwidth considerations rather than the physics of moving film. Two standards emerged: NTSC in much of the Western Hemisphere and PAL in the rest of the world. NTSC was designed to display 60 images per second on a CRT display (for obscure technical reasons, this was changed to 59.94 images per second when the NTSC standard was extended to support color broadcasts) and PAL was designed to display 50 images per second. As with shuttered film projectors, this presented images near or above the flicker fusion rate. In both cases, not enough broadcast bandwidth was available to transmit complete images of sufficient resolution at this rate. As a result, images are transmitted in *interlaced* format, with alternating horizontal image lines transmitted in one *field* and then the remaining horizontal image lines transmitted in the following field. These are usually referred to as the *odd* and *even* fields, with the odd field including every other line starting at the first, and the even field containing the remaining lines. The term *frame* is used to refer to a consecutive pair of fields, which, between them, contain the whole image. This produces visually acceptable imagery much of the time, but noticeable flicker-related artifacts occur with thin horizontal lines or horizontally moving, high-contrast vertical edges.

The incompatible frame rates between film and analog broadcast television make it difficult to convert movies to video. The most common solution for NTSC is to use *3:2 pulldown*, in which consecutive frames of the film are alternately transferred to three or two consecutive video fields. Twenty-four film frames thus fill up 60 video fields ($12 \times 3 + 12 \times 2$). One significant problem with 3:2 pulldown is that 40% of the frames contain one film image in the first interlaced field and a different film image in the second interlaced field, sometimes producing distracting artifacts. Various tricks are used in some DVD players and high-end television monitors to undo the damage done by 3:2 pulldown. Converting film for use in PAL broadcasts is most easily done by duplicating each film frame in the two interlaced fields of a broadcast frame, letting the television version of the film run 4% faster than the director intended. Pitch-shifting is sometimes done with PAL conversions so that the sound is perceptually less distorted than would otherwise be the case.

High-definition television (HDTV) and digital transmission are substantially changing the nature of displayed video in numerous ways, including some that directly affect motion perception. The HDTV standard includes multiple formats. Three initially became popular: The 480i format roughly approximated the NTSC standard in terms of nominal resolution and the use of interlace encoding. The 720p format increased nominal resolution by 50% over the NTSC standard (and increased actual resolution *much* more than this over the NTSC over-the-air broadcast standard), moved to a 16:9 aspect ratio from NTSC's 4:3 aspect, and used a noninterlaced encoding in which a full distinct image is displayed every 1/60th of a second. (The p stands for *progressive scan*, as distinct from interlace.) The 1080i format increased the nominal resolution further, but used interlacing to keep transmission bandwidth requirements similar to 720p. More recently, television monitors have been marketed capable of 1080p, meaning the nominal spatial resolution of 1080i, but without interlacing. The original standard envisioned frame/field rates of 60 Hz. As of this writing, some monitors are being marketed with a 120 Hz frame rate. No transmission sources operate at this bandwidth, but there are ways of interpolating a lower bandwidth signal to potentially take at least some advantage of these faster displays.

A theoretical analysis predicts that moving to progressive scan should reduce apparent motion artifacts, and, indeed, such displays sometimes look better than their interlaced relatives. Complicating the effects of video standards, however, is the varying nature of displays themselves. CRT displays, by their nature, have a dark interval between when a given location on the screen is refreshed with a new image. While the NTSC field refresh rate of 60 Hz is (just) above the flicker-fusion rate for most viewers, 60 Hz is still capable of producing visual fatigue. As a result, many CRT displays used as computer monitors were run at higher refresh rates, typically combined with the use of progressive scan. This is not an issue for LCD monitors and similar technologies, since if properly operating these displays have little or no flicker.[2]

Film and video cameras require a finite time to acquire a single image frame. If there is motion between the camera and what is being imaged, motion blur will result. This is actually a good thing, as long as the blur is not too severe, since it reduces the high space-time frequencies that might otherwise alias into the window of visibility, making the moving imagery seem more natural than would otherwise be the case. Computer graphics animations typically are not generated with motion blur. The resulting moving imagery may therefore not look as natural as film or video. To make the apparent motion in such animations look more like real motion, either the frame rate needs to be increased or motion blur needs to be simulated as part of rendering (Korein & Badler, 1983; Potmesil & Chakravarty, 1983; Watson et al., 1986).

For interactive computer graphics, it is important to distinguish between the frame rate of the display and the rate at which new images are generated by the rendering process. In many situations, the time to generate a new frame of imagery is substantially greater than the 15 ms needed to keep up with a 60 Hz display. In such cases, the same generated frame will be shown multiple times. This can still produce an acceptable sense of natural motion, as long as care is taken to avoid space-time frequencies that result in visible artifacts. In practical terms, update rates as slow as 10 Hz might appear fairly natural if image plan velocities and spatial detail are low. Such low update rates affect latency, however, and so should be avoided when rapid response control is needed. In fact, many gamers insist that an update rate substantially *faster* than the display's ability to refresh images is essential, so that the portion of the display being refreshed has the most recent imagery possible.

5.7 Suggestions for Further Reading

Between them, these two chapters in the same volume provide a reasonably comprehensive coverage of two-dimensional motion processing in the human visual system:

---

[2]DLP displays intrinsically flicker, but at a rate far above the flicker-fusion threshold.

Anstis, S. (1986). Motion perception in the frontal plane: Sensory aspects. In K. R. Boff, I. Kaufman, & J. P. Thomas (Eds.), *Handbook of perception and human performance: Vol. 1. Sensory processes and perception* (chap. 16). New York: Wiley.

Mack, A. (1986). Perceptual aspects of motion in the frontal plane. In K. R. Boff, I. Kaufman, & J. P. Thomas (Eds.), *Handbook of perception and human performance: Vol. 1. Sensory processes and perception*(chap. 17). New York: Wiley.

There is an extensive literature on apparent motion but few articles that provide comprehensive coverage of those aspects of the topic directly related to film and to video displays. Research articles relevant to apparent motion in such displays:

Adelson, E. H., & Bergen, J. R. (1985). Spatiotemporal energy models for the perception of motion. *Journal of the Optical Society of America A, 2*(2), 284–299.

Watson, A. B., Ahumada, A. J., Jr., & Farrell, J. E. (1986). Window of visibility: A psychophysical theory of fidelity in time-sampled visual motion displays. *Journal of the Optical Society of America A, 3*(3), 300–307.

6

Stereo and Accommodation

No other source of information about layout has been more studied than binocular disparity...

—Cutting and Vishton (1995)

Some people presume the term *3D vision* to be synonymous with *stereo vision*. While there are many other ways in which the visual system is able to estimate the three-dimensional spatial structure of the visible environment, information obtained from overlapping views acquired by the two eyes is a primary source of depth perception. The geometry underlying stereo vision is straightforward, though substantial complexities are involved in the required visual processing. This chapter covers the basics of stereo vision and also the visual information associated with *accommodation* (focus) of the eyes. Accommodation is a source of depth information in its own right. More importantly, however, accommodation and stereo interact in a way that has important implications for stereo image displays.

As important as binocular stereo is to depth perception, a substantial portion of the population has partial or complete stereoblindness. Exact numbers are difficult to know, since data are limited, qualitatively different types of stereo deficits may be involved (Richards, 1971), and the prevalence of stereoblindness increases with age (G. S. Rubin et al., 1997). Richards (1970) found that 4% of a sampling of MIT students could not fuse random dot stereograms (see Section 6.2.2) and another 10% had difficulty interpreting the images in terms of the three-dimensional structure that corresponded to the stimulus. Many people with stereoblindness are unaware of the deficit, since they can still perceive accurate depth due to the many other nonstereo cues involved in space perception.

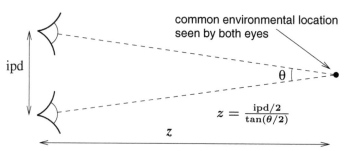

Figure 6.1

The angle between lines of sight intersecting at the same environmental location can be used to determine the distance to that location.

6.1   The Geometry of Stereo Vision

Stereo vision is based on geometric *triangulation*. Lines of sight from the two eyes to the same environmental location can be intersected to determine the location of the intersection point relative to the location of the eyes. Figure 6.1 illustrates the situation when the point of interest is directly in front of the viewer. The eyes are separated by an *interpupillary distance* (ipd), which, in adults, averages a bit over 6 cm. The two lines of sight differ in orientation by an angle θ. (Some authors use the term *binocular parallax* when referring to this angle, though others associate a different meaning with the term *parallax*.) The smaller the value of θ, the farther away the intersection point. The distance from the midpoint of the eyes to the intersection point is represented by z.

From simple trigonometry,

$$z = \frac{\text{ipd}/2}{\tan(\theta/2)} \quad , \quad \theta = 2\tan^{-1}\left(\frac{\text{ipd}}{2z}\right) . \tag{6.1}$$

When the intersection point is directly in front of the viewer, each eye is angled in from straight ahead by $\theta/2$. The relationship between z and θ is mathematically more complex when the intersection point is to the side, but the values are similar.

Figure 6.2 shows a plot of the intersection angle as a function of distance to the intersection point. The intersection angle drops sharply for about half a meter from the head, and then it changes much more slowly as distance increases further. The changing relationship between the intersection angle and distance has important implications for the ability of the visual system to accurately recover larger distances. This becomes particularly apparent if the rate at which the angle changes with distance is examined

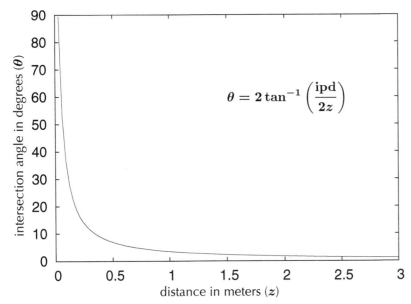

Figure 6.2

Intersection angle θ as a function of distance (see Figure 6.1).

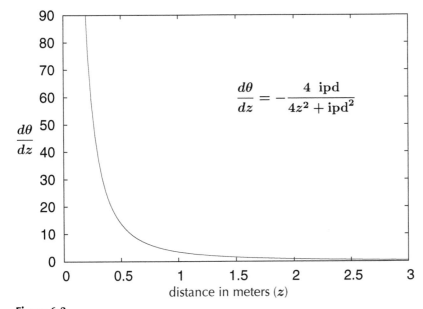

Figure 6.3

Rate of change of intersection angle as a function of distance.

over a range of distances:

$$\frac{d\theta}{dz} = -\frac{4 \text{ ipd}}{4z^2 + \text{ipd}^2} \, .$$

(6.2)

In Figure 6.3, $\frac{d\theta}{dz}$ is plotted as a function of z. The rate of change of θ approaches 0 beyond about 2 m, indicating that the visual system will necessarily have reduced sensitivity to differences in distance beyond that point. At even larger distances, changes in z produce changes in θ that will be too small to be useful.

6.2   Depth from Triangulation in the Visual System

Two quite distinct problems must be solved by the visual system in order to determine the distance to an environmental location, as in Figure 6.1 and Equation (6.1). First of all, the two lines of sight actually have to be aimed at the same point. The second problem involves determining the actual angles of the two lines of sight and using this information to infer the depth.

6.2.1   The Correspondence Problem

Figure 6.4 shows views of a collection of objects (a Holmes stereoscopic viewer, plus a number of stereo pair view cards) from two offset positions, one representing what the left eye would see and the other representing what the right eye would see. If two lines of sight intersect at the same point on a visible surface, then the corresponding retinal images will be

(left-eye view)   (right-eye view)

Figure 6.4

Binocular stereo: a view from the left and right eyes.

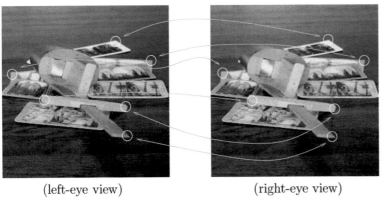

(left-eye view)   (right-eye view)

Figure 6.5

A small sampling of the correspondences in Figure 6.4.

of the same surface, viewed from slightly different orientations—and in the case of viewing directions to the side, slightly different distances. Except in unusual cases, the change in viewing position is slight, and the appearance of the surface in the two views will be similar.

A major challenge in determining depth from stereo is to make sure that the two lines of sight used in the computation shown in Equation (6.1) really do point toward the same physical location in the world. This is known as the *stereo correspondence problem*. To solve the correspondence problem, the visual system must find a pair of retinal image regions, one for each eye, that are sufficiently similar that they likely correspond to the same external location. Figure 6.5 shows examples of some of the correspondences in Figure 6.4. The visual system requires many more correspondences in order to construct a three-dimensional view from images of this sort. A matching criteria that is too strict would result in the visual system being unable to find sufficient matches to perceive depth. A matching criteria not strict enough leads to incorrect matches resulting in incorrectly perceived depth (Figure 6.6).

The relationship between interpupillary distance and depth adds additional complications. If *ipd* were to be reduced, the range of distance over which $\frac{d\theta}{dz}$ is large enough to indicate visual sensitivity to depth differences decreases from what is shown in Figure 6.3. Increasing *ipd* increases the range over which depth differences can be perceived, but decreases the visual similarity between the views from each eye of a nearby common location, since the difference in the orientation of the views increases. While the eye spacing in humans of about 6 cm is constrained by head size, it also turns out to be well tuned to using stereo over and a bit beyond reaching space.

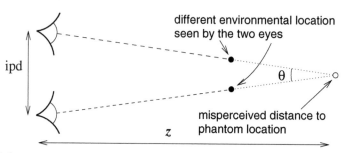

Figure 6.6

Depth is misperceived if the lines of sight from the two eyes are directed at different environmental locations.

Though the correspondence problem has been studied extensively in both the vision science and computer vision communities, the way in which the visual system establishes stereo correspondences largely remains an open question. Various matching criteria have been proposed, differing in the associated image properties that are utilized and in other constraints used to eliminate incorrect matches. One set of theories hypothesizes that the establishment of stereo correspondences happens early in the visual system's processing of the retinal image, with matching based on some sort of image-similarity metric (Figure 6.7, left). This ordering allows depth information to contribute to other forms of image feature extraction relevant to subsequent visual processing. Many of the methods reviewed in Scharstein and Szelisk (2002) fall into this category. There is another pos-

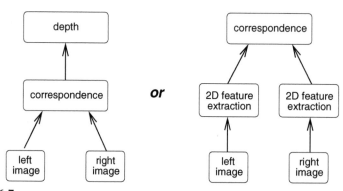

Figure 6.7

Theories of stereo correspondence determination differ on whether matching is based on features extracted from each eye individually or whether it is based on comparisons of the raw imagery itself.

sibility (Figure 6.7, right), involving extraction of individual features from each retinal image and then a subsequent feature matching step. The advantage here is that appropriately chosen features may have characteristics usable in similarity matching that are less sensitive to small changes in the orientation of view than are simple image patches. Features of this sort that have been considered include individual pixels (e.g., Marr & Poggio, 1976), localized point features (e.g., Barnard & Thompson, 1980), edges (e.g., Marr & Poggio, 1979), and more-complex features (e.g., D. G. Jones & Malik, 1992).

Many theories of stereo presume that image or feature similarity alone is not sufficient to resolve ambiguities associated with the process of determining correspondences and that, as a result, additional constraints must be brought to bear on the problem. Marr and Poggio (1976) list two such constraints: *continuity*, which presumes that surfaces are cohesive and smooth, resulting in nearby surface points having similar intersection angles between lines of sight except at surface boundaries, and *uniqueness*, which limits line of sight from one eye to a single corresponding line of sight in the other eye. One problem for theories built from these constraints is that it is possible to determine the depth of stacked, semitransparent surfaces using stereo (Prazdny, 1985). For such surfaces, intersection angles are not spatially homogeneous, and a single line of sight from one eye can be associated with multiple surfaces, each generating an intersection with a different line of sight from the other eye.

6.2.2   Random Dot Stereograms

In 1971, Bela Julesz described a way of producing a pair of patterns that, when viewed normally, appeared to have no structure whatsoever, but had a clear three-dimensional structure when viewed such that one pattern was visible only in the left eye, and the other pattern was visible only in the right eye. Figure 6.8 shows how to produce a simple version of these *random dot stereograms*. First, background and foreground images are created by randomly placing dots of a fixed size on a contrasting background. Separate left- and right-eye images are then constructed by superimposing the foreground pattern on the background in two different, horizontally offset positions. Because the foreground and background patterns have identical texture properties and match in color and brightness, the outlines of the foreground are not visible in the two final images, shown at the bottom of Figure 6.8. When viewed separately by the two eyes, the bottom pair of images in Figure 6.8 will appear as either a square floating above a background surface or as a square aperture through which a more distant surface is seen, depending on the sign of the offset used when superimposing the foreground pattern. (Constructing random dot stereograms involving

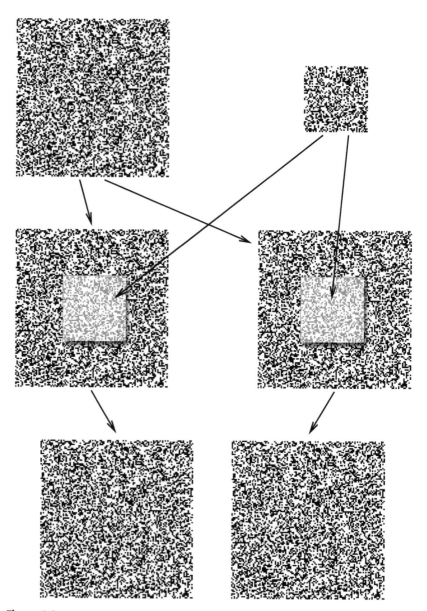

Figure 6.8

Simple random dot stereograms can be produced by randomly placing dot patterns on an image to create background (upper left) and foreground (upper right) images, and then superimposing the foreground image on the background at two different, horizontally offset positions (middle row). The result is two apparently featureless images, which, when viewed individually by the left and right eyes, produce a perception of a three-dimensional pattern (bottom row).

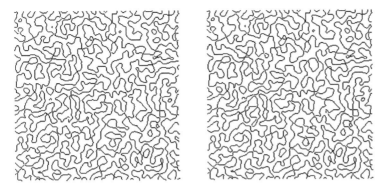

Figure 6.9

Low spatial frequency contours in Figure 6.8, showing that feature-based correspondence is possible even with random dot patterns.

surfaces that are not parallel to the display surface is quite a bit more
complicated.)

There are a number of options for viewing stereo pairs such as shown
at the bottom of Figure 6.8. Easiest for most people are *Lorgnette viewers*,
which are inexpensively available from many sources. Some people are
able to cross their eyes while looking at patterns of this sort, producing the
appearance of three images rather than two. The central image will be a
combination of the two actual images and will appear in 3D, but with the
left- and right-eye views swapped, which reverses the sign of the apparent
depth difference. A very few people will be able to relax their eyes in
such a way that they are not converged, again producing the appearance
of a merged image between the two "real" images, but this time without
swapping left and right images. Viewing stereo pairs without the aid of a
viewer is called *free fusing*.

While random dot stereograms are often offered as evidence that the
visual system can establish stereo correspondences without any preceding
feature extraction from the individual left- and right-eye images, the situation is not so simple. Even the apparently random images in Figure 6.8
have structure when appropriately band-pass filtered (D. G. Jones & Malik, 1992). The perception of depth in random dot stereograms may well be
based on such extracted features, rather than the dot images themselves.
Figure 6.9 shows the two random dot stereograms shown at the bottom of
Figure 6.8, processed through a zero-crossing edge detector (Marr & Hildreth, 1980). The structure of Figure 6.8 is still preserved, and, in fact,
this image pair can also be seen in depth using Lorgnette viewers or free
fusing.

6.2.3   Color and Stereo Vision

The similarity metric used by the visual system to determine correspondences is largely driven by the luminance properties of the two retinal images. Similarity in color seems to have little influence on whether or not features in each eye are matched (C. Lu & Fender, 1972). This is consistent with the claim by Livingstone and Hubel (1987) and others that the neural mechanisms in the visual system that process depth and movement are separate from those associated with color perception, though color can affect correspondence under some circumstances (den Ouden, van Ee, & de Haan, 2005; Stuart, Edwards, & Cook, 1992). Likewise, dissimilarity in color is not an impediment to correspondence. This is why colored glasses can be used to create stereo displays (see Section 6.4.1). Left- and right-eye images are superimposed in the same display or on the same printed page, each in a separate color, typically red and green, red and cyan, or red and blue. The combined image is viewed using glasses with one lens in one of the image colors and the other lens in the other color. As a result, each eye sees only the intended image. The visual system has no difficulty in combining the two dissimilarly colored images into a single, three-dimensional percept.

6.2.4   Da Vinci Stereopsis

The information that binocular stereo provides about depth is most often discussed in terms of intersecting lines of sight from the two eyes to points corresponding to the same environmental surface location. In addition, however, the visual system is also able to exploit situations in which environmental surface locations seen in the view from one eye are *not* visible in the other eye. Da Vinci (1566/1970) described how the portion of a background surface seen behind a foreground object is different when viewed from the two eyes. This can be used to infer depth information, an effect that is now referred to as *da Vinci stereopsis* (Nakayama & Shimojo, 1990).

At the left edge of a nearer occluding surface, a portion of the more distant background will be visible in the left eye but not the right (Figure 6.10(a)). Similarly, at the right edge of a nearer occluding surface, a portion of the more distant background will be visible in the right eye but not the left (Figure 6.10(b)). These patterns provide an effective ordinal cue for depth (Anderson & Nakayama, 1994). The unmatched regions always correspond to the partially occluded, and therefore more distant, surface. It is similar, at least in terms of geometry, to the accretion and deletion of surface texture due to motion, described in Chapter 11.

As shown in Figure 6.10, a background region visible in the left eye but not in the right will appear to the left of the boundary of the occluding surface (Figure 6.10(a)) while a background region visible in the right eye

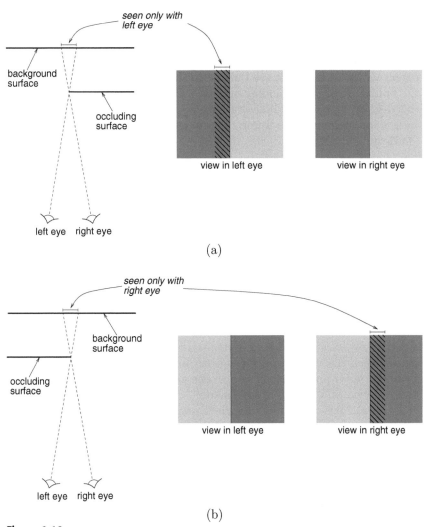

Figure 6.10

Da Vinci stereopsis: unmatched image regions can provide information about depth ordering at occlusion boundaries. (a) At the left edge of an occluding surface, a portion of the more distant background will be visible in the left eye but not the right eye. (b) At the right edge of an occluding surface, a portion of the more distant background will be visible in the right eye but not the left eye.

but not in the left will appear to the right of the boundary of the occluding surface (Figure 6.10(b)). The constraints of real-world geometry preclude both a background region visible in the left eye but not in the right appearing to the right of the boundary of the occluding surface, and a background region visible in the right eye but not in the left appearing to the right of the boundary of the occluding surface. The visual system is sensitive to this distinction and has difficulty forming a stable image when one of the cases impossible in the real world is generated using a stereoscopic display (Nakayama & Shimojo, 1990).

6.2.5   Determining the Directions of Lines of Sight

The determination of depth based on lines of sight from the two eyes that intersect at a common environmental point requires knowing the angle between these two lines of sight, as shown in Figure 6.1 and Equation (6.1). In the human visual system, two very different mechanisms are combined in making this measurement. One involves sensing the pointing direction of the eyes relative to the head. The other compares the retinal locations in the two eyes of the projection of a single environmental feature.

The term *vergence angle* (or sometimes *convergence*) specifies the angular difference between the pointing directions of the two eyes. If the left and right eyes are fixated on a common environmental point in front of the viewer, then the vergence angle can be used to determine absolute depth as in Figure 6.1 and Equation (6.1). The human visual system does in fact use vergence as a source of information about depth (Foley, 1980; Mon-Williams & Tresilian, 1999), though there is controversy over the accuracy with which depth can be determined by vergence alone. Also, as predicted by Equation (6.2), vergence is only useful as a depth cue for distances within a few meters of the head. Vergence is referred to as an *ocularmotor* or *extraretinal* source of information about depth, indicating that it is one of the few cues providing information relevant to spatial vision that is based in a fundamental way on sensory information other than retinal images.

The vergence angle of the eyes when fixated on a common point in space is only one of the ways that the visual system is able to determine depth from binocular stereo. A second mechanism involves a comparison of the retinal images in the two eyes and does not require information about where the eyes are pointed. A simple example demonstrates the effect. Hold your arm straight out in front of you, with your thumb pointed up. Stare at your thumb and then close one eye. Now, simultaneously open the closed eye and close the open eye. Your thumb will appear to be more or less stationary, while the more distant surfaces seen behind your thumb will appear to move from side to side (Figure 6.11). The change in retinal

(left-eye view)   (right-eye view)

Figure 6.11

Binocular disparity. The view from the left and right eyes shows an offset for surface points at depths different from the point of fixation.

position of points in the scene between the left and right eyes is called *disparity*.

Given both corresponding retinal locations and the vergence angle of the eyes, it is possible to determine the angle of intersecting lines of sight, as in Figure 6.1 and Equation (6.1), and thus compute the distance z from head to environmental location. As with convergence, the sensitivity of binocular disparity to changes in depth decreases with depth. If eye pointing angles are not known, then, for locations approximately in front of the viewer, disparities are a source of distance information relative to the distance to the fixation point. Once correspondences have been established, the relative positions on which particular points in the world project onto the left and right retinas indicate whether the points are closer than or farther away from the point of fixation. *Crossed disparity* occurs when the corresponding points are displaced outward relative to the fovea, and indicates that the surface point is closer than the point of fixation, while *uncrossed disparity* occurs when the corresponding points are displaced inward relative to the fovea, and indicates that the surface point is farther away than the point of fixation (see Figure 6.12).

Figure 6.12 shows crossed and uncrossed disparities defined relative to the projection of the fixation point. More generally, disparity indicates depth relative to the *horopter*, defined as the locus of points in the world projecting onto corresponding retinal locations and thus generating zero disparity. Crossed disparities indicate that the surface point generating the disparity is closer than the horopter; uncrossed disparities indicate that the surface point generating the disparity is farther away than the

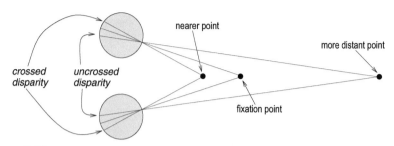

Figure 6.12
Near the line of sight, surface points nearer than the fixation point produce disparities in the opposite direction from those associated with surface points more distant than the fixation point.

horopter. The horopter is not a fixed distance away from the eyes but rather is a curved surface passing through the point of fixation. Because of the relationship of crossed and uncrossed disparities to the horopter, disparity is usually considered a relative depth cue, distinct from vergence.

There is a limit to the maximum range of retinal disparity values that the human visual system can place into effective correspondence (Howard, 2002). If disparities exceed this range, double vision (*diplopia*) occurs. The range of disparity over which correspondence is possible is called *Panum's fusional area*. It is defined by the angular difference between the point at which diplopia first occurs in crossed disparities and the point at which it first occurs in uncrossed disparities, and so is associated with a range of disparities around the horopter. Specifying the actual extent of Panum's fusional area is complicated by the fact that it is dependent on spatial frequency, retinal distance from the fovea, and a variety of other factors, in addition to being subject to individual differences. The disparity limit for placing high spatial frequency patterns into correspondence might be as low as ten arc minutes, while low-frequency patterns can have disparity differences of several degrees and still be fusible (Schor, Wood, & Ogawa, 1984). Furthermore, not all disparities that can be fused are viewable without discomfort. *Percival's zone of comfort*, which specifies the range of disparities that can be viewed over significant periods of time without distress, is about a third of Panum's fusional area (D. M. Hoffman, Girshick, Akeley, & Banks, 2008).

Retinal disparity has both a magnitude—typically specified in terms of visual angle—and a direction. *Horizontal disparity* is in the direction parallel to the direction of offset of the two eyes. *Vertical disparity* is in the direction orthogonal to this direction and the facing direction. Informally, for the head held level, horizontal disparity is in the left-right direction, and vertical disparity is in the up-down direction. Many discussions of binocular disparity implicitly or explicitly assume that horizonal disparity is the property used to determine depth. While horizontal disparities are larger in magnitude than vertical disparities for the same pair of corresponding points, vertical disparity is non-zero for corresponding surface points over much of the visual field. To see this, consider binocular viewing of a short vertical line segment, positioned to the right of the facing direction. The distance from the left eye to the line is longer than the distance from the right eye to the line, resulting in the retinal projection of the line in the left eye having a smaller vertical extent that the retinal projection of the line in the right eye. Since the projection of the endpoints of the line in the left eye are closer together than the projection of the same points in the right eye, one or both of the corresponding retinal locations will necessarily differ in vertical position.

Mathematically, under a broad range of circumstances, evaluating both horizontal and vertical disparities is sufficient to determine absolute depth to visible environmental locations without extraretinal information about the vergence angle of the eyes (Longuet-Higgins, 1982; Mayhew & Longuet-Higgins, 1982). The human visual system appears to use both extraretinal information about vergence and vertical disparity to determine absolute depth, but the relative contribution of the two depends on the visible field of view (M. F. Bradshaw, Glennester, & Rogers, 1996; B. J. Rogers & Bradshaw, 1995). Ocularmotor-determined vergence angle contributes to absolute depth determinations across a wide range of fields of view, but has the greatest effect when the view of the environment is narrow. Vertical disparity seems to require a field of view greater than about 20° to be effective in providing the scaling information needed to determine absolute depth.

The perception of depth from stereo is affected by contrast and contours in a manner similar in some ways to brightness (see Chapter 3). The Craik-O'Brien-Cornsweet effect, in which contrast in a visual property across a contour dominates the perception of the magnitude of the property on either side of the contour, is present for stereo and a number of other visual cues in addition to brightness (Anstis, Howard, & Rogers, 1978). The effect is far stronger for vertically oriented disparity discontinuities than for horizontally oriented discontinuities (B. J. Rogers & Graham, 1983), suggesting that it is disparity estimation that is being affected, rather than a more general representation of depth.

6.3   Accommodation and Blur

In common with other imaging systems involving conventional lenses, the sharpness of retinal images varies with the distance from the eye to the surface under view (Marcos, Moreno, & Navarro, 1999; B. Wang & Ciuf-freda, 2004). At any given point in time, the eye has a focal distance that will produce the maximum sharpness in the retinal image. Surfaces closer to and farther from this distance will be seen less clearly, with the rate at which distance affects sharpness characterized by the *depth-of-field*. The optical properties of the eye can be modified to optically focus at different distances, a process referred to as *accommodation*. Unlike cameras, focusing in the human eye is accomplished by distorting the shape of the lens at the front of the eye rather than moving fixed-shape lenses with respect to a focal plane. Most people have increasing difficulty focusing over a range of distances as they get beyond about 45 years old.

The vision system has access to information from the muscles in the eye that affect focus. As a result, accommodation is a potential source of depth information, at least at near distances. There is an interaction between accommodation and convergence in the human visual system: accommodation is used to help determine the appropriate vergence angle, while the vergence angle is used to help set the focus distance (Howard, 2002). This helps the visual system when there is uncertainty in setting either accommodation or vergence.

Accommodation in principle can support depth perception either directly, through an association between the muscle forces acting on the lens of the eye, or indirectly, by biasing vergence and thus affecting the scaling of depth as derived from disparity. The evidence suggests that accommodation is, at best, a weak depth cue (Fisher & Ciuffreda, 1988; Ritter, 1977; Wallach & Norris, 1963; Watt, Akeley, Ernst, & Banks, 2005), though there is substantial variability in the reports of its effect. Mon-Williams and Tresilian (2000) argue that accommodation can be used to determine ordinal depth when no other depth cues are available, but otherwise has little effect on depth perception.

Those not familiar with the specifics of visual perception sometimes confuse depth estimation from accommodation with depth information arising out of the blur associated with limited depth-of-field in the eye. The accommodation depth cue, which arises from the focusing of the eye, can only provide information about the distance to that portion of the visual field that is in focus. It does not depend on the degree to which other portions of the visual field are out of focus, other than that blur is used by the visual system to adjust focus. Blur is affected by how far a surface location is away from the focal distance, but blur does not indicate if the imaged surface is nearer or farther than the focal distance. Furthermore, blur discrimination in the human visual system is poor (Mather & Smith, 2002), and the magnitude of blur is of limited use in determining even distance relative to the focal distance unless it can be scaled by information about depth-of-field. For these reasons, Mather and

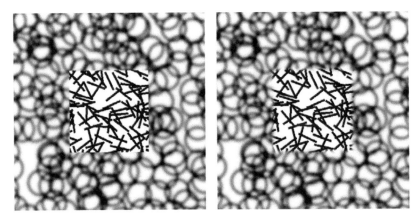

Figure 6.13
Does the central square appear in front of the pattern of circles or is it seen as appearing through a square hole in the pattern of circles? The only difference in the two images is the sharpness of the edge between the line and circle patterns (Marshall et al., 1996, used by permission).

Smith assert that "blur is best viewed as a relatively coarse, qualitative depth cue."

Depth-of-field-related blur does seem to provide a degree of ordinal depth information (Marshall, Burbeck, Arely, Rolland, & Martin, 1996). In Figure 6.13, the perception of the depth ordering at a boundary is affected by the sharpness of the boundary relative to the sharpness of the surfaces to either side. A sharp boundary is seen as attached to the sharper of the two surfaces, making that surface appear in front of the more blurred surface. A blurred boundary appears to be part of the blurred surface, making that surface appear in front and also demonstrating that the depth ordering is not a function of the degree of blur alone.

Another striking instance of blur affecting space perception is what is often informally referred to as the *tilt-shift effect*. In this effect, a variable pattern of blur across an image of a large-scale scene combines with perspective cues for relative depth to generate a sense that the image is actually of a small-scale model (R. T. Held, Cooper, O'Brien, & Banks, 2010; Okatani & Deguchi, 2007). Figure 6.14 shows an example. While there has been little formal perceptual study of the tilt-shift effect, it appears to require a scene with strong perspective cues indicating an obliquely viewed ground plane. A blur pattern is applied such that one portion of the image is unblurred, with the magnitude of blur in the remainder of the image consistent with the perspective-indicated relative depth difference from the unblurred area. (A web search for the terms "tilt shift Photoshop" will

Figure 6.14

An example of the tilt-shift effect. The upper image is of a real scene. The lower image, which appears to be of a miniaturized model, was created from the upper image using simulated lens blur consistent with a narrow depth-of-field.

produce many pages explaining how to create images of these sorts from standard photographs.)

6.4   Issues Specific to Computer Graphics

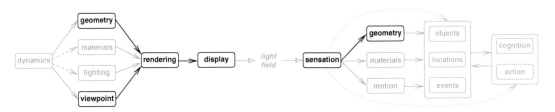

Stereoscopic depth perception requires convergence and disparity. While these are a natural consequence of viewing the three-dimensional world, the stereo cues available when viewing a displayed image specify the depth to the display surface, not the scene portrayed on that surface (see Chapter 12). To overcome this, stereoscopic display devices must display separate images to the two eyes, with the images differing in ways that approximate the convergence and disparity that would arise from viewing the actual physical environment being portrayed.

6.4.1   Displaying Images in Stereo

Figure 6.15 shows a *stereogram*, which is produced by taking a picture of the same scene from two camera positions, offset horizontally by a small distance. Specialized cameras exist for taking both images at once, though with a great deal of care and little motion in the scene it is possible to shoot the first image, move the camera slightly to the side, and then shoot the second image. In Figure 6.15 the two images are placed side to side so that the picture taken from the left camera position is to the left and the picture taken from the right camera position is to the right. If the left image is seen only by the left eye and the right image is seen only by the right eye, both retinal images will be similar but with disparity corresponding to depth in the original scene. The result, for those not affected by stereoblindness, will be that the visual system will perceive a single image, with a strong sense of three-dimensionality.

Most people will be unable to view the stereograph in this way without aid. To have each image fill the field of view of one eye, it is necessary to get so close to the pictures that only the severely nearsighted will be able to focus on them. For those who can make out the images up close, accommodation cues will couple with vergence in a way that crosses the eyes, complicating the eye positioning needed to keep each picture in view of

Figure 6.15

Photographically produced stereogram. The two images were taken from horizontally offset camera positions and are intended to be viewed separately by the left and right eyes.

only one eye. It is this second problem that makes free fusing, as described in Section 6.2.2, so difficult.

Charles Wheatstone (1838) constructed the first device to aid in viewing images stereoscopically. The *Wheatstone stereoscope* used mirrors oriented at 45° to the viewer's facing direction to provide binocular viewing of two images placed to either side of the viewer (see Figure 6.16). Because of the mirrors, the images needed to be right-left reversed. Wheatstone's article describing the stereoscope included a page of hand-drawn figure pairs that could be viewed in the device. The use of mirrors in the Wheatstone

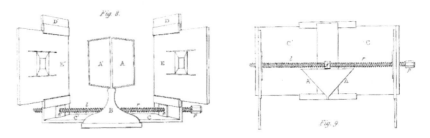

Figure 6.16

Wheatstone stereoscope (from Wheatstone, 1838).

Figure 6.17

Stereoscopic viewers: (a) Hubbard folding, (b) Lorgnette, (c) Holmes,
(d) anaglyphic, and (e) View-Master.

stereoscope allows the two images being viewed to be placed a significant
distance from the eyes without overlapping each other due to the increased
image size needed for more distant viewing. This is compatible with the
smaller vergence angle associated with viewing more distant objects in the
natural world. The Wheatstone design is still used in some perception
experiments exploring stereopsis and in some radiologic applications, but
it is too cumbersome for casual use.

Eleven years after Wheatstone's published description of his mirror-
based stereoscope, Sir David Brewster demonstrated an alternative design
that dispensed with mirrors and instead had users look straight ahead at a
pair of images, with each eye looking through a lens (Brewster, 1856). The
lenses served to magnify the images, so small pictures looked bigger. More
importantly, they affected the focus information so that accommodation
signaled the pictures as being farther away than they really were. This
causes the eyes to point in a less-converged orientation, and thus individually point toward the intended pictures. While Wheatstone and Brewster
are probably best known for the viewers that they designed, both contributed significantly to the theory of stereo vision (Wade & Ono, 1985).
Brewster's design was popularized by Oliver Wendell Holmes (1859), and
Holmes stereoscopes are still in common use. Figure 6.17 shows some of
the many types of stereoscopes used today for viewing image pairs of the
form shown in Figure 6.15, plus the ubiquitous View-Master viewer and its
reels of image pairs.

Stereoscopes require a relatively precise alignment between images and viewer optics, and cannot easily support stereo viewing over a wide field of view. Both of these constraints pose problems for images projected on movie screens, displayed on computer monitors, or appearing in large format on the printed page. In all these cases, a different mechanism is used to allow left and right eyes to view separate and distinct images. The basic idea is to overlap (*multiplex*) left and right images on the same display surface and then have viewers wear goggles that can separate out the two images and allow each to be seen only by the appropriate eye.

The most common of these systems is *anaglyphic stereo*, in which left-eye and right-eye images are displayed in separate colors, and glasses are worn with colored lenses corresponding to the left- and right-eye images. Anaglyphic stereo takes advantage of the relative insensitivity of the visual system to color in establishing correspondences. Different-colored features in the left-eye and right-eye images can be matched easily, as long as they have similar shape and contrast. The effectiveness of anaglyphic stereo depends in part on the colors chosen, since that determines how much of the image intended for one eye leaks over into the other eye's view. To date, no clear standard has emerged. Much of the continuing popularity of anaglyphic stereo is due to the fact that images can be viewed on any color-capable display device using inexpensive colored glasses.

If properly prepared, anaglyphic images can convey some sense of natural color even through the colored glasses, though the effect is imperfect. Full-color stereo images can be obtained by overlaying left- and right-eye images on a display surface such that each has a different polarization. Both linear and circular polarization can be used, but circular polarization produces less variability when the user's head is tilted. For linear polarization, left/right images use polarizations with orthogonal orientations. For circular polarization, left/right images use polarizations of opposite direction. Viewing such images with glasses having the appropriate polarization results in the desired three-dimensional effect. Polarization stereograms cannot be presented on conventional display devices. One common way to use this method is to have two projectors, each with the appropriate filter over its lens, carefully aligned to project overlapping images. This also requires a special screen, since conventional projection screens will change the polarization characteristics of the light that they reflect.

A popular way to display full-color stereograms on computer monitors is to use *field-sequential stereo* (often called *active stereo*), in which left and right images are displayed sequentially in time, in consecutive video fields. *Shutter goggles* are worn by the viewer, and an active liquid crystal system alternates passing light through the left and right eyes in sync with the alternating projection of left and right images. Synchronization is achieved by having the display system or video source generate a signal that is sent to the shutter goggles, usually using some wireless transmission mechanism. Field-sequential stereo works well, particularly with monitors having a high refresh rate. A monitor refresh rate $\geq$120 Hz results in a flicker rate for each eye of $\geq$60 Hz, which, for most people, will not be noticeable (Chapter 5).

Four different technologies are in current use for projecting 3D images in theaters. They vary substantially in terms of the impact on theater operators, but, marketing claims aside, there are as yet no controlled studies showing a clear choice in terms of the perceptual fidelity of the 3D experience. The RealD system uses field-sequential alternating circular polarization and passive polarized goggles, resulting in a single projector system that does not need active shutter goggles or carefully registered dual projectors (Cowan, 2008). As with all systems using polarized stereo projection, a special screen is required to preserve the intended polarization. An alternate polarization approach (IMAX and Christie 3D) uses two projectors, one for each eye. This provides increased brightness over single-projector solutions and, in the case of IMAX, has the potential for increased resolution when film-based projection is used. As with RealD, a special screen is required. Dolby 3D uses a variation on anaglyphic stereo, called *wavelength multiplex visualization* (Jorke, Simon, & Fritz, 2008). Each eye is covered by a filter passing three narrowly tuned spectral bands: one in the red region, one in the green region, and the third in the blue region. The frequency tuning of these notch filters is slightly offset for the two eyes, with the left eye seeing a different portion of the red, green, and bluish spectrums than the right eye. The images intended to be seen by the left and right eyes are run through the same sets of filters and then simultaneously projected on the screen. The result is that the left and right eyes are presented with distinct images, each with sufficient spectral variability to see the full range of perceptible colors due to the trichromatic property of human color vision (see Chapter 4). No special screen is required. The XpanD system uses field-sequential projection combined with shutter goggles actively synchronized to the projection system. These goggles are substantially more expensive than the passive goggles used in the polarization-based systems, but the approach avoids the need for special polarization-preserving screens.

One problem with all of these display technologies is that accommodation is fixed at a distance dependent on the distance to the display surface and any intervening optics, while the vergence needed to bring left- and right-eye images into correspondence varies. In the real world, accommodation and vergence covary with distance (see Section 6.3). The accommodation-vergence conflict in stereo displays can lead to visual fatigue and worse, particularly as viewing time increases (D. M. Hoffman et al., 2008; Wann, Rushton, & Mon-Williams, 1995; Wann & Mon-Williams, 1997). It is important to note that depth-of-field blurring techniques

(Barsky & Kosloff, 2008; Hillaire, Lécuyer, Cozot, & Casiez, 2008), on their
own, do not alleviate this problem; however, in principle, low-latency stereo
rendering coupled with very rapid eye tracking of both eyes might help.

6.4.2   3D Film

Stereo animations using mechanically displayed flip cards date back to the
1850s. By the 1890s multiple suggestions for stereo motion pictures had
been proposed. The first 3D feature film, *The Power of Love*, was shown
in 1922. (For a history of 3D film, see Zone, 2007.) Since that time, there
have been periodic renaissances of stereo in film, usually associated with a
combination of technological advances, market forces, and occasionally art
(Mendiburu, 2009). A major peak in the popularity of 3D film occurred
in the 1950s, including *The Creature from the Black Lagoon* and many
other releases, both more and less noteworthy. The early 21st century has
seen yet another revival, enabled by the increasing use of digital projection
technology in theaters and a number of other factors.

The display of 3D images in movie theaters presents three significant
perceptual challenges. The range of seating positions means that the geometric relationships projected onto viewers' retinas will vary substantially
throughout the audience. Since the left and right imagery is either captured
by cameras or synthesized by computer graphics rendering, the relationship between left and right camera geometry is not bound by the geometric
relationships of the viewers' left and right eyes. This provides degrees of
freedom to the 3D cinematographer well beyond what is available in 2D
film making, an added flexibility that can be used for better or worse (often
the latter). Finally, the screen itself can interfere with stereo perception in
ways that can be perceptually significant.

There will be, at most, one location in a theater where the visual angles
of images projected on the screen match the visual angles apparent from
the location of the camera. From any other location, shapes will be distorted, and the visual extent of objects will be wrong. As discussed much
more completely in Chapter 12, the visual system is relatively effective at
compensating for these shape distortions when viewing images displayed
on a screen or other flat surface, but often misjudges the scale of size and
distance. There is some evidence that the visual system may be more sensitive to the effects of viewpoint location when viewing stereo images than
when viewing conventional 2D displays (R. T. Held & Banks, 2008). The
problem is that with stereo, viewing from the "wrong" vantage point will
not only affect the visual angles of the projected image, but will also distort
disparity and vergence.

In stereo vision, the eyes are a fixed distance apart, and the visual system has access to their pointing directions. In 3D film, whether acquired

photographically or produced using computer graphics, there is complete flexibility with regards to camera (real or virtual) spacing and pointing direction. As a result, vergence and disparity for a viewer watching the projected image may be *very* different than for a viewer looking at the corresponding physical environment from the camera location. Used well, this can allow the 3D cinematographer to manipulate perceived size and distance. Used less well, size and distance will be misperceived in unintended ways (e.g., producing a toy-like appearance similar to that seen in Figure 6.14). Used even less well, audiences will get a headache.

In 3D film, the screen distance between corresponding points in the left-eye and right-eye images is called *parallax*. The parallax associated with a corresponding pair of points is said to be positive if the retinal projection of those points results in uncrossed disparity for a viewer fixated on a point on the actual screen surface. Negative parallax generates crossed disparity for a viewer fixated on a point on the screen. The viewer's retinal disparity for this same set of corresponding points is a function of the viewer's distance from the screen and eye vergence angle. It is important that camera spacing and pointing be done in a manner that results in a range of image parallax (the *parallax budget*) that, when viewed from any seat in the theater, results in retinal disparities well within Panum's fusional area.

If the optical axes of the two cameras are parallel, all parallax will be nonpositive. If it is desirable to spread the parallax budget over both positive and negative values, postproduction image shifting can be used. Converging the two cameras will also result in positive and negative screen parallax, but now there will also be vertical distortions that will affect vertical disparity. Whether or not this affects perception is likely a function of the angular extent of the screen as seen by the viewer (M. F. Bradshaw et al., 1996; B. J. Rogers & Bradshaw, 1995), though few if any systematic studies have been done to evaluate the way in which manipulations that change camera convergence or parallax affect perception in theater-like displays. To complicate things further, some 3D films are made with dynamically changing camera spacing or convergence within a single scene. The minimum suggested viewing angle for movie theater seats is variously listed at ranging from about 25° to about 35°, close to the critical field of view of 20° for vertical disparity to have a significant effect. This suggests that there is likely to be a complicated relationship between theater dimensions, seating location, and production design as they affect stereo perception in 3D film.

A perceptual conflict occurs when an object with negative screen parallax gets too close to the screen boundary, an effect referred to as a *paradoxical window* (Lipton, 1982) or *stereoscopic window violation* (Mendiburu, 2009). Figure 6.18 illustrates the problem. Figure 6.18(a) shows a displayed surface point near the left edge of the screen with a screen parallax

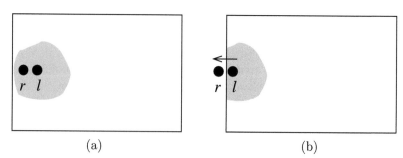

(a)   (b)

Figure 6.18

A perceptual conflict occurs when an object with negative screen parallax gets too close to the screen boundary: (a) left- and right-eye views within frame, (b) right-eye view moves out of frame.

indicating that it is located in depth in front of the screen. In this situation, the left-eye view of the point appears on the screen to the right of the right-eye view of the same point. Now consider what happens if the point moves to the left relative to the screen, due either to object or camera motion. As shown in Figure 6.18(b), the right-eye view of the point will disappear before the left-eye view of the same point. The left-eye view of the surface point that is no longer visible to the right eye is seen to the right of the boundary associated with the disappearance of the surface point in the right-eye view, a situation which cannot occur in the real world, as indicated in Section 6.2.4.

In some cases, the paradoxical window effect will not produce a noticeable visible conflict. These include rapid motion of foreground objects into or out of the frame, and darker foreground objects that produce relatively little contrast with the screen frame (Lipton, 1982). In other circumstances, the paradoxical window effect can be perceptually disturbing. Careful composition of the scene can avoid situations in which an object presented with negative parallax moves out of the field of view. Another option is to put dark strips at the sides of the projected image, arranged to give negative parallax to the sides of the strips such that the screen edges appear to float forward toward the same perceptual depth as the object that would otherwise cause the conflict.

It is possible to synthesize stereo images from imagery originally acquired with a single camera, thus converting a film from 2D to 3D. This can be done using ad hoc methods that cut up individual frames into objects that should appear at different depths and then making an image pair by differentially shifting parts of the original image to produce the appropriate parallax, generating a 3D model of the original scene and then reprojecting the original image to generate left-eye and right-eye views, or exploiting the parallax associated with translational camera motion by using original image frames taken at different times as a single left/right image pair (Mendiburu, 2009).

6.4.3   Autostereoscopic, Accommodative, and Volumetric Displays

All of the stereo display devices discussed above require specialized viewing equipment and suffer from problems due to vergence-accommodation conflict. A number of technologies under development remove one or both of these limitations.

Autostereoscopic displays present different images to the two eyes without the need for specialized glasses (Dodgson, 2005). One approach, also used in 3D postcards, is to divide the display surface into narrow strips and then use optical techniques to change the set of strips that is visible from different viewing positions. If the viewer is aligned properly with the display, the viewing angle associated with the left eye sees one set of strips while the viewing area of the right eye sees a different set of strips.

Accommodative displays allow for stereo viewing in which vergence and focus are approximately matched. This reduces eye strain due to vergence-accommodation conflict, and potentially increases the accuracy of depth perception. One approach to accommodative displays is to blend images from multiple displays involving different optical path lengths (Akeley, Watt, Girshick, & Banks, 2004). Another approach is to construct a display with each pixel covered by a lens having a focal length adjustable under computer control (S. Liu, Hua, & Cheng, 2010).

Volumetric displays present images in a true, three-dimensional space, rather than displaying 2D images to each eye to simulate stereo viewing (Favalora, 2005; A. Jones, McDowall, Yamada, Bolas, & Debevec, 2007). As a result, vergence and disparity cues are more natural and match accommodation, though both are relative to the display volume, not necessarily the scene being displayed. Some volumetric technologies display a true, three-dimensional structure, with the changes in viewing angle associated with head movement resulting in appropriate visual changes to background surfaces at occlusion boundaries. Other approaches to volumetric displays are more correctly described as $2\frac{1}{2}$-D systems, with visual errors at occlusion boundaries resulting in a lack of da Vinci stereopsis and visual artifacts during head motion.

6.4.4   Visually Immersive Virtual Environments

Immersive virtual environments are computer interfaces that provide a user with the sensory experience of being in a simulated space. The term *virtual reality* is often used to describe such systems, though with variable

Figure 6.19

Head-mounted display (left); user wearing HMD in tracked space (right).

usage in both technical and popular media. Most immersive virtual environment displays are primarily or exclusively visual, though additional sensory modalities are needed to provide a compelling experience of being in the simulation (Whitton, 2003). Work on virtual environments dates back at least to Heilig (1960, 1962) and Sutherland (1965, 1968). One essential component to effective visually immersive displays is that what is seen must change appropriately as the user moves (see Chapter 11). This is typically implemented by coupling the CG viewpoint used in the simulation to a head tracker worn by the user. While head tracking is almost certainly more important to achieving immersion than is binocular stereo, a large number of visually immersive virtual environment systems use both.

Two quite different classes of display systems are used in visually immersive virtual environments. One approach is to use multiple screen-based displays surrounding the user (Cruz-Neira, Sandin, & DeFanti, 1993). These provide a wide field of view and a sense of being truly surrounded by the simulated space, but they severely limit mobility. Mobility is increased at the cost of limited field of view and other ergonomic problems by using a head-mounted display (HMD). An HMD is a helmet worn by a user that places a video screen in front of each eye to provide a stereo display system. A tracking system determines the position and orientation of the helmet so that the viewpoint used to generate the computer graphics can be updated in a manner consistent with the user's actual movements (Figure 6.19.)

Most HMDs have limited fields of view, typically 20°–40° horizontally. In some HMDs, *partial overlap* stereo is used to extend the horizontal field of view. This involves rendering the computer graphics with the virtual cameras *di*verged, such that when distant surfaces are viewed, only a portion of the two images overlap. Optics are then used to appropriately position the images relative to the eyes so that when the user's eyes are pointed straight ahead the left eye is aimed at a point right of center on the left image and the right eye is aimed at a point left of center on the right image. An overlap of 50% is common, resulting in a 50% gain in horizontal field of view. With partial overlap, only the central portion of the rendered view is visible in both eyes and hence perceivable in stereo. In addition, many users see a visually distracting bar, seemingly close in front of their nose.

6.5   Suggestions for Further Reading

Any text on visual perception will have a chapter on stereo vision, though the coverage varies substantially in the amount of detail included. The following includes a good discussion of the topic, many examples presented as anaglyphs, and its own set of colored glasses:

Frisby, J. P., & Stone, J. V. (2010). *Seeing: The computational approach to biological vision* (2nd ed.). Cambridge, MA: MIT Press.

The most complete coverage available of human binocular stereo perception:

Howard, I. P. (2002). *Seeing in depth: Vol. 1. Basic mechanisms.* Toronto, Ontario: I Porteous.

Howard, I. P., & Rogers, B. J. (2002). *Seeing in depth: Vol. 2. Depth perception.* Toronto, Ontario: I Porteous.

The classic work by Julesz should be required reading for anyone interested in the development of theories of human stereo vision:

Julesz, B. (1971). *Foundations of cyclopean perception.* Chicago: University of Chicago Press.

Between them, these three books cover the history and technology of 3D film:

Lipton, L. (1982). *Foundations of the stereoscopic cinema: A study in depth.* New York: Van Nostrand. Available from http://www.stereoscopic.org/library/

Zone, R. (2007). *Stereoscopic cinema and the origins of 3-D film, 1838–1952.* Lexington, KY: University Press of Kentucky.

Mendiburu, B. (2009). *3D movie making: Stereoscopic digital cinema from script to screen.* Burlington, MA: Elsevier.

III

Surfaces and Movement

7

Perspective

An excellent way to learn about the importance of perspective in visually conveying information about depth is to stroll through the Uffizi Gallery in Florence, Italy (Figure 7.1). The exhibits are organized chronologically, starting in the 13th century. The early paintings have an obvious two-dimensional appearance to them, though there are a few examples in this pre-Renaissance period of attempts to break the perception of what was represented on the canvas from the flatness of the canvas itself. In one case, a small subcanvas protrudes from the main surface. In others, illustrations of interposition (partial occlusion) are used to create a stacking effect in

Figure 7.1

Statues of Leon Alberti and Leonardo da Vinci outside of the Uffizi Gallery in Florence, Italy.

which one entity is seen nearer than another, but without any clear sense of the depths involved. From there, the gallery tour progresses to the Renaissance, where the perspective-based visual cues of depth scaling, foreshortening, and convergence of parallel lines are increasingly used to give a rich sense of spaciousness to the art.[1] The development of methods for incorporating mathematically correct perspective into paintings occurred

---

[1] Along the way, note Raphael's *Leo X and Cardinals*, which includes excellent renderings of complex indirect lighting and material properties.

Figure 7.2

Examples of linear perspective.

over much of the 15th century. Currently available English translations of key work from this period include Alberti (1435/1991) and da Vinci (1566/1970).

Perspective effects are pervasive in our visual world and provide a wealth of information about spatial layout (Sedgwick, 1983, 1986). These effects include object size scaled by distance, the convergence of parallel lines, the ground plane extending to a visible horizon, position on the ground plane relative to the horizon, and more (Figure 7.2). While the Renaissance had to struggle to understand the mathematics of perspective and its implications on drawing, perspective transforms are now an integral part of any 3D graphics systems (Roberts, 1965). This chapter provides an overview of the nature of perspective projection and its utility in providing information about size and distance. Additional information relating to perspective can be found in Chapters 8, 11, and 12.

7.1   The Nature of Perspective

Images are formed when light reflected from the environment is *projected* onto a two-dimensional imaging surface. For this chapter, we will assume visual images are produced by a *point projection* process in which visible rays of light all pass through a common projection point and fall on a flat image plane. This is usually a reasonable approximation for conventional

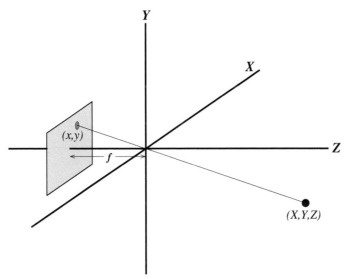

Figure 7.3

Simplified coordinate system for describing the effects of perspective projection, with image plane aligned with the (X, Y) plane of the world coordinate system.

cameras, though the resulting mathematics does not accurately describe the human eye with its large aperture lens, curved retina, and multiple sources of optical distortion. Nevertheless, the formalism gives intuition as to the nature of perspective effects and is much easier to illustrate on the (flat) printed page than would be a formalism that more accurately represented the actual optics and geometry of the eye.

We will further simplify the mathematics by assuming that image and world coordinate systems are aligned as shown in Figure 7.3. Locations in the environment will be specified by the three-dimensional coordinates (X, Y, Z). Locations on the image plane will be specified by the two-dimensional coordinates (x, y). In this simplified formulation, the image plane will be aligned with the world coordinate system such that the x, y plane is parallel to the X, Y plane, and the image plane is offset a distance f from the origin of the world coordinate system, where f is called the *focal length*. The origin of the (X, Y, Z) coordinate system is called the *center of projection* (*CoP*) or *optical center*. In this model, all lines of sight associating an (x, y) location in the image with a (X, Y, Z) location in the world pass through the point of projection. The Z-axis constitutes the *optical axis* of this system. This formalism has several annoying properties. As with actual imaging systems, the x and y coordinates of a projected point have opposite signs from the corresponding X and Y world locations. This

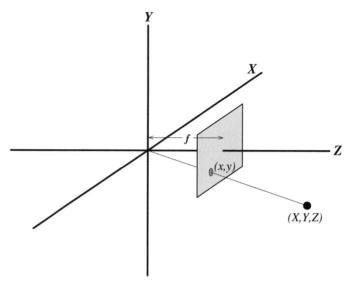

Figure 7.4

Treating the image plane as if it was in front of the point of projection eliminates the sign reversal for world and image coordinates.

can be fixed by artificially reversing the signs of the x and y values, effectively putting the image plane in front of the point of projection (see Figure 7.4), which is the convention we have used below. Additionally, if the coordinate system is right-handed, then at least one of the X-, Y-, or Z-axes will point in a direction not corresponding to the natural meanings of "right," "up," and "forward." This commonly causes confusion when creating graphics programs in low-level tool kits such as OpenGL.

For the coordinate system shown in Figure 7.3, with the convention that the x and y values have the sign of the corresponding X and Y locations, the image-plane location of a world point at (X, Y, Z) is specified by

$$x = f\frac{X}{Z} \ , \quad y = f\frac{Y}{Z} \ . \tag{7.1}$$

For two locations approximately equal distance along the Z-axis from the imaging device

$$\Delta x = x_i - x_j = \frac{f}{Z}(X_i - X_j) = \frac{f}{Z}\Delta X \ ,$$

$$\Delta y = y_i - y_j = \frac{f}{Z}(Y_i - Y_j) = \frac{f}{Z}\Delta Y \ . \tag{7.2}$$

If the distance Z to an object in the environment is fixed, the size of the projection of the object on the image plane *increases* with the focal length f.

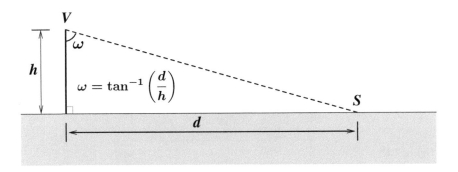

Figure 7.5
The angle between the line of sight from a vantage point V (a distance h from a surface) to a point S on that surface, relative to the line of sight normal to the orientation of the surface.

This is the principle behind telephoto photographic lenses, with increasing focal length linearly related to magnification. For fixed f, the size of the projection of a world object on the image plane *decreases* with increasing distance Z from the imaging system. This scaling effect provides almost all of the information about spatial layout that arises due to perspective. Most directly, it creates a relationship between object size and object distance (see Section 7.3). It also causes the familiar appearance of parallel lines converging in the distance, as in Figure 7.2.

An infinite plane, viewed from a vantage point above the plane, will have a visible *horizon*. Figure 7.5 shows the angle ω between a line of sight to the nearest point on an infinite surface and the line of sight to a point a distance d from that nearest surface point. For a vantage point V, a distance h from the surface, ω is given by the relationship

$$\omega = \tan^{-1}\left(\frac{d}{h}\right) . \tag{7.3}$$

As $d \to \infty$, $\omega \to 90°$, regardless of the magnitude of h. All lines of sight with $\omega < 90°$ intersect the surface or some object on or above the surface. All lines of sight with $\omega > 90°$ fail to intersect the surface, whether or not other objects are present. The view from all unobstructed lines of sight with $\omega = 90°$ is split by surface and nonsurface, thus forming the horizon. One consequence of this is that two lines of sight from the same vantage point to distinct points on the horizon can be used to determine the orientation of the surface in the coordinate system used to define the lines of sight. Computationally, the surface normal is given by the normalized cross product of the pointing vectors of the lines of sight.

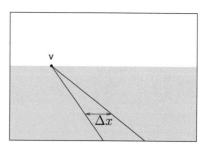

Figure 7.6

Parallel lines on a planar surface that are not perpendicular to the Z-axis project to converging lines in an image of the surface.

Under the perspective model used in this section, involving point projection onto a flat image plane, a line on a planar surface projects to a line in the image. Figure 7.6 shows the image of an infinite planar surface with two parallel lines, a distance ΔX apart, oriented such that the horizon of the surface is parallel with the Y-axis. From Equation (7.2), the distance between the projection of the lines in the image is given by $\Delta x = \frac{f}{Z}\Delta X$, where Z is the distance from the viewpoint to the actual world location of the lines. As $Z \to \infty$, $\Delta x \to 0$. The consequence of this is that the image of parallel lines on an obliquely viewed, infinite surface converge to a point. This point is called the *vanishing point* of the lines, and lies on the horizon of the surface.

If there are multiple families of parallel lines on the same flat surface, with the families differing in orientation on the surface, there will be multiple vanishing points, one for each family of lines. All of these vanishing points will lie on a single *vanishing line*. If the parallel lines are on an infi-

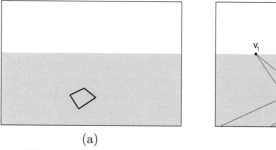

(a)   (b)

Figure 7.7

(a) Markings on an infinite flat surface, made up of two pairs of parallel lines.
(b) The vanishing points of the two sets of parallel lines.

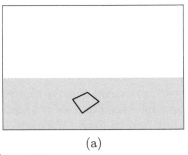 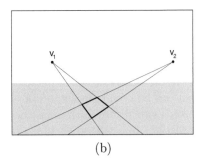

(a)   (b)

Figure 7.8

(a) Two pairs of parallel lines on a flat surface of finite extent. (b) The vanishing points of the two sets of parallel lines, which no longer correspond to the visible edge of the surface.

nite surface, the vanishing line will correspond to the visible horizon of that surface (Figure 7.7). If parallel lines appear on a surface of finite extent, the vanishing points no longer lie on the visible edge of the surface (Figure 7.8). Multiple sets of parallel lines still define a vanishing line, which is

Figure 7.9

Circular patterns on a flat surface that is viewed obliquely project to ovals. Under perspective projection, the amount of distortion varies over the image, since the angle of the line of sight relative to the surface normal is not constant.

sufficient to determine the orientation of the finite surface. Distinguishing between the vanishing line for a surface and the visible edge of the surface is critical when determining the orientation of the surface if the surface is relatively small.

Another way in which perspective affects projected images in a manner that can be used to assist in inferring properties of environmental geometry is often called *foreshortening*, though that term is used to refer to a variety of distinct but related effects. If a surface pattern is viewed obliquely, the pattern is compressed along the direction of tilt by a factor given by the cosine of the angle between the line of sight and the surface normal. Figure 7.9 provides an example, with circular patterns foreshortened into ellipses due to oblique viewing. The compression of the projected image along the axis of tilt is not actually a perspective effect, since it is not related to the geometry shown in Figure 7.3 or the distance scaling of Equation (7.1). However, when viewing a flat surface, the amount of foreshortening varies over the image due to changing directions of the lines of sight. This can be clearly seen in Figure 7.9, where the more distant markings are more squished due to the increasingly oblique angle that the lines of sight make with the surface.

7.2   Interposition

Equation (7.1) is incomplete, in that not all surface points in the world are actually projected onto the image plane of an imaging system. Much of the world will be outside of the field of view of the imaging system, which is determined by the extent of the image plane that is sensitive to incident light. Even for (X, Y, Z) locations within the field of view, however, many such locations will not be visible because they will be hidden by nearer surfaces. For opaque surfaces, Equation (7.1) needs to be qualified when applying it to image formation by specifying that the image energy projected onto the image plane is a function of the energy emitted by the *closest* surface along the corresponding line of sight. The situation is much more complex for translucent materials, but it will still be the case that nearer objects still partially or completely hide (*occlude*) farther objects along a single line of sight.

The visual cue for depth associated with occlusion is called *interposition*. Interposition provides ordinal information for depth ordering but gives no indication of the magnitude of the depth difference. Likely the most important visual information for interposition in the absence of stereo or motion comes from junctions where edges associated with surface boundaries come together. T-junctions seem to be particularly important. In Figure 7.10(a), the lighter-colored blob appears to be clearly in front of the

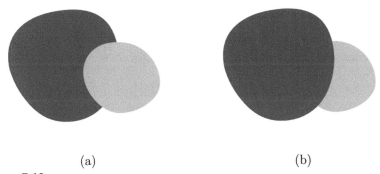

(a)   (b)

Figure 7.10

Interposition provides a visual indication that an image region corresponds to one world entity closer to the viewpoint than a second world entity corresponding to an adjacent image region. (a) Lighter colored blob is in front of darker blob. (b) Lighter colored blob is behind darker blob. In both cases, T-junctions provide critical information about depth ordering.

darker-colored blob, while the situations are reversed in Figure 7.10(b). A major source of visual information for this depth ordering comes at the intersections of the boundaries of the two blobs. More can be found about the importance of junctions in Chapter 3. While there is much theoretical support for the importance of junctions in perceiving depth and many examples involving line drawing images, attempts by the computer vision community to develop methods able to reliably detect junctions in real imagery have met with, at best, limited success (see Apostoloff & Fitzgibbon, 2005; Stein & Hebert, 2009).

7.3   The Relationship between Size and Distance

For an object substantially farther away from the viewpoint than the size of the object itself, the relationships indicated in Equation (7.2) can be rewritten in terms of visual angle in one of two ways:

$$s \approx 2d \tan \left(\frac{\theta}{2} \right) \tag{7.4}$$

or

$$d \approx \frac{1}{2} s \cot \left(\frac{\theta}{2} \right) , \tag{7.5}$$

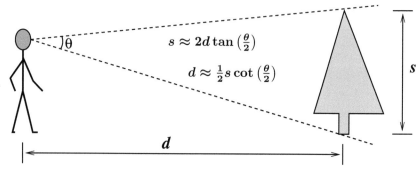

$$s \approx 2d \tan\left(\tfrac{\theta}{2}\right)$$

$$d \approx \tfrac{1}{2}s \cot\left(\tfrac{\theta}{2}\right)$$

Figure 7.11

The size-distance relationship allows the real-world size of an object to be determined based on the visual angle subtended by the object and its distance from the viewer. Likewise, the distance to an object can be determined based on the visual angle subtended by the object and its known actual size.

where s is the size of an object, defined as the extent perpendicular to the line of sight; d is the distance of the object from the viewer; and θ is the visual angle subtended by the object (see Figure 7.11). Together these are known as the *size-distance relationship*, with Equation (7.5) also referred to as *Emmert's law* (Boring, 1940; Epstein, Park, & Casey, 1965; Kilpatrick & Ittelson, 1953). In principle, by knowing the retinal size of a visible object, it is possible to determine the size of the object in the world (or, more accurately, the extent of the object perpendicular to the line of sight) given its distance, or to determine the distance to the object given its physical size. Figure 7.12 shows a practical application of the size-distance relationship.

Figure 7.12

A practical example of the size-distance relationship. These cards are passed out at Katmai National Park in the US, in an effort to avoid both having visitors harass the brown bears and having the brown bears eat the visitors. The figure is printed to scale.

The original support for Emmert's law came from experiments in which people looked at a pattern for a time sufficient to produce an afterimage, then judged the apparent size of the afterimage while looking at another surface. The apparent size of the pattern was found to be proportional to the distance to the surface, consistent with Equation (7.4). Holway and Boring (1941) showed that the physical sizes of two circular patterns could be accurately compared when the two patterns were presented at distances varying by as much as a factor of ten if visual information was available indicating the distance from the viewer to each pattern. When visual information for distance to one of the patterns was eliminated, matching was consistent with the retinal size of the pattern (the proximal stimulus) rather than the physical size of the pattern (the distal stimulus). Reducing but not eliminating depth information produced comparisons that were between the distal and proximal values.

The converse effect involves the relationship between actual and retinal size affecting perceived distance, as shown in Equation (7.5). Figure 7.13 is an illustration of *relative size*, which is one example of size affecting perceived distance. The figure should be viewed with one eye, looking through a rolled-up piece of paper so that no part of the page other than the two ellipses and the surrounding white space is visible. This will remove visible indicators of depth other than the appearance of the ellipses themselves.

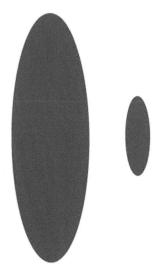

Figure 7.13

An example of relative size affecting distance perception, best viewed through a rolled-up sheet of paper that hides everything but the two ellipses.

Figure 7.14

Familiar size can affect distance perception if the retinal image is recognized as
an object of a known real world size. As with Figure 7.13, this figure should
be viewed through a rolled-up sheet of paper that hides everything but the two
images of people.

Viewed in this manner, most people will have the sense that the ellipse on
the right is farther away than the ellipse on the left. This is consistent with
Equation (7.5) if the visual system is acting as if the two patterns arose
from the projection of objects of similar actual size, but different distances
from the viewer.

Figure 7.14 shows a pattern similar to that in Figure 7.13, except that
the two entities present are easily recognized as people, likely to have similar
real-world sizes. Viewed through a rolled-up piece of paper as was done
for Figure 7.13, many people will have an increased sense of depth for
Figure 7.14 compared with Figure 7.13. This is an example of *familiar size*,
in which the perception of distance predicted by Equation (7.5) exploits
information about the actual size *s* of an object in the world, based on
recognizing the object and knowing its likely real dimensions (Ittelson,
1951; Yonas, Pettersen, & Granrud, 1982). Figure 7.15 is an example of
a popular class of optical illusions, in which familiar size is put in conflict
with other visual cues to distance.

The degree to which familiar size actually affects perception of distance
has been controversial, with a number of researchers providing evidence
that apparent distance is affected far more by relative size than familiar,

(a)   (b)

Figure 7.15

A conflict between familiar size and other depth cues. (a) Perspective and familiar size cues are consistent. (b) Perspective and familiar size cues are inconsistent.

known size (e.g., Epstein, 1961). C. B. Hochberg and Hochberg (1952) found no differences in perceived distance when pictures of an adult and child were viewed under conditions such that both produced similarly sized retinal images. Gogel (1976) argued that familiar size affects verbal descriptions of distance much more than a nonverbal measure involving motion parallax, suggesting a cognitive influence on the former. However, in an experiment in which a combination of relative and familiar size was compared with relative size alone, Yonas et al. (1982) found that adults and seven-month-old babies saw depth differences between two patterns only when familiar size was present, while five-month-old babies made no distinction between the two conditions.

Another potential confound in the studies of the perception of size and distance is the *specific distance tendency* (Gogel, 1969; Gogel & Tietz, 1973; Philbeck & Loomis, 1997). When visual cues for depth are weak or absent, target locations often appear to be at a distance of 2 m–4 m from the viewer, regardless of their actual location. This can cause an overestimation of nearer distances and an underestimation of farther distances. The impact of the specific distance tendency on real-world perception, where there are typically a rich set of depth cues available, is unknown.

7.4   Size and Shape Constancy

During real-world viewing of situations such as depicted in Figure 7.2, similarly sized objects at substantially different distances from the viewer appear to be this same size, despite the fact that their retinal sizes will differ by the same ratio as their distances from the viewer. This is an example of *size constancy*. When a rich set of visual cues for spatial layout are present, we see the distal size of objects and not the extent of the proximal stimulus (e.g., Epstein, 1961). Our perception of size is dominated by the actual physical size, and we often have almost no conscious awareness of the corresponding retinal size of objects, though under some circumstances it is possible to force judgments toward retinal size (Carlson, 1960; Gilinsky, 1955). Size constancy is less effective when looking at pictures, such as the printed Figure 7.2, for reasons discussed in Chapter 12.

A variety of mechanisms have been suggested to account for size constancy, none of them sufficient on its own to explain the empirical data. The size-distance relationship almost certainly plays a part. Familiar size likely does as well, though the supporting evidence is less clear. Another possibility involves the visual properties of the ground texture occluded by an object (J. J. Gibson, 1950a).

Size constancy is rarely exact, with both underestimation and overestimation of actual size occurring in many circumstances. Size constancy often fails completely at longer distances. When looking down at the ground from an airplane, houses, vehicles, and the like look small, even though we know their actual size. To get a sense of the complexity of size constancy, hold your two hands out in front of you, one at arm's length and the other at half that distance away from you, as shown in Figure 7.16(a). Your two

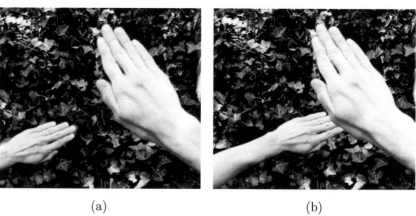

(a)   (b)

Figure 7.16

(a) Size constancy makes hands positioned at different distances from the eye appear to be nearly the same size, even though the retinal sizes are quite different. (b) The effect is less strong when one hand is partially occluded by the other, particular when one eye is closed.

Figure 7.17

Distinctly different 2D shapes can appear equivalent if they have an equivalent 3D interpretation (after J. J. Gibson, 1950a).

hands will look almost the same size, even though the retinal sizes differ by roughly a factor of two. The effect is much less strong if the nearer hand partially occludes the more distant hand, as in Figure 7.16(b), particularly if you close one eye (Gregory, 1997).

The visual system also exhibits *shape constancy*, where the perception of geometric structure is closer to actual object geometry than might be expected, given the distortions of the retinal image due to perspective (Figure 7.17). As with size constancy, shape constancy benefits from visual information for depth (e.g., Gogel, 1965; Vishwanath, Girshick, & Banks, 2005). The recovery of 3D shape from oblique views is also aided if the actual shapes have strong symmetries (King, Meyer, Tangney, & Biederman,

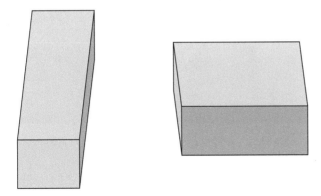

Figure 7.18

Identical 2D shapes can appear distinctly different if they have different 3D interpretations (after Shepard, 1981).

1976). Not only does shape constancy make dissimilar projected patterns look similar, but it can also make identical projected shapes look strikingly dissimilar, as in Figure 7.18, where the top surfaces of the two objects are identical in their shape on the printed page, except that one is rotated with respect to the other.

7.5   The Importance of the Ground Plane

J. J. Gibson (1950b) hypothesized that "there is literally no such thing as a perception of space without the perception of a continuous background surface." Gibson called this hypothesis the *ground theory* of space perception, distinguishing it from an *air theory* of perception arising from laboratory experiments using isolated objects free of a visible background surface. Human perception evolved in a terrestrial world, and Gibson's approach to vision was based in fundamental ways on the nature of that world.

7.5.1   Surface Contact

Figure 7.19 provides a compelling illustration of the way the vision system uses perspective-based information about surfaces to infer depth to objects appearing to rest on those surfaces. In the left image of the figure, two objects appear to be in contact with a flat support surface, with one being closer to the viewpoint than the other. In the right image, it is seen

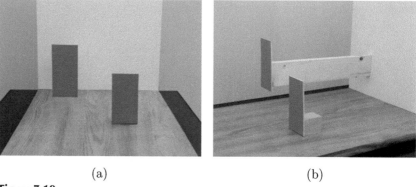

(a)   (b)

Figure 7.19

(a) Both rectangular objects appear in contact with a wooden support surface, with the left object seeming to be farther away than the right object. (b) The actual configuration, in which both rectangular objects are the same distance from the camera in (a), and the left object is *not* in contact with the support surface. (Motivated by a similar demonstration in J. J. Gibson, 1950a.)

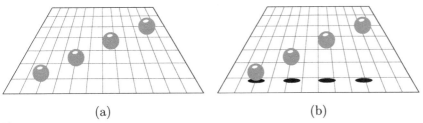

(a) (b)

Figure 7.20
Shadows can indirectly function as a depth cue by associating the depth of an object with a location on the ground plane. (a) The spheres appear to be receding in depth and in contact with the ground plane. (b) Shadows suggest that the spheres are floating above the ground plane, all at the same depth. (After Kersten et al., 1997).

that actually one of the objects is substantially above the support surface, and that both are the same distance from the viewpoint used for the left image. Two points are key about this phenomenon: (1) the left object is seen in contact with the support surface, even when it is not, and (2) the depth of the left object is consistent with the (incorrectly) perceived contact location.

Objects need not be seen to be in direct contact with a ground plane for the ground plane to affect the perception of distance to the object. Perceived distance to objects is influenced by the ground plane when they appear to be supported by other objects that in turn appear to be in contact with the ground, though the effect varies with the height of the supporting objects (Meng & Sedgwick, 2001, 2002). Cast shadows can have the effect of making the casting object appear to be at the depth associated with where the shadow is positioned on the ground plane, rather than at that portion of the ground plane occluded by the object, as is the case in Figure 7.19(a) (Kersten, Mamassian, & Knill, 1997; Yonas, Goldsmith, & Hallstrom, 1978). In Figure 7.20(a), the spheres appear to be in contact with the ground plane as in Figure 7.19(a), and as a result, appear to be receding in depth. In Figure 7.20(b), all but the left sphere are seen floating above the ground plane, with a perceived depth consistent with the location of the shadows on the ground plane. More can be found about this in Chapter 9.

The perception of distance to objects is affected by surfaces with which the objects are in contact, even if those surfaces are not the ground plane or part of objects that are in turn in contact with the ground. In Figure 7.21(a) the upper dot appears farther away than the lower dot, consistent with both dots being located on a receding surface seen from a location above the surface. (As with many of the other figures in this chapter, Fig-

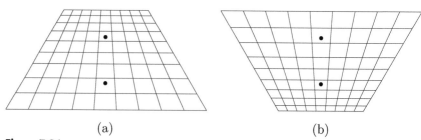

(a)   (b)

Figure 7.21

Relative depth between two surface locations is affected by whether the locations
are seen to be on a (a) floorlike or (b) ceilinglike surface.

ure 7.21 is most effective when viewed monocularly through a tube formed
by a rolled-up piece of paper, so as to remove nonperspective cues for spatial structure.) In Figure 7.21(b) the upper dot appears closer than the
lower dot, consistent with both dots being located on a receding surface
seen from a location below the surface (Epstein, 1966). Distance perception to ceiling locations can be nearly as accurate as distance perception to
locations on the floor (W. B. Thompson, Dilda, & Creem-Regehr, 2007),
though the information from floor locations dominates that from ceiling locations when the two are placed in conflict (Bian, Braunstein, & Andersen,
2005, 2006) and other spatial judgments may be easier for floor locations
relative to ceiling locations (McCarley & He, 2000).

7.5.2 Surface-Related Information for Distance and Size

There are two classes of mechanisms by which depth can be inferred for
locations on a planar surface viewed in perspective. One possibility is that
the pattern of markings on the surface itself is used as a reference for distance. The other is that perspective information is used to estimate the
orientation of the surface with respect to the viewer, after which trigonometric properties are used to determine depth.

The projection of an obliquely viewed surface marked with a regularly
distributed pattern will exhibit a *texture gradient*, with the scale of the
pattern changing with viewing distance (see Chapter 8). For visual textures
made up of distinctive, isolable patterns, relative distances between pairs
of points on the surface can be found by counting the texture elements on
a line between the two points (J. J. Gibson, 1950a; Sedgwick, 1983, 1986).
Support for the use of ground surface texture in distance estimation comes
from studies that show that while distance estimates are accurate when
the region between the viewer and a target location is uniformly textured,
accuracy decreases if there is a gap or obstruction between the viewer and

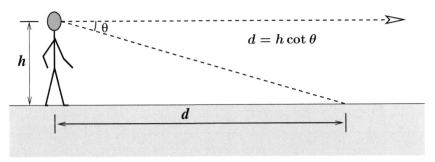

Figure 7.22

The horizon-distance relation, in which distance to locations on the ground plane can be determined by the cotangent of the angle of declination from the horizon to the target, scaled by eye height.

the target location, or if the intervening distance consists of two distinct texture patterns (He, Wu, Ooi, Yarbrough, & Wu, 2004; Sinai, Ooi, & He, 1998).

For an observer standing on an effectively infinite ground plane, the distance d to locations on the ground can be computed using the *horizon-distance relation* (also called the *angle of declination*):

$$d = h \cot \theta \,, \tag{7.6}$$

where θ is the angle of declination from the horizon to the line of sight to the target location and h is the viewer's eye height, as shown in Figure 7.22 (Sedgwick, 1983). One consequence of this relationship is that *height in the visual field* can be used to determine relative depth to locations on a horizontal ground plane, with more distant locations appearing above nearer locations, as in Figure 7.21(a). Empirical evidence for the use of height in the visual field as a depth cue in the absence of any visual context such as a textured ground plane or a visible horizon is mixed. In pictures, it seems to have a relatively weak effect (Dunn, Gray, & Thompson, 1965; Epstein, 1966). For targets in the real world that are small points of light in an otherwise dark room, the effect is much stronger, though subject to a systematic bias at longer distances (Ooi, Wu, & He, 2006). Under normal viewing conditions with a clearly visible ground plane, the horizon-distance relation supports accurate distance judgments out to at least 20 m (Gardner & Mon-Williams, 2001; Grutzmacher, Andre, & Owens, 1997; Ooi, Wu, & He, 2001).

A relationship similar to Equation (7.6) allows determination of the size of objects in the vertical dimension, when those objects are situated on a

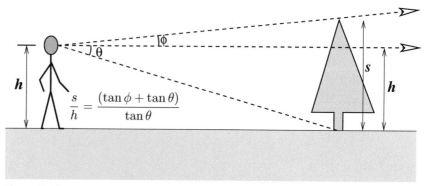

Figure 7.23
The horizon ratio allows determination of the vertical extent of an object based
the viewer's eye height and the angles from the horizontal to the top and bottom
of the object.

ground plane:

$$\frac{s}{h} = \frac{(\tan\phi + \tan\theta)}{\tan\theta} \, , \tag{7.7}$$

where s is the vertical extent of the object, h is the eye height of the
viewer, θ is the angle of declination as in Equation (7.6), and ϕ is the
angle of elevation or declination from the horizon to the top of the object
(Figure 7.23). This is called the *horizon ratio* (Sedgwick, 1983, 1986).
When the vertical extent of the object is relatively small compared with
the viewing distance, Equation (7.7) can be simplified and reformulated:

$$s = h\frac{s_p}{h_p} \, , \tag{7.8}$$

where s is the vertical extent of the object, h is the eye height of the
viewer, s_p is the proximal vertical extent (visual angle) of the full object,
and h_p is the proximal vertical extent (visual angle) of that portion of
the full object below the horizon. As indicated by Equation (7.8) the
distal vertical extent (actual height) of the object is given by the ratio of
total proximal vertical extent to proximal vertical extent below the horizon,
scaled by eye height. This can, in principle, be used to determine the actual
size of the object based only on visual information plus known eye height,
without any explicit recovering of distance. Without information about eye
height, the horizon ratio can be used to compare the vertical extent of two
or more objects. Figure 7.24(a) schematically shows the size comparisons
that are possible using the horizon ratio. Objects i and k are taller than
the eye height involved in this view, while object j is shorter. In terms

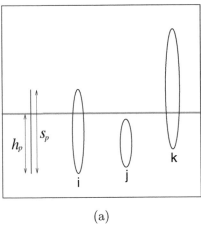
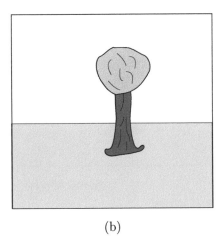

(a)   (b)

Figure 7.24

(a) The horizon ratio can be used to determine vertical size by comparing the visible portion of an object below the horizon to the total vertical visible extent of the object. (b) A sketch of the horizon ratio in practice.

of relative size, object j is shorter than object i, which in turn is shorter than object k. Figure 7.24(b) is a sketch of the horizon ratio in practice. If this view occurred for a standing adult viewer and the tree was on a flat, extended ground plane, the height of the tree would be approximately 5.5 m. In practice, of course, flat, extended ground planes are relatively rare. There has been relatively little study of the degree to which the horizon ratio is actually used in human vision, and results have been mixed (e.g., Bertamini, Yang, & Proffitt, 1998; Bingham, 1993; S. Rogers, 1996).

For an infinite, horizontal ground plane, the angles of declination and elevation in Equations (7.6)–(7.8) are the same if measured with respect to the visible horizon or with respect to a direction normal to the direction of gravity. These two possible frames of reference diverge if the ground plane is truncated or is not level with respect to gravity (Sedgwick, 1983, 1986). Evidence for the use of gravity-relative angle of declination comes from experiments in which distances are judged to locations on a level ground plane while wearing prisms, as shown in Figure 7.25. Base-up prisms bend light in a manner such that the line of sight to viewed target locations on the ground appears to be lower than it would be without the prisms. This increases the angle of declination with respect to gravity. It does not change the angle of declination with respect to other visual information such as the horizon, since the whole of the visual field is alerted by the prisms. Similarly, base-down prisms decrease the angle of declination with respect to gravity, but not the angle of declination with respect to visual

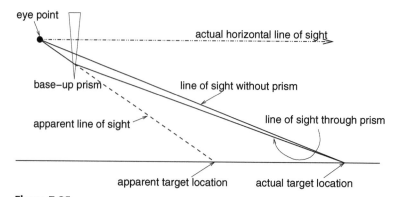

Figure 7.25

Wearing prism goggles changes the angle of declination between gravity-relative horizontal and the effective line of sight to locations on the ground.

frames of reference. Distance judgments to locations on the ground are in fact underestimated when wearing base-up prisms and overestimated when wearing base-down prisms (Gardner & Mon-Williams, 2001; Grutzmacher et al., 1997; Ooi et al., 2001). Wearing base-up prisms causes distance judgments to locations on the ceiling of an indoor room to be overestimated, as would also be predicted from this analysis (W. B. Thompson et al., 2007).

Evidence also exists for the influence of visible frames of reference on the horizon-distance and horizon-ratio relations. Messing and Durgin (2005) found an effect on distance judgments in the expected direction using a virtual reality display when the visual horizon was raised, while leaving unchanged the angle of declination relative to gravity for target locations. Ozkan and Braunstein (2010) demonstrated that size judgments varied as a function of the visual angle between target objects on the ground and a visual indication of the ground horizon, influenced by both the explicit visible boundary of the ground surface and the implicit horizon defined by the vanishing line of surface markings.

Little is known about how the visual system measures the angles in the horizon-distance and horizon-ratio relationships. These angles might be sensed based on some combination of retinal extent, eye pointing directions obtained from ocularmotor information, or head pointing obtained from proprioception. We do know that when the field of view is restricted to approximately 40°, head movement is required in order to determine accurately scaled distances (Creem-Regehr, Willemsen, Gooch, & Thompson, 2005). For smaller fields of view, the head movement to visually scan across the ground surface from the viewer's feet to the object seems to be important in accurately judging distance (Wu, Ooi, & He, 2004).

7.5.3 Eye-Height Scaling

The horizon-distance relation can be used to determine absolute distance if eye height is correctly used in scaling. Likewise, correct eye-height scaling, together with the horizon ratio, can support accurate size judgments. The degree to which eye-height scaling is actually used in distance and size judgments is still not clear, particularly for situations involving other-than-normal, standing eye height. Surreptitious manipulations of eye height involving people looking through a peephole into a room with a different floor height from the room they were standing in showed an effect in the predicted direction on determinations of whether or not an aperture is wide enough to walk through, or a step low enough to step on, and on reports of perceived height, but not on reports of perceived width or perceived distance expressed as an interval (Warren & Whang, 1987; Wraga, 1999a). Wraga showed that judgments of object height were of similar accuracy for standing and seated observers unable to see the floor immediately in front of them, but it is not clear if this was due to the influence of visual indicators of eye height, such as the visual scale of floor texture, or nonvisual proprioceptive information about posture. When standing on level ground, accurate distance judgments do not require viewers seeing their feet or the floor region immediately around where they are standing (Creem-Regehr et al., 2005), though when standing on a platform raised above the ground surface on which distance judgments are to be made, a visual indication of the distance to that surface may affect judgments of distance to locations on that surface away from the location of the viewer (Sinai et al., 1998). Dixon, Wraga, Proffitt, and Williams (2000) showed that eye-height scaling effects seem to have much less effect when looking at pictures than when looking at the real world (or at least a simulation of real-world viewing).

7.6 Issues Specific to Computer Graphics

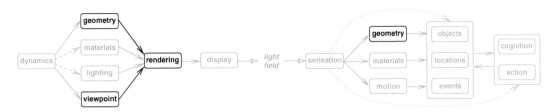

Correct handling of perspective and occlusion are ubiquitous features in all modern computer graphics rendering systems, though nonperspectively correct texture mapping can still be found in older hardware and software. Accurate perspective in computer graphics is a good thing, since so many

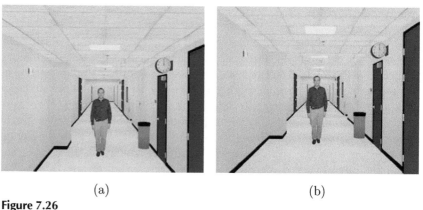

(a)   (b)

Figure 7.26

The interaction between rendered eye height, familiar size, and the horizon ratio.
(a) Rendered eye height corresponding to a standing adult. (b) Rendered eye
height corresponding to 80% of a typical standing adult eye height.

other sources of information about the spatial structure of the world are
lacking or less effective compared to real-world viewing. Despite this, outside of the film industry it is often the case that little attention is paid
to texturing and viewpoint manipulations that can affect space perception
when computer graphics is viewed. Overly simplified geometry, overde-
pendence on texture mapping as a substitute for explicit geometry, and
image-based rendering can reduce the number and nature of interposition
cues. Limitations on graphical realism might affect familiar size judgments,
but there is, as yet, little or no research on this. The lack of effective
shadowing and global illumination can affect the appearance of contact
and thus surface-related distance judgments. Ground surface textures of
inappropriate scale or appearance have the potential to distort distance
judgments.

Perhaps most significantly, viewpoints and rendered fields of view are
often chosen in computer graphics with little regard for either how a viewer
would be looking at a physical instantiation of the rendered scene or how
the observer would be looking at the display surface on which the rendered
scene is shown. As an example, Figure 7.26 shows how an interaction between rendered eye height, familiar size, and the horizon ratio can lead to
an unrealistic-looking image when the viewpoint is set too low. In Figure 7.26(b), the person is obviously too big, even in the small-size printed
image. Chapter 12 contains an extensive discussion of other issues associated with the rendered viewpoint not appropriately matching the viewer's
position relative to the display surface.

7.7   Suggestions for Further Reading

For the most complete coverage in a single source of the topics in this chapter,
see one of the following:

Sedgwick, H. A. (1983). Environment-centered representations of spatial
layout: Available information from texture and perspective. In J. Beck, B.
Hope, & A. Rosenfeld (Eds.), *Human and machine vision* (pp. 425–458).
Orlando, FL: Academic Press.

Sedgwick, H. A. (1986). Space perception. In K. Boff, L, Kaufman, & J.
Thomas (Eds.), *Handbook of perception and human performance* (Vol. 1, pp.
21:1–21:57). New York: Wiley-Interscience.

8

Texture

The English word *texture* has a common etymology with the word *textile*. Within the context of visual perception, the term *texture* refers to surface appearance characterized by a regular pattern distributed over the surface. Figures 8.1 and 8.2 show examples of visual textures, both artificial and naturally occurring. The regularity associated with a visual texture can be highly structured, as in a brick wall, or more random, as in the view of a grassy field. Visual textures play several important roles in perception (Landy & Graham, 2004). Most obviously, recognizable textures can indicate the materials composing an object's surfaces. Even when visual textures cannot be identified as a specific material, they may provide information about

Figure 8.1

Visual texture can provide information about surface shape.

the material properties of a surface. Surfaces in the world are often made of different materials, and so visual texture can often be used to organize a two-dimensional view of the world into different regions likely to correspond to different objects or object parts. Finally, variability in visual textures over the two-dimensional, projected view of the world often provides evidence for aspects of the three-dimensional geometric structure of the corresponding surfaces in the world, as shown in Figure 8.1.

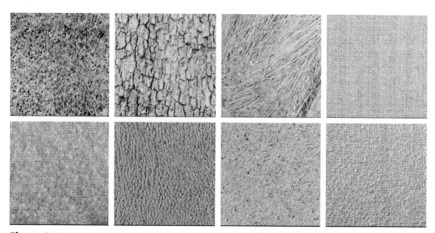

Figure 8.2
Eight different visual textures.

8.1   Characterizing Information About a Visual Texture

To exploit the information available in visual textures, the perceptual system must extract characterizations of the optical variability of the textures that correlate with material and geometric properties of the environment under view. This is a problem that has been studied extensively in both the vision science and computer vision communities. Historically, two ways of characterizing visual textures were common: *structural* and *statistical*.

Structural descriptions involve a specification of individual subpatterns making up a texture (called *texture elements*, *textels*, or *textons*) and an indication of how the subpatterns are replicated over the image region corresponding to the surface (e.g., Beck, 1982; J. J. Gibson, 1950a; Julesz, 1981). Several of the texture patterns shown in Figure 8.2, as well as the texture in Figure 8.5(a) fit well within this formulation. Structural characterizations might be adequate for many manmade and some naturally occurring materials, though automatic extraction of texture elements has proven difficult and many visual textures lack easily distinguishable subparts.

Visual textures can also be characterized statistically, either using conditional distributions of nearby image locations (e.g., Haralick, 1979; Julesz, 1975; A. P. Witkin, 1981) or in terms of their spatial frequency distribution (e.g., Bovik, Clark, & Geisler, 1990; Chen, 1982; Knutsson & Granlund, 1983). Statistical approaches assert that the important perceptual qualities of a given texture are captured by a set of parameters measuring aspects of the brightness distribution of the texture. Statistics that have been used include first-order measures of the overall brightness variability, second-order measures characterizing the joint distribution of brightness at nearby image locations, and a variety of higher-order measures. For example, fine-scale textures will typically have less correlation between nearby image locations than will coarser textures, while correlation in oriented textures will have a nonuniform distribution as a function of direction. Within the context of a spatial frequency framework, fine-scale textures will typically have more high-frequency content than coarser textures, while oriented textures will have a nonuniform distribution of spatial frequency energy with respect to orientation. Simple power-spectrum approaches to texture analysis have proven moderately successful for some automated image analysis applications, but don't adequately account for the human ability to discriminate some textures but not others. While these statistical measures have played an important role in the investigation of human vision, they are more successful at characterizing the perception of the artificial patterns often used in perception experiments than they are at characterizing how people see real-world textures.

More recently, the limitations of models of texture perception that depend on explicit extraction of texture elements or on statistical or spatial frequency properties of intensity distributions can be overcome with multistage models that first apply local filters sensitive to small-scale intensity patterns and then look for distinctive patterns in the spatial distribution of the outputs of these filters (Bergen & Adelson, 1988; Malik & Perona, 1990). For example, the model described in Malik and Perona (1990) first processes the original brightness distribution with local, linear filters motivated by the responses of certain types of neurons in area V1 of the visual cortex. These filters are sensitive to circularly symmetric blobs of various sizes and to eccentric patterns of differing sizes and orientations. The outputs of these linear filters are then run through a second, nonlinear filtering step to account for the effects of contrast reversals on the output of the linear filters and to suppress outputs of the initial filters unlikely to be associated with meaningful differences in the visual properties of the original pattern. In the final step, a measure of the spatial variability of the processed filter outputs is computed, leading to an indication of the boundaries between two perceptually distinct textures. An illustration of such a model is shown in Figure 8.3.

More recently, these multistage, filter-based models have been extended in ways reminiscent of structural descriptions using texture elements. The original structural models of texture appearance were based on local features (textons), described in terms of distinctive small-scale shape properties (Julesz, 1981). These models were sufficient to characterize visual similarities and differences in the appearance of artificially created patterns featuring well-separated texture elements made up of simple line segments,

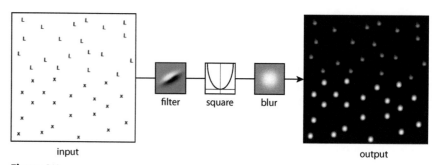

input   output

Figure 8.3
Two textures can be discriminated by simple filtering models. The input image is passed through a filter (in this case, tuned to diagonal features). The output is rectified and blurred to identify regions of the image that are rich in diagonal features. This process responds more strongly to the Xs than the Ls, leading to a higher response to one texture than the other. This can be used to discriminate the two textures.

but were inadequate in accounting for the visual perception of more-natural imagery. A more powerful alternative is to define textons in terms of the output of a collection of linear filters, such as those used in Malik and Perona (1990). For a representative set of training images, each cluster of similar filter outputs is presumed to be a texton, able to serve as a prototype of a visually distinct texture (Cula & Dana, 2004; Leung & Malick, 2001; Varma & Zisserman, 2005).

The effect of variations in illumination and viewing direction on visual textures is significantly different depending on whether the surface being viewed is smooth, with the texture pattern due only to spatial variability in reflectance, or whether the surface has small-scale geometry, in which case, appearance is also affected by specularities, shadows, and occlusion (Leung & Malick, 2001). To achieve a degree of invariance to illumination and viewing direction, many of the filter-based models determine textons based on clusters of feature responses evaluated over images of different materials, with multiple images involving different lighting and viewing direction for each material. Only feature properties that are stable across these variations of lighting and viewing direction generate compact clusters.

8.2 Classification and Discrimination

The ability of people to recognize a specific material type from visual texture alone is quite variable. The problem is well illustrated in Figure 8.2, where it is easy to tell that the textures are different but difficult to tell

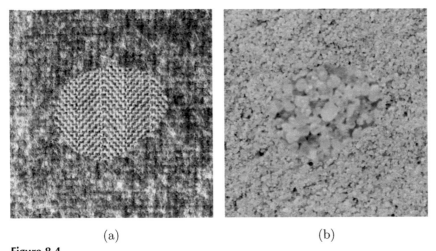

(a)   (b)

Figure 8.4

Visually distinct textures providing a sense of two-dimensional spatial organization. (a) Two different materials. (b) Identical materials except for scale.

what many of them are. Manmade materials often exhibit properties that make them easier to identify than naturally occurring textures (e.g., the images of various fabrics making up some of the textures in Figure 8.2). Even when visual textures are not identifiable as a specific material, they can still provide information about more generic material properties (see Chapter 10). While visual recognition by people based on texture has received relatively little study, there is an extensive literature on texture-based recognition in the computer vision literature (e.g., Haralick, 1979; Mao & Jain, 1992; Randen & Husøy, 1999; Weszka, Dyer, & Rosenfeld, 1980), and automated classification of visual textures has been done with some success in applications ranging from medical radiology to remote sensing.

People are quite good at discriminating between two or more different textures, even when visual identification of the individual textures is difficult. This is important in establishing the two-dimensional spatial organization of a scene. In Figure 8.4(a), not only is it clear that two distinct textural patterns are present, but the boundary between the two patterns is also quite apparent. Figure 8.4(b) shows two textures that are identical except for scale. The boundary between the two textures now involves no overall change in brightness or contrast and is hence less distinct, but the image still visually organizes into two regions.

The visual prominence of the boundary between two textures is not well predicted by the subpatterns making up the texture, as shown in

(a)   (b)

Figure 8.5

(a) A composite of three textures, in which one boundary is much more prominent than the other. (b) Individual textels making up the three textures. (After Beck, 1982.)

Figure 8.5. Most viewers will agree that the pattern of tilted Ts at the left of Figure 8.5(a) is quite distinct from the pattern of upright Ts at the center of Figure 8.5(a), while the boundary between the upright Ts and the Ls is much less distinct. When seen in isolation, as in Figure 8.5(b), however, the tilted and upright Ts look more similar to each other than the upright T looks to the L.

The effect shown in Figure 8.5 occurs in the real world, not just in psychology labs. In many instances, camouflage depends on the object to be hidden having a visual texture that is difficult to distinguish from other immediately surrounding surfaces, even though it is distinctly different under close examination (see Figure 8.6 and Color Plate V). Partly, this keeps the camouflaged surfaces from being correctly recognized as to material type. More importantly, however, is that the camouflaged surface be such that it doesn't lead to a strong sense of spatial organization. When this is the case, there is no visual information as to the presence of an object, much less silhouette information for the shape of the object.

A number of different perceptual studies have been conducted to characterize the nature of texture discrimination in the human visual system

Figure 8.6

An example of natural camouflage. (See Color Plate V.)

(e.g., Gurnsey & Browse, 1987; Kröse, 1987; Landy & Bergen, 1991; Noth-durft, 1990, 1991; Wolfson & Landy, 1995). However, specific predictions arising out of the various computational theories for texture discrimination have only rarely been evaluated with rigorous perceptual experimentation. At least in the case of textures differentiated by differences in dominant orientation, visual discrimination may not correspond to large spatial gra-dients in the sorts of features used in the multistage, filter-based models (Ben-Shahar, 2006).

8.3 Perception of Three-Dimensional Surface Structure from Visual Texture

The size-distance relationship holds for visual textures as well as for single, distinct objects. As a result, the distance to an identifiable texture with known and familiar texture-element size and distribution on a surface can be estimated based on the retinal image size and distribution of the com-ponents making up the texture. This effect has received little study in the perception community, though it relates to work on image statistics done in computer vision (Torralba & Oliva, 2002).

Visual texture is a strong cue for surface orientation. When a textured surface is viewed from an oblique angle, the projected view of the texture is distorted relative to the actual markings on the surface. By measuring these distortions as they appear in the retinal image, the visual system can construct an estimate of the orientation of the corresponding surface in the world. Surface orientation relative to the viewer is often characterized in terms of *slant* and *tilt*, particularly when analyzing the effects of surface shape on visual texture (Stevens, 1981). The slant of a point on a surface is the angle between the line of sight to that point and the surface normal at the point. A slant of $0°$ indicates a surface that is perpendicular to the line of sight. A slant approaching $90°$ indicates that the surface is being viewed from a highly oblique angle. Tilt refers to the orientation of the projection of the surface normal onto a plane perpendicular to the line of sight. Informally, it is the direction in which the surface falls away from the viewer the fastest. Figure 8.7 shows examples of five different surface orientations involving differences in both slant and tilt.

Two quite distinct types of distortions occur in the view of surface tex-tures as a function of the orientation of the surface (J. J. Gibson, 1950a, 1950b; Knill, 1998a). The strengths of both are affected by the amount of slant, with the orientation of the distortion a function only of tilt. One type of distortion comes from the foreshortened effect that is directly re-lated to the angle between the surface and the line of sight (Knill, 1998b; A. P. Witkin, 1981). The other type of distortion arises from perspective-

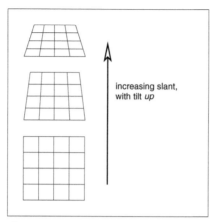
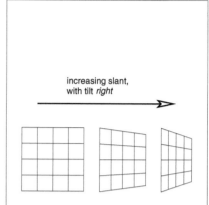

Figure 8.7

Surface orientation is often characterized in terms of slant and tilt.

projection viewing and is due to the scaling of retinal size with the reciprocal of distance from the viewer (J. J. Gibson, 1950a, 1950b). The visual distortions due to perspective are thus not a direct consequence of the surface being slanted relative to the line of sight; but rather, they are due to there being spatial variability in depth when there is nonzero slant.

Compared with viewing a surface perpendicular to the line of sight, oblique viewing produces a compression of the retinal image along the direction of tilt, with the ratio of projected to actual size along the direction of tilt proportional to the cosine of the slant angle. For visual textures, this distorts both the appearance of texture elements and the distribution of texture elements. For example, Figure 8.8 shows the projected view of a surface marked with uniform-size circular dots, oriented perpendicularly to the line of sight. Figure 8.9 shows the projected view of the same surface, except slanted 60° away from the line of sight. The circles now appear as ellipses, with the ratio of the minor to major axes equal to the cosine of the slant (0.5). The horizontal density of dots remains the same as in Figure 8.8, but the dot density in the vertical direction is doubled.

Foreshortening of texture elements and element distributions provide the most information about surface tilt and slant when the pattern on the actual surface is *isotropic*, meaning that the aspects of brightness distributions used to determine element shape and spacing are insensitive to rotations of the surface itself. To see why this is so, imagine that a surface was marked with the (nonisotropic) pattern shown in Figure 8.9. Viewing such a surface oriented perpendicularly to the line of sight would result in visual information identical to that seen when viewing a surface with the isotropic markings shown in Figure 8.8, slanted at 60°. Absent additional

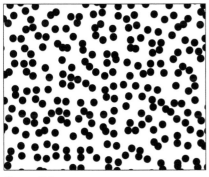

Figure 8.8

A textured surface marked with circular dots, oriented perpendicular to the line of sight.

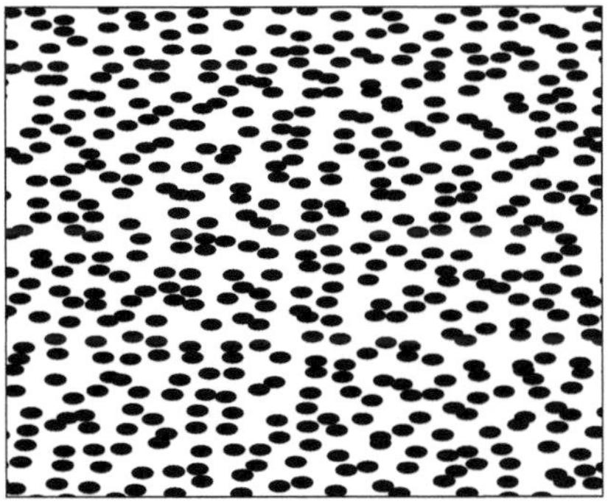

Figure 8.9

The same surface as in Figure 8.8, but with a 60° slant relative to the line of sight.

information, the visual system has no way of confirming that the surface markings are actually isotropic, and empirical evidence is, so far, inconclusive as to whether or not the perception of surface orientation based on textures acts as if the visual system is presuming isotropy (Knill, 1998b; Rosenholtz & Malik, 1997).

Figure 8.10 shows the effect of perspective on the appearance of visual texture. Again, the pattern on the surface is made up of circular dots, distributed in a random but isotropic manner, and the surface is slanted at 60°, though the geometric field of view is significantly greater than in Figure 8.9. (The *geometric field of view* is the field of view of the virtual

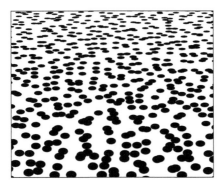

Figure 8.10

A surface marked with circular dots and slanted 60° relative to the line of sight, with significant perspective effects apparent.

camera used in the rendering process.) Because distance from the viewpoint to the surface increases with height in the image, the size of the dots and the spacing between dots in the perspective projection decreases. This change was described by J. J. Gibson (1950b) as a *texture gradient*. Inferring surface slant and tilt from texture gradients requires that it be possible to locally determine some measure of *texture density* relating to either texture element size or spacing or to some more statistical or spatial frequency characterization relating to element size or distribution, and then computing a spatial gradient of this measure. The magnitude of the gradient is related to the surface slant. In practice, however, there are theoretical limitations to this approach (Stevens, 1981), and empirical evidence suggests that human vision is poor at utilizing texture gradients for estimating slant (Epstein & Park, 1964; Knill, 1998b).

For texture gradients to be an effective indicator of surface tilt and slant, the size and distribution of texture elements over the actual surface cannot vary over the surface. (Formally, the statistical properties of the texture on which perception of texture gradients is based should be stationary with respect to position on the surface.) If this is not the case, then the cause of observed variability in texture element size or density in the retinal image cannot be uniquely identified as arising from the distortion of markings that occurs as part of the perspective projection, rather than arising from variability in the markings on the surface itself.

In addition to exhibiting a texture gradient, the projected dots in Figure 8.10 appear as ellipses. Moreover, the amount of compression of the ellipses varies from top to bottom in the image. This is because the lines of sight to locations on a planar surface viewed in perspective will vary with location over the projected image, with the range of orientations the same as the field of view. While the perception literature typically draws a sharp distinction between foreshortening and perspective as sources for visual information about tilt and slant, the two effects are both manifested in perspectively projected images. The relative weighting of foreshortening effects and perspective-induced texture gradients appears to be a function of the field of view and the orientation of the surface (Knill, 1998b; Todd, Thaler, & Dijkstra, 2005). The reason that Figure 8.9 shows foreshortening but little texture gradient, whereas Figure 8.10 shows both, is that Figure 8.9 was created with a geometric field of view of 5°, while Figure 8.10 was created with a geometric field of view of 45°. The narrow field of view in Figure 8.9 means that the variation in depth over the image, relative to the average distance to the surface, is small, limiting depth-determined changes in texture element size and spacing. (Even though the geometric fields of view in the two figures are very different, the figures are displayed at the same size on the page. See Chapter 12 for more on this issue.)

In everyday common experience, we notice that slanted surfaces appear steeper than they actually are (J. J. Gibson, 1950b). A number of explanations have been proposed for this phenomenon. The cosine relationship between slant and changes to the retinal image favors slopes being seen as roughly perpendicular to the line of sight. For example, for an observer looking horizontally at a surface actually tilted at 45°, the shape of texture elements will only be foreshortened by 30%. If the visual system assumes a more linear relationship between foreshortening and slant than is trigonometrically valid, the surface will look steeper. A second class of explanations is based on presumptions about the mechanisms used by the visual system to infer slant from the resulting patterns of light on the retina and the observation that these mechanisms become less reliable at highly oblique viewing angles (Turner, Gerstein, & Bajcsy, 1991). Finally, it has been suggested that subjective slant underestimation is associated with complex aspects of perception and action (Proffitt, Bhalla, Gosswiler, & Midgett, 1995).

More-distant terrain surfaces often look steeper than nearer surfaces, though there has been very little formal study of this phenomenon. In principle, the visual information for surface slant is independent of the distance to the surface, as long as the angular extent of the visible surface remains constant. One likely reason for more distant surfaces looking steeper is that the visible angle subtended by more distant surfaces is typically smaller than for nearer surfaces, and reductions in field of view are known to affect perception of slant (Knill, 1998c). Also, it is important to note that, unlike the artificial patterns used in most perception experiments, visual textures exist at a wide range of scales on most naturally occurring surfaces. Due to limitations in acuity (and image resolution in computer graphics), fine-scale texture properties may be visible on closer surfaces that are not visible on more distant surfaces. This can change apparent texture element size, shape, and distribution on a viewed surface in ways not well described by just foreshortening and perspective. These effects have been little studied in vision science.

So far, all of the discussion about perceiving surface orientation from visual texture has implicitly presumed that the geometry of the physical surface under view is flat, or at least smooth. An additional form of visual distortion occurs when surfaces with distinct three-dimensional surface relief are viewed obliquely (Leung & Malik, 1997). In this case, protrusions in the surface will partly occlude other parts of the surface. In addition, because of the nature of perspective projection, the more distant the protrusion, the more of it that will be occluded by protrusions at nearer distances. This is caused by an interaction between variability in the angle of the line of sight to individual surface locations over the field of view, and the occlusion of portions of one protrusion by another protrusion im-

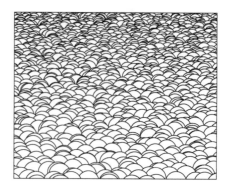

Figure 8.11

A surface made up of three-dimensional spheres, viewed in perspective, showing the effect of fine-scale variations in surface geometry on visual texture.

mediately in front. A greater portion of the more-distant protrusions are occluded because the line of sight is more oblique. This changes the visible shape of each protrusion. For example, the surface shown in Figure 8.11 is composed of uniform-size, randomly distributed, intersecting spheres. A texture gradient is clearly apparent. Also apparent is that more of each individual sphere is visible in the lower portion of the figure than in the upper portion of the figure. If the protruding elements vary in color or brightness over the height of the element, it will also cause a change in the overall color or brightness of the image with increased distance along lines of sight to the slanted surface. Very little is currently known about if or how this effect might be used by the human vision system to determine slant. (See Saunders, 2003, for one relevant study.)

8.4   Issues Specific to Computer Graphics

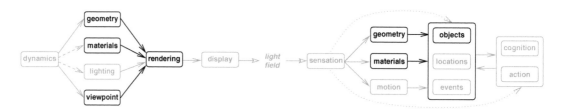

The term *texture* has a more general meaning in computer graphics than it does in visual perception. In computer graphics, *texture maps* are image-like data that are registered with a piece of surface geometry and used to modulate some aspect of the surface as it affects the rendering process. Most often, texture maps are used to apply surface markings to geometry by affecting the color and reflectivity of the surface. Texture mapping can also be used to locally modulate surface normals (*bump mapping*) or surface geometry (*displacement mapping*). When the texture maps themselves ·consist of regular patterns regularly distributed over the texture image, the result of texture mapping is a rendered image that includes visual textures as described in this chapter. However, texture mapping can also be used to apply patterns to a surface intended to be evocative of geometric detail, such as a photograph of the side of a building used as a texture map applied to a planar facet of the CG building model. When texture maps consist of visual textures, they can result in rendered images that potentially exhibit some or all of the perceptual effects described above. The details of texture mapping are complicated, and some of those details can affect visual classification, discrimination, and perception of surface geometry in significant ways.

8.4.1   Distortions Arising out of the Texture Mapping Process

The resolution of a texture map image can be higher than the resolution of that texture as it will appear on the screen due to either the original texture map image being of too high a resolution or because it is applied to a distant surface and then perspectively projected. In such cases, some sort of *minification* process has to occur during texture mapping, by which the high-resolution texture map is coarsely sampled to match the final screen resolution. Texture images are often dominated by high spatial frequencies and so are subject to aliasing when they are sampled in this manner. Figure 8.12 shows a high-frequency texture map consisting of vertical black and white bars, applied to a flat surface oriented perpendicularly to the line of sight. Figure 8.13 shows the same surface with the same texture map applied, but with an oblique viewing angle. The surface looks as expected in the lower part of the figure, where perspective projection results in a need for magnifying the texture. Higher up in the figure, however, *moiré patterns* appear. The high spatial frequencies of the texture map image have been undersampled, resulting in the appearance of *aliased* lower-frequency artifacts on the screen.

Mipmapping, most often thought of as a technique for minimizing the temporal scintillation that frequently occurs with high spatial frequency texture maps, can also be used to reduce spatial aliasing. Figure 8.14 shows a rendering identical to Figure 8.13, except that mipmapping of texturing has been enabled. The moiré patterns have been suppressed, but so has any sense of the texture continuing out to the horizon. Figure 8.15 was rendered identically to Figure 8.14, except that anisotropic filtering was enabled. Now, the texture is apparent at farther surface distances. Anisotropic filtering is increasingly available in computer graphics systems

Figure 8.12

A high-frequency square-wave texture map, viewed perpendicularly to the surface.

Figure 8.13

The same texture map as in Figure 8.12, but viewed from an oblique angle.

Figure 8.14

The same texture map and viewing angle as in Figure 8.13, but with mipmapping enabled.

Figure 8.15

The same texture map and viewing angle as in Figure 8.13, but with both mipmapping and anisotropic filtering enabled.

specifically to deal with preserving detail and minimizing artifacts with texture mapped surfaces viewed obliquely.

The effects shown in Figures 8.13–8.14 can significantly affect texture gradients in rendered images. As a result, they can significantly affect apparent surface orientation. To facilitate accurate perception of three-dimensional surface structure, it is therefore important to choose texture map images appropriately and pay careful attention to the use of mipmapping and anisotropic filtering.

8.4.2   Rendering Visual Textures Arising from Rough Surfaces

As indicated in Section 8.3, the appearance of visual texture arising from surfaces that are rough can be significantly affected by variations in the directions of illumination and viewing. Conventional texture mapping onto flat polygons cannot reproduce these effects. Bump maps (Blinn, 1978), displacement maps (Cook, 1984), relief textures (Oliveira, Bishop, & McAllister, 2000), and a variety of related techniques can be used to produce more-realistic renderings in these cases by modifying shading, warping geometry, and—in some cases—introducing appropriate small-scale occlusions. The *bidirectional texture function* (BTF) is a more general solution for dealing with textures that change appearance as a function of illumination and viewing directions, though it comes at substantial computational cost (Dana, van Ginneken, Nayar, & Koenderink, 1999). As with the bidirectional reflectance distribution function (BRDF), values of the BTF at a particular surface location are indexed by the direction of incident illumination and viewing direction. However, whereas the indexed value in a BRDF is a simple reflectance, values of the BTF are whole image patches.

8.4.3   Scaling of Textures and Perception of Spatial Organization

Figures 8.16 and 8.17 illustrate how texture mapping can affect the perceptual spatial organization of a scene. Figure 8.16 shows a rendering of a cube sitting on top of a support surface. Both the cube and the support surface are texture mapped using a pink noise image, with the two texture maps differing only in average brightness. (Lighting further affects the brightness of the various surfaces.) Figure 8.17 is a rendering identical to Figure 8.16, except that the scale of the texture applied to the support surface is different.[1] In Figure 8.17, the cube seems to float above the support surface, and the overall appearance seems unnatural. In Figure 8.16, the cube looks more like it is resting on the surface, though since the textures of the cube

---

[1] Technically, the two images differ only in how the texture coordinates of the support surface are specified.

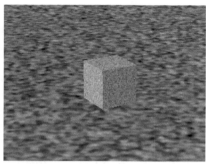

Figure 8.16

A cube on a planar surface, both with random-noise textured surfaces that differ only in brightness.

Figure 8.17

The same situation as in Figure 8.16, but with the texture of the support surface having a different scale.

faces and the support surface are now more similar, the cube is less easily distinguished from the surface on which it is resting.

The effects shown in Figures 8.16 and 8.17 occur with some frequency in practice. Often, generic tilable textures are used to pattern surfaces with little or no consideration of how the scale of the texture map image corresponds to the scale of the geometry to which it is applied. Even when the scales are correctly matched, the resolution of some texture maps may be too low, resulting in a need for magnification that results in a blurry appearance. This is common in flight simulators and similar applications, such as Google Earth. A similar phenomenon can occur in image compositing if the images involved are not appropriately matched. In all of these cases, it is important to match the texture statistics as they will appear in the final image, not as they are manifested in texture maps or source images for composites.

8.4.4   Choosing Textures to Aid in Shape Perception

Relatively little research has been directed at the problem of choosing textures in computer graphics applications with the intent of facilitating shape perception. The problem is complicated for complex sculpted surfaces by the difficulty in controlling perceptually relevant aspects of textures as they are applied to such surfaces. Kim, Hagh-Shenas, and Interrante (2004) describe an approach in which anisotropic texture maps with strong oriented structure are applied to curved surfaces in a manner that locally aligns the orientation of the texture with the directions of principle curvature of the surface. For some textures and viewing conditions, this appears to increase the accuracy of shape perception.

Figure 8.18

The two larger images were produced from the corresponding smaller images by the texture synthesis process described in Efros and Leung (1999). (© 1999 IEEE.)

8.4.5   Texture Synthesis

Understanding the basis on which the perceptual system discriminates between visual textures is also essential in creating effective *texture synthesis* systems, which can fill holes in textured surfaces and create large textured surfaces from smaller examples (see Figure 8.18). Two general approaches exist. Parametric approaches determine the statistics of a source texture and use these to iteratively modify the statistics of a random noise pattern until they are sufficiently close (Heeger & Bergen, 1995; Portilla & Simoncelli, 2000). The advantage of such methods is that they build an explicit model of the texture, so that the contributions of given statistics to the appearance of the texture can be assessed and, in principle, varied. This can also provide some insights into the features that are important for human texture perception. However, they can have many thousands of parameters, and still do fail to reproduce certain textures, especially those with clearly defined texture elements. By contrast, nonparametric methods take pixels or patches of pixels from a source texture and tile and blend them into a new pattern without visible artifacts (Efros & Freeman, 2001; Efros & Leung, 1999). Nonparametric approaches can create very compelling textures for a wide variety of sources. However, they provide little insight into the features that the visual system uses for texture discrimination, and do not provide parameters for tweaking the appearance of the texture. Ultimately, the successes and failures of both approaches depend on ensuring that the newly generated texture patterns and the original patterns have similar statistical properties for those statistics that relate to texture discrimination, without introducing artifacts that appear as boundaries.

8.5   Suggestions for Further Reading

A good overview of texture perception, along with a comprehensive bibliography:

> Landy, M. S., & Graham, N. (2004). Visual perception of texture. In L. M. Chalupa & J. S. Werner (Eds.), *The visual neurosciences* (pp. 1106–1118). Cambridge, MA: MIT Press.

The classic reference introducing the concept of texture gradients:

> Gibson, J. J. (1950). *The perception of the visual world.* Cambridge, MA: Riverside Press.

9

Illumination, Shading, and Shadows

Every opaque body is surrounded and its whole surface enveloped in
shadow and light.
—Leonardo da Vinci (1566/1970)

Illumination is to the eyes what air is to the lungs. Everything that we see, we see ultimately because it is illuminated by some source of light, whether it be the sun, a candle, or light reflected from nearby surfaces. By changing the illumination conditions, it is possible to considerably alter the subjective appearance of an object, as can be seen in Figure 9.1. Unsurprisingly, artists are acutely aware of this and have a sophisticated vocabulary for describing the qualities of lighting and its effects within a scene. Painting, sculpture, photography, and architecture all use light in a variety of ways to create moods, to mold the spaces between things, and to draw attention to or conceal details.

Though illumination is what enables vision at all, it is paradoxically considered to be something of a nuisance for a visual system trying to reconstruct the outside world. It is important to remember that perception evolved primarily to guide actions: to help us acquire food, navigate, and use tools. Because we cannot act on light, most of the time illumination is not the most important property of the scene. The visual system is generally more interested in recognizing objects and reconstructing the shapes and positions of surfaces in three-dimensional space. Thus, the large variations in illumination that occur in the natural environment (e.g., indoors versus outdoors, or across shadow boundaries) are a problematic source of variation in the image that makes estimating the intrinsic properties of objects more difficult.

One consequence of this is that relatively little research has been conducted on the perception of illumination or shading per se. Rather, most

Figure 9.1

Three photographs of a textured candle under different illumination conditions, from left to right: collimated, hemispherical diffuse, and Ganzfeld illumination. (From the Utrecht Oranges Database; Pont & Koenderink, 2003; reproduced with permission.)

research that involves illumination is concerned with the contribution that illumination makes (for better or worse) to the perception of other aspects of the scene: 3D shape, surface reflectance, object identity, and space. The interaction of light with surfaces creates shadows and shading patterns that provide a rich source of information about the physical properties of the scene. In this chapter, we will introduce some of the contexts in which illumination, shading, and shadows play a major role in visual perception, and discuss some of the implications for computer graphics.

9.1   Physical Properties of Illumination and Shading

What is illumination? In everyday speech, *illumination* usually refers to a source of light, such as a lightbulb or the sun. In computer graphics, light arriving at a surface directly from such light sources is referred to as *direct illumination*. Direct illumination is relatively easy to compute but, on its own, leads to unnatural-looking images. This is because in natural scenes, light from primary sources generally interacts with the scene many times before reaching the eye. It is scattered by dust particles and water droplets as it passes through space and reverberates between surfaces, reflecting many times before reaching the eye. This scattering and interreflection effectively fill space with light, so that in a typical scene almost all points in space receive light from multiple directions. From the point of view of a surface within the scene, all of the incoming light is treated the same way, so properly speaking, all of this light should be considered illumination. In computer graphics, these additional, nonlocal effects are called *global illumination*. Global illumination is much more expensive to compute but leads to radically more lifelike renderings.

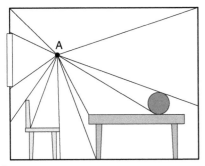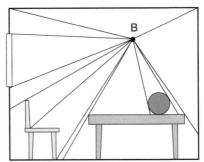

Figure 9.2

Gibson's ambient optic array consists of the set of all rays converging on each point in space. When the observer moves from location A to location B, the incident pattern transforms in a way that carries information both about the structure of the scene and about the observer's motion.

The physicist Gershun (1936/1939) formalized the idea of space filled with light with the concept of the light field, which is a function describing the amount of light traveling in every direction through every point in space. Later, the psychologist J. J. Gibson (1979) developed a very similar intuition, called the *ambient optic array* (Figure 9.2). He argued that as organisms move through their environment, they continuously sample the highly structured ambient field of light. For each vantage point in space, the surfaces in the environment create a unique set of solid angles that converge on that point. As the organism moves, the pattern of solid angles transforms continuously, providing visual information both about the structure of the surrounding world and about the movements of the organism itself. It is worth mentioning that this concept is related to certain image-based computer graphics techniques, such as *unstructured lumigraphs*, in which new views of a scene are approximated from a set of photographs taken at locations in the scene. However, this kind of sampling of the light field is not the usual meaning of the word *illumination* in perception research. From a perceptual point of view, the most important aspects of illumination relate to how it interacts with and reveals the properties of surfaces in the scene. Light passing through some distant point in empty space cannot be perceived directly. Instead, illumination can only have an impact on our sense organs through its interactions with surfaces and media that spray some of the ambient light back toward our eye.

When a surface is placed in a light field, it reflects some proportion of the incident light. For typical diffuse surfaces, each point on the surface integrates the light arriving from all directions,[1] weighted by the relation-

---

[1] For a point on a surface, this is actually the hemisphere of directions above the tangent plane of the surface.

ship between the surface's three-dimensional orientation and the illumination. This relationship creates continuous variations of intensity—known as *chiaroscuro* or shading—in the image which provide a powerful source of information about the scene, particularly for curved surfaces. In this section, we will discuss some of the physical properties of illumination and shading, focusing on diffuse (matte) surfaces, and in the following section discuss how these relate to the perception of 3D shape.

What structures can the light field take on, and what consequences do these have for shading and perception? To keep things simple, we will start by considering the pattern of light converging on a single point in space. By contrast, the complete light field is made up of an infinite number of such samples, taken at each location in space, and therefore represents the way that lighting conditions change continuously through space.

The light arriving at a single point from all directions can be captured in a spherical image and is often called a *light probe* in the computer graphics literature. Each pixel in the image represents a different incident direction on the sphere, and the intensity of the pixel represents the amount of light arriving along that direction. In practice, light probes are typically projected onto a two-dimensional map (see Section 9.1.4).

9.1.1   Collimated Illumination and the Cosine Law

Arguably, the most important simple model of lighting is *collimated illumination*, in which the light field consists of perfectly parallel rays arriving from a certain direction (Figure 9.3). This is sometimes known as *direc-*

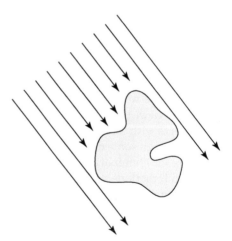

Figure 9.3
Collimated illumination consists of parallel rays.

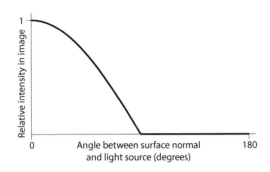

Figure 9.4

A golf ball, sprayed with matte paint and viewed under collimated illumination. Note the hard, completely black shadows, where the surface normal faces away from the direction of the light. (From the Utrecht Oranges Database; Pont & Koenderink, 2003; reproduced with permission.)

tional illumination in computer graphics, or *point source at infinity* in computer vision. In terms of the light-probe representation, the image would consist of a Dirac delta function, with the entire light probe black except for a single, infinitely narrow peak. Geometrically, this kind of illumination occurs with a light source at infinite distance from the scene, although it can also be approximated by passing light through a collimator, such as a matte black honeycomb. Rays that are not parallel to the tubes of the honeycomb are absorbed, leaving only parallel rays to pass through. Probably the most commonly occurring natural approximation to collimated light is moonlight on a cloudless night.

What effects does collimated illumination have on the appearance of objects in the scene? Consider a planar patch of diffuse surface under collimated illumination. When the patch directly faces the light source (i.e., when the surface normal is parallel to the illumination direction), the surface receives the highest possible radiant flux and thus the patch appears bright in the image. As the surface is slanted away from this direction, the intensity of the surface decreases steadily until the surface normal is perpendicular to the illumination direction, at which point the surface appears black in the image. For an ideal Lambertian surface, the falloff in intensity is a simple clipped cosine function, as shown in Figure 9.4. This is known as the *cosine law for shading*, and is the basis of many important algorithms for recovering 3D shape from shading. The function is clipped at zero, because for angles larger than 90° the surface receives no light and therefore reflects no light. This means that under collimated lighting, substantial portions of a typical object can be in complete shadow, therefore providing no information to the visual system. The regions of the object that receive light have the highest contrast shading of any illumination, and the transition between shaded and shadowed portions of the object—known as the *body shadow*—is abrupt for collimated illumination. For these reasons, collimated light is generally considered to be the hardest and most unforgiving illumination in artistic contexts: it is high contrast; it reveals surface relief; and it creates sharp, dark shadows and bright, localized highlights.

Despite the fact that it is neither common in the real world nor visually appealing, collimated shading is widely used in computer science, because it is very simple to compute. Because there is only one incident direction, it is not necessary to evaluate the costly integration of illumination across all incident directions. Furthermore, in some circumstances, more complex illumination conditions can be approximated as the sum of multiple directional sources, each of which is rapidly computed.

9.1.2   Ambient Illumination and Vignetting Effects

At the opposite extreme of illumination conditions is spherically constant illumination, in which the same amount of light arrives from every direction in the light probe, as depicted in Figure 9.5. In psychology, this is known as a *Ganzfeld* (from the German, meaning "whole field"), while in computer graphics, it is called *ambient illumination* or the *ambient term*. Although physically simple, we almost never encounter such illumination in the natural environment, except perhaps in a "polar whiteout" or dense fog. An example of a golf ball under uniform illumination is shown in Figure 9.6.

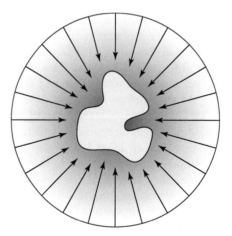

Figure 9.5
Ganzfeld illumination, in which light arrives equally from all directions.

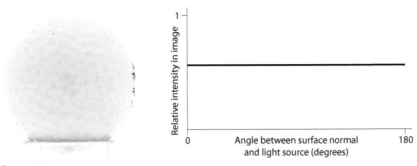

Figure 9.6

A golf ball under Ganzfeld illumination. Note the low contrast in the shading (the black features on the right-hand side are ink markings). In direct illumination, the ambient term is a constant. (From the Utrecht Oranges Database; Pont & Koenderink, 2003; reproduced with permission.)

Research scientists at NTT Communications in Japan developed a light chamber with diffusers and rounded corners, which could produce almost perfect Ganzfeld illumination. Takeuchi and Matsuoka (2002) studied how this type of illumination affects the appearance of objects. Under Ganzfeld illumination, convex objects look extremely unnatural and flat, and may even appear to be self-luminous. There are no shadows, convex surfaces are uniform intensity (i.e., without shading), glossy surfaces appear matte, and small variations in pigmentation across a surface become highly salient. Indeed, the researchers found that experimental participants would sometimes make large misjudgments of material properties, such as mistaking a block of copper for wood due to the absence of luster and the visible graining in the metal. Simple local shading methods in computer graphics often approximate natural illumination as a sum of ambient (i.e., constant intensity) and directional terms, although this is a poor model of shading in the real world.

There is, however, one very important aspect of shading that is most easily understood with ambient illumination, and that is the global illumination effect known as *vignetting*. So far we have only considered how exposed, planar patches of surfaces respond to light. However, when the surface geometry is complex, some parts of the surface may block light from other parts of the surface. Consider, for example, a patch of surface located in a concavity, as shown in Figure 9.7. As mentioned earlier, the intensity of the patch in the image depends on the amount of light arriving at the patch, integrated across the entire hemisphere of directions around that point. When the point is located in a concavity, some of the directions are blocked off, so that the total amount of light incident on the point is

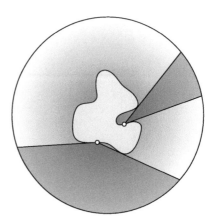

Figure 9.7

Vignetting occurs when a point on the surface can only "see" a small portion of the surrounding illumination due to occlusion by other parts of the object. This is approximated in ambient occlusion shading.

less than when the surface patch is fully exposed. This vignetting effect causes creases, hollows, and other concavities in the surface to be a darker shade in the image, leading to a second type of form-revealing chiaroscuro effect. Unlike local shading, vignetting is blind to surface orientation per se, depending solely on the semilocal geometry of the surface. In computer graphics applications, this global illumination effect is often approximated using *ambient occlusion*, in which the proportion of the surrounding environment that is visible to each point on the surface is precomputed and used to scale the ambient illumination term. Although ambient occlusion is not a complete, physically correct estimate of global illumination, it nevertheless imparts a realistic appearance to objects with complex geometries by providing the visual shading cues associated with vignetting. Very little is known about how the visual system uses this type of shading to estimate shape, although it has been suggested that the brain could use the heuristic that "dark is deep" (Langer & Bülthoff, 2000)—in other words, that darker intensities in the image tend to be deeper in concavities. We discuss this in more detail below.

9.1.3   Diffuse Illumination

Between the two extremes of collimated and Ganzfeld illumination are a wide variety of *diffuse illumination* conditions. In some cases in computer graphics, diffuse illumination is created with area sources; in others, it emerges automatically by evaluating a full global illumination solution, in which surfaces provide secondary illumination for one another.

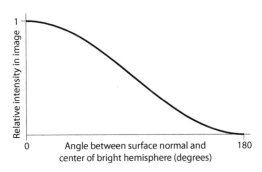

Figure 9.8

Hemispherical diffuse illumination. (From the Utrecht Oranges Database; Pont & Koenderink, 2003; reproduced with permission.)

One simple, direct model of diffuse illumination is the *hemispherical-diffuse* model—also known as the *overcast sky* or *cloudy day* model—in which the upper and lower hemispheres of the light probe are both uniform intensity. The upper hemisphere is brighter than the lower, because in the real world, the sky is almost always brighter than the ground. For a convex Lambertian surface under such illumination, the function relating image intensity to the angle between the surface normal and the center of the bright hemisphere (i.e., straight up into the sky) is a *raised cosine*, as shown in Figure 9.8. This means that all points on a convex object receive at least some light, even those with normals that point away from the sky. Consequently, there are no harsh black shadows, shading gradients are low contrast, surface relief is concealed, and highlights are broad and smooth, giving objects a "soft," "forgiving," and "neutral" appearance. It is little surprise that photographers often use light boxes, light tents, and other overwhelmingly diffuse illuminations for product shots and portraits. Unlike global illumination solutions, the raised-cosine model allows local shading to be computed as efficiently as with directional illumination, because again, there is no need to integrate across all incoming directions. Although only a cartoon of illumination conditions in the real world, objects appear more natural under hemispherical-diffuse lighting than under collimated lighting, and it is surprising that the raised-cosine shader is not used more frequently in real-time applications.

9.1.4   Real-World Illumination and Image-Based Lighting

So far we have discussed simple artificial models for representing illumination conditions. However, as noted earlier, illumination in the real world arises from the interaction of light with all surfaces in the surrounding scene, which can be highly complex. Imagine, for example, the illumina-

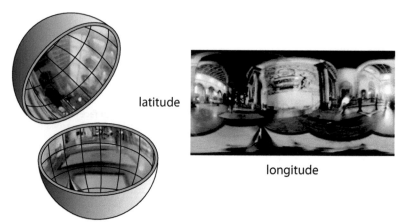

latitude

longitude

Figure 9.9

A light probe captures the light arriving from every direction on the sphere surrounding a point in the real world. To visualize this, we can project it into two dimensions, here using the Lambert cylindrical equal-area projection. (Light probe image from Debevec, 1998; reproduced by permission from Paul Debevec). (See Color Plate VI.)

tion in a forest where light breaks unevenly through the canopy and reflects from leaves and bark of many different colors.

The illumination arriving at a location in a real scene can be captured photographically and used to render synthetic objects, a process known as *image-based lighting* (Debevec, 1998). In practice, real-world light probes can be created by photographing a mirrored sphere (under orthographic viewing, a specular hemisphere reflects rays from all surrounding directions due to the angle-doubling nature of specular reflection); or by stitching together several images taken with a fish-eye lens; or by using a dedicated panoramic camera, which scans the entire sphere around the head of the tripod. The result is a light probe that captures the full complexity of the light arriving at that point in the world. Image-based lighting creates images of objects that look almost exactly as they would appear if they were placed in that location in the real scene, leading to renderings of extraordinary realism. Consequently, the technique has become a de facto standard in the movie industry. An example of one of Paul Debevec's light probes, captured from Galileo's tomb from the Santa Croce in Florence, Italy, is shown in Figure 9.9 and Color Plate VI.

Real illuminations can be highly complex, with structures that occur at many scales. For example, a cloudless sky tends to have very smooth intensity gradients, while the leaves in the forest are details that occur at a fine spatial scale. The multiscale nature of natural illuminations can be represented by decomposing the light probe data using spherical harmonics, which is analogous to Fourier decomposition applied to functions on a sphere. With spherical harmonics, low-order harmonics represent the slowest gradients, while higher-order harmonics represent fine spatial details.

Not all these features are equally important for the appearance of objects. The fine details of the patterns are important for specular surfaces, but they do not play a role in diffuse shading. Interestingly, Ramamoorthi and Hanrahan (2001a, 2001b) have proven that the appearance of a diffuse object can be almost perfectly reconstructed using only the first nine spherical harmonic coefficients of the light probe. This means that for diffuse shading, the full variety of all possible real-world illumination conditions can be represented very compactly. It has been suggested that the human visual system might also represent complex illumination conditions using low-order spherical harmonic approximations (Doerschner, Boyaci, & Maloney, 2007).

Capturing illuminations from the real world has also allowed us to study the statistical variation of natural illumination patterns across different scenes. This has revealed some important regularities that the visual system can exploit for estimating properties of the scene. Probably the most obvious and well-known regularity of illumination in the real world is that in both indoor and outdoor environments, more light tends to come from above than below. It has been argued for several hundred years that the visual system can use this to disambiguate ambiguous images, a process commonly called the *light-from-above assumption* or *light-from-above prior* (Benson & Yonas, 1973; Berbaum, Bever, & Chung, 1983, 1984; Brewster, 1826, 1832, 1847; von Fieandt, 1949; Hagen, 1976; Hershberger, 1970; Hess, 1950; Ramachandran, 1988; Rittenhouse, 1786; although, see also Koenderink, van Doorn, Kappers, te Pas, & Pont, 2003; B. Liu & Todd, 2004).

Specifically, in the absence of cast shadows, shading information is ambiguous about whether a surface is convex or concave. However, if the visual system assumes that light comes from above, then the brightest pixels in the image are more likely to be facing upward, while darker pixels face downward. This assumption allows the visual system to resolve the convex/concave ambiguity and arrive at a unique estimate of shape. For example, in Figure 9.10, the relief patterns are identical except for the direction of the intensity gradients. On the left, the dark portions of the image tend to be seen as protruding, and the light as receding, because of the organization of the intensity gradients. By contrast, on the right, the opposite is the case. Turning the image upside down should reverse this effect.

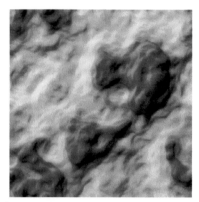 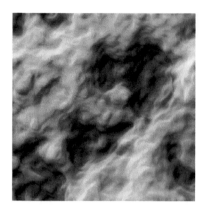

Figure 9.10

The light-from-above assumption and the perception of convexity. These two patterns are identical except for the direction of the intensity gradients in the image. Most people see the dark patches in the image on the left as hills, while on the right they appear to be valleys.

Bizarrely, there is also experimental evidence that the light from above prior is actually slightly biased to the left-hand side; that is, participants have a slight preference for illumination coming from above-left (Mamassian & Goutcher, 2001). The reason for this is still a matter of controversy. It may be caused by an underlying physiological difference in processing between the two cerebral hemispheres (many cognitive processes are lateralized, or carried out predominantly on one side of the brain, to some degree). Alternatively, it has been suggested that the left bias might be caused by the fact that interiors such as classrooms and offices are often arranged so that light strikes the page from the left-hand side, so that the right-handed majority do not cast shadows onto the page they are working on. Irrespective of the cause, it is interesting to speculate about potential uses of this bias in computer graphics, particularly for nonphotorealistic rendering.

Natural illumination patterns contain many other statistical regularities. Dror, Willsky, and Adelson (2004) studied the intensity distributions, spatial frequency content, and marginal and joint wavelet coefficient distributions of light probes. They found that, in many respects, the statistics of light probes resemble those of other natural images. This has consequences for the appearance of shaded and glossy objects. Fleming, Dror, and Adelson (2003) compared human perception of surface gloss under natural and artificial illuminations. They found that participants were better at judging the surface reflectance properties of spheres rendered under real-world light probes than under simple synthetic illuminations, such as point sources or random noise illumination models. They argued that the intensity distribution of natural illuminations is particularly important for shading and the perception of gloss. Specifically, illumination in the natural environment has a very high dynamic range of intensities. Light that comes from direct sources, such as the sun, is often many orders of magnitude brighter than secondary reflections. However, direct sources generally make up only a small proportion of pixels in the light probe. Thus, the intensity histograms of natural illumination patterns tend to be heavily skewed, with only a few directions much brighter than the rest. This causes clear shading patterns and bright highlights that are important for the perception of both shape and surface reflectance properties. This is discussed in greater detail in Chapter 10.

As discussed in Section 9.1, the statistics of illumination also vary from point to point within a scene. The light field fills the entire space of a scene, such that the appearance of a surface varies depending on both how it is oriented and where it is placed. Mury, Pont, and Koenderink (2007) have measured how the low-order properties of the light field vary from location to location in a variety of different indoor and outdoor scenes. They developed a custom high dynamic range photometer called a *plenopter* (after the *plenoptic function* of Adelson & Bergen, 1991), which consists of 12 photosensitive cells, arranged in a dodecahedron, to collect light arriving from all incident directions. They used the measurements to estimate the low-order spherical harmonic coefficients at various positions within the light field. As mentioned above, these low-order terms are sufficient to determine the appearance of a Lambertian surface. They found that in the scenes they measured, the light field varied smoothly from position to position, indicating that a sparse sampling is sufficient to approximate the entire light field quite well, as intervening locations can be interpolated from the samples. They also found that the light field is dominated by the geometrical structure of the scene, such as the position of sources and surfaces, rather than by the materials they are made of. This was confirmed by showing that extremely simple analytical models capture many of the properties they observed in natural scenes. The fact that the low order properties of the light field are well organized and simple suggests that the visual system might be able to represent them, albeit approximately. We discuss some of the experimental evidence that suggests that humans can indeed estimate variations in the illumination throughout a scene, in Section 9.5.

9.2   Shape from Shading

In the preceding sections we have considered a number of physical properties of illumination and shading. However, as indicated in the introduction to this chapter, most perception research deals not with the perception of illumination or shading per se, but rather with how these factors affect the perception of the intrinsic properties of surfaces, such as their reflectance or 3D shape. In the following sections we will outline some of the key problems that this poses to the visual system. We start by considering how illumination and shading affect the perception of shape.

As we have seen, when light interacts with surfaces, it creates form-revealing chiaroscuro patterns in the image, which the visual system can use to estimate 3D shape. This is known as *shape from shading*. How the brain solves shape from shading remains a deep mystery for vision research. Unlike stereopsis, motion parallax, and a number of other depth cues, the relevant image information that the brain uses and indeed which properties of shape are represented are still topics of controversy.

9.2.1   Theoretical Work on Shape from Shading

One of the reasons that human shape from shading is poorly understood is that it is a very difficult problem from a theoretical perspective. Under arbitrary illumination conditions and with arbitrary surface reflectance properties, recovering shape from shading is undercconstrained. In other words, the image information alone does not uniquely specify the underlying geometry. When viewing a patch of surface, the intensity in the image depends on the illumination, the local orientation of the surface, and its reflectance properties. In order to solve for any one of these factors, the brain would need to know the other two, which is what makes the problem undercconstrained.

To overcome this fundamental ambiguity, computational shape-from-shading algorithms often impose certain restrictions on the illumination conditions, the reflectance properties, or the geometry of the object. For example, it is common to assume that the surface is Lambertian with uniform albedo, or that illumination is collimated. When such constraints are imposed, the problem becomes tractable, or at least less hopeless. However, human shape from shading does not appear to be restricted in this way. We rarely experience any problems inferring the shape of objects, irrespective of their reflectance properties or the illumination conditions (Figure 9.11). It is this flexibility that separates human shape from shading from state-of-the-art computer algorithms.

Computational approaches to estimating shape from shading typically start with the *reflectance map* (Horn, 1977; Horn & Brooks, 1989; Horn & Sjoberg, 1979). Under direct illumination, the intensity of a surface patch in the image depends on its orientation relative to the light source, as well as its reflectance properties, which determine how light is reflected from the surface. The reflectance map is a two-dimensional function that cap-

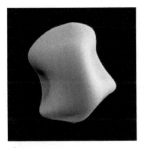 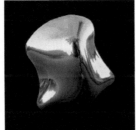 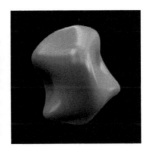

Figure 9.11

The three objects have identical shape but different surface reflectance properties and are viewed under different illuminations. Despite the fact that there is no context to provide additional information, we experience little problem in perceiving the 3D shape of these objects.

tures these relationships. It relates the image intensity to three-dimensional surface orientation, under the assumption that shading is completely local (i.e., no shadows, interreflection, vignetting, or translucency), so that each surface orientation yields a unique intensity in the image. Specifically, we can represent any visible surface normal using two parameters (such as slant and tilt, or by using the partial derivatives of the depths relative to the image plane). These are the two axes of the reflectance map. Each point in the map contains an intensity value, which tells us how bright a pixel in the image would appear if it imaged a surface patch with the corresponding orientation. Thus, the reflectance map combines information about surface reflectance properties and illumination conditions in a single function. An example reflectance map—in this case for a Lambertian surface under collimated illumination—is shown in Figure 9.12.

The reflectance map can be thought of as a simple forward model for rendering an image of an object with specific lighting and shading properties. Given a 3D model—or rather, given a pixel map containing the surface normals at each visible point on the model—we can create a rendering as follows: For each pixel in the image, we read out the corresponding surface normal. These two numbers act as indices into the reflectance map. We then look up the intensity stored in the corresponding location in the reflectance map, and place that value in the pixel from the image. When applied to all pixels, the result is a rendering of the object with the corresponding reflectance and illumination conditions.

The problem for shape from shading, as it is normally posed, is the need to invert this rendering process. In other words, given an intensity value from a given pixel, we want to know what the corresponding surface orien-

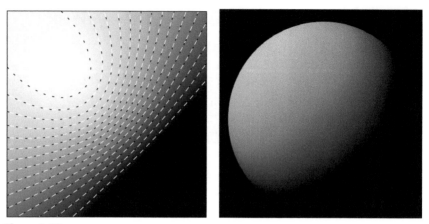

Figure 9.12

The reflectance map for a Lambertian surface under collimated illumination. Image intensity is plotted as a function of the surface normal. Dashed lines indicate isophotes, or lines of constant intensity (left). A sphere rendered with this reflectance map (right).

tation is. It is easy to see that this is an ill-posed task, because intensity is a single scalar value, while surface orientation requires two parameters. Thus, for any given intensity value, there is a whole family of different surface orientations that could have produced that intensity. For example, in Figure 9.12, each of the dashed isophote lines in the reflectance map indicates the one-parameter family of different surface orientations that correspond to a given image intensity for this reflectance map. To recover the unique surface normal corresponding to a given image intensity, the visual system would have to combine measurements from multiple locations to find a set of mutually consistent estimates, under certain assumptions about the geometry of the surface, such as smoothness. Many methods and constraints have been proposed for doing this, although how these potential constraints relate to human shape from shading has not been tested extensively.

To make matters worse, this assumes that we know the reflectance map. However, the human visual system typically does not know a priori what the reflectance and illumination conditions are. As stated above, these other scene properties also need to be inferred from the image. Thus, it seems quite unlikely that human shape from shading operates according to the same principles as traditional shape-from-shading algorithms.

One alternative is that human shape from shading does not rely on an estimate of the reflectance map, or indeed on the relationship between image intensity and surface orientation per se. That is, instead of explicitly estimating or assuming the properties of the reflectance map, the visual system might instead use some other image quantity that is indicative of shape properties while being relatively unaffected by changes in the illumination or reflectance properties.

Several authors have identified higher-order quantities in shading patterns that are systematically related to geometrical properties. For example, Koenderink and van Doorn (1980) identified a number of invariants that are related to 3D shape based on the structure (e.g., topological properties) of the *isophotes* in the image. Isophotes are curves of constant image intensity, which are influenced by both the illumination and 3D shape. Rather than using the raw image intensities to estimate surface orientation directly on a pixel-by-pixel basis, the visual system could estimate geometrical properties related to curvature based on the patterns of the isophotes across space.

Fleming, Torralba, and Adelson (2004, 2009) have suggested that the visual system could use image filters tuned to different image orientations (see Chapter 3) to estimate local surface curvature properties. This is related to the suggestion that isophotes are the key image quantity, because orientation-sensitive filters respond most strongly when aligned with isophotes, and most weakly when isophotes cut across them. The key intuition is that when a surface is weakly curved, the image gradients tend to be shallow, leading to weak responses from filters. By contrast, when the surface is more strongly curved, the responses are stronger. In particular, when a surface patch is anisotropic (i.e., when it is weakly curved in one direction and more strongly curved in the orthogonal direction, like a cylinder), the shading patterns tend to run along the direction of weakest curvature (see Figure 9.13). This is most clear with cylindrical specular surfaces, such as a polished faucet or chair leg. If you look carefully at such an object, you will notice that the reflections run along the length of the cylinder in parallel stripes. If you rotate the object, the stripes rotate with it, irrespective of the orientation of features in the surrounding world. Oriented filters that are aligned with the direction of minimum curvature respond strongly, while filters that cut across the shading or reflections respond weakly. This means that the visual system could use the relative strengths of the filter responses to estimate the direction of minimum surface curvature, as well as the ratio of minimum to maximum curvature, at each point on the surface. Together, these relationships suggest that the key mapping in shape from shading may not be between *image intensity* and *surface orientation*, but rather between *image orientation* and *surface curvature* properties. Fleming et al. showed how this relationship may account for our surprising ability to estimate the shape of perfectly specular surfaces even when the illumination conditions are unspecified.

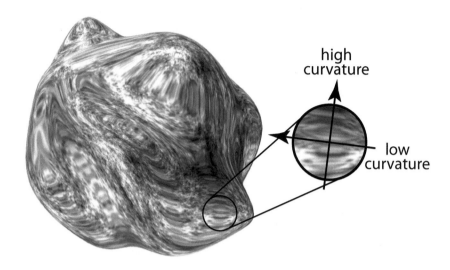

Figure 9.13

A specular surface. In the close-up, notice that the reflections appear stretched out into parallel streaks along the direction of minimum surface curvature.

The idea of a mapping between image orientation and surface curvature has also been exploited in nonphotorealistic rendering by artificially exaggerating the relationship to enhance local shape features (Vergne, Pacanowski, Barla, Granier, & Schlick, 2009). They found that exaggerating the mapping led to substantial improvements in the depiction of surface details. This relationship between image orientations and view-dependent measures of surface curvature is also the basis for the apparent-ridges method for rendering line drawings (T. Judd, Durand, & Adelson, 2007).

9.2.2   Shape-from-Shading Ambiguities

The simultaneous effects of shape, reflectance, and illumination on the image lead to a number of important ambiguities in the perception of shape from shading. As we have already seen, for shallow surfaces under directional illumination, there is a convex/concave ambiguity. A bright feature in the image must be pointing at the light source, but it is unclear whether the light source is, for example, above or below the surface and, consequently, whether the surface is facing up or down. When applied to all locations simultaneously, this leads to a global convex-concave ambiguity. In practice, it is worth noting that context usually resolves this ambiguity.

Cast shadows, interreflections, and other cues to the direction of the light source, as well as a bias for globally convex surfaces, mean that in the real world we rarely make mistakes about whether a shape points in or sticks out.

There is also an ambiguity between changes in surface reflectance and changes in surface orientation. When presented with a given discontinuity in intensity in the image (e.g., a light-dark edge), one possible interpretation is that it might be due to a change in the surface albedo, which scales the overall amount of light reflected from the surface. However, an alternative explanation of the edge could be that the surface contains a discontinuity in three-dimensional orientation—that the surface suddenly points away from the light—which would scale the overall amount of light incident on the surface. These two alternative causes can yield exactly the same change in intensity in the image and therefore can be impossible to distinguish locally. We discuss this in more detail below.

A third important ambiguity was described by Belhumeur, Kriegman, and Yuille (1999). They showed mathematically that, under collimated illumination, a given pattern of intensities in the image is consistent with a whole family of different scenes that are related to one another by affine transformations—shearing and scaling. This is called the *bas-relief* ambiguity. In short, the intuition is as follows: A given shading gradient could be caused by a shallow surface with glancing illumination (which causes strong gradients) or by a deeper surface under illumination that comes from closer to head-on (which causes weaker gradients). This bas-relief ambiguity applies to the entire scene—that is, all surface patches and the illumination considered together. As we shall see, it plays a role in several perceptual problems, including both estimating shape and estimating the direction of the light source.

Together, these ambiguities and the limited success of computer vision algorithms suggest that shape from shading is a challenging problem for the human visual system. Despite this, we rarely experience problems telling 3D shape from a photograph of an object. How well does human shape from shading work?

9.2.3 Experiments on Shape from Shading in Humans

Early work on human shape from shading focused on simple shapes, such as ellipsoids and cylinders, under simple illumination conditions. For example, Todd and Mingolla (1983) showed participants' renderings of cylindrical surface patches under collimated illumination. They asked the participants to rate the curvature of the surface with reference to five physical cylinders that were visible throughout the experiment. They varied the light-source direction and the reflectance properties of the surface to measure how these

other factors affected shape judgments. They found that participants' ratings of curvature increased monotonically with the simulated curvatures,
although the matte surfaces were rated as substantially flatter than they
really were, while the shiny surfaces were seen as having higher curvature
than the matte ones. Interestingly, they also asked participants to judge
the direction of illumination and found that participants were better at
judging the direction of illumination than they were at estimating the surface curvatures, and that the judgments were unaffected by the shininess
of the surface. The authors argue that shape-from-shading models that
make restrictive assumptions about light direction and Lambertian surface
reflectance cannot account for the data.

H. H. Bülthoff and Mallot (1988) presented participants with computer
renderings of ellipsoids with different aspect ratios, and asked participants
to adjust stereoscopic depth probes to report the perceived shape of the
objects. In some of the conditions, the shaded surfaces were presented
stereoscopically, so that task was effectively trivial, as participants simply
had to set each probe to the same disparity as the corresponding surface
location. However, in other conditions, the shaded surfaces were presented
without stereoscopic cues. They found, like Todd and Mingolla (1983),
that participants tended to underestimate the depths of the surface, suggesting that shading, when in conflict with other cues, is only a relatively
weak cue to 3D shape. However, it is important to note (as the authors
do) that there is something quite unnatural about adjusting probes in
stereoscopic depth to match the apparent depths produced by a monocular shape cue. At no depth setting would the probes appear to lie on
the surface itself; they would always float in front of the pictorial plane.
This may account for the participants' reluctance to set the probes to large
disparities.

One of the most important innovations in the study of shape from shading was the development of the *gauge-figure task*. In a landmark study,
Koenderink, van Doorn, and Kappers (1992) for the first time presented
participants with complex 3D shapes under natural illumination conditions, and measured in detail what they perceived. In order to do this,
they asked participants to adjust the 3D orientation of small "gauge figure" probes. These probes consisted of a circular disk with a small stick
that pointed out perpendicularly from the center of the figure on one side,
like a sundial or an old-fashioned drawing pin. The participants's task was
to rotate the gauge figure in three-dimensions so that the disk appeared
to lie in the local tangent plane (i.e., flush with the surface), while the
needle stuck out perpendicularly from the surface (i.e., along the surface
normal). By measuring the perceived surface orientation at many locations
across the surface, it is possible to reconstruct the shape perceived by the
participants.

Koenderink et al. (1992) found that participants' settings across the surface were generally internally consistent; that is, the probe settings could be combined to reconstruct a global estimate of perceived shape without large residual errors. They also found that the perceived shape correlated very well with the real shape in the sense that points that are closer to the viewer on the surface appeared closer in the reconstruction. However, they found that repeated measurements across participants, or by a given participant across multiple sessions, differed from one another significantly. Importantly, they found that the different reconstructions were systematically related to one another by an affine transformation. This is important given the bas-relief ambiguity, described in Section 9.2.2, which suggests that shape from shading can be solved only up to an affine transformation. It shows that the participants effectively have a perceptual free parameter, which varies from session to session, in which they specify by some unknown process what the affine scaling of the shape is. Adding other cues, such as binocular stereopsis, can help resolve the ambiguity, and this explains why we generally do not experience the ambiguity in everyday life.

In subsequent studies using the gauge-figure task, Mamassian and Kersten (1996) used the participants' gauge-figure settings to infer where the participant believed the light source was. The authors asked participants to set gauge figures for a croissant-shaped object and, based on the results, argued that there was little evidence that shading played a role in determining the participants' estimate of shape. Instead, they argued that the contour of the object was probably the most important cue. While this may well be true for the simple geometry used in this experiment, it is also clear that shading can provide unique additional sources of information about 3D curvature in other circumstances. For example, Koenderink, van Doorn, Christou, and Lappin (1996b) directly compared gauge-figure settings for shaded images of sculptures of human torsos with those for simple line drawings of the same sculptures. They found that while settings were good with the contours, they were substantially better when the shading cue was also present. More recently, in a direct comparison of various line drawing rendering methods, Cole et al. (2009) found that for shapes with simple geometry, shading provides little additional improvement in gauge settings beyond what was provided by contours. This was particularly the case for geometry that consisted of planar and curved surface patches joined by sharp creases (i.e., orientation discontinuities), such as machined engine parts. By contrast, for irregular smoothly curved surfaces—like bones or potatoes—the shading provided additional information that made the gauge settings more reliable and accurate.

Several authors have also measured how illumination affects the perception of shape from shading. Koenderink, van Doorn, Christou, and Lappin (1996a) measured the effects of changing the direction of illumination on the perception of complex shape, again using gauge-figure judgments of torso sculptures. They found that changing light direction caused subtle distortions of perceived shape in which the shapes were somewhat elongated in the direction of the light source. Similarly, Caniard and Fleming (2007) found that with simpler geometries, changing the illumination direction can lead to quite-substantial changes in perceived shape. When participants were asked to distinguish between subtly different shapes, the large changes in the image caused by illumination changes dominated the weak differences due to the geometry.

In general, the effects of illumination direction on perceived shape depend on the geometry. When the surface is smooth, with relatively low curvature, the image gradients are shallow. Under these conditions, changing the illumination direction has a large effect on the orientation of image gradients, leading to misperception of the principle curvature directions. When shading gradients are aligned with shape features, the shading enhances the features; by contrast, when shading runs perpendicularly to the shape features, it tends to wash out their contrast, weakening the perceived curvatures along those directions. It is interesting to speculate how these effects could be exploited in rendering.

In most of the experiments we have considered so far, the illumination was dominated by a directional term. How well can we perceive shape from shading under diffuse illumination conditions? Diffuse shading is a particularly interesting test case for theories of shape from shading, because the chiaroscuro is due primarily to vignetting effects, rather than the cosine shading law. In other words, the relationship between image intensity and surface orientation breaks down, to be replaced by a relationship between image intensity and the degree of self-occlusion. In principle, participants could use a heuristic that darker pixels are deeper in the surface, which is sometimes called the "dark is deep" heuristic. Langer and Bülthoff (2000) presented participants with irregularly rippled surfaces under both directional and diffuse illumination, and asked the participants to distinguish whether specific surface locations (indicated by dots) were local convexities or concavities. They found that participants were just as good at the task under diffuse illumination as they were with collimated lighting when the illumination came from above. When the illumination came from below, the participants were actually below chance performance, indicating that they perceived the local concavities as convexities and vice versa, as we discussed above. They also compared judgments of depth with judgments of image brightness, to test whether participants used the "dark is deep" heuristic. They found that brightness and depth judgments did indeed correlate, but that participants actually did better than would be predicted by this heuristic, indicating that human shape estimation is more sophisticated than previously thought.

9.3   Illumination and the Intrinsic Properties of Surfaces

As we have seen, light bounces all over the place before it reaches the eyes. This means that the input to the visual system—the intensities in the retinal image—are a complex combination of many physical properties of the scene. The image of a surface, for example, depends on the lighting, the reflectance attributes of the surface, and its three-dimensional orientation. The goal of vision is to recover the intrinsic physical properties of surfaces and objects from the retinal image. Somehow the visual system has to separate the retinal image intensities into these distinct physical causes.

For a diffuse surface, if we ignore color, the amount of light reaching the eye is $L = I \cdot R$, where I is the total incoming illumination (taking into account the angle relative to the light source) and R is the reflectance or albedo of the surface (which is the proportion of incoming light that the surface reflects). Because R is an intrinsic property of the surface, it is often argued that this is the quantity that the visual system is trying to estimate; that is, the visual system is trying to solve $R = L/I$. Expressed in words, the visual system is trying to recover the reflectance by discounting or compensating for the contribution of the illumination to the retinal luminance. This is difficult because, in general, I is unknown. Thus, there are an infinite number of combinations of I and R that result in a given value of L.

The fact that the visual system is interested in intrinsic properties of surfaces, rather than retinal intensities, is demonstrated in many compelling illusions. For example, in Adelson's "checker-shadow" illusion (Figure 9.14), most observers find it hard to believe that the tiles labeled A and B are actually the same intensity in the image. We have an overwhelming impression that B is a lighter shade of gray than A. You can check for yourself that they are, in fact, the same shade by cutting holes out of a sheet of paper and placing the sheet so that it covers the surroundings. At first, this seems like a huge illusion: why do we see two identical patches so differently from one another? However, it is important to understand that what we experience is the result of the human visual system trying to estimate the intrinsic properties of surfaces, and getting the answer right. Although A and B project the same retinal intensity, this is not a physical quantity of interest to the visual system. Instead the visual system attempts to recover the reflectances corresponding to A and B, which are indeed different: A is painted a dark shade of gray but illuminated brightly, while B is a light shade of paint, but is dim because it is in the shadow. Thus, this is not really an illusion (in the sense of misperception) at all.

The key issue facing the visual system, therefore, is how to distinguish which variations in image intensity are due to changes in the illumination from those that are due to changes in the intrinsic pigmentation of the

Figure 9.14

Ted Adelson's *checker-shadow* Illusion. The checks labeled A and B are actually the same shade of gray in the image. However, we don't see it that way. (© 1995, Edward H. Adelson.)

surfaces. How the visual system achieves this is still not understood. One of the most common suggestions is that spatial variations in illumination are generally slower (i.e., lower spatial frequency) than changes in pigmentation. This suggests that the visual system should filter out very low spatial frequencies to remove the spatial variations that are due to lighting, and indeed there is evidence that this plays a role in surface appearance. However, there are many cases, such as abrupt shadows, in which simple filtering operations cannot account for our perception.

Indeed, it is difficult to argue that the visual system fully "discounts" or filters out changes in illumination, because we are visually aware of shadow boundaries and shading patterns. This suggests that instead of removing the effects of illumination, the visual system separates intensity changes into distinct causal layers. Barrow and Tenenbaum (1978) suggested that the visual system could split the image into maps that represent the separate contributions of illumination and pigmentation to the observed image intensity, as depicted in Figure 9.15. This is known as *intrinsic image analysis*.

Gilchrist et al. (1999) have suggested that the visual system segments the visual field into regions (called *frameworks*), within which the illumination is approximately constant. They argued that the visual system estimates the relative albedos of different surfaces within each framework by taking the ratio of their intensities. This works because if the illumina-

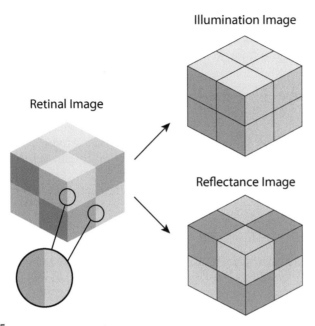

Figure 9.15

Intrinsic image analysis. The retinal image is decomposed into two hypothetical layers, each representing a distinct physical cause in the scene. Note local edges are ambiguous. The two circled edges have identical intensity profiles, but different physical causes: one is due to shading; the other is due to pigmentation. (Figure inspired by similar figures by Ted Adelson.)

tion is roughly constant within each framework, then the ratio of intensities reliably indicates the ratio of surface reflectances (effectively, I is assumed to be constant so $L \propto R$). However, the ratios do not specify the absolute reflectance values of the patches within each framework, only their albedos relative to one another. In other words, a ratio specifies that one surface is, for example, twice as reflective as another, but not whether the two are white and mid-gray, or mid-gray and black. In order to overcome this, Gilchrist et al. suggest that the visual system uses a simple heuristic in order to *anchor* its scale of reflectance values: it assumes that the brightest surface within each framework is white, and works out the other surfaces based on the ratios relative to this. Thus, this theory accounts for both the visible differences in illumination across the boundaries between frameworks, and the discounting of the illuminant within each framework. Unfortunately, however, the theory does not explain how the visual system parses the scene into illumination frameworks in the first place. A number of general organizational principles have been suggested, but there still exists no model that can take as input an image and return as output a segmentation into frameworks.

9.4   Global Illumination and the Light Field

So far almost all of the illumination and shading phenomena that we have discussed are *local*; that is, they refer to the light arriving at a single point in space, rather than to the way that light is distributed through space, interacting with multiple surfaces in the scene. In this section we discuss some of the properties of lighting and shading that occur when we consider the interactions between surfaces and the passage of light through space.

9.4.1   Interreflections and Mutual Illumination

Arguably the most important difference between local and global illumination is the interreflection of light between surfaces. In some scenes—such as cloisters and long, windowless corridors—almost all of the visible surfaces are illuminated only indirectly, via light that is reflected from other surfaces. Mutual illumination is particularly visible where surfaces are close to one another, such as the corners of rooms, or when objects are in contact with one another. In these cases light bounces back and forth between the surfaces, causing a subtle mingling of colors. A very reflective surface can cast a visible reflex onto a nearby object, almost like a spotlight. It is worth noting that interreflections therefore tend to somewhat counteract the vignetting effect that occurs in concavities. Some of these effects are visible in Figure 9.16 and Color Plate VII.

Surprisingly little is known about how the visual system handles mutual illumination. It is clear that global illumination renderings look noticeably more realistic than renderings that feature only direct illumination. However, it is unclear whether this is because the visual system explicitly estimates the interactions between surfaces—and therefore notices when they are missing or wrong—or whether it is simply that global illumination effects tend to create certain gradients and other statistical image properties in the rendering, which causes the image to more closely resemble the statistics of images in the real world.

One of the most important demonstrations that interreflections play a role in the estimation of surface lightness was by Gilchrist and Jacobsen (1984). They created two identical model rooms and painted one uniform white and the other uniform black. They then illuminated the two rooms with carefully controlled lighting so that the average intensity of the two scenes was the same, and asked participants to look through a peephole and report what shade of paint they thought the rooms were painted with.

Figure 9.16

On the left, the Cornell Box is rendered with only direct illumination; on the right, a full global illumination rendering is shown. Interreflections have a substantial effect on the appearance of the scene. (See Color Plate VII.)

This is an interesting comparison because the direct shading of a black and a white surface are simply scaled versions of one another. If the white surface reflects five times as much light as the black, then every point on the surface should be five times as bright as the corresponding point on the black surface. Once the experimenters had normalized for this by scaling the intensity of the illumination, then the direct shading should render the two rooms indistinguishable, if the participants relied on direct illumination alone to judge the surface albedo. However, this is not what they found. The participants correctly reported seeing the white room as white, while the black room, which was illuminated with much more intense lighting, was seen as middle gray. How were the participants able to distinguish the shades of paint? The important insight is that although the direct shading differs only by a multiplicative scaling, the indirect illumination is quite different for black and white rooms. In a black room, there is less interreflection between surfaces, and thus the shadows remain dark and there are no reflexes. By contrast, in the white room, reflections between surfaces make the light field more diffuse, leading to reflexes; brighter shadows; and a softer, lower contrast appearance overall. Evidently, the human visual system can use this information for inferring that the paint must be reflecting more light. Exactly how this is computed from the image, however, remains a mystery.

A second elegant demonstration that the visual system knows how to interpret mutual illumination was developed by Bloj, Kersten, and Hurlbert (1999). They exploited a well-known ambiguous three-dimensional figure called the Mach card, which consists of a single piece of cardstock folded into a V and placed facing the viewer like an open book (i.e., with the central fold more distant than the edges). Our perception of the Mach card is bistable; that is, the interpretation spontaneously flips with prolonged viewing. It can either be seen as concave like it really is, or convex like a roof. Bloj et al. modified the Mach card by painting one of the two sides pink. The mutual illumination between the two halves of the card causes the white side to be illuminated with pink light, which makes it look as if it has a slightly pinkish tinge. The experimenters then used a special optical device for swapping the two eyes' views. This has the effect of reversing the binocular depth information, thereby encouraging the participants to misperceive the shape of the card as convex instead of concave. They found that when the perceived shape of the object reversed, the white side changed appearance from a subtle pink to a deep magenta color. This occurs because in the convex interpretation, the two sides of the card are seen as facing away from each other. Therefore, the visual system can no longer attribute the pinkish tinge to mutual illumination. Instead, it interprets the pink as belonging to the intrinsic color of the card. The fact that we do not make this mistake when the card is correctly perceived as concave demonstrates that the visual system knows that it must "discount" or compensate for the effects of secondary reflections coming from nearby surfaces. In subsequent research, Doerschner, Boyaci, and Maloney (2004) have shown that the visual system also takes into account the angle between two surfaces when compensating for the mutual illumination. However, they also found that this compensation is only partial, in the sense that we attribute a proportion of the color of the secondary illumination to the surface itself.

9.4.2   Participating Media and Atmospheric Effects

So far, all of the effects that we have considered in this chapter assume that light travels through a vacuum. In empty space, light travels in straight lines, and the intensity does not vary along the length of the ray. However, in our natural environment, light travels through air, which often contains small particles of dust, smoke, and water. These refract, scatter, and absorb light as it moves through the medium, leading to a wide variety of atmospheric effects, such as the blue color of the midday sky and the reds of sunset, as well as mist and fog, crepuscular rays (sometimes called "God rays" in computer graphics) and lunar coronae, or even the rather more mundane look of a smoky pub or dingy puddle.

Very little is known about the effects of participating media on perception. Certainly, exotic atmospheric effects like aurora borealis and nacreous clouds are encountered so rarely by most humans that it is unlikely that

Figure 9.17
An example of aerial perspective, in which contrast is reduced as a function of distance.

we have any special mechanisms for interpreting them. Even rainbows are generally perceived to be physical sources of light located in the sky, rather than as the passage of light through intervening droplets. Although beautiful to look at—and sometimes nontrivial to simulate—most of these phenomena are not considered to be particularly important by perception researchers.

By contrast, probably the most important effect of participating media, such as fog or haze, is the more down-to-earth fact that image contrast decreases systematically as a function of distance through the medium. Near objects are clearly visible, while distant surfaces, such as mountains or skyscrapers, appear washed out and often somewhat bluish due to Rayleigh scattering (see Figure 9.17). This atmospheric scattering produces a depth cue called *aerial perspective* (da Vinci, 1566/1970), which the visual system could, in principle, use to facilitate the perception of distance. Unfortunately, although systematic, the precise degree of contrast reduction varies with the time of day and atmospheric conditions, so it cannot provide stable, metric information about distances. However, it has the advantage that it is most effective over very large distances, which is the complement of other depth cues, such as binocular parallax, which tend to provide the most reliable depth information at near distances. Aerial perspective makes large scenes appear more realistic; however, little is known about how it interacts with other depth cues, such as linear perspective, in the estimation of very large distances.

9.5   Experiments on Human Estimation of Illumination

As we have seen, the light field can be complex, and provides important
sources of information about surface reflectance and 3D shape. But how
well can observers estimate the illumination itself? Most experimental work
on surface reflectance estimation and color constancy has focused on how
well the observer can ignore or discount the illuminant to achieve stable
estimates of surface properties. In these experiments, participants are typically presented objects or patterns under different illumination conditions
and are asked, through a variety of psychophysical procedures, to report the
intrinsic colors of the surfaces despite the differences in the image caused
by the lighting. In many cases, the scenes consist of simple co-planar surfaces, so that the only aspect of the illumination that participants have to
account for in making their settings is the overall intensity. However, some
researchers have also used the participants' responses to infer more complex
aspects of the illumination conditions the observer believes are present in
the scene. For example, in one set of studies (Bloj et al., 2004; Ripamonti et
al., 2004), the experimenters asked observers to identify the surface albedo
of a card when it was presented at various orientations relative to the
dominant light source in the scene. They found that the perceived albedo
varied as a function of the orientation (i.e., the participants did not perfectly discount the illuminant). Additionally, they found that the pattern
of responses varied substantially from participant to participant. However, they then used the participants' settings to infer the parameters of a
simple illumination model (point source plus ambient term) that would correspond to the errors in albedo judgments. In other words, they estimated
which illumination conditions would be consistent with the errors that the
participants made. They found that the pattern of errors could be well
predicted using such an illumination model. More importantly, they also
found that the errors made by individual participants, as well as the differences in responses between participants, corresponded to only relatively
small errors in the estimated position and brightness of the point source
term. This suggests that participants were able to estimate the properties of an unseen light source quite accurately when asked to judge surface
albedo. Similar experiments using computer graphics simulations instead
of real scenes reached similar conclusions (Boyaci, Doerschner, & Maloney,
2006; Boyaci, Maloney, & Hersh, 2003). Other experimenters (Mamassian
& Kersten, 1996) have used participants' estimates of 3D shape to infer the
perceived position of a point source.

More recently, researchers have started to ask how well participants
can estimate illumination properties directly, as opposed to inferring them
indirectly from other judgments. For example, Koenderink et al. (2003)
showed participants patches of surface texture with mesoscale relief, which

had been photographed under collimated illumination from different directions, and asked the participants to judge the direction of the illumination.
Specifically, they presented participants with a rendered hemisphere and
asked them to adjust the direction of the illumination in the rendering to
match what they saw in the photographs. They found that participants
were generally quite good at estimating the azimuth of the illumination—
that is, the orientation of the illumination in the image plane—but only
up to a 180° ambiguity. In other words, participants could tell that the
illumination orientation was—for example—diagonal in the image, to an
accuracy within a range of around 15°, but they could not tell whether
the light was coming from above-left or bottom-right. This makes sense
because the surface relief is subject to a convex/concave ambiguity. Specifically, shallow relief viewed head-on generally does contain strong cues that
allow the visual system to tell whether a given feature is a bump or a crater
in the surface. When the participants get the sign of the depth relationships in the surface relief wrong (i.e., they believe bumps are really craters
and vice versa), then their inferences about the illumination direction are
correspondingly wrong by 180°. As mentioned above, when observers are
uncertain about the sign of surface relief, they tend to assume that light
comes from above. The authors found that the overwhelming majority of
the participants' settings were biased toward seeing light as coming from
above, which is consistent with previous findings on the light-from-above
prior. By contrast to the azimuth, participants were much worse at estimating the elevation of the illumination (the extent to which the lighting was
coming from a grazing angle as opposed to head-on, parallel to the surface
normal). This makes sense as there is an additional ambiguity relating the
magnitude of the depth variations to the elevation of the light source, which
is related to the bas-relief ambiguity mentioned in Section 9.2.2. Specifically, a given shading gradient in the image could be caused by shallow
surface relief under glancing illumination, or by deeper relief illuminated
from nearly head-on. Indeed, other studies have shown that participants
tend to confound surface relief with the angle of incidence (Ho, Landy,
& Maloney, 2006). This fundamental uncertainty about the cause of image gradients shows up in participants' settings, which were more broadly
distributed across elevations than across azimuths. Pont and Koenderink
(2007) found that the difference in accuracy between azimuth and elevation estimates also holds for solid, roughly spherical objects with various
surface textures. They tested this using images from the Utrecht Oranges
database (Pont & Koenderink, 2003), as shown in various figures in this
chapter.

So far the experiments we have described deal mainly with the intensity
and direction of illumination. However, as we saw earlier in the chapter,
the light field can be much more complex than this. What additional

aspects of the light field can human observers estimate? In a second experiment, Pont and Koenderink (2007) showed participants' renderings of smooth Lambertian spheres. One of the spheres had illumination conditions that were chosen by the computer; the other could be adjusted by the participant. This time, in addition to adjusting the orientation of the illumination, participants could also move a slider to adjust the directedness or diffuseness of the illumination. The participants' task was, again, to set the lighting so that the two spheres appeared to be illuminated the same way. They found that participants were able to match the diffuseness of the illumination accurately but with rather large variance, which suggests some degree of uncertainty. They also found that there were interactions between different parameters of the illumination. When the lighting was highly directed (i.e., close to collimated), participants were better at setting both the azimuth and polar angle of the direction. This makes intuitive sense, because direction of illumination is better defined when the illumination is less diffuse. More interestingly, they also found that participants' estimates of diffuseness was affected by the polar angle of the illumination. When illumination came from behind the object, participants overestimated the directedness of the lighting, and when the illumination came from in front, they tended to see it as more diffuse than it really was.

The light fields considered so far consisted of only a single dominant direction. However, in the real world, illumination can arrive simultaneously from multiple directions. Doerschner et al. (2007) tested whether participants can compensate for illumination arriving from two collimated sources from different directions simultaneously. They found that participants could indeed adjust albedo as a function of surface orientation while accurately taking into account the presence of two light sources. They argue that this is surprising given that in the world in which we evolved, we only experienced one dominant light direction at a time (i.e., the sun or the moon). However, it is important to remember that secondary illumination from other surfaces can come from arbitrary directions, and this may explain why we are able to compensate for multiple simultaneous light directions.

Finally, we should also consider the perception of variations in the light field from location to location and across time. Snyder, Doerschner, and Maloney (2005) simulated a scene consisting of two rooms, one in front of the other, arranged such that the rear room was visible through an open doorway in the back wall of the front room. The rear room was brightly illuminated, while the nearer room was more dimly illuminated. Thus, the intensity of the light field varied substantially when moving from the back of the rear room, through the doorway to the front of the near room. They simulated a card floating in space at different depths in the rooms using stereoscopic presentation, and asked participants to match the apparent albedo of the card. If participants were aware of the changes in the light field across the scene, they should adjust the target to different luminances to achieve constant apparent albedo: the patch should be darker in the dimmer illumination, and brighter in the brighter room to achieve a constant surface appearance. They found that the participants could indeed partially adjust for the predominant illumination at different depths within the scene. Interestingly, when the experimenters added a number of mirrored (specular) spheres throughout the scene, performance improved substantially. These spheres effectively acted as light probes for different points in the scene, which could—in principle—specify the way that the light is changing through space. However, it was unclear before this experiment whether participants could actually use this information to improve their estimates of the lighting.

The Snyder et al. (2005) study investigated the perception of changes in illumination intensity across space; however, this tells us little about the perception of higher-order properties, such as the direction of illumination at different points in the scene. To address this, Koenderink, Pont, van Doorn, Kappers, and Todd (2007) showed participants photographs of scenes with certain canonical light field structures. The scenes included, for example, collimated illumination, or a source in the center of the scene (sometimes called "nativity scene" illumination, in reference to paintings in which the infant Christ at the center of the painting is the primary source of light in the scene). Superimposed on the photographs were renderings of a Lambertian spherical probe stimulus, which could be adjusted by the participants. Their task was to adjust the properties of the illumination for the probe so that it matched the illumination for that point in the scene. Participants could adjust the intensity, direction, and diffuseness of the lighting. The authors found that settings made by different participants were very similar to one another and were highly repeatable across sessions. They also found that the settings correlated relatively well with the true illumination conditions at the various locations in the scene, with one notable exception: when the probe was placed within the volume of a shadow cast by objects in the scene. This is interesting, as it shows that while participants are able to represent the general trends of illumination within a scene, certain effects are perceived to occur on the illuminated surfaces themselves, rather than in the unpopulated space of the scene.

Gerhard and Maloney (2010) have shown that we can also compensate for temporal variations in lighting. They showed participants stereoscopic images of convex and concave pyramids under illumination that consisted of a mixture of both collimated and diffuse components. They then changed the scene in one of two ways: they either rotated the direction of the collimated lighting by a small amount, or they kept the lighting fixed and modified the albedo of the surfaces in a way that produced similar effects on the luminance ratios across edges in the scene, but was not consistent with a change in the lighting. They asked participants to detect whether the change was due to a change in lighting or not, and found that participants were exceedingly accurate at the task. They could distinguish real changes in lighting from the "fakes" when the light moved by just five degrees or so. This suggests that participants can be extremely good at detecting subtle changes in lighting conditions over time.

9.6   Cast Shadows

When objects are placed in a strongly directional light field, such as a spotlight, they tend to cast shadows onto surfaces in the surroundings. Cast shadows are actually volumes. This can be seen directly when there is participating medium, such as mist or smoke. However, we typically only experience shadows on a *receiving surface*—that is, the surface for which the light source is occluded by the shadow-casting object. Depending on the number of light sources, single objects can cast multiple shadows that can overlap to different extents on the receiving surface. There are a number of properties of natural shadows that are worth noting because they have direct consequences for perception.

9.6.1   Shadows and Image Contrast

First, almost by definition, shadows are darker than their surroundings. This may seem obvious, but it imposes constraints on the polarity of image contrasts across the shadow boundary. The visual system is acutely aware of this. One of the reasons that the faces in photographic negatives are hard to recognize is that the shadows that the human visual system naturally tends to ignore, become salient and distracting.

The visual system's tacit assumption that shadows are dark appears to be hard-wired, in a way that other properties of the visual field are not. One interesting piece of evidence for this was revealed in a phenomenological study by Anstis (1992). For extended periods, he used a modified video camera to view the world in photographic negative—that is, with the intensities in the image inverted so that the darkest portions of the image appeared bright and the brightest regions appeared dark. (See also Section 18.3.2.) This is analogous to a famous experiment (G. Stratton, 1897) in which, for a week, the experimenter wore goggles that flip the image of the world upside down. In that experiment—despite extreme disorientation initially—by the end of the week, the experimenter's brain had partially compensated for the inversion, allowing him to perform many tasks practically normally. By contrast, in Anstis' photographic-negative experiment, Anstis reported never becoming accustomed to the inversion of intensities.

He found that shadows were salient and distracting, and that recognizing faces was difficult. The whole world looked unreal, and the participant experienced many confusions about the cause of bright and dark patches in the world. For example, the participant reports, "When I watched people swimming in the pool I noticed that when swimmers kicked up foam, the water appeared to turn black as though ink was momentarily mixed into it, but disappeared when the disturbance subsided and the water fell back into the pool." This suggests that contrast polarity plays a major role in our ability to distinguish illumination variations from pigmentation variations.

At the same time, shadows are rarely truly black, as light usually arrives from additional directions other than the occluded light source. Indeed, only in the case of a truly collimated light field with no interreflections would shadows be completely black. A shadow reduces the intensities associated with surface colors in a multiplicative way; i.e., a shadow reduces the incoming light by a fixed proportion, so the outgoing light also reduces by the same ratio. One consequence of this is that Michelson contrast is preserved across shadow boundaries (see Chapter 2). Wallach (1948) argued that the visual system could use the contrast ratio across image contours to estimate the relative albedo of two surfaces.

9.6.2   Shadow Boundaries: The Penumbra

A second important characteristic of natural shadows is that they typically have a blurry fringe, or *penumbra*. This is caused by the fact that even highly directional illumination is rarely truly collimated. Because light sources are somewhat extended, light rays graze the casting object's perimeter at a range of angles, leading to a gradient of intensity in the

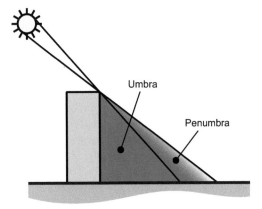

Figure 9.18
Extended sources cause a blurry fringe at the edge of cast shadows.

neighborhood of the shadow's edge (Figure 9.18). The size of the penumbra varies depending on the light source and the distance between the casting object and the receiving surface. The penumbra tends to be narrowest when the light source is small in area and the casting object is close to the receiving surface.

Penumbras play an important role in perception: they give the visual system a vital clue that a transition in intensity in the image is actually caused by a shadow (i.e., a change in illumination) rather than a change in the intrinsic pigmentation of the object. Of course, it is possible to carefully paint a surface with a graded change in surface color, resembling the penumbra of an object. However, under most circumstances, fuzzy intensity changes are more likely to be due to shadow boundaries than to the surface albedo. This is particularly the case when there are some spatial variations in the pigmentation (i.e., a texture), because the penumbra produces a gradient that is common across the different surface colors.

A powerful demonstration that the visual system can use the penumbra and the contrast polarity at edges to tell if they are shadow boundaries was developed by Ewald Hering (1874/1964). The demonstration works as follows: Take an object, such as a mug, and place it on a piece of uniform paper. Now illuminate the object with a spotlight so that it casts a shadow onto the sheet of paper. As expected, the shadow looks like a change in the illumination on the sheet of paper, which appears to be all the same shade of white. Now, with a thick black marker—wide enough to cover the penumbra of the shadow—trace carefully around the boundary of the shadow. Once you have finished, stand back and look at the shadow. Most observers agree that the shadow no longer looks like a shadow. Instead, it looks like a patch that is made of a different shade of pigment, as if someone had cut out a shadow-shaped piece of dark-gray paper and placed it on the white paper. Two effects are responsible for the illusion. First, by using the thick marker, the edge of the shadow is made perfectly sharp instead of blurred, which removes the cue from the penumbra that the change in intensity is actually a shadow boundary. Secondly, and perhaps more importantly, the black marker changes the contrast polarity at the edge of the shadow. Instead of a transition from bright (outside the shadow) to dim (inside the shadow), the marker creates two transitions: one from bright (outside the shadow) to black (marker), and a second one from black (marker) to dim (inside the shadow). It is this second transition, from black to dim, that is inconsistent with a real shadow edge, as shadows are always darker than their immediate surroundings. Thus, the visual system vetoes the interpretation of a shadow, and interprets the shadow as a change in surface pigmentation. This demonstration works best when you try it yourself, but when set up correctly, it also powerfully confirms the

Figure 9.19

The position of the spheres is identical in the two images. However, by changing the location of the cast shadows, the spheres appear to be either lying upon or floating above the ground plane. (After Kersten et al., 1997.)

phenomenological distinction between extrinsic illumination and intrinsic pigmentation.

9.6.3 Shadows and Distance Perception

Another important property of shadows is the spatial relationship between the casting object and the receiving surface (see Section 7.5.1). If the casting object is in contact with the receiving surface, the shadow abuts the casting object. By contrast, if the object is moved away from the receiving surface, the cast shadow separates from the casting object in the image. This means that the relationship between objects and their shadows can

Figure 9.20

A surface with a drop shadow. Changing the separation between the surface and the shadow makes the surface appear to float further in front of the background. Kersten, Knill, Mamassian, and Bülthoff (1996) showed that continuously changing the offset of the shadow leads to an impression of the surface moving in depth, even though its retinal projection does not change.

provide useful information about the depth of the casting object (Yonas et al., 1978). Figure 9.19 shows an example of this by Kersten et al. (1997). The spheres lie on a straight line in the image. However, by altering the separation between the spheres and their shadows, the spheres can be made to appear to float above the ground plane. Shadows and interreflections can be a powerful indicator of contact between two surfaces, an effect that is also known as *visual glue* (Madison, Thompson, Kersten, Shirley, & Smits, 2001; W. B. Thompson, Shirley, Smits, Kersten, & Madison, 1998). This effect is also exploited in the creation of "drop shadows" (Figure 9.20). Kersten et al. (1996) showed that continuously changing the breadth of a drop shadow can induce a vivid impression of motion in depth, even though the object that casts the shadow does not actually move at all in the image.

9.6.4 Shadows and the Properties of an Unseen Light Source

Shadows can also provide several sources of information about the position and properties of the light source. First, as we have mentioned, the size of the penumbra is affected by how extended the light source is: collimated light produces no penumbra, while large light sources—such as a light box—produce fuzzy, diffuse shadow boundaries. Second, the size of a shadow is affected by the relative distances of the casting object to the light source and the receiving surface (Figure 9.21). When the object is much closer to the receiving surface than to the light source, the shadow is approximately the same size as the casting object. By contrast, as the object gets closer to the light source and further from the receiving surface, the shadow increases in size. Thus, if an object casts a large shadow, the light source must be small and close, even if it cannot be seen directly.

Third, the direction and length of a shadow are informative about the azimuth and elevation of the light source, respectively. If an object and its shadow are on the ground plane and the horizon is visible, it is—in

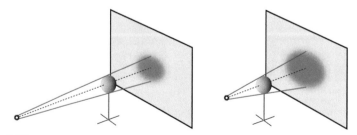

Figure 9.21

The size of a cast shadow depends on the relative distances of the source, the shadow-casting object, and the receiving surface.

principle—possible to work out where the light source must be, using simple perspective geometry. Pont et al. (2009) have shown that participants make systematic errors when judging the directions of shadows from visible light sources; however, at a coarse level of analysis, participants clearly have some intuition about how shadows are affected by the position of light sources in the scene. When the light source is very distant, the shadows cast by multiple objects will tend to be close to parallel. By contrast, when shadows diverge substantially, the light source must be close. However, very little is known about the extent to which the visual system uses this information in building its representation of the light field.

9.7   Issues Specific to Computer Graphics

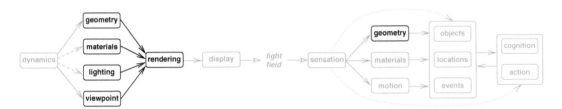

One issue that is of enormous practical importance to the movie industry is the extent to which we are sensitive to inconsistencies in illumination. Photo-compositing plays a major role in modern movie making, and, if not done correctly, it can lead to visually apparent inconsistencies in lighting conditions that undermine the illusion of a single, coherent scene. How good are human observers at detecting inconsistencies in lighting? Ostrovsky, Cavanagh, and Sinha (2005) have suggested that under some circumstances we are remarkably poor at detecting large inconsistencies. They provide some example images in which large and noticeable shadows point the wrong direction relative to the rest of the scene. There are also many cases in fine art in which painters illuminated individuals within the painting inconsistently. To study this systematically, the authors presented participants with arrays of objects with different orientations suspended in space. All of the objects except for one were illuminated consistently, and the participants' task was to find the "odd man out" as quickly as possible. The authors found that participants were slow and inefficient at finding the inconsistent target, suggesting that the visual system can tolerate large inconsistencies in illumination of 90°. Consistency of illumination is also used in image forensics for identifying images that have been doctored or composited (M. K. Johnson & Farid, 2007).

9.8   Suggestions for Further Reading

A beautifully illustrated description of how complex illumination and shading can be in the real world:

Koenderink, J. J., & van Doorn, A. J. (2003). Shape and shading. In L. M. Chalupa & J. S. Werner (Eds.), *The visual neurosciences* (pp. 1090–1105). Cambridge, MA: MIT Press.

A classic text on the physics of illumination:

Moon, P. H., & Spencer, D. E. (1981). *The photic field.* Cambridge, MA: MIT Press.

Key issues caused by illumination for the perception of surface albedo:

Adelson, E. H. (2000). Lightness perception and lightness illusions. In M. Gazzaniga (Ed.), *The new cognitive neurosciences* (2nd ed., pp. 339–351). Cambridge, MA: MIT Press.

A lucid review of experiments on human perception of the light field:

Maloney, L. T., Gerhard, H. E., Boyaci, H. & Doerschner, K. (2010). Surface color perception and light field estimation in 3D scenes. In L. R. Harris & M. Jenkin (Eds.), *Vision in 3D environments* (pp. 65–88). Cambridge, UK: Cambridge University Press.

Plate I

The visible spectrum, with wavelengths indicated in nanometers. (From the Wikimedia Commons.)

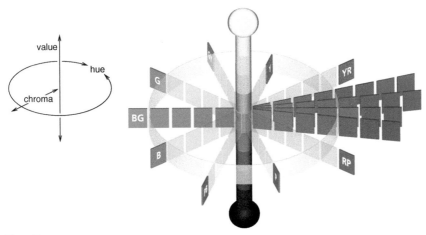

Plate II

The Munsell color system, which represents apparent color in terms of *value, hue,* and *chroma*, using a cylindrical coordinate system. (Figure on right courtesy of X-Rite, Inc.)

Plate III

Which color is closer in appearance to red: green or violet?

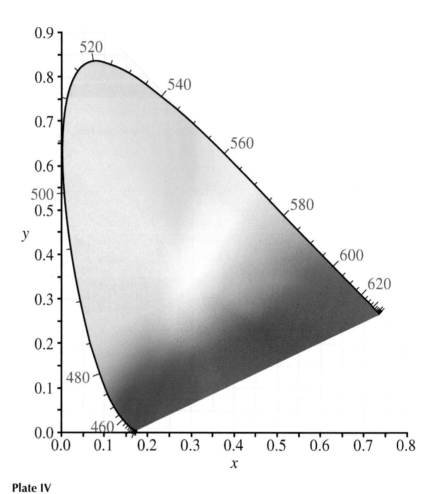

Plate IV

CIE x, y color space. The outer curved boundary shows the x, y values for pure spectral colors, with the wavelength shown in nanometers. (From the Wikimedia Commons.)

Plate V

An example of natural camouflage. (See Figure 8.6.)

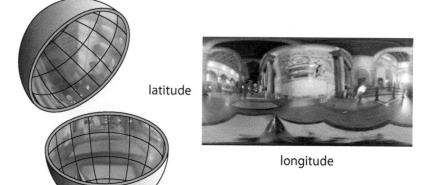

latitude

longitude

Plate VI

A light probe captures the light arriving from every direction on the sphere surrounding a point in the real world. To visualize this, we can project it into two dimensions, here using the Lambert cylindrical equal-area projection.(Light probe image from Debevec, 1998; reproduced by permission from Paul Debevec). (See Figure 9.9.)

Plate VII

On the left, the Cornell Box is rendered with only direct illumination; on the right, a full global illumination rendering is shown. Interreflections have a substantial effect on the appearance of the scene. (See Figure 9.16.)

Plate VIII

Photographs of two spheres in two different contexts. We easily identify the spheres across changes in the illumination, and easily distinguish between the two spheres. (From Fleming et al., 2003.) (See Figure 10.2.)

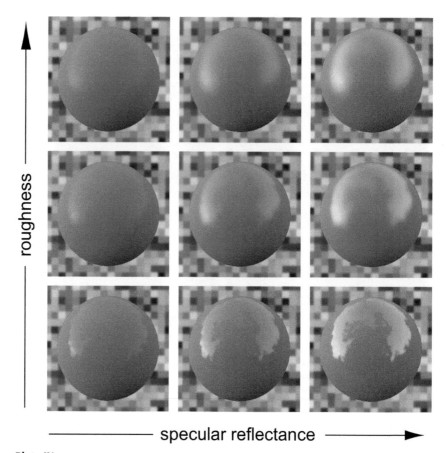

Plate IX

Renderings of a sphere with different parameters of the Ward reflectance model. By varying the parameters, a wide range of different surface appearances can be simulated. (From Fleming et al., 2003.) (See Figure 10.4.)

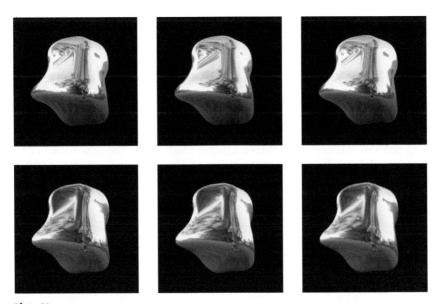

Plate X

A stereoscopic version of Hartung and Kersten's (2003) sticky reflections effect. In each row, the stereopairs formed by the left and middle images are for cross fusion, while the stereopairs formed by the middle and right images are for uncrossed fusion. Having fused the two images, the top object should appear lustrous like a metallic surface, while for the lower object, the reflections should slowly appear more like patterns painted onto the surface. (See Figure 10.12.)

Plate XI

The highlights in the image are highly localized, and yet the impression of glossiness spreads across the entire surface. When when the highlights are removed, the object appears matte. (From Adelson, 2001.) (See Figure 10.15.)

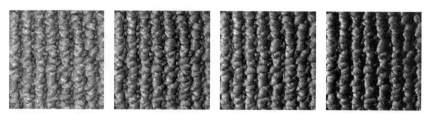

Plate XII

Examples of a BTF with different lighting conditions. The appearance of the material changes depending on the lighting and viewpoint, much like a BRDF. (Images from the Bonn BTF database by Reinhard Klein and colleagues, `http://btf.cs.uni-bonn.de/download.html`, Müller et al., 2005.) (See Figure 10.23.)

Plate XIII

La Pietà by Michelangelo. Solid marble can be made to connote different materials depending on the shape of the surface. (Image © 2005 Stanislav Traykov; reproduced with permission from the author.) (See Figure 10.24.)

10

Perception of Material Properties

As we go about our daily lives, we interact with a huge variety of different materials—most of which have distinct and easily recognizable visual appearances. At a glance we can tell the difference between dough, wood, soap, soil, bronze, silk, skin and countless other kinds of "stuff." Without touching an object, we usually have a clear idea of what it would feel like just by looking at it: we can tell whether it would be hard, rough, crumbly, malleable, slimy, smooth, or mushy, for example.

Estimating the physical properties of things can be vital for many biological tasks, such as determining whether potential food is edible, or working out whether a patch of ground is safe to tread on. Moreover, material appearance and the look and feel of things can also have profound impact on how much we value them (think of sumptuous textiles, glossy car paint, sparkling jewelry, and lustrous consumer electronics, for example). In the film industry, artists and animators go to great lengths to get materials right, as they are widely considered to be crucial to the realistic appearance of scenes and characters.

Clearly, the visual appearance of materials plays a very important role in perception. Despite this, research on material perception (at least in the widest sense) is in its relative infancy. Human and computer vision research has traditionally focused on *object recognition* (see Chapter 15) as one of the key goals of vision, and tended to somewhat ignore the equally important goal of *material recognition*. However, not all of the stuff in our environment is actually organized into discrete objects. Snow, sand, mud, water, fluff, and sky are all examples of stuff that is just "stuff." It doesn't really make sense to think of them as distinct objects—it is generally more useful to define them by what they are made of and how they appear. Based on our everyday experience, our ability to recognize different kinds of materials probably rivals our ability to recognize objects, as can be seen

Figure 10.1

Close-up photographs of several different materials with distinctive visual appearance. We are good at recognizing different types of materials by sight.

in Figure 10.1. In this figure, without any context, we can easily identify the different materials and make judgments about their properties, such as whether they are soft or dry or smooth.

Material perception poses many fascinating questions. What gives a particular material its distinctive visual appearance? Which visual features does the brain use to identify and represent different materials? How does the visual system estimate the physical properties of materials from ambiguous image data? At present, we are only just beginning to answer these questions.

In this chapter, we will focus mainly on the various ways in which light interacts with different materials, leading to appearance properties such as albedo, glossiness, and translucency. These are the aspects of material appearance that are deeply related to shading and rendering, and are also the areas in which most research on human perception has been conducted. However, at the end of the chapter we will also briefly discuss some of the other important aspects of material perception, such as the ways that different materials move and change shape or appearance in response to forces and the passage of time. These are the areas of material perception related to the simulation of fluid flow, deformable objects, cloth dynamics, and weathering. These processes are poorly understood but surely play a critical role in the characteristic visual qualities of many materials.

10.1   What Makes Material Perception Difficult?

Before discussing what gives materials their distinctive appearances, and how the brain might go about estimating these, it is useful to remind ourselves what makes material perception challenging.

Suppose you are presented with two spheres with different material appearances, as shown on the left side of Figure 10.2 and Color Plate VIII.

Figure 10.2

Photographs of two spheres in two different contexts. We easily identify the spheres across changes in the illumination, and easily distinguish between the two spheres. (From Fleming et al., 2003). (See Color Plate VIII.)

One sphere has a highly polished surface, like chrome, and the other is made of a pearlescent white material. Because the two surfaces appear so different from one another, it can be hard to appreciate what might be difficult about estimating reflectance properties from the retinal image. However, it is important to remember that the input to the visual system is highly ambiguous. The intensities in the image are a complex and unknown combination of many distinct physical processes, including the lighting, material properties, object geometry, and effects of participating media. In order to recover the intrinsic material properties of the surface—and identify which sphere is mirrored and which one is pearlescent—the visual system somehow has to disentangle these various contributions from one another.

One reason this is difficult is that the image of a given material can change dramatically depending on the context. For example, the image of the mirrored sphere consists of nothing more than a distorted reflection of the world surrounding it. Therefore, when it is moved from one context to another, the image that the sphere presents to the visual system changes dramatically, as can be seen in the right column of Figure 10.2. Indoors, an object will tend to reflect walls and furniture, whereas outside, the image of the object will be filled with distorted reflections of trees and clouds. This means that the visual system cannot recognize materials by simply matching the image against a stored template. Somehow, the visual system has to abstract what is common to the appearance of the sphere across these different contexts.

To make matters worse, a mirrored sphere could, in principle, be made to take on any arbitrary appearance simply by placing it in a carefully contrived context so that it reflects certain intensities into the eye. For example, by placing the chrome sphere in a specially designed scene consisting of carefully chosen, smooth image gradients, it could be made to produce exactly the same pattern of pixels as one of the pearlescent objects. Because the images would be identical, the visual system would have no way to tell the difference. However, we do not have to go to such extremes to encounter problems. It turns out that on a pixel-by-pixel basis, the image of the mirrored and matte spheres on the left (same illumination) are actually more similar to one another than the two images of the chrome surface in different contexts. This occurs because the positions of the highlights and dark regions are the same when the illumination is the same.

This is the fundamental ambiguity facing the visual system: identical materials can create very different images, and very different materials can create surprisingly similar images. Under arbitrary viewing conditions, the image would be completely ambiguous, and the visual system would have no way of knowing which aspects of the image are due to the material, and which are due to lighting, geometry, or other effects. Throughout this chapter we will discuss numerous cues that the brain could use to distinguish whether a given feature in the image is due to pigmentation, highlights, shadows, or some other cause. Thus, distinguishing the true causes of different image features is a key theme in material perception, which we revisit many times in this chapter. For example, if a given image feature is a highlight, it means the surface is glossy. By contrast, if the same feature is actually a surface marking, then the surface is more likely to be matte and textured. However, local image features are generally highly ambiguous in isolation. The visual system must somehow integrate information across the image to arrive at a unique estimate of the surface properties.

10.2   Estimating Material Properties: Two Approaches

How can the visual system overcome these ambiguities and estimate material properties? Broadly speaking, two general approaches have been suggested. The first is inverse optics, which is the idea that the visual system explicitly estimates and discounts the contributions of illumination and geometry to the observed intensity values. According to this line of reasoning, the visual system "runs physics in reverse" to accurately model the physical properties of the scene, reconstructing the positions of light sources, the surface geometry, and the physical reflectance parameters of the surface from the image. In order to estimate the reflectance of the spheres in Figure 10.2, the visual system would model the scene surrounding the spheres, estimate that the surface is spherical, and use this information to factor out the contributions of lighting and geometry to the image. What is left over once these other factors are removed would be the intrinsic reflectance properties of the object.

The main advantage of such an approach is that the visual system would theoretically end up with a *physical* model of the scene, much like a scene description in computer graphics. The main disadvantage is that the visual system is faced with a "chicken and egg" problem: in order to estimate and discount the lighting, the visual system would need to estimate and discount the *reflectance*—but this is exactly what we are trying to work out in the first place! To get around this problem, inverse optics models often invoke some kind of a priori assumptions about the properties of the world. For example, it is common to assume that the illumination is collimated, or that the surface reflectance is uniform and Lambertian (i.e., completely matte). This makes the problem tractable but limits the range of viewing conditions and physical properties that can be recovered from the image. (See Chapter 9 for more discussion about inferring properties of Lambertian surfaces.)

An alternative approach to inverse optics would be to identify image measurements that are diagnostic of material properties, but which remain roughly invariant across changes in the illumination. That is, if there are certain image features that reliably correlate with a given material across a range of viewing conditions, then the visual system could use these measurements to recognize the material. This way, rather than explicitly estimating and discounting the effects of the illumination on the image, the visual system would try to ignore them; and rather than explicitly estimating physical reflectance parameters, the visual system would recognize materials by representing their typical appearance in the image. We can call this the *image statistics* approach. The logic underlying such an approach is discussed below.

When we posed the problem in Section 10.1 of estimating material properties from the image, we argued that under arbitrary viewing conditions the image is ambiguous. However, in the natural world, viewing conditions are *not* completely arbitrary. As discussed in Chapter 9, in the real world, illumination conditions are shaped by the environment, leading to certain statistical regularities that are generally well conserved from scene to scene. These statistical regularities in the world mean that a given material tends to present certain statistical regularities in the image. For example, consider a glossy surface under various illumination conditions. Although the precise positions of highlights and shadows can vary completely from scene to scene, certain features of the reflections (such as the average contrast or blurriness of the highlights) generally remain more constant. Thus, a given material will tend to produce certain telltale statistical signatures in the image, which the visual system could use to recognize different materials. This approach has the disadvantage that the visual system could be fooled when the assumed statistics of the world are infringed. For example, when light comes from below (a relatively rare occurrence) instead of above (the norm), the shading of the object may be misperceived, leading to errors in both shape and material perception. Despite this, the image statistics approach has the advantage of being able to handle arbitrary material properties: as long as a material exhibits distinctive image features, the visual system can learn these to recognize the material. Indeed, the fact that we can rapidly learn to recognize materials with novel appearances, such as compact discs or exotic gemstones, suggests that the visual system is not stuck with a simple parametric model of reflectance properties.

In the rest of the chapter we will describe various aspects of material appearance and how the visual system might estimate these properties from the image.

10.3   Surface Reflectance and the BRDF

The optical properties of materials can be extremely complex and are affected by processes at a wide range of physical scales, from the orbitals of single electrons to mesoscale surface relief that can be felt with the fingertips. Broadly, it can be useful to divide the light interactions that determine material appearance into *local* and *nonlocal* effects. Local effects are those for which each point of the surface can be treated in isolation, whereas nonlocal effects involve interactions between spatially separated parts of the material, which we will discuss later in the chapter. The appearance of many complex materials, such as textiles and skin, is determined by both local and nonlocal effects. However, to keep things simple, we will start by

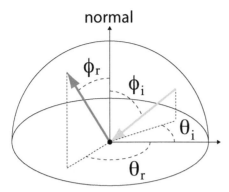

Figure 10.3
The BRDF describes the light reflected in every direction from a surface as a
function of light arriving from every direction. We use two parameters—θ_i and
ϕ_i—to represent incoming directions, and two parameters—θ_r and ϕ_r—to represent the outgoing directions. Thus, the BRDF is a four-dimensional function.

considering smooth, opaque surfaces without any texture. These can be
described well by purely local interactions with light.

When light strikes such a surface, only two things can happen: the light
can be absorbed, or it can be reflected in some direction. The light that is
absorbed never reaches the eye, so it has little impact on perception, except
to determine the overall blackness of the material. The light that reflects
from the surface can be sprayed out in complex patterns, which determine
the appearance of the surface. The amount of light reflected depends on
both the incoming direction and the reflectance properties of the surface.
To fully describe how a surface reflects light, we need to represent the
amount of light reflected in every direction as a function of the amount of
light arriving from every direction. This function is called the *bidirectional
reflectance distribution function* (BRDF). Ignoring effects of wavelength
(i.e., color properties), the BRDF is a function of four parameters, as shown
in Figure 10.3. It is the difference in BRDF that is responsible for the
different appearances of metal, plastic, and paper.

In theory, the BRDF can be arbitrarily complex up to the constraints
imposed by certain physical laws, such as *energy conservation* (i.e., a surface can't reflect more light in total than is incident upon it) and *Helmholtz
reciprocity* (i.e., all ray trajectories can be traversed in either direction).
The BRDFs of some synthetic materials, such as modern textiles, car
paints, and holograms, are carefully crafted to achieve particular effects.

When a high degree of accuracy is required, or when the reflectance
properties are highly complex, the complete four-dimensional BRDF can be

approximated using measurements from real samples of materials, usually gathered with a goniospectrometer. This is a device for taking calibrated images of a sample of the material under a dense sampling of different lighting directions. The captured data are tabulated and can be interpolated during rendering to achieve highly accurate simulations of local reflectance properties.

However, in practice, it is often not necessary to use such a detailed representation of the BRDF. Indeed, empirical BRDFs are often undesirable because they take up lots of memory, and they cannot be easily tweaked or

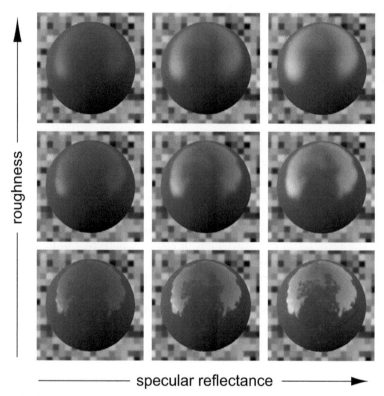

Figure 10.4

Renderings of a sphere with different parameters of the Ward reflectance model. By varying the parameters, a wide range of different surface appearances can be simulated. (Fleming, R. W., Dror, R. O., & Adelson, E. H. (2003). Real-world illumination and the perception of surface reflectance properties. *Journal of Vision*, 3, 347–368. © 2003. Reproduced with permission of Association for Research in Vision & Ophthalmology via Copyright Clearance Center.) (See Color Plate IX.)

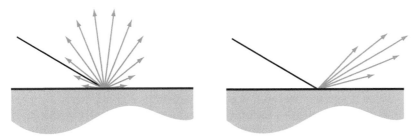

Figure 10.5
Ideal Lambertian (left) and specular (right) reflection. Depending on the roughness of the surface, the specular lobe may be somewhat spread, as depicted here,
leading to blurrier reflections.

adjusted to create novel material appearances. Thus, it is more common to
use analytical BRDF models, which can approximate a wide range of common materials quite well with only a handful of parameters. By varying
the parameters of such a model, a continuous range of different material
appearances can be simulated, as shown in Figure 10.4 and Color Plate IX.
More-complex multi-layer models, such as car paints or varnished surfaces,
can be approximated by superimposing several layers of the model with
different parameter settings. Many parametric models can be found in the
computer graphics literature, each designed to capture a different range
of optical phenomena, such as anisotropic effects (Ward, 1992) or highly
rough diffuse materials (Oren & Nayar, 1995). Parametric models have the
advantage that appearance can be designed from scratch and continuously
adjusted by the user.

One aspect that almost all models share is a separation of the BRDF
into *diffuse* and *specular* components. These two types of reflection are
contrasted in Figure 10.5. Diffuse reflection occurs when incoming light is
sprayed back out of the surface broadly in all directions. Purely diffuse
surfaces appear matte, like chalk or matte paint. The simplest type of
diffuse reflection is Lambertian reflection. Lambertian surfaces have the
special property that their intensity in the image depends only on the angle
of the surface relative to the light source. Thus, a given surface patch
appears equally bright from any viewpoint. Ignoring wavelength effects,
Lambertian materials differ from one another by only a single parameter:
the proportion of light reflected—which is called the *diffuse reflectance*, or
albedo. Different values of albedo lead to surfaces with different shades of
gray.

Specular reflection, by contrast, is ideal mirror reflection, which follows
Hero's law: the angle of reflection is equal to the angle of incidence relative
to the surface normal. Specular reflection creates a virtual image of the

world, leading to a characteristic lustrous, mirrorlike appearance. Common examples of highly specular materials include polished metals and minerals. When the surface is not perfectly smooth, the specular reflection may be somewhat spread out, leading to blurrier reflections, as depicted in Figure 10.5.

When a surface has both specular and diffuse components, it appears glossy, and in some cases the only reflections that are clearly visible are the light sources. These are commonly called *specular highlights*. With these physical principles in mind, in the following sections we will consider the perception of diffuse and glossy surfaces.

10.4   Matte Materials: Albedo and Lightness Constancy

For historical reasons, the overwhelming majority of material-perception research deals with the perceived albedo of diffuse surfaces, such as patches of paper. In psychology, the subjective impression that a surface is a particular shade of gray is called *lightness*. In everyday life, we are extremely adept at estimating surface albedo across changes in the lighting conditions. This is called *lightness constancy* and is widely considered to be a major challenge for the visual system (Brainard, 2003; von Helmholtz, 1878/1925; Hering, 1874/1964; Hurlbert, 1998; Maloney, 1999). It is commonly argued that to achieve lightness constancy, the brain must estimate and discount the contribution of the illuminant to the retinal image intensities.

Lightness can be contrasted with *brightness*, which is the subjective impression that a patch in the image is a certain intensity. It is important to understand that these two things are not the same. Consider, for example, the image in Figure 10.6. The entire card appears to be made out of the same material. That is, it all appears to be the same lightness. At the same time, we are clearly aware that the two sides are not the same intensity in the image. We see one side as being more dimly illuminated, and therefore less bright, in the image. In other words, the lightness is uniform, but the brightness is not. Experiments show that participants can separate these two simultaneous experiences (Arend & Reeves, 1986; A. D. Logvinenko & Maloney, 2006; A. Logvinenko, Petrini, & Maloney, 2008; Tokunaga, Logvinenko, & Maloney, 2008). Thus, although lightness constancy involves compensating for illumination variations, the brain clearly does not filter them out completely. Instead, what the brain does is probably closer to intrinsic image analysis (see Chapter 9). In other words, it separates the image intensities into distinct physical causes, isolating the variations that are due to albedo changes from those that are due to shading and illumination.

Figure 10.6

An image of a gray card under a cast shadow. The entire card appears to be the same lightness. At the same time, we also perceive a difference in brightness on either side of the shadow boundary.

In the laboratory, lightness perception is often studied using co-planar surface patches, such as different shades of gray paper. For example, in a classic experiment, E. H. Land and McCann (1971) created a display consisting of many rectangular papers of different sizes and many different shades of gray. Such stimuli are commonly referred to as Mondrian displays, after their passing resemblance to the abstract paintings by the Dutch artist. In Land and McCann's experiment, the display was illuminated by a fluorescent tube that was placed close to the bottom of the display, so that there was a clear shading gradient from bottom to top. They carefully adjusted the illumination so that the luminance of a high-reflectance patch at the top of the display matched the luminance of a low-reflectance patch at the bottom. They found that despite the fact that the two regions were identical in terms of luminance, the high-reflectance region looked substantially lighter than the low-reflectance region, indicating that we have lightness constancy: when judging the properties of the paper, we estimate the albedo, despite differences in image intensity. The authors developed a theory for lightness constancy called Retinex (because it was thought to involve mechanisms in both the retina and cortex) which involves integrating the contrast ratios across edges to discount the intensity shallow gradients caused by shading. Edwin Land, who was also the inventor of the Polaroid camera, was a superb showman who challenged audiences' intuitions about color vision by demonstrating how color sensations are independent of the wavelength distribution in the image. He took monochrome photographs of scenes through three different-colored filters and then projected the resulting color channels back through corresponding filters. A key demonstration was when he projected two of the images through their filters, but one image was projected without any filter (e.g., the green and blue images would be projected through green and blue filters, but the red channel would be shown without any red filter). Despite the fact that only two color channels were present, a wide range of colors were experienced, including colors that "belong to" the missing channels, such as pinks and reds (although not the entire gamut was experienced). In reality, this is simply a vivid demonstration that the visual system estimates the intrinsic color (i.e., albedo) of surfaces, rather than just the spectrum of light entering the eye. The information that the visual system uses to estimate reflectance is necessarily spatial, involving comparisons between different regions. It was the contrasts from neighboring regions that induced an impression of red or pink in the corresponding regions.

10.4.1   Simultaneous Contrast and Low-Level Accounts of Lightness Perception

Under simple conditions (distant or diffuse lighting, no shadow-casting objects), a diffuse surface appears as a single intensity in the image. As we have already implied, a uniform gray patch in the image, taken in isolation, is completely ambiguous: it could be a white surface under dim illumination, or a black surface under bright illumination. Therefore, in order to estimate lightness, the visual system compares regions to their surroundings. A famous demonstration of the effects of the surroundings on appearances is simultaneous contrast, which is depicted in Figure 10.7. Figure 10.8 shows how shading can affect simultaneous contrast. Figure 10.8(a) appears to be a shaded bar surrounded by a near-uniform brightness rectangle. In fact, as shown in Figure 10.8(b), the bar is of uniform brightness, and it is the larger rectangle that is shaded.

Simultaneous contrast is sometimes explained as the result of a low-level sensory mechanism called *lateral inhibition*, which enhances contrast and suppresses the response of cells to regions of uniform or slowly changing intensity. This has the side effect of filtering out low spatial frequencies from the image. The reason this might be useful for lightness constancy is that illumination changes tend to be slower gradients in the image than pigmentation changes. Therefore, if the visual system filters these out, it will be effectively discounting the illuminant.

According to this explanation of simultaneous contrast, in Figure 10.7, if the visual system enhances the contrast of the central squares relative

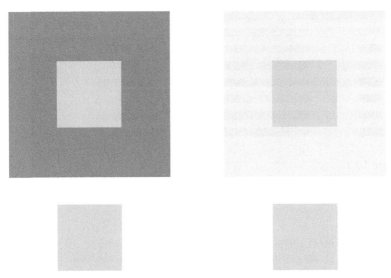

Figure 10.7
Simultaneous contrast. In the top two images, the central squares appear to have different brightnesses. They actually have the same intensity, as shown in the lower two images.

(a)   (b)

Figure 10.8
Simultaneous contrast occurs with smoothly varying surroundings as well. (a) A constant-intensity inner bar surrounded by a smoothly varying intensity outer rectangle. (b) The inner bar seen against a uniform background.

to the background, then the square on the dark background will appear brighter than it actually is, while the square on the bright background will appear darker than it actually is, which is what we experience. However, local, low-level filtering accounts of lightness constancy like this also predict that we should see fringing artifacts around all edges in the image, whereas—in fact—we see each region in the display as completely uniform brightness. To account for this, a number of researchers have suggested that the filtering is followed by a processing stage in which the brain actively fills in the regions between edges with uniform brightness, perhaps

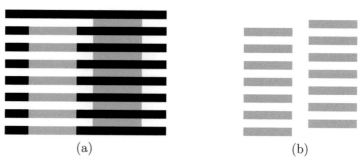

(a)   (b)

Figure 10.9

The Munker-White illusion. The small rectangles in (a) are all the same shade of gray, as can be seen in (b).

by some form of diffusion process (Gerrits & Vendrick, 1970; Grossberg & Mingolla, 1985a, 1985b; Paradiso & Nakayama, 1991). However, this proposal remains controversial, and physiological evidence has not been forthcoming. Furthermore, there are a number of configurations in which simple contrast enhancement actually predicts the *opposite* of what we perceive. For example, in the Munker-White illusion (Figure 10.9), neutral gray rectangles are embedded in elongated strips in an alternating pattern. When the rectangles are embedded in the dark strips, only the short edges are surrounded by black, while the long edges are surrounded by white. Thus, the rectangles are flanked by more white than black, and contrast enhancement would predict that the rectangles should appear darker. In fact, they appear lighter than their counterparts embedded in the white stripes. This suggests that spatial organization in the image also plays an important role. In other words, the visual system segments the image into meaningful units or groups before comparing intensities to estimate albedo. For nearly a hundred years, researchers have tried to articulate the Gestalt grouping principles that the visual system uses for selecting which image regions to compare and integrate to arrive at lightness estimates. A number of sophisticated models exist that can predict grouping and lightness percepts for many artificial configurations (Anderson, 1997, 2003; Gilchrist et al., 1999; Grossberg & Mingolla, 1985a, 1985b; Rudd, 2001). However, these typically do not generalize well to real-world images.

10.4.2   The Gelb Effect and Lightness Anchoring

When observers are shown an isolated patch in a dark void, it appears white, irrespective of its true reflectance. This is called the *Gelb effect*. When a lighter patch is placed next to the first one, the new patch appears white, and the original patch appears darker. It is possible to repeat

Figure 10.10

The snake illusion (Adelson, 2000). The diamonds are all the same shade of gray. On the left, they appear slightly different from one another. However, on the right they appear substantially different from one another, despite the fact that the local context is identical in the two cases.

this with a series of cards of increasing albedo: each time a new card is added, the previous cards appear darker, and the newest appears white. As discussed in Chapter 9, Gilchrist et al. (1999) have used this and other demonstrations to argue that the visual system estimates lightness by *anchoring* the brightest visible element to white, and estimating the lightness of other patches relative to this anchor. This is based on two tacit assumptions. The first is that all patches that are being compared are under the same illumination. The second is that the distribution of reflectances in the world is roughly constant from scene to scene. This is potentially problematic, as it means that the visual system would not be able to distinguish between two scenes with differing average reflectance, which Gilchrist himself has shown is possible (see Chapter 9).

There is evidence that lightness perception involves parsing the scene into regions of different illumination level. For example, consider the *snake illusion* (Adelson, 2000), shown in Figure 10.10. All four diamonds in the images are the same shade of gray. While this is clearly visible in the left pair, on the right most people experience a strong difference in apparent lightness between the diamonds. This is particularly surprising given that the local neighborhood of the diamonds (i.e., the intensity of the immediate surroundings) is identical in the two cases. Thus, local contrast effects cannot explain the phenomenon. This suggests that the estimation of albedo involves segmenting the scene into regions along boundaries where prevailing illumination conditions differ from one another. Later in the chapter, we discuss how locations where several contours meet (so-called *contour junctions*) are very important for identifying transparent layers. Similarly, contour junctions also provide important information for parsing the image into regions with different illumination levels.

10.5   Specular Reflection and Glossiness

As mentioned in Section 10.3, specular surfaces exhibit highlights and mirrorlike reflections. For many aspects of visual processing, specular reflections are considered to be something of a nuisance: they are often very bright, high-contrast features that are not fixed to the surface, so they can cause problems for stereopsis, estimating diffuse reflectance, setting visual sensitivity (exposure), and tracking object motion. However, they can tell us about how shiny a surface is, and they have several important properties that assist in material perception. In this section we will review many of the cues that the visual system can use for recognizing specular reflections and then using them to estimate glossiness.

10.5.1   Highlights and Color

For most dielectric materials (i.e., nonconductive materials that can be polarized by an electric field, such as plastics), specular reflection is spectrally neutral (i.e., the same color as the light source), whereas for some metals—such as gold or copper—it is not. This gives these metals their distinctive colors. Based on the fact that dielectric specular reflections are neutral, it has been suggested that the visual system could use them to estimate (and therefore discount) the spectrum of the illuminant for color constancy (D'Zmura & Iverson, 1993a, 1993b, 1994; D'Zmura & Lennie, 1986; H.-C. Lee, 1986; J. N. Yang & Maloney, 2001; Zickler, Mallick, Kriegman, & Belhumeur, 2008). The visual system may also use the color consistency between highlights and other cues to the lighting to tell whether a given patch in the image is a highlight or a surface marking (Nishida et al., 2008).

10.5.2   The Fresnel Effect

Another important physical property of specular reflection from dielectrics is the Fresnel effect, which is the tendency for surfaces to be more specular at glancing angles. Even ordinary paper, which appears almost completely matte when viewed head-on, appears somewhat glossy when viewed at grazing angles. You can see this for yourself by putting a sheet of paper on the windowsill. When you stand next to the windowsill and view the paper from above, it does not look as bright and shiny as when you put your eye as close as possible to the level of the windowsill so that you view the sheet at a grazing angle. Note that in both cases the incident light is the same; the difference has to do with the grazing view angle. Almost nothing is known about the perceptual consequences of the Fresnel effect, apart from anecdotal observations that it makes renderings of some glossy materials appear more realistic. For example, the Fresnel effect is particularly important in simulating car paint. Without it, the paint tends to look like plastic. The fact that the Fresnel effect does affect the apparent material quality of the glossy surfaces suggests that the visual system takes into account the relationship between the contrast of specular reflections and the geometry of the surface.

10.5.3 Motion Properties of Specular Reflections

One of the most important properties of specular reflections is that they are *view dependent*. In other words, the position of a highlight on a surface depends not only on the light source and surface normal, but also on the position of the viewer. Therefore, unlike texture markings or diffuse shading, highlights move relative to the surface whenever the object or viewer moves. Highlights tend to slide rapidly across regions of low curvature, and move more slowly across regions of high curvature (Koenderink & van Doorn, 1980). This provides a motion cue that the visual system can use to distinguish between matte surface markings and specular reflections. If a feature moves relative to the surface, then it must be a specular reflection rather than a texture marking. Hartung and Kersten (2003) have shown that the visual system uses this information to distinguish between matte and shiny surfaces. They rendered objects with the specular reflections artificially "stuck" to the surface during object motion. When the objects are viewed statically, they appear shiny, because the reflections look completely normal. However, when the object rotates, the reflections rotate with the object as if attached to the surface like texture markings, instead of sliding over the surface the way real specular reflections would. This makes the reflections appear to be matte surface markings painted onto the surface, which causes the material appearance of the entire object to change from lustrous to matte. Thus, optical flow can provide a powerful source of information for distinguishing between matte and shiny surfaces.

10.5.4 Stereoscopic Properties of Specular Reflections

Another consequence of view dependency is the unusual binocular depth placement of specular reflections. Unlike texture markings or shading, when reflections are viewed stereoscopically, they are generally not located on the physical surface in depth. They fall behind convex surfaces and in front of concave surfaces, as shown in Figure 10.11. A. Blake and Bülthoff (1990) have shown that the visual system uses the stereoscopic depth of features to identify that they are actually highlights. They manipulated the stereoscopic depth of the highlights in renderings of surfaces, and observed the effects on perceived glossiness. They found that when highlights are artificially placed at the same depth as the surface, they appear to be surface markings, and when placed in front of convex surfaces, they appear

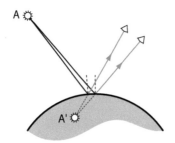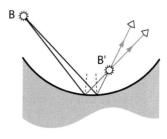

Figure 10.11

The image location of specular highlights relative to the surface is generally different for the two eyes. Therefore, when the visual system fuses the two images, the reflections do not fall on the surface in depth. For convex surfaces, the reflection generally falls behind the surface, whereas for concave surfaces, the reflection falls in front of the surface. (Figure after A. Blake & Bülthoff, 1990.)

to be a cloud or haze floating in front of the object. In both cases, because the highlight is not interpreted as a specular reflection, the surface no longer appears glossy.

A version of this effect is shown in Figure 10.12 and Color Plate X. For each row, the left and middle images constitute a stereo pair appropriate for cross-eyed viewing while the middle and right images constitute an equivalent stereo pair appropriate for uncrossed fusion, most easily done using a Lorgnette viewer or a similar apparatus. The object shown on the top row has normal binocular disparities, so it should appear lustrous, like chrome. However, for the object shown on the bottom row, the specular reflections have been artificially placed at the same stereoscopic depth as the surface. With prolonged viewing, the lustrous appearance that we see when viewing the single images fades, and we experience the reflections as if they were painted on the surface, making it look matte. This is effectively a stereoscopic version of the motion effect by Hartung and Kersten (2003).

10.5.5   Binocular Luster

One other stereoscopic effect is worth noting. Texture markings on a surface tend to be visible to both eyes, and are mainly horizontally separated in the two retinal images because the two eyes are horizontally separated in the head. However, specular reflections are not subject to these constraints because they are derived from the surface normal and the features in the surrounding world. A given feature may be reflected from a surface many times, or visible to only one eye, or separated vertically as well as horizontally in the two eyes. This makes it hard—or, in some cases, impossible—for the visual system to match certain features in the two

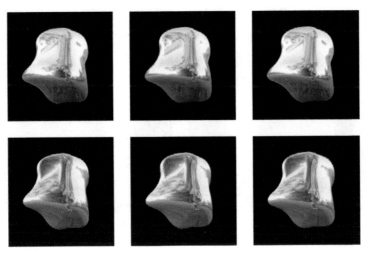

Figure 10.12

A stereoscopic version of Hartung and Kersten's (2003) sticky reflections effect. In each row, the stereopairs formed by the left and middle images are for cross fusion, while the stereopairs formed by the middle and right images are for uncrossed fusion. Having fused the two images, the top object should appear lustrous like a metallic surface, while for the lower object, the reflections should slowly appear more like patterns painted onto the surface. (See Color Plate X.)

eyes. When the visual system cannot fuse features from the two eyes, we experience an effect called *binocular rivalry*, in which there is intermittent perceptual switching between the two eyes' images, as if they were competing for consciousness. Specular objects tend to create patches in the image that are rivalrous, and this leads to *binocular luster* (Anstis, 2000; von Helmholtz, 1878/1925), which is an important part of specular appearance under natural viewing conditions. Even patches of uniform gray can appear somewhat glossy by making them rivalrous (e.g., by making them different contrasts).

10.5.6 Specular Highlights and Image Intensity

Despite the importance of motion and stereoscopic cues, we can also easily recognize glossy surfaces in single, static images. How does the visual system do this? One of the most important sources of information comes, of course, from highlights—which are reflections of primary light sources. Highlights are generally much brighter than diffuse surface markings because the reflection is more focused. This means that the visual system can use the sheer intensity of an image feature as a cue that the feature might

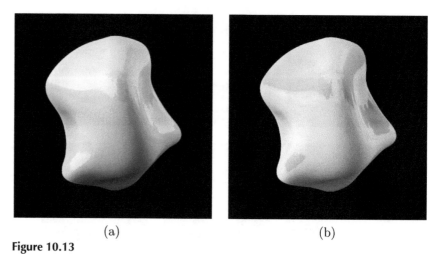

(a)   (b)

Figure 10.13

(a) An image with the appearance of a glossy surface. (b) If the intensities of the specular component are inverted, the surface no longer looks glossy, and the negative highlights appear more like stains.

be a highlight rather than texture or shading.

The visual system expects highlights to be at least as bright as their surroundings in much the same way as it expects shadows to be darker than their surroundings (see Chapter 9). In Figure 10.13, we invert the contrast polarity of the specular reflections compared to the diffuse shading in the image (i.e., the specular component is effectively a photographic negative of the surrounding world). Doing this largely eliminates the impression that the surface is glossy, because the highlights are darker than their surroundings and look like patches of matte pigment instead of reflections.

The importance of bright highlights can also be expressed statistically in terms of the intensity distribution of the image. Glossy surfaces tend to have positively skewed intensity histograms, with most pixels of low or intermediate intensity (due to shading and shadows) and only a small proportion of very bright pixels (due to the highlights). By modifying the intensity histogram of such an image, it is possible to make the surface appear to be more or less glossy. Specifically, making the histogram more positively skewed makes the surface appear more glossy, whereas reducing or reversing the skew tends to make it appear more matte (Motoyoshi, Nishida, Sharan, & Adelson, 2007). You can try this for yourself with photo-editing software. For example, using the Curves function in Adobe Photoshop, it is possible to change the shape of the intensity distribution to exaggerate or suppress the brightest portions in the image. An example is shown in Figure 10.14. Motoyoshi et al. showed participants patches of dif-

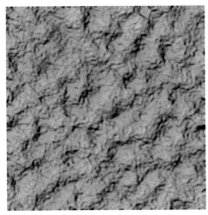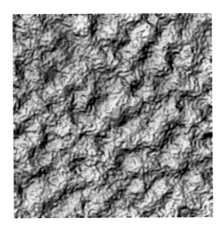

Figure 10.14
These two images are derived from the same source image. The one on the left was passed through a compressive nonlinearity so that the intensity histogram is slightly negatively skewed. The one on the right was passed through an expansive nonlinearity, so the histogram is positively skewed. This affects the apparent glossiness of the surface.

ferent surfaces and found that judgments of glossiness correlated with the skewness of the intensity histogram. They suggested that the visual system may contain mechanisms for measuring the skewness of the histogram. To support this claim, they used an adaptation paradigm. The logic of an adaptation experiment is that with prolonged stimulation, cells that are sensitive to a particular stimulus tend to habituate, leading to weaker responses. When a neutral stimulus is shown after adaptation, we experience an aftereffect, as in the waterfall illusion (see Chapter 1). Motoyoshi et al. created such an effect by adapting participants with images that had certain intensity distributions. After adaptation, participants were asked to judge the glossiness of a surface that had intermediate glossiness. They found that with appropriate adaptation they could make this neutral stimulus appear to be either more or less glossy. They used this result to argue that the brain must contain mechanisms tuned to the intensity distribution, and that these mechanisms play a role in judgments of glossiness.

The positive skew in the histogram of glossy surfaces is related to the fact that illumination intensities are heavily skewed in the natural world (Dror et al., 2004; Fleming et al., 2003). As described in the previous chapter, for most incoming directions, light arrives from secondary reflections, while only a few directions bring light from primary light sources. Nevertheless, when a glossy object is placed close to a light source, the highlights can cover a large proportion of the surface, leading to a negatively skewed histogram. As you might expect, under these conditions, the surface also looks extremely glossy, suggesting that although a positively skewed intensity histogram tends to make surfaces look glossy, it is not a necessary condition for perceiving gloss. Furthermore, we can recognize highlights in low-contrast images, even when they are clipped to the same intensity as other bright portions of the image. Thus, the bright regions are not the only features that the brain uses for recognizing specular surfaces. The visual system can also use reflections of other objects as a cue that a surface is specular. In complex natural environments, specular surfaces tend to be covered in reflections of different intensities. When reflections are not very bright, they behave like a transparent layer overlaid on the surface—we can see the texture patterns of the underlying surface through the highlights. They add intensity to the patterns visible through them, which makes the texture locally brighter and lower contrast. Interestingly, this means that some of the cues that are used for identifying transparent layers can also be used for identifying specular reflections (see Section 10.6). One of the outstanding theoretical challenges is to understand how the visual system integrates the information from all these different intensities and regions into an impression of a homogeneous surface.

10.5.7 Propagation of Glossiness from Local Highlights

Because light sources are often relatively compact, highlights tend to be localized in the image. Beck and Prazdny (1981) made the interesting observation that even very local highlights can make a large change to the appearance of a whole surface. They took a photograph of a glossy jug with a localized highlight and modified it to remove the highlight (this can be done by taking the photograph through a polarizing filter or, nowadays,

Figure 10.15

The highlights in the image are highly localized, and yet the impression of glossiness spreads across the entire surface. When when the highlights are removed, the object appears matte. (From Adelson, 2001.) (See Color Plate XI.)

with photo-editing software). Without the highlight, the visual system has no information that the jug is specular, and it appears uniformly matte. By adding the localized highlight back into the image, the entire surface takes on a glossy appearance, as if the effects of the highlight propagate across the image. A version of this effect is shown in Figure 10.15 and Color Plate XI. Berzhanskaya, Swaminathan, Beck, and Mingolla (2002) measured the strength of the effect by asking participants to judge the glossiness of the surface at different distances from the highlight. They found that the effect of the highlight diminishes with distance but nevertheless spreads far over the surface.

10.5.8   Highlights and Surface Shape

Another important property of highlights—and of specular reflections in general—is that they tend to be elongated along the direction of least curvature on the surface.[1] For example, the reflections in a cylindrical faucet look like parallel stripes that run along the length of the cylinder (Fleming et al., 2004). If you pay attention to glossy surfaces around you, you will notice that the highlights and reflections are often highly distorted in a way that is systematically related to the surface shape. The visual system expects reflections to be stretched and compressed in a way that is consistent with the 3D shape of the object. When highlights are artificially stretched along other directions, they tend to look like texture markings or spotlights projected onto the surface, and the object appears matte (Beck, Prazdny, & Ivry, 1984; Todd, Norman, & Mingolla, 2004). An interesting exception to this is when the BRDF is anisotropic (e.g., brushed aluminum). Depending on the direction of the anisotropy, highlights and reflections can be stretched out in arbitrary directions. At present no research has been conducted on how the visual system handles such surfaces.

10.5.9   Consistency between Shading and Highlights

The way that an object is illuminated determines how both diffuse shading and highlights are located relative to the surface. Thus, in the real world, the position of highlights tends to be consistent with the shading in certain ways. For example, suppose you are looking at a glossy sphere illuminated by a single point source. The peak intensity of the shading and of the highlight will generally not occur at the same location in the image (this would only happen if lighting arrives along the line of sight). Nevertheless, they are systematically related to one another. The highlight would never occur in the shadows, or on the opposite side of the object from the

---

[1]Strictly speaking, it is not the *intrinsic curvature* of the surface that is important, but a view-dependent quantity that depends mainly on the second derivatives of the surface depth relative to a given viewpoint.

diffuse peak. When the geometry and illumination are simple, the visual system can detect inconsistencies between shading and highlights. When this occurs, the highlight is not interpreted as a specular reflection, and the surface tends not to look as glossy. Thus, the consistency of shading and highlights is another cue that the visual system uses for recognizing glossy surfaces.

10.6   Transparency and Translucency

So far, all of the materials we have discussed are opaque, which means that all the important optical effects occur at the surface itself, and no light passes through the object. However, the appearance of many materials, such as milk, wax, glass, and water results from the fact that light passes through the materials. How does the visual system estimate the properties of transparent and translucent materials, such as these?

10.6.1   Perceptual Transparency and Scission

Gestalt psychologists in the early twentieth century noticed that by juxtaposing several opaque papers in certain configurations, they could create a compelling illusion of seeing one surface *through* another, as shown in Figure 10.16. This is impressive because somehow the visual system is able to split a single intensity value into two distinct causal layers with different material properties: an opaque background layer with a certain lightness, and a foreground layer with a different lightness and opacity. This process of splitting intensities into distinct layers is sometimes called *scission*

Figure 10.16

Four image regions look opaque when separated (right), but appear transparent when placed next to one another (left).

(Anderson, 1997; Kanizsa, 1955; Koffka, 1935; Metelli, 1974). The patterns are consistent with a very simple physical model of transparency—similar to neutral density filters—in which the transparent layer is infinitely thin and both transmits and reflects some proportion of the incident light. By varying the gray values of the different regions, it is possible to make the illusory transparent layer take on a range of different qualities, from opaque to transparent, and from dark to light. Scission is crucial to estimating the properties of the layers.

Subsequent research (Beck et al., 1984; Beck & Ivry, 1988; Gerbino, 1994; Metelli, 1974; Robilotto, Khang, & Zaidi, 2002; Singh & Anderson, 2002) has tried to characterize exactly which image quantities determine the perceived properties of the transparent surface. For example, Singh and Anderson have argued that the visual system estimates the opacity of the transparent layer by measuring the Michelson contrast of the intensities in the transparent region and comparing it to Michelson contrast of the surroundings.[2] When the difference in contrast is small, the transparent layer tends to appear highly transparent; when the difference in contrast is large, it tends to appear more opaque.

10.6.2 Geometric and Photometric Constraints

In order for scission to occur, certain conditions in the image have to hold. These can broadly be separated into *geometric* and *photometric* conditions. The geometric conditions are essentially that there must be consistency and continuity between the patterns visible outside and inside the transparent region. For example, if there are stripes in the background, the stripes should remain the same size and orientation when seen through the transparent layer, so that there are no discontinuities as they pass under the transparent surface. This makes sense, because thin transparent films cannot change the orientation or size of patterns visible through them.

Of course, it is physically possible that the stripes in the background could change from one orientation to another, and that this change just so happens to line up with the border of the transparent layer. However, this would be a *nongeneric* configuration, because the alignment of the features in the near and far layers is unlikely to occur by chance. The tiniest perturbation would change the qualitative structure of the image, so that the discontinuities in the background would no longer be aligned with the boundary of the transparent layer. The visual system, seeking the most probable explanation for the image, therefore rejects the interpretation that there is a second physical layer that "just so happens" to be aligned with

---

[2]Michelson contrast is a measure of contrast that is normalized by the average intensity: $L_{max} - L_{min}/L_{max} + L_{min}$, where L_{max} and L_{min} are the maximum and minimum luminances in the area of interest.

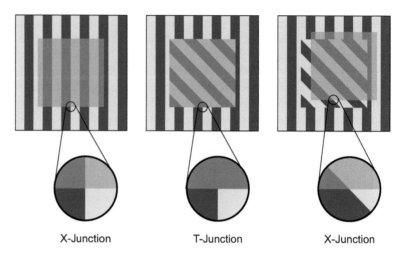

| X-Junction | T-Junction | X-Junction |

Figure 10.17

Geometric constraints for scission. A transparent layer in front of some stripes (left). Note that the contours are continuous across the boundary of the transparent layer, leading to X-junctions. If the change in contrast is accompanied by a break in the contours, this creates T-junctions, and the low contrast region is not interpreted as a transparent layer, even though—in theory—there could be change in the background that happens to align with the edge of the transparent surface (center). If we shift the transparent layer, then the configural conditions are no longer infringed, X-junctions reoccur, and the surface appears transparent again (right).

the changes of the pattern in the background.

These geometrical constraints have consequences for local image features at the boundary of the transparent surface. When a contour in the background layer passes underneath the boundary of the transparent overlay, the two contours form a local contour junction—specifically, an X-junction—in the image. Manipulations that break the X-junctions (so that they become T-junctions) or add orientation discontinuities to them tend to reduce the sense of transparency (see Figure10.17).

In addition to the geometric constraints, certain photometric constraints have to be satisfied. For a given legal spatial configuration, only certain combinations of intensities are consistent with transparency. For example, a transparent overlay cannot increase the contrast of patterns seen through it. Likewise, it cannot change the contrast polarity: if a feature in the background is darker than its surroundings, it cannot become lighter than its surroundings when viewed through a transparent layer. Together, these rules can be captured by the ordinal relationships of intensities occurring

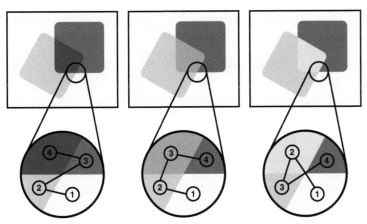

Figure 10.18
Photometric cues to transparency. X-junctions occur when a contour in the background passes underneath a transparent surface. Depending on the ordinal relationship between the intensities in the junction, it can be consistent with either surface being in front, or only one surface, or neither surface. (Figure adapted from Beck & Ivry, 1988).

at X-junctions (Adelson & Anandan, 1990; Beck & Ivry, 1988), as shown in Figure 10.18. These photometric and geometric rules for scission help the visual system to distinguish whether a given intensity change in the image is due to paint, shadow, or transparency.

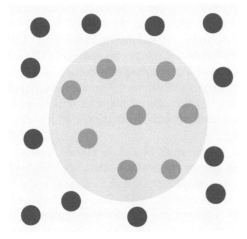

Figure 10.19
Fuchs' transparency, in which there are no X-junctions.

Although X-junctions are a useful way of visualizing the constraints on perceived transparency, it is worth noting that we can also see transparency without any X-junctions in the image, as shown in Figure 10.19. This is known as *Fuchs' transparency* (Fuchs, 1923a, 1923b).

10.6.3   Solid Transparent Objects

So far, the type of transparency we have considered is based on a very simple physical model in which the image intensity is a linear combination of light reflected from the foreground and background layers. Many processes in the world behave this way, including shadows, highlights, stains, gauze screens (like a mosquito net), and thin neutral density filters. However, ironically, the model is a very poor approximation of light transport through chunks of real transparent stuff, such as glass or ice. The way that light interacts with these materials has profoundly different consequences for the image cues that the brain can use to recognize such materials.

The first important difference is that when light strikes a real transparent object, some of the light is reflected specularly from the surface, leading to clearly visible specular highlights. Specularities play an important role in the appearance of solid transparent objects by providing information about the 3D shape of the surface and making the object appear more solid. The higher the refractive index of the material, the greater the specular reflection. Thus, the shininess of transparent surfaces is also informative about the optical density of the material.

The remaining light passes through the surface into the body of the object, refracting as it does so. The refracted rays travel through the object until they reach another location on the surface, at which point—depending on the angle relative to the surface normal—they either refract out of the object, or undergo total internal reflection (TIR) and reflect back into the body of the material. Rays can undergo TIR multiple times before reemerging from the object. Because refraction is wavelength dependent, some transparent objects, such as cut gemstones, sparkle various colors when moved relative to the light. This is an important part of their visual appeal and differs from specular reflections, which are usually spectrally neutral.

When a solid transparent object is viewed against a textured background, refraction causes the features that are visible through the object to appear displaced and distorted in the image (Figure 10.20). The extent of the distortion is determined by the refractive index of the material: the higher the refractive index, the greater the amount of distortion. This is somewhat similar to the distortions that occur with specular reflections, except that the relationship between the distortions and the geometry of the object is different. While specular distortions depend only on the cur-

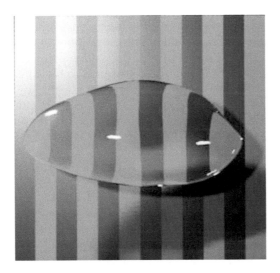

Figure 10.20
A refractive pebble viewed against a stripy background. Note that the stripes are distorted when viewed through the pebble, and that this interrupts the X-junctions at the edge of the object.

vatures of the reflecting surface, refractive distortions depend on the thickness of the object as well as the curvatures on both the front and rear surfaces. Importantly, the distortions caused by refraction can infringe the geometrical constraints described above, which apply only to the simple, linear model of transparency. Despite this, we clearly see solid transparent objects as transparent.

Because the distortions depend on the object's refractive index, the visual system can use the degree of distortion to estimate the refractive index of the material. However, the magnitude of distortion is also affected by additional properties of the scene that are not related to the material per se. For example, the thickness of the refractive object and the distance between the object and the background also affect how patterns are distorted by the object. This means that the cues to refractive index provided by distortion are ambiguous. Fleming et al. (unpublished) have shown that participants' judgments of refractive index are affected by the degree of distortion, but that the visual system does not correctly compensate for additional contributions to the distortions observed in the image. In other words, it uses the distortion cue heuristically, at face value, rather than correctly inverting optics to estimate the refractive index of the material.

Another perceptually important parameter of solid transparent materials is the opacity, which determines the proportion of light absorbed as it passes through the material. The absorption determines the darkness and color of the material, making, for example, bottle glass appear green, or amethyst purple. The amount of darkening and color saturation depends on the thickness of the piece of material, so to estimate the intrinsic properties of the material, the visual system would have to take the geometry of the object into account. To date, no perceptual research has been conducted on how the visual system estimates transmissivity of solid transparent objects.

10.6.4   Subsurface Scattering and Translucent Materials

In English, we use the word *translucent* (in contrast to *transparent*) to describe materials such as wax, jade, and frosted glass, which visibly transmit light but in such a way that we cannot see patterns clearly through them. Translucency plays an important role in the appearance of many materials, including milk, leaves and human skin. It gives these materials a characteristic softness or glow that is crucial to their distinctive look.

Translucency has two basic physical causes. In the case of materials like frosted glass, the blurriness of the refracted light is caused by single scattering at the surface of the object. Specifically, because the surface is rough at a microscopic scale, the light is refracted in a distribution of different directions, much like the effects of surface roughness on the specular lobe of the BRDF (Figure 10.5). Once inside the object, the refracted rays travel unimpeded, and thus they behave just like in normal transparent materials. If you take a frosted glass marble and moisten it so that the microscopic scratches and pocks are glazed over, the marble appears much less translucent and much more transparent. If you chip it, the underlying transparent material is revealed.

The second type of translucency is due to subsurface scattering (Figure 10.21). This occurs when the light is continuously scattered and absorbed as it passes through the material, which acts like a participating medium (see Chapter 9). The result is that light diffuses through the material, filling it with light and generally reemerging from the surface of the object at a location distant from where it entered. Because the scattering occurs throughout the material and not just at the surface, if you take a chunk out of the material, it still looks translucent, unlike frosted glass.

To fully describe the sub-surface scattering properties of a material requires the *bidirectional scattering surface reflectance distribution function* (BSSRDF), which describes how much light emerges from a point within the medium in every direction, as a function of the light arriving at that point from every direction. In computer graphics, this is usually approximated using a low-parameter model, and the resulting (highly complex) light transport within the medium is evaluated efficiently using a diffusion-

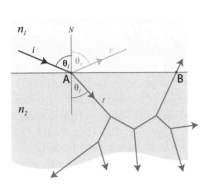 

Figure 10.21

Subsurface light scattering causes rays that arrive at point A to exit at a distant point B. This leads to the characteristic soft, glowing appearance of translucency. Also shown is specular reflection and refraction occurring at the surface.

based approximation developed by Jensen and Buhler (2002). The most important parameters of the BSSRDF model are the scattering and absorption coefficients, which determine the proportion of light scattered and absorbed as it passes through a unit distance of the medium. The pattern of scattering is usually modeled with the Henyey-Greenstein phase function, which essentially describes how much light is scattered in each direction.

The perceptual appearance of a material varies as a function of these parameters in a way that is highly nonlinear and which is still not fully understood. Perceptually, the most important intuitive dimensions of translucency appear to be similar to those used to describe linear transparency models (i.e., *opacity* and *lightness*). However, there are clearly additional perceptual dimensions as well.

How does the visual system estimate the properties of translucent materials? As we have suggested many times throughout this chapter, it is useful to contrast two alternative approaches: inverse optics and image heuristics. Given the complexity of light transport through translucent materials, it is highly unlikely that the visual system can fully invert the optics, tracing diffusion gradients in reverse to estimate the parameters of the BSSRDF. Instead, it seems more likely that the brain picks up on a number of image measurements that correlate with changes in translucency, under a wide range of typical viewing conditions. Fleming and Bülthoff (2005) studied various low-level image cues that the visual system could use to estimate properties of subsurface scattering materials. They found that the simple intensity and contrast statistics of the kind that are thought to be important in linear transparency models are insufficient for explaining the perception of translucency. Instead, they suggested that the visual system parses the shading patterns of the object to determine which regions would be in shadow if the object were opaque. If the visual system can identify regions of the object that only receive light that has bled through the object, then it is possible to approximately estimate the degree of translucency based on the distribution of intensities in this region. Consistent with this idea, they found that changes in illumination direction have large effects on perceived translucency. Specifically, they found that objects look substantially more translucent when illuminated from behind than from in front. Intuitively, this makes sense because when an object is illuminated from behind, the front surface is only visible because of the light that has transmitted through the object. By contrast, when the object is illuminated from in front, the light scatters back toward the viewer without passing deeply into the material, so the shading patterns are less diagnostic of the subsurface scattering properties; the shading looks more like standard diffuse shading.

10.7   Texture and Surface Relief

The materials that we have considered so far are homogeneous with no spatial variations. However, the distinctive appearances of many materials, such as granite, Dalmatian fur, or wood bark, result largely from spatial variations in surface properties. Even many surfaces that at first glance appear to be uniform—especially organic ones—actually have subtle variations in pigmentation or surface relief. It is well known that renderings without textures tend to appear lifeless and artificial.

Texture is such an important aspect of perception, and is related to so many different aspects of visual information processing, that we have dedicated an entire chapter to it (see Chapter 8). However, here it is worth briefly considering some of the aspects of texture perception that are directly related to material recognition.

Textures can broadly be separated into two distinct physical processes. One is variation in the *optical properties* of the material; the other is variation in the *mesoscale geometry* of the surface. Many natural materials contain both processes, and in some cases they are correlated with one another. An example is shown in Figure 10.22, in which the natural pigmentation of the starfish texture occurs in the concavities of the surface. However, more generally, cracks and crevices tend to accumulate dirt, which makes them darker, while exposed features are more likely to be buffed smooth, which can make them glossier. Thus, although pigmentation and relief are distinct processes, they often have related effects on appearance. In turn,

Figure 10.22
A close-up of some texture on the back of a starfish. Note that the convexities are
light colored, while the concavities are dark. Thus, shading and albedo variations
correlate for this texture.

this means that in some cases, the visual system may confound the two in
its representation of a given texture.

From a physical point of view, optical variations can be captured with a
spatially varying bidirectional reflectance distribution function (SVBRDF),
which is simply a map of the local BRDF at each position on the surface.
A more complete representation of a texture is the bidirectional texture
function (BTF). Like a BRDF, the BTF captures the appearance of a
patch of material from a dense sampling of view directions and lighting
directions, except that the sample is a patch of texture instead of uniform
material. This is important (and differs from a SVBRDF) because not all
appearance effects in textures are local. For example, surface relief leads
to self-occlusion at glancing angles, which affects how neighborhoods of
the material appear in the image, due to self-shadowing and other effects.
The BTF also captures the semilocal effects of subsurface scattering and
interreflections. If the BRDF changes arbitrarily from position to position,
the SVBRDF or BTF could be very high-dimensional functions. However,
natural textures tend to have a high degree of redundancy with properties
changing slowly, allowing efficient compression. An example BTF is shown
in Figure 10.23 and Color Plate XII.

Figure 10.23

Examples of a BTF with different lighting conditions. The appearance of the material changes depending on the lighting and viewpoint, much like a BRDF. (Images from the Bonn BTF database by Reinhard Klein and colleagues, `http://btf.cs.uni-bonn.de/download.html`, Müller, Meseth, Sattler, Sarlette, & Klein, 2005.) (See Color Plate XII.)

Most work on texture perception has focused on spatially varying pigmentation, some has considered mesoscale geometry, and almost no work has been conducted on the full appearance as represented with the BTF.

10.7.1   Texture Space

Similar textures often appear to be related to one another along meaningful perceptual dimensions. For example, if you have a dozen or so patches of leather, the textures will tend to have similar colors, the patterns of cracks may fall along a continuum of spatial scales, and they may appear more or less regular. Given two similar textures, it is usually possible to imagine what an intermediate texture would look like. This kind of observation has led to the idea that there may be a perceptual *texture space* in which all textures could be embedded, much as there is a color space, which arranges different colors systematically within three dimensions. There have been a number of attempts to identify the basic dimensions, or features, of this texture space (Rao & Lohse, 1992, 1996). Experimenters find that there are at least a few dimensions along which all textures appear to be comparable: the spatial scale, overall orientation, degree of regularity versus randomness, and so on. However, when we consider the huge variety of all possible textures, it becomes apparent that there are potentially an infinite number of dimensions, depending on which features we choose to pay attention to. The features that are natural to use for comparing two texture patches vary, depending on which textures are to be compared. When two samples are very different from one another, it is not easy to intuit what an intermediate texture would look like. Thus, rather than there being a single monolithic texture space with fixed cardinal dimensions, it may be that texture space is organized locally, with different features taking precedence depending on the samples. It is also worth noting that the fact that color space has three dimensions is determined by the cone-response functions at the very front end of visual processing. By contrast, the arbitrary number of dimensions that would be required to describe all possible textures would depend on the features extracted by subsequent processing. Parametric models for texture analysis and synthesis, such as Portilla and Simoncelli (2000), can have many thousands of dimensions. While they are highly expressive, there are still many textures—particularly those composed of clearly visible, discrete units (e.g., beans, bricks, or chainmail)—that such models do not capture well.

10.7.2   Surface Roughness and Illumination

As we have indicated, surface relief is an important aspect of many natural textures. It can also be very important for determining how we handle different surfaces, as it affects the friction and harshness of the surface. Consequently, we are quite good at distinguishing surface texture, and particularly roughness, haptically (Katz, 1925; Lederman, 1981; Lederman & Abbott, 1981; Lederman, 1983). In the visual domain, surface relief produces shallow shading patterns that depend on the profile and amplitude of the relief. The contrast of these shading patterns increases with the amplitude of the relief, so contrast can be used as a cue to surface roughness. However, texture contrast is also affected by the angle of illumination: grazing angles cause high contrasts with larger cast shadows. This means that contrast is an ambiguous cue. Ho et al. (2006) studied how the perceived roughness of materials varies as a function of the illumination conditions. They found that when textures are illuminated head-on, they tend to appear less rough than when illuminated at glancing angles. This makes intuitive sense, as suggested, because the contrast and size of local cast shadows within the texture increase as light arrives from grazing angles. Thus, the visual system does not correctly compensate for changes in illumination when judging surface relief.

As mentioned in Chapter 9, Koenderink, Pont, and colleagues (Koenderink et al., 2003; Koenderink, van Doorn & Pont, 2007; Pont & Koenderink, 2005, 2007) have shown that texture shading effects can also provide information about the illumination conditions, and that participants can use this information for estimating the light-source direction. Padilla, Drbohlav, Green, Spence, and Chantler (2008) presented participants with real-time renderings of surfaces that were generated from a two-parameter random noise model for rough surfaces. The textures had an amplitude spectra of the form $1/f^\beta$—in other words, with a power-law falloff as a function of spatial frequency. They varied the amplitude and β parameters to create a range of different surface appearances, and asked participants to judge the apparent roughness. Specifically, they presented participants with two patches in each trial: one had parameters chosen by the computer (the Test stimulus), and the other could be adjusted by the participant (the Match stimulus). The Test stimulus varied in both amplitude and β, while the Match could only be adjusted in terms of amplitude. The participants' task was to adjust the amplitude of the Match surface until it appeared to be the same roughness as the Test, despite any differences in the falloff parameter. They found that participants' settings increased with increasing amplitude but that the β parameter also affected judgments of roughness, so that surfaces with shallower falloff were seen as rougher than surfaces with a sharper falloff. This suggests that roughness is likely to be a multidimensional perceptual quantity and that participants conflate high-frequency content with amplitude. The authors also presented a simple filter-based model that fit the responses well, suggesting that low-level image measurements could play an important role in the estimation of surface relief.

10.8   3D Shape, Deformations, and the Perception of Material Properties

In this chapter we have focused almost exclusively on the optical properties of materials, such as translucency, glossiness, and texture, which result from the way that light interacts with different materials. As we have seen, two objects that have the same overall shape can appear to be made of completely different materials, depending on the mesoscale surface relief and the ways in which light reflects from or passes through the material. However, the converse is also the case. Objects with identical optical properties can appear to be completely different materials, depending on their 3D shape. Classical sculptors take advantage of this. They take a block of uniform material—such as clay, marble, or wood—and shape it to create the appearance of a range of different materials. This can be seen, for example, in Figure 10.24 and Color Plate XIII, *La Pietà* by Michelangelo. By modeling the undulations of drapery or the smooth form of skin, sculptors are able to connote many different material appearances. Of course, we do not actually believe that the marble is made of cloth or skin anymore than we believe the objects depicted in a painting are real. However, the fact that we can recognize the different materials in the sculpture based entirely on changes in shape suggests that 3D form can itself be a powerful source of information about material properties.

The fact that we can recognize materials from their 3D shape has at least two distinct causes. The first is simply the fact that, statistically, different objects tend to be made out of specific materials. For example, furniture, machine parts, and fruit and vegetables are all made of distinctly

Figure 10.24

La Pietà by Michelangelo. Solid marble can be made to connote different materials depending on the shape of the surface. (Image © 2005 Stanislav Traykov; reproduced with permission from the author.) (See Color Plate XIII.)

different kinds of stuff. The mapping is not always one-to-one (for example, chairs can be made out of wood, metal, textiles, and other materials), but, statistically, the brain can learn that some materials correlate more often than others with particular shapes. Of course, when the correlations are infringed, we can be tricked—for example, by wax fruits or by a novelty brick that is actually made of sponge. However, in general, the correlations are reliable, and thus the brain can use them to make inferences about material properties. There is evidence that the visual system uses object identity to recognize materials. For example, Hansen, Olkkonen, Walter, and Gegenfurtner (2006) presented participants with photographs of various fruits and vegetables on a computer monitor and asked them to adjust the color of the images until they appeared completely neutral gray. They found that participants made small but highly systematic errors in making their settings. Specifically, the participants perceived the images to be neutral gray when they were actually weakly colored along the hue direction opposite (on the hue circle) to the typical color of the specific fruit or vegetable. That is, for example, the participants set the orange to a slightly purplish color, and the banana to a slightly bluish color. This suggests that there is a small but measurable memory color effect, in which the observers' judgments of neutral gray are affected by the remembered color associated with the object.

The second reason that 3D shape can indicate material properties is more subtle, and applies not only to familiar objects but also to novel ones. Different substances have very different internal structures and physical properties, such as hardness, elasticity, and viscosity. These properties determine the way that different materials organize themselves into certain shapes and respond to external forces. For example, solids may be malleable, like lead, or fracture in response to stress, like glass. In contrast, liquids tend to flow. However, the precise way in which they flow depends on their viscosity, or viscoelastic properties; compare, for example, the different ways that milk, honey, and ketchup flow. Physically complex materials, such as fabrics, can have different response properties, depending on the fibers and the ways that they are woven together. For example, satin is "slinky," while wool tends to be "springy." Thus, although we cannot see the internal structure of different materials directly, they cause the materials to organize themselves into distinctly different shapes, patterns, and movements, which we can use to infer their properties. Figure 10.25 shows simulations of two viscoelastic fluids with different physical

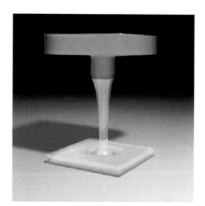 

Figure 10.25

Simulations of viscoelastic fluid flow created using the algorithm described by Goktekin et al. (2004). Even though these are static images and the materials have identical optical properties, we have a clear impression of the differences in their physical properties because of the shapes that they adopt in response to gravity. Little is known about how the visual system achieves this. (Images used by permission of T. Goktekin, A.W. Bargteil, and J.F. O'Brien.)

parameters, created using the method described in Goktekin, Bargteil, and O'Brien (2004). The fluids have identical optical properties, but because of the differences in viscoelasticity, they flow differently, leading to distinctive shapes that are highly informative about their properties. Even in a static snapshot of the flow, as shown here, we can clearly see the difference between their viscosity, and we have certain expectations about how they would move or respond if we touched them.

To date, very little is known about how the visual system uses shape cues for estimating material properties. Given how complex the processes are physically, it seems rather unlikely that the visual system inverts the kinematics of complex motions to infer the intrinsic parameters of the materials. Instead, it seems more plausible that the visual system abstracts from the retinal data a number of statistical shape and motion properties that correlate with physical processes. For example, as discussed in Chapter 18, it is known that the brain can recognize many aspects of human motion from highly reduced motion stimuli called *point light walkers*, which consist of a small number of points attached to the limbs. Observers can recognize the gender and even the mood of the actor, as well as recognizing familiar individuals from the trajectories of just a handful of points moving on a screen. This suggests that the visual system is extremely good at extracting information from spatiotemporal velocity and acceleration profiles. It seems plausible that a similar mechanism could be used for recognizing the statistical motions associated with different fluids, textiles, or other deforming materials. If true, this means that it might be possible to create convincing simulations of particular materials based solely on the statistics of motion, rather than by modeling the underlying physics.

10.8.1 Transformations, Mechanical History, and Aging

It is important to note that the shape of an object generally does not depend solely on its material composition. It also depends on the series of forces and processes that have been applied to the material over time, such as biological growth, artificial manufacture, or simply random events. Together with the intrinsic properties of the material, these forces and processes mold and model objects to give them their distinctive shapes.

Some combinations of material and manufacturing processes make it very hard to tell at a glance what exactly has been done to the material to shape it into a particular object (e.g., a die-cast metal toy). However, for some other combinations of materials and transformations, such as a crumpled tin can, we seem to be able to simultaneously infer something about the material, based on the way it is bent and deformed, and about the forces or processes applied to the object. It is as if the shape of the object is the product of both its intrinsic material properties and the history

Figure 10.26

We see the shape of this object as having being caused by a particular type of transformation, in this case twisting.

of actions applied to it, and the brain can separate these two contributions from the final, observed shape. There is an interesting analogy here, for the separation of image intensities into distinct physical causes, that we encountered several times throughout this chapter. Much as we can separate a patch of gray pixels into a combination of illumination and reflectance (or background and transparent overlay), so too, we can separate a given shape into the combination of its intrinsic material properties and the extrinsic forces that have been applied to it—its mechanical history. In Figure 10.26, we do not simply see the object as a set of isolated surface locations with certain curvatures and normals. We also see that the shape as a whole has been created by a twisting process. The brain somehow organizes the features of the shape into an interpretation of the processes that created it.

Leyton (1992) has developed a theory of how the visual system could infer forces from shape, based upon the local symmetry axes of the object. The theory does not make distinctions between different material properties, so we will not describe it in detail. However, in brief, he argues that local asymmetries in a shape provide visual evidence that a force has been applied to the object, acting along the local symmetry axis. For example, if the shape contains a protrusion, it is likely that some process, such as biological growth, has acted along the symmetry axis of the protrusion to cause it to stick out from the rest of the object. He has shown how more-complex actions, such as squeezing and twisting, can be built out of patterns of simpler forces acting along the local symmetry axes of the object. It is interesting to speculate how such a theory could be extended to enable the estimation of material properties from 3D shape as well.

The mesoscale texture and optical properties of materials also change over time as objects age. Some of these changes are quite subtle, such as when soup gets cold and develops a slightly opaque skin; others are much more dramatic, such as when iron rusts or fruit goes moldy. There are many processes that cause material appearance to change over time: oxidization, weathering and erosion, biological decay, patination, and just the general accumulation of scratches and dust over time. In computer graphics, some work has attempted to simulate the processes of aging and weathering (Dorsey, Edelman, Jensen, Legakis, & Pedersen, 1999; Dorsey & Hanrahan, 1996; Dorsey, Rushmeier, & Sillion, 2007; Gu et al., 2006; J. Lu, Georghiades, Rushmeier, Dorsey, & Xu, 2005; Rushmeier, 2009; Sun, Sunkavalli, Ramamoorthi, Belhumeur, & Nayar, 2007), but very little is known about how the human visual system recognizes the effects of aging on appearance.

Given the wide variety of different processes, it might seem intuitively that there cannot be one single mechanism for recognizing aging. However, Gu et al. (2006) showed, interestingly, that many different aging processes share something in common. They collected a database capturing the appearance of various materials at different stages in time. In general, the aging process progresses at different rates at different locations on the surface, leading to an increase in the spatial variation, or texture, over time. For example, as a banana ripens, it develops dark spots as different parts of the surface age at different rates. Importantly, however, Gu et al. found that the progression through color space is rather well conserved across locations within a given sample; the difference between different locations is simply the *rate* at which the color changes. This suggests, first, that the presence of texture could itself be a cue to aging. Indeed, it is no coincidence that many cosmetics are designed to reduce the apparent variations in skin pigmentation across the face, which tend to accumulate with age. Secondly, it also suggests that the visual system might be able to distinguish imperfections that are due to aging processes from textures that are due to the intrinsic patterning of the surface by comparing the distribution of colors across the surface. Yoonessi and Zaidi (2010) presented participants with patches of texture from the aforementioned database Gu et al., and asked them to recognize the materials. They found that participants were better at recognizing materials when they were shown multiple snapshots at different points in the time course, and that performance also substantially increased when the images were shown in color, rather than grayscale. This suggests that the human visual system uses color information and the way color changes to identify different materials. The way that materials change is, therefore, an important part of their appearance.

10.9   Issues Specific to Computer Graphics

One aspect of material perception that has immediate practical impor- tance for end-users of computer graphics is the intuitive parameterization of shaders. To achieve a given material appearance, the user must se- lect an appropriate model and modify the parameters to hone in on the desired look. However, as mentioned several times in this chapter, the models are generally based on the underlying physical properties rather than parameters that directly determine appearance in the image. Unfor- tunately, varying these parameters often does not lead to intuitive, percep- tual uniform changes in appearance. To address this, some researchers have attempted to measure the perceptual scales associated with the physical parameters of the model so that the parameters can be rescaled, leading to more intuitive changes in the image. For example, Pellacini, Ferwerda, and Greenberg (2000) used a psychophysical method called multidimensional scaling to measure the perceptual similarity between different samples of objects rendered with the Ward BRDF (Ward, 1992). Using this data, they suggested a perceptual reparameterization of the model to enable more in- tuitive navigation. Ngan, Durand, and Matusik (2006) have proposed a metric for automatically identifying perceptual scales of BRDFs and use this to facilitate navigation not only within a given BRDF model but also for transitions between models.

Further research along these lines is required to understand how percep- tual metrics work more generally, and to apply these to costly simulations such as fluid flow and cloth dynamics, where the cost to the user of trying out different variations is large.

10.10   Suggestions for Further Reading

A statement of many of the challenges posed by materials for human and machine vision systems, this thought-provoking essay raises many issues that are yet to be addressed by the field:

Adelson E. H. (2001). On seeing stuff: The perception of materials by hu- mans and machines. In B. E. Rogowitz & T. N. Pappas (Eds.), *Proceedings*

SPIE Human Vision and Electronic Imaging VI, (Vol. 4299, pp. 1–12). Bellingham, WA: SPIE.

The problem of separating the image into distinct physical causes is laid out very clearly in this reading:

Adelson, E. H., & Pentland, A. P. (1996). The perception of shading and reflectance. In D. Knill & W. Richards (Eds.), *Perception as Bayesian Inference* (pp. 409–423). New York: Cambridge University Press.

11

Motion of Viewer and Objects

Every photographer is aware that even a slight movement of his camera during exposure will shift the image on the film, for it ruins his picture. The same kind of shifting of the image on the retina occurs all the time during vision, with the difference that vision is enriched rather than spoiled.

—J. J. Gibson (1950a)

While Gibson's references to film may seem a bit archaic in a world of digital cameras and vibration-control lenses, his essential point is still clear. Retinal motion is almost always present and almost always informative. We are active observers of our world, often in motion. The resulting visual changes provide us with key information about our movement through the world, the geometry of the environment through which we are moving, and potential hazards with which we are in imminent danger of collision. Objects moving within the environment are frequently of importance to us. Their visual motion draws our attention, and often can provide information about their shape.

Chapter 5 dealt with the visual system's processing of two-dimensional visual motion, introducing the concept of optic flow as the representation of the information that is directly extracted from a time-varying view of the world. This chapter covers how the visual system interprets optic flow to determine properties of geometry and movement. Chapters 17 and 18 deal with more-complex cognitive aspects of the perception of visual motion.

11.1 Relative Motion, Optic Flow, and Frames of Reference for Describing Movement

Time-varying changes in the retinal image occur due to time-varying changes in the geometry, materials, lighting, or viewpoint of the environment under view. The discussion in this chapter is limited to changes due to either the viewer moving through the world or objects in the world moving with respect to the viewer and each other. The optic flow generated by such movements is a function of the *relative* changes in position between the eyes and viewed locations in the environment, regardless of whether it is the viewer or objects that are moving. This is a potential source of confusion. The frame of reference used to specify viewer and environmental locations and movement is important in interpreting visual motion. Motion can be specified with respect to multiple different frames of reference, fixed to the eye, head, body, environment, or objects in the environment. The ease with which the relationship between movement and geometry can be related to retinal optic flow varies between these different representations.

As in Chapter 7, we will use a formulation involving a perspective projection onto a planar imaging surface, indexed by the two-dimensional coordinates (x, y) having a common origin and axis alignment with world coordinates (X, Y, Z) (see Figure 7.3). We will further assume that the focal length f is 1.0, since this removes clutter in the math. By similar triangles, the actual (x, y) values can be divided by the actual f to simulate this effect with no loss of information. For the purposes of this chapter, we will ignore issues associated with the aperture problem and the movement of untextured, homogeneous surfaces, and presume that optic flow is in fact the projection onto the image plane of three-dimensional relative-movement vectors for each visible point in the environment.

The origin of the coordinate system used in this formulation is fixed to the point of projection, with the Z-axis aligned with the optical axis of the imaging system. As a result, all relative motion between the imaging system and an environmental point P at location (X_P, Y_P, Z_P) appears as temporal changes in X_P, Y_P, and Z_P. The instantaneous relative velocity between P and the imaging system is the first temporal derivative of (X_P, Y_P, Z_P), which we will denote as (X'_P, Y'_P, Z'_P). To determine the optic flow associated with this motion, we need to know how (X'_P, Y'_P, Z'_P) projects onto (x'_P, y'_P), where (x_P, y_P) is the image-plane location of the projection of P. Most authors use the notation (u, v) to refer to (x', y'), with u specifying the flow magnitude in the x direction and v specifying the flow magnitude in the y direction, and we will do so here as well.

Perspective projection affects the relationship between (X'_P, Y'_P, Z'_P) and (u_P, v_P) in a manner similar to that affecting spatial locations and intervals. In particular, the magnitude of flow, $\|(u_P, v_P)\|$, due to the projection of a point P moving with respect to the imaging system, is related to the magnitude of the velocity of P, $\|((X'_P, Y'_P, Z'_P)\|$, by scaling factors associated with the image location (x_P, y_P), the reciprocal of depth $\frac{1}{Z}$, and a foreshortening scaling factor—which is the sine of the angle between the line of sight to P and the direction of (X'_P, Y'_P, Z'_P).

The location and movement relative to the eye of points on object surfaces are easily and naturally represented in this formulation. Object movement relative to the head, the whole body, or to some environmentally defined frame of reference requires a coordinate transform. For an observer moving through a stationary environment, this formulation restates the situation as the environment moving past a stationary observer. An added complication arises when describing not just the instantaneous movement of a single point relative to the eye, but instead describing the movement of whole objects relative to the observer. Two distinctly different problems occur with describing rotations. The first, not covered here, involves the actual specification of the rotation in terms of matrix transformations, Euler angles, pitch/roll/yaw, or a variety of other formulations, each with its own advantages and disadvantages. The second relates to the coordinate system used to represent movement. All common specifications of movement involving rotations consist of some combination of rotation around the origin of the coordinate system and a possible translation. The specification of the translational component of such movement depends in a critical way on the origin of the coordinate system used. As an example of this complication, consider representing the motion of a cylinder rotating around its axis. In a coordinate system centered on the cylinder, the movement is a pure rotation with no translational component. If the rotation is instead described with respect to a coordinate system with an origin elsewhere, then an additional compensating translation is required in the representation to keep the center of the cylinder at a fixed location. In both cases the actual motion is the same, but the description of the motion is quite different. This is more than just a notational annoyance, since perception of rotational motion is affected by the coordinate system presumed by the visual system at a given instance.

11.2   Viewer Motion

The visual motion that occurs when an observer moves through the environment provides four distinct sorts of information. First, along a particular line of sight, the angular velocity of a location in the world relative to the direction of movement is inversely proportional to the distance to the location (von Helmholtz, 1878/1925). This provides a powerful source of information about the geometry of the world. Depth is often much more apparent if we are moving than if we are totally still. Second, visual motion provides information about the heading direction of physical motion, independent of all other perceptual cues (Loomis & Beall, 1998). The importance of this for locomotion is indicated by evidence that visual indication of heading often dominates proprioceptive and vestibular information for self-movement. Third, the ability to identify objects moving in the world is important in a number of ways for our survival. Vision is able to identify moving objects, even when the observer is also moving. Finally, visual motion can signal impending collision between the viewer and some other entity in the world, another obviously important feature facilitating survival.

11.2.1 The Relationship between Viewer Motion, Scene Geometry, and Optic Flow

In the coordinate system used here and in Chapter 7, the center of projection of the image system is fixed at the origin, with viewer motion through the world represented as world motion relative to the viewer. As a result, the instantaneous velocity V of the imaging system relative to an otherwise static world can be specified by translation velocity T and rotational velocity ω around the origin:

$$V = -T - \omega \times r \,, \tag{11.1}$$

where

$$T = (U, V, W)^T \,, \quad \omega = (A, B, C)^T \,. \tag{11.2}$$

In this formulation, the optic flow (u, v) at the image-plane location (x, y) corresponding to the projection of a point in the world $P = (X, Y, Z)$ is given by (Bruss & Horn, 1983)

$$u = u_t + u_r \,, \quad v = v_t + v_r \,; \tag{11.3}$$

$$u_t = \frac{-U + xW}{Z} \,, \quad v_t = \frac{-V + yW}{Z} \,; \tag{11.4}$$

$$u_r = Axy - B(x^2 + 1) + Cy \,, \quad v_r = A(y^2 + 1) - Bxy - Cx. \tag{11.5}$$

There are several notable points about these expressions that are of significance in interpreting information about the geometry of the world and the viewer's movement through that world. First of all, the optic flow can be factored into two components: one due only to translational velocity and another due only to rotational velocity (Equation (11.3)). The translational component of flow at a particular image location (x, y) is dependent on the translational velocity of the imaging system, the image location, and the reciprocal of the distance along the Z-axis to the world point imaged at (x, y). The rotational component of flow at a particular image location (x, y) is dependent on the rotational velocity of the imaging system and the image location. In particular, the rotational component of flow is not a function of the geometry of the world under view! To see this, consider optic flow specified in a spherical coordinate system. The angular velocity of the viewing system will produce an exactly opposite angular velocity in the optic flow. As a result, the component of optic flow due to rotation of the imaging system is fully specified by the rate of rotation, without regard to the distance to visible surfaces. This is not the same thing as saying optic flow due to rotation never provides information about the geometry of the world. Rather, it is the case that the optic flow generated by the rotation of the imaging system *around its point of projection* is uninformative about the geometric properties of the world.

11.2.2 The Special Case of No Rotation

For pure translational motion of the imaging system, the resulting optic flow is a function solely of (u_t, v_t), and so the magnitude of flow is proportional to $\frac{1}{Z}$ plus a term dependent on location in the image. Figure 11.1 provides two examples, with Figure 11.1(a) showing the flow resulting from forward motion and Figure 11.1(b) showing the flow resulting from sideways motion. The scaling of flow by $\frac{1}{Z}$, called *motion parallax*, is clear. Also clear is that flow magnitude does not lead directly to distance, but is also affected in a rather complex way by the direction of translational motion. Motion parallax is a powerful cue to relative depth, particularly for sideways motion (B. Rogers & Graham, 1979). For sideways translation, over a local area the larger the magnitude of optic flow the closer the associated surface point. In principle, motion parallax could also provide information about absolute distance to environmental locations if the speed

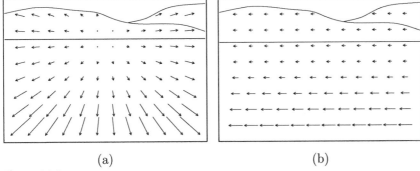

$$\text{(a)} \qquad\qquad\qquad\qquad \text{(b)}$$

Figure 11.1

The optic flow generated by movement over a ground plane, with the viewing direction slightly down from the horizontal. (a) Forward movement parallel to the ground plane. (b) Sideways movement to the right, parallel to the ground plane.

of sideways motion were available to the perceptual system. In practice, there is evidence that motion parallax is, at best, a weak cue for absolute distance, even when viewers move sideways under their own power, particularly for actual distances beyond a few meters (Beall, Loomis, Philbeck, & Fikes, 1995; Degelman & Rosinski, 1979; Ono, Rivest, & Ono, 1986), but more study of this issue is needed.

For the same special case when there is translational motion but no rotational motion of the imaging system, the resulting optic flow is zero at the image location given by

$$(x, y) = \left(\frac{U}{W}, \frac{V}{W} \right) . \tag{11.6}$$

For image coordinates normalized such that the effective focal length is 1.0, the line of sight corresponding to the (x, y) image location given in Equation (11.6) is parallel to the direction of translational motion $T = (U, V, W)^T$. If $W > 0$, corresponding to movement being at least partially forward with respect to the pointing direction of the imaging system, this (x, y) image position is called the *focus of expansion* (FOE), with nonzero flow values all oriented radially away from the FOE. In the case where $W < 0$, corresponding to movement being at least partially backward with respect to the pointing direction of the imaging system, the location of zero flow is called the *focus of contraction*, with other image locations having associated flow values that are oriented toward the focus of contraction. Because of these relationships, the focus of expansion or focus of contraction provides information sufficient to determine the direction of translation of

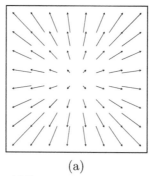 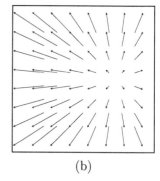

(a)   (b)

Figure 11.2

The focus of expansion is a visual indication of the direction of translational motion. (a) Forward movement toward a surface oriented perpendicularly to the line of sight. (b) The same situation, but with movement forward and slightly to the right.

the imaging system, presuming that no rotation is occurring at the same time.

Figure 11.2 provides two examples. In both cases, the viewpoint is pointed toward a flat surface perpendicular to the optical axis of the imaging system. Figure 11.2(a) shows the flow resulting from motion directly forward. Figure 11.2(b) is the flow resulting when movement is forward and to the right, as signaled visually by the rightward shift of the focus of expansion. The focus of expansion can also be seen in Figure 11.1(a), slightly above the center of the image because the direction of view is slightly down from the direction of translation. There is no apparent focus of expansion in Figure 11.1(b) because under planar projection the pure sideways motion puts the line of sight corresponding to the direction of movement an infinite distance from the center of the image and thus outside of the field of view.

11.2.3   The General Case of Eye or Viewer Motion Involving Both Translation and Rotation

The relationship between movement, the geometry of the world, and optic flow is considerably more complex when both translation and rotation of the imaging system are occurring. Two distinct situations can lead to combined translational and rotational motion. One is associated with movement along a curvilinear path. The other occurs due to eye rotations, even when the viewer is otherwise moving in a straight line. Such eye rotations are common when a moving viewer fixates at a particular surface point as motion is occurring. Figure 11.3 shows the flows resulting from the same motions and geometry as in Figure 11.1, except that eye rotations are introduced to keep optic flow zero at the center of the field of view. The

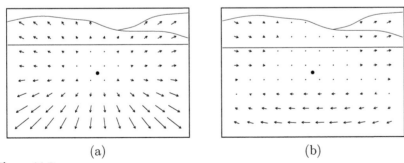

(a)   (b)

Figure 11.3

Optical flow generated as in Figure 11.1, except that eye is fixated on ground surface. (a) Forward movement parallel to the ground plane. (b) Sideways movement to the right, parallel to the ground plane.

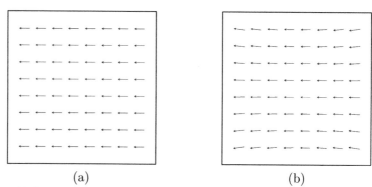

(a)   (b)

Figure 11.4

The optic flow generated by movement while looking at a flat surface, perpendicular to the line of sight. (a) Sideways movement to the right. (b) Rotational movement to the right.

direct relationship between flow magnitude and relative depth no longer holds, and the simple pattern of flow expanding from a focus of expansion corresponding to the direction of movement, as in Figure 11.1(a), is gone.

A mathematical analysis shows that in general, both the translational velocity T and rotational velocity ω can still be recovered in this case (Bruss & Horn, 1983). However, the ability to accurately determine the parameters of motion is intrinsically sensitive to noise in the recovery of optic flow values, particularly in the absence of depth variability and for narrow fields of view (Adiv, 1989). This can be seen in Figure 11.4. When facing a surface oriented perpendicularly to the optical axis, and so having constant Z in the coordinate system used for Equations (11.1)–(11.5), translational motion to the side produces a flow pattern very similar to rotation around the center of the imaging system with no translation.

There is substantial evidence that people can judge their heading direction based on visual motion even in the presence of rotation (e.g., Li & Warren, 2000; Royden et al., 1994; Warren & Hannon, 1988). Researchers disagree, however, on whether this requires nonvisual information about eye rotation or if, instead, recovery of heading can be done from retinal image motion alone. For example, Royden et al. provide support for the claim that heading judgments are more accurate for real eye movements rather than for eye movements simulated on a visual display. Li and Warren argue that retinal optic flow alone is sufficient for the recovery of heading, but that extra retinal information about eye motion can also be used by the perceptual system in the determination of heading. Also relevant to the recovering of heading is the demonstration in Warren, Morris, & Kalish (1988) that accuracy improves with speed and texture density.

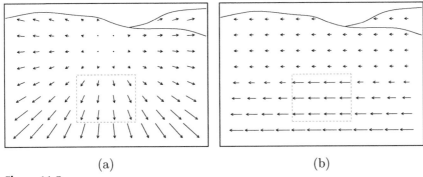

(a)   (b)

Figure 11.5

The same motion and geometry as in Figure 11.1, except for the addition of a vertically oriented rectangular surface positioned on the ground plane near the viewer.

In Equation (11.4), (u_t, v_t) varies discontinuously with (x, y) if, and only if, Z varies discontinuously with (x, y). In Equation (11.5), (u_r, v_r) varies continuously with (x, y) and is not dependent on Z. As a result, for viewer motion through an otherwise static world, spatial discontinuities over the image in optic flow necessarily correspond to discontinuities in depth. Figure 11.5 provides an example. The motions and world geometry are the same as in Figure 11.1, except that there is a vertically oriented rectangular surface positioned on the ground plane near the viewer, as indicated by the dotted rectangle. For both forward and sideways motion, there is a sharp change in optic flow at the top of this added surface due to the change in depth between the surface and the ground plane. No such discontinuity in flow occurs at the bottom of the added surface, since the Z values to the bottom of the surface and the contact points on the ground plane are the same. The differences between flow at the sides of the added surface and ground plane flow immediately adjacent in the image gradually increase from bottom to top, as would be expected from the geometric structure. This association between discontinuities in flow and discontinuities in depth occurs whether or not rotation of the imaging system is present.

In addition to discontinuities in optic flow indicating surface boundaries, the nature of the difference in flow values across such discontinuities can aid in heading determination in the presence of rotation (Reiger & Lawton, 1983, 1985). Consider the difference in the flow value on either side of a discontinuity, with the sides being labeled l and r for convenience:

$$u^d = u^{(l)} - u^{(r)} , \quad v^d = v^{(l)} - v^{(r)} . \tag{11.7}$$

Since the rotational component of flow is independent of scene structure and necessarily varies slowly over the field of view,

$$u_r^d = v_r^d \approx 0 \ . \tag{11.8}$$

From Equations (11.3) and (11.4), at flow discontinuities

$$u^d \approx u_t^d = \left(\frac{1}{Z^{(l)}} - \frac{1}{Z^{(r)}} \right) (-U + xW) \ ,$$

$$v^d \approx v_t^d = \left(\frac{1}{Z^{(l)}} - \frac{1}{Z^{(r)}} \right) (-V + yW) \ . \tag{11.9}$$

Similar to the situation in Equation (11.6) and the discussion that follows on the focus of expansion, the values of (u_d, v_d) across flow discontinuities point toward or away from the direction of translational motion. Unlike the situation with flow itself, however, the orientation of the difference of flow values yields the direction of translational motion even when rotation is present, though in this case additional information is required to determine if the translational motion is toward or away from this line of sight. Evidence is mixed as to whether or not differential flow plays a role in heading determination in people (Ehrlich, Beck, Crowell, Freeman, & Banks, 1998; Li & Warren, 2000).

If there are one or more objects in the view that are moving with respect to the world at large, the instantaneous relative motion of each with respect to the image system can be characterized by separate values for T and ω. This complicates the problem of determining heading. If the visual system analyzes the global pattern of optic flow to estimate heading detection, the estimate will be biased by flow values associated with objects moving relative to the environmental frame of reference. In fact, visual-heading judgments seem to be relatively insensitive to the effects of moving objects, except for objects subtending a relatively large angle and crossing the observer's path of movement (Royden & Hildreth, 1996).

11.2.4 Vection

The term *vection* refers to the illusion of self-motion in circumstances where the viewer is not actually moving (Andersen, 1986; Dichgans & Brandt, 1978). Usage of the term is often limited to the perception of self-motion based on visual stimuli alone, but some consider vection to potentially involve auditory or noninertial proprioceptive cues as well. The classic example of vection is the *railroad car illusion*.[1] This illusion involves sitting

---

[1] The decline of rail service in the United States may be making this a less-compelling example for some readers.

(a)   (b)

Figure 11.6

Optokinetic drum, made using a vertically striped, rotatable curtain. (a) A person about the enter the drum. (b) The curtain surrounding the person. (Photographs courtesy of John Rieser and Bobby Bodenheimer.)

in one stationary car, looking out at a different stationary car on an adjacent track. Often, when the other car starts to move, there is a strong sense that it is remaining stationary while the car you are sitting in is starting to move in the opposite direction. The perception of relative motion is correct, but absolute motion with respect to the world frame of reference is misperceived.

The majority of perceptual studies of vection have addressed *circular vection*, which involves the sense of rotating around a vertical axis centered on the viewer's body. A compelling sense of circular vection can be obtained from standing inside a rotating *optokinetic drum* (Figure 11.6). The optokinetic drum is a cylindrical surface marked with a distinctive pattern—often vertically oriented black-and-white stripes. The drum completely surrounds the viewer. In the version shown in Figure 11.6, the drum is a fabric curtain, lifted to allow the viewer to enter and then lowered when the drum is in operation. When the drum starts to spin, the viewer experiences several seconds in which the drum is seen (correctly) as moving. After a few seconds, the typical viewer will experience a short period of disorientation, followed by the sensation that he or she is rotating inside of the drum, which now appears to be stationary with respect to the world at large. The sense of movement is absolutely compelling, even though it is the viewer who is actually stationary. It is also as effective at triggering motion sickness as is real motion!

It is commonly believed that circular vection requires visual motion in peripheral vision (e.g., Brandt, Dichgans, & Koenig, 1973). The actual situation seems to be more complicated. The ability of a rotating visual pattern to stimulate a compelling sense of self-rotation in a stationary observer appears to depend on an interaction between the spatial frequency of the pattern and whether it is viewed in central or peripheral vision (Palmisano & Gillam, 1998), with vection most compelling for moving high spatial frequency patterns in central vision and low spatial frequency patterns in peripheral vision. A number of authors have suggested that this may be due to two separate perceptual processes at work, one operating on central vision and the other operating on peripheral vision (Andersen & Braunstein, 1985; Palmisano & Gillam, 1998). Circular vection is facilitated if the visual stimuli contains patterns stationary with respect to the viewer when these patterns are seen as being in front of a pattern moving with respect to the viewer. It is inhibited in the reverse condition when the visual stimuli contains patterns stationary with respect to the viewer, which are seen as being behind a pattern moving with respect to the viewer (Brandt, Wist, & Dichgans, 1975; Howard & Howard, 1994; Ohmi, Howard, & Landolt, 1987).

A visually induced sense of translational motion (*linear vection*) can also occur, due either to observing actual surfaces moving toward or away from the viewer or to animated patterns with optic flow consistent with such movements (Andersen, 1986; Berthoz, Pavard, & Young, 1975; Dichgans & Brandt, 1978). The railroad car illusion is an example of linear vection. Anecdotal evidence suggests that linear vection is more difficult to achieve under laboratory conditions than is rotational vection, but few if any studies have documented this under controlled conditions. As with rotational vection, linear vection can be triggered by either central-field or peripheral moving visual patterns (Andersen & Braunstein, 1985), and is facilitated by visually stationary foreground patterns (Ohmi & Howard, 1988).

One difficulty in studying vection in a controlled manner is that there are few objective measures that can be used to quantify perceived self-motion. As a result, most evaluations of vection are based on subjective reports of a sense of movement. These include simple responses about whether or not a sense of self-movement occurred at all, along with quantitative measures of onset time, duration, velocity, and the degree of believability of the effect. Several more objective measures have been used, such as pointing toward previously seen targets after viewing a vection display (Lepecq, Jouen, & Dubon, 1993), but these measures are often unable to clearly distinguish between the perception of self-motion and the perception of world motion.

11.2.5 Visual Control of Postural Stability

Standing upright is a challenging motor control problem, since it involves the balancing of an inverted, articulated pendulum with a compliant linkage (Lakie, Caplan, & Loram, 2003). Maintaining postural stability requires information about postural sway. In people, this information comes from vestibular, proprioceptive, and visual sources—all of which assist in what we informally think of as balance. Surprising to many people is the dominant role that vision plays in this process. We can stand in the dark or with our eyes closed, showing that vision is not required for balance. However, stability is noticeably impacted when visual information is degraded or removed (Edwards, 1946; H. A. Witkin & Wapner, 1950).

The importance of vision in maintaining postural stability becomes clearer when vision and other senses relevant to balance are placed in conflict. Perhaps the most famous example of this is the *swinging-room experiment* (D. N. Lee & Aronson, 1974; D. N. Lee & Lishman, 1975). In this experiment, a structure having front and side walls and a ceiling was suspended on long ropes just above a stationary floor. The length of the ropes was such that when the structure was swung forward or backward, the resulting motion was predominately parallel to the floor. When infants from age 13 to 16 months stood in the center of the structure facing the closed end and then the structure was moved, most swayed or fell in the direction of the structure's movement (D. N. Lee & Aronson, 1974).

The direction of actual sway was consistent with the infants' interpreting the visual information as an indication that they were swaying in a direction opposite the direction of motion of the structure. They responded to this (incorrect) perception of self-movement with motor control activities generating a compensating body torque toward the direction of the motion of the structure. Since they were, in fact, in balance at the time, they became unbalanced and swayed or fell in the direction of structure movement. Adults, standing on either a narrow beam or in one of two different postures aimed at increasing postural instability, exhibited similar behavior when placed in a similar structure that was continuously oscillating (D. N. Lee & Lishman, 1975).

11.2.6 Perception of Speed of Movement and Time-to-Collision

Optic flow is insufficient in and of itself to determine the translational speed either of the viewer moving through the world or of moving objects in the world. To see this, consider the monocular optic flow produced by relative motion between the viewer and the environment, as specified by Equations (11.1)–(11.5). Now consider the flow $(u^{(\alpha)}, v^{(\alpha)})$ resulting when both the instantaneous translational velocity of the relative motion between viewer and environment and the scaling of the environment itself are multiplied by some positive scaling constant α:

$$T^{(\alpha)} = (\alpha U, \alpha V, \alpha W)^T \,, \qquad (11.10)$$

$$u_t^{(\alpha)} = \frac{-\alpha U + x\alpha W}{\alpha Z} = u_t \,, \quad v_t^{(\alpha)} = \frac{-\alpha V + y\alpha W}{\alpha Z} = v_t \,. \qquad (11.11)$$

Rotational flow (u_t, v_r) remains the same, since rotational flow at a given image location is a function only of rotational velocity, which is not affected by the scaling of translational velocity. Whatever the scaling of the speed of translational motion, the optic flow stays the same as long as the size of the environment is comparably scaled. As a result, optic flow alone cannot be used to uniquely determine the speed.

In principle, actual speed can be determined if optic flow is augmented by distance information. It is likely that in practice recovery of speed is idiosyncratic to specific situations and actions. For example, speed estimation associated with ball catching almost certainly involves different processes than speed estimation associated with driving. More importantly, for many activities it is less important to know actual speeds than it is to know the time before some critical event is going to occur. When crossing the street as a pedestrian, knowing the speed of approaching vehicles is less important than knowing how much time you have to get to the other side without getting run over.

Under some conditions, optic flow contains sufficient information to determine time-to-collision with an environmental location, even when no information is available about speed or distance. If relative motion is limited to constant speed translational movement and ϕ is the visual angle subtended by an entity in the environment on a collision course with the viewer, then time-to-collision t_{toc} is given by the relationship

$$t_{toc} = \frac{\phi}{\frac{d\phi}{dt}} \,. \qquad (11.12)$$

David Lee has called this value τ (D. N. Lee, 1976; D. N. Lee & Reddish, 1981), though Lee more commonly defines ϕ as the visual angle from a location of interest to the focus of expansion. The value τ becomes an imperfect predictor of time-to-collision when acceleration is occurring or motion is along a curved trajectory. Furthermore, τ is also not really a predictor of time-to-collision, but rather it is a predictor of time to closest approach. As a result, τ can indicate an imminent collision in situations in which the viewer will actually pass to the side of the object (see Section 11.3.3). There is disagreement on whether τ-like measures are actually used for determination of impending contact with environmental locations, or if such judgments also use explicit information about distance (Schiff & Detwiler, 1979; Tresilian, 1991; Wann, 1996).

11.2.7 Non-optic Flow Information for the Perception of Self-Motion

All of the discussions so far in this chapter have presumed that information about optic flow comes directly from changes in the retinal image, as described in Chapter 5, and that it is optic flow that leads to the perception of heading and the control of posture. The actual situation seems to be more complicated. According to van den Berg and Brenner (1994), stereo viewing improved perception of heading when the visual stimulus did not represent a surface but was rather a cloud of dots, similar to the effect of driving in a snowstorm. J. W. Kelly, Loomis, and Beall (2005) used stereo to manipulate the three-dimensional appearance of a random dot pattern without changing the two-dimensional optic flow generated by the pattern, in the process modifying the effectiveness of visual control of postural stability. This provides evidence that optic flow is not sufficient on its own for this purpose. Loomis, Beall, Macuga, Kelly, and Smith (2006) and Macuga, Loomis, Beall, and Kelly (2006) showed that optic flow specified only by changing disparity values, with monocular views being only scintillation noise, still supported the determination of heading and several actions, such as ball catching and the avoidance of moving obstacles, indicating that optic flow is not necessary for these tasks. Mohler et al. (2007) showed that the recalibration resulting from a mismatch between visual and biomechanical indicators of locomotion speed (see Chapter 13) was affected by changed visual indications for velocity even when the magnitude of optic flow was held constant, indicating that the effect is not controlled purely by optic flow alone.

11.3   Object Motion

The visual motion generated by the movement of individual objects provides three sources of useful information about the world under view. First, as with viewer motion, object motion leads to visual information about both the nature of the motion and the geometry of the object. Ullman (1979) refers to this as *structure from motion* (SFM). Second, also as with viewer motion, discontinuities in optic flow are always associated with significant properties of the scene; but when moving objects are possible, interpreting such flow discontinuities becomes more complex. Finally, the ability to detect entities moving with respect to the world at large is important in the performance of many actions, some of them critical to survival.

11.3.1   Structure from Motion

In describing the information available from visual motion associated with
an object moving relative to a viewer, it is often most intuitive to use
a coordinate system centered on the object, rather than centered on the
viewer, as in Section 11.2. In such a representation, the translational motion of compact objects provides limited information about the geometric
structure of the objects unless the objects are large, since the variability
in optic flow due to the perspective-related variability in depth is small
relative to the average depth. Rotation of the object around its center, on
the other hand, generates significant variability in optic flow when the axis
of rotation is not parallel to the line of sight. This occurs because of two
effects, both related to the imaging process that projects three-dimensional
velocities of surface points onto two-dimensional optic flow on the retina.
First, the relative magnitude of 3D surface-point motion is dependent on
the distance of the surface point from the axis of rotation. The second
effect is due to the foreshortening that occurs when the 2D velocities of
surface points are projected to two-dimensional optic flow on the retina.
Such rotations change the 3D velocities of surface points on the object over
time in such a way as to cause large changes in the magnitude of the associated optic flow. Object rotation around an axis other than around the
line of sight is referred to as *rotation in depth*, since the rotation causes
changes over time in the distance from the viewpoint to surface locations.
In the special case of object rotation around the line of sight, the velocity of surface points is always perpendicular to the line of sight, resulting
in a situation where no foreshortening occurs as long as the visual angle
subtended by the object is relatively small. In this case, the resulting
flow is independent of the geometric structure of the object, except for its
silhouette.

Figures 11.7–11.9 illustrate these effects. Figure 11.7(a) shows the optic
flow generated by a cylinder oriented vertically and rotating around its
axis. Figure 11.9(a) is a plot of the resulting flow along a horizontal image
line. Figure 11.8(a) shows the optic flow generated by a plane oriented
perpendicularly to the line of sight and rotating around a vertical axis
in the plane, with Figure 11.9(b) a plot of the resulting flow. The two
flow patterns are dramatically different, reflecting the significant differences
in geometry. Figures 11.7(b) and 11.8(b) show the same geometry but
this time rotating around an axis coincident with the optical axis of the
imaging system. As described above, the flow patterns are, in this case,
identical .

The differences between the information about scene geometry available
due to viewer motion and due to object motion are frequently confusing.
In Section 11.2, we argued that only translational motion produces pat-

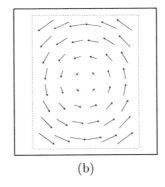

(a)   (b)

Figure 11.7

Optic flow of a cylindrical surface with its axis orientated vertically. (a) Rotating around its axis. (b) Rotating around the optical axis.

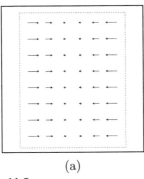
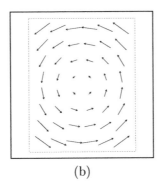

(a)   (b)

Figure 11.8

Optic flow of a planar surface with its orientation perpendicular to the optic axis. (a) Rotating around a vertical axis in the surface plane. (b) Rotating around the optical axis.

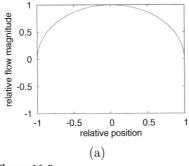
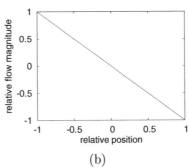

(a)   (b)

Figure 11.9

Optic flow as a function of horizontal image location for an object rotating around a vertical axis through its center. (a) Cylinder (Figure 11.7(a)). (b) Plane (Figure 11.8(a)). Maximum magnitude normalized to 1.0.

terns of optic flow dependent on the geometric structure of surfaces in view, with rotations producing flow independent of scene geometry. Here, we are arguing that the flow produced from object translation is of little use in perceiving surface geometry, whereas rotations produce significant geometry-related changes in flow. The confusion comes about because of the different frames of reference that are used. Optic flow generated by relative motion between the imaging system and surfaces is uninformative about surface geometry when the relative motion is a rotation around the optical axis of the imaging system. Object rotation around an axis through the center of the object, when expressed in a coordinate system with its origin at the center of the imaging system, becomes a combination of translation and rotation, as described in Section 11.1. The presence of translation in this imaging-system-centered coordinate system means that a relationship will exist between flow and object geometry.

One of the first demonstrations that the visual system could infer 3D structure from 2D visual motion associated with object rotation was the *kinetic depth effect* of Wallach and O'Connell (1953). They used a small light source to project shadows of objects onto a translucent screen and then had people observe the shadows from the other side of the screen. Both solid objects and bent-wire objects were used. When some of the objects were rotated, a strong sense of three-dimensionality was apparent from the view of the generated shadows. The same experiment can be repeated by casting a shadow generated by a bent paper clip onto a white surface under direct sunlight, or another collimated illumination source, and then rotating the paper clip. As with the original Wallach and O'Connell result, only some shapes will generate shadows that appear to move in three dimensions, an effect related—at least in part—to the aperture problem described in Chapter 5.

The mathematics underlying the recovery of geometric structure from visual motion has received extensive study in the computer vision community (Longuet-Higgins & Prazdny, 1980; Ullman, 1979; and many more-recent papers). Multiple methods described in terms of both optical flow and discrete point correspondences have been proposed, and substantial debate has occurred about the minimal conditions and assumptions necessary to unambiguously determine three-dimensional object geometry. The relevance of this work to understanding human vision is not clear, since perception based on visual motion is not always consistent with the mathematical predictions (Braunstein, 1976; Todd, 1984).

As indicated above for an object rotating around an axis coincident with the line of sight, the resulting optic flow is not dependent on the geometric structure of the object, and thus object shape cannot be uniquely recovered from such flow patterns. Despite this, some flow patterns resulting from rotation around the line of sight do appear as distinctly three dimensional.

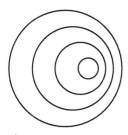

Figure 11.10

The stereokinetic effect.

Figure 11.10 is one example of this *stereokinetic effect* (Musatti, 1924; Proffitt, Rock, Hecht, & Schubert, 1992). If the pattern is rotated around the center of the outer ring, it will look like a rotating 3D cone or funnel, slightly tilted away from the line of sight.

In the stereokinetic effect, the visual motion is consistent with multiple geometric shapes, and the surprise is that it is the 3D shape that is usually seen. A more striking example of the perception of structure from motion mathematically inconsistent with the optic flow from which it arises is that a rectangular strip of uniformly translating texture seen through an aperture can appear as a cylinder rotating around an axis perpendicular to the line of sight, particularly if the strip of moving texture is surrounded by stationary texture (Ramachandran, Cobb, & Rogers-Ramachandran, 1988; Royden, Baker, & Allman, 1988). A possible reason for this and similar illusions is that part of the information for structure from motion comes for surface boundaries, not just variations in flow over surfaces (W. B. Thompson, Kersten, & Knecht, 1992).

11.3.2   Dynamic Occlusion

As shown in Section 11.2.3 for viewer motion through an otherwise-static world, spatial discontinuities over the image in optic flow necessarily correspond to discontinuities in depth. If objects moving with respect to the environment at large are present, discontinuities in flow can also occur across boundaries separating views of two surfaces moving with respect to one another. Thus, when moving objects are possible, spatial discontinuities in optic flow are necessarily associated with depth discontinuities or the boundaries of independently moving objects. Either case is ecologically significant. One of the reasons that visual motion is such a powerful cue for spatial organization is that discontinuities in flow are always associated with important properties of either the geometry of the world or the movement of objects, whereas discontinuities in properties such as brightness, color, and texture have many more possible causes.

Flow discontinuities are associated with the progressive occlusion or disocclusion of a more-distant surface by a nearer surface, except in the special case of flow on either side of a flow discontinuity being parallel to the orientation of the boundary itself. Two separate mechanisms seem to be involved in the perception of these *dynamic occlusion boundaries*. The appearance or disappearance of visible surface texture (called the *accretion* or *deletion* of texture) gives direct evidence of dynamic occlusion (Kaplan,

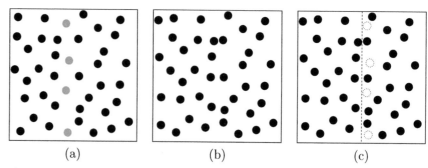

(a)   (b)   (c)

Figure 11.11

An example of texture deletion. (a) Image at time t_1. (b) Image at time t_2, with some of the texture elements now occluded. (c) If the occluded texture elements are known to be associated with the left surface, this is an indication that the left surface is moving behind the right surface.

1969). Figure 11.11 provides an example. Figures 11.11(a) and 11.11(b) show two textured surfaces moving toward each other at two instances in time, t_1 and t_2. Between t_1 and t_2, the four dots shown in gray in Figure 11.11(a) disappear. (The dots are marked in gray for convenience in understanding the figure; they need not be visually distinctive for there to be a clear sense of texture deletion.) The deletion of texture in Figure 11.11(b) is an indication of dynamic occlusion but in and of itself does not indicate which side of the boundary corresponds to the occluded surface. The differentiation between the occlud*ing* and occlud*ed* sides of the boundary becomes possible if optic flow or other means can be used to associate the disappearing texture with a surface to one or the other side of the boundary, as indicated in Figure 11.11(c) (Mutch & Thompson, 1985). An analogous situation occurs when surfaces are moving away from one another, leading to accretion of visible surface texture.

A second mechanism for detecting and interpreting dynamic occlusion boundaries is based directly on optic flow, augmented with information about how the boundary itself is moving in the retinal image. The relationship between the optic flow to either side of the boundary and the flow of the boundary is governed by the *boundary flow constraint*, which states that near the boundary the flow of the occluding surface will be the same as the flow of the boundary (W. B. Thompson, Mutch, & Berzins, 1985). Figures 11.12 and 11.13 provide illustrations. Figure 11.12 shows dynamic occlusion, with two surfaces moving toward each other. In Figure 11.12(b), the boundary is moving with the right surface, indicating that the right surface is moving in front of the left surface. Figure 11.12(c) shows the situation in which the left surface is moving in front of the right surface.

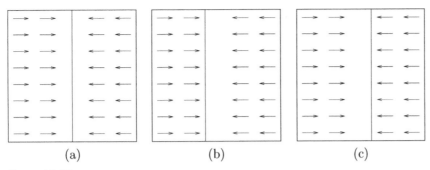

Figure 11.12

Boundary flow. (a) Two surfaces moving toward each other, with the arrows indicating optic flow values at particular view locations. (b) The boundary moving consistent with the optic flow of the right surface, indicating that the right surface is progressively occluding the left. (c) The boundary moving with the left surface, indicating that it is progressively occluding the right.

Figure 11.13 shows the corresponding situations when the two surfaces are moving away from one another. The visual system is able to exploit the boundary flow constraint to disambiguate between occluding and occluded surfaces and dynamic occlusion and disocclusion boundaries, even in the absence of deletion or accretion of surface texture (Yonas, Craton, & Thompson, 1987).

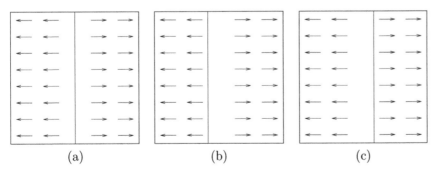

Figure 11.13

Boundary flow in the case of disocclusion. (a) Two surfaces moving away from each other. (b) Left surface in front. (c) Right surface in front.

11.3.3 Moving-Object and Collision Detection

An imaging system stationary in the world can easily detect moving objects, since only they will generate image motion. This observation underlies one class of motion-detection methods used in video surveillance. However, it is worthless for people, since eye rotations and head motions generate substantial retinal motion even when everything visible in the world is stationary. A key problem for biological vision is to detect entities moving with respect to the world at large, ignoring visual motion due only to the observer's movements.

A number of classes of theories have been proposed to account for moving-object detection from a moving observer. Most common in the perception literature are methods based on identifying localized regions of optic flow that are distinct in some set of specific properties from the surrounding flow (e.g., Brenner & van den Berg, 1996; Ölveczky, Baccus, & Meister, 2003). Proposals for criteria allowing discrimination between object and background flow include size and surroundedness of regions of similar motion, patterns in the flow fields themselves, depth, extraretinal information about eye rotation, and a variety of other factors. The psychophysics supporting these models of moving-object detection is most often done with stationary observers looking at animations on computer monitors, and the degree to which this applies to natural, wide field of view viewing by an observer moving normally through a realistic environment remains an open question.

A second approach to detecting moving objects is based on finding patterns of optic flow inconsistent with the patterns of flow that can arise from an observer moving through a static environment (e.g., Irani & Anadan, 1998; W. B. Thompson & Pong, 1990). Compared to the methods described above, these typically involve a more global analysis of the flow field and are specified in terms of more precise constraints on the flow as-

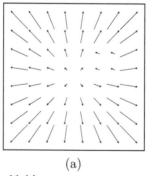
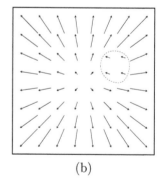

(a)   (b)

Figure 11.14

Detecting moving objects from optic flow, as in (a). For pure translational motion, the region circled in (b) necessarily corresponds to an object moving with respect to the background.

sociated with observer motion. A simple example of this approach, which is only effective if either there is no eye rotation or the effects of eye rotation have been factored out of the flow field in some manner, is to note that the flow field resulting from pure translational motion through a static environment is oriented radially from a focus of expansion or contraction (see Section 11.2.2). Flow vectors violating this orientational constraint must have arisen from independently moving objects, as illustrated in Figure 11.14. A number of more powerful (and more complicated) methods have been proposed to deal with the general motion case. While these global approaches to moving-object detection have the potential for more precision and accuracy than does local flow discrimination, little empirical evidence has been offered that they are actually utilized in biological vision systems.

One aspect of moving-object detection also involves aspects of the perception of time-to-collision. As mentioned in Section 11.2.6, τ and similar visual cues for time-to-collision don't actually indicate if contact will occur, or if instead the object will pass to the side of the observer or the observer will pass to the side of the potential obstacle. For constant translational motion of both viewer and moving objects, a method of collision detection long known to mariners is potentially relevant: "If the bearing becomes constant and the distance is decreasing, the two vessels are on collision courses...." (Bowditch, 1802; W. B. Thompson & Kearney, 1986). The utility of this relationship to more general motion and its use in biological vision systems have received little, if any, systematic study.

11.4   Issues Specific to Computer Graphics

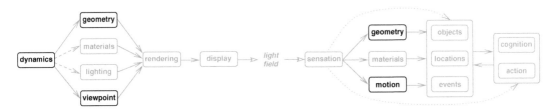

The strength of visual motion as a cue for the geometric structure of the world under view makes it particularly important in computer graphics. Graphical displays usually lack binocular stereo; are limited in field of view; suffer from multiple limitations as described in Chapter 12; and, in many other ways, are much less effective than the real world in generating an accurate sense of depth and spatial organization. Visual motion can compensate for many of these shortcomings, which is one of the reasons for the pervasiveness of dolly shots in film.

There are, however, a number of potential problems in using visual motion in computer graphics, beyond the two-dimensional image motion perception issues discussed in Chapter 5. If motion is specifically intended to increase the sense of spatial structure, animators and designers of visualization interfaces need to know which combinations of types of motion, perspective, field of view, and observer and object frames of reference actually do provide information about depth. In addition, the motions specified in rendering have to appear natural (see Chapters 17 and 18). Less recognized is that the sensitivity of the visual system to discontinuities in optic flow puts a premium on creating graphical renderings with small- and large-scale occlusion boundaries that are comparable to the real world. This requires an appropriate combination of detailed explicit geometry and tools such as displacement maps and relief textures. Also, while the importance of visual motion and interactivity are widely noted in the computer graphics and visualization communities, interactivity does not necessarily improve vision-based comprehension in all cases (see Chapter 13).

The perception of heading depends in a central way on perspective effects. If the viewpoint used to generate a perspective rendering does not match the viewpoint from which the rendering is viewed, heading perception will be in error. (The related problem of viewpoint mismatch in static images is discussed in depth in Chapter 12.) This can have important implications for applications such as vehicle simulators. Incorrect viewing locations have little effect on τ-based estimates of time-to-collision but can bias estimates that involve distance perception as part of the process. Structure from motion for rotating small objects is relatively insensitive of the location of the viewpoint.

Motion parallax and perception of heading play a central role in visually immersive virtual environments, often called "virtual reality" systems. Such systems track head position so that the computer graphics displayed to the user are updated in a manner consistent with the user's own motions (Sutherland, 1965, 1968). Done correctly, this provides a strong sense of movement through a geometrically complex environment (Hettinger, 2002). Done incorrectly, it quickly makes users sick. The most compelling sense of moving through a simulated virtual world comes from multimodal sensory interfaces that combine visual motion, head tracking, and other inertial, auditory, and vibrational cues (L. R. Harris, Jenkin, & Zikovitz, 2000; Riecke, Feuereissen, & Rieser, 2009; Whitton, 2003).

11.5   Suggestions for Further Reading

Gibson's book covers many of the concepts central to the perception of viewer motion and environmental structure based on optic flow:

Gibson, J. J. (1950). *The perception of the visual world.* Cambridge, MA: Riverside Press.

Two overviews of visual control of locomotion and determination of heading—the first providing an overview of the problem and including a discussion of the nonvisual sources of information that are relevant, and the second describing the role played by optic flow:

Loomis, J. M., & Beall, A. C. (1998). Visually controlled locomotion: Its dependence on optic flow, three-dimensional space perception, and cognition. *Ecological Psychology, 10*(3–4), 271–285.

Warren, W. H. (2008). Optic flow. In T. D. Albright & R. Masland (Eds.), *The senses: A comprehensive reference: Vol. 2. Vision II* (chap. 12). San Diego, CA: Academic Press.

Two overviews of recovering object shape from visual motion, the first concentrating on phenomenology and the second on computational issues:

Braunstein, M. L. (1976). *Depth perception through motion.* New York: Academic Press.

Ullman, S. (1979). *The interpretation of visual motion.* Cambridge, MA: MIT Press.

The best example of the railroad car illusion in film, plus a variety of examples of false perspective:

Davison, J., & Lowry, H. (Producers); Abrahams, J., Zucker, D., & Zucker, J. (Directors) (1984). *Top Secret!* [Motion picture]. United States: Paramount.

12

Pictorial Space

In 1435, the Renaissance scholar Leon Battista Alberti published *Della pittura* (*On Painting*), a treatise formally describing the principles of creating perspectively correct paintings (Alberti, 1435/1991). In this work, Alberti utilized a metaphor that is now referred to as *Alberti's window*: "When [painters] go around a surface with lines and then fill the described places with colors, nothing is to be sought more than that on this one surface are represented many forms of surfaces, and not otherwise than if this surface, which they work on with colors, were wholly transparent and so glass like that the entire visual pyramid passed through it" (Greenstein, 1997). Alberti goes on to suggest a method for constructing perspectively correct paintings involving "a veil ... set up between the eye and the object to be represented, so that the visual pyramid passes through the loose weave of the veil," with the painting copied from the image on the veil rather than the view of the three-dimensional object itself.

In his notebooks, Leonardo da Vinci (1566/1970) suggested a similar procedure for drawing a place accurately: "Have a piece of glass ... [placed] between your eye and the thing you want to draw. ... [W]ith a brush ... draw upon the glass that which you see beyond it."[1] Modern retellings of this technique presume that the light reaching the eye is unchanged if the glass is colored to exactly match the color of the world originally seen through the glass. A major goal of computer graphics can be thought of as producing the colored window without actually having the equivalent real-world view available.

In fact, however, the painted glass does not generate exactly the same light field as that emanating from the world seen through an empty frame instead of the glass. This has profound perceptual implications, partic-

---

[1] This idea is closely related to the *camera obscura*.

303

ularly for space perception. Views of display surfaces such as computer monitors, projection screens, photographs and other print media, and the "painted glass" described above—no matter how carefully constructed— differ from views of the real world in at least two important ways:

1. Critical depth cues to the structure represented in a displayed image are missing, and there is a conflation of spatial perception of graphical images on the display surface and of the display surface itself.

2. There is often a mismatch between the viewer's position relative to the display surface and the rendered viewpoint.

Vision scientists refer to the perception of images of the three-dimensional world, as opposed to the perception resulting from directly viewing the real world represented in those images, as *perception of pictorial space*, or sometimes *picture perception* (S. Rogers, 1995). While perception of pictorial space has received substantial theoretical and empirical study, the topic is only briefly covered in basic visual perception texts.

12.1   Missing and Conflicting Spatial Cues

> *[H]uman vision involuntarily strikes some kind of "compromise" between the* flatness *of the picture surface and the* relief *due to monocular cues.*
>
> —Koenderink, van Doorn, and Kappers (1994)

The term *pictorial information* refers to depth cues involving occlusion, shading, geometric perspective, and aerial perspective.[2] These are the sources of spatial information in a static image that can be utilized by a person viewing the image monocularly from a stationary viewpoint. Though not considered a pictorial cue in the perception literature, in the context of computer graphics, video, and film, object motion can be included in the discussion of pictorial cues as they relate to the perception of pictorial space. Unlike the real world, however, the nonpictorial cues of stereo, accommodation, and head-movement-induced motion parallax do not provide information for the spatial structure of the environment represented in the picture, but instead indicate the spatial structure of the surface on which the picture is drawn. The field of view captured in the picture is necessarily much less than the near-180° horizontal field of view of the human visual system. Viewing is passive, whereas in the real world vision is facilitated

---

[2]Note the confusion between the terms *pictorial perceptual cues* and *perception of pictorial space*. The first refers to the spatial information conveyed by a picture about the pictured space. The latter refers to the totality of the perceptual experience relating to spatial structure when viewing a picture.

by directed gaze and body motion. Spatial and temporal resolution and dynamic range in graphical media is typically significantly limited relative to the real world. Despite all this missing or restricted information, pictures and computer graphics displays can create a compelling sense of the three-dimensional spatial structure of a pictured space (Ames, 1925; Eaton, 1919; Koenderink, 1998; Koenderink et al., 1994; Schlosberg, 1941).

12.1.1   Conflicting Cues for Represented and Pictorial Surfaces

While stereo, accommodation, and head-movement-induced motion parallax do not contribute to the perception of the structure of the represented scene, they still function to provide depth information when viewing a picture. Stereo and head-movement-induced motion parallax exploit trigonometric constraints from multiple spatial (stereo) or temporal (motion parallax) viewing locations. They are sufficient for the unambiguous recovery of depth to a surface under view, if that surface is within the effective range of the cue and if there are distinct markings on the surface. Over sufficiently short ranges, accommodation might also provide information about surface depth. Importantly, for stereo and motion parallax it matters only that the surface be marked; the nature of the markings doesn't matter as long as they do not have a geometric structure leading to aperture ambiguity. Accommodation also does not depend on the nature of surface markings, as long as the markings are not blurred edges confusable with out-of-focus sharp edges. As a result, the information available from stereo, accommodation, and motion parallax is determined by the location of the physical display surface, not the depicted scene drawn on that display surface. The same is true for pictorial information for the location and orientation of the borders of the display surface, which also are unaffected by the pictorial information within the picture or display itself (Eby & Braunstein, 1995).

What, then, do people "see" when they look at a picture or image display? Stereo and head-movement-induced motion parallax provide the visual system with an indication of the true location of the display surface, independent of the nature of the picture drawn on that surface (as long as *some* picture is drawn on the surface). The pictorial cues conveyed by the picture itself provide the visual system with an indication of the relative location of whatever is being pictured, assuming that the picture is drawn in a perspectively correct manner. Almost never are these two classes of information for depth consistent with one another. Despite this, there is no strong subjective sense of multiple and incompatible surfaces under view. Rather, if a pattern drawn on the display surface has strong pictorial cues for three-dimensional shape, we usually see something close to that three-dimensional shape, unless we attend to the display surface itself, in which case we see the shape and location of that surface instead (see Polanyi, 1970).

This is not to say, however, that the pictured three-dimensional shapes are seen exactly as would be the corresponding real-world scene. Rather, the depths that are seen in such a situation tend to be somewhere between the depths indicated by the pictorial cues in the drawn pattern on the display surface and the distance to the display surface itself. When looking at a picture or computer display, this often results in a sense of scale smaller than intended, since the display surface is closer than the depicted objects. On the other hand, seeing a movie in a big-screen theater produces a more compelling sense of spaciousness than does seeing the same movie on television, even if the distance to the TV is such that the visual angles are the same, since the movie screen is farther away. In the case of big-screen movies, the depth cues to the distant screen make the depicted scene seem farther away than is the case with the nearer screen (Ames, 1925; T. L. Yang, Dixon, & Proffitt, 1999). If the angular extent is the same in both cases, big-screen viewing will produce a sense that the depicted objects are larger due to the size-distance relationship.

Figure 12.1 illustrates this effect. The figure shows the image of two pennies, one drawn at twice the size of the other. Alternately look with both eyes at the smaller penny on the left from a distance of about 35 cm ($13\frac{3}{4}$ inches) and the larger penny on the right from a distance twice as far away. It may help to cover whichever penny you are *not* looking at with one of your hands. Which drawing looks bigger? Almost everyone will say the right penny, which of course *is* larger. Note, though, that the ratio of drawn size to viewing distance in both cases is the same, making the visual angles the same. It is the size-distance relationship that makes

Figure 12.1

Alternately look with both eyes at the left image from a distance of 35 cm ($13\frac{3}{4}$ inches) and the right image from a distance of 70 cm ($27\frac{1}{2}$ inches), covering up the alternate image in each case. Which looks larger?

us "see" something close to the correct size and not confuse angular visual extent with actual distal extent. Exactly the same thing is happening with viewing a movie on a small-screen display versus a big-screen theater, except that the theater screen is beyond the effective range of stereo as an absolute distance cue, so the disparity between the appearance of size is not as great as it is for Figure 12.1 viewed from less than a meter away.

It has long been known that the sense of spaciousness in pictures increases when they are viewed with one eye closed (Ames, 1925; da Vinci, 1566/1970; Koenderink, 1998; Pirenne, 1970; Schlosberg, 1941). This is almost certainly due to the fact that monocular viewing removes the stereo cue for the flatness of the picture surface itself. By reducing this conflict with the pictorial information conveyed by the picture about the depicted scene, the pictorial information conveys a stronger sense of depth about the scene. The sense of depth can be further increased by looking at the picture through some sort of *viewing tube*. The viewing tubes used in perception experiments are positioned in a fixed location relative to the picture, so they not only restrict viewing to one eye but also eliminate head-motion-induced motion parallax. A similar effect can be achieved looking through a rolled-up piece of paper or even looking through a circle formed by your fingers, though in these cases some motion parallax information for the flatness of the picture is likely to be present. Most of the discussions of viewing tubes in the perception literature concentrate on the fact that they eliminate or reduce conflicting information about pictorial depth due to stereo and motion parallax. Another effect of viewing tubes is that they often hide the edges of the picture under view, thus eliminating cues for flatness due to the borders of the picture.

12.1.2   Reduced Field of View

In addition to missing and conflicting nonpictorial information for the spatial structure of pictured scenes, the field of view in pictures is usually significantly restricted compared to real-world viewing. Perspective information for depth involving inferences about vanishing lines and points requires a wide field of view so that the projection of parallel lines in the environment onto the picture plane results in lines in the picture with distinctly different orientations. Perspective information for depth directly or indirectly involving the size-distance relationship requires visible objects at distinctly different distances from the observer, which becomes less likely as the field of view is decreased.

Empirical evidence exists that reducing the field of view represented in a picture reduces perceived depth with both picture viewing and viewing of the real world (e.g., Hagen, Jones, & Reed, 1978). In the real world, the effect of restricting field of view on distance judgments to locations on the ground plane is greater if head motions are restricted (Creem-Regehr et al., 2005; Wu et al., 2004). It is not clear what the implications of this are for normal picture perception, since in picture perception the viewing direction associated with the pictured scene is fixed, but viewer head motion is not.

12.1.3   Limited Resolution and Dynamic Range

The brightness and dynamic range of light in the real world are impossible to re-create using any current display technology. Resolution of rendered images is also often less than the finest detail perceivable by human vision. Lightness and color constancy are much less apparent in pictures than in the real world, likely because the visual system attempts to compensate for variability in the brightness and color of the illumination based on the ambient illumination in the viewing environment rather than the illumination associated with the rendered image. This is why the realistic appearance of color in photographs depends on film color balanced for the nature of the light source present when the photograph was taken and why realistic color in digital photography and video requires a white-balancing step. While much is known about how limitations in resolution, brightness, and dynamic range affect the detectability of simple patterns, almost nothing is known about how these display properties affect spatial vision, recognition of material properties, or object identification.

12.2   Incorrect Viewpoint

A picture of objects in perspective will look more lifelike when seen from the point from which the objects were drawn.

—Leonardo da Vinci (1566/1970)

Confounding the analysis of perspective in pictorial perception is the fact that two perspective projections are involved: one associated with the original generation of the picture and the other associated with the viewing of the picture. The first of these is fixed at the time that the image is created. The second is dependent on the relationship between the viewer's location and the surface on which the picture is presented. Pictorial perception is like looking through Alberti's window only when the viewpoint with respect to the picture itself results in a projection on the retina equivalent to what would occur if the viewer were at the viewpoint from which the picture was generated.

12.2.1   Determining the Correct Location for Viewing a Picture

For reasons of conceptual and mathematical simplicity, we will assume that the picture and its view are both produced using planar projection.

In fact, some imaging devices (e.g., fish-eye lenses, various methods for creating panorama images) and painting styles (e.g., multiple perspective) involve other perspective models, and the human eye implements a distinctly nonplanar projection due to the curvature of the retina. As discussed in Chapter 7, planar projections are characterized by a center of projection (CoP) that can be thought of as a viewpoint location, a viewing direction and an image-plane orientation (the direction corresponding to "up" in the image), and a focal length. The center of projection of an acquired or synthesized image is sometimes referred to as the *station point* of the image (Sedgwick, 1980). All physically realizable planar-projection imaging devices also have an *image plane* of finite extent that can be characterized in terms of its physical size relative to the focal length or as an angular field of view.[3]

It is often said that a picture produced by perspective projection should be viewed from its center of projection in order for the viewing of the picture to produce a retinal image with equivalent geometric structure to the retinal image resulting for directly viewing the pictured scene. This is both confusing and, in one sense, partially incorrect. Conventional photographs are taken from a specific location in the real world, and so their center of projection is defined in that world. Perspectively correct paintings also have a viewpoint location (CoP) in the physical or imaginary world being depicted. Computer graphics generated using perspective projection have a viewpoint (CoP) located in the model being rendered. Of course, in all these cases the appropriate location for viewing the picture is defined with respect to the picture, not the real or virtual world depicted in the picture. In the case of paintings, the Alberti's-window metaphor leads directly to the fact that the preferred viewing location is the position relative to the canvas used as the vantage point when creating the painting. Things are not so simple for photographs, since the photograph under view will almost certainly be blown up from the image on the film plane and may be cropped as well, meaning that the geometry of patterns on the picture is not an exact match for the geometry originally imaged on the film plane. Computer graphics are even more complicated, since the "image plane" is virtual and can be specified in a variety of different ways depending on the software system used.

In an attempt to avoid contributing to this confusion, we will use the term *perspective-preserving pictorial viewpoint* (PPPV) to signify the viewpoint relative to the surface on which a picture appears that results in the

---

[3]Polar-coordinate representations of the light field at the point of projection have the advantage of eliminating the need to consider focal length or the limitations of a finite image plane. They also simplify the mathematics for a few—but only a few—computations that relate properties of the light field to the scene geometry that generated the light field. J. J. Gibson's (1979) concept of the *optic array* is one such polar representation.

depicted picture projecting to the same retinal image as would the original scene viewed at the CoP used to generate the picture. The key property of the perspective-preserving pictorial viewpoint in terms of pictorial depth cues is that it causes both relative and absolute visual angles to be preserved. The line of sight from the CoP used to generate the picture to any visible location, expressed in polar coordinates relative to the optical axis of the projection used to generate the picture, will be the same as the line of sight from the perspective-preserving pictorial viewpoint to the corresponding pictured location, relative to the optical axis of the projection characterizing how the picture is viewed.

The two perspective projections involved in pictorial perception each have an associated field of view, and they need not be the same. One of these is determined by the perspective-projection process involved in generating the picture and the extent of image plane onto which the external three-dimensional scene is projected. This is often referred to as the *geometric field of view*. A 35 mm film camera with a 50 mm lens results in a geometric field of view in the long orientation of the image of approximately 39.6°.[4] This value is independent of how the resulting picture is viewed, but is affected by cropping of the picture. The other field of view relevant to pictures and other displayed images specifies the viewing angle subtended by the borders of the picture or displayed image itself. In computer graphics, this is sometimes called the *display field of view*. The display field of view is solely a function of the picture size and the location of the viewer relative to the print or screen.

It is relatively straightforward to determine the geometrically optimal viewing position from which to observe a picture when the picture was created such that the image plane is perpendicular to and centered on the line of sight. In such circumstances, the pictorial cues in the picture related to perspective will be correct only if the picture is viewed from a position that is along a line going through the center of the picture and perpendicular to the picture surface, at a distance that makes the geometric and displayed fields of view the same. The analysis is far more tedious if the acquired or generated image is cropped off-center before display, or if the real or virtual image plane is not normal to the line of sight, as is often the case for head-tracked display systems (see Section 12.4).

It is useful to separate the effects of an incorrect viewing location into two categories. One considers viewing at a location along an axis with its origin at the center of the picture and oriented normal to the picture surface, but from a distance that does not match geometric and displayed

---

[4]Determining the geometric field of view for digital cameras is complicated by the fact that there is no standard image-plane size for these devices.

fields of view. The other involves viewing from a location not on the normal axis going through the picture center.

12.2.2   Incorrect Viewing Distance

Viewing a picture from a viewing distance that results in a display field of view larger than the geometric field of view will produce a magnified image. A display field of view smaller than the geometric field of view will produce a minified image. The former occurs when viewing from too close to the picture relative to the PPPV, the latter when viewing from too far away. Magnification and minification affect the visual information supporting relative and familiar size judgments, producing a multiplicative scaling of these depth cues with indicated depth inversely proportional to the increase in magnification. They can also affect perceived surface slant (see page 313) and thus affect depth judgments for objects in contact with the ground plane or another support surface. Figure 12.2 provides an example. The figure simulates viewing the same picture from two different viewing distances, with the image on the right showing the equivalent of half the viewing distance as the image on the left. Even in this simulation, to most viewers absolute distances in the right image look closer than distances to the same locations in the left image. Relative depths are also compressed in the image on the right compared to the left. If this were an actual picture viewed from two different viewing distances, distance perception to the pictorial surface would also affect distance perception to the pictured scene (see Section 12.1.1), further increasing the sense that locations on the nearer and projectively larger view were closer than for the more-distant and projectively smaller view.

Figure 12.2
Two views of the same picture: far viewing distance (left) and near viewing distance (right).

Figure 12.3

Wide-angle (left) and telephoto (right) view of the same scene as pictured in Figure 12.2.

The effect of picture viewing distance on perceived depth is related to the differences in perceived depth between wide-angle and telephoto images of the same scene, though the situations differ in one important respect. Figure 12.3 shows wide-angle and telephoto views of the same scene as depicted in Figure 12.2. In this case, the differences in the sense of absolute depth between the two images and the sense of depth compression in the right image compared to the left are even more striking. While the two images shown in Figure 12.2 differ only in 2D scale, the images shown in Figure 12.3 differ both in 2D scale and in geometric field of view. The wider

Figure 12.4

Manipulations of camera-object distances can strongly affect size perception in picture perception.

geometric field of view in the left image in Figure 12.3 provides additional perspective cues for the spaciousness of the scene.

Figure 12.4 shows what some might consider a practical application of this effect. The fish are the same in both pictures. The difference in apparent size comes about because the relative camera-object distances are manipulated in ways that are both inconsistent with the picture viewing distance and largely unnoticed because of the incomplete depth information that is available.

Controlled experiments confirm that magnification and minification affect people's distance judgments (e.g., Bengston, Stergios, Ward & Jester, 1980; Kuhl, Thompson, & Creem-Regehr, 2006; Lumsden, 1983; O. W. Smith, 1958) though the specific mechanism by which they operate is not known. Objects and locations in magnified views look closer than in minified views, though most experiments report that the magnitude of changes is less than the scale change between the two cases. Judgments of depth intervals are also compressed in magnified views compared with minified views. Magnification and minification of a picture change perspective cues for object shape, and—at least for rectilinear shapes—people seem to notice if the magnification or minification (or equivalently, viewing distance of the picture) does not correspond closely to the projection involved in creating the picture (Nicholls & Kennedy, 1993).

Magnification and minification, whether caused by changes in viewing distance to a picture or changes in the geometric field of view of the picture-generation process, can also change visual information for perspective-indicated surface horizons (the implied vanishing line) and thus affect judgments of surface slant (Farber & Rosinski, 1978; Lumsden, 1980; Sedgwick, 1991). Figure 12.5 illustrates the effect. Two views of the same wall are shown: the one on the left taken with a wide-angle lens and the one on the

Figure 12.5

Two views of a brick wall, both involving the same 45° slant of the wall relative to the viewing direction, with a wider-angle lens used for the left image than for the right (after Lumsden, 1980).

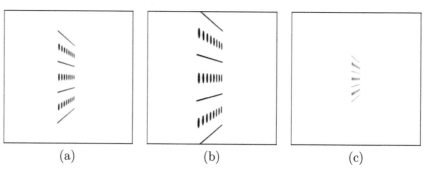

(a)   (b)   (c)

Figure 12.6

(a) A perspective-projection picture of a textured surface with its surface normal slanted away from the line of sight by 80°. (b) The picture shown in (a), magnified by 50%. (c) The picture shown in (a), minified to half its original size.

right taken with a telephoto lens. The viewing direction in both cases was 45° relative to the orientation of the wall. The perceived slant is noticeably greater in the wide-angle view than in the telephoto view. Magnification and minification do not affect visual cues for texture slant involving foreshortening.

Figure 12.6 provides an illustration of the mechanism underlying this effect and also shows how minification and magnification differentially affect perspective and foreshortening cues for surface slant. Figure 12.6(a) shows a computer-graphics-generated textured surface with an orientation of 80° to the line of sight. (The image was generated with a geometric field of view of 30° horizontally and vertically. Printed in this size, it is hard to get close enough to match this to the display field of view.) Figure 12.6(b) shows the image of the textured surface in Figure 12.6(a), magnified by 50%. This is equivalent to halving the viewing distance to Figure 12.6(a). Figure 12.6(c) shows the image of the textured surface in Figure 12.6(a), shrunk in size by 50%. This is equivalent to increasing the viewing distance to Figure 12.6(a) by a factor of 1.5.

The original textured surface contained three lines of circular dots. These have been foreshortened in all three images, but while the resulting ellipses have different sizes in the three views, they all have the same aspect ratio and so convey equivalent information about surface slant. The same is not true for the vanishing point implied by the projection of parallel lines in the original texture. Compared with Figure 12.6(a), the vanishing point is farther from the center of the picture in Figure 12.6(b) and closer to the center of the picture in Figure 12.6(c). For convenience in this example, the orientation of the parallel lines on the texture has been matched with the direction of tilt so that the lines of sight to the various vanishing points are indicators of the perspective-specified surface slant. In particular, the perspective information indicates that the surface in Figure 12.6(b) is less steeply slanted than the surface in Figure 12.6(a), while the surface in Figure 12.6(c) is more steeply slanted than the surface in Figure 12.6(a).

12.2.3 Off-Axis Viewing

Viewing a picture from a location not on the normal axis going through the picture center is variously characterized in terms of translating the viewing location parallel to the picture plane, or rotating the viewpoint around the center of the viewed image while keeping the viewing distance to the image center constant. Off-axis viewing can have a substantial effect on the visual information for surface slant. Figure 12.7(a) shows a picture of a textured surface tilted 40° to the right. Figure 12.7(b) shows the picture resulting from viewing the picture in Figure 12.7(a) from a location 40° to the left of center. The visual information indicates a steeper surface slant, but much less than the visual information for slant in Figure 12.7(c), which shows a picture of a textured surface tilted 80° to the right.

Figure 12.8 shows the effect of moving the viewpoint for viewing a picture in a direction perpendicular to the direction of surface slant in the picture. Figure 12.8(a) shows a picture of a textured surface tilted up by 40°. Figure 12.8(b) shows the picture resulting from viewing the picture in Figure 12.8(a) from a location 40° to the left of center. Figure 12.8(c) shows a picture of a textured surface tilted up by 40° and rotated to the right by 40°. Figures 12.8(b) and 12.8(c) show very different sorts of distortion compared to Figure 12.8(a).

While Figures 12.7 and 12.8 show that substantial changes in the visual cues for surface slant occur with off-axis viewing, one of the surprises in the

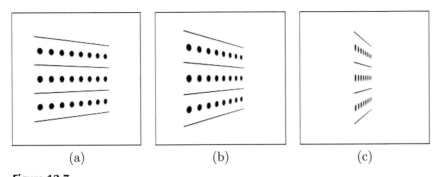

(a)   (b)   (c)

Figure 12.7

(a) A picture of a textured surface tilted 40° to the right. (b) A view of (a) from 40° to the left. (c) A picture of a textured surface tilted 80° to the right.

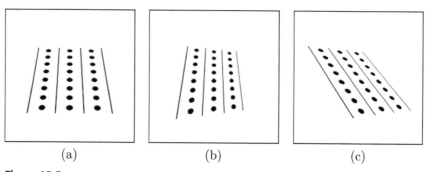

(a)   (b)   (c)

Figure 12.8

(a) A picture of a textured surface tilted up 40°. (b) A view of (a) from 40° to
the left. (c) A picture of a textured surface tilted up 40° and rotated to the right
by 40°.

perception of pictorial space is how little these are noticed in actual off-axis
viewing conditions. Figure 12.9 shows an example. Hold the upper image
in the figure at a distance so that it is twice as far from your eyes as the
width of the image, which will correspond to the PPPV for the geometric
field of view of the original photograph. Look at the upper picture with
the picture held perpendicular to the line of sight and with the picture
rotated 45° around the vertical axis such that the right edge is nearer. The
picture will look little different in either orientation, even though at the
45° orientation the retinal image is approximately that shown in the lower
image, which *does* look seriously distorted.

There is dispute about the degree to which off-axis viewing of a picture
results in a distorted perception of the scene depicted in the picture (see
S. Rogers, 1995). Also, different aspects of space perception seem to be
affected differentially by off-axis viewing (Goldstein, 1987). Nevertheless,
it is clear from viewing the top image in Figure 12.9 at various orientations that the visual system is less sensitive to the geometric distortions
that occur in such circumstances than would be predicted by a simple
analysis of the changes in projected image. Theories for why this is so
fall into one of three categories: insensitivity to the changes in projected
image, shape constancy, or compensation for the changes in projected
image.

The first of these potential explanations presumes that viewing is usually done from near the PPPV of the picture or displayed image, the resulting geometric distortions are small, and the human visual system is
inexact in its measurements of local geometry relative to spatial perception and so unaffected by these small distortions (Cutting, 1987). The
amount of distortion does in fact vary nonlinearly with the angle of off-axis

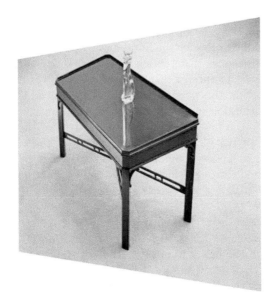

Figure 12.9
A picture with strong rectilinear structure, with a geometric field of view such
that the perspective-preserving pictorial viewing distance is twice the picture
width (above). An approximation to the retinal image resulting from viewing
the picture above from 45° to the side (below). (After Vishwanath et al., 2005.)

viewing, with most measures of the amount of change obeying something like a cosine law. However, the degree of off-axis viewing is often large, and the extreme changes in the projection of the top image in Figure 12.9 between straight-on viewing and viewing at a 45° angle argue against an account of insensitivity to viewing angle that depends on changes being small.

A second possibility is that the perceived shape of objects and spatial relationships in pictures viewed away from the PPPV is aided by familiarity with the shapes and expectations about the regularity and symmetry of the geometry (Busey, Brady, & Cutting, 1990; Wallach & Slaughter, 1988). Figure 12.9 can be used to provide evidence against this theory. Look at the upper image again from the same distance both straight ahead and rotated 45°, but now with one eye closed and the other eye looking through your circled forefinger or a rolled-up piece of paper. Under monocular viewing, the view of the figure tilted by 45° looks distorted, though unless you are very careful adjusting the viewing aperture, the apparent distortion will not be as great as shown in the lower image. The increase in perceived distortion under monocular viewing would not occur if the visual system were compensating for off-axis viewing based on familiarity with projected shapes and geometric relations.

A final class of theories for the limited perceptual effect of off-axis viewing of pictures presumes that the visual system is explicitly compensating for the slant of the picture or display surface. Some of these theories are based on extracting the perspective-preserving pictorial viewpoint from perspective information in the picture itself. Others involve using binocular disparity or the projected shape of the edges of the picture to infer the orientation of the pictorial surface relative to the viewer. The perceptual differences between binocular and monocular off-axis viewing of Figure 12.9 provide strong evidence that stereo vision plays an important role in compensating for the effects of viewing a picture from other than the ideal vantage point.

Vishwanath et al. (2005) describe an experiment that suggests that at least for slant perception, stereo-based compensation for off-axis viewing is done based on the orientation of the line of sight to each local area of interest, rather than based on some global recovery of the orientation of the display surface with respect to the viewer. This theory has an interesting corollary. Pictures created with a wide geometric field of view (typically greater than about 40°) often look distorted, even when viewed from the perspective-preserving pictorial viewpoint (Pirenne, 1970). Vishwanath et al. argue that this occurs because, for regions of the viewed picture far from its center, there is a substantial angle between the line of sight and the local surface normal, causing incorrect compensation as if viewing was off-axis.

12.2.4   Eye-Height Scaling

As indicated in Chapter 7, eye-height scaling is one of the few ways that
absolute (as opposed to relative) distance can be determined from visual
information. That chapter indicates that empirical evidence relevant to the
use of eye-height scaling in human visual perception is quite limited. This
sparseness of evidence does not mean that eye-height scaling is not used,
only that it remains largely an open question. Even less is known about the
effect, if any, of eye-height scaling on the perception of pictures. Photographers and cinematographers sometimes position their cameras at heights
distinctly different from normal standing eye height, but little controlled
experimentation has been done on how this quantitatively affects perception. Likewise, while the effect of off-axis viewing positions of pictures on
perception of slant and spatial organization has been studied, little is known
about how it affects perception of size. One study that has investigated
the effect of eye-height scaling on absolute size perception concluded that
eye-height scaling did not have an effect when participants were viewing a
desktop computer monitor (Dixon et al., 2000). It would be reasonable to
presume that the same is true when viewing a conventional picture, but it
is likely that the experiment remains to be done.

12.3   Is Picture Perception Learned?

One of the common questions asked by students in perception classes is
whether pictorial perception is learned or innate. Sometimes the question is asked with specific reference to line drawings (see J. J. Gibson,
1951), sometimes with respect to all pictorial depictions. A closely related
question is whether the perception of pictorial space involves mechanisms
distinct from the perception of the real world. Not surprisingly, this is a
difficult question to answer empirically, and much of the "evidence" supporting one particular position or another is anecdotal (see Miller, 1973).
There are, however, a number of reasonably well-controlled experiments
that shed light on the matter.

J. Hochberg and Brooks (1962) described an experiment in which, except for six "accidental" exceptions, for the first 19 months of one child's
life, the child was not allowed to see pictures. The child was then presented
with pictures of objects, including both photographs and line drawings. His
naming responses to these pictures were near perfect.[5]

Deregowski, Muldrow, and Muldrow (1972) reported on an experiment
in which members of the Me'en tribe in Ethiopia were shown pictures

---

[5] J. Hochberg and Brooks (1962) state: "The constant vigilance and improvisation
required of the parents proved to be a considerable chore from the start—further research
of this kind should not be undertaken lightly."

Figure 12.10

Two of the three pictures used in Deregowski et al. (1972) to explore picture recognition in a population unfamiliar with viewing pictures. (Courtesy of Pion Limited, London.)

printed in black ink on a type of cloth familiar to the participants. Figure 12.10 shows two of the three pictures that were used. Even though the participants had either very limited or no prior experience with pictures, their ability to describe the depicted animals and scenes was good, though significant time and effort was involved on their part. From this, Deregowski et al. drew the conclusion that pictorial perception is possible without prior experience, but is not as easily done as perception of the real world.

In a review article, Bovet and Vauclair (2000) argued that children as young as two or three months old are able to recognize what is depicted in a picture, but that prior exposure to pictures makes the task easier for both children and adults. The same article surveys an extensive collection of research articles on picture perception in animals ranging from nonhuman primates to guppies. Results on pictorial perception in animals are inconsistent, and this remains—at least partly—an open question. Importantly, Bovet and Vauclair emphasize that pictorial perception is not an all-or-nothing capability, but rather there are different aspects of picture perception that may be differentially affected by prior experience.

12.4   Issues Specific to Computer Graphics

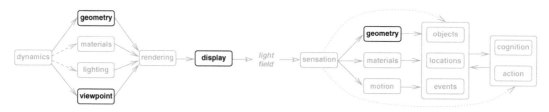

Computer-graphics-generated imagery is almost always presented on some sort of display surface, such as printed media, a computer monitor, or a projection screen. As a result, the perception of the scenes depicted in computer graphics generated imagery is subject to the same distortions involving missing and conflicting spatial cues and mismatched viewpoints as other pictorial media. There are, however, aspects of picture perception that are unique to computer graphics, either because of the flexibility provided by computer generation of images or because of the sorts of display devices commonly used to present computer graphics imagery.

12.4.1   Missing and Conflicting Spatial Cues

As with the viewing of other pictorial material, perception of the distance to the display surface and display frame will affect perception of distance to entities in the depicted scene. This is particularly true for images viewed on a computer monitor at normal viewing distances. At these distances, binocular stereo, motion parallax, and accommodation are all effective at indicating the distance to the display surface. The positioning of the display in the workspace also likely contributes to a sense of the display surface being close to the observer.

The subjective sense of spaciousness in a rendered scene viewed on a computer monitor can be increased by putting a frame in front of the monitor, with the frame sized such that it hides the frame of the monitor itself. Unlike the actual monitor frame, if this new frame is sufficiently far from the display surface it won't be perceived as part of that surface and so won't contribute to the confound between distance to the display and distance to the scene pictured on the display. This still leaves confounding information from stereo, but the effect is sufficiently beneficial that it is sometimes used in perception experiments presented on computer monitors.

The most direct way to reduce conflicting information for depth is to display the pictorial information in stereo. This requires that the viewer's eyes be presented with separate images that are appropriate to the slightly offset viewing positions associated with each eye. Chapter 6 describes a number of technologies that make this possible. A second and complementary way to reduce conflicting information for depth in computer graphics displays is to hide or remove visual information for the edge of the display surface and for the rest of the viewing environment other than the display surface—an approach known as *visual immersion*. Head-mounted displays (HMDs) do this using optics that create, with varying degrees of success, the sense of looking at the display surfaces through viewing tubes that are completely separate from the images being displayed. Alternately, projection screens can be arrayed around the viewer, filling the viewer's field of view. The best known of these surrounding screen displays is the CAVE (Cruz-Neira et al., 1993).

It is possible that the apparent distortion arising from viewing pictures displayed with a very wide field of view (Pirenne, 1970; Vishwanath et al., 2005) might be reduced by using curved display screens, since lines of sight toward the screen would be more closely normal to the screen orientation than is the case for flat screens far away from the center. While claims have been made about the perceptual superiority of curved screens, more study is required to know the importance of this effect.

12.4.2   Incorrect Viewpoint

Except in the case of computer generated films and other "artistic" uses of computer graphics, it is often the case that little concern is given to where to place the center of projection for rendering and how to adjust the viewing frustum. As a result, mismatches between the projection used to create an image and the retinal projection of that image from wherever it is actually viewed are common. In general, the center of projection for rendering should be chosen in a purposeful manner, with particular care that the eye height makes sense. The viewing frustum should be set so that the geometric field of view and the display field of view will be approximately matched. Matching the geometric and display fields of view is particularly important with HMDs, since mismatches are known to change distance perception (Kuhl, Thompson, & Creem-Regehr, 2006).

When viewing computer graphics displays, the visual system compensates for the effect of the perspective distortions due to off-axis viewing on perception of slant and shape in the same manner as for other types of pictures. Banks, Rose, Vishwanath, and Girshick (2005) offer the following advice, meant to be applicable to the choice of seating locations in a movie theater but applicable to many other viewing situations as well: "[A] binocular viewer, sitting sufficiently close to the screen to estimate its slant from disparity, will not experience noticeable distortions because of the ability to adjust for obliqueness of view. However, a variety of circumstances should make distortions due to viewing obliqueness noticeable: sitting at the edge of the theater such that slant of the movie screen exceeds 45°, or sitting obliquely and far from the screen such that slant from disparity is unreliable. Furthermore, viewers with deficient binocular vision are more likely to experience distortions from oblique viewpoints."

The recent reemergence of 3D movies and visualization systems may increase the sensitivity to viewing location. Under conventional viewing conditions, if the viewer is not sitting at the perspective-preserving pictorial viewpoint, information about the slant of the screen coming from binocular stereo and other sources helps preserve a near-correct perception of slant and shape. With 3D display devices, however, the stereo information now corresponds to the depicted scene, not the display surface. This may cause distorted slant and shape perception when sitting at other than the perspective-preserving pictorial viewpoint (R. T. Held & Banks, 2008).

Viewer movement presents special challenges for a computer graphics display system. If it is desired that viewer movement be accompanied by appropriate motion parallax, then a tracking system must be used to determine the viewer's head location and update the rendering center of projection. For head-mounted displays, viewing direction must also be tracked, something not required in screen-based displays. If a viewer moves while wearing a head-mounted display, the relationship between the center of projection of the rendered image and how the displayed image is viewed is unchanged, since the user is wearing the display. For screen-based systems, however, this relationship changes. Often, this is compensated for by warping the viewing frustum to account for off-axis viewing and changes in viewing distance to the screens. Whether or not this is a good idea depends in part on the level of visual immersion in the display, since other compensation mechanisms are active in nonimmersive viewing.

12.5   Suggestions for Further Reading

An excellent and comprehensive overview of issues relating to pictorial perception:

Rogers, S. (1995). Perceiving pictorial space. In W. Epstein & S. Rogers (Eds.), *Perception of space and motion* (pp. 119–163). San Deigo, CA: Academic Press.

A recent article covering compensation for off-axis viewing:

Vishwanath, D., Girshick, A. R., & Banks, M. S. (2005). Why pictures look right when viewed from the wrong place. *Nature Neuroscience, 8*(10), 1401–1410.

Two books covering older, but still relevant, work on the perception of pictorial space:

Pirenne, M. H. (1970). *Optics, painting & photography.* Cambridge, UK: Cambridge University Press.

Hagen, M. A. (Ed.). (1980). *The perception of pictures I: Alberti's window: The projective model of pictures.* New York: Academic Press.

IV

Perception of Higher-Level Entities

13

Spatial Orientation and Spatial Cognition

Consider the task of exploring a new city by foot. As you view the surroundings and walk on the streets, you receive many sources of information for where you are in the environment, but still may find it difficult to find your way back to your hotel. *Spatial orientation* is a term describing humans' understanding about where they are positioned and oriented relative to objects in their environment (Rieser, 1999) and is critical for everyday spatial goals of navigating and acting in one's environment. Staying oriented requires the use of reference systems often referred to as *spatial frames of reference*. A spatial frame of reference is a means of representing locations relative to some spatial framework. The *egocentric* reference frame defines locations relative to the viewer and may be further subdivided into spatial relations with respect to the viewer's body parts, such as eye, head, and body coordinate systems. The *allocentric/exocentric* reference frame defines relationships relative to something other than the viewer. This includes *object-relative* judgments based on the intrinsic coordinate system of the object or the relation between two objects, and the *environment-centered*, or *geocentric*, reference frame defining spatial relations with respect to features of the environment, such as up/down with respect to gravity, magnetic compass directions, and landmarks. Broadly, *spatial cognition* includes the acquisition, manipulation, and representation of knowledge about spatial objects and environments.

13.1   Divisions and Information for Space Perception

One way to characterize the spatial environment is through divisions of
space that differentiate between graded egocentric regions that extend from
a viewer's near to far. Cutting and Vishton (1995) defined three regions
of space in the context of relevant cues for distance perception (see Figure 13.1 for two of the three). According to this classification, *personal
space* is the area that extends just out to approximately two meters beyond the viewer. Within this space close to the observer, "primary depth
cues" of binocular disparity, accommodation, and convergence are most
informative, along with depth information from occlusion and relative size.
Action space extends from the boundary of personal space to approximately
30 meters, distances over which one could act (such as walk, throw, etc.)
over a short time frame. The effectiveness of the primary depth cues is
reduced, leading to more reliance on occlusion, relative size, familiar size,
and motion parallax, as well as the related cues of linear perspective, height
in the field, and horizon ratio. *Vista space* extends out beyond 30 meters,
where pictorial cues of aerial perspective and texture gradient gain importance. Distance perception within personal and action space has been
studied extensively, whereas much less work has investigated perception

(a)   (b)

Figure 13.1

Defining regions of space with respect to distance from the observer. (a) Personal
space. (b) Action space.

of vista spaces. A recent study suggests that vista space may be further subdivided into near vista space—up to about 75 meters, which appears to be perceptually compressed—and farther vista space, in which distances tend to be perceived as farther than the actual distance (Daum & Hecht, 2009).

The validity of the distance-cue-defined divisions of space is reinforced by converging ideas of spatial divisions into near and far that are based on mostly neuropsychological models. These models have defined *periper-sonal* and *extrapersonal* spaces, functionally specified as the space within reach of the viewer versus the space beyond what is reachable (Grusser, 1983; Previc, 1998). Recent work has suggested that the boundary between peripersonal and extrapersonal space is malleable and may be influenced by manipulations of one's own representation of the body. For example, some neuropsychological patients with spatial neglect show a lack of aware-ness of the left side of space specific to their own reachable space. Berti and Frassinetti (2000) showed that when a neglect patient used a handheld wand that extended their reachable space, the space of neglect was also ex-tended. A related finding showed that when healthy adults extended their reach with a tool, their subsequent distance judgments changed, suggesting that distance perception is scaled to the body's ability to act (Witt, Prof-fitt, & Epstein, 2005). Other models of spatial thinking also support this concept of multiple spaces defined around the body. Tversky (2003) cate-gorized space of the body as the understanding of positions and relations of body parts, space around the body as the space within which one can immediately see and reach things, and space of navigation as space that is explored and too large to see all at once.

13.2   Distance Perception and Ways to Measure It

As is clear from the previous chapters in this book, there are many sources of information available for depth perception that contribute to a repre-sentation of spatial layout. Much of the history of visual space perception involves the use of psychophysical methods to measure visually perceived space to map the correspondence between physical properties and percep-tual experience. Some approaches use controlled, reduced-cue settings in order to define the information and mechanisms used in distance percep-tion (Gogel, 1990; Sedgwick, 1986). The advantage of this methodological approach is that single sources of information may be isolated and their importance for space perception determined. Other approaches use full-cue settings (Loomis, Silva, Fujita, & Fukusima, 1992), which allow for more-naturalistic spatial environments that may more easily generalize to realistic visual-perception processes.

Determining the best way to evaluate distance perception is quite difficult, given that there is no direct way to measure what someone "sees." Estimates of distance can be made in multiple ways, and an analysis of the measures and the behavioral outcomes is important to consider. Distance measures can be concerned with absolute distances, reflecting a metric scale of the space (e.g., three meters); relative distances, specified as comparisons with other locations (e.g., location X is twice as far as location Y); or ordinal distances, which reflect depth ordering—but not the magnitude of the difference—between two locations.

Traditionally, magnitude estimation and verbal judgments have been used to assess the scaling of egocentric distance (Da Silva, 1985). Magnitude estimations involve the observer giving a number as a response about distance in the context of a standard stimulus that is presented. The standard could be a metric unit (such as 30 m) or an arbitrary unit (such as 10). Verbal reports require the observer to give a metric number about the absolute distance, sometimes also in the context of a reference unit. Other types of judgments about distance have involved bisection tasks—in which the viewer sets an indicator to mark the center of an interval, or matching tasks—in which an interval in one plane is matched to an interval in another plane.

It has been established over many investigations that egocentric absolute distance judgments made by stationary observers within action space are fit well by linear functions, although the slope of the function varies as a function of the type of distance estimation. When verbal reports are used, the average slope is about .80, suggesting some response compression, whereas estimations by visually directed actions (discussed below) tend to show slopes closer to 1.0 (Loomis & Philbeck, 2008). However, after about a century of research on distance perception, it still remains an important and open question of what sources of information are used for distance perception and how they are combined (Cutting & Vishton, 1995), and whether visual space perception is "veridical" or correctly perceived (Loomis et al., 1992). Loomis et al. (1992) present two criteria for evaluating the veridicality of space perception. The first is the linearity of the function relating perceived absolute distance to physical distance. The second is the perceptual equality of equal physical intervals. It has been suggested that this second criteria has not been upheld from experiments comparing intervals in the frontal and sagittal (depth) planes (Loomis et al., 1992; Toye, 1986; Wagner, 1985). A depth foreshortening has been well established, with frontal intervals appearing larger than sagittal ones (Wagner, 1985), as indicated by an interval matching task. Interestingly, this is not a function of the distinction between indication of egocentric and exocentric intervals per se. Philbeck, O'Leary, and Lew (2004) examined a walking-based measure of exocentric distances and found no depth foreshortening, compared to the large amount of depth compression of ex-ocentric extents found in verbal reports or frontal matching.

Several concerns about increased variability and cognitive biases result-ing from instructions and expectations have been raised in the context of verbal reports and magnitude estimations. One particular issue is how to instruct participants to indicate their perception of space. Researchers have used instructions that include "apparent" or "phenomenal" versus "objec-tive" or "physical," but it is not clear that this eliminates the intrusion of cognitive factors (Carlson, 1977). Measuring distance perception with more indirect measures could help to avoid the problem of expectations (Loomis & Philbeck, 2008). Indirect measures take advantage of the co-variations of perceptual variables, known as *percept-percept couplings*. For example, the relationship between size and distance is such that perceived size s can be computed based on angular size θ and perceived distance d: $s \approx 2d \tan(\theta/2)$ (see Section 7.3). Thus, judgments of size can reflect an observer's perceived distance and may be a useful way to indirectly reveal perceived distance while avoiding confounds and/or variability associated with knowledge or expectations. However, a different theoretical account of size perception suggests that size can be directly perceived (J. J. Gibson, 1950b) and that no mediating perceptions, such as perceived distance, are necessary. In support of this, it has been found that a manipulation of eye height that influenced aperture size judgments did not influence perceived distance (Warren & Whang, 1987).

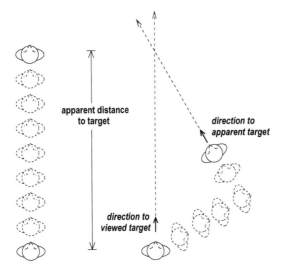

Figure 13.2

Two versions of visually directed walking tasks: direct and indirect blind walking.

An alternative, and now dominant, way of measuring distance perception is through *visually/perceptually directed action* (see Figure 13.2). It has been well established over the last 20 years that observers are very good at walking to previously viewed target locations without vision to distances of about 20 meters. In contrast to other measures described above, people show a remarkable accuracy at this *blind walking* task with little systematic bias in full-cue environments (Loomis et al., 1992; Rieser, Ashmead, Talor, & Youngquist, 1990; Thomson, 1983). In this task, observers view a target stimulus in the environment, close their eyes (usually with a blindfold), and walk to the target location. It is generally believed that viewers update their self-location with respect to the environment as they walk with eyes closed. In other words, during blind walking they keep track of the changing representation of the environment with respect to their own body location. This claim is further supported by the performance seen in triangulation tasks, in which an indirect path of locomotion to the target is required. For example, in *triangulation by walking*, the observer walks on an oblique path and, at a signal, turns and walks a couple of steps in the direction of the target. The direction of walking is used to triangulate the perceived location of the target. A version of this task called *indirect walking* requires the viewer to turn and walk all the way to the target location. In another variation, *triangulation by pointing*, an observer points to the target either during or after walking along a path away from the target. The general accuracy of these tasks, despite their unpredictability in path of movement, suggests that viewers are able to maintain and update their spatial orientation with dynamic movement (see Section 13.3).

13.3   Dynamic Spatial Orientation

How is it that we are able to keep track of locations in space as we move, or as objects move, and maintain the representation of a stable world? There are multiple sources of information that allow for *spatial updating*—the process of updating representations of locations in the environment with respect to the self. Often, dichotomies of terms are described to reflect the types of cues or sources of information specifying self-movement. Taken from the nonhuman animal literature on navigation, *allothetic* refers to external information for spatial orientation, including visual, auditory, olfactory, or tactile cues for spatial position. *Ideothetic*, or internal, information includes efference from the motor system's intended act, afference feeding back from the joints and muscles, and vestibular signals associated with linear and angular accelerations. Spatial updating may be position based, relying on landmarks or other environmental cues. Updating may also rely on *path integration*—the process of integrating velocity- or acceleration-based signals for self-motion from allothetic (such as visual flow) and ideothetic sources, to estimate current self-position and orientation (Loomis, Klatzky, Golledge, & Philbeck, 1999; Mittelstaedt & Mittelstaedt, 1982). Path integration is often tested with a return-to-origin task, in which the observer is led blindfolded along an outbound path of a typically small number of segments and turns and is then asked to turn and walk back to the origin of the path without any additional information from environmental cues (e.g., Klatzky et al., 1990). Although some animals, such as rodents, are very skilled at path integration, humans typically show large errors when navigating by path integration alone (see Loomis et al. (1999) for further analysis of error patterns).

The imprecise return-to-origin performance seen in typical human path-integration tasks stands in contrast to the generally accurate visually directed action tasks described in Section 13.2, where locomotion also occurs without visual feedback. A difference is the nature of the visually directed task, based on an initial perception of target location within an environment and the viewers' goal to update their mental representation of their own self-position with respect to the remembered environment. Rieser (1999) outlines a theory of dynamic spatial orientation that accounts for the abilities of humans to maintain their spatial orientation while walking without vision. Intuitively, observers learn over time the consistent covariation between their actions and their perception of the environment as they navigate through space. For example, as you walk along a straight path given a certain pace, there is a consistent, corresponding environmental flow (visual, or other sensory) that moves by you. Forward walking results in translations in perspective, and turning your head and body results in rotations in perspective (in the opposite direction). We rely on this perception-action coupling even when "perception" of environmental information is absent (i.e., when one's eyes are closed). Thus, one's eyes-closed representation of the environment is updated with self-movement corresponding to the learned perception-action relationship.

Empirical studies have shown evidence for this claim using an adaptation paradigm that tested blind walking to targets before and after an intervention that manipulated the coupling between walking and visual flow (Pick, Rieser, Wagner, & Garing, 1999; Rieser, Pick, Ashmead, & Garing, 1995). Rieser et al. (1995) created a mismatch between visual and biomechanical information for self-movement by having observers walk on a gym treadmill that was pulled by a tractor at a rate either faster or slower than their rate of walking. The effect was a *recalibration of locomotion*, in which post-test blind walking behavior was changed relative to the pre-test. After experiencing a visually faster condition, observers then stopped short of the target when walking without vision. The visually slower condition similarly led to an overshoot of the target distance. These, and other related results (Durgin et al., 2005; Kuhl, Creem-Regehr, & Thompson, 2008; Mohler et al., 2007), suggest that the blind walking task is performed by spatially updating one's representation of the environment in a way that is calibrated by one's perception of self-motion. Perception of self-motion can be informed by multisensory information, including vision and audition, proprioception (limb position), and vestibular (acceleration) and motor signals.

13.4   Perceptual Adaptation

The compelling findings resulting from the calibration-of-locomotion research show how adaptable humans are. Perceptual adaptation is a change in perception or perceptual-motor coordination that occurs as a result of discrepancies between different sensory modalities (Welch, 1986). These effects can be distinguished from sensory adaptation effects, which are short-lived and result from prolonged normal sensory stimulation from a single modality. Sensory adaptation is experienced as a reduction of intensity of a stimulus feature, such as color, orientation, or motion, because of fatigue of specific sensory neurons. It is also associated with the experience of perception of an "opposite" feature. For example, after fixating on a leftward-oriented line, a vertical line will be perceived as oriented to the right.

A classic example of perceptual adaptation is the change in perceptual-motor behavior seen from viewing and acting on the world through prisms. When viewing an object through prisms that shift the visible world laterally, one's reach toward that object with eyes closed will show an error corresponding to the discrepancy between the visual and actual location of the target. Practice with eyes open reaching to the target will quickly reduce the error, demonstrating the *reduction effect*. Furthermore, once adaptation has occurred, removing the prisms will lead to reaching errors in the opposite direction, demonstrating the *negative aftereffect*. This negative aftereffect is considered strong evidence that perceptual adaptation has occurred, since it cannot be explained by conscious correction of an action.

It is a difficult and important question to consider what is actually adapting in these types of scenarios—visual experience or motor movements? Some well-known "self-experiments" were conducted by G. M. Stratton (1896) and later Kohler (1962), in which the experimenters wore inverting (180° displacement) prisms for about a week and noted their perceptual experiences of adaptation. While their behavior improved dramatically over days—showing impressive performance on complex tasks such as reading, writing, and walking—it is not clear that they ever *experienced* a right-side-up world, although subjective statements do indicate that the world sometimes "looked correct." Furthermore, there are many examples of the related phenomenon of *visual capture*, suggesting the powerful effect of visual information on felt position of the body. In conditions in which a person's visual and proprioceptive information for limb position are in conflict, after a brief interval of limb movement the experience of felt limb position corresponds to the visual, rather than proprioceptive, position of the limb (Hay, Pick, & Ikeda, 1965).

The experimental paradigm developed by von Helmholtz (1878/1925) creates situations in which observers are tested on a perceptual response, then exposed to some *rearrangement* period, and then tested again on the same perceptual response. Much subsequent research using wedge prisms followed this paradigm to establish and test the parameters involved in the adaptation process to lateral shifts in the visual world (R. Held & Freedman, 1963; R. Held, Efstathiou, & Greene, 1966). These studies found that the negative aftereffect (1) is a negatively accelerating function with time that asymptotes after about 35 trials, (2) transfers across hands and eyes in some circumstances, (3) is inhibited by delays of feedback, and (4) is facilitated by active movement but can occur when limbs are passively moved during the rearrangement period as well. (See Welch, 1986, for more in-depth presentation of experimental findings). What do these patterns of results say about the visual-experience-versus-motor-response question? While there are purely visual effects associated with wearing prisms, it is generally believed that these types of negative aftereffects are due to the pairing and relearning of visual motor relationships and are best obtained and revealed through active motor responses. However, the fact that adaptation effects sometimes generalize beyond the specific eye or limb that is adapted suggests broader adaptation of visual space perception that may be tied to perceived head or eye position (C. S. Harris, 1980). We further consider these points about generalization of adaptation effects in Section 13.9.

13.5 Imagery and Spatial Transformations

Abilities involving mental imagery extend beyond the processes of online spatial updating during walking, as described in Section 13.4, to include both object-based and egocentric mental transformations of space. These processes are thought to underlie many common activities, such as action planning, object recognition, spatial reasoning, and problem solving. Most individuals find it quite easy to imagine vivid visual images of objects (e.g., a dalmatian) or spaces (e.g., the layout of your bedroom). Phenomenologically, the experience is one of a "picture in the head," and the problem

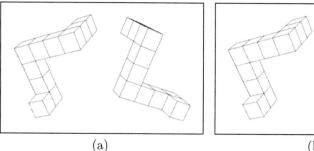 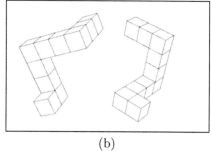

(a)   (b)

Figure 13.3

Figures similar to those used by Shepard and Metzler (1971). (a) Objects are
the same except for rotation. (b) Objects are different.

facing psychologists for many years has been to define the representations
that give rise to this experience.

The central debate that emerged in the 1970s was whether visual mental images are "special" in the sense that they are supported by pictorial
representations, different from languagelike descriptions (Kosslyn, 1994).
One side of the argument suggested that the representations of visual images are *analog*, or isomorphic, meaning that they preserve the visual-
spatial relations of the real stimulus. The *propositional* side of the argument posited that although we may have the mental experience of images,
there is no need to consider an explanation that differs from an abstract
proposition (Pylyshyn, 1973). While there is still some form of the debate
today (Pylyshyn, 2003), there is much evidence from cognitive and more
recent functional neuroimaging approaches in support of the analog model
(Kosslyn, 1994).

The study of mental transformations, specifically the task of *mental rotation*, provided initial support for the analog, picture-metaphor theory of
imagery. Shepard and Metzler (1971) created stimuli of three-dimensional
objects made out of cube figures (see Figure 13.3). Pairs of these rotated
objects were presented to an observer, who was asked to determine whether
the objects were identical or mirror images. This is considered an object-
based transformation in which spatial orientation is represented relative
to intrinsic axes of the object. Response time to determine whether the
pairs were the "same" or "different" was measured. The findings were
striking, showing a remarkably systematic linear increase in response time
with increasing angular difference, analogous to a physical rotation of the
object in space. This monotonic rotation function was upheld for rotations
in the picture plane and in depth. Since then, many studies have examined the processes involved in mental rotation using two-dimensional and

three-dimensional objects (Just & Carpenter, 1985; Pani & Dupree, 1994; Shepard & Cooper, 1986), as well as hands, feet, and bodies (Parsons, 1987a, 1987b, 1994). (See Section 13.5.1 for discussion of egocentric transformations.) Other forms of object-based imagery tasks require inspection of images. The logic is that if images have analog properties, then the time required to inspect or *mentally scan* across the image should vary as a function of the properties of the image. Several well-known studies demonstrated this predicted pattern of response time, requiring observers to learn a simple map and then imagine moving from one point to another along the map (Kosslyn, Ball, & Reiser, 1978). For example, the participant is told to imagine a spot on the map moving from the "tree" to the "rock." Response times increased with the distance of the path required. Together, object rotation and translation task performance suggests that mental images are represented in a way that preserves the functional relationships of 3D space. They are not really pictures in the head but are represented in an analogous way.

13.5.1   Object-Based versus Viewer-Based Transformations

It is useful to return to the notion of reference frames in comparing the abilities and processes involved in imagined spatial transformations (Wraga, Creem, & Proffitt, 1999; Zacks & Michelon, 2005). In an object-based transformation, as described above, the reference frame of the object moves relative to a stationary, egocentric reference frame and environmental reference frame. An egocentric, or viewer-based, transformation involves the transformation of the body (or part of the body) relative to stationary objects and environmental reference frames.

   The ability to imagine egocentric transformations may specifically facilitate planning of actions and predicting or understanding others' behavior. Experiments using pictures of body parts, such as hands and feet, have demonstrated that individuals rely on representations of their own bodies to solve tasks involving orientation decisions. Pictorial representations of rotated hands were presented to observers, who were asked to judge whether the image presented was a right or left hand (see Figure 13.4). Response times for indicating the decision were highly correlated with the time required to explicitly imagine a limb movement. Both the handedness judgment and the imagined limb movement were related to ratings about how awkward it was to move into a given limb orientation and to the time required to physically move to a given hand position (Parsons, 1987b, 1994). Results such as these suggest that the *body schema*, including knowledge of body-part relations and dynamic representations of body position, influences mental transformations of some types of objects.

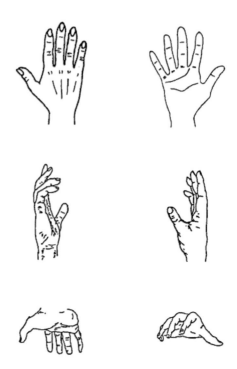

Figure 13.4

Pictorial representations of rotated hands, presented to observers for judgments about whether the image represented a right or left hand. (From Parsons, L. M., 1994, Temporal and kinematic properties of motor behavior reflected in mentally simulated action, *Journal of Experimental Psychology: Human Perception and Performance, 20*, 709–730; Reprinted with permission from the American Psychological Association.)

Related work has examined the question of how individuals spatially update the locations of objects or parts of objects within an environment after imagined spatial transformations, and whether there are differences in imagining changes in layout given object-based and viewer-based transformations. Given an object or array of objects, consider two possibilities for representing a changing layout relative to the viewer. One could imagine a viewer-based transformation, in which an observer imagines a change in their own perspective. For example, imagine that you are giving directions to a friend who is facing you, and you describe the route from their facing direction instead of your own. Alternatively, one could imagine an object-based transformation, in which the object rotates and the observer's viewing direction/position remains constant. Several lines of research have suggested that while different imagined transformations share

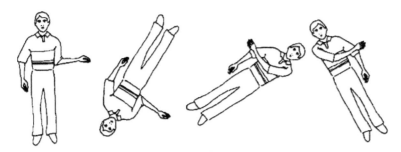

Figure 13.5

Examples of same-different and left-right tasks with body figures. (Reprinted with permission from Zacks, J., Mires, J. Tversky, B., & Hazeltine, E., 2002, Mental spatial transformations of objects and perspective, *Spatial Cognition and Computation, 2*, 315–322; © 2002 Elsevier.)

similar spatial-processing resources, there are some important distinctions both in behavior and in the neural mechanisms proposed to support behavior (Zacks & Michelon, 2005). Presented with the task of naming an object in a given location after a specified imagined transformation, observers are better (revealed through faster and more accurate responses) given viewer-based versus object-based transformations (Simons & Wang, 1998; Wraga, Creem, & Proffitt, 2000). Distinct from the body-part transformations described above, perspective transformations involving changes in viewing direction appear less constrained by biomechanical movement constraints or the possibility of actual movement (Creem, Wraga, & Proffitt, 2001; Creem-Regehr, Neil, & Yeh, 2007). However, there is an advantage for perspective transformations when they are tied to rotations around the viewer's principal axis, perpendicular to the ground plane (Creem et al., 2001).

There is also an apparent flexibility in the ability to choose and use reference frames in spatial-transformation tasks. One example of this is a paradigm that presented line drawings of several human bodies, each with one hand outstretched (see Figure 13.5) and required two types of spatial judgments: a same-different judgment determining whether the two figures presented were the same (only rotated), and a left-right judgment asking whether the figure's extended hand was a left or right hand (Zacks, Mires, Tversky, & Hazeltine, 2002; Zacks, Rypma, Gabrieli, Tversky, & Glover, 1999). Distinct behavioral performance was found for the two tasks. The same-different task showed a monotonic increase in response time with increasing orientation disparity, following earlier object-based mental rotation tasks. In contrast, the handedness-decision task showed a flat response time function, attributed to a viewer-based transformation of the body used to solve the task. Other work has manipulated the strategies used to mentally rotate non-body figures, showing that performance and brain-activation patterns are dependent on the strategies learned (Kosslyn, Thompson, Wraga, & Alpert, 2001; Wraga, Thompson, Alpert, & Kosslyn, 2003).

Finally, there are differences to consider between translational and rotational transformations. Computationally, updating one's spatial location during translational movement requires information about distances to environmental locations; spatial updating during rotational movement does not. The reason for this is that the angular velocity of the view of distant locations during translational motion is a function of distance, with the viewing directions to locations farther away rotating more slowly relative to the direction of heading than the view of nearer locations. For rotations, on the other hand, changes in the pointing direction to distant locations is only a function of the amount of rotation that the viewer undergoes. Paradoxically, in terms of behavioral performance, people generally show greater difficulty in spatial updating of the location of objects during rotation compared to translation, particularly when information for self-movement is not provided (see Section 13.5.2).

13.5.2   The Role of Physical Movement

While humans clearly have the ability to imagine spatial transformations, the ability to physically move in space has important consequences for understanding spatial layout (Creem-Regehr, 2004). Research that has directly compared imagined and real movements in the context of spatial updating typically claims that automatic updating of spatial locations occurs with self-movement, leading to more efficient and superior performance. In these types of tasks, an observer learns a layout of objects and then is asked to physically face a new direction or to remain stationary but imagine the same transformation, and subsequent memory for the object location is tested with an eyes-closed pointing measure. Particularly for rotational self-movement, additional time was needed for the imagined movement, and the time increased as a function of the amount of rotation required (Rieser, 1989). Similar to the imagined movement results, the importance of physical self-movement is seen in situations in which visual information for self-movement is provided without corresponding vestibular, proprioceptive, or efferent information from the body. This can be done by using virtual environments in which optic flow patterns are manipulated so that an observer may navigate through an environment with a control device, such as a joystick, while physically maintaining the same location or viewing direction (Chance, Gaunet, Beall, & Loomis, 1998; Klatzky, Loomis, Beall, Chance, & Golledge, 1998). Notably, virtual environment conditions that do not allow for physical turning of the body have led to large systematic errors in spatial updating.

An important role for physical self-movement in spatial transformations has also been demonstrated in situations in which physical movement influences the process of mental rotation. The physical rotation of a knob or joystick during an object mental rotation task facilitates performance when the direction of physical rotation is compatible with the mental-rotation direction compared to when they are incompatible directions (Wexler, Kosslyn, & Berthoz, 1998; Wohlschläger & Wohlschläager, 1998). These types of findings have implications for the level of motor processing involved in mental transformations and ways that physical interaction might aid in visualization applications in which object-orientation decisions are required.

13.6   Spatial Knowledge and Memory

While many of the concepts of spatial orientation described so far in this chapter seem to deal with more transient or "online" types of spatial processing, we must also consider the important role of long-term spatial memory. For example, how do you remember the location where you parked your car earlier in the day or the location of a particular building on campus? These types of questions rely on *spatial knowledge*, defined as a representation of the environment in memory and a hypothetical multidimensional construct (Golledge, 1999). Spatial knowledge is created by integrating different sources (visual, motor, kinesthetic) of information as well as higher-level goals of the observer (Gallistel, 1990; Gillner & Mallot, 1998). Intuitively, it is difficult to describe memory for spatial locations without adopting a frame of reference. The building may be specified with respect to the observer (e.g., in front of me), other buildings (e.g., between the library and the bookstore), or the campus (e.g., at the northwest corner).

Critical to learning and memory for locations is a spatial reference system (Bryant, Tversky, & Franklin, 1992; McNamara, 2003). McNamara proposes that an environment has an intrinsic structure, such as the layout of buildings with respect to each other, that is encoded by establishing a spatial reference system. This reference vector, providing a dominant orientation of the environment, is influenced by a number of different cues, such as egocentric experience (e.g., how the environment was first viewed), the extrinsic structure or shape of the environment, and intrinsic properties of the objects themselves within the environment. The use of a spatial reference system leads to orientation-dependent memory representations with the initial learning position as a dominant. Many studies have supported this general notion, typically testing people's memory of a previously learned layout with a task called *judgment of relative direction* (JRD), in which observers are asked to imagine themselves at a given object location and adjust a pointer on a dial, typically presented on a computer screen to point to another named object. For example, instructions might be given to "Imagine you are standing at the shoe facing the lamp. Point to the clock" (see Figure 13.6). Earlier work demonstrated dominance of the experienced viewpoint on spatial memory, similar to the viewpoint dependency seen in object recognition. In other words, people were faster to respond—and more accurate—when their imagined facing direction at test was parallel to the learned view of the environment than when tested at an unfamiliar view (Shelton & McNamara, 1997). More-recent work has shown an interaction between the reference frame of the viewer's initial viewing position and the shape of the environmental layout. Facilitated responses were found only when the observer's learning perspective was aligned with the environment's dominant long axis (Shelton & McNamara, 2001). Furthermore, studies have found a combined influence of egocentric perspective and the environment's intrinsic structure, such as the symmetrical structure of a layout of objects, or instructions to group the objects in a certain way (Mou & McNamara, 2002; Mou, Zhao, & McNamara, 2007). Given that real-world environments often have features that provide both extrinsic and intrinsic structures, there have been investigations of memory

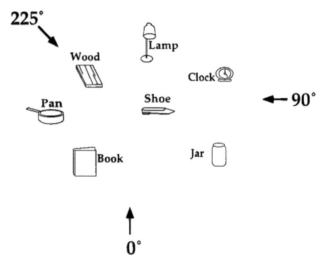

Figure 13.6

Schematic drawing of JRD test of spatial memory. (Reprinted with permission from Shelton, A. L., & McNamara, T. P., 2001, Systems of spatial reference in human memory, *Cognitive Psychology*, *43*(4), 274–310; © 2001 Elsevier.)

performance when these reference systems are put in conflict (J. W. Kelly & McNamara, 2008). In these circumstances, spatial memories are shown to be influenced by the initial egocentric viewpoint, with no influence of the other spatial frameworks. Thus, when viewing an environment, egocentric experience appears to be a strong influence on the reference system relied on in spatial memory.

13.6.1   Learning and Representing Spatial Environments

The paradigm described above to test spatial memory focuses on one way to learn the spatial layout of an environment: viewing it from single or multiple perspectives. Broadly we may think about learning an environment through (1) ground-level experience traveling in that environment or (2) a "bird's-eye" overhead perspective or symbolic model, such as a map. This distinction is referred to as route-based versus survey knowledge, respectively (Golledge, 1999). Route learning involves learning through a sequence of actions, updating segments and angles of a desired path. A global structure of the space may be formed by integrating specific routes, features, and landmarks from different experiences. Survey learning relies on a perspective that is external to the space from a fixed orientation, providing more-direct access to global or configurational structure of the space (Shelton & McNamara, 2004). Siegel and White (1975) proposed a classic framework for acquiring spatial knowledge that involves a progression of stages from (1) knowledge about discrete landmarks to (2) route knowledge based on sequences of landmarks to (3) metrically scaled, integrated survey knowledge. It has been shown more recently that the acquisition of landmark, route, and survey knowledge may occur more continuously, rather than in a sequential process (Ishikawa & Montello, 2006). The term *cognitive map* is used frequently both in nonhuman animal contexts, where the term originated (Tolman, 1948), and in the human spatial memory literature. Generally, it refers to an internal configurational representation of spatial information consisting of landmarks, paths, areas or regions, and some three-dimensional characteristics of surfaces (Golledge, 1999). The cognitive-map system allows organisms to locate themselves in places, remember spatial locations, and traverse from one place to another (Nadel, 1999). This internal representation may be externalized in a number of different response measures, such as verbal directions of routes, Euclidean distance estimation, estimates of direction through pointing, reproducing learned routes, or recognition of scenes or sequences of route segments (see Kitchin, 1996). There has been limited investigation about how well the measures reflect spatial knowledge as well as how consistent they are (Allen, Kirasic, Dobson, Long, & Beck, 1996; Kitchin, 1996), which makes comparisons across studies more difficult.

Investigations of how well people can access their cognitive maps of spatial layout have examined both behavioral and neural mechanism differences as a function of different types of spatial learning. Some have shown that extensive route learning leads to similar spatial memory performance as does limited map learning (Thorndyke & Hayes-Roth, 1982), but others suggest that the development of survey knowledge from repeated route learning is not automatic (Taylor, Naylor, & Chechile, 1999). A study directly comparing spatial-memory tasks with virtual environment movies filmed from route or survey perspectives found evidence for both general viewing-orientation effects and memory effects specific to the mode of learning (Shelton & McNamara, 2004). Participants learned text or visually presented routes or maps. They were tested on a scene-recognition task in which images of routes or maps were presented on a computer screen, and the participants decided whether the images came from the learned environment or a distractor environment. Results showed that participants performed best when the test images matched the learning perspective (route or survey) as well as the learning orientation, similar to the viewpoint-dependent representations described earlier. The orientation effects, however, were different in the two learning conditions. For route learning, the orientation advantage was linked to a particular leg of the path, whereas in survey learning there was only an advantage for the initial viewing orientation. Furthermore, when a nonvisual test of JRD was used instead of scene recognition, benefits of initial learning orientation were not specific to the leg of the path for either route or survey learning. These results suggest that in addition to a difference in encoding, the way spatial memory is tested may also influence the way spatial representations are accessed.

13.7   The Process of Wayfinding: A Summary

Wayfinding is the purposeful goal of moving from an origin to a destination that cannot be directly perceived by the traveler (Allen, 1999; Golledge, 1999) and involves many of the concepts defined under the heading of *spatial orientation* outlined in this chapter. In humans this involves selecting a route and finding one's way along it. This begins with an anchor point, or *home base*, that can be kept track of by memory of an outbound route, memory of relative locations using landmarks, use of path integration in spatial updating, or use of a bird's-eye view to define a layout context. Choices of specific routes can be influenced by goals, familiarity, and environmental structure. Experience with a route can be used to cognitively construct a configuration of spatial layout. Knowledge of the location and orientation of one's own body relative to locations of nearby objects is one important component. Both self-to-object and object-to-object relations are likely formed. One way to conceptualize these different sets of relations is to understand that the self-to-object encoding allows for quick sensorimotor transformations that are updated with self-movement. The object-to-object relations remain preserved in the cognitive-map representation, independent of a change in body position or perspective (Sholl, 1996). However, different theories exist as to the nature of orientation-independent versus orientation-dependent spatial-memory representations. The issue of how humans combine cognitive representations of spatial layout with external aids such as maps, verbal descriptions, and signs to assist in wayfinding, is also important. There are considerable individual differences both in how people assess their competency in wayfinding as well as in strategies that may be used, which are discussed in Section 13.8.

13.8   Individual Differences

Individual differences in spatial orientation and spatial cognition are important to consider in that they may inform us about the processes underlying behavior. At the same time, understanding differences among individuals may help to facilitate or inform skilled task performance that is relevant to real-world goals. From an everyday perspective, it may seem obvious that people differ in some aspects of spatial abilities—those functions related to the representation and processing of spatial information. Some people are experts in skilled movements such as dance; others find it difficult to navigate with a map. But from a cognitive perspective, the dominant approach has been to average data across individuals to draw conclusions about averages and populations, rather than to examine the differences. Spatial-abilities research has, however, had a history of assessing individual differences, stemming from the presence of relevant spatial tasks on standardized tests used to evaluate professional abilities and intelligence (Hegarty & Waller, 2005). This *psychometric* approach uses statistical methods, such as factor analysis or multidimensional scaling, to identify how abilities are related to each other (e.g., Lohman, 1988). In the following two sections we consider individual differences in two domains of spatial abilities that are relevant to the goals of spatial orientation: spatial visualization and environmental spatial abilities.

13.8.1   Spatial Visualization Abilities

Spatial visualization ability underlies the representation and manipulation of spatial forms (Hegarty & Waller, 2005; Keehner & Khooshabeh, 2005). This ability is directly related to the task of mental rotation. The mental rotations test (MRT) is a paper-and-pencil mental rotation task using Shepard and Metzler block stimuli (Vandenberg & Kuse, 1978). This task has been shown to produce a large gender difference, with men performing close to one standard deviation above the average performance of women (Voyer, Voyer, & Bryden, 1995). Given this strong effect of gender, there are often claims about a general notion of males having superior spatial abilities compared to females. It becomes clear that this claim is limited, however, when one considers (1) how different strategies may influence performance and (2) that this large effect does not generalize across many other spatial tasks. One more useful way of analyzing spatial visualization ability is to identify the cognitive processes that may be underlying performance on this type of task (Hegarty & Waller, 2005). Speed of processing has been identified as a significant source of individual differences in spatial visualization. Furthermore, it has been shown that low-spatial-ability individuals have more difficulties in maintaining an image and transforming it. This behavior may be accounted for by differences in working memory and/or executive control, which function both to maintain information and manage and coordinate task goals (Miyake, Rettinger, Friedman, Shaw, & Hegarty, 2001). Another beneficial approach is to determine the differences between spatial visualization tasks that may, on the surface, seem similar. For example, Kozhevnikov and Hegarty (2001) showed that the ability to mentally rotate an object and the ability to mentally reorient the imagined self (perspective taking) are separable spatial abilities (see also Hegarty & Waller, 2004). Finally, it is useful to consider how allowing additional information—such as interactivity or dynamic visual images (Keehner, Khooshabeh, & Hegarty, 2008) or providing a real world context—may improve spatial visualization ability.

13.8.2   Environmental Spatial Abilities

Environmental spatial abilities refer to tasks of wayfinding, navigation, and representation of large-scale environments, in contrast to the "small-scale" or visual-form tasks that characterize spatial visualization. These abilities typically involve movement of an observer through an environment and require the integration of spatial information over time and perspectives (Hegarty & Waller, 2005). As such, they seem quite different from the types of spatial abilities measured in paper-and-pencil tests. In general, there have been fewer investigations of individual differences in environmental tasks. However, one approach has been to examine how well the traditional psychometric tests of spatial visualization predict performance on large-scale environmental tasks. Research generally shows that there are weak correlations between psychometric measures of spatial ability and environmental spatial tasks (Allen et al., 1996; Hegarty, Richardson, Montello, Lovelace, & Subbiah, 2002). Others have studied the relationship of gender and wayfinding, finding that after learning a route by map or direct experience, males tend to rely on compass direction, and females are more likely to attend to landmarks (Lawton, 1994).

A different approach to individual differences in large-scale space has been to examine how self-report measures of *sense of direction* predict environmental spatial ability. Hegarty et al. (2002) developed the Santa Barbara Sense of Direction Scale (SBSOD) and studied the relationship between these self-report measures and different measures of spatial cognition, including pointing to landmarks in different-scale environments, blindfolded spatial updating, and environmental learning from different media. Using a seven-point rating system for agreement or disagreement, the scale presented statements such as "I am very good at giving directions" and "I usually let someone else do the navigational planning for long trips." The results showed that SBSOD is highly correlated with the ability to update one's position in an environment with self-movement. The results also showed a stronger relationship between self-reported sense of direction and measures of spatial knowledge that are based on direct navigation in an environment compared to that of self-reported sense of direction and forms of spatial knowledge acquired from maps, video, or virtual environments. Consistent with other findings, the SBSOD was unrelated to psychometric tests of spatial abilities. It is an interesting finding in itself that people seem to have an accurate idea of their own skills involving sense of direction and that this clearly predicts performance on environmental spatial tasks. Together, the findings indicate distinctions between small- and large-scale spatial abilities directly related to a distinction between tasks which are object-based and those that involve an egocentric updating of an observer in an environment. This reinforces the idea that spatial abilities involve multiple constructs that should not be assumed to all correlate with each other (Hegarty, Montello, Richardson, Ishikawa, & Lovelace, 2006).

13.9   Issues Specific to Computer Graphics

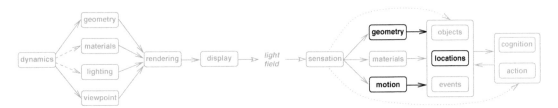

Many of the topics presented in this chapter involve real-world viewing situations in which perceivers act in and remember spaces. These spatial functions are critical for daily activities in natural environments, but how do they generalize to graphical environments? The following sections introduce issues of perception of scale, visualization, and learning and navigation within the context of computer graphics displays.

13.9.1   Scale and Spatial Cognition in Computer Graphics

For many applications of computer graphics, it is important for users to perceive an accurate sense of the scale and spatial layout depicted in the displayed imagery. This is especially salient for applications such as architectural or educational systems, where scale is critical to the experience. Evaluating the accuracy of space perception is difficult, since (as we have seen within this chapter) we must rely on behavioral measures to assess what is perceived.

Sections 13.2 and 13.3 describe issues relating to response measurement in distance perception and spatial-orientation tasks. One important question is whether the outcomes of the measures in the real world generalize to spatial environments presented in computer graphics. This question must be further qualified by the fact that results seen in immersive displays, such as a head-mounted display (HMD), may be different from those in nonimmersive displays, such as a conventional computer monitor.

Immersive virtual environment (IVE) systems are computer interfaces that provide users with the sensory experience of being in a simulated space. These systems often consist of an HMD that allows users to view and move within a computer-generated environment but can also include other devices, such as CAVE-like displays. Given the importance of self-motion to spatial orientation and spatial cognition functions, IVEs have the potential to provide a realistic means of learning and interacting with large-scale environments useful for applications in training, education, and rehabilitation. However, while visually directed actions indicating distance perception are accurate in the real world, at least out to distances of several tens of meters, the same is not true in HMD virtual environments. Numerous studies have found that actions are performed in HMD virtual environments as if distances were perceived as smaller than intended (Loomis & Knapp, 2003; Sahm, Creem-Regehr, Thompson, & Willemsen, 2005; W. B. Thompson et al., 2004) (see Table 13.1). Much research has been directed at determining the causes of this distance-compression effect. There is evidence that at least in isolation, compression of distance judgments is not due to issues involving binocular stereo (Willemsen, Gooch, Thompson, & Creem-Regehr, 2008), restricted field of view (Creem-Regehr et al., 2005; Knapp & Loomis, 2004), motion parallax (Beall et al., 1995), or image quality (W. B. Thompson et al., 2004). Physical properties of an HMD may influ-

Study	Distances	CG	Task
Witmer and Sadowski (1998)	4.6m–32m	85%	Treadmill walking
Loomis and Knapp (2003)	5m–15m	42%	Triangulated walking
Durgin et al. (2002)	2m–8m	65%	Direct walking
W. B. Thompson et al. (2004)	5m–15m	44%	Triangulated walking
Sahm et al. (2005)	3m–6m	70%	Direct walking
Sahm et al. (2005)	3m–6m	70%	Throwing
Richardson and Waller (2007)	3m–6m	56%	Direct walking
Richardson and Waller (2007)	3m–6m	54%	Triangulated walking

Table 13.1
Distance judgments based on viewing computer graphics (CG) generated imagery using visually immersive displays are compressed. The percentages indicate the overall ratio of perceived distance to actual distance.

ence the effective scale of virtual space, but this only partially accounts for the results that have been observed (Willemsen, Colton, Creem-Regehr, & Thompson, 2009). Other suggestions have been made that cognitive effects, such as expectations about room size or explicit feedback about responses, may affect the scaling of actions in virtual environments (Foley, 2007; Interrante, Anderson, & Ries, 2006a, 2006b; Interrante, Ries, Lindquist, & Anderson, 2007; Richardson & Waller, 2005). The systematic differences in absolute distance perception between real and virtual environments also generalize across response measures. While much of the work has involved visually directed walking measures, distance compression is also seen in visually directed throwing (Sahm et al., 2005) and verbal reports (Kunz, Wouters, Smith, Thompson, & Creem-Regehr, 2009).

There has been considerably less examination of the scaling of other spatial dimensions in virtual environments. Size perception has been investigated but much less so than distance perception. The effects on absolute size perception of the eye height used for rendering and the level of visual immersion have been explored using verbal reports and hand position to match virtual object heights (Dixon et al., 2000). For standing observers viewing scenes rendered from the correct eye height and viewed in a full-immersive HMD system, judgments were accurate. Reduced immersion and manipulation of rendered eye height both reduced accuracy. The effects of scene complexity (Kenyon, Sandin, Smith, Pawlicki, & DeFanti, 2007; Luo, Kenyon, Kamper, Santin, & DeFanti, 2007) and stereo and motion parallax (Kenyon et al., 2007) on size perception in screen-based systems have been explored using a task in which the size of a virtual image of a familiar object was adjusted so that it appeared to match the size of a real version of the object. T. L. Yang et al. (1999) used an ingenious experimental design that simulated nonimmersive viewing using an immersive HMD to probe how specific aspects of visual immersion affected perception of a particular size property.

Beyond the issues associated with perceiving scale, computer graphics displays provide a mechanism for spatial learning and navigation outside of a real-world situation. One important question has been how virtual environment navigation may differ between a desktop and a head-mounted display. While there are several notable differences between the types of displays, one important factor is the lack of body-based cues for self-movement when using desktop navigation. While navigating with a manual device, such as a joystick or keyboard, provides visual information for self-movement, there is no accompanying motor, vestibular, or proprioceptive information. Many researchers have examined the effectiveness of desktop spatial learning of graphical environments, using paradigms that later test the effects of spatial learning in the real world. There are mixed results as to the effectiveness of desktop spatial navigation. In general, there is increased difficulty in learning spatial layout with desktop navigation (Ruddle, 2001), although some have found relatively similar post-learning estimates of route and survey knowledge after desktop (versus HMD) navigation (Ruddle, Payne, & Jones, 1999; Ruddle & Peruch, 2004). There is also evidence that observers use visual landmarks when they are available (Foo, Warren, Duchon, & Tarr, 2005) and that some spatial updating may occur with visual rotation of an environment without accompanied physical movement (Riecke, Cunningham, & Büulthoff, 2006). Despite these examples, there is strong evidence for the importance of body-based cues for self-movement in more complex navigation and updating tasks. Performance is overall better given physical movement within an HMD virtual environment compared to visual navigation alone, and body-based information for rotation is particularly important (Chance et al., 1998; Klatzky et al., 1998; Ruddle, 2009; Ruddle & Lessels, 2006; Wraga, Creem-Regehr, & Proffitt, 2004). The nature of the type of movement (e.g., translation and/or rotation) and the influence of realism of the graphics are variables that should also be considered.

Adaptation and recalibration mechanisms are also relevant for spatial orientation in computer graphics displays. People easily adapt to changing circumstances, and effects of adaptation may or may not be similar in graphics as in the real world. Studies of perceptual-motor recalibration have been conducted using graphical displays in immersive virtual environment settings allowing for a direct manipulation of the information specifying visual and biomechanical self-motion. Both large-screen and head-mounted displays have shown effects comparable to those initially demonstrated in the real world for gain changes in rotation or translation (Kuhl et al., 2008; Mohler, Creem-Regehr, & Thompson, 2006; Mohler et al., 2007). It has also been demonstrated that walking for just a few minutes with eyes open within an HMD virtual environment leads to adaptation and subsequent changes in behavior indicating scale (Mohler et al., 2006; Richardson & Waller, 2007). Adaptation effects that could be associated with inherent conflicts in cues due to geometric distortions in HMDs have also been examined. It is possible that changes in distance estimations found by manipulating graphics (Kuhl, Thompson, & Creem-Regehr, 2009) could change over time due to adaptation to the conflicting visual and nonvisual cues for distance. However, there was no evidence of these types of adaptation effects happening over a five minute period (Kuhl et al., 2009).

13.9.2   Visualization in 3D Computer Graphics Applications

The design of effective visualizations is as much a challenge for cognitive science as for computer and information science.

—Mary Hegarty

Individual differences in spatial visualization abilities demonstrate the need to consider how well three-dimensional information is conveyed in applications using external visualization tools—visual-spatial representations presented on a computer screen. While advances in computer graphics, such as sophisticated rendering methods and hardware, have increased the use of complex 3D graphics in applications like architecture and medicine, the effectiveness of these visualizations for the human observer must be considered. The presentation of 3D models that can then be rotated on a computer screen provides a way to off-load effortful cognitive processes of mental transformations by allowing interactivity and/or dynamic motion displays (Gordin & Pea, 1995). This idea follows a framework of some embodied or grounded cognition models where motor processes supplement the internal cognitive processing required and facilitate performance (Wilson, 2002). However, there are inconsistent results from research on the effectiveness of interactivity in spatial tasks—sometimes the ability to interact with the visualization improves performance, and sometimes it does not. One reason for this may be that allowing interactivity does not ensure that users will know how to interact with the visualization and use it effectively (Keehner, Hegarty, Cohen, Khooshabeh, & Montello, 2008). In a task involving rotation and inference about a cross-section of a model, it was shown that what mattered most was seeing task-relevant information, regardless of whether this was obtained actively through interaction or passively through viewing alone. Thus, although research in psychology would suggest potential advantages of adding motor control to graphical visualizations, more evaluation is needed as to what is critical for effective use.

Spatial-orientation decisions may be particularly difficult in graphical displays because of ambiguities in spatial frames of reference. Frames of reference are critical for representing and manipulating spatial forms and environments. Typical 3D modeling programs do not provide an onscreen environmental frame of reference for objects being modeled and may lead to difficulties maintaining orientation within 3D space. As is seen in much of the spatial orientation research above, spatial encoding with respect to the egocentric frame of reference tends to dominate spatial representations. We are helped by moving around in the world and in this way can easily update orientation. However, desktop-based modeling programs and applications do not allow for feedback about the observer's position in space, and controlling virtual viewpoints in relation to an object can be a challenging task for new users of graphical 3D environments (Khan, Mordatch, Fitzmaurice, Matejka, & Kurtenbach, 2008). Some advances have been made in implementing tools that could support effective reference systems (Fitzmaurice, Matejka, Mordatch, Khan, & Kurtenbach, 2008; Khan et al., 2008; Stull, Hegarty, & Mayer, 2009), although more work is needed.

13.10   Suggestions for Further Reading

A detailed analysis of ways to measure space perception:

> Loomis, J. M., & Philbeck, J. W. (2008). Measuring spatial perception with spatial updating and action. In R. L. Klatzky, B. MacWhinney, & M. Behrmann (Eds.), *Embodiment, ego-space, and action.* New York: Taylor & Frances.

An edited volume that has several important theoretical views on spatial cognition:

> Golledge, R. G. (Ed.) (1999). *Wayfinding behavior: Cognitive mapping and other spatial processes.* Baltimore, MD: Johns Hopkins University Press.

A review of the classic mental imagery debate:

> Kosslyn, S. M. (1994). *Image and brain: The resolution of the imagery debate.* Cambridge, MA: MIT Press.

14

Perception and Action

We are told that vision depends on the eye, which is connected to the brain. I shall suggest that natural vision depends on the eyes in the head on a body supported by the ground, the brain being only the central organ of a complete visual system.

—J. J. Gibson (1979)

The terms *perception* and *action* are used together in perceptual theory to include a number of different perspectives on how perceptual and motor processes are linked together. While the actions or responses made in the environment might at first seem distinct from the topics in perception that you have considered so far that deal with *incoming* visual information, it is important to consider how action provides critical information for perception. There are several theoretical views that describe the nature of the relationship between perception and action, considering action as essential for perception, as an integrated component of perception, and even as a form of perception. At the same time, actions may reveal visual processing in different ways than seen in other non-movement-based responses. As these different views are described, it also becomes apparent that there are different ways to define *perception*. Most common to perception textbooks is a definition of conscious sensory experience, or one's awareness of the world. This awareness can then be revealed through psychophysical methods, measuring the relationship between properties of the environment and a viewer's experience. However, it is also the case that sensory information may be processed in ways that do not allow for conscious experience (see also Chapter 16). Whether or not this visual processing without awareness should be considered perception is debatable. Models that closely link action and perception must question whether actions can be equated with perception—and if not, what distinguishes action from perception?

14.1   Ecological Approach to Perception

The phrase *perception and action* is probably best known for its association with J. J. Gibson's (1950a, 1979) ecological approach to perception. Gibson's approach argued for the importance of a moving observer and the abundant amount of information in the environment for perception. A dominant view in perception emphasizes perception as a complex process of inference, necessary because of the ambiguity in the retinal image when an observer views the environment from a stationary viewpoint. However, the ecological approach emphasized that there was enough information in the environment itself to specify accurate perception. Gibson proposed a theory of *direct perception* in which perception was defined as the act of picking up information; the information in the environment was *unambiguous* given movement of the viewer and constraints of regularities in the environment (see also Runeson, 1988). Thus, there was no need to consider the additional information added by the visual system.

What about the environment is perceived? J. J. Gibson (1979) proposed that information was directly perceived from the optic array, the structure created by surfaces, textures, and contours of the environment. As an observer moves, changes that occur in the optic array provide the information for perception. *Invariant information* in a scene is the information from surfaces that remains constant over change. Gibson wrote that invariants provide information for perceptual constancies. Chapters 5 and 11 presented the concept of optic flow, the pattern of motion produced at a moving point of observation during locomotion. In optic flow, we may consider two types of information: *perspective structure*, the egocentric distances and directions that continually change with locomotion, and *invariant structure*, the environmental information that does not change with the moving point of observation. In order to extract what is constant over change, change is needed. This change comes from a moving observer.

14.1.1   Visual Control of Action

From the ecological approach to perception, changing optic flow patterns are a critical source of information for perception of self-motion and the control of action. As described in Chapter 11, an example of the powerful influence of vision on posture and balance is demonstrated in the swinging-room experiment (D. N. Lee & Aronson, 1974) and other related findings (Stoffregen, Smart, Bardy, & Pagulayan, 1999). In an optic flow field, the focus of expansion (FOE) (see Chapter 11) corresponds to one's current direction of self-motion, or *heading*, and numerous experiments have demonstrated that people can judge their heading based on optic flow at an accuracy of about 1° (Lappe, Bremmer, & van den Berg, 1999; W. H. War-

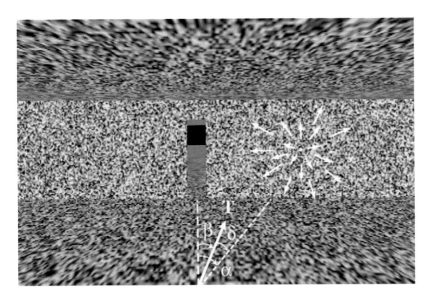

Figure 14.1

Optic flow was manipulated in a virtual environment. Heading direction specified by optic flow is displaced (δ) from the actual direction of walking (T). Normally locomotion produces optic flow with an FOE in the direction of walking.
(Reprinted by permission from Macmillan Publishers Ltd: Warren, W. H., Jr.,
Kay, B. A., Zosh, W. D., Duchon, A. P., & Sahuc, S., 2001, Optic flow is used to
control human walking, *Nature Neuroscience*, *4*(2); © 2001.)

ren, 2004). Much additional research has examined the question of whether
optic flow is used for everyday actions involved in navigation, such as steering to a goal, avoiding obstacles, and avoiding collisions. While optic flow
information could be used, a question from the ecological viewpoint has
been, *is* it used? For steering to a stationary goal, there is evidence that
people use both optic flow (the visual direction of the target relative to
heading specified by the flow) and egocentric direction (the visual direction of the target relative to the felt direction of travel), depending on the
amount of visual surface structure available (Warren, Kay, Zosh, Duchon,
& Sahuc, 2001; Rushton, Harris, Lloyd, & Wann, 1998). Figure 14.1 shows
an example of how the FOE can be displaced from the direction of walking
to test whether optic flow or egocentric direction is used for goal-directed
walking. Other studies on intercepting a moving target found reliance solely
on egocentric direction of the target and not on optic flow (Fajen & Warren, 2004). These differences are attributed to a distinction in underlying
control strategies characterized within a framework of *behavioral dynamics*,

the adaptive, coordinated behavior of an agent and its environment (Fajen & Warren, 2007; W. H. Warren, 2006).

14.1.2   Affordances

For the ecological approach to perception, *perception is for action*. Thus, the concept of *affordances* was defined by J. J. Gibson (1979) as the opportunities for action provided by the environment. Organisms perceive objects and the environment in the context of how they can act with them given the environmental conditions and the capabilities of the actor. For example, stairs afford climbing, and gaps afford passing through—constrained by the nature (e.g., the size of the body, limbs, hands) and the goal of the individual. Consistent with his view of direct perception, Gibson argued that affordances are not based on cognitive processing but are directly perceived from the information available to the viewer. Furthermore, affordances have *meaning* without a process requiring cognitive mediation because they describe what individuals can do (and cannot do) in their environment (Fajen, Riley, & Turvey, 2008). Many perceived affordances, including passability, step-on ability, sit-on ability, and reachability, have been examined in empirical research. It has been shown that accurate perception of affordances is based on body-scaled information. In other words, affordances are scaled to information intrinsic to the observer, such as leg length or shoulder width. Eye-height-scaled optical information (see Chapters 7 and 12) is one important source of information used for perceived affordances. In one classic study on affordances using apertures, Warren and Whang (1987) showed that individuals can determine from a distance if it is possible to walk through narrow apertures without turning their shoulders to fit through. Their experimental manipulations demonstrated that observers' passability judgments were based on body-scaled eye-height information and that the ratio of passable width to shoulder width was constant across different-sized individuals. Several other studies have also shown the dynamic body-scaled nature of affordances by manipulating intrinsic body information in some way. For example, a raised *false floor*, which reduced specified eye height (the viewer was unaware of the manipulation), was used in Warren and Whang's aperture study described above. Viewers judged narrower apertures to be passable with reduced eye height from the raised false floor, providing evidence for the use of eye-height scaling in perceiving affordances. In another example, Mark (1987) manipulated body size by having observers make sitting and climbing judgments while wearing 10 cm-high blocks on their feet. This initially caused overestimations of the maximum riser height that they could climb and underestimations of the maximum seat height they could sit on. Over trials, they *retuned* their responses to gradually return to accurate judgments of action capability, even without performing the actual action.

14.2 Separate Systems for Perception and Action

Despite the phenomenology of a unified visual experience, the visual system has classically been defined by two broad subsystems, one for object recognition and one for spatial localization (R. Held, 1968; Schneider, 1969; Trevarthen, 1968; Ungerleider & Mishkin, 1982). Well known for their distinction of the two cortical visual systems, Ungerleider and Mishkin (1982) labeled two anatomical streams projecting from the primary visual cortex. The ventral stream, projecting to the inferior temporal cortex, was identified as subserving object-based tasks such as discrimination and recognition, and the dorsal stream, projecting to the posterior parietal cortex, was identified for spatial localization. (*Ventral* and *dorsal* are terms used in anatomical descriptions of the brain, referring to lower and upper parts, respectively). Much of the organization of higher-level vision has been based on this *what* versus *where* distinction.

More recently, Milner and Goodale (1995) proposed a functionally defined theory that broadly redefined the roles of the two visual systems, emphasizing a distinction based on awareness or recognition (*what*) versus visuomotor control (*how*) (see also Goodale & Milner, 1992). This view of separable systems of "vision for perception" versus "vision for action" is also referred to as the *two-visual-systems theory*, and follows a similar distinction made earlier by Bridgeman, Lewis, Heit, and Nagle (1979) between *cognitive* and *sensorimotor* systems. A significant difference between the two-visual-systems theory and the traditional dichotomy between object and spatial processing is the focus on the response goal of the observer. The two-visual-systems theory maintains that a single, general-purpose representation of objects or space does not exist. Instead, the visual system is defined by the requirements of the output that each stream subserves. Thus, separate visual systems are defined for conscious visual experience (perception) and visuomotor transformation (action). The systems are differentiated along functional dimensions involving frames of reference and time. It is proposed that the *what* system forms enduring representations of the visual world in both egocentric and viewer-invariant frameworks that promote an awareness of the world's persistent structure. In contrast, the *how* system transforms information about the location, orientation, and size of objects in egocentric coordinates, online in real time, for action tasks such as pointing, reaching, and grasping. Much of the initial evidence in support of this theory came from neuropsychological patients who showed a functional loss of specific perceptual behavior corresponding to a specific area of brain damage. The well-studied patient, D.F., who had significant damage to her *what* system, failed to consciously discriminate simple shapes and orientations perceptually, while her ability to guide actions toward these stimuli remained intact. It is important to note that both perception and action responses in these assessments are made *manually*. For judgments of shape and size, D.F. was asked to indicate the width of an object by matching it to the width between her thumb and forefinger—a task that she performed at chance. In contrast, when asked to reach for the same object, her grip size was appropriate to the dimensions of the object.

Much of the behavioral evidence (and controversy) with healthy individuals in support of the two-visual-systems theory has come from studies using visual illusions. These studies claim that visually guided actions fail to reflect the subjective experience of illusory effects, in contrast to non-action-based perceptual judgments, which reveal the perceived illusion. Haffenden and Goodale (1998) demonstrated such a distinction using the *Ebbinghaus/Titchener circles illusion*, in which observers typically report that a circle surrounded by smaller circles appears larger than the same size circle surrounded by larger circles. In this experiment, perceptual judgments about a disk surrounded by smaller or larger disks showed the typical contextual effect of the surround. In contrast, the grip aperture used to grasp the center disk was unaffected by the illusion. In this study, there is a subtle distinction between the perceptual task, which was a manual estimation task requiring the observer to adjust the interval between their thumb and index finger to match the size of the target disk, and the action task, which was an actual grasp of the disk (see Figure 14.2). Similar results have been obtained from other illusions, such as the Muller-Lyer and Ponzo illusions (Carey, 2001; Glover, 2004), and have been cited as evidence of dissociations between conscious perception and visually guided action. Nevertheless, there is debate as to whether these performance differences truly reflect dissociations between perception and action systems, or rather are the result of other attentional or task-specific effects (Franz, 2001; Smeets & Brenner, 2006). Thus, the status of the claims of perception-action dissociations with illusions remains controversial.

Real-world environment-based tasks have also been used to support a distinction between perceptual awareness of space and actions directed toward space. For example, Proffitt et al. (1995) demonstrated that perception of geographical slant was overestimated in verbal reports and visual matching measures (adjusting a disk to the cross-section of the hill). In contrast, an action-based measure involving manually adjusting a board was more accurate. Supporting the dissociation, manipulations of behavioral potential (e.g., fatigue, wearing a backpack) influenced the perceptual

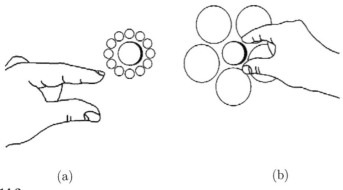

(a)   (b)

Figure 14.2

Representation of (a) perceptual matching and (b) grasping measures of the Ebbinghaus/Titchener circles illusion. (Reprinted from Carey, D. P., 2001, Do action systems resist visual illusions? *Trends in Cognitive Sciences, 5*, 109–113; with permission from Elsevier.)

judgments but not the haptic judgments. Studies of egocentric distance perception have found underestimation of matching or verbal report measures but more accurate action-based responses such as walking without vision to previously viewed targets (Andre & Rogers, 2006). The finding that one response type is more accurate than another could be interpreted with the view that the different responses are controlled by separable underlying representations. However, another possible account is that a common underlying representation informs two differently calibrated responses (Philbeck & Loomis, 1997), as discussed further in Section 14.3.

14.3   Integrated Perception and Action Systems

It may seem somewhat difficult to reconcile evidence for separate systems for perception and action with the evidence for perceptual-motor recalibration described in Chapter 13, in which there is a close coupling between perception and action. This integration is important to consider in interpreting the results of action-based measures used to reveal distance perception (see also Chapter 13). An integrative view of perception and action can be characterized by a research approach that uses action-based responses to reveal perceptual representations. While it does not exclude the possibility that separate representations inform different responses in some circumstances, the approach focuses on how certain actions are valid measures of perceived distance and does not make the distinction between perceptual representations for awareness and action. For example, Philbeck and Loomis (1997) assessed distance perception in both full-cue and reduced-cue environments using two different measures: verbal reports of target distance and blind walking to targets. There was a close covariation of these two responses: both measures reflected accurate distance perception under full-cue conditions, and both measures were similarly biased in a reduced-cue viewing condition (see also Hutchison & Loomis, 2006). In another example, Ooi et al. (2006) demonstrated that an action-based judgment involving blind walking combined with gesturing to indicate perceived target location and judgments of perceived target shape were both consistent with an intrinsic bias in the implicit understanding of the ground surface. Similarly, ground-plane interruptions influence both blind walking and perceptual-matching tasks in analogous ways (He et al., 2004). These studies rely on the use of percept-percept couplings, such as size-distance invariance, to demonstrate that perception and action-based judgments rely on a common internal representation. The logic is that cue manipulations that affect distance judgments should also influence size judgments in a similar way. Loomis and Philbeck (2008) have proposed a model that accounts for the differences between perceptual judgments and actions without appealing to different representations or visual systems (see also Philbeck & Loomis, 1997). In this model, percepts from different sensory modalities converge on a single representation that is then transformed for different types of responses. It is at the level of this output transform that differences in judgments arise.

The evidence for the Loomis and Philbeck (2008) model of a single perceptual representation informing action and non-action-based judgments comes primarily from judgments directed toward objects in action or extrapersonal space. Consistent with this, the evidence in support of separable visual systems for perception and action comes predominantly from studies testing perception in near or peripersonal space. This does not negate the two-visual-systems hypothesis of separable systems for perception and action but instead can be used to point out several important differences between actions carried out within peripersonal space and actions carried out within extrapersonal space. Actions performed in farther-away spaces require longer time frames of several seconds, rather than the milliseconds that most actions in reachable space require to complete. Actions such as locomotion involve the dynamic updating of space with self-movement. Also, these actions likely rely on different depth cues than those thought to guide actions within reachable distances. These differences are supported by evidence from brain-damaged patients that blind-walking tasks do not require the same brain regions (parietal or dorsal stream) that are required in near-distance actions, such as reaching and grasping (see Section 14.4).

The debate about single versus multiple perceptual representations informing spatial judgments is difficult to resolve. As stated above, the finding of differences as a function of the response measure used could be interpreted as a result of processing of separate visual systems for awareness and action. This reasoning follows the logic that manipulating one variable and finding two different patterns of results suggests a dissociation of processes. However, another plausible form of the multiple representation view suggests that different internal representations are attributed to task-specific selections of visual information rather than to the processing of two separate systems. In other words, the task itself might lead to differential attention to or weighting of visual cues and, subsequently, a different perceptual representation compared to another response task. Finally, response differences could be attributed to a single representation model. In this account, different indications of perception may be a result of either calibration of responses or postperceptual judgment processes. Future research in this area is needed to help resolve this theoretical debate.

14.4   Reaching and Grasping

While much of the discussion so far on acting in spaces has dealt with *action spaces* (in which we walk), many everyday tasks are performed within *personal*, or *near*, spaces (in which we can reach, such as grabbing a cup of coffee or picking up a pen to write). This seemingly automatic task requires perception of the distance to the target as well as the properties of the target, such as size and weight, and a generation of motor commands to initiate and complete the action. Reaching and grasping are visually guided action tasks that have been studied in a number of different ways relating to visual perception.

One question brings us back to space perception and how to define the information used to guide reaching. Many investigations of perception within reaching space have shown distortions in the perception of egocentric distance and shape using non-action based judgments such as verbal reports (Todd, Tittle, & Norman, 1995). These findings stand in contrast to the common observation that people are experts at skilled reach-to-grasp movements. Laboratory experiments also support this claim, showing that adults can reach and grasp objects with high accuracy and precision even without a view of their hands during the movement. Reaching has been shown to be more systematic and much less variable as a response measure than other measures, such as verbal reports (Pagano & Bingham, 1998). However, it is also true that reaching measures indicating perceived distance, size, and shape become increasingly less accurate and precise over time, particularly under monocular viewing (Bingham & Pagano, 1998; Mon-Williams & Bingham, 2007; Wickelgren & Bingham, 2000). Bingham and Pagano (1998) have argued that a distinguishing feature used for egocentric distance while reaching is the feedback used to calibrate visual information (see also Bingham, Bradley, Bailey, & Vinner, 2001). Similar to the recalibration research discussed in Chapter 13 (e.g., Rieser et al., 1995), feedback about the outcomes of reach and grasp movements is important to the accuracy of behavior. The calibration of reaching distance has been examined by researchers (e.g., Bingham & Pagano, 1998; Bingham et al., 2001) by restricting viewing conditions (e.g., monocular viewing, direction of head movement). In general, drift in reaching responses increases when feedback and visual information are restricted. When calibration information is provided, performance improves, even in situations of poor visual information. In one experiment examining the influence of head movements on monocular reaching, it was shown that reaching was more accurate and precise given forward versus side-to-side movement that generated motion parallax (Wickelgren & Bingham, 2000). For both of these head-movement conditions, accuracy and precision decreased when haptic feedback from the object was removed, but the deterioration was greater for the side-to-side movement. More recently, Mon-Williams and Bingham (2007) distorted the haptic feedback obtained during grasping of visible objects. They used a real-world experimental setup with a mirror, which allowed a haptic target to be moved to provide distorted haptic feedback as an observer viewed their hand grasping an object. The results showed that reaches calibrated to the distorted haptic information and that the calibration generalized across different reach distances.

It is also important to consider the common everyday task of grasping an object to use it in some way. This relates back to the concept of affordances but has been studied in ways that extend beyond J. J. Gibson's (1979) view of direct perception. While all objects do have affordances that may guide behavior based on object structure and relevant goals, recent research suggests that the action representation for familiar objects such as tools extends beyond their visual structure and relies also on known function (Creem & Proffitt, 2001; Frey, 2008; S. H. Johnson & Grafton, 2003). These studies suggest that the visual processing of tools is "special" in the way that it involves both conceptual knowledge about the object and representations for action.

The nature of tools as action-relevant objects has been examined in different experimental paradigms investigating how the action system may be recruited when viewing objects. In one series of studies, observers were asked to make decisions about visually presented tools (such as whether the object was natural or manufactured; or upright or upside down) with action-based responses that matched or did not match the objects. For example, a fry pan might have been presented with the handle facing to the right, and the observer would respond to the upright/upside-down question with their right or left hand (see Figure 14.3). The results showed

Figure 14.3

Examples of objects presented with specific handle orientations, upright and inverted. Photographs of objects such as these were used in Tucker and Ellis (1998). (Images courtesy of Michael J. Tarr, Center for the Neural Basis of Cognition and Department of Psychology, Carnegie Mellon University, http://www.tarrlab.org/.)

response-compatibility effects, finding that when the responses matched the characteristics of the object (i.e., right hand with a handle in the right-facing direction), then responses were faster, even though the response measure itself was irrelevant to the task dimension (e.g., judgment of upright versus upside down) (Tucker & Ellis, 1998). These results support the claim that viewing tools automatically activates motor representations, or in other words, the action system is recruited even in an object-based task (Tucker & Ellis, 1998, 2001). There is a growing literature of functional neuroimaging studies that also supports this claim (Creem-Regehr, Dilda, Vicchrilli, Federer, & Lee, 2007; Grezes, Tucker, Armony, Ellis, & Passingham, 2003; Lewis, 2006).

14.5   Embodied Perception

Theories of embodied cognition suggest that cognition is grounded in bodily states, action simulation, and sensory-motor systems (Barsalou, 2008). The common-coding hypothesis (Prinz, 1990) fits well into the embodied cognition framework, suggesting that the same representational systems are shared between perception and action. According to this theory, these systems are shared because actions are coded in terms of their associated distal perceptual events or outcomes. In other words, actions are associated with perceivable events. Actions are performed in the context of goals that affect the environment and are accompanied by corresponding sensory and motor feedback about these effects. Likewise, when an observer perceives events resulting from an action, motor representations are activated. Thus, associations between body movements and perceptual consequences are activated even when overt actions are not performed (Hommel, Musseler, Aschersleben, & Prinz, 2001). Behavioral evidence for this common-coding system comes from studies that ask individuals to recognize the perceptual outcomes of their own actions. For example, individuals have been shown to be able to better recognize their own pen trajectories in writing than others' and to predict the landing position of a dart when viewing their own throwing movements more accurately than when watching others' throwing movements (Knoblich & Flach, 2001; Knoblich & Prinz, 2001).

Interest in the shared representations for perception and action has grown with the identification of *mirror neurons* in the monkey premotor cortex. These neurons were identified as having the unique property of showing activity both when the monkey would perform an intentional hand movement (such as grasping an object) and when the monkey would observe another monkey or human perform the hand movement (Rizzolatti & Craighero, 2004). Since the initial identification of these neurons in monkeys, there has developed a large body of evidence in humans that there are also shared neural systems for overt action and the observation of others' actions (S. Blakemore & Frith, 2005; Buccino et al., 2001). The presence of a mirror system in observers could serve multiple purposes for perception. Some have proposed that the mirror system facilitates an action understanding, which can aid in planning our own actions and interpreting the actions of others (Jeannerod, 2001). Others have extended these ideas further to suggest that the mechanisms underlying the observation of actions are related to concepts in social psychology such as imitation, empathy, self-awareness, and agency (Decety & Jackson, 2004). Issues such as these are further discussed in Chapter 18.

The influence of visual body-based effects on spatial actions near the body has also been studied in the context of embodied perception. Subjectively, *visual capture* is described as the feeling of one's limb in a location that corresponds to the visual, rather than proprioceptive, position of the limb (see also Chapter 13). A striking example of this is the powerful effect of mirrors on neuropsychological patients who have disorders of body perception, such as phantom limb pain. These patients may view their intact limb in a mirror, move it systematically, and experience it as a substitute for their missing limb (Ramachandran & Rogers-Ramachandran, 1996). N. P. Holmes, Crozier, and Spence (2004) demonstrated the use of a similar mirror illusion to examine the influence of visual-proprioceptive conflict on pointing to external targets in healthy adults. Participants reached to a target with their unseen right arm while looking at a mirror reflection of their left arm. Their reaching behavior indicated an influence of vision on proprioceptive information for arm position, showing pointing errors that increased as the discrepancy between the visual and proprioceptive hand position increased. These and related results (N. P. Holmes & Spence, 2006) are important because they demonstrate not only that vision affects awareness of felt body position but also that this can influence spatial localization to targets in peripersonal space. The *rubber hand illusion* shows a similar visual-capture effect, in which a visible fake hand is stroked simultaneously with an unseen real hand and a person feels (and acts) as if the stroking is occurring at the location of the fake hand (Botvinick & Cohen, 1998). This effect has also been demonstrated recently in virtual environments (Slater, Perez-Marcos, Ehrsson, & Sanchez-Vives, 2008) and with full bodies (Lenggenhager, Mouthon, & Blanke, 2009; Lenggenhager, Tadi, Metzinger, & Blanke, 2007; Petkova & Ehrsson, 2008). The effects of visual capture are one demonstration of a broader idea that the perception of one's own body schema is influenced by multiple sensory modalities, extending the classic neurological definition which involved primarily unconscious proprioception.

A related theory of embodied perception posits that bodily states affect not only the processes of action but also those of perception (Proffitt, 2006). Proffitt (2006) has proposed that non-optical variables such as physiological potential, energetic costs, and intention influence perceptual awareness and that this serves as important information for action planning. The studies described in Section 14.2 on geographical slant perception support this view. Although measures of geographical slant perception as described in Section 14.2 show a distinction between perception and action, this model suggests that both systems subserve a similar goal of assessing the potential to act and the costs of these actions. Converging evidence for this view comes from effects of perceived effort and emotion on judgments of distance (Proffitt, Stefanucci, Banton, & Epstein, 2003; Stefanucci, Proffitt, Clore, & Parekh, 2008). More work is needed to specify the mechanisms in which physiological systems or cognitive factors could influence perceived space, given controversy and conflicting results surrounding this view (Durgin et al., 2009; Hutchison & Loomis, 2006; Woods, Philbeck, & Danoff, 2009).

14.6   Issues Specific to Computer Graphics

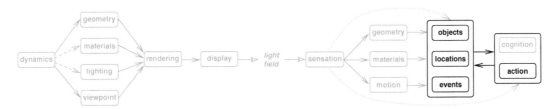

Applied tasks that involve interacting with images within near or reachable spaces have become increasingly common in domains such as medicine and education. For example, laparoscopic surgery requires precise manual performance through a small incision while viewing the image of interest on a screen displaced from the patient. Conventional ultrasound displays use the same technique of portraying anatomical data on a displaced screen (Klatzky, Wu, Shelton, & Stetton, 2008). Perception-action approaches may be able to inform these applications, leading to more effective interfaces. One such line of research has examined the effectiveness of *augmented reality* visualization in ultrasound (Klatzky et al., 2008). Augmented reality is a form of virtual environment in which a viewer sees the real-world environment with virtual-graphical objects inserted into the environment (Azuma, 1997). The technique of real-time tomographic reflection (RTTR), or "sonic flashlight," allows an ultrasound image to appear as a virtual slice at the tip of an ultrasound transducer, providing binocular depth cues. Thus, the virtual slice on a target body is perceived with appropriate orientation and depth using an egocentric frame of reference. A significant difference between this type of display and conventional ultrasound is that actions can be directly guided to the actual location on the body in ultrasound-guided surgery. Researchers have studied how motor skills may be differently learned in conventional versus sonic-flashlight methods of ultrasound. A study by Wu, Klatzky, Shelton, and Stetten (2005) showed greater accuracy in spatial representation of targets and in accessing targets given the direct, augmented reality display. While there are clear advantages to the direct-action ultrasound-guided surgery method, it is also important to consider how perception-action theory could inform learning to act with conventional imaging displays that are not co-located with a patient's body. These types of spatial representations have been labeled as *cognitively mediated* because they are based on spatial information that is specified in a way that does not have a one-to-one correspondence with a visually defined location (Wu, Klatzky, & Stetten, 2008). Understanding the effects of the feedback provided and the nature of recalibration will help to inform training for more effective use (Mohler et al., 2006).

As seen in some of the research described above, haptic information is also a significant factor in the accuracy of visually guided manual actions. This suggests the importance of multisensory information for perception within spaces close to the body in the context of graphical displays. Interestingly, while there are apparent distortions in space perception in virtual environments in near space as seen in action space (see Chapter 13), these distortions seen in reaching distances are in the opposite direction. Reaching in virtual environments tends to overshoot targets, as compared to the underestimation of distances that occurs beyond a couple of meters. One explanation for the overestimation of judgments of near distances is that the accommodative distance of most virtual displays is well beyond reaching distance (see Chapter 6). This was tested in a study in which -2 Diopter lenses were worn within the HMD to reduce the accommodative distance in the virtual environment. As a result, the focal distance was approximately equal to the virtual target distance presented. The results of this manipulation showed a reduction in the overestimation, as predicted (Bingham et al., 2001).

Visual information for body parts may influence space perception in virtual environments. Keehner (2008) found that in a task designed to mimic laparoscopic surgery conditions, there were significant effects of viewing one's own hand from a certain perspective. A back view of the left hand (as if viewing from the left) helped all participants on a maze performance task. However, a palm view of the hand (as if viewing from the right) impaired performance, particularly for low-spatial-ability individuals. These results are suggestive of an embodied perspective within this task, as the palm view was inconsistent with the users' internal representation of their hand position. The influence of perspective on a body or body part may influence space perception more broadly. Work with visual avatars, or digital representations of the body (Bailenson & Blascovich, 2004), in graphics environments can be informed by the study of visual perspective taking and embodied perceptual representations.

It is also relevant to consider the importance of action-based responses conveyed in this chapter. Regardless of different theoretical views about whether actions are informed by different visual systems than perception, or whether they are the same as perception, it is clear that actions provide a relatively unbiased and precise way to measure space perception. However, there may be limitations to the use of executed actions, given some   . types of graphical displays. While direct actions work well in immersive HMD environments, they may not make sense cognitively in screen-based displays. Other tasks that are based in action representations, such as the perceived affordances described above, may be a useful approach to the study of space perception. These tasks rely on plans to act but do not necessarily require overt action. Similarly, tasks of imagined movement (as described in Chapter 13) may also serve the same purpose.

14.7   Suggestions for Further Reading

James J. Gibson's last book and complete description of the ecological approach to perception:

> Gibson, J. J. (1979). *The ecological approach to visual perception*. Boston: Houghton Mifflin.

Milner and Goodale's first book on the two-visual-systems hypothesis, and a revised view 13 years later:

> Milner, A. D. & Goodale, M. A. (1995). *The visual brain in action*. Oxford, UK: Oxford University Press.

Milner, A. D. & Goodale, M. A. (2008). Two visual systems re-viewed. *Neuropsychologia, 46*(3), 774–785.

A good edited volume on embodied perception:

Knoblich, G., Thornton, I. M., Grosjean, M., & Shiffrar, M. (Eds.). (2006). *Human body perception from the inside out*. New York: Oxford University Press.

15

Object and Scene Recognition

Introductory textbooks on visual perception often state that the two main goals of the visual system are the visual guidance of action and the identification of objects (see Chapter 14). This chapter focuses specifically on the latter goal, though of course the two are related to one another. The discussion begins by outlining the problems inherent in a visual system that attempts to recognize environmental objects, and then covers several possible solutions proposed for these problems. It is important to note that these solutions take into account many of the visual processes covered in previous chapters, such as frames of reference and viewpoint, as well as determination of contours and occlusion. Overall, object recognition is a complex process (or set of processes) that builds on those lower- or middle-level visual processes that precede them. However, which processes are included in recognition and how they operate are still under debate. Much of the research on object recognition has been done by the computer vision community, as will become apparent throughout this chapter. While this has had significant influence on psychology research, many of the computer-vision-based theories of object recognition have not yet been evaluated as to their ability to account for human performance.

15.1   The Problem of Object Recognition

Object recognition involves establishing a mapping from the retinal image to an object categorization. Our perceptual system might classify a view of the world as corresponding to a chair, a building, a Jaguar XK-E, or Grandpa George. Figures 15.1–15.4 illustrate some of the complexities that complicate this process. Depending on the circumstances, the two images in Figure 15.1 should be recognized as a fork and spoon, as silverware, or

Figure 15.1
Objects must be recognizable at multiple levels of categorization.

Figure 15.2
Object recognition must (usually) be invariant to viewing conditions.

Figure 15.3
Invariance to viewpoint fails under some circumstances.

Figure 15.4
We can often recognize unfamiliar instances of familiar categories of objects.

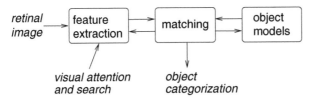

Figure 15.5

The basic components of the object recognition process.

as both silverware and a particular kind of silverware. The two images shown in Figure 15.2 should both be recognized as mugs, even though the difference in viewpoint generates significant differences in the images. A quick glance at Figure 15.3 shows that the visual system is not always invariant to viewpoint, as can be confirmed by turning the page upside down. In Figure 15.4, we recognize a vehicle-like object, even though we have likely never seen this particular view of a vehicle before.

To recognize an object, an observer must determine whether the features of the potential object in the environment match those of the representation that may be stored for a similar object already in memory. Figure 15.5 shows the major components likely to be part of a recognition system. A *feature extraction* process is required to transform the patterns of brightness, color, and perhaps motion in the retinal image into a form useful for matching against *object models*. It also seems likely that object recognition involves matching extracted features to more generalized *scene models* in order to establish a context for more focused perception of objects, as described in Section 15.3. Most existing theories of object recognition utilize some form of the types of features described in Chapter 3. Many of these theories presume that only features associated with a single object are extracted by this process, though little is yet known about how this *segmentation* process might be accomplished to allow for recognition of objects in the presence of background clutter. A *matching* process evaluates the similarity between features extracted from the retinal image and object descriptions, which need to be stored in memory and accessible to the recognition process. The matching process reaches a decision about whether or not sufficient similarity exists to constitute a match—and if so, which object category should be assigned to the view. The interaction between feature extraction and matching is shown as bidirectional, since the matching process may provide top-down control of which features are extracted. Finally, visual attention and search can direct the feature extraction process to a particular location in the view and particular sorts of image properties. Multiple theories have been proposed by both the human vision and computer vision communities as to the nature of the extracted features, the nature of the models, and the nature of the matching process, with the actual operation of the human visual system when performing object recognition tasks still largely an open question.

Object localization utilizes the grouping and figure/ground processes described in Chapter 3. These processes organize primitive image features into regions, surfaces, and shapes likely to correspond to a single object or a significant portion of an object. Object localization also depends in critical ways on visual attention and search (Chapter 16). Segregating most images into regions corresponding to individual objects based only on low-level image features is not possible, and so the object localization and visual search processes are likely influenced in a top-down manner by the matching processes.

Shape is often considered to be the most important property for determining to which category an object belongs. As a result, the feature-extraction process is usually thought of as inferring shape descriptions from views of the world that can be matched in some manner to object models also describing shape. How does the visual system determine whether two shapes are equivalent, especially when the shape that is presented to us may be oriented differently in space than that which is stored in memory? What are the components into which a shape can or should be analyzed? Is it possible that objects are not decomposed into their shape parts, but rather may be represented holistically?

Marr and Nishihara (1978) list three criteria that shape representations used in object recognition must have: accessibility, scope and uniqueness, and stability and sensitivity. *Accessibility* refers to the feasibility of extracting the specified shape information from the retinal image. While this may seem an obvious requirement, a number of theories of object recognition presume feature extraction likely to be infeasible for real-world images. *Scope* refers to the generality of the representation. Many theories of object recognition presume shape representations that are limited to only a portion of the real-world objects recognizable by the visual system. *Uniqueness* in a representation means that the same shape always has the same description. A representation of shape has *stability* if similar shapes result in similar descriptions. The use of stable representations allows the recognition system to be tolerant of small variations in the actual or apparent shape of an object. Simultaneously, shape representations need to have *sensitivity* to shape differences that matter when distinguishing between objects of similar overall shape.

A central problem in object recognition, as is the case with many other aspects of visual perception covered in this book, is that the retinal image is a two-dimensional pattern of image intensities, while objects are almost always three-dimensional volumetric entities. Despite the large amount of perceptual research done on object recognition, there is still substantial disagreement over whether the shape descriptions involved are 2D, 3D, or some combination of the two. Features extracted from the retinal image might be two-dimensional properties such as contour shape, or might be three-dimensional surface properties inferred from stereo, motion, perspective, shading, and the like. An object model in memory might capture the full 3D geometry of the object or might be closer in nature to views of the object. The shape representations output by the feature extraction process need not correspond to those used to represent object models, but they do have to be sufficiently compatible for efficient and accurate matching to be possible.

Shape representations also require a frame of reference, which are often categorized as either *viewpoint-dependent* or *viewpoint-invariant*. In the case of appearance-based features, viewpoint-dependent, viewer-centered coordinate systems are often most natural. This is particularly true for models of recognition that exploit information about how a particular object is likely to be viewed. In contrast, three-dimensional shape descriptions represented in a viewpoint-invariant, object-centered coordinate system facilitate recognition of objects from unfamiliar viewpoints.

The matching process must generate a measure of similarity between representations of the object under view and some subset of the object models in memory. The intrinsic computational complexity of this task is such that some combination of parallel processing and careful selection of candidate models is almost certainly required. Determining shape similarity is particularly complicated if the shape primitives or frames of reference are different for extracted features and object models. Since extracted features and models in memory will rarely be an exact match, the matching process needs to both decide if any matches exist and decide how to respond to situations in which multiple different object models have high similarity to the extracted view features. As with any signal detection problem, there is a trade-off between accuracy and efficiency, and a need to balance false-positive and false-negative errors.

One major source of difficulties that must be overcome in object recognition is the variability in the image projected on the retina due to distance, size, viewpoint, illumination, and more. The feature extraction and matching processes, together with the nature of the object models used, must somehow achieve invariance to these changes in viewing conditions. Perceptual constancy for brightness, color, size, and shape can help. This may not be enough, however. A coffee mug that has fallen on its side is perceived to be the same object as that which is standing upright. Even more striking is that the cat that is lying down is still perceived to be the same as when it is standing up, despite gross differences in the overall shape of the cat in each situation. Somehow, shape descriptions and shape matching must be tolerant of such visual changes.

Adding to the complexity of object recognition, multiple sorts of categorizations need to be made. Biederman (1987) argued that there are important differences between the mechanisms used to recognize count-noun entities, which have distinct boundaries, and mass-noun entities, which are without such boundaries and to which the indefinite article or a number cannot be applied in linguistic descriptions. "Chair," "building," "Jaguar XK-E," and "Grandpa George" are all examples of count-noun entities. "Air" and "water" are examples of mass-noun entities. Most research on object recognition has dealt with count noun categories. Much less is known about perception of mass-noun categories, a topic partially covered in Chapter 10. Object categorizations almost always exist within a hierarchical taxonomy. "My house" is a subordinate category of "building," "car" is a superordinate category of "Jaguar XK-E."

Rosch, Mervis, Gray, Johnson, and Boyes-Braem (1976) define *basic-level categories* as containing objects that are similar in shape, motor interaction, and attributes. For example, all cats have similar shapes, even if they are different breeds. Also, most people interact with cats by petting them. Finally, cats have other attributes common among members of the basic-level category, such as whiskers, pointy ears, and a tail. A *subordinate category* is a category somewhere in the taxonomic subtree below the basic-level node. "Siamese" is a subordinate category of "cat." Recognizing exemplars in this category requires an understanding of subtle differences between Siamese cats and other cats. A *superordinate category* is an ancestor of the basic-level category. "Animals" is a superordinate category description for "cats." Different recognition processes may be involved for each level of categorization. Furthermore, the majority of theories about object recognition are explicitly or implicitly targeted toward identification of basic-level categories.

15.2   Possible Approaches to Object Recognition

Possible approaches to object recognition are often organized into classes based on the nature of the shape features used and the manner in which insensitivity to viewpoint is achieved. Four such classes are commonly discussed, though several other possibilities appear in the literature. *Structural-decomposition* approaches use three-dimensional shape models represented as a collection of constituent parts defined in terms of generic shape primitives, typically represented in an object-centered coordinate system, along with a mechanism for inferring such descriptions from views of the object. *Characteristic-views* approaches use two-dimensional object models representing expected views of objects from prototypical viewpoints. Some methods involve a combination of these. While most empirical support

favors structural decomposition, characteristic views, or a combination of
the two as being the best accounts of how object recognition functions in
the human visual system, two other approaches have also received substantial attention. *Alignment* approaches transform candidate object models
in ways aimed at matching a sparse set of image features, and then more
completely match the transformed models to the actual view. Methods
based on *invariant properties* use shape features intrinsically insensitive to
variability in viewpoint. It is important to note that while the issue of viewpoint invariance has dominated much of the research on object recognition,
invariance to background clutter, lighting, and occlusion is also critical to
real-world performance.

15.2.1   Structural Decomposition

Structural decomposition presumes that the visual system characterizes
shape for object recognition in terms of three-dimensional components that
can be used to build any 3D object in the environment. Thus, the process
of object recognition would involve identifying the parts of the object and
then determining the relationships between the parts in order to recognize
the complex object as a whole. Several of the early theories of object recognition involving structural decomposition used some form of *generalized
cylinders* as shape primitives (Binford, 1971; Brooks, 1983). Generalized
cylinders are defined by an axis, which may be curved, and a cross-section
which need not be a fixed circle (Figure 15.6). They are particularly well
suited to biological shapes. They can also be easily organized into hi-

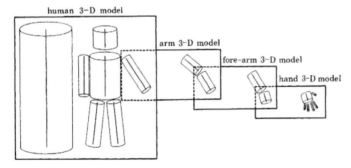

Figure 15.6

Generalized cylinders are well suited for representing many biological shapes
and certain other types of objects. (Figure 3 from Marr, D., & Nishihara, H.
K. (1978), Representation and recognition of the spatial organization of three-
dimensional shapes, *Proceedings of the Royal Society of London B, 200*(1140),
269–294. Used by permission.)

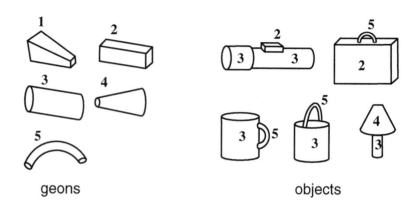

geons   objects

Figure 15.7

Examples of individual geons and simple objects made up of two or three geons. (Adapted from Biederman, Cooper, Hummel, & Fise, 1993; used courtesy of Irv Biederman.)

erarchical shapes, which facilitates simultaneously achieving stability and sensitivity in object recognition (Marr & Nishihara, 1978).

A more general set of geometric primitives is used in the theory of *recognition-by-components* (RBC) proposed by Biederman (1985, 1987). Biederman's RBC theory termed these volumetric parts *geons*, short for geometric ions. The full set of 36 geons proposed by Biederman includes shapes like cylinders, pyramids, and blocks. Biederman asserts that this subset of volumetric objects can be combined to make up nearly all of the objects that we can recognize. Figure 15.7 illustrates a portion of the set of geons, along with examples of object shapes that can be described as collections of geons.

One of the important aspects of the RBC theory is the idea that geons are shapes that exhibit a great deal of projective invariance, meaning that they can be recognized over a wide range of viewpoints. For example, a pyramid looks like a pyramid from almost every viewpoint, except for a few that occur only rarely in natural environments. Therefore, geons have contours with properties that are preserved in both the 3D structure of the object and in most 2D projections onto the retina. These *nonaccidental properties*, as they are often called, allow the visual system to determine which geons are present in an object regardless of viewpoint, and to determine their placement relative to each other. Given these nonaccidental properties, the RBC approach directly addresses the stability problem by claiming that geons can be identified across a variety of viewpoints, illumination conditions, and distances, resulting in reliable recognition.

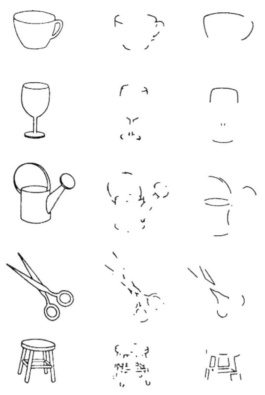

Figure 15.8

The objects on the right are harder to recognize because the geons are not identifiable. (From Biederman, I., 1987, Recognition-by-components: A theory of
human image understanding, *Psychological Review*, *94*(2), 115–147; reprinted
with permission from the American Psychological Association.

Biederman claims, in what he calls his "principle of componential recovery," that object recognition is fast and accurate when the geons in an
object and the configurational arrangement of those geons are both easily
identifiable (Biederman, 1987, 1995; Biederman & Cooper, 1991). The presumption is that in most natural viewing conditions, neither occlusion nor
atypical viewpoints will seriously impede the ability to recover geon types
and their arrangements.

Support for this comes from experiments such as illustrated in Figure 15.8. The left column in the figure shows intact line drawings of objects
representable using a relatively small number of geons. The line drawings
in the middle column of Figure 15.8 were produced from those in the left
column by deleting portions of contours in a way that still allowed for

identification of the individual constituent geons. The images shown in the right column had similar amounts of contour deletion, but done in a way that made it difficult to parse the line drawing into a geon structure. Recognition accuracy was relatively high for the drawings in the middle column, even for relatively short viewing times. Recognition accuracy was much worse for images in the right column, even with exposure times of five seconds.

In the RBC model, geons are extracted based on contour information. Additional support for RBC, or at least support for RBC and other models based on contours, comes from experiments that compare object recognition based on photographs of objects to equivalent line drawings of the same objects. For example, Biederman and Ju (1988) found little difference in classification accuracy in two different types of tasks between color photographs of everyday objects against a white background and equivalent line drawings that provided no shading or texture cues. No significant differences were found between objects where object color might provide evidence for identity (e.g., silverware) and objects where color was likely to be uncorrelated with identity (e.g., a chair).

In geon-based theories of object recognition, *binding* refers to the process by which the geons in an object are related or conjoined to make up a more complex object. For example, a coffee mug is a curved cylinder bound to the side of a wider cylinder. Traditional solutions to the binding problem have included different units for representing each relationship among the parts (Hinton, McClelland, & Rumelhart, 1986). However, in very complex objects, the number of relationships among parts that need to be represented can grow exponentially. Hummel and Biederman (1992) proposed a neural network model for object recognition that allowed for the same units to be involved in the binding of different parts. In this manner, conjunctions of parts in different objects could be represented by the same network and a fewer number of units, given that their binding properties were more dynamic. Binding occurs when units that represent different attributes of an object temporally synchronize their outputs (von der Malsburg, 1987). The advantage of proposing synchrony is that it is biologically plausible, since neurons are known to exhibit temporal synchrony. Training the model resulted in the ability to recognize objects from line drawings, even when the objects had been altered due to translations, scale, rotations, and mirror-reversals. Interestingly, the model performed well even when it had been trained with only one view of an object. According to Hummel and Biederman (1992), performance of the system conformed to the behavioral data collected from laboratory studies with humans.

While there is ample empirical support for the recognition-by-components theory as an account of visual object recognition, there are limitations to the model as well. First, identification of natural objects

may not be easy to accomplish with geons. Consider a tree or a flower. It
is not clear which geons could be conjoined to produce an adequate representation allowing for the recognition of all trees or even some flowers. All of
the parts of a flower (e.g., the petals or the stamen) do not easily map onto
geons. Geons seem to make sense if we are trying to explain recognition of
manmade objects, but they do not fit as easily into a recognition model for
some natural objects. Moreover, people are able to discriminate between
horses and donkeys despite very similar constructions of geons. The RBC
theory does not easily account for the ability to perceive differences among
these subordinate categories. Finally, geons cannot easily represent other
subordinate categorizations, such as differences among faces. (See Chapter 18 for more on face recognition.) Even with a larger set of geons (up to
108 have been proposed by some), there is no way to account for the fine
discriminations between parts needed to differentiate faces. Furthermore,
many of the models that have been proposed typically discriminate between
only a small number of geons (e.g., eight geons rather than a larger set).
Thus, this limits our ability to really understand whether the RBC approach requires or utilizes the full set of geons that Biederman proposed on
a regular basis. An alternative approach presented in the following section
does not fall victim to these shortcomings, but may have its own.

15.2.2   Characteristic Views

Section 15.2.1 presented evidence suggesting that object recognition requires three-dimensional information to be stored as the comparison template that is structural in nature and does not include information specific
to a particular viewpoint. However, in this section, we will present evidence that shows that human (and monkey) object recognition can be
strongly viewpoint-dependent. Single, individual viewpoints, even though
they are two-dimensional in nature and variable in their properties, can
provide enough information to recover three-dimensional regularities in an
object, which can lead to recognition. The simplest of these approaches
is *template matching*, which uses actual images as the object models and
uses an image-similarity metric for matching. Figure 15.9 provides an example in which two different templates are used to recognize faces in an
image. While template matching has been used with some success in certain computer vision applications, it is too limited on its own to account
for humans' object recognition abilities. However, more-sophisticated models that involve mechanisms by which recognition is based on referencing
stored viewpoints of objects have proven quite successful in accounting for
behavioral data.

Template-like object recognition can obtain a degree of invariance to
viewpoint by using multiple templates, each corresponding to a possible

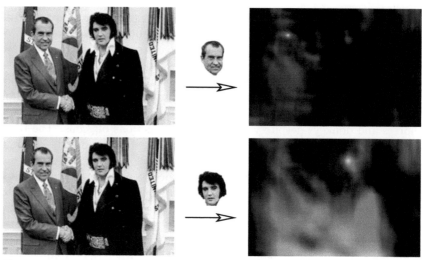

Figure 15.9

Image-based template matching, with two different templates applied to the same image. The white spots in the right images indicate the locations of best match. (Original image from the National Archives and Records Administration.)

view. Chakravarty and Freeman (1982) developed a 3D object recognition technique that uses characteristic views to discover the identity of the object (see also Chakravarty, 1982; Lavin, 1974). The views are derived from the set of all possible images that an object can project onto the retina from an infinite number of perspectives. These views are classified into a set of topological equivalence classes, thereby producing the characteristic views for which the approach is named. Linear transformations produce the varying views of the object within each equivalence class. The model determines the silhouette of the object through edge detection and then matches that to the stored characteristic views, resulting in object recognition and also an output of the position and orientation of the object. An obvious disadvantage to this approach is that occlusion can derail the determination of the silhouette, making recognition much more difficult.

Koenderink and van Doorn (1976, 1979) introduced a similar approach, which they termed *aspect graphs*. Their approach took into account that from almost any viewpoint of an object, a small movement of the object does not greatly affect our ability to recognize it. Object recognition is successful because of the similarities in the topological structure of an object (i.e., its aspects) that are preserved across small changes in viewpoints. Models can be constructed to recognize an object by taking into account the way an object could change its projection due to motion and how that relates to the aspects of the object that could be visible at any given time. In other words, an object representation is an aspect graph, with the aspects forming the nodes of the graph, and possible changes in perspective due to motion forming the arcs of the graph. Thus, a complete inventory of all possible views of an object is stored in the graph, with the size of the graph being related to the complexity of the shape it represents.

Related to the characteristic-views approach of Chakravarty and Freeman (1982) is the concept of *canonical views*, which are defined as prototypical views or preferred views of objects. If 30 people were asked to imagine a car or an apple, then it is likely that they would imagine the object from very similar viewpoints, suggesting that a canonical view of that object exists. The notion of canonical views was first mentioned by Palmer, Rosch, and Chase (1981). They conducted a series of experiments to determine if canonical views existed and whether they were consistent both within participants and across them. In their first experiment, they asked participants to rank many different photographs of 15 objects for their level of "goodness." In the second experiment, participants described the mental image that came to mind when an object was verbally presented to them (see also Chapter 13, Section 13.5, for a discussion of visual imagery). In the third experiment, participants were asked to position an object in the most appropriate way in order to take a picture of it for a brochure or advertisement. Interestingly, there was consistency both within and across participants for the three tasks. Most participants preferred an off-axis viewpoint (i.e., a three-quarters view of the object), which also allowed for the most surfaces of the object to be visible. These experiments shaped the criteria that is now considered to be the most important in identifying a canonical view. More recently, Verfaillie and Boutsen (1995) had participants rate the level of goodness in a paired comparison task. Eleven computer-generated images were constructed for each of 70 objects. Participants were asked to choose which viewpoint they liked better when presented with two of the images produced from a single object. They replicated the findings of Palmer et al.—that people prefer a three-quarter viewpoint aligned to the object's major axis. These findings have obvious implications for understanding how people may mentally scan images in the brain, given that their initial image of the object may conform to a canonical perspective.

These approaches are based directly on the view of the object being identified and do not require that the 3D structure of the viewed object be recovered. Upon first consideration, a potential problem arises with these approaches. Namely, to support a viewpoint-dependent system for object recognition, the visual system would have to store numerous viewpoint-dependent representations for each object. This could lead to copious numbers of templates being stored in memory, and therefore the suitable indexing system for referencing all of these representations would be cumbersome. However, much of the research has shown that this approach does not need to rely upon a large number of stored viewpoints. In other words, this storage problem can be resolved if there is a means of relating one image or viewpoint to another, effectively generalizing from a familiar view to an unfamiliar view. Thus, the number of viewpoints needed for recognition is dependent upon the shape of the object. For example, if an object has sharp-bounded contours (e.g., right-angled corners), then an average of only three views need to be stored in order to recognize it. Under some circumstances, even two stored views may be sufficient (Ullman & Basri, 1991; Ullman, 1998). Recognition, then, occurs when transformations of the viewpoint-dependent representation are performed in order to align or equate the stored viewpoint with the to-be-recognized viewpoint. These transformational processes include translations and rotations, as well as dilatations (Willems & Wagemans, 2001). All of these processes incur a cost for recognition assuming a large angular difference in viewpoint between the stored representation and the currently viewed object.

Psychophysical evidence further supports the notion that canonical views stored as representations may underlie object recognition. First, the angle of orientation of the to-be-recognized object can predict the amount of time it will take to recognize the object and the likelihood of correct recognition. As the view of the object departs from the angle of orientation of the trained or canonical viewpoint, the time taken to recognize the object is increased and correct recognition decreases (H. H. Bülthoff & Edelman, 1992; Jolicouer, 1985; Tarr & Pinker, 1989). Second, even if participants are trained on novel objects with rich 3D information, their representations are not necessarily 3D in nature. Sinha (1995) trained participants using a 3D model and then varied the structure of the object at test time by showing either a similar or dissimilar 3D shape and a similar or dissimilar two-dimensional view of the object. The findings showed that viewpoint was more important for recognition than the similarity of the 3D information. Evidence from Tarr and Pinker (1989) further suggests a reliance on two-dimensional representations rather than three-dimensional representations. They showed that participants who trained with many two-dimensional views of an object had improved recognition compared to those who trained with limited number of views.

Computer models have been developed to recognize an object using a two-dimensional approach through active shape matching (Lades et al., 1993). Shape matching involves constructing a nonlinear image of a to-be-recognized stimulus that is then compared to the stored image for an object. Fit of the stimulus to the stored view is measured by determining the distance that a point in the viewed image must travel in order to correspond with a similar feature in the stored representation. The points in the image can be like Gabor patches, termed *jets* (Lades et al.), or can be regions of the scene, like ovals for the eyes (Yuille, 1991).

The evidence that supports viewpoint-dependent representations is quite compelling; however, this approach is not without weaknesses. One of the arguments against the approach is that people have no problem recognizing that novel objects are 3D but this begs the question of how that recognition occurs when no stored 2D views for a novel object exist in memory. Also, many of the models for this approach are limited in their scope. The models can recognize rigid objects by matching 2D views but fail to recognize objects that often deform, like the human body. Finally, the situations in which view-based theories have been very successful in recognizing objects are when the objects are identical but vary in viewpoint. The approach does not address the problem of classifying examples of entry-level categories, such as chairs or houses. One could imagine that categorizing a 19th-century Victorian as a house would be very different than classifying one built in the 1960s. How would viewpoint-dependent theories account for our ability to easily categorize these houses upon first sight? Explaining this ability is a real problem for image-based approaches.

15.2.3   Alignment

Structural-decomposition theories of object recognition presume that generality comes from the use of 3D object models represented in terms of abstract, predefined building blocks and explicit connections between these building blocks, combined with an image-to-model matching process that is largely insensitive to viewpoint. One significant problem with this class of theories is that the use of a small set of volumetric primitives and relationships limits the ability to represent many types of object geometry critical to identification. Furthermore, the recognition of model primitives based on contours in the view is subject to many sources of error. Theories involving some form of characteristic views avoid both of these limitations. Since the models are two-dimensional views, they can represent arbitrary (two-dimensional) geometry and are not restricted to representations involving a limited set of primitives. The fact that models and views are both image-like means that matching is straightforward, at least in principle. A significant difficulty with these approaches is generality. Achieving viewpoint invariance, particularly for complex objects, can involve the need to have a large number of views in memory and an efficient recall mechanism for accessing views that are potentially relevant in a given instance. Invariance to geometric distortions of a prototype object and to variations in materials and lighting is even harder to achieve.

The alignment method for object recognition hypothesizes an approach with the potential to address all of these limitations (Lowe, 1985; Ullman, 1989, 1996). Alignment methods presume that object models are represented in terms of explicit detailed geometry and an associated set of transformations that can map model geometry into a form equivalent to potential views of the corresponding object. Recognition proceeds in two stages. In the first stage, a transformation is estimated for each model that plausibly brings the model into correspondence with the view. In the second stage, each of the transformed models is compared to the view to determine the goodness of match. In the case of two-dimensional models, allowable transformations might consist of 2D rotations, scale changes, and perhaps more-complex deformations. For three-dimensional models, the transformations usually include general 3D rotations. While the need to solve for transformations might seem to be prohibitively complex, under a broad range of circumstances the transformations can be estimated based on a sparse set of feature correspondences between view and model. This is even true for 3D models, where the transformation needs to account for the pose of the model relative to the viewed object. In this way, alignment methods are similar to the structural decomposition approach of Biederman (1985, 1987). The important difference is that the models are not constrained to be made of geons, or other predefined primitives, and relationships between features are described in terms of low-level, generic geometry, rather than high-level, abstract geometric predicates. Matching of the view to transformed models is based on predicting the view from the transformed model, and so has similarities to the matching process for characteristic views. Empirical investigations of the role alignment might actually play in human vision have been limited, but it can be argued that the findings of Tarr and Pinker (1989) provide support for the existence of alignment-like processes in visual object recognition.

15.2.4   Invariant Properties

The recognition of three-dimensional objects from the two-dimensional projections on the retina might be accomplished through identification of projective invariants. These invariants are those aspects of an object that are preserved when its three-dimensional structure is projected onto a two-dimensional surface. For example, parallel lines remain parallel from all viewpoints when a book is projected onto a two-dimensional surface, and a transformed circle often takes on the shape of an ellipse. Imagine taking a round coin and tilting it slowly away from you. As you do, the coin takes on an elliptical shape from your viewpoint, which increases with degree of tilt. In order to recognize the object as a circular coin, the visual system has to determine the degree of tilt and the foreshortening of the object to determine its overall shape (Cutting, 1986; Rivlin & Weiss, 1997).

According to Palmer (1989), transformations can occur that preserve the *objective shape* of the object. This shape, he claims, is a property of the object that should be considered to be like its objective size or orientation. The objective (or invariant) shape of the object will not change when it is translated to another position, when it is rotated, when it is dilated, or when it is reflected (e.g., through the creation of mirror images of the object). Moreover, these transformations could be applied to two objects (either 2D or 3D), and as long as the transformations can be reversed and the objects brought into correspondence, then they will be perceived as having the same objective shape.

15.2.5   Hybrid Approaches

Changes in viewpoint can impact both viewpoint-dependent and viewpoint-independent object recognition, though in somewhat different ways. Furthermore, visual properties that characterize object structure need to be identified for both approaches in order to recognize objects across varying viewpoints. Ullman (1996) argued that parts of objects may be stored in memory, in addition to representations of the whole object, though these representations are likely separate. If both representations were found to exist in memory, then this would suggest that the two theories need not be mutually exclusive. Also, it would be logical to think that both representations may exist in the visual system in order to be applied in different situations. Obviously, view-specific representations lend themselves to problems that involve recognizing the same object from different perspectives. In contrast, structural decomposition models seem better suited for categorizing entry-level exemplars (rather than a Victorian house versus a 1960s abode). Both viewpoint-dependent and viewpoint-independent models may work together to achieve object recognition that can be quick (when relying on stored views) or slow (when relying on matching to parts) (see Hummel & Stankiewicz, 1996).

Recent research has tried to integrate these theories into a more coherent model that incorporates both structural invariance and viewpoint dependence across a variety of situations. For example, Foster and Gilson (2002) claim that both view-dependent and structural-invariance representations are used for object recognition. In their experiment, they asked participants to discriminate between two 3D objects (they looked like volumetric wire frames) that were rotated from one another at a randomly chosen degree. The objects had not been seen before and were presented simultaneously. Each object was computer generated to differ in structure, namely by the number of the parts, the curvature of the parts, the length of the parts, and the angle of the juncture of the parts. They found that participants had a harder time detecting metric properties (curvature, length, angles) of the objects than the number of parts. However, the ability to discriminate the objects did not differ based on these metric properties, only on the rotational differences between the two objects. Recognition of similarity was incredibly reliable when the angular orientation differed by 45° or less. Overall, Foster and Gilson showed evidence for differences in recognition based on parts and on viewpoint in one experimental paradigm.

Fragment-based approaches achieve viewpoint-invariance by using object models made up of a collection of subimages of small-scale features of objects of interest (Bart, Byvatov, & Ullman, 2004; Ullman, Vidal-Naquet, & Sali, 2002). Generality is obtained by allowing for multiple different subimages to characterize the same object feature. Image fragments are a richer representation of visual structure than simple image contours, but simpler and so more robust to variability than characteristic views of complete objects. An additional advantage of the fragment-based approach is that it does not depend on a prior segregation of the view into distinct objects, and so is able to combine segmentation of the view into distinct objects and recognition into a single process (Ullman, 2007). Some empirical support exists for the use of fragments in human object recognition (Hegdé, Bart, & Kersten, 2008).

Serre, Wolf, Bileschi, Riesenhuber, and Poggio (2007) describes an approach similar in some ways to the fragment-based model of object recognition, and which uses computational mechanisms that are biologically motivated. Simple, base-level image features are organized hierarchically in a manner that provides a degree of tolerance to changes in scale and variability in position. The intent is to provide a balance between sensitivity and stability. Performance on simulations is promising, but as with most computer vision approaches to object recognition, we know little about how well they describe the way in which human object recognition actually works.

15.3   Scene Perception and the Role of Context in Object Recognition

Sometimes a thing in front of you is so big you don't know whether to comprehend it by first getting a dim sense of the whole and then fitting in the pieces or by adding up the pieces until something calls out what it is.

—Maclean (1976)

An observer is rarely tasked with identifying a single object. Most environments contain multiple objects, which can either complicate or enhance the ability to recognize that a specific object is present. Interestingly, recognition of the type of environment that one is in can facilitate the ease and speed with which an object is identified in that scene. A brief glimpse of an environment can result in a basic-level categorization of the scene (Potter, 1976) and even an understanding of the spatial layout of the environment (Schyns & Oliva, 1994). Not surprisingly, this quick evaluation of the scene can lead to predictions about objects that may or may not be present. In the following sections we will discuss processes involved in scene recognition, with a particular focus on research that has utilized information about a scene to aid in object recognition.

15.3.1 Scene Recognition

So far, this chapter has concentrated on the identification of isolated, named objects with well-defined extent—what Biederman (1987) referred to as "count-noun entities." The visual system is also very effective at recognizing the overall nature of a scene based on very quick glances. Properties such as the general type of object present, the general category of environment, the overall geometric scale of the visible space, navigability, and more can be detected in views as short as 20 ms–70 ms (Greene & Oliva, 2009; Thorpe, Fize, & Marlot, 1996). This rapid recognition of scene properties occurs even for cluttered scenes containing many individual objects. It is possible for presentation times as short or shorter than those required to recognize individual, simple objects presented against a white background.

Until recently, most models of how overall scene properties were recognized presumed that scene recognition followed the recognition of individual objects in the scene and the determination of the spatial organization of those objects. The ability to recognize scene properties very quickly suggests that a different process may be at work. Evidence is emerging that the visual system determines the global structure of a scene *prior* to determining properties of individual parts of the scene (Kimchi, 1992; Navon, 1977). Oliva and Torralba (2006) proposed that global and local spatial frequency features (such as described in Chapters 3 and 8), which can be rapidly computed by the visual system, are sufficient to determine a wide variety of whole-scene properties. The processes they described are not dependent in any way on explicitly identifying individual objects in the scene or on any direct extraction of spatial information about the scene by any of the mechanisms previously described in this book.

While most of the work on scene perception focuses on semantic categories of scenes, a similar global/local feature analysis may lead to a determination of the overall scale of a scene without any determination of the depth to specific locations in the scene (Torralba & Oliva, 2002). This is possible because the distribution of local spatial frequencies in a scene systematically varies as a function of viewpoint, perspective, and content in a manner correlated with scale. Hoiem, Efros, and Hebert (2007) demonstrated a computer vision algorithm capable of partitioning an image based on 3D scene orientation using an approach similar to this.

15.3.2 Objects in Context

An ongoing challenge for vision scientists is to implement a visual system akin to the one in humans that can classify objects autonomously in indoor or outdoor environments. This requires the models to be able to (1) autonomously build an object-classification database sufficient to identify a number of objects found in these environments and (2) use this database to autonomously search the environment for objects. Overall, this problem involves recognizing not only one object in a scene but also a variety of objects that may co-occur in certain environments. Moreover, these objects may be cluttered in the scene, with plenty of occlusion and differences in illumination making recognition very difficult.

Cognitive and perceptual psychologists have suggested that a potential solution for this problem could involve a classification system that acknowledges correlations among objects present in certain environments. If the model knows that it is searching an office environment, then all of the objects in the scene become a source of information that can help to recognize an object that may be especially occluded. Those objects that are consistent with an office environment (e.g., computer, bookshelf, chair, desk) have been shown to be recognized more quickly than objects not consistent with the scene (e.g., a bed) (Oliva & Torralba, 2007; Palmer, 1975). Just as faces generally appear as a certain configuration of parts, so too does the location of objects in a scene. Imagine your office, and then imagine your friend's office. In both contexts, it is more likely that the computer monitor would be on top of the desk rather than underneath it. Recent research has shown that we implicitly learn these relationships even from an early age (Fiser & Aslin, 2001, 2005). The information needed for this *contextual cueing* is often acquired without explicit attention (Chun & Jiang, 1998).

In computer vision, objects in an image are commonly located using a window that is slid across the scene in order to classify each area under the window as background or object. This technique has been successful at identifying objects such as cars and faces (Forsyth & Ponce, 2003). The state-of-the-art in computer vision now includes the use of contextual information—termed *global scene representations*—to improve the efficiency of these local approaches (Oliva & Torralba, 2001). These models take the low-level features in the scene (edges) and predict whether the scene is of an indoor, outdoor, urban, etc. setting. Once this prediction is made, the contextual information associated with that type of scene can be used as a complement to the object recognition processes to determine the likelihood that a given object is in the environment. Many of these algorithms can correctly predict whether an object is in the scene without ever localizing the object itself (Torralba, 2003; Torralba & Oliva, 2003).

Divvala, Hoiem, Hays, Efros, and Hebert (2009) attempted to better define the concept of context in the service of building more generalizable models for accomplishing object recognition. They objectively evaluated what is meant by *context* in a standardized setting, examined different ways of using those contexts to improve object recognition performance, and also proposed new algorithms for using context to recognize objects. Another model suggests visual systems can use both low-level, bottom-up processes and high-level, top-down processes to understand a scene. Specifically, Yuille and Kersten (2006) proposed a model for the visual system in which low-level cues (such as edges detected in the scene) are evaluated to offer up a proposal of what is in the scene, which is then verified by a high-level process. Such a system allows for rapid scene detection, even in the face of inexperience with the low-level features of the scene.

15.4   Issues Specific to Computer Graphics

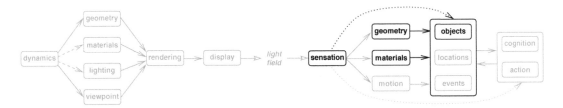

It is obviously important to construct video or digital displays that help observers recognize objects when depicted in real-world scenes (video), on desktop or other screen-based displays, and in immersive or virtual environments. When objects are depicted by computer graphics, the information that is used to recognize them may be degraded (lighting, color, texture, etc.), making the object more difficult to correctly identify. An important question becomes, what should be modeled in order to ensure successful recognition? Also, are there trade-offs when using the different approaches in models?

As indicated above, much remains to be learned about how object recognition functions in the visual system. Further complicating the situation, very different mechanisms may be involved in recognition for basic-level, superordinate, and subordinate object categories. Thus, it is difficult to make general statements about how computer graphics can best facilitate object recognition. Perhaps the best advice that can be given is that geometric models, materials, lighting, and rendering methods all need to support the appearance in rendered images of both the local features associated with most structural decomposition theories and the more holistic look required for methods dependent on characteristic views to succeed. The emerging evidence for the importance of spatial frequency features and other image statistics in scene and object recognition presents additional challenges for computer graphics, since few if any graphics systems are designed to control these properties of the generated image.

Also, graphic artists should be sensitive to depicting objects from a viewpoint that may be quite different from the usually seen orientation. The unusual-views problem also arises for computer-simulated object recognition models. Airport baggage security systems are an obvious everyday application for these types of programs. The TSA has a strong interest in being able to automate the review of bags and their contents in security lines. Obviously, the recognition program should be able to identify whether there is a gun in a bag, but if the gun is in a nontypical orientation, will the program be less than reliable? Industrial applications also have to deal with the problem of object recognition given the need for automating certain tasks, like the ability of a robot to remove the correct object from a bin of objects quickly and effectively. Computer simulations that address this problem (under restricted viewing conditions) have been proposed by psychologists (Huttenlocher & Ullman, 1990; Lowe, 1985). In these simulations, the input image depicts a bin full of objects (usually similar objects). The task of the simulation is to determine how many individual objects are in the bin and to which direction they are oriented. First, the simulation finds the edges in the scene using a luminance edge algorithm developed by Marr and Hildreth (1980). Then the simulation takes a basic wireframe model of the object in the bin and uses it to determine the orientation of the potential objects in the bin (now represented as edges only). This wireframe model is three-dimensional. It is matched to the edge segments depicted in the scene, and a correspondence between the edges and potential three-dimensional objects in the bin is calculated. Thus, if all edges are not found in the scene, top-down processes can be used based on the stored 3D wireframe model to determine the location and position of the objects in the bin.

Nonphotorealistic rendering (NPR) is a computer graphics approach based on imitating pen-and-ink drawing or painting techniques of artists and illustrators, rather than approximating the actual view of a physical environment (B. Gooch & Gooch, 2001). Many of the NPR methods that are intended to produce technical illustrations (as used in manuals, encyclopedias, and textbooks) highlight edges while reducing the dynamic range and detail of surface shading (e.g., DeCarlo & Santella, 2002; A. Gooch, Gooch, Shirley, & Cohen, 1998; Raskar & Cohen, 1999). While the perceptual motivation for this is rarely argued in the NPR literature, this approach is consistent with structural decomposition models of object recognition, such as Biederman's geons, which base recognition primarily on the silhouettes of object parts rather than the shading, color, or texture of object surfaces.

Finally, techniques related to scene recognition can be used to assist in filling in image holes when unwanted content has been removed and to ameliorate the related problem of *retargetting* images for presentations involving significantly different display sizes or aspect ratios. For example, Hays and Efros (2007) describe an algorithm that can recover missing image pieces or objects in a scene by mining a large database of preexisting images of similar scenes, rather than just basing the image completion on the image being manipulated. A key step is using scene-recognition techniques to find alternative images that are semantically appropriate in the context of the manipulation.

15.5 Suggestions for Further Reading

An edited volume on object recognition, particularly useful for its coverage of viewpoint-dependent methods:

Tarr, M. J., & Bülthoff, H. H. (Eds.). (1999). *Object recognition in man, monkey, and machine*. Cambridge, MA: MIT Press.

A discussion of object recognition and other issues in high-level vision:

Ullman, S. (1996). *High-level vision: Object recognition and visual cognition*. Cambridge, MA: MIT Press.

Comprehensive coverage of object recognition modeling, with an examination of neuroscience and psychological findings as well:

Edelman, S. (1999). *Representation and recognition in vision*. Cambridge, MA: MIT Press.

16

Visual Attention and Search

Even in things that are plainly visible you can note that if you do not direct the mind, the things are, so to speak, far removed and remote for the whole time.

—Lucretius (1st century BC/1965)

How do observers organize the world into objects and events to be perceived? Even if you are reading this chapter in a quiet setting in the library, consider all of the visual (and other sensory) information around you, such as people, books, and furniture—as well as what is in the immediate surround on your desk, such as a pen, notebook, and water bottle. Visual scenes present much more information to the visual system than could be processed at one time. This chapter focuses on the processes of *attention* that are needed to select only some of a scene for further processing. We emphasize topics in *selective attention*—rather than other related topics such as divided attention and multiple types of attentional resources—because of their direct relevance to visual perception and computer graphics.

In vision, there are at least two important goals that are served by attentional mechanisms that are critical to perceptual experience: (1) selecting relevant information and ignoring irrelevant information, and (2) modulating this selected information in the context of the specific situation (Chun & Wolfe, 2001). Essentially, we focus on some parts of a scene to the exclusion of others. There are some aspects of attention that are built in to our visual systems. For example, high visual acuity is restricted to the foveal region, or center of fixation. Beyond factors defined by physiology, the control of selective attention is described by two different types of processes that work together. Bottom-up, or *exogenous*, attention is involuntary and automatic, driven by an external stimulus by certain features, such as changes in color or motion. Top-down, or *endogenous*, attention

393

is under voluntary control of the observer, a goal-driven process thought to be more effortful. Eye movements are important to selection processes, but it is also important to consider that attention is more than moving the eyes. We can attend to locations that we are not looking at, and we can look at things without attending to them.

16.1   Bottom-Up and Top-Down Processing

Regarding how attention shifts, there is a long history of discussion and thought, from the ancient Greek philosophy of Aristotle to 17th-century Descartes, who defined a distinction between voluntary "attention" and involuntary "admiration" (Hatfield, 1998). Several early psychologists known for their work in visual perception also made significant contributions to the understanding of attentional control. Notable psychologists include von Helmholtz (1878/1925) with his studies on attention shifting, and James (1890) with his distinction between "active" and "passive" attention. The Gestalt psychologists (e.g., Wertheimer, Koffka, Kohler) also distinguished between the attention drawn to a perceptual object in a stimulus-driven way and the attention that results from voluntary control (R. D. Wright & Ward, 2008).

It is now a well-developed concept in attention research that attentional processes are both stimulus driven (bottom-up) and goal driven (top-down). Evidence for goal-driven, intention-controlled attention comes from laboratory tasks that instruct viewers to follow a goal (e.g., identify a letter in a display while ignoring others) or respond after a cue (e.g., location-cueing paradigms described in more detail below). Stimulus-driven attention, or *attentional capture*, has been studied in terms of two different categories of stimulus properties: visual attributes and abrupt visual onset (Egeth & Yantis, 1997). Feature singletons are stimuli that differ in one or more visual attributes—such as color, orientation or motion—and have been shown to be subjectively salient and detected efficiently during search (Treisman, 1980). However, there has been a debate over whether singletons capture attention in a stimulus-driven way, without an influence of top-down control. Some have argued in favor of capture, with singletons showing that attention may be drawn to the salient cue even when irrelevant to the task; others have found no support for this claim, showing that the saliency of singletons (even visual motion) did not influence a goal-directed task (Hillstrom & Yantis, 1994). Abrupt visual onset of a stimulus is also considered important for stimulus-driven attention (Yantis & Jonides, 1990), particularly when a stimulus is presented in peripheral vision. However, similar to the singleton research, attentional capture from abrupt onset can also be modulated by task goals. Together, a body of work suggests that both stimulus properties and observer goals influence how attention is directed. One theory that has addressed the dual nature of attentional control is the *guided search model* (Wolfe, 1994). In this model, both top-down and bottom-up activation are combined to influence visual search for a stimulus, and efficiency of a search is influenced by how much bottom-up stimulus information guides attention to targets or away from distractors (see also Section 16.4).

16.2   Eye Movements

There are two broad classes of eye movements, both important to an understanding of visual attention. *Saccadic eye movements* are rapid eye movements used to bring images to the fovea. Saccades are natural, subjectively effortless ballistic eye movements made quickly and periodically at about three times per second (Kowler, 1995). The typical velocity of the eye movement is about 700°–900°/second (an average saccade during reading would last about 25–30 ms), and durations of fixation between saccades are about 250–300 ms. It is during these fixation periods that the majority of visual perception occurs. In fact, there is evidence that visual and some cognitive processing are shut down during saccades, a phenomenon known as *saccadic suppression*. For example, classic work by Bridgeman, Hendry, and Stark (1975) showed that a target displaced during a saccade went undetected by observers. In this study, observers were asked to make eye movements to different fixation points while a stimulus was moved at unpredictable times, and to respond when they saw a stimulus "jump." Target detection was suppressed if the displacement occurred right before the saccade and, maximally, during the eye movement. Interestingly, it has also been shown that pointing behavior to a target displaced during the saccade was accurate to the changed location, despite failure to consciously detect the change (Bridgeman et al., 1979). This result was interpreted in support of separable visual systems for perception and action, as described in Chapter 14. More-recent studies have demonstrated *change blindness* (see also Section 16.5.1) during saccades, in which a change in a scene that occurs during the saccade goes unnoticed (Henderson & Hollingworth, 2003). Smooth-pursuit eye movements are smooth and continuous movements, slower than saccades (maximum of 100°/second) and requiring constant feedback from the image for correction. They serve the function of preventing rapid motion of the retinal image, allowing a moving object to stay focused on the retina. Smooth eye movements require both sensory information for tracking as well as cognitive processes of expectations and selective attention in order to successfully maintain a focused, stable image of a moving stimulus (Kowler, 1995).

Eye-tracking technologies can determine the direction and time of foveal fixation. Modern *eye trackers* are camera-based systems that compute the location of the center of the pupil by using the reflection of light from the eye. Standard methods use a fixed-head tracking system, which provides a precise way of transforming eye orientation into world coordinates. More recently, mobile eye-tracking systems have been developed that allow free movement of the head and body so that eye movements may be measured in more-naturalistic tasks, such as driving and other complex skills. However, a limitation associated with this is the reduced accuracy in measurement.

Many would argue that the study of visual attention cannot be accomplished without the study of eye movements, given the close link between the control of attention and control of gaze (Henderson, 2006). While it is the case that attention can be directed independently of eye movements, they are also naturally linked. One area of research performed on eye movements and visual cognition is the viewing of natural scenes. In complex scenes, attention is directed to specific stimulus-based and goal-relevant locations through gaze control (Henderson, 2003). Figure 16.1 presents a representative eye-movement path over a complex natural scene. Henderson (2007) describes eye fixation as either "pulled" by stimulus properties or "pushed" by goal-directed behavior to a particular scene location. The

Figure 16.1

Distributions of fixations over a scene. (From Henderson, J. M., 2007, Regarding scenes, *Current Directions in Psychological Science, 16*, 219–222; © 2007 Association for Psychological Science, reprinted by Permission of SAGE Publications.)

"pulling" of fixations has been investigated by analyses of image properties at fixations, showing that image statistics are correlated with fixation
locations. Research has found high spatial frequency content and edge density to be greater at fixations compared to unfixated patches (Henderson,
2003).

A second way to examine the stimulus-driven approach to fixations has
been through the creation of *saliency maps*, which identify regions of a
scene that are different from the surrounding area in image dimensions
such as color, contrast, intensity, and orientation on a number of different
spatial scales (Itti & Koch, 2001). The high salient points on the map serve
as predictors in a model about how gaze will be distributed in the scene
and can be compared with observed eye fixations.

The "pushing" toward scene locations comes from knowledge and memory for a scene as well as the goals of the viewer. Active task goals have

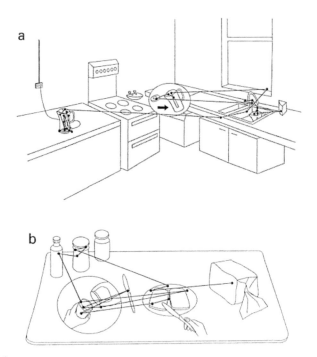

Figure 16.2
Sequence of fixations in (a) tea and (b) sandwich making. (Reprinted from Land,
M. F., & Hayhoe, M., 2001, In what ways do eye movements contribute to every-
day activities? *Vision Research*, *41*, 3559–3565; © 2001, with permission from
Elsevier.)

a strong influence on gaze fixation. Numerous studies on tasks, ranging from driving to hand washing to making sandwiches, show that fixations are tightly linked to relevant areas in the scene as well as relevant actions, such as reaching and grasping (see Figure 16.2). It has been shown that fixations during real-world active tasks, such as the task of making tea, are less strongly tied to visual saliency (Hayhoe, 2009). A current research question is how best to model the combination of knowledge structures and image properties (Henderson, 2007).

One question explored with eye fixations in both active and passive scene-perception research is the extent to which *visual memory* representations are formed during movements of gaze and how much these inform the programming of later gaze fixation. For active, natural tasks, there is

Figure 16.3

View (top) of the virtual environment in Aivar, Hayhoe, Chizk, and Mruczek (2005), with the toy model on the top, the resource area on the right, and the workspace on the left. Close-up of the model (bottom-left) and location of pieces in the resource area (bottom-right). (Aivar, M. P., Hayhoe, M. M., Chizk, C. L., & Mruczek, R. E. B. (2005). Spatial memory and saccadic targeting in a natural task. *Journal of Vision*, 5, 177–193. © 2006. Reproduced with permission of Association for Research in Vision & Ophthalmology via Copyright Clearance Center.)

evidence that people use memory in programming saccadic eye movements. Some of the recent work on this topic has been carried out in immersive virtual environments with mobile head trackers. For example, in one study, participants were asked to build a copy of a toy model in a virtual environment (Aivar et al., 2005). The virtual environment presented the model at the top, a resource area on the right that had a spatial arrangement of the toy pieces, and a workspace area on the left where the toy would be built (see Figure 16.3 for the virtual environment display). Participants first had experience with a single spatial arrangement in the resource area. After this, when they reached for a piece and then fixated in the workspace, the spatial arrangement was changed in the resource area. When participants looked back to the resource area for another piece, they fixated first on the initial location of the piece rather than its current, visually specified location. This pattern of results suggests that a representation of the spatial structure of the environment was stored across fixation, and that saccades were at least partially driven by memory for location and not by the visual stimulus in the scene.

16.3   Selective Attention

As stated in the introduction to this chapter, we are constantly overloaded with more sensory information than can be processed at one time. Selective attention is the ability to select some of the information for further processing while excluding irrelevant information. We are often successful at this process, but it is also important to consider that attentional mechanisms may be—on one hand—too selective by ignoring information that is relevant, or—on the other hand—ineffective at filtering out information irrelevant to the task (Strayer & Drews, 2007). Both of these could have implications for what is "seen." Furthermore, individuals do not always have a good *metacognitive* understanding of the effects and limitations of attention, meaning that they do not have knowledge about how attentional processes may influence perception and cognition (Varakin, Levin, & Fidler, 2004).

16.3.1   Early versus Late Selection

Given the need for selection, an obvious question becomes, when does the selection occur? This question has received a considerable amount of investigation. Early selection theories argued that unattended information is not processed beyond initial sensory features (e.g., Broadbent, 1958). Late selection theories argued that since a goal of selective attention is to focus on relevant information and filter irrelevant information, there must be some mechanism to process the information to determine what is relevant.

However, the notion of late selection then poses a problem for the purpose of selection itself, which is to avoid processing irrelevant information. Thus, a debate emerged early in cognitive science about whether selection occurred early or late in the process (much of this work occurred with auditory perception). It is now generally believed that there is a middle ground between these strong views. Unattended information is not processed to the same degree as attended information, but it is not completely filtered either (Chun & Wolfe, 2001; Pashler, 1998; Treisman, 1960).

16.3.2   Attentional-Cueing Paradigm and Space-Based Attention

One dominant way to study spatial attention is based on a cueing task paradigm in which viewers are asked to respond with a button press to the onset of stimulus, which is preceded by a visual cue. The cue could be in various forms and is intended to draw attention to a location in space (see Figure 16.4). In the original paradigm by Posner et al. (1978), a cue was presented in the center of the visual field prior to the test stimuli. The cue was either a left- or right-facing arrow or a neutral plus sign, indicating that the stimulus would appear on the left or right side of the fixation point (80% of the time) or that it was equally likely to appear on either side. Observers kept their eyes fixated on a central fixation point. The results of this experiment showed that time to respond to a test stimulus that was consistent with the cue (valid trial) decreased compared to the neutral trials, and time to respond to the stimulus when it was inconsistent with the cue (invalid trial) increased. Using this paradigm, researchers developed

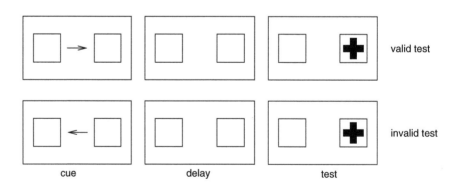

Figure 16.4

Representation of the attentional-cueing paradigm of Posner, Nissen, and Ogden (1978).

a model of three operations required to shift attention to a new location. These include (1) disengagement of attention from an object, (2) movement of attention, and (3) engagement of attention to a new object. Performance of brain-damaged patients on the attentional-cueing task supported the notion that these three operations are mediated by three different brain areas (Posner & Raichle, 1994; Posner, Walker, Friedrich, & Rafal, 1984). Well known as a metaphor for how spatial attention works is the *spotlight theory*. In this analogy, attention is a spotlight that enhances processing at a given location. This suggests a moving area of attention in space that can account for the general facilitation and inhibitory effects seen in the cueing-paradigm results. The *zoom lens theory* modified the spotlight theory, emphasizing not only the spatial location but also a change in the size or extent of the focus of attention. The change in "zoom" is thought to be accompanied by a change in the amount of visual detail available within the region of attention. A wider zoom is associated with poor resolution, whereas a more narrow scope would improve the spatial resolution.

16.3.3   Object-Based Attention

In addition to space-based theories of attention, there is evidence in support of object-based attention. This account differs from space-based accounts of attention by suggesting that attention selects an object, rather than a location, in space. Studies demonstrating object-based attention show that there are performance advantages for tasks which require decisions about attributes that are part of the same object, rather than parts of separate objects, even when they occupy the same location in space. For example, Baylis and Driver (1993) presented a stimulus which could be interpreted as two objects (black figures) or a single object (white figure), depending on the perceptual grouping (see Figure 16.5). The task was to determine the height of the apexes formed from the angled white center figure. Responses were faster when the figure was perceived to be one white object instead of two black objects.

Spatial-cueing paradigms as described in Section 16.3.2, are also used to examine how object-based attention may be used (Egly, Driver, & Rafal, 1994). In this method, two parallel rectangles were presented, and a target could appear in either end of either rectangle. A location at one of the ends of the rectangles was cued. Viewers were fastest in detecting targets in the cued location, supporting space-based attention. However, they were also faster at detecting a target at the opposite end of the *same* rectangle that was cued compared to a target at equal distance inside another rectangle, supporting object-based attention. More-recent work studying this same-object advantage has examined the factors that define what an object is (Ben-Shahar, Scholl, & Zucker, 2007; Moore & Fulton, 2005) and the nature

Figure 16.5

An example of object-based attention. The decision about height of apex was faster when the display was perceived as one object (white) compared to two objects (black). (Adapted from Baylis, C. G., & Driver, J., 1993, Visual attention and objects: Evidence for hierarchical coding of coding of location, *Journal of Experimental Psychology: Human Perception and Performance*, *19*(3), 451-470, Figure 2; used with permission from the American Psychological Association.)

of the mechanisms that would support both location- and object-based attentional selection (Zemel, Behrmann, Mozer, & Bavelier, 2002).

Furthermore, object-based accounts of attention help to explain some of the phenomenology of how one can be attending to a spatial location but still not detect the presence of an object. In *inattentional blindness*, an object that is not attended to is not noticed. In other words, the phenomenon may be thought of as "looking without seeing" (Mack & Rock, 1998). Early demonstrations of inattentional blindness were carried out with a method of superimposing two videos—one showing two people playing a hand game and the other showing three people passing a basketball. Viewers were asked to attend to one of the videos and make a response. During this period of attending to one of the games, an unexpected event occurred in the unattended video (such as a woman carrying an umbrella walking through the basketball game scene). Surprisingly, most viewers failed to notice the unexpected event (Neisser & Becklen, 1975). These demonstrations were more recently replicated and expanded upon by Simons and Chabris (1999), who presented a stimulus of two teams of people in white and black shirts passing basketballs. The task was for the participant to count the number of passes of a certain team. In one version, during the attended event, a person wearing a gorilla suit walked into the middle of the group, faced the camera and thumped its chest, and walked out. Again, about half of the participants in the study failed to notice the gorilla (see Figure 16.6). For more examples of inattentional blindness in real-world settings, see `http://www.simonslab.com/videos.html`, as well as the recent "invisible gorilla" blog, `http://theinvisiblegorilla.com/blog/`.

Other results supporting inattentional blindness come from the use of the inattention paradigm of Mack and Rock (1998), originally developed to

Figure 16.6
A frame from the "gorilla" video of Simons and Chabris (1999). (Figure provided by Daniel Simons.)

ask which visual features could be perceived without attention. Their task presented a cross figure and required participants to decide whether the vertical or horizontal line was longer. On inattention trials, an unexpected shape appeared near the cross, and participants were asked about various properties of the stimulus, such as the color and shape. Performance on these trials was compared to divided-attention trials in which the participant knew about the possibility of an additional object appearing in the display. The results showed that single sensory properties such as color could be identified on inattention trials, but shape could not. Surprisingly, about 25% of the participants did not perceive any stimulus at all! Overall, this paradigm has established that simple objects are not easily detected when they are not attended to.

16.3.4   Attention to Multiple Targets

Much of the work described in this chapter so far examines the critical function of attending to a single location or object. However, it is also necessary in our everyday lives to accomplish sustained attention to several dynamic objects in the environment at one time. A task named *multiple-object tracking* (MOT) has been used experimentally to test the abilities and limitations of maintaining attention on more than one object (Pylyshyn & Storm, 1988). In a representative task, a group of identical-feature objects (such as a simple shape) appears on a screen and then a subset of these objects are identified as targets to track as they move among the other objects. After all of the objects stop moving, the observer is asked to identify the original targets. A number of studies have shown that there are performance limitations on this task. Accuracy of choosing the correct targets decreases with increasing numbers of objects, increasing speed of object motion, and closer spacing of objects (Alvarez & Franconeri, 2007; Franconeri, Lin, Pylyshyn, Fisher, & Enns, 2008; Intriligator & Cavanagh, 2001). While it is useful to define these limits on object tracking for applications involving multiple target search, recent approaches have also worked to propose a common explanation for observed performance decrements. One explanation may be that the visual system has a limited ability to individuate objects that are in close proximity, termed a *crowding effect*. Consistent with this mechanism based on the spatial resolution of visual attention, Franconeri, Jonathan, and Scimeca (2010) showed that when object spacing was controlled for, viewers could track many objects as well as they could track a single object, and that speed was also not a significant predictor of performance. Multiple-object-tracking research has also helped to define what is meant by *object-based attention*, providing alternative ways to test the phenomenon (Scholl, 2009). For example, it has been shown that object-based attention can be influenced by cues of connectedness and curvature discontinuities (Scholl, Pylyshyn, & Feldman, 2001), and that it is constrained by object cohesion (vanMarle & Scholl, 2003).

16.3.5 Attention Can Enhance Perception

Given that behavior changes in numerous ways with attention, it is an important question to ask whether attention influences the *appearance* of a stimulus or simply the *response* to the stimulus due to other attentional factors. Several different studies have tested the effects of involuntary (exogenously cued) attention on object appearance using a methodology that required comparative judgments of two stimuli with a judgment that was not the dimension of interest, to avoid cognitive biases that might be associated with emphasizing the specific dimension. For example, the researchers were interested in whether attention influenced perceived contrast between gratings but asked observers to report the orientation of the stimulus that was higher or lower in contrast, rather than to make a judgment about perceived contrast directly. Given two physically identical contrast gratings, observers were more likely to report the orientation of the cued grating than that of the one that was not cued, indicating greater perceived contrast for the attended stimulus. Using this type of paradigm, it has been shown that attention enhances perceived contrast (Carrasco, Ling, & Read, 2004), color (Fuller & Carrasco, 2006), and a number of other perceived object dimensions. More recently, similar effects of attention on perceived contrast (T. Liu, Abrams, & Carrasco, 2009) and spatial frequency (Abrams, Barbot, & Carrasco, 2010) have been found using a voluntary (endogenous) task. Thus, a body of work suggests that attending to an object can change the viewer's basic sensory experience of that object.

16.4 Visual Search

Visual search is ubiquitous in everyday behavior. Search tasks include finding car keys in a drawer, a friend in a crowd, or a feature on a radiology scan. Visual search in the psychology laboratory involves task paradigms that present a target to be found among a set of distractors. The efficiency, or how easily the target is detected, serves as the performance measure. It is important to consider how the process of search relates to the concepts already described in selective attention. The study of visual search has been concerned with several questions that cross domains of perception, attention, and memory.

The most well-known theory for visual search is the feature integration theory (FIT) (Treisman, 1980). In FIT, visual search tasks are described as requiring either "preattentive" or "focused attention" stages of processing. Preattentive search is accomplished without attention for a target defined by a single basic feature, such as color or orientation. Given a display such as an O among distracting items of T, the phenomenon of *visual pop-out* would occur for the O (see Figure 16.7). Behaviorally, it was shown that

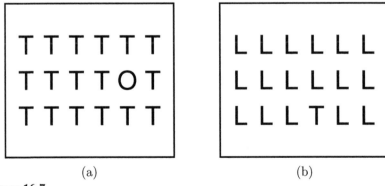

(a)   (b)

Figure 16.7

(a) Visual pop-out, where the target O is distinguished from the distractors (Ts) by only one feature (curved versus straight lines). (b) A visual search for target T among Ls is harder, since it requires a conjunction of features (configurations of horizontal and vertical lines).

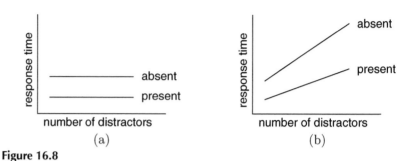

Figure 16.8

(a) In parallel search, response time does not increase as a function of number of distractors in the display. (b) In serial search, response time increases linearly with increasing number of distractors.

the pop-out effect occurred regardless of the number of distractor items in the display, and it was argued that this stage of search involved *parallel processing* of the entire visual field at one time. In contrast, searching for a target that shares features with the distractors, such as a T among Ls, requires focused attention—an effortful search performed with serial processing in which a sequence of attentional fixation was needed. Patterns of response times associated with parallel and serial searches confirmed this distinction. For parallel search, response time remained constant as a function of number of distractors. For serial search, response time increased as a function of the number of distractors (see Figure 16.8). The nature of the search as self-terminating also led to the prediction that response time for finding a "present" target would be faster than that for determining that the target was "absent."

The term *integration* in feature integration theory further suggests that there must be a mechanism for putting together individual features into visual objects. This process is called *binding*. Treisman (1980) proposed that attention to specific spatial locations is required to conjoin individual features into objects. Thus, a conjunction search involving focused attention was required for finding a target that was defined by a conjunction of features. The FIT also predicted that features in the preattentive stage of processing may not be correctly conjoined. This prediction was shown in the phenomenon of *illusory conjunctions*, which were demonstrated with a paradigm showing that when items defined by two features (such as color and shape) were flashed on a screen quickly, there were memory errors in reporting the conjoined features. For example, if a red S, blue T, and green X were presented, participants might report having seen a blue S and a red T. There have been a number of revised theories relating to the FIT since it was first proposed (Treisman & Sato, 1990; Wolfe, 2003, 1994).

16.4.1   Practice and Consistency

Although "preattentive" search was used by Treisman (1980) to refer to
the automatic processing that occurs prior to attention, another way to
enable automatic and less effortful processing is through practice. In human information-processing, there is a broad distinction between two types
of processing, *automatic* and *controlled*. Automatic processes are fast, activated without active control, and are free of the capacity limitations of
attention. Controlled processes are slow, effortful, and require attentional
control. Classic studies on practice in visual search showed that human
performance can improve with practice given one type of training but not
others (Shiffrin & Schneider, 1977). With *consistent mapping* training in
which the observer's mapping of stimulus response stays the same over
time, performance may become automatic. However, with *varied mapping*
training in which the stimulus response mapping varies across trials, auto-
maticity does not develop and controlled processing is required. This was
shown experimentally with tasks such as always searching for the same target (consistent mapping) compared to tasks where the target on one trial
becomes the distractor on another (varied mapping). The same types of
consistency effects apply to real world design such as maintaining a consistent spatial layout on a visual display used across different interfaces.
Importantly, as tasks become more automatic, more attentional resources
may be available for performing other tasks at the same time.

16.4.2   Working Memory

The construct of working memory has also played an important role in
models of visual search. *Working memory* refers to the process of active
maintenance and manipulation of information when it is no longer present
in the environment (Postle, 2006). Generally, working memory is associated with our abilities to use top-down control in goal-driven tasks (Kane,
Bleckley, Conway, & Engle, 2001) and is therefore likely linked with visual
selective attention. Many models of visual search processing include visual
working memory as an important part of the process, serving to maintain
a template of the target and therefore biasing perception of target features that are relevant for the task goal (Desimone & Duncan, 1995), or—
after selection of the target—maintaining that target object representation
(Treisman & Sato, 1990). To test these models, researchers have examined
whether holding information in working memory influences search performance, following the logic that if visual search relies on working memory,
search should be impaired when working memory is taxed. Results from
recent investigations have shown that a concurrent, visual object working
memory task interferes with visual search for a target only when the target changes from trial to trial; given a stable visual target, visual search

appears to require minimal object working memory resources (Woodman, Luck, & Schall, 2007). However, holding spatial locations in working memory does interfere with visual search (Woodman & Luck, 2004). While it is clear that there are important interactions between visual working memory and visual attention, the relationship is complex and may be best understood by examining specific task distinctions (for a review, see Awh, Vogel, & Oh, 2006).

16.5   Other Failures of Visual Awareness

As can be seen in the phenomenon of inattentional blindness, described in Section 16.3.3, viewers are unaware of significant portions of the visual world, and this awareness is likely influenced by attention. The following sections describe two other examples of circumstances in which what is presented to the visual system is not equivalent to what is perceived.

16.5.1   Change Blindness

Although we often notice changes in our environment that are signaled by transients of motion or sound, there are circumstances in which visual changes that occur during a disruption go unnoticed. The failure to detect substantial visual changes is known as *change blindness*. As described in Section 16.2, one disruption that occurs naturally and often in visual perception is the saccade. A number of laboratory studies have shown that visual environmental changes that occur during a saccade are not detected. But change blindness effects generalize beyond saccade studies. In a classic study using a "flicker" paradigm, photographs of a real-world scene were presented in a repeated way so that a significant change to the image occurred on every other image (Rensink, O'Regan, & Clark, 1997). The images appeared for 240 ms, with an 80 ms gray screen presented in between each image. The original and modified images were repeated until the viewer reported the change. Viewers rarely detected the change on the first cycle of images and often required extended viewing (over tens of seconds) in order to notice and report the change. Other work has used motion picture clips to demonstrate a similar effect, where a primary actor or object in the scene changed during a "cut" to a different view, and only about one-third of the viewers noticed the change (Levin & Simons, 1997). Even in a real-world setting on a college campus, it was shown that people failed to detect the change of a person while talking with the person! Simons and Levin (1998) had an experimenter initiate a conversation with a naive pedestrian on campus. During the conversation, two other experimenters, carrying a door, walked in between the conversation, and while the initial experimenter was occluded by the door, another experimenter replaced him and continued the conversation with the pedestrian. This real-world substitution of experimenters went unnoticed.

Attention researchers have examined several different explanations for this striking phenomenon in order to explain the nature of the effect. One possibility is that there is little or no visual memory for scenes, so that visual details of individual objects in a scene cannot be preserved. In this view, when attention is withdrawn from an object (due to a disruption, such as a saccade, blank screen, or even a door), the gist or meaning of a scene may remain, but representations of visual details are lost (O'Regan & Noë, 2001; Rensink, 2002; Wolfe, 1998). The assumption is that visual memory is *transient*. In contrast, others have demonstrated that there are robust visual memories for objects in scenes when attention is withdrawn, so it is difficult to use a failure to form or retain a visual representation as a complete explanation (Hollingworth, 2006). Instead, it may be that there is a failure to compare representations of attended objects pre- and post-change. Evidence for intact pre-change representations has been shown in studies in which a cue directed attention to the change location after a change occurred (Hollingworth, 2003). In these cases, change detection was improved, showing that there must have been an enduring memory of the initial object available for comparison. In support of this idea, other studies demonstrated that even when change blindness was demonstrated and observers were unaware of a change, they were still able to accurately pick out objects that were in pre- and post-change scenes (Mitroff, Simons, & Levin, 2004).

16.5.2   Attentional Blink

Another example of a failure to perceive is thought to be a result of temporal constraints on attention. We are generally very good at perceiving visual stimuli at rapid speeds of presentation. However, given rapidly presented targets, there is a brief time—after perceiving a target—in which the next target will not be perceived. This failure to perceive the second item within about a half second of the first is called *attentional blink*, named after the idea that an actual blink of the eye also prohibits perception (Shapiro, Raymond, & Arnell, 1997). The attentional blink is typically studied in a specific type of search task called *rapid serial visual presentation* (RSVP). In this task, a viewer is presented with a sequence of visual stimuli and given a specific type of target to report, such as the letters in a series of numbers and letters. One dominant explanation of the failure to detect the target is that attention is completely captured for the first target and then unavailable for the next target. As has been proposed in inattentional blindness—without attention, there is no conscious perception of a visual object.

16.6   Issues Specific to Computer Graphics

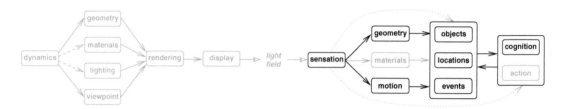

16.6.1   Attention and Effective Displays

After becoming more familiar with effects of inattentional blindness and change blindness, it should not be surprising that failures in visual awareness could also have some negative implications for perception in human-computer interfaces. One implication has to do with viewers' lack of understanding about their limitations in visual awareness. Creators and users of graphics displays may have overestimations of their abilities to detect information, or intuitive ideas about the presentation of effective displays that may not correspond to research findings on selective attention. For example, there is a general belief that turning information into visual forms is most effective for communicating that information. Varakin et al. (2004) call this an "illusion of visual bandwidth." Visual displays may facilitate cognitive performance in circumstances where critical information can be conveyed by a single feature. In one example, anesthesiologists showed more-rapid responses with a graphical display that changed the shape of an object representing a heart during a heart attack (Agutter et al., 2003). However, there are several reasons to question generalized statements about benefits of visual displays of information. These include (1) the breadth or extent of attention to be allocated at one time; (2) the effectiveness of certain features at capturing attention; and (3) the extent to which attention leads to deep or meaningful processing of information.

Practical questions involve how best to attract attention to parts of a display. Transient or abrupt changes may seem to be a good solution, but, as seen from some of the research described, these changes may be masked by saccades or by cognitive factors, such as task goals or expectations about where to look. Furthermore, even if attention is directed to a given location, this does not guarantee a complete and in-depth representation of a stimulus. One example is the abundant use of pop-up Internet advertisements, which—in different circumstances—could (1) fail to be salient enough to attract attention (Varakin et al., 2004) or (2) act in an intrusive way by diverting attention from the primary task (Sagarin, Britt, & Heider, 2003).

One type of display that should be considered in the context of visual awareness and attention is an augmented-reality head-up display (HUD). These displays are designed to provide additional information for navigation and control on the windshield of a vehicle (such as a plane or car), so that the user can more effectively monitor the external environment. As might be expected, despite the advantages of additional useful information presented within the user's field of view, there are also likely consequences associated with dividing attention, integrating the display and the environment, and the frames of reference to be attended to (Wickens, Vincow, & Yeh, 2005). For a pilot, for example, the HUD works to guide attention to a particular part of the environment with some type of marker on the display. This method integrates screen-based and world-based frames of reference and could help in detection of unexpected events, but has also been shown to make pilots less aware of events that were outside of their immediate cognitive context (Wickens & Long, 1995). Augmented-vision displays in development for aiding people with low vision (Apfelbaum, Apfelbaum, Woods, & Peli, 2008) simultaneously present two different views to one or both eyes. Experiments carried out with these displays have replicated inattentional blindness effects with the ball-throwing task described in Section 16.3.3.

Furthermore, a construct directly related to attention and the human factors of displays is the *useful field of view* (UFOV), defined as the region in the visual field over which a viewer can process visual information at a single glance, with no further eye or head movements (Ball, Beard, Roenker, & Griggs, 1988; A. B. Sekuler, Bennett, & Mamelak, 2000). The UFOV relates to one's ability to perform everyday actions, such as driving and walking, among visual distractors, such as cluttered scenes. Assessment typically involves a task that measures the ability of a viewer to localize a single target in the periphery in the presence of distractors while performing another attention-demanding task in central vision. Significant variation has been found in the size of the UFOV across individuals and task factors, including reduced UFOV, in older versus younger adults. It has also been shown that UFOV can improve with practice.

16.6.2   Perceptually Based Rendering

Approaches informed by models of visual attention have been directed toward the goal of rendering high-fidelity, complex scenes in computer graphics. Given that high-fidelity rendering is computationally expensive, several methods have been used to selectively render some parts of the scene at the expense of others. These methods are based on several of the concepts covered in this chapter. Initial work with selective rendering was based on the premise that detailed vision only occurs in the fovea, so that graphics

presented in the periphery could be presented at lower quality and go unnoticed by the viewer. If the goal is to direct computational effort at the
regions of the scene on which the viewer will fixate, what best determines
where these locations will be? Certain features of the scene will attract
attention in a bottom-up manner, but, as we have seen, this may not always predict where attention will be directed. Top-down task goals are
also important, particularly in their influence on realistic action sequences.

One approach has been to model task-level saliency—and not only
bottom-up saliency maps (Cater, Chalmers, & Ledda, 2002; Cater,
Chalmers & Ward, 2003). By providing specific task goals, Cater, Chalmers,
and Ward (2003) aimed to test whether they could elicit inattentional blindness for low-quality rendering even at points of fixation. Their task was to
count the number of teapots in a computer generated office scene. There
were three levels of resolution quality of the office scene: entire high quality
(sampling resolution of 3072×3072), entire low quality (sampling resolution
of 1024×1024), and selective quality (the majority of the scene was rendered in low quality, except for 2° visual angle centered on each teapot).
The results showed that viewers consistently failed to notice any difference between the high-quality and selective-quality image. Eye-tracking
data were also obtained, confirming that fixations were made both on the
target teapots (high quality) and nontarget objects (low quality). The results suggest that the phenomenon of inattentional blindness may work to
allow selective rendering even when low-quality images are targets of fixation. Related work has developed a selective guidance system (Sundstedt,
Debattista, Longhurst, Chalmers, & Troscianko, 2005) that produces an
importance map to direct the rendering. The importance map is a combination of a task map (which models the effect of top-down, goal-directed
attention) and a saliency map (which models bottom-up, feature-driven
attention). In an animated walk-through of an office corridor, observers
were asked to count the number of fire-safety items. As in the previous
work, observers were not able to detect differences in the rendering quality of the high-quality and selective-quality scenes. There are important
questions still left unanswered by this approach, such as how best to measure detectability of change, and the relative benefits and costs of these
computational savings.

16.6.3   Video Game Effects on Selective Attention

A focus of this chapter has been on the effects of selective attention on
visual perception, and particularly the perception of computer graphics.
As a final thought, it is interesting to reverse the relationship and consider
how interacting with computer graphics may influence attention. Green
and Bavelier (2003, 2006) have examined the effects of playing action video

games on components of perception, attention, and perceptual learning (see also Green, Li, & Bavelier, 2009). For visual attention, action video games seem an ideal test—they require the processing of multiple items simultaneously and the selection of relevant information. Could action-video-game experience actually enhance attentional resources and/or spatial selection? Green and Bavelier (2006) addressed this question by testing video-game players (VGPs) and non-video-game players (NVGPs) on two attentional paradigms. First, with a paradigm that varies perceptual load (high versus low number of distractors), they found that the VGPs had an increase in attentional resources available. Second, with the useful field of view (UFOV) task, they measured the ability to allocate attention throughout the visual field. The results showed an enhancement in spatial attention at both central and peripheral locations for VGPs compared to NVGPs. In addition, a third experiment showed that training of NVGPs increased their performance on the UFOV task as well, showing improvement in allocating spatial attention. The take home message—playing video games is not just a mindless activity; instead, it could be a useful way to increase one's visual attentional processing!

16.7   Suggestions for Further Reading

Accessible reading on topics in visual attention:

> Hayhoe, M., & Ballard, D. (2005). Eye movements in natural behavior. *TRENDS in Cognitive Sciences*, *9*(4), 188–194.

> Simons, D. J., & Rensink, R. A. (2005). Change blindness: Past, present, and future. *TRENDS in Cognitive Sciences*, *9*(1), 16–20.

A thorough review of visual attention:

> Egeth, H. E., & Yantis, S. (1997). Visual attention: Control, representation, and time course. *Annual Review of Psychology*, *48*, 269–297.

17

Event Recognition—Inanimate

As we have seen, the visual system is involved in identifying objects (see Chapter 15) and guiding actions (see Chapter 14). In this chapter, we will explore how the visual system helps us understand events that unfold over time with inanimate objects. It especially addresses how the visual system understands and interprets actions or events that may occur outside of our bodies. An essential distinction to make here is that events are not just actions. Actions imply an actor, but events can also occur without an immediate actor, as when a candle blows out in the wind (Zacks & Tversky, 2003). Surprisingly, the visual system seems to play an important role in our understanding of events like the collision between two objects. In other words, we can actually see if a collision is natural or unnatural. This recognition does not always occur and may depend on the complexity of the physics behind an event, but the fact that the naturalness and physical dynamics of the event may be interpreted by the visual system suggests it performs very high-level processes.

In addition to recognizing the physical dynamics of an event, the visual system also seems to parse events into separate spatiotemporal entities. For example, watching someone bake a cake involves understanding when the baker is performing one step rather than another. When does the baker mix the dry ingredients, and is that action distinct from when the baker combines the wet ingredients? The visual system seems to aid in our recognition of the parts of events like baking a cake, a process also known as *event parsing*, or *event segmentation*. The larger process that involves recognizing these spatiotemporal wholes of an event and their characteristics as they occur over time for an observer is often termed *event perception*. This chapter discusses event perception as it relates to inanimate objects and events not involving action of the perceiver. The study of events as they occur in animate objects (biological motion) will be the topic of Chapter 18.

17.1 Types of Events

We will begin our discussion of event perception by defining the word *event* as it relates to the topic of this chapter. Much of the research covered in previous chapters has contributed to our definition of events. For example, events may have parts, which would make the processes behind recognizing an event very much like recognizing an object (think back to the recognition-by-components theory discussed in Chapter 15; see also Biederman, 1987). For events, these parts could be defined by space (grasp the cup on the table; then lift it to your mouth), by time (first, move the cup here; then move it there), or by conceptual goals (once you have moved the cup, pour in the coffee). Thus, we perceive the world as composed of distinct events in addition to individual objects (Barker, 1963). In addition to having parts, events should have a perceived beginning and end (akin to an edge for an object, but possibly more subjective) to be perceived as separate from other events that may be unfolding over time (Kurby & Zacks, 2008; Zacks & Tversky, 2003).

Furthermore, events can also be defined as changes to the surfaces in the world, such as translations, rotations, collisions, and deformations—which again returns us to previous discussions of perception of motion and objects from other chapters. J. J. Gibson (1979) originally proposed this idea, though many of his contemporaries have also provided experimental evidence to suggest that these surface changes can be directly perceived by the visual system (Bingham & Wickelgren, 2008). Early work suggested that perceivers poorly understand events like two balls colliding or a rock splashing into a pond (McCloskey, 1983), but later work has shown that there are some events that we can reliably understand and others for which our understanding is much weaker (Gilden & Proffitt, 1989; Proffitt & Gilden, 1989). We will begin our examination of event perception by discussing this research in more detail.

17.2 Perceiving Natural Events

Research on understanding events originated with studies done by Michotte (1946/1963), which examined simple interactions between two objects. Examples included one object *launching*, *triggering*, or *entraining* another (see Figure 17.1 for examples of these and other events). Michotte questioned why and when one object was perceived as causing another to move. Depicting the objects simply as squares, he showed participants different events occurring over time. The participants were asked to discuss what took place or occurred in the displays. The results nicely identified many variables relevant for determining whether one object causes another to

Figure 17.1

Examples of events involving interactions. (Reprinted from Scholl, B. J., & Tremoulet, P. D., 2000, Perceptual causality and animacy, *Trends in Cognitive Sciences*, 4(8), 299–309; © 2000, with permission from Elsevier.)

move in specific ways. The examples given will pertain to the perception of launching, but the same variables can be manipulated in different ways to produce a perception of triggering or entraining.

Michotte found that one of the most important variables in the perception of causation is timing. The motion of one square needs to set into motion the other square within 200 ms of a collision for causation to be perceived reliably. The direction of motion is also important. If square x is perceived to launch square y, then the direction of y should be approximately the same as the direction that x was moving. Also, if y is perceived to be launched by x then it must move more slowly than or at approximately the same speed as x, but never faster. Michotte's seminal work paved the way for other researchers to explore our ability to perceive the natural dynamics in an event. It also spawned an important research question that continues to animate the field: how much is our understanding of events dependent upon our experiences in the world?

Many contemporary studies have extended the work of Michotte in various ways (for a review, see Scholl & Tremoulet, 2000). For example, researchers have shown that launching can be replicated with illusory motions, like apparent motion (Gordon, Day, & Stecher, 1990). This is of obvious importance for conveying causal interactions in animations. Others constructed displays that expanded Michotte's displays to include such interactions as *pulling*, *disintegrating*, and *bursting* (White & Milne, 1997, 1999). Moreover, some of the contemporary studies have adopted different methodologies for assessing the perception of the displays. For example, in the studies conducted by White and Milne (1997, 1999), the researchers asked participants to rate three different statements that described the event in the displays (one involved causality, another emphasized no interaction, and the last described the items moving on their own), rather than directly obtaining perceptual reports, as in Michotte's studies. Finally, recent studies have shown that these percepts (such as launching) seem to occur across cultures (Morris & Peng, 1994) and emerge in infancy, even before language is learned (Leslie, 1982; Leslie & Keeble, 1987).

Michotte's work was also extended by researchers interested in addressing the question of how people perceive the nature of physical events. His initial studies spawned an area of research now called *intuitive physics* (or *naive physics* by some). The first set of studies on this topic was done by Runeson (1977), in which he more closely examined how people interpreted the collision between two objects. Runeson asked participants to view a collision and then decide which object was heavier given the outcome of the collision. The findings showed that participants seemed able to determine the weight of the object through watching the dynamics of the collision.

Further work, however, suggested that people may not be able to actually perceive information about the mass of the objects involved in a collision (Gilden & Proffitt, 1989). Gilden and Proffitt investigated a variety of collision types and determined that participants seemed to use two types of heuristics to make a decision about the mass of the objects involved in the collision. First, participants appeared to use what the researchers termed a *ricochet* heuristic. (A heuristic is a simple rule, like a shortcut or a rule of thumb that participants use to reason about an event.) Simply put, if x hits y and x moves backward at a higher velocity than the forward motion of y, then y is heavier than x. They also found that participants

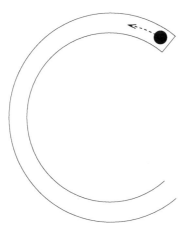

Figure 17.2

In the C-shaped tube problem, participants are given a figure like this and asked to draw the trajectory that the ball will take upon exiting the tube. (After McCloskey, Caramazza, & Green, 1980.)

used what they called a *clobbering* heuristic to interpret some collisions. For this heuristic, if x hits y and y is catapulted off in the same direction that x was moving, then x is interpreted as being heavier than y. Their findings also showed that when these two heuristics conflicted in a given dynamic event, participants had a very hard time deciding which ball was heavier. This inability to resolve the conflicting heuristical information is inconsistent with a purported direct ability to perceive mass. Instead, the conflict suggests that participants were not simply seeing the mass— they were performing cognitive processes to reason about the weight of the objects after the collision was perceived.

Other intuitive physics research has used static descriptions of events to understand how people perceive event dynamics. McCloskey et al. (1980) described an event (a ball rolling through a C-shaped tube) to college-aged students and then asked them to predict (by drawing) the trajectory that the ball would take when it exited the tube (see Figure 17.2). The correct answer is that the ball should travel in a straight path after exiting the tube, because no force is acting on the ball once it leaves the tube. One-third of the students, however, claimed that the ball would continue to travel in a curved path. Examination of other events that involved predicting path trajectories also resulted in one-third of college students predicting erroneous paths.

This research begged the question of why these erroneous judgments would occur if the visual system is sensitive to the dynamics of collisions.

Some researchers suggested that these biases in judgment simply resulted from problems with higher-level cognitive responses, rather than a visual misinterpretation of the event dynamics. One possible way of addressing this issue would be to show people alternative responses and ask them to choose one (this test would be more visual in nature than McCloskey et al., 1980, drawing test). Kaiser, Proffitt, and Anderson (1985) asked participants to predict the trajectory of the ball in the C-shaped tube task using both a static representation of the problem (similar to the previous research) and a series of videos that depicted possible trajectories occurring in real time. Their findings showed that even though people predicted incorrectly in the static version of the problem (replicating the finding of McCloskey et al.), they correctly identified the straight trajectory in the dynamic versions. Overall, their results suggest that the visual system may be more sensitive to natural events that unfold over time.

Nonetheless, further work revealed that perceiving the nature of dynamic events may not always be possible, even when the events are shown in video format rather than static. These studies demonstrated that people have a hard time perceiving the principles of physics known as *conservation of angular momentum* and *the effects of distribution of mass in objects* (wheels in this case) on the speed at which they will roll down an incline (Proffitt, Kaiser, & Whelan, 1990). Surprisingly, when participants were asked to predict which wheel would arrive at the bottom of the ramp first, they were unable to do so, even after watching computer animations of examples of angular momentum. The wheels differed in their visual properties and the distribution of mass, but Proffitt et al. hypothesized that participants (college-aged students) should have been able to discover that more mass on the outside of the wheel made the wheel roll more slowly. Their participants were unable to interpret this law of dynamics from the visual dynamic displays. Even more interesting is that physics professors at the University of Virginia (where these studies were run) were not much better at predicting which wheel would win the race (when only allowed to watch the animations and not solve the problem by hand).

These disparate findings—that people can only sometimes visually understand the dynamics of an event—prompted researchers to identify which variables reliably predict when the visual system can successfully interpret the dynamics of an event. Proffitt and Gilden (1989) attributed the differences in success rates to differences in the perception of two kinds of motions: particle motion and extended body motion. Particle motion is motion that is produced when there is a change in the position of an object that is dependent upon the location of its center of mass only (no other variables are relevant). Extended body motion results from a change in the position of an object that is related to other variables, such as the distribution of mass in the object, its size, and its orientation in space (e.g., rolling wheels, liquid displacements, collisions). In nature, the same object can undergo both types of motions. A ball being dropped is an example of particle motion, and a ball being rolled down a ramp is an example of extended body motion. However, Proffitt and Gilden showed that the visual system seems to be better at interpreting the former (particle motion) as compared to the latter (extended body motion), providing an excellent way of characterizing the events and predicting success.

17.3   Event Recognition and Segmentation

Section 17.2 discussed the research on understanding how people perceive the nature of dynamic events. In this section, we will review how people recognize and parse events like baking a cake. As an overview, event segmentation can be both fine-grained and coarse-grained (Zacks, Tversky, & Iyer, 2001; see Figure 17.3). For example, in cake baking one could decide that mixing the ingredients is one part of the event and putting it in the oven is another part. This would be a somewhat coarse-grained analysis of the parts. A fine-grained segmentation might parse the event more finely (temporally or conceptually) to include parts such as (1) mixing the dry ingredients and (2) mixing the wet ingredients. The fact that parsing an event can include both specific and broad parts is not surprising given that actions are often hierarchically divided into goals and subgoals.

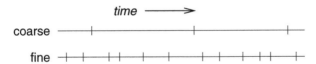

Figure 17.3
Coarse-grained event segmentation includes fewer breakpoints (represented as vertical lines in this diagram) over time than does fine-grained segmentation. (After Zacks, Tversky, & Iyer, 2001.)

17.3.1   Measuring Event Segmentation

In contrast to object parts, which are segmented in space, event parts seem to be segmented more in time. Therefore, initial studies on event segmentation asked participants to naturally parse events (in other words, to determine the boundaries of events) that they watched unfold time. Newtson (1973) pioneered this work by asking participants to watch a video of an event and to press a button whenever they felt one unit of the event had ended and a new one had begun. He termed the points in time that participants tapped the button as *breakpoints*. An analysis of these breakpoints both within participants and across participants revealed that participants often identify segments based on the completion of goals in an event or on large changes in the physical pose of the actor. Zacks, Tversky, and Iyer (2001) replicated Newtson's findings using a between-participants design (for more discussion of their results, see below). Together, these results suggest that the choice of boundaries for events is similar across people and that these choices are consistent within the same person. Furthermore, the level (either coarse- or fine-grained) at which people place these boundaries will vary with their understanding of the event, such that little understanding results in more fine-grained boundaries (Newtson, 1973; Vallacher & Wegner, 1987).

Newtson and Engquist (1976) then tested whether the loss of breakpoint information in a film would result in poorer memory and comprehension of the film's events. When brief deletions of the film occurred at a breakpoint, participants were more likely to notice them. Also, participants asked to reorder the slides in a slide show to represent the temporal sequence of an event, recalled more when the slides represented breakpoints in the event rather than nonbreakpoints. Recognition for the breakpoints in an event was also better when compared to recognition of nonbreakpoints.

More recently, Zacks, Tversky, and Iyer (2001) replicated the effects of Newtson and Engquist (1976) with a slightly different experimental paradigm. Their goal was to determine whether event perception should be considered a purely bottom-up process (driven by the perceptual stimuli only) or if it also involved top-down, cognitive influences. To test this notion, they asked participants to segment four videos that differed in familiarity to the observer (making the bed, doing the dishes, fertilizing a houseplant, and assembling a saxophone). The participants were asked to segment the videos in a coarse-grained way and a fine-grained way over two different experimental sessions, with a delay in between. They found that participants' chosen boundaries were similar, regardless of whether they delineated large boundaries or small ones. Also, the large boundaries were very likely to correspond with some of the small boundaries, suggesting a hierarchical structure to the boundary choices. Furthermore, one group of participants was asked to describe the units as they made their boundary choices. This group was more likely to show a hierarchical structure in their boundary choices, likely due to how they cognitively interpreted the event while segmenting. Their results suggest that both bottom-up and top-down processes can influence event segmentation.

Most of the previously discussed methodologies examined qualitative or subjective reports of event boundaries. Others have conducted quantitative analyses of event segmentation. For instance, Zacks (2004) showed that segmentation of simple, animated events was related to changes in the acceleration of the objects and their positions relative to one another. Hard,

Tversky, and Lang (2006) took abstract versions of films that depicted one object "chasing" another and two objects playing "hide-and-seek" (both based on the famous Heider and Simmel (1944) movies designed to study the activation of anthropomorphic descriptions when watching simple moving geometric figures) and played them forward and backward for participants, effectively manipulating the interpretability of the films in the process. If top-down processes are necessary to identify breakpoints, then playing the film backward should make the breakpoints more difficult to pinpoint. Top-down processing was also strengthened by having some participants watch and describe a narrative for the video before segmentation was assessed. Thus, participants who watched the film for the first time while identifying breakpoints should have been less able to interpret the events, possibly influencing their ability to segment it hierarchically. Their findings did not support this hypothesis. Those participants who were familiar with the films did not choose breakpoints that were significantly different from that of those for whom the films were novel. Moreover, watching the film played backward did interfere with cognitive interpretations of the events but did not greatly alter the hierarchy of the segmentations. Again, these findings suggest that participants segment events with an objective, physical means whether or not an interpretation is available.

More indirect measures confirmed the notion that event segmentation is ongoing and automatic. Zacks, Braver, et al. (2001) asked participants to passively view movies while their brain activity was recorded using functional magnetic resonance imaging (fMRI). Participants were then asked to segment the videos into both fine- and coarse-grained units, which were used for analysis in the passive viewing session. The results showed that areas in the frontal lobe were activated a few seconds before the boundaries and that this activation lasted until a few seconds after the boundary. Of particular interest is that participants only passively viewed the events in the scanner, but their brain activity suggested that they were automatically detecting the breakpoints during passive viewing. Further study has shown that another area that activates for breakpoints is the human MT complex, which is involved in analyzing motion in a scene (Speer, Swallow, & Zacks, 2003). Taken together, these neuroscientific results suggest that event segmentation is an automatic, perceptually driven process that may rely specifically on motion processing in the visual system.

17.3.2   Why Is Event Segmentation Useful?

Across studies, assessments of event segmentation show that observers tend to segment based on a hierarchical structure for the event. The event boundaries, or breakpoints, correspond to subgoals, which—when combined—make up the larger goal of the event or activity. This hierarchical structure allows for fine-grained segmentations of the event to be clustered into larger coarse-grained segmentations of the event. Both behavioral and neuroscience experiments suggest that the perceptual system may spontaneously segment events into parts.

A question that follows from these studies is this: why would event segmentation be automatic and useful? Segmentation is an adaptive and important process for the perceptual system for several reasons (Kurby & Zacks, 2008; Zacks & Tversky, 2003; Zacks & Swallow, 2007). First, event segmentation allows us to have a more coherent understanding of what is occurring in the world. Specifically, event segmentation is a way of simplifying the large number of events that may occur at any moment. Through this simplification, which has sometimes been termed *chunking*, the steps of a complicated procedure or event can be better understood and more likely to be remembered (Gobet et al., 2001). In other words, the ability to recognize what is going on may be related to how an observer has parsed the units of that event. Recognition may also be more effective when an event has been segmented because the observer will be more likely to relate the current event to previous stored knowledge, such as schemas for events (Bartlett, 1932; Rumelhart, 1980). Relating ongoing events to knowledge about other previous activities increases comprehension of an event. This increased comprehension due to event segmentation is evident not only in events like baking a cake but also in learning motor skills (Zacks & Tversky, 2003). Better comprehension of an event also promotes anticipation of future actions and events. This ability, importantly, permits the perceiver to better predict when to act, where to act, and how to act, increasing effectiveness in the control and execution of previously learned actions. Overall, this body of research suggests that event segmentation is an important perceptual process because it enables the observer to relate ongoing activities to prior knowledge while also increasing the ability to learn new skills. As Zacks and Tversky (2001) aptly state, "An inability to perceive events as such would be even more debilitating than an inability to perceive objects."

17.4 Event Recognition: Interactions between Vision and Audition

We have already seen that the perceptual system is involved in perceiving the natural dynamics of an event, as well as segmenting more-complex events into parts. This section will discuss research showing that when the outcome of an event is ambiguous, the perceptual system will combine or use information from many senses to resolve this ambiguity in understanding or recognizing the event. Although Michotte (1946/1963) conducted

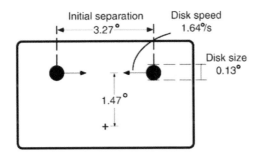

Figure 17.4

Configuration of visual stimulus for R. Sekuler, Sekuler, and Lau (1997) and Watanabe and Shimojo (2001). (From Watanabe, K., & Shimojo, S., 2001, When sound affects vision: effects of auditory grouping on visual motion perception, *Psychological Science, 12*(2), 109–116; © 2001 American Psychological Society, reprinted by permission of SAGE Publications.)

some initial studies on audio-visual interactions in perceiving causality (the sound was produced by an electrically controlled hammer in an enclosed box), technical issues prohibited additional work after obtaining variable results. Thus, the research on audio-visual interactions in the perception of causality is still nascent, and the field is ripe for development.

One of the earliest studies on this topic showed that information from two senses can be used to resolve ambiguity in the perception of an event (R. Sekuler et al., 1997). R. Sekuler et al. presented participants with an ambiguous display that involved two identical target disks moving toward one another, coinciding, and then moving apart (see Figure 17.4). However, the direction at which they moved after coinciding was varied in order to make the movement of the disks more ambiguous. The disks either paused for a second or two at the point of coincidence or moved continuously throughout the event. The authors found that participants perceived the display as representing a collision (e.g., that the two small disks seemed to bounce off each other) if a click occurred at or near the point of collision. Surprisingly, even when the sound occurred as much as 150 ms after the visual collision, it still produced a perception of bouncing. Finally, in an ingenious control study, the authors tested whether or not the perception of bouncing was due to some generalized attention effect heightened by the onset of the sound near the visual event. Interestingly, in a condition in which the sound was on until the collision occurred (heightening attention at the time of the event, but not being ecologically plausible in terms of natural collisions), participants were not more likely to perceive bouncing as compared to a control in which no sound was presented. Thus, only sound onset, not offset, predicted the perception of collision.

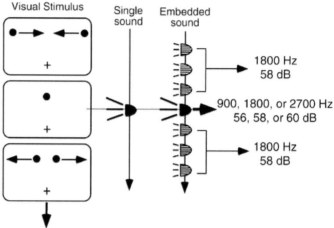

Figure 17.5

Experimental paradigm used in Watanabe and Shimojo (2001). (From Watanabe, K., & Shimojo, S., 2001, When sound affects vision: effects of auditory grouping on visual motion perception, *Psychological Science, 12*(2), 109–116; © 2001 American Psychological Society, reprinted by permission of SAGE Publications.)

Continuing this work, Watanabe and Shimojo (2001) questioned whether the influence of a coincident sound on the perception of bouncing, as discussed in the R. Sekuler et al. (1997) studies, could be attenuated by the presentation of a similar sound before and after the coincident sound (termed *auditory flankers*). They argued that the presentation of the auditory flankers reduced the saliency of the coincident sound and, in turn, the perception of the visual event as a bounce (see Figure 17.5). However, differing acoustic properties of flankers from those of the target sound (such as a different pitch for the flankers as compared to the target sound) recovered the perception of bouncing.

Other work has shown that causality can be perceived in visuo-auditory displays when the visual and auditory portions of the event are not temporally synchronous. Guski and Troje (2003) set a surface in motion in a video after either visual, auditory, or both events occurred. In the visual-only condition, the visual event (the surface being set in motion) was followed by a blink of the screen. In the audio-only condition, the visual event was followed by a collision sound. In the final condition, both a blink and a sound occurred when the surface was set in motion. Participants gave ratings of the degree of causality that they perceived between the two events for each condition. Guski and Troje systematically varied the delay between the onset of the additional information (blink, sound, or both) and the visual event itself. They found that causality was perceived when temporal synchrony existed between the visual event and the blink or sound, but that the additional information (the blink, sound, or both) did not have to perfectly overlap with the occurrence of the visual event. In fact, when the sound occurred about 50 ms after the visual event, participants perceived it as more causal. This finding is not surprising, given that sound waves travel at slower rates than light waves. Overall, their findings support a role for audition in perceiving visual events.

As a final thought, recent work has also postulated that visual events can influence the perception of auditory signals. Schutz and Lipscomb (2007) had participants view movies of a professional marimba player striking a key with either a long stroke or short stroke. The auditory information that accompanied the video was exactly the same in both video conditions. However, participants rated the sound produced by the long stroke as longer than that produced by the short stroke. This finding was the first to show that a visual event could alter the perception of an auditory event in an ecologically valid task. In fact, the authors recommend the use of these visual strokes in performances to influence the experience of the audience.

17.5 Issues Specific to Computer Graphics

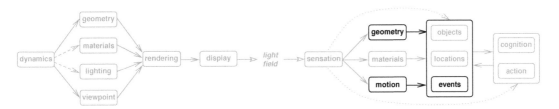

Animators and moviemakers need to tell their viewers a coherent story. In addition to the story itself, it is important that the visual information emphasize the correct partitioning of the story line into events and that the underlying causality of these events be clear.

17.5.1 Parsing of Events in Film and Simulations

An important issue for animators and others working in film is how to guide the experience of the viewer to be consistent with the intention of the moviemaker. Boltz (1992) found that memory for that which occurred in a feature film is better when there are no breaks such as commercials in the feature film. If breaks must occur, such as on commercial television, then viewers will be most likely to remember events in the film if the breaks occur at event boundaries. This idea can also be applied to static displays conveying an event unfolding in time, like a comic. McCloud (1993) argued that comic creators can control how time is segmented by manipulating the placement and graphic features of panels in comic strips. The panels that contain the thoughts or statements made by the actor in the comic are separated from each other by frames, which represent the passage of time through space.

The parsing of events is also important for remembering previously explored spaces, especially in simulations. Radvansky and Copeland (2006) hypothesized that event boundaries could be introduced in virtual environments in order to increase the likelihood of remembering objects within the virtual scene. Specifically, they found that when participants walked through a virtual door, they were less likely to remember objects in the room that they just exited. They argued that the door represented an event boundary in the exploration of the virtual environment that served to segment memory for objects in one room from memory for objects in another room.

17.5.2   Perceptual Fidelity of Animations

There are obvious trade-offs for computer graphics when deciding whether an animation application should render a collision between two objects in a physically correct way. The costs can include computational limitations in rendering the complexity of the animation (O'Sullivan & Dingliana, 2001) and an inability to portray or render a very specific animation (Barzel, Hughes, & Wood, 1996). Thus, quite often computer graphics are rendered such that the animation seems plausible, rather than being completely accurate in terms of the physics of the simulation (O'Sullivan, Dingliana, Giang, & Kaiser, 2003; Barzel, 1997). However, some research has shown that users are sensitive to decreases in the accuracy of motions portrayed in physical simulations (Oesker, Hecht, & Jung, 2000; Stappers & Waller, 1993). Knowledge about perception of events could be helpful when deciding whether to render an animation that is plausible or accurate.

Few computer animation researchers have questioned whether saving computational power by rendering a plausible animation reduces the perceptual fidelity of the dynamics of the animation. O'Sullivan et al. (2003) evaluated the fidelity of physically based animations by determining the thresholds at which observers were sensitive to anomalies in these displays. For example, one of the variables they tested was the time at which a ball is launched after it is hit. They repeatedly tested observers to determine which differences in time they could reliably detect. From the sensitivity experiments, the researchers were able to identify probability functions that could objectively evaluate the fidelity of novel physical animations. These algorithms allow computer graphics researchers to render animations that adhere to the visual sensitivity of human observers, while still being efficient in terms of rendering costs.

Nusseck, Lagarde, Bardy, Fleming, and Bülthoff (2007) have also studied the effect of elasticity on the ability of humans to predict the actions of objects for later interaction. *Elasticity* is defined as the deformation and recovery of an object in response to stress. Nusseck et al. used an animation of a ball bouncing, in which the ball was dropped at a particular location and then bounced a certain number of times in the animation based on its elastic properties. Participants viewed the same event over multiple trials in which the elasticity of the ball was varied. Most balls bounced twice, but the most elastic ball only bounced once, and the least bounced three times. Participants rated the elasticity of the ball (using a seven-point Likert scale) in each animation at four time points. The researchers found that people did not identify elasticity by the first time point but could reliably differentiate elasticity by the second time point. However, in a follow-up experiment, participants were not able to set a paddle at the point at which it would intercept the bouncing balls. These findings suggest that people can discover the elastic properties of the balls visually, but that these properties may not inform plans for interactions with the balls. The authors argue that this result is important for the construction of design interfaces that may portray animations requiring action on the part of the user. If the user will not use the properties of the object to predict action, then computing costs could be reduced by rendering less realistic physical simulations.

Most of the research presented in this chapter on the perception of causality has involved only a few simple objects in the portrayal of events. However, everyday events can be quite complex and can occur in many different contexts. Not surprisingly, both psychologists and computer scientists have begun to examine the effect of context on the perception of causality in physical events. Scholl and Nakayama (2002) varied the context given during a collision event to examine whether the context could influence causality in the target event. The displays were similar to those used in the original Michotte (1946/1963) studies on launching. Participants were told to watch the target event and rate it for causality. However, on some trials, a second set of objects were included in the scene, and these objects acted in a manner similar to the target objects (e.g., object A launched object B in the target event, and object C launched object D in the contextual event). There were also trials in which a single object was included with the target event, but it simply moved in a straight line across the screen and changed color at the point at which the target event (launching) occurred. In both of these conditions, participants were told to rate only the target event for causality. In the contextual condition that included another launch, participants reported 92.1% of the target events as causal. Interestingly, when the context was a single moving object, participants reported that only 5% of the target events were causal. Thus, the context in which the event took place influenced the interpretation of the event.

The influence of context on the perception of causality has interesting implications for rendering animations that include physical events. Reitsma and O'Sullivan (2009) found an effect of scenario on the perception of animations. In their studies, participants watched animations of a collision in a snooker simulator (snooker is like billiards) or an abstract scenario and were asked to indicate whether the event was realistic or if an error in the animation was present. The snooker simulation was considered to be more realistic than the abstract scenario, but the motions portrayed in both were exactly the same. As hypothesized, the scenario had a large effect on participants' tolerance for errors in the animation, such that errors were less tolerated in the abstract scenario than in the more realistic snooker scenario. The results suggest that the realism with which a scenario is rendered makes errors in the target event less detectable. Thus, graphics researchers could implement more-realistic scenarios to accommodate less-realistic dynamics, at least in some cases.

17.6   Suggestions for Further Reading

A historical work on event perception:

> Michotte, A. E. (1963). *The perception of causality* (T. R. Miles & E. Miles, Trans.). New York: Basic Books. (Original work published 1946)

A comprehensive and interesting review of the intuitive physics literature:

> Proffitt, D. R., & Kaiser, M. K. (1995). Perceiving events. In W. Epstein & S. Rogers (Eds.), *Perception of space and motion* (pp. 227–261). New York: Academic Press.

An edited volume on the topic of understanding events and event segmentation:

> Shipley, T. F., & Zacks, J. M. (Eds.). (2008). *Understanding events: From perception to action.* New York: Oxford University Press.

18

Event Recognition—Biological

This chapter focuses on biological events, distinct from the previous chapter on inanimate events. There are several reasons why we include a separate chapter on biological events. Most obviously, the kinematics and dynamics of biological motion are unlike the movement of almost any inanimate object. For vertebrates, biological motion is constrained by complex kinematic linkages formed by bones and joints. Human vision has a special sensitivity for such motions, involving specialized mid- and high-level processing mechanisms. More broadly, many would argue that the human ability to perceive human form and motion is "special," different from the processes used to perceive nonhuman events (see Section 18.4). Important to this discussion is the question of how both motion and form contribute to the perception of biological events. Much of the psychology research in this area has focused on motion mechanisms, with an emphasis on point-light displays that lack information for form. We begin with an overview of the perception of point-light displays. Subsequent sections introduce perceptual work in character animation that have the flexibility to manipulate appearance, emphasizing interactions between form and motion. We also include a discussion of face perception, since this too is highly specialized in humans.

18.1 Perception of Point-Light Displays

It always evokes the same spontaneous response after the first one or two steps: this is a walking human being! The observer has the freedom neither to combine the moving points in other groupings by an act of concentration nor to see these elements just as a series of unrelated points in motion.

—Johansson (1973)

Humans have the impressive ability to perceive the complex events inherent in human movement. Decades ago, Gunnar Johansson (1973) demon-

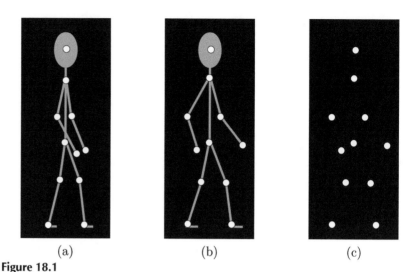

   (a)   (b)   (c)

Figure 18.1

Point-light walker displays. (a–b) Lights are attached to the head and major joints of a person walking across a dark room. The moving lights create a strong appearance of human movement, even when the person's body cannot be seen and only the lights are visible. (c) A static view of the lights produces little sense of human form.

strated this ability by creating displays of point lights attached to the joints on the body. As the quote above suggests, there is an immediate and seemingly automatic perception of moving point-light displays as human forms. These *point-light walkers* have sparked an abundance of research (a count of more than 500 publications as of five years ago; Thornton, 2006b) on what is referred to as *perception of biological motion*. Biological motion described generally is the movement of living organisms, although most of the research involving the perception of biological motion has focused on human forms. The BioMotionLab has an interactive website to demonstrate how compelling point-light walkers can be: http://www.biomotionlab.ca/Demos/BMLwalker.html.

Human point-light stimuli are dynamic displays of the kinematics of human motion without other information for human form. Johansson (1973) is well known for establishing the technique of creating point-light walker displays by placing lights on the head and major joints of the individual and filming the individual while acting. The result was a pattern of dots that, when moving, were easily interpreted as specific actions. In contrast, when presented as a stationary pattern of lights, no human form is perceived (see Figure 18.1). This is one example of structure from motion, as the structure of human form is not perceived without motion. It is different, however, from the methods described in Chapter 11 in that it is specialized to the unique nature of biological movement. More recently, other techniques have been used to create these types of displays (Thornton, 2006a). These techniques include (1) creating algorithms to model the cyclical movement of the limbs (Cutting, 1978; Hodgins, O'Brien, & Tumblin, 1998); (2) the addition of points to film footage of human or animal motion; and (3) motion capture, in which markers attached to a moving body are tracked over time (see Section 18.5.1).

What has intrigued researchers since Johansson's early displays has been the vivid perception of human (or animal) characteristics conveyed in point-light displays. Observers easily determine the gender and identity of point-light walkers (Cutting & Kozlowski, 1977; Kozlowski & Cutting, 1977). Categories of actions are also readily perceived, although actions such as walking and climbing are recognized better (faster and more accurately) than social actions such as dancing (Dittrich, 1993). Interactions between individuals and emotional implications of actions have also been shown to be readily perceived (Dittrich, Troscianko, Lea, Barrett, & Gurr, 1996). Furthermore, the ability to perceive biological motion from point-light displays develops early, with studies showing that infants as young as three months old can discriminate a canonical walking form from one in which phase relations among the elements representing the joints had been perturbed (Bertenthal, Proffitt, & Kramer, 1987). Between the ages of three and seven months, infants become sensitive to global human body structure (Pinto, 2006). While most work suggests that preferences for biological motion displays do not emerge in humans until about three months of age, a recent study found that two-day-old infants showed a preference for a point-light display of a walking hen in comparison to random dot motion or the inverted hen figure in motion (Simion, Regolin, & Bulf, 2008), similar to findings in newly hatched chicks (Regolin, Tommasi, & Vallortigara, 2000).

Point-light displays can be manipulated in both spatial and temporal ways in order to test abilities and accounts of perception of biological motion. Spatial manipulations involve removing specific points, shifting positions of the dots, and altering depth relations of individual dots. Temporal manipulations involve varying display duration, varying smoothness of motion by the addition of interframe delays, and modifying the temporal profile of dot trajectories (Thornton, 2006a). Overall, perception of biological motion even with such manipulations is quite robust, although variables such as location of the points relative to the joints, distortions in phase relations of the moving dots, and orientation of the figure matter significantly. A common way to measure detection and recognition of point-light displays is to immerse the biological motion figure in a mask of identical dots. These masking elements differ from the figure of interest only in their motion characteristics. One example is that of scrambled walkers, created to leave local motion trajectories the same as the coherent figure of interest, but with a random offset added.

18.2   What Makes Biological Events Compelling?

Given the compelling phenomenology of biological motion, researchers have examined the mechanisms of motion and form perception that might be involved. Within the basic perception domain, much of this work has involved point-light displays and thus has focused on issues related to local and global motion analyses. Local motion signals come from the change in position of each point-light over time. Global motion information may be described as the changes of structural information of the body posture over time (Lange, Georg, & Lappe, 2006). In addition, across basic and applied approaches, other higher-level perceptual mechanisms have been examined, such as the specialized mechanisms for perceiving human form and the influence of variations in the appearance of characters.

18.2.1   Local and Global Motion Processing

Despite the complexity of biological motion stimuli, there has been a considerable amount of investigation in support of local analyses of motion in point-light displays (Cutting, 1981; Johansson, 1973; Neri, Morrone, & Burr, 1998). Mather, Radford, and West (1992) demonstrated evidence in support of low-level motion processing by varying the time interval between frames of dots presented. It was argued that since low-level processes operate over very short time intervals (approximately 50 ms), increasing the interframe interval should influence observers' abilities to perceive biological motion if low-level processes are important. If higher-level motion processing (which operates at longer time frames) is used, there would be no predicted difference. The results showed an advantage in performance for shorter time increments, supporting the claim of the use of low-level motion processes. However, other work showed that much longer interframe intervals could be used (up to 120 ms), and human motion was still perceived, suggesting additional higher-level mechanisms (Thornton, Pinto, & Shiffrar, 1998). Mather et al. (1992) also varied the contrast in point-light sequences so that there were reversals of intensity of each dot on a frame-by-frame basis. Performance was poor with the contrast reversal, also in support of low-level motion processes. Another method used to demonstrate the reliance on local motion of individual dots is a scrambled-motion technique in which local motion of the point-light display is intact, but individual dot trajectories are randomly displaced, disrupting structural information. Using this method, Troje and Westhoff (2006) found that direction of the walker was still perceived with either spatial or temporal scrambling.

However, it has also been shown that local motion analysis does not fully explain visual perception of human movement. Casile and Giese (2005) found evidence for the use of mid-level motion features (optic flow fields) in detecting human walker figures and walking direction. They extracted mid-level motion features from normal and point-light stimuli and designed a novel point-light stimulus that combined the extracted dominant motion features with coarse positional information. They showed that the novel stimulus was perceived as a human walker and that walking direction was recognized, even though inconsistent with the kinematics of human walking. Psychophysical data were supported by a neural model that exploited these critical motion features and led to overall good recognition rates. One salient effect seen with perception of human body movement has been termed the *inversion effect*, showing that performance in detecting and recognizing human movement is impaired when the display is inverted with respect to the viewer's head position (Bertenthal & Pinto, 1994; Pavlova & Sokolov, 2000; Troje, 2003). The effect suggests that perception of point-light displays of human action is orientation dependent in an egocentric coordinate frame. Given that the local information is consistent for upright and inverted figures, this argues that there is a higher-level configural effect contributing to perception of human movement. The inversion effect and assumptions about configural processing are consistent with the research on face perception (see Section 18.3.2).

As described so far, a review of the psychology literature on perception of biological motion shows that point-light walker displays created from real human movement convey natural biological motion, despite the lack of information for the form of the body. Point-light stimuli are perceived easily and immediately as human forms, with more complex properties such as sex and identity of the individual, meaningful actions, emotion, and social interaction also often apparent. For computer graphics, it is important to ask, given that the form of humanoid characters is provided (unlike the point-light walkers), when is their motion perceived to be biological? This is an important question for many applications using animated characters, such as film, games, education, and training.

When viewing animation of computer graphics characters, motions that seem "wrong" may be obvious to detect. However, determining what matters for perceiving natural biological motion in character animation and how to best evaluate perception of natural motion are both difficult endeavors. Humanoid characters may be manipulated both for their appearance and for their motion, and both may matter for the perceptual experience of what is judged as "natural." From point-light research, there is evidence indicating that temporal manipulations of motion have significant effects on perception of biological motion. For example, Hill and Pollick (2000) used an exaggeration technique to vary point-light displays of right-arm movement in a sequence of picking up, drinking from, and putting down a glass. The technique involved a key-frame approach in which the arm-movement sequences were divided into movement segments based on velocity profiles of the wrist. The durations of movement segments were scaled relative to average values so that there would be both negative and positive exaggeration of the time of the motion segment. Participants first learned to associate the unmanipulated arm-movement sequences with individuals. Then, they were presented with both the learned movements and the exaggerated motion sequences and asked to identify the individual learned in the first part of the study. The results showed greater sensitivity for identifying the individuals with the positive exaggerated motion and lower sensitivity for the negative exaggeration, compared to no exaggeration. In other words, viewers were actually better at recognizing the identity of the new figures with exaggerated movement compared to those that they had originally learned. This study provided evidence that temporal information was used to discriminate among people. These results are also consistent with face-caricature effects seen when facial features are exaggerated.

18.2.2   Interaction of Form and Motion

Because of the nature of point-light displays, the influence of bodily structure on perception of biological motion has been limited to studies of the influence of form that do not involve high-level appearance manipulations. In contrast, much of what we know about the influence of appearance on perception of biological events comes from investigations of perception of animated characters. Despite limited form information in point-light displays, many claim that perception of the form as a body contributes significantly to the perception of biological motion. For example, Lange et al. (2006) have shown that observers can discriminate human motion by matching the stimulus dots in a single frame to a human-body-posture template. They provide evidence that global motion information is derived from analyzing the change in a figure over time, not from local motion. Other work has shown differences between human motion and other motion displays specifically by manipulating characteristics that leave individual dot motions intact but disrupt the hierarchy or structure of the human form. This work has shown that while people can learn to discriminate these "arbitrary" motion sequences among a mask of randomly moving dots, they do not show the typical inversion effects (i.e., advantage for perceiving the upright figure) for nonbiological motion (Hiris, Humphrey, & Stout, 2005). A manipulation that altered depth relations of individual dots in a stereoscopic display also showed the influence of higher-level infor-

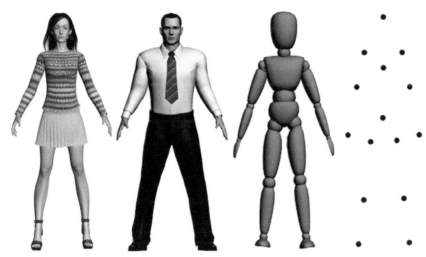

Figure 18.2

Varying appearance of animated models: woman, man, androgynous figure, point-light walker. (Images courtesy of Rachel McDonnell.)

mation for form, as the depth-scrambled displays that affected local motion were still perceived as human figures (I. Bülthoff, Bülthoff, & Sinha, 1998).

More extensive work on the interaction of form and motion has been conducted in the context of perception of characters in computer graphics animation where there is the opportunity to manipulate appearance. Given the temporal-exaggeration effects shown with point-light walkers as described in Section 18.2.1, one might expect a dominance of temporal motion information on perception of animated character actions as well. McDonnell, Jörg, Hodgins, Newell, and O'Sullivan (2009) examined human computer graphics models and varied both the form of the models and their animated walks in order to determine whether form or motion would dominate in perceiving the sex of the character. The characters were animated through motion capture of three males and three females walking. They then modified the animations to create three additional walks that were "neutral" to the sex of the character. They also varied the appearance of the model to convey a man, woman, androgynous figure, and a point-light walker (see Figure 18.2). The viewers' task was to rank the sex of the character from 1 to 5, very male to very female. In a second experiment, a variety of models were presented, ranging from a model with exaggerated male features to a neutral androgynous body to a model with exaggerated female features. Their results showed that both appearance and motion influenced the perceived sex of the character. With neutral walks, appearance dominates. With an androgynous body, motion domi-

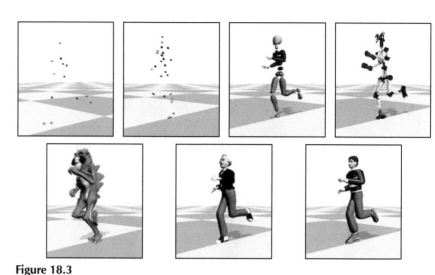

Figure 18.3

The characters used in Chaminade, Hodgins, and Kawato (2007) as a test of uncanny valley effects with character body motion. (© Carnegie Mellon University, used by permission.)

nates. Thus, they suggest that for clear male versus female perception of characters, both the body model and biological motion should be specific to the sex.

Another related study on perceiving animated character actions investigated the perception of computer graphics characters as they become increasingly anthropomorphic (i.e., humanlike), using both perceptual measures and brain imaging (Chaminade et al., 2007). The *uncanny valley* effect was first hypothesized by Mori (1970) in the context of observers' emotional responses to robots as they are made more humanlike. Observers had an increasingly positive response as robots were made to more closely resemble humans in appearance and in motion, but only up to a point—beyond which a repulsive response occurred, described as a sense of eeriness. As the characteristics of the robot became less humanlike, there was again an increase in positive emotional response. Thus, the uncanny valley represents a negative evaluation of artificial beings as they become more similar to—but not exactly like—humans. In Chaminade et al. (2007), animated characters were varied on the dimensions of the humanoid appearance (point-light displays, ellipse model, robot, alien, clown, or human jogger; see Figure 18.3) and the way they were animated (motion capture or key-frame animation). Viewers were asked to label whether a character's running motion was "biological" or "artificial." While the largest effect on labeling was a result of the animation technique (motion capture was rated more biological than key frame), there was also an effect of the humanlike appearance of the characters. Consistent with the emotional responses of the uncanny valley, the perceptual evaluation showed a *reduced* tendency to label full anthropomorphic characters as having "biological" movement.

18.3   Perception of Faces

18.3.1   Facial Expressions

The face is particularly important for understanding the emotional states of people around us. The face contains a large number of muscles that when contracted or extended in different patterns can form a wide variety of emotional expressions. An interest in understanding emotional expressions conveyed by the face dates back to Darwin's (1872) book entitled *The Expression of the Emotions in Man and Animals*. Darwin believed that emotional expressions had evolved because they were integral to the survival of a species. For example, if one member of a species displayed fear in his facial expression, the rest of the group might surmise that a predator was nearby and act accordingly. Individuals in the group could also convey their emotional state and thus change the way that other members in the group might act toward them. In other words, emotional expressions were considered to be an important mechanism for communication in many species.

Darwin claimed that these emotional expressionswere instinctual and genetically inherited. Thus, many psychologists did not pursue research related to emotional expressions until 40 years ago, because they believed these expressions to be universal rather than learned. Research done by Ekman (1973) has shown that facial expressions in humans are similar from culture to culture, providing further evidence for a genetic predisposition for displaying certain emotions. At the same time, another group of researchers led by Izard (1971) were exploring similar hypotheses about expressions across cultures. In the end, both groups found a consistent relationship between the labeling of different emotional expressions in many cultures. The results suggested a clear connection between facial expressions and emotions across different languages and cultures.

Further work by Izard (1977) has examined whether facial expressions also contribute to our subjective experience of the emotion itself. In her facial-feedback hypothesis, Izard claims that when people contract their muscles to form an emotional expression, this action contributes to them feeling that emotion. In fact, one could assume an expression, and this would produce feelings associated with the emotion being expressed. For example, research has shown that when people are asked to spontaneously exhibit an emotional expression, their physiological arousal increases in relation to the type of emotion being expressed (Ekman, Levenson, & Friesen, 1983). Thus, people who are asked to display a fear expression show a concurrent increase in their arousal level that is somewhat indicative of actually feeling fear.

18.3.2 Face Recognition

For a variety of reasons, recognizing a face is very similar to recognizing the posture or shape of a body. First, face recognition involves performing within-category discrimination (or what we termed subordinate categorization in Chapter 15) of a symmetric, natural object whose movement is constrained by muscles and tendons. Second, faces all contain the same essential features, such as eyes, a nose, a mouth, and ears. Thus, the recognition of faces could be considered as similar to the recognition of bodies but may differ from object recognition given that objects do not have to be symmetrical and need not possess the same features across exemplars of a category.

Thus, many psychologists have questioned whether the processes that underlie facial recognition are the same as those used for object recognition. Early theorists postulated that face processing was more sequential in nature than object-recognition processes. J. L. Bradshaw and Wallace (1971) found that participants were faster at deciding whether mug shots were different if more differences were present in the face itself. In other words, when the eyes, mouth, and nose were very different across the shots, judgments of similarity were performed more quickly because it was easier to locate a feature that differed through sequential scanning of the face. Continuing this research, Sergent (1984) showed that recognizing that two faces were different was fastest when the chins of the faces differed (as compared to differences in other singular features). However, if additional feature differences were present in addition to different chins, then even faster decisions were possible. The results suggested that there may be an interaction between facial features when performing recognition tasks; however, more importantly, Sergent discovered that these interactions disappeared when the faces were inverted (presented upside down).

The overall reduction of recognition due to inversion was evidence for a more holistic or configural process underlying the identification of faces. Tanaka and Farah (1993) tested this hypothesis by scrambling the features in faces and then asking participants to remember those scrambled faces. Such a manipulation, they argued, should disrupt face recognition if holistic processes underlie recognition, but should not disrupt recognition if sequential processes were at work. Importantly, Tanaka and Farah also asked participants to recall individual features in normal faces as a con-

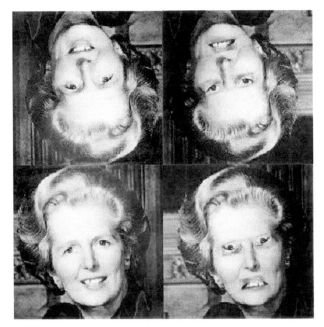

Figure 18.4

The Thatcher illusion: when inverted, the odd orientations of the parts are not easily detected. (From P. Thompson, 1980; courtesy of Pion Limited, London.)

trol. Their findings showed that if the nose was in a new location, then recognition performance was disrupted. Consistent with Sargent's findings, this performance decrement disappeared when the scrambled faces were inverted. Taken together, these findings argue for a strong dependency on the upright orientation of faces in order for recognition to occur. This orientation dependency does not seem to be present in object recognition, which suggests that there are different processes that underlie face recognition (Yim, 1969). Whether this different processing also underlies the recognition of human bodies is still under debate.

Further work showed that the individual features of faces may not be perceived as upright or inverted when in the context of an inverted face. The famous Thatcher illusion, discovered by P. Thompson (1980), clearly demonstrated that participants were unaware of odd configurations of facial features when examining a picture of Thatcher that was inverted (see Figure 18.4). The results of this experiment provided further support that configural processing is used to recognize faces.

Researchers then began to question whether faces were "special" types of objects, given the different processes that underlie face recognition in comparison to object recognition. Another consideration is the extensive experience that people have in discriminating faces across their lifespan. Thus, is it just extensive experience in recognizing faces that leads to configural processing? Diamond and Carey (1986) proposed testing this question by examining recognition of faces and dogs in dog-show judges and breeders. Dog breeders were chosen as participants given their extensive experience in recognizing a different category of objects: dogs. Interestingly, the results among dog breeders revealed impaired recognition of dogs when the images of the dogs were inverted. Again, these results suggest that frequent exposure to a particular category of stimuli results in an inversion effect.

Gauthier and Tarr (1997) followed this work by training participants to be experts at recognizing a novel class of objects called *Greebles* (see Figure 18.5; see also Gauthier, Williams, Tarr, & Tanaka, 1998). These stimuli are similar to faces because they have the same number of features and are

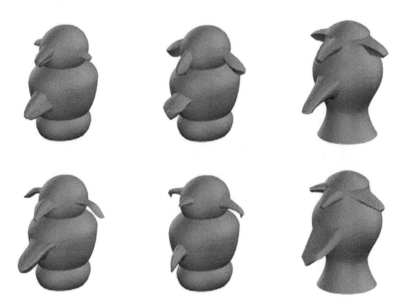

Figure 18.5

Examples of Greebles. The first two columns represent different exemplars from one family, while the last column represents two exemplars from a different family. (Images courtesy of Michael J. Tarr, Center for the Neural Basis of Cognition and Department of Psychology, Carnegie Mellon University, `http://www.tarrlab.org/`.)

Figure 18.6
Photographic negation (left) results in slower or inaccurate recognition of faces.

symmetrical. However, the visual system processes Greebles as if they were objects (not faces), without expertise in discriminating them. After extensive training, which involved being able to discriminate between different Greeble families at a certain criterion, participants were asked to recognize features of Greebles both in isolation and in their normal configurations. As hypothesized, performance was much better when the parts were presented in the trained configuration, but only when they were also presented in an upright orientation. This evidence suggests that expertise in recognizing certain types of objects is due to configural processing. Moreover, cognitive neuroscience evidence demonstrates that prosopagnosics—certain brain-damaged patients who have lost only the ability to recognize faces— are able to recognize particular features of faces in isolation but are unable to recognize a face as a whole object (de Haan, Young, & Newcombe, 1987). These patients also do not show a decrement in performance when faces are inverted. Thus, the face is a stimulus that may require different processes for recognition than objects.

There are other features that are also important for face recognition which are directly relevant to computer graphics researchers: pigmentation and shading. When these cues are removed from a face, then the face is much harder to recognize. For example, photographic negation interferes with face recognition (Galper & Hochberg, 1971; see Figure 18.6). Also monochrome (black-and-white) faces for which shading is preserved are much easier to recognize than traced drawings of faces that include only information about the edges of the face (Davies, Ellis, & Shepherd, 1978). Even though the configuration of these faces is preserved, recognition is not as successful when illumination and information about shape from shading is reduced.

18.4   Why Are Biological Events Special?

It is clear from the abundance of perceptual science research on both biological motion perception and face perception that humans show high levels of sensitivity and expertise for biological events. The "special" nature of this processing is likely a result of several factors. One important factor is the direct experience that we have with our own bodies and self-movement. As described in Chapter 14, there is a good amount of evidence in support of the idea that the representations used for acting are shared with those used in perceiving actions (Hommel et al., 2001). Thus, the motor experience of carrying out our own body movements, such as walking, influences the ability to perceive others' body movements. Support for this claim comes from behavioral studies showing that one's ability to discriminate biological motion is influenced by one's own actions (Jacobs & Shiffrar, 2005) and that people are better able to recognize their own movements or more-familiar actions compared to others' actions or unusual actions (Jacobs, Pinto, & Shiffrar, 2004; Knoblich & Prinz, 2001). These effects are attributed to an unconscious motor simulation process (Jeannerod, 2001), in which the motor system that is typically used in action execution is also used for perception of action. It is also clear that the extensive experience that human observers have with bodies and faces is associated with configural (holistic rather than part-based) processing that differs from the processing of nonbiological objects.

Furthermore, the unique processes of biological-event perception may stem from our existence as social organisms, where understanding others' actions is critical to social interactions with others. While it may seem intuitive that facial expressions serve an important role in conveying the internal states of others, body movements also serve this function. Humans have a remarkable ability to perceive emotion and action intention from displays of human body motion. Emotions such as surprise, fear, anger, and joy are readily perceived with individual point-light actions (Dittrich et al., 1996; Pollick, Paterson, Bruderlin, & Sanford, 2001) as well as with interpersonal actions such as two point-light actors engaged in a dialogue (Clarke, Bradshaw, Field, Hampson, & Rose, 2005). It is also the case that viewing dynamic bodies and faces can influence the viewer's own emotional state and subsequent actions (Niedenthal, 2007). This type of "social contagion" has been attributed to a framework of embodied cognition (see also Chapter 14) in which there exists a close link between one's own sensory-motor experiences and understanding of others outside of oneself. Thus, our ease of perceiving biological events may not be simply a result of familiarity and experience with these types of events but also may be attributed to a fundamental need to understand actions, intentions, and mental states of others.

18.5   Issues Specific to Computer Graphics

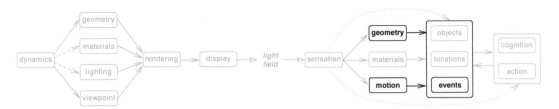

As briefly introduced throughout this chapter, there are several different commonly used techniques in character animation that are used in practice and research. We begin this section with a short overview of computer animation to provide a context for how methods of animation might influence the perception of biological events specific to computer graphics. Computer animation is an extremely complicated process, and the descriptions that follow leave out many important issues. More comprehensive coverage of computer animation can be found in the textbooks listed in Section 18.6. We follow this brief review with a discussion of some of the relevant research relating to objective measurement of perception of animated bodies and faces.

18.5.1   Computer Animation

In computer graphics, rigid body motion of solid objects can be easily specified by simple transformations applied to the geometric primitives that compose the surface of an object. The complexity of biological motion precludes direct control of surface geometry in all but the simplest of situations. Instead, animated characters are *rigged* with a control structure having a manageable number of degrees of freedom. The animator manipulates these controls, and an automatic process then updates the detailed geometry as appropriate. Not surprisingly, the most common way in which the bodies of vertebrate characters are controlled uses a *skeletal rig*, consisting of a set of rigid links connected by revolute or spherical joints, together with a procedure for controlling a deformable surface skin based on the configuration of the skeleton. Metalevel controls are often used, both to simplify the process of defining joint angles and to add additional constraints to the possible motions. Rigging is also used for facial animation, but the complexity of facial motions is such that facial rigs can be significantly more complicated than skeletal rigs used to control body motions.

Three classes of techniques are used in computer animation to control rig parameters and thus the overall motion of characters. In *key-frame* animation, the animator specifies important aspects of the position and pose of characters at critical frames in a motion sequence. A process then generates the intermediate frames by smoothly interpolating rigging controls between the key frames. Key-frame animation, which has its roots in hand-drawn animation, allows the animator extensive creative control over character motions and expressions. Key-frame animation can also be used to manipulate nonbiological entities in an animation. *Performance capture* (often called *mocap* or *motion capture*) uses actors to control animated characters. Motion capture systems measure the three-dimensional position of multiple points on the actor's body over time. These point locations are mapped onto a skeletal model using the process of *inverse kinematics*. The skeletal model drives the animation of the graphical character. Performance capture can create highly accurate motions but limits the ability to perturb motions for artistic reasons. *Procedural animation* uses some form of algorithmic control of characters and inanimate animation. This can range from simple ad hoc methods (as in some video games), to goal-directed behavior (as used in crowd scenes), to sophisticated physical simulations.

Across the different techniques of computer animation, what remains critical is the perceptual experience of the viewer. Animation has the potential to create a believable character that has a personality within a context. However, attaining this goal requires a careful consideration of how the motion fits with a character and a story. For example, realistic motion is likely best paired with a realistic object, but cartoony or more caricatured motion might be necessary for a highly caricatured object. Furthermore, thoughts and intentions associated with movement may be effectively conveyed with subtle actions, such as eye or head movement, which help to answer "why" the action is there (Lasseter, 2001). These types of considerations are important for biological events that rely on the kinematics of human movement, but also inform the creation of nonkinematic biological events where both appearance and motion help to convey a personified character. For example, Disney/Pixar's *Cars* characters have facial configurations and expressions that engage viewers to respond to them in humanlike ways, despite their lack of biological motion and structure.

18.5.2   Character Animation: Bodies

Researchers in applied perception and computer graphics have examined how certain techniques of character animation can affect the perception of human motion. In key frame animation, one factor that has implications for resource allocation is the pose update rate used—the frequency of the individual simulation steps displayed. The pose update rate can vary significantly depending on the type of application. Determining the minimal pose update rate sufficient for the perception of smooth biological motion is important to achieving perceptually effective computer animations. Attempts have been made to identify the importance of factors of appearance and motion on perceived smoothness of animated characters (McDonnell, Newell, & O'Sullivan, 2007). Viewers were asked to give a forced-choice response to the presentation of animated characters as "smooth" or "jerky," and a threshold for 80% probability of acceptance as smooth was calculated for characters that varied in aspects of walk complexity, leg-cycle rates, and linear velocity. This type of quantitative approach to evaluating perception of animation has advantages for providing guidelines for optimizing real-time character simulation based on these types of properties.

With motion capture techniques of character animation, additional editing of the data can often lead to the perception of unnatural motion. One approach to measure sensitivity to errors in edited mocap of human ballistic motions was conducted by Reitsma and Pollard (2003). Human jumping motion was modified by adding in a fixed change in velocity to either horizontal or vertical motion early in the flight phase. Viewers categorized the viewed motion of the humanoid characters as perceived as either an "error" or not, and also ranked their confidence. From these decisions, a level of acceptable error could be calculated, and an error metric was defined that could be used to predict perceptual effects of physics errors that might result in processed motion.

In sum, none of the different techniques of character animation are guaranteed to result in the perception of natural biological motion (Forsyth, Arikan, Ikemoto, O'Brien, & Ramanan, 2006). Furthermore, there is a complex interaction between the animation methods and manipulations of variables of form and motion. Past and current theory and research in perception and neuroscience has led to perceptually informed manipulations. Evaluation of objective perception of biological motion has shown to be useful in determining the benefits and costs of different approaches and can also lead to predictive models about sensitivity to motion errors.

18.5.3   Character Animation: Faces

Modeling facial movements has become a popular topic in character animation over the past 20 years (see Figure 18.7). Applications for facial modeling include entertainment, video games, telepresence, education, and training applications. The complexity of animating faces can be understood by considering the increasing number of factors that must be taken into account when attempting to model facial expressions. These factors include, but are not limited to, the speed of the facial movements, the complexity of the facial movement, and the realism of motion of the face

Figure 18.7
Computer animated avatar faces performing seven basic peak expressions. (From Griesser, Cunningham, Wallraven, & Bülthoff, 2007. © 2007 Association for Computing Machinery, Inc. Reprinted by permission.)

(Noh & Neumann, 1998). Many models have been proposed as possible solutions to the problem of facial animation. Similar to animations for movements of the body, movements of the face and head are most often modeled by shape-based systems (somewhat analogous to key-frame rendering), skeleton-muscle systems (physically based rendering), and motion capture (performance-driven rendering). All of these systems have produced successful and believable facial animations of characters in recent movies. Thus, we will discuss the underlying principles for each model in turn, while also presenting some of the advantages and disadvantages to each approach.

The first three-dimensional facial animation was developed by Fred Parke (1972) while at the University of Utah. His model contained a mesh of 3D points that made up the face and could be controlled by a set of parameters to conform the face to different shapes. For example, some of the points controlled the relative location of the eye or lip corners and could be altered to create new 3D models of a head or new facial expressions on the same head. In fact, many of the actions that are performed by the model to create facial expressions, such as raising the lip corners, were based on those outlined by Ekman (1973). Parke's model represents an instance of shape-based systems that model the facial mesh and then approximate changes in the parameters of the model over time to animate the face. After the locations of points in these meshes have been identified, they are blended together into submeshes (also known as shapes) (Joshi, Tien, Desbrun, & Pighin, 2003). Unfortunately, identifying the mesh points that correspond to specific emotional expressions requires intensive labor on the part of the animation team, akin to developing the key-frames and interpolating them in key frame modeling. Moreover, once the points have been identified, they do not generalize to other characters or faces easily.

Thus, some researchers began exploring physically based models for facial animation that had the obvious benefit of generalizing across characters that may possess differently sized or shaped faces. These skeletal-muscle systems simulate the actions of bones, tissues, muscles, and skin in a manner that is consistent with the anatomy of the human body. The first skeletal-muscle system was developed by Platt and Badler (1981). Using a model that followed the mass-spring principle of muscle fibers, they were able to simulate realistic movements of muscles in the face. However, their model was computationally expensive. Waters (1987) attempted to alleviate some of this computational expense by refining the definitions for the muscles to include only the nature of their actions (linear, sheet, etc.), rather than being dependent on the underlying bone structure. This adaptation to the physically based models had the added benefit of allowing these models to be applied to a diverse array of facial shapes and sizes. Almost all of the more recent facial animation models that include physically realistic simulations are based at least indirectly on Waters' original work. These models are complex and can sometimes be computationally expensive, given the physics that must be simulated for them to be effective. However, facial action units identified by Ekman (1973) have been applied in these models to reduce their complexity (Sagar, 2006). Some of these models have been used to create characters in recent films such as *Monster House* and *King Kong*. In fact, the short film presented at SIGGRAPH in 1985 entitled *Tony de Peltrie* was one of the first animation films to include a character with emotional expressions modeled using a physically based system.

There are obvious advantages to simulating the physics of facial animations in terms of realism, but, as stated above, these techniques can be computationally expensive. Another method that has developed to model animations using realistic motion is often termed *motion capture* or *performance-driven models*. For these models, cameras are placed around a human face that is fitted with sensors or reflectors which are captured by the cameras as they move over time. Thus, a participant makes various facial expressions, and the cameras take rapid snapshots or videos of the locations of the sensors over time. This change in position over time can be imported into a computer model that is then used to simulate the same motion in a 3D, computer-generated face. Early versions of motion capture were developed to try to enhance key-framing techniques (Parke & Waters, 1996). L. Williams (1990) was the first to use static images from motion capture in modeling faces, and Guenter, Grimm, Wood, Malvar, and Pighin (1998) updated this technique to utilize video streaming. This technique was used to animate the characters seen in the movie *The Polar Express*. Though this film was extremely popular and used nearly 150 sensors for capturing motion, some of the critics claimed that the realism of the character animation was insufficient to convey the true emotional expression (an example of the uncanny valley problem as described in Section 18.2.2). Thus, the difficulties that this area has faced include dealing with data that sometimes have noise and vibration which require cleaning and retuning of the sensor locations once they are transported to the modeling algorithm.

When dealing with video streaming, these errors can increase with time. More-recent films, like *The Matrix Reloaded*, have been more successful at conveying realistic facial motion using motion capture techniques with high-definition cameras. Recent work in this field has demonstrated capture without sensors in order to use the video for texture and lighting information in the model (Zhang, Snavely, Curless, & Seitz, 2004).

Most importantly for this chapter, computer graphics researchers have realized that using objective perceptual metrics to evaluate the effectiveness of facial animations and expressiveness is imperative. Moreover, these metrics can then be used to inform future iterations of the animation models. For example, the FacePEM model developed by Deng and Ma (2008) used objective measures of perception to enhance a hybrid facial animation model that included real facial-motion analysis and statistical learning techniques. In essence, facial animations were constructed using motion capture and then were presented to viewers who reported on the type of emotion being expressed and its level of expressiveness. These data were analyzed, and the statistical outcomes were used to modify the animations such that they better conveyed emotional expressions. Objective perceptual evaluations have also been used to determine whether isolated regions of the face (eyebrows, eyes, mouth) can be animated in an avatar to reliably produce particular emotional expressions (Griesser et al., 2007). Findings showed that disgust, sadness, and happiness were more reliably perceived in these animations than surprise, confusion, and fear.

18.6   Suggestions for Further Reading

A comprehensive review of biological motion perception:

> Blake, R. & Shiffrar, M. (2007). Perception of human motion. *Annual Review of Psychology, 58,* 47–73.

Two textbooks covering computer animation, both biological and inanimate, with the first emphasizing higher-level concepts and including many examples from animated films, and the second emphasizing algorithms and lower-level detail:

> Kerlow, I. (2009). *The art of 3D computer animation and effects* (4th ed.). Hoboken, NJ: Wiley.

> Parent, R. (2007). *Computer animation: Algorithms and techniques* (2nd ed.). San Francisco, CA: Morgan Kaufmann.

Bibliography

Abrams, J., Barbot, A., & Carrasco, M. (2010). Voluntary attention increases perceived spatial frequency. *Attention, Perception, & Psychophysics, 72*(6), 1510–1521.

Addams, R. (1834). An account of a peculiar optical phaenomenon seen after having looked at a moving body, etc. *London and Edinburgh Philosophical Magazine and Journal of Science, 5*, 373–374.

Adelson, E. H. (2000). Lightness perception and lightness illusions. In M. Gazzaniga (Ed.), *The new cognitive neurosciences* (2nd ed., pp. 339–351). Cambridge, MA: MIT Press.

Adelson, E. H. (2001). On seeing stuff: The perception of materials by humans and machines. In B. E. Rogowitz & T. N. Pappas (Eds.), *Proceedings SPIE Human Vision and Electronic Imaging VI* (Vol. 4299, pp. 1–12). Bellingham, WA: SPIE.

Adelson, E. H., & Anandan, P. (1990). Ordinal characteristics of transparency. In *Proceedings AAAI Workshop on Qualitative Vision* (pp. 77–81). Menlo Park, CA: AAAI Press.

Adelson, E. H., & Bergen, J. R. (1985). Spatiotemporal energy models for the perception of motion. *Journal of the Optical Society of America A, 2*(2), 284–299.

Adelson, E. H., & Bergen, J. R. (1986). The extraction of spatio-temporal energy in human and machine vision. In *Proceedings Workshop on Motion: Representation and Analysis* (pp. 151–155). Los Alamitos, CA: IEEE.

Adelson, E. H., & Bergen, J. R. (1991). The plenoptic function and the elements of early vision. In M. S. Landy & J. A. Movshon (Eds.), *Computational models of visual processing* (pp. 3–20). Cambridge, MA: MIT Press.

Adelson, E. H., & Movshon, J. A. (1982). Phenomenal coherence of moving visual patterns. *Nature, 300*, 523–525.

Adelson, E. H., & Pentland, A. P. (1996). The perception of shading and reflectance. In D. Knill & W. Richards (Eds.), *Perception as Bayesian inference* (pp. 409–423). New York: Cambridge University Press.

Adiv, G. (1989). Inherent ambiguities in recovering 3-D motion and structure from a noisy flow field. *IEEE Transactions on Pattern Analysis and Machine Intelligence, 11*(5), 477–489.

Agutter, J., Drews, F., Syroid, N., Westenskow, D., Albert, R., Strayer, D., et al. (2003). Evaluation of a graphical cardiovascular display in a high fidelity simulator. *Anesthesia & Analgesia, 97*(5), 1403–1413.

Aivar, M. P., Hayhoe, M. M., Chizk, C. L., & Mruczek, R. E. B. (2005). Spatial memory and saccadic targeting in a natural task. *Journal of Vision, 5*(3), 177–193.

Akeley, K., Watt, S. J., Girshick, A. R., & Banks, M. S. (2004). A stereo display prototype with multiple focal distances. *Proc. SIGGRAPH '04, Transactions on Graphics, 23*(3), 804–813.

Alberti, L. B. (1991). *On painting* (M. Kemp, Ed. & C. Grayson, Trans.). London: Penguin Classics. (Original work published 1435)

Allen, G. L. (1999). Spatial abilities, cognitive maps, and wayfinding. In R. G. Golledge (Ed.), *Wayfinding behavior* (pp. 46–80). Baltimore: Johns Hopkins University Press.

Allen, G. L., Kirasic, K. C., Dobson, S. H., Long, R. G., & Beck, S. (1996). Predicting environmental learning from spatial abilities: An indirect route. *Intelligence, 23*(2), 327–355.

Alvarez, G. A., & Franconeri, S. L. (2007). How many objects can you track?: Evidence for a resource-limited attentive tracking mechanism. *Journal of Vision, 7*(13), 14:1–14:10.

Ames, A., Jr. (1925). The illusion of depth from single pictures. *Journal of the Optical Society of America, 1*(2), 137–148.

Andersen, G. J. (1986). Perception of self-motion: Psychophysical and computational approaches. *Psychological Bulletin, 99*(1), 52–65.

Andersen, G. J., & Braunstein, M. L. (1985). Induced self-motion in central vision. *Journal of Experimental Psychology: Human Perception and Performance, 11*(2), 122–132.

Anderson, B. L. (1997). A theory of illusory lightness and transparency in monocular and binocular images: The role of contour junctions. *Perception, 26*(4), 419–453.

Anderson, B. L. (2003). The role of occlusion in the perception of depth, lightness, and opacity. *Psychological Review, 110*(4), 785–801.

Anderson, B. L., & Nakayama, K. (1994). Toward a general theory of stereopsis: Binocular matching, occluding contours, and fusion. *Psychological Review, 101*(3), 414–445.

Andre, J., & Rogers, S. (2006). Using verbal and blind-walking distance estimates to investigate the two visual systems hypothesis. *Perception & Psychophysics, 68*(3), 353–361.

Angelaki, D. E. (2004). Eyes on target: What neurons must do for the vestibuloocular reflex during linear motion. *Journal of Neurophysiology, 92*(1), 20–35.

Anstis, S. (1986). Motion perception in the frontal plane: Sensory aspects. In K. R. Boff, I. Kaufman, & J. P. Thomas (Eds.), *Handbook of perception and human performance: Vol. 1. Sensory processes and perception* (chap. 16). New York: Wiley.

Anstis, S. (2000). Monocular lustre from flicker. *Vision Research, 40*(19), 2551–2556.

Anstis, S. M. (1992). Visual adaptation to a negative, brightness-reversed world: Some preliminary observations. In G. A. Carpenter & S. Grossberg (Eds.), *Neural networks for vision and image processing* (pp. 1–14). Cambridge, MA: MIT Press.

Anstis, S. M., Howard, I. P., & Rogers, B. (1978). A Craik-O'Brien-Cornsweet illusion for visual depth. *Vision Research, 18*(2), 213–217.

Apfelbaum, H. L., Apfelbaum, D. H., Woods, R. L., & Peli, E. (2008). Inattentional blindness and augmented-vision displays: Effects of cartoon-like filtering and attended scene. *Opthalmic and Physiological Optics, 28*(3), 204–217.

Apostoloff, N., & Fitzgibbon, A. (2005). Learning spatiotemporal T-junctions for occlusion detection. In *Proceedings Conference on Computer Vision and Pattern Recognition* (pp. 553–559). Los Alamitos, CA: IEEE.

Arend, L., & Reeves, A. (1986). Simultaneous color constancy. *Journal of the Optical Society of America A, 3*(10), 1743–1751.

Auerbach, E., & Wald, G. (1954). Identification of a violet receptor in human color vision. *Science, 120*(3115), 401–405.

Awh, E., Vogel, E. K., & Oh, S. H. (2006). Interactions between attention and working memory. *Neuroscience, 139*(1), 201–208.

Azuma, R. T. (1997). A survey of augmented reality. *Presence: Teleoperators and Virtual Environments, 6*(4), 355–385.

Baddeley, R. (1997). The correlational structure of natural images and the calibration of spatial representations. *Cognitive Science, 21*(3), 351–372.

Bailenson, J. N., & Blascovich, J. (2004). Avatars. In W. S. Bainbridge (Ed.), *Encyclopedia of human-computer interaction* (pp. 64–68). Great Barrington, MA: Berkshire.

Ball, K. K., Beard, B. L., Roenker, D. L., & Griggs, D. S. (1988). Age and visual search: Expanding the useful field of view. *Journal of the Optical Society of America A, 5*(12), 2210–2219.

Banks, M. S., Rose, H. F., Vishwanath, D., & Girshick, A. R. (2005). Where should you sit to watch a movie? In *Proceedings SPIE/IS&T human vision & electronic imaging conference* (Vol. 5666, pp. 316–325). Bellingham, WA: SPIE.

Barker, R. G. (1963). The stream of behavior as an empirical problem. In R. G. Barker (Ed.), *The stream of behavior* (pp. 1–22). New York: Appleton-Century-Crofts.

Barnard, S. T., & Thompson, W. B. (1980). Disparity analysis of images. *IEEE Transactions on Pattern Analysis and Machine Intelligence, 2*(4), 333–340.

Barrow, H. G., & Tenenbaum, J. M. (1978). Recovering intrinsic scene characteristics from images. In A. Hanson & E. Riseman (Eds.), *Computer vision systems* (pp. 2–25). New York: Academic Press.

Barrow, H. G., & Tenenbaum, J. M. (1981). Computational vision. *Proceedings of the IEEE, 69*(5), 572–595.

Barsalou, L. W. (2008). Grounded cognition. *Annual Review of Psychology, 59*, 617–645.

Barsky, B. A., & Kosloff, T. J. (2008). Algorithms for rendering depth of field effects in computer graphics. In *Proceedings 12th WSEAS International Conference on Computers* (pp. 999–1010). Stevens Point, WI: World Scientific and Engineering Academy and Society (WSEAS).

Bart, E., Byvatov, E., & Ullman, S. (2004). View-invariant recognition using corresponding object fragments. In *Proceedings European Conference on Computer Vision* (pp. 152–165). Berlin: Springer.

Bartlett, F. C. (1932). *Remembering: A study in experimental and social psychology.* New York: Macmillan.

Bartz, D., Cunningham, D., Fischer, J., & Wallraven, C. (2008). The role of perception for computer graphics. In *Proceedings Eurographics (State-of-the-Art Reports)* (pp. 65–86). Aire-la-Ville, Switzerland: Eurogaraphics Association.

Barzel, R. (1997). Faking dynamics of ropes and springs. *IEEE Computer Graphics and Applications, 17*(3), 31–39.

Barzel, R., Hughes, J. F., & Wood, D. N. (1996). Plausible motion simulations for computer graphics animations. In *Proceedings Eurographics Workshop on Computer Animation and Simulation*. Aire-la-Ville, Switzerland: Eurogaraphics Association.

Bayes, T. (1763). An essay towards solving a problem in the doctrine of chances. *Philosophical Transactions of the Royal Society, 53*, 370–418.

Baylis, G. C., & Driver, J. (1993). Visual attention and objects: Evidence for hierarchical coding of location. *Journal of Experimental Psychology: Human Perception and Performance, 19*(3), 451–470.

Baylor, D. A. (1987). Photoreceptor signals and vision. *Investigative Ophthalmology & Visual Science, 28*(1), 34–49.

Beall, A. C., Loomis, J. M., Philbeck, J. W., & Fikes, T. G. (1995). Absolute motion parallax weakly determines visual scale in real and virtual environments. In *Proceedings of the SPIE* (Vol. 2411, pp. 288–97). Bellingham, WA: SPIE.

Beck, J. (1982). Textural segmentation. In J. Beck (Ed.), *Organization and representation in perception* (pp. 285–318). Hillsdale, NJ: Lawrence Erlbaum.

Beck, J., & Ivry, R. (1988). On the role of figural organization in perceptual transparency. *Perception & Psychophysics, 44*(6), 585–594.

Beck, J., Prazdny, K., & Ivry, R. (1984). The perception of transparency with achromatic colors. *Perception & Psychophysics, 35*(5), 407–422.

Beck, J., & Prazdny, S. (1981). Highlights and the perception of glossiness. *Perception & Psychophysics, 30*(4), 407–410.

Belhumeur, P., Kriegman, D., & Yuille, A. (1999). The bas-relief ambiguity. *International Journal of Computer Vision, 35*(1), 33–44.

Ben-Shahar, O. (2006). Visual saliency and texture segregation without feature gradient. *Proceedings of the National Academy of Sciences, USA, 103*(42), 15704–15709.

Ben-Shahar, O., Scholl, B. J., & Zucker, S. W. (2007). Attention, segregation, and textons: Bridging the gap between object-based attention and texton-based segregation. *Vision Research, 47*(6), 845–860.

Benson, C. W., & Yonas, A. (1973). Development of sensitivity to static pictorial depth information. *Perception & Psychophysics, 13*(3), 361–366.

Berbaum, K., Bever, T., & Chung, C. S. (1983). Light source position in the perception of object shape. *Perception, 12*(4), 411–416.

Berbaum, K., Bever, T., & Chung, C. S. (1984). Extending the perception of shape from known to unknown shading. *Perception, 13*(4), 479–488.

Bergen, J. R., & Adelson, E. H. (1988). Early vision and texture perception. *Nature, 333*, 363–364.

van den Berg, A. V., & Brenner, E. (1994). Why two eyes are better than one for judgments of heading. *Nature, 371*, 700–702.

Berkeley, G. (1709). *An essay towards a new theory of vision.* Dublin: Aaron Rhames.

Berlin, B., & Kay, P. (1969). *Basic color terms: Their universality and evolution.* Berkeley: University of California Press.

Bertamini, M., Yang, T. L., & Proffitt, D. R. (1998). Relative size perception at a distance is best at eye level. *Perception & Psychophysics, 60*(4), 673–682.

Bertenthal, B. I., & Pinto, J. (1994). Global processing of biological motions. *Psychological Science, 5*(4), 221–225.

Bertenthal, B. I., Proffitt, D. R., & Kramer, S. J. (1987). Perception of biomechanical motions by infants: Implementation of various processing constraints. *Journal of Experimental Psychology: Human Perception and Performance, 13*(4), 577–585.

Berthoz, A., Pavard, B., & Young, L. R. (1975). Perception of linear horizontal self-motion induced by peripheral vision (linearvection) basic characteristics and visual-vestibular interactions. *Experimental Brain Research, 23*(5), 471–489.

Berti, A., & Frassinetti, F. (2000). When far becomes near: Remapping of space by tool use. *Journal of Cognitive Neuroscience, 12*(3), 415–420.

Berzhanskaya, J., Swaminathan, G., Beck, J., & Mingolla, E. (2002). Highlights and surface gloss perception (VSS abstract). *Journal of Vision, 2*(7), 93.

Bian, Z., Braunstein, M. L., & Andersen, G. J. (2005). The ground dominance effect in the perception of 3-D layout. *Perception & Psychophysics, 67*(5), 801–815.

Bian, Z., Braunstein, M. L., & Andersen, G. J. (2006). The ground dominance effect in the perception of 3–D scenes is mainly due to the characteristics of the ground surface. *Perception & Psychophysics, 68*(8), 1297–1309.

Biederman, I. (1985). Human image understanding: Recent research and a theory. *Computer Vision, Graphics, and Image Understanding, 32*(1), 29–73.

Biederman, I. (1987). Recognition-by-components: A theory of human image understanding. *Psychological Review, 94*(2), 115–147.

Biederman, I. (1995). Visual object recognition. In S. F. Kosslyn & D. N. Osherson (Eds.), *An invitation to cognitive science: Vol. 2. Visual cognition* (2nd ed., pp. 121–165). Cambridge, MA: MIT Press.

Biederman, I., & Cooper, E. E. (1991). Evidence for complete translational and reflectional invariance in visual object priming. *Perception, 20*(5), 585–593.

Biederman, I., Cooper, E. E., Hummel, J. E., & Fise, J. (1993). Geon theory as an account of shape recognition in mind, brain and machine. In *Proceedings British Machine Vision Conference* (pp. 175–186). London: Springer-Verlag.

Biederman, I., & Ju, G. (1988). Surface versus edge-based determinants of visual recognition. *Cognitive Psychology, 20*(1), 38–64.

Binford, T. O. (1971). Visual perception by computer. In *Proceedings IEEE Conference on Systems and Controls*. Los Alamitos, CA: IEEE.

Bingham, G. P. (1993). Perceiving the size of trees: Biological form and the horizon ratio. *Perception & Psychophysics, 54*(4), 484–495.

Bingham, G. P., Bradley, A., Bailey, M., & Vinner, R. (2001). Accommodation, occlusion, and disparity matching are used to guide reaching: A comparison of actual versus virtual environments. *Journal of Experimental Psychology: Human Perception and Performance, 27*(6), 1314–1344.

Bingham, G. P., & Pagano, C. C. (1998). The necessity of a perception-action approach to definite distance perception: Monocular distance perception to guide reaching. *Journal of Experimental Psychology: Human Perception and Performance, 24*(1), 145–168.

Bingham, G. P., & Wickelgren, E. A. (2008). Events and actions as dynamically molded spatiotemporal objects: A critique of the motor theory of biological motion perception. In T. F. Shipley & J. M. Zacks (Eds.), *Understanding events: From perception to action* (pp. 255–286). New York: Oxford University Press.

Blake, A., & Bülthoff, H. H. (1990). Does the brain know the physics of specular reflection? *Nature, 343*, 165–168.

Blake, R., & Shiffrar, M. (2007). Perception of human motion. *Annual Review of Psychology, 58*, 47–73.

Blakemore, C., & Campbell, F. W. (1969). On the existence of neurons in the human visual system selectively sensitive to the orientation and size of retinal images. *Journal of Physiology, 203*(1), 237–260.

Blakemore, S., & Frith, C. (2005). The role of motor contagion in the prediction of action. *Neuropsychologia, 43*(2), 260–267.

Blinn, J. F. (1978). Simulation of wrinkled surfaces. *Proc. SIGGRAPH '78, Computer Graphics, 12*(3), 286–292.

Bloj, M., Ripamonti, C., Mitha, K., Hauck, R., Greenwald, S., & Brainard, D. H. (2004). An equivalent illuminant model for the effect of surface slant on perceived lightness. *Journal of Vision, 4*(9), 735–746.

Bloj, M. G., Kersten, D., & Hurlbert, A. C. (1999). Perception of three-dimensional shape influences colour perception through mutual illumination. *Nature, 402*, 877–879.

Bolles, R. C., Baker, H. H., & Marimont, D. H. (1987). Epipolar-plane image analysis: An approach to determining structure from motion. *International Journal of Computer Vision, 1*(1), 7–55.

Boltz, M. (1992). Temporal accent structure and the remembering of filmed narratives. *Journal of Experimental Psychology: Human Perception and Performance, 18*(1), 90–105.

Boring, E. G. (1940). Size constancy and emmert's law. *The American Journal of Psychology, 53*(2), 293–295.

Botvinick, M., & Cohen, J. (1998). Rubber hands 'feel' touch that eyes see. *Nature, 391,* 756.

Bovet, D., & Vauclair, J. (2000). Picture recognition in animals and humans. *Behavioral Brain Research, 109*(2), 143–165.

Bovik, A. C., Clark, M., & Geisler, W. S. (1990). Multichannel texture analysis using localized spatial filters. *IEEE Transactions on Pattern Analysis and Machine Intelligence, 12*(1), 55–73.

Bowditch, N. (1802). *American practical navigator.* Newburyport, MA: Blunt.

Boyaci, H., Doerschner, K., & Maloney, L. T. (2006). Cues to an equivalent lighting model. *Journal of Vision, 6*(2), 106–118.

Boyaci, H., Maloney, L. T., & Hersh, S. (2003). The effect of perceived surface orientation on perceived surface albedo in three-dimensional scenes. *Journal of Vision, 3*(8), 541–553.

Braddick, O. (1974). A short-range process in apparent motion. *Vision Research, 14*(7), 519–527.

Bradshaw, J. L., & Wallace, G. (1971). Models for the processing and identification of faces. *Perception & Psychophysics, 9*(5), 443–448.

Bradshaw, M. F., Glennester, A., & Rogers, B. J. (1996). The effect of display size on disparity scaling from different perspective and vergence cues. *Vision Research, 36*(9), 1255–1264.

Brainard, D. H. (2003). Color appearance and color difference specification. In S. K. Shevell (Ed.), *The science of color* (2nd ed., pp. 191–216). Washington, DC: Optical Society of America.

Brandt, T., Dichgans, J., & Koenig, E. (1973). Differential effects of central versus peripheral vision on egocentric and exocentric motion perception. *Experimental Brain Research, 16*(5), 476–491.

Brandt, T., Wist, E. R., & Dichgans, J. (1975). Foreground and background in dynamic spatial orientation. *Perception & Psychophysics, 17*(5), 497–503.

Braunstein, M. L. (1976). *Depth perception through motion.* New York: Academic Press.

Brenner, E., & van den Berg, A. V. (1996). The special role of distant structures in perceived object velocity. *Vision Research, 36*(23), 3805–3814.

Brewster, D. (1826). On the optical illusion of the conversion of cameos into intaglios, and of intaglios into cameos, with an account of other analogous phenomena. *Edinburgh Journal of Science, 4,* 99–108.

Brewster, D. (1832). *Letters on natural magic.* London: John Murray.

Brewster, D. (1847). On the conversion of relief by inverted vision. *Transactions of the Royal Society of Edinburgh, 15,* 657–662.

Brewster, D. (1856). *The stereoscope: Its history, theory, and construction, with its application to the fine and useful arts and to education.* London: John Murray.

Bridgeman, B., Hendry, D., & Stark, L. (1975). Failure to detect displacement of the visual world during saccadic eye movements. *Vision Research, 15*(6), 719–722.

Bridgeman, B., Lewis, S., Heit, G., & Nagle, M. (1979). Relation between cognitive and motor-oriented systems of visual position perception. *Journal of Experimental Psychology: Human Perception and Performance, 5*(4), 692–700.

Broadbent, D. E. (1958). *Perception and communication.* London: Pergamon Press.

Brooks, R. A. (1983). Model-based three-dimensional interpretations of two-dimensional images. *IEEE Transactions on Pattern Analysis and Machine Intelligence, 5*(2), 140–150.

Bruss, A. R., & Horn, B. K. P. (1983). Passive navigation. *Computer Vision, Graphics, and Image Processing, 21*(1), 3–20.

Bryant, D., Tversky, B., & Franklin, N. (1992). Internal and external spatial frameworks for representing described scenes. *Journal of Memory and Language, 31*(1), 74–98.

Buccino, G., Binkofski, F., Fink, G. R., Fadiga, L., Fogassi, L., Gallese, V., et al. (2001). Action observation activates premotor and parietal areas in somatotopic manner: An fMRI study. *European Journal of Neuroscience, 13*(2), 400–404.

Bülthoff, H. H., & Edelman, S. (1992). Psychophysical support for a two-dimensional view interpolation theory of object recognition. *Proceedings of the National Academy of Sciences, USA, 89*(1), 60–64.

Bülthoff, H. H., & Mallot, H. A. (1988). Integration of depth modules: Stereo and shading. *Journal of the Optical Society of America, 5*(10), 1749–1758.

Bülthoff, I., Bülthoff, H. H., & Sinha, P. (1998). Top-down influences on stereo-scopic depth-perception. *Nature Neuroscience, 1*(3), 254–257.

Burton, G. J., & Moorhead, I. R. (1987). Color and spatial structure in natural scenes. *Applied Optics, 26*(1), 157–170.

Busey, T. A., Brady, N. P., & Cutting, J. E. (1990). Compensation is unnecessary for the perception of faces in slanted pictures. *Perception & Psychophysics, 48*(1), 1–11.

Byrne, A., & Hilbert, D. R. (Eds.). (1997). *Readings on Color: Vol. 2. The science of color.* Cambridge, MA: MIT Press.

Campbell, F. W., & Green, D. G. (1965). Optical and retinal factors affecting visual resolution. *The Journal of Physiology, 181*(3), 576–593.

Campbell, F. W., & Gubisch, R. W. (1966). Optical quality of the human eye. *The Journal of Physiology*, *186*(3), 558–578.

Campbell, F. W., & Robson, J. G. (1968). Application of Fourier analysis to the visibility of gratings. *The Journal of Physiology*, *197*(3), 551–566.

Caniard, F., & Fleming, R. W. (2007). Distortion in 3D shape estimation with changes in illumination. In *Proceedings 4th Symposium on Applied Perception in Graphics and Visualization* (pp. 99–105). New York: ACM.

Canny, J. (1986). A computational approach to edge detection. *IEEE Transactions on Pattern Analysis and Machine Intelligence*, *8*(6), 679–698.

Card, J. (1955, October). Silent film speed. *Image*, *4*(7), 55–56.

Carey, D. P. (2001). Do action systems resist visual illusions? *Trends in Cognitive Sciences*, *5*(3), 109–113.

Carlson, V. R. (1960). Overestimation in size-constancy judgments. *The American Journal of Psychology*, *73*(2), 199–213.

Carlson, V. R. (1977). Instructions and perceptual constancy judgments. In W. Epstein (Ed.), *Stability and constancy in visual perception: Mechanisms and processes* (pp. 217–254). New York: Wiley.

Carrasco, M., Ling, S., & Read, S. (2004). Attention alters appearance. *Nature Neuroscience*, *7*(3), 308–313.

Casile, A., & Giese, M. A. (2005). Critical features for the recognition of biological motion. *Journal of Vision*, *5*(4), 348–360.

Cataliotti, J., & Gilchrist, A. (1995). Local and global processes in surface lightness perception. *Perception & Psychophysics*, *57*(2), 125–135.

Cater, K., Chalmers, A., & Ward, G. (2003). Detail to attention: Exploiting visual tasks for selective rendering. In *Proceedings Eurographics workshop on rendering* (pp. 270–280). Aire-la-Ville, Switzerland: Eurogaraphics Association.

Cavanagh, P. (1992). Attention-based motion perception. *Science*, *257*(5076), 1563–1565.

Cavanagh, P., & Mather, G. (1989). Motion: The long and short of it. *Spatial Vision*, *4*(2/3), 103–129.

Chakravarty, I. (1982). *The use of characteristic views as a basis for recognition of three-dimensional objects* (Tech. Rep. No. IPL-TR-034). Troy, NY: Rensselaer Polytechnic Institute, Image Processing Lab.

Chakravarty, I., & Freeman, H. (1982). Characteristic views as a basis for three-dimensional object recognition. In *Proceedings Society for Photo-Optical Instrumentation Engineers Conference on Robot Vision* (Vol. 336, pp. 37–45). Bellingham, WA: SPIE.

Chalmers, A., McNamara, A., Daly, S., Myszkowski, K., & Troscianko, T. (2000). *Image quality metrics.* ACM SIGGRAPH Course Notes.

Chaminade, T., Hodgins, J., & Kawato, M. (2007). Anthropomorphism influences perception of computer-animated characters' actions. *Social Cognitive and Affective Neuroscience*, *2*(3), 206–216.

Chance, S. S., Gaunet, F., Beall, A. C., & Loomis, J. M. (1998). Locomotion mode affects the updating of objects encountered during travel: The contribution of vestibular and proprioceptive inputs to path integration. *Presence: Teleoperators and Virtual Environments*, *7*(2), 168–178.

Chen, C. H. (1982). A study of texture classification using spectral features. In *Proceedings International Conference on Pattern Recognition* (pp. 1074–1077). Washington, DC: IEEE Computer Society.

Chun, M. M., & Jiang, Y. (1998). Contextual cueing: Implicit learning and memory of visual context guides spatial attention. *Cognitive Psychology*, *36*(1), 28–71.

Chun, M. M., & Wolfe, J. M. (2001). Visual attention. In E. B. Goldstein (Ed.), *Blackwell handbook of perception* (pp. 272–310). Malden, MA: Blackwell.

Clarke, T. J., Bradshaw, M. F., Field, D. T., Hampson, S. E., & Rose, D. (2005). The perception of emotion from body movement in point-light displays of interpersonal dialogue. *Perception*, *34*(10), 1171–1180.

Clowes, M. B. (1971). On seeing things. *Artificial Intelligence*, *2*(1), 79–116.

Cole, F., Sanik, K., DeCarlo, D., Finkelstein, A., Funkhouser, T., Rusinkiewicz, S., et al. (2009). How well do line drawings depict shape? *Proc. SIGGRAPH '09, Transactions on Graphics*, *28*(3), 28:1–28:9.

Cook, R. L. (1984). Shade trees. *Proc. SIGGRAPH '84, Computer Graphics*, *18*(3), 223–231.

Cornsweet, T. N. (1970). *Visual perception.* New York: Academic Press.

Cowan, M. (2008). *REAL D 3D theatrical system: A technical overview.* www.edcf.net. European Digital Cinema Forum.

Craik, K. J. W. (1996). *The nature of psychology: A selection of papers, essays, and other writings* (S. L. Sherwood, Ed.). New York: Cambridge University Press.

Creem, S. H., & Proffitt, D. R. (2001). Grasping objects by their handles: A necessary interaction between cognition and action. *Journal of Experimental Psychology: Human Perception and Performance*, *27*(1), 218–228.

Creem, S. H., Wraga, M., & Proffitt, D. R. (2001). Imagining physically impossible transformations: Geometry is more important than gravity. *Cognition*, *81*(1), 41–64.

Creem-Regehr, S. H. (2004). Remembering spatial locations: The role of physical movement in egocentric updating. In G. Allen (Ed.), *Human spatial memory: Remembering where* (pp. 163–189). Mahwah, NJ: Lawrence Erlbaum.

Creem-Regehr, S. H., Dilda, V., Vicchrilli, A., Federer, F., & Lee, J. N. (2007). The influence of complex action knowledge on representations of novel graspable objects: Evidence from fMRI. *Journal of the International Neuropsychological Society*, *13*(6), 944–952.

Creem-Regehr, S. H., Neil, J. A., & Yeh, H. J. (2007). Neural correlates of two imagined egocentric spatial transformations. *Neuroimage*, *35*(2), 916–927.

Creem-Regehr, S. H., Willemsen, P., Gooch, A. A., & Thompson, W. B. (2005). The influence of restricted viewing conditions on egocentric distance perception: Implications for real and virtual environments. *Perception*, *34*(2), 191–204.

Cronin, T. W., & Marshall, N. J. (1989). A retina with at least ten spectral types of photoreceptors in a mantis shrimp. *Nature*, *339*, 137–140.

Cruz-Neira, C., Sandin, D., & DeFanti, T. A. (1993). Surround-screen projection-based virtual reality: The design and implementation of the CAVE. In J. T. Kajiya (Ed.), *Proceedings of SIGGRAPH 93, Computer Graphics Proceedings, Annual Conference Series* (pp. 135–142). New York: ACM Press.

Cula, O. G., & Dana, K. J. (2004). 3D texture recognition using bidirectional feature histograms. *International Journal of Computer Vision*, *59*(1), 33–60.

Cunningham, D. W., & Wallraven, C. (2011). *Experimental design: From psychophysics to user studies*. Natick, MA: A K Peters/CRC Press.

Cutting, J. E. (1978). A program to generate synthetic walkers as dynamic point-light displays. *Behavior Research Methods & Instrumentation*, *10*(1), 91–94.

Cutting, J. E. (1981). Coding theory adapted to gait perception. *Journal of Experimental Psychology: Human Perception and Performance*, *7*(1), 71–87.

Cutting, J. E. (1986). *Perception with an eye for motion*. Cambridge, MA: MIT Press.

Cutting, J. E. (1987). Rigidity in cinema seen from the front row, side aisle. *Journal of Experimental Psychology: Human Perception and Performance*, *13*(3), 323–334.

Cutting, J. E., & Kozlowski, L. T. (1977). Recognizing friends by their walk: Gait perception without familiarity cues. *Bulletin of the Psychonomic Society*, *9*(5), 353–356.

Cutting, J. E., & Vishton, P. M. (1995). Perceiving layout and knowing distance: The integration, relative potency and contextual use of different information about depth. In W. Epstein & S. Rogers (Eds.), *Perception of space and motion* (pp. 69–117). New York: Academic Press.

Da Silva, J. A. (1985). Scales for perceived egocentric distance in a large open field: Comparison of three psychophysical methods. *American Journal of Psychology*, *98*(1), 119–144.

da Vinci, L. (1970). *The notebooks of Leonardo da Vinci* (Vol. 1). New York: Dover Press. (Original work published 1566)

Daly, S. (1993). The visible difference predictor: An algorithm for the assessment of image fidelity. In A. B. Watson (Ed.), *Digital images and human vision* (pp. 179–206). Cambrige, MA: MIT Press.

Dana, K. J., van Ginneken, B., Nayar, S. K., & Koenderink, J. J. (1999). Reflectance and texture of real-world surfaces. *ACM Transactions on Graphics*, *18*(1), 1–34.

Darwin, C. (1872). *The expression of emotion in man and animals*. New York: Philosophical Library.

Daum, S. O., & Hecht, H. (2009). Distance estimation in vista space. *Attention, Perception, & Psychophysics*, *71*(5), 1127–1137.

Davies, G., Ellis, H., & Shepherd, K. (1978). Face recognition accuracy as a function of mode of representation. *Journal of Applied Psychology*, *63*(2), 180–187.

De Valois, R. L., & De Valois, K. K. (1993). A multi-stage color model. *Vision Research*, *33*(8), 1053–1065.

Debevec, P. E. (1998). Rendering synthetic objects into real scenes: Bridging traditional and image-based graphics with global illumination and high dynamic range photography. In M. Cohen (Ed.), *Proceedings of SIGGRAPH 98, Computer Graphics Proceedings, Annual Conference Series* (pp. 189–198). Reading, MA: Addison Wesley.

Debevec, P. E., & Malik, J. (1997). Recovering high dynamic range radiance maps from photographs. In T. Whitted (Ed.), *Proceedings of SIGGRAPH 97, Computer Graphics Proceedings, Annual Conference Series* (pp. 369–378). Reading, MA: Addison Wesley.

DeCarlo, D., & Santella, A. (2002). Stylization and abstraction of photographs. *Proc. SIGGRAPH '02, Transactions on Graphics*, *21*(3), 769–776.

Decety, J., & Jackson, P. L. (2004). The functional architecture of human empathy. *Behavioral and Cognitive Neuroscience Reviews*, *3*(2), 71–100.

Degelman, D., & Rosinski, R. (1979). Motion parallax and children's distance perception. *Developmental Psychology*, *15*(2), 147–152.

Deng, Z., & Ma, X. (2008). Perceptually guided expressive facial animation. In *Proceedings ACM SIGGRAPH/Eurographics Symposium on Computer Animation* (pp. 67–76). Aire-la-Ville, Switzerland: Eurogaraphics Association.

Deregowski, J. B., Muldrow, E. S., & Muldrow, W. F. (1972). Pictorial recognition in a remote Ethiopian population. *Perception*, *1*(4), 417–425.

Desimone, R., & Duncan, J. (1995). Neural mechanisms of selective visual attention. *Annual Review of Neuroscience, 18*, 193–222.

Diamond, R., & Carey, S. (1986). Why faces are and are not special: An effect of expertise. *Journal of Experimental Psychology: General, 115*(2), 107–117.

Dichgans, J., & Brandt, T. (1978). Visual-vestibular interaction: Effects on self-motion perception and postural control. In R. Held & H. W. Liebowitz (Eds.), *Handbook of sensory physiology* (Vol. 8, pp. 756–795). New York: Springer-Verlag.

Dittrich, W. H. (1993). Action categories and the perception of biological motion. *Perception, 22*(1), 15–22.

Dittrich, W. H., Troscianko, T., Lea, S. E. G., Barrett, J., & Gurr, P. R. (1996). Perception of emotion from dynamic point-light displays represented in dance. *Perception, 25*(6), 727–738.

Divvala, S. K., Hoiem, D., Hays, J. H., Efros, A. A., & Hebert, M. (2009). An empirical study of context in object detection. In *Proceedings IEEE Conference on Computer Vision and Pattern Recognition* (pp. 1271–1278). Los Alamitos, CA: IEEE.

Dixon, M. W., Wraga, M., Proffitt, D. R., & Williams, G. C. (2000). Eye height scaling of absolute size in immersive and nonimmersive displays. *Journal of Experimental Psychology: Human Perception and Performance, 26*(2), 582–593.

Dodgson, N. A. (2005). Autostereoscopic 3D displays. *Computer, 38*(8), 31–36.

Doerschner, K., Boyaci, H., & Maloney, L. T. (2004). Human observers compensate for secondary illumination originating in nearby chromatic surfaces. *Journal of Vision, 4*(2), 92–105.

Doerschner, K., Boyaci, H., & Maloney, L. T. (2007). Testing limits on matte surface color perception in three-dimensional scenes with complex light fields. *Vision Research, 47*(28), 3409–3423.

Dorsey, J., Edelman, A., Jensen, H. W., Legakis, J., & Pedersen, H. K. (1999). Modeling and rendering of weathered stone. In A. Rockwood (Ed.), *Proceedings of SIGGRAPH 99, Computer Graphics Proceedings, Annual Conference Series* (pp. 225–234). Reading, MA: Addison Wesley.

Dorsey, J., & Hanrahan, P. M. (1996). Modeling and rendering of metallic patinas. In H. Rushmeier (Ed.), *Proceedings of SIGGRAPH 96, Computer Graphics Proceedings, Annual Conference Series* (pp. 387–396). Reading, MA: Addison Wesley.

Dorsey, J., Rushmeier, H., & Sillion, F. (2007). *Digital modeling of material appearance.* San Francisco, CA: Morgan Kaufmann.

Dror, R. O., Willsky, A., & Adelson, E. H. (2004). Statistical characterization of real-world illumination. *Journal of Vision, 4*(9), 821–837.

Dulac, N., & Gaudreault, A. (2005). Heads or tails: The emergence of a new cultural series, from the phenakistiscope to the cinematograph. *Invisible Culture: An Electronic Journal for Visual Culture*, *8*. (`http://www.invisibleculture.rochester.edu/in_visible _culture/Issue_8/issue8_dulac-gaudreault.pdf`)

Dunn, B. E., Gray, G. C., & Thompson, D. (1965). Relative height on the picture-plane and depth perception. *Perceptual Motor Skills*, *21*(1), 227–236.

Durgin, F. H., Baird, J. A., Greenburg, M., Russell, R., Shaughnessy, K., & Waymouth, S. (2009). Who is being deceived? The experimental demands of wearing a backpack. *Psychonomic Bulletin & Review*, *16*(5), 964–969.

Durgin, F. H., Fox, L. F., Lewis, J., & Walley, K. A. (2002, Nov). *Perceptuomotor adaptation: More than meets the eye.* Paper presented at the 43rd annual meeting of the Psychonomic Society, Kansas City, MO.

Durgin, F. H., Pelah, A., Fox, L. F., Lewis, J., Kane, R., & Walley, K. A. (2005). Self-motion perception during locomotor recalibration: More than meets the eye. *Journal of Experimental Psychology: Human Perception and Performance*, *31*(3), 398–419.

D'Zmura, M., & Iverson, G. (1993a). Color constancy: I. basic theory of two-stage linear recovery of spectral descriptions for lights and surfaces. *Journal of the Optical Society of America A*, *10*(10), 2148–2165.

D'Zmura, M., & Iverson, G. (1993b). Color constancy: II. results for two-stage linear recovery of spectral descriptions for lights and surfaces. *Journal of the Optical Society of America A*, *10*(10), 2166–2180.

D'Zmura, M., & Iverson, G. (1994). Color constancy. III. general linear recovery of spectral descriptions for lights and surfaces. *Journal of the Optical Society of America A*, *11*(9), 2389–2400.

D'Zmura, M., & Lennie, P. (1986). Mechanisms of color constancy. *Journal of the Optical Society of America A*, *3*(10), 1662–1672.

Eaton, E. M. (1919). The visual perception of solid form. *British Journal of Opthalmology*, *3*(8), 349–363.

Eby, D. W., & Braunstein, M. L. (1995). The perceptual flattening of three-dimensional scenes enclosed by a frame. *Perception*, *24*(9), 981–993.

Edelman, S. (1999). *Representation and recognition in vision.* Cambridge, MA: MIT Press.

Edwards, A. S. (1946). Body sway and vision. *Journal of Experimental Psychology*, *36*(6), 526–535.

Efros, A. A., & Freeman, W. T. (2001). Image quilting for texture synthesis and transfer. In E. Fiume (Ed.), *Proceedings of SIGGRAPH 2001, Computer Graphics Proceedings, Annual Conference Series* (pp. 341–346). Reading, MA: Addison Wesley.

Efros, A. A., & Leung, T. K. (1999). Texture synthesis by non-parametric sampling. In *Proceedings IEEE International Conference on Computer Vision* (Vol. 2, pp. 1033–1038). Washington, DC: IEEE Computer Society.

Egeth, H. E., & Yantis, S. (1997). Visual attention: Control, representation, and time course. *Annual Review of Psychology, 48*, 269–297.

Egly, R., Driver, J., & Rafal, R. D. (1994). Shifting visual attention between objects and locations: Evidence from normal and parietal lesion subjects. *Journal of Experimental Psychology: General, 123*(2), 161–177.

Ehrlich, S. M., Beck, D. M., Crowell, J. A., Freeman, T. C. A., & Banks, M. S. (1998). Depth information and perceived self-motion during simulated gaze rotations. *Vision Research, 38*(20), 3129–3145.

Ekman, P. (1973). Cross-cultural studies of facial expression. In P. Ekman (Ed.), *Darwin and facial expression: A century of research in review* (pp. 169–222). New York: Academic Press.

Ekman, P., Levenson, R. W., & Friesen, W. V. (1983). Autonomic nervous system activity distinguishes among emotions. *Science, 221*(4616), 1208–1210.

Epstein, W. (1961). The known-size-apparent-distance hypothesis. *The American Journal of Psychology, 74*(3), 333–346.

Epstein, W. (1966). Perceived depth as a function of relative height under three background conditions. *Journal of Experimental Psychology, 72*(3), 335–338.

Epstein, W., & Park, J. (1964). Examination of Gibson's psychophysical hypothesis. *Psychological Bulletin, 62*(3), 180–196.

Epstein, W., Park, J., & Casey, A. (1965). The current status of the size-distance hypotheses. *Psychological Bulletin, 58*(6), 491–514.

Eskicioglu, A. M., & Fisher, P. S. (1995). Image quality measures and their performance. *IEEE Transactions on Communications, 43*(12), 2959–2965.

Fairchild, M. D. (2005). *Color appearance models* (2nd ed.). Hoboken, NJ: Wiley.

Fajen, B. R., Riley, M. A., & Turvey, M. T. (2008). Information, affordances, and the control of action in sport. *International Journal of Sport Psychology, 40*(1), 79–107.

Fajen, B. R., & Warren, W. H. (2004). Visual guidance of intercepting a moving target on foot. *Perception, 33*(6), 689–715.

Fajen, B. R., & Warren, W. H. (2007). Behavioral dynamics of intercepting a moving target. *Experimental Brain Research, 180*(2), 303–319.

Farber, J., & Rosinski, R. R. (1978). Geometric transformations of pictured space. *Perception, 7*(3), 269–282.

Favalora, G. E. (2005). Volumetric 3D displays and application infrastructure. *Computer, 38*(8), 37–44.

Fennema, C. L., & Thompson, W. B. (1979). Velocity determination in scenes containing several moving objects. *Computer Graphics and Image Processing*, *9*(4), 301–315.

Ferwerda, J. A. (2003). Three varieties of realism in computer graphics. In *Proceedings SPIE human vision and electronic imaging* (pp. 290–297). Bellingham, WA: SPIE.

Ferwerda, J. A. (2008). Psychophysics 101: How to run perception experiments in computer graphics. In *ACM SIGGRAPH course notes* (pp. 87:1–87:60).

Ferwerda, J. A., Pattanaik, S. N., Shirley, P., & Greenberg, D. P. (1996). A model of visual adaptation for realistic image synthesis. In H. Rushmeier (Ed.), *Proceedings of SIGGRAPH 96, Computer Graphics Proceedings, Annual Conference Series* (pp. 249–258). Reading, MA: Addison Wesley.

Ferwerda, J. A., Shirley, P., Pattanaik, S. N., & Greenberg, D. P. (1997). A model of visual masking for computer graphics. In T. Whitted (Ed.), *Proceedings of SIGGRAPH 97, Computer Graphics Proceedings, Annual Conference Series* (pp. 143–152). Reading, MA: Addison Wesley.

von Fieandt, K. (1949). The phenomenological problem of light and shadow. *Acta Psychologica*, *6*, 337–357.

Field, D. J. (1987). Relations between the statistics of natural images and the response properties of cortical cells. *Journal of the Optical Society of America A*, *4*(12), 2379–2394.

Fiser, J., & Aslin, R. N. (2001). Unsupervised statistical learning of higher-order spatial structures from visual scenes. *Psychological Science*, *12*(6), 499–504.

Fiser, J., & Aslin, R. N. (2005). Encoding multielement scenes: Statistical learning of visual feature hierarchies. *Journal of Experimental Psychology: General*, *134*(4), 521–537.

Fisher, S. K., & Ciuffreda, K. J. (1988). Accommodation and apparent distance. *Perception*, *17*(5), 609–621.

Fitzmaurice, G., Matejka, J., Mordatch, I., Khan, A., & Kurtenbach, G. (2008). Safe 3D navigation. In *Proceedings Symposium on Interactive 3D Graphics and Games* (pp. 7–15). New York: ACM.

Fleet, D. J., & Jepson, A. D. (1990). Computation of component image velocity from local phase information. *International Journal of Computer Vision*, *5*(1), 77–104.

Fleet, D. J., & Langley, K. (1994). Computational analysis of non-Fourier motion. *Vision Research*, *34*(22), 3057–3079.

Fleming, R. W., & Bülthoff, H. H. (2005). Low-level image cues in the perception of translucent materials. *ACM Transactions on Applied Perception*, *2*(3), 346–382.

Fleming, R. W., Dror, R. O., & Adelson, E. H. (2003). Real-world illumination and the perception of surface reflectance properties. *Journal of Vision*, *3*(5), 347–368.

Fleming, R. W., Torralba, A., & Adelson, E. H. (2004). Specular reflections and the perception of shape. *Journal of Vision*, *4*(9), 798–820.

Fleming, R. W., Torralba, A., & Adelson, E. H. (2009). *Shape from sheen* (Tech. Rep. No. MIT-CSAIL-TR-2009-051). MIT.

Foley, J. M. (1980). Binocular distance perception. *Psychological Review*, *87*(5), 411–434.

Foley, J. M. (2007). Visually directed action: Learning to compensate for perceptual errors (VSS abstract). *Journal of Vision*, *7*(9), no. 416.

Foo, P., Warren, W. H., Duchon, A., & Tarr, M. J. (2005). Do humans integrate routes into a cognitive map? Map- versus landmark-based navigation shortcuts. *Journal of Experimental Psychology: Learning, Memory, and Cognition*, *31*(2), 195–215.

Forsyth, D. A., Arikan, O., Ikemoto, L., O'Brien, J., & Ramanan, D. (2006). Computational studies of human motion: Part 1, Tracking and motion synthesis. *Foundations and Trends in Computer Graphics and Vision*, *1*(2/3), 77–254.

Forsyth, D. A., & Ponce, J. (2003). *Computer vision: A modern approach*. Upper Saddle River, NJ: Prentice Hall.

Foster, D. H., & Gilson, S. J. (2002). Recognizing novel three-dimensional objects by summing signals from parts and views. *Proceedings of the Royal Society of London, B*, *269*(1503), 1939–1947.

Franconeri, S. L., Jonathan, S. V., & Scimeca, J. M. (2010). Tracking multiple objects is limited only by object spacing, not by speed, time, or capacity. *Psychological Science*, *21*(7), 920–925.

Franconeri, S. L., Lin, J., Pylyshyn, Z. W., Fisher, B., & Enns, J. T. (2008). Multiple object tracking is limited by crowding, but not speed. *Psychonomic Bulletin & Review*, *15*(4), 802–808.

Franz, V. H. (2001). Action does not resist visual illusions. *Trends in Cognitive Sciences*, *5*(11), 457–459.

Frey, S. H. (2008). Tool use, communicative gesture and cerebral asymmetries in the modern human brain. *Philosophical Transactions of the Royal Society B*, *363*(1499), 1951–1957.

Frisby, J. P., & Stone, J. V. (2010). *Seeing: The computational approach to biological vision* (2nd ed.). Cambridge, MA: MIT Press.

Fuchs, W. (1923a). Experimentelle untersuchungen über die änderung von farben unter dem einfluss von gestalten. *Zeitshcrift für Psychologie*, *92*, 299–325.

Fuchs, W. (1923b). Untersuchungen über das simultane hintereinandersehen auf derselben sehrichtung. *Zeitschrift für Psychologie*, *91*, 195–235.

Fuller, S., & Carrasco, M. (2006). Exogenous attention and color perception: Performance and appearance of saturation and hue. *Vision Research*, *46*(23), 4032–4047.

Gallistel, C. R. (1990). *The organization of learning*. Cambridge, MA: MIT Press.

Galper, R. E., & Hochberg, J. (1971). Recognition memory for photographs of faces. *American Journal of Psychology*, *84*(3), 351–354.

Gardner, P. L., & Mon-Williams, M. (2001). Vertical gaze angle: Absolute height-in-scene information for the programming of prehension. *Experimental Brain Research*, *136*(3), 379–385.

Gauthier, I., & Tarr, M. J. (1997). Becoming greeble experts: Exploring mechanisms for face recognition. *Vision Research*, *37*(12), 1673–1682.

Gauthier, I., Williams, P., Tarr, M. J., & Tanaka, J. (1998). Training greeble experts: A framework for studying expert object recognition processes. *Vision Research*, *38*(15–16), 2401–2428.

Georgeson, M. A., & Sullivan, G. D. (1975). Contrast constancy: Deblurring in human vision by spatial frequency channels. *Journal of Physiology*, *252*(3), 627–656.

Gepshtein, S., & Kubovy, M. (2007). The lawful perception of apparent motion. *Journal of Vision*, *7*(8), 1–15.

Gerbino, W. (1994). Achromatic transparency. In A. L. Gilchrist (Ed.), *Lightness, brightness and transparency* (pp. 215–255). Hove, England: Lawrence Erlbaum.

Gerhard, H. E., & Maloney, L. T. (2010). Detection of light transformations and concomitant changes in surface albedo. *Journal of Vision*, *10*(1), 1–14.

Gerrits, H. J. M., & Vendrick, A. J. H. (1970). Simultaneous contrast, filling-in process, and information processing in man's visual system. *Experimental Brain Research*, *11*(4), 411–430.

Gershun, A. (1939). Svetovoe pole (English: The light field) (P. Moon & G. Timoshenko, Trans.). *Journal of Mathematics and Physics*, *18*(2), 51–151. (Original work published 1936)

Gibson, J. J. (1950a). *The perception of the visual world*. Cambridge, MA: Riverside Press.

Gibson, J. J. (1950b). The perception of visual surfaces. *American Journal of Psychology*, *63*(3), 367–384.

Gibson, J. J. (1951). What is a form? *Psychological Review*, *58*(6), 403–412.

Gibson, J. J. (1979). *The ecological approach to visual perception*. Boston, MA: Houghton Mifflin.

Gibson, S., & Hubbold, R. J. (1997). Perceptually-driven radiosity. *Computer Graphics Forum*, *16*(2), 129–140.

Gilchrist, A. L., & Jacobsen, A. (1984). Perception of lightness and illumination in a world of one reflectance. *Perception*, *13*(1), 5–19.

Gilchrist, A. L., Kossyfidis, C., Bonato, F., Agostini, T., Cataliotti, J., Li, X., et al. (1999). An anchoring theory of lightness perception. *Psychological Review*, *106*(4), 795–834.

Gilden, D. L., & Proffitt, D. R. (1989). Understanding collision dynamics. *Journal of Experimental Psychology: Human Performance and Perception*, *15*(2), 372–383.

Gilinsky, A. S. (1955). The effect of attitude upon the perception of size. *The American Journal of Psychology*, *68*(2), 173–192.

Gillner, S., & Mallot, H. A. (1998). Navigation and acquisition of spatial knowledge in a virtual maze. *Journal of Cognitive Neuroscience*, *10*(4), 445–463.

Glover, S. (2004). Separate visual representations in the planning and control of action. *Behavioral and Brain Sciences*, *27*(1), 3–78.

Gobet, F., Lane, P. C. R., Croker, S., Cheng, P. C.-H., Jones, G., Oliver, I., et al. (2001). Chunking mechanisms in human learning. *Trends in Cognitive Sciences*, *5*(6), 236–243.

Gogel, W. C. (1965). Equidistance tendency and its consequences. *Psychological Bulletin*, *64*(3), 153–163.

Gogel, W. C. (1969). The sensing of retinal size. *Vision Research*, *9*(9), 1079–1094.

Gogel, W. C. (1976). An indirect method of measuring perceived distance from familiar size. *Perception & Psychophysics*, *20*(6), 419–429.

Gogel, W. C. (1990). A theory of phenomenal geometry. *Perception & Psychophysics*, *48*(2), 105–123.

Gogel, W. C., & Tietz, J. D. (1973). Absolute motion parallax and the specific distance tendency. *Perception & Psychophysics*, *13*(2), 284–292.

Goktekin, T., Bargteil, A. W., & O'Brien, J. F. (2004). A method for animating viscoelastic fluids. *Proc. SIGGRAPH '04, Transactions on Graphics*, *23*(3), 463–468.

Goldsmith, T. H. (1990). Optimization, constraint, and history in the evolution of eyes. *The Quarterly Review of Biology*, *35*(3), 281–322.

Goldstein, E. B. (1987). Spatial layout, orientation relative to the observer, and perceived projection in pictures viewed at an angle. *Journal of Experimental Psychology: Human Perception and Performance*, *13*(2), 256–266.

Goldstein, E. B. (2009). *Sensation and perception* (8th ed.). Belmont, CA: Wadsworth.

Golledge, R. G. (1999). Human wayfinding and cognitive maps. In R. G. Golledge (Ed.), *Wayfinding behavior: Cognitive mapping and other spatial processes* (chap. 1). Baltimore, MD: Johns Hopkins University Press.

Gooch, A., Gooch, B., Shirley, P., & Cohen, E. (1998). A non-photorealistic lighting model for automatic technical illustration. In M. Cohen (Ed.), *Proceedings of SIGGRAPH 98, Computer Graphics Proceedings, Annual Conference Series* (pp. 447–452). Reading, MA: Addison Wesley.

Gooch, A. A., Olsen, S. C., Tumblin, J., & Gooch, B. (2005). Color2gray: Salience-preserving color removal. *Proc. SIGGRAPH '05, Transactions on Graphics*, *24*(3), 634–639.

Gooch, B., & Gooch, A. A. (2001). *Non-photorealistic rendering*. Natick, MA: A K Peters.

Goodale, M. A., & Milner, A. D. (1992). Separate visual pathways for perception and action. *Trends in Neuroscience*, *15*(1), 20–25.

Gordin, D. N., & Pea, R. D. (1995). Prospects for scientific visualization as an educational technology. *The Journal of the Learning Sciences*, *4*(3), 249–279.

Gordon, I., Day, R., & Stecher, E. (1990). Perceived causality occurs with stroboscopic movement of one or both stimulus elements. *Perception*, *19*(1), 17–20.

Green, C. S., & Bavelier, D. (2003). Action video games modify visual selective attention. *Nature*, *423*, 534–537.

Green, C. S., & Bavelier, D. (2006). Effect of action video games on the spatial distribution of visuospatial attention. *Journal of Experimental Psychology: Human Perception and Performance*, *32*(6), 1465–1468.

Green, C. S., Li, R., & Bavelier, D. (2009). Perceptual learning during action video games. *Topics in Cognitive Science*, *2*(2), 1–15.

Greene, M. R., & Oliva, A. (2009). The briefest of glances. *Psychological Science*, *20*(4), 464–472.

Greenstein, J. M. (1997). On Alberti's "sign": Vision and composition in quattrocento painting. *Art Bulletin*, *79*(4), 669–698.

Gregory, R. L. (1997). *Eye and brain: The psychology of seeing* (5th ed.). Princeton, NJ: Princeton University Press.

Grezes, J., Tucker, M., Armony, J. L., Ellis, R., & Passingham, R. E. (2003). Objects automatically potentiate action: An fMRI study of implicit processing. *European Journal of Neuroscience*, *17*(12), 2735–2740.

Griesser, R. T., Cunningham, D. W., Wallraven, C., & Bülthoff, H. H. (2007). Psychophysical investigation of facial expressions using computer animated faces. In *Proceedings 4th Symposium on Applied Perception in Grapics and Visualization* (pp. 11–18). New York: ACM.

Grossberg, S., & Mingolla, E. (1985a). Neural dynamics of form perception: Boundary completion, illusory figures, and neon color spreading. *Psychological Review*, *92*(2), 173–211.

Grossberg, S., & Mingolla, E. (1985b). Neural dynamics of perceptual grouping: Textures, boundaries, and emergent segmentations. *Perception & Psychophysics, 38*(2), 141–171.

Grusser, O. J. (1983). Multimodal structure of the extrapersonal space. In A. Hein & M. Jeannerod (Eds.), *Spatially oriented behaviors* (pp. 327–352). New York: Springer-Verlag.

Grutzmacher, R. P., Andre, J. T., & Owens, D. A. (1997). Gaze inclination: A source of oculomotor information for distance perception. In *Proceedings 9th International Conference on Perception and Action (Studies in Perception and Action IV)* (pp. 229–232). Hillsdale, NJ: Lawrence Erlbaum.

Gu, J., Tu, C., Ramamoorthi, R., Belhumeur, P., Matusik, W., & Nayar, S. K. (2006). Time-varying surface appearance: Acquisition, modeling, and rendering. *Proc. SIGGRAPH '06, Transactions on Graphics, 25*(3), 762–771.

Guenter, B., Grimm, C., Wood, D., Malvar, H., & Pighin, F. (1998). Making faces. In M. Cohen (Ed.), *Proceedings of SIGGRAPH 98, Computer Graphics Proceedings, Annual Conference Series* (pp. 55–66). Reading, MA: Addison Wesley.

Gurnsey, R., & Browse, R. A. (1987). Micropattern properties and presentation conditions influencing visual texture discrimination. *Perception & Psychophysics, 41*(3), 239–252.

Guski, R., & Troje, N. F. (2003). Audiovisual phenomenal causality. *Perception & psychophysics, 65*(5), 789–800.

Guzman, A. (1968). Decomposition of a visual scene into three-dimensional bodies. In *Proceedings Fall Joint Computer Conference* (pp. 291–304). New York: ACM.

de Haan, E. H. F., Young, A. W., & Newcombe, F. (1987). Face recognition without awareness. *Cognitive Neuropsychology, 4*(4), 385–415.

Haffenden, A. M., & Goodale, M. A. (1998). The effect of pictorial illusion on prehension and perception. *Journal of Cognitive Neuroscience, 10*(1), 122–136.

Hagen, M. A. (1976). The development of sensitivity to cast and attached shadows in pictures as information for the direction of the source of illumination. *Perception & Psychophysics, 20*(1), 25–28.

Hagen, M. A. (Ed.). (1980). *The perception of pictures i: Alberti's window: The projective model of pictures.* New York: Academic Press.

Hagen, M. A., Jones, R. K., & Reed, E. S. (1978). On a neglected variable in theories of pictorial perception: Truncation of the visual field. *Perception & Psychophysics, 23*(4), 326–330.

Hansen, T., Olkkonen, M., Walter, S., & Gegenfurtner, K. R. (2006). Memory modulates color appearance. *Nature Neuroscience, 9*(11), 1367–1368.

Haralick, R. M. (1979). Statistical and structural approaches to texture. *Proceedings of the IEEE*, *67*(5), 786–804.

Hard, B. M., Tversky, B., & Lang, D. S. (2006). Making sense of abstract events: Building event schemas. *Memory & Cognition*, *34*(6), 1221–1235.

Haro, G., Bertalmío, M., & Caselles, V. (2006). Visual acuity in day for night. *International Journal of Computer Vision*, *69*(1), 109–117.

Harris, C. S. (1980). Insight or out of sight? two examples of perceptual plasticity in the human adult. In C. S. Harris (Ed.), *Visual coding and adaptability* (pp. 95–149). Hillsdale, NJ: Erlbaum.

Harris, L. R., Jenkin, M., & Zikovitz, D. C. (2000). Visual and non-visual cues in the perception of linear self motion. *Experimental Brain Research*, *135*(1), 12–21.

Hartung, B., & Kersten, D. (2003). How does the perception of shape interact with the perception of shiny material? *Journal of Vision*, *3*(9), 59.

Hatfield, G. (1998). Attention in early scientific psychology. In R. D. Wright (Ed.), *Visual attention* (pp. 3–25). New York: Oxford University Press.

Hay, J. C., Pick, H. L., Jr., & Ikeda, K. (1965). Visual capture produced by prism spectacles. *Psychonomic Science*, *2*(8), 215–216.

Hayhoe, M., & Ballard, D. (2005). Eye movements in natural behavior. *TRENDS in Cognitive Sciences*, *9*(4), 188–194.

Hayhoe, M. M. (2009). Visual memory in motor planning and action. In J. R. Brockmole (Ed.), *The visual world in memory* (pp. 117–139). New York: Psychology Press.

Hays, J., & Efros, A. A. (2007). Scene completion using millions of photographs. *ACM Transactions on Graphics*, *26*(3), No. 4.

He, Z. J., Wu, B., Ooi, T. L., Yarbrough, G., & Wu, J. (2004). Judging egocentric distance on the ground: Occlusion and surface integration. *Perception*, *33*(7), 789–806.

Hecht, S., Shlaer, S., & Pirenne, M. H. (1942). Energy, quanta, and vision. *The Journal of General Physiology*, *25*(6), 819–840.

Heeger, D. J., & Bergen, J. R. (1995). Pyramid-based texture analysis/synthesis. In R. Cook (Ed.), *Proceedings of SIGGRAPH 95, Computer Graphics Proceedings, Annual Conference Series* (pp. 229–238). Reading, MA: Addison Wesley.

Hegarty, M., Montello, D. R., Richardson, A. E., Ishikawa, T., & Lovelace, K. (2006). Spatial abilities at different scales: Individual differences in aptitude-test performance and spatial-layout learning. *Intelligence*, *34*(2), 151–176.

Hegarty, M., Richardson, A. E., Montello, D. R., Lovelace, K., & Subbiah, I. (2002). Development of a self-report measure of environmental spatial ability. *Intelligence*, *30*(5), 425–447.

Hegarty, M., & Waller, D. (2004). A dissociation between mental rotation and perspective-taking spatial abilities. *Intelligence*, *32*(2), 175–191.

Hegarty, M., & Waller, D. (2005). Individual differences in spatial abilities. In P. Shah & A. Miyake (Eds.), *Handbook of higher-level visuospatial thinking* (pp. 121–169). New York: Cambridge University Press.

Hegdé, J., Albright, T. D., & Stoner, G. R. (2004). Second-order motion conveys depth-order information. *Journal of Vision*, *4*(10), 838–842.

Hegdé, J., Bart, E., & Kersten, D. (2008). Fragment-based learning of visual object categories. *Current Biology*, *18*(8), 597–601.

Heider, F., & Simmel, M. (1944). An experimental study of apparent behavior. *The American Journal of Psychology*, *57*(2), 243–259.

Heilig, M. L. (1960). *Stereoscopic-television apparatus for individual use.* (U.S. patent 2,955,156)

Heilig, M. L. (1962). *Sensorama simulator.* (U.S. patent 3,050,870)

Held, R. (1968). Dissociation of visual functions by deprivation and rearrangement. *Psychologische Forschung*, *31*(4), 338–348.

Held, R., Efstathiou, A., & Greene, M. (1966). Adaptation to displaced and delayed visual feedback from the hand. *Journal of Experimental Psychology*, *72*(6), 887–891.

Held, R., & Freedman, S. J. (1963). Plasticity in human sensorimotor control. *Science*, *142*(3591), 455–462.

Held, R. T., & Banks, M. S. (2008). Misperceptions in stereoscopic displays: A vision science perspective. In *Proceedings Symposium on Applied Perception in Graphics and Visualization* (pp. 23–32). New York: ACM.

Held, R. T., Cooper, E. A., O'Brien, J. F., & Banks, M. S. (2010). Using blur to affect perceived distance and size. *Proc. SIGGRAPH 2010, Transactions on Graphics*, *29*(3), 1–16.

von Helmholtz, H. (1925). *Treatise on physiological optics* (J. P. C. Southall, Trans.). Rochester, NY: Optical Society of America. (Original work published 1878)

Henderson, J. M. (2003). Human gaze control during real-world scene perception. *Trends in Cognitive Sciences*, *7*(11), 498–504.

Henderson, J. M. (2006). Eye movements. In C. Senior, T. Russell, & M. S. Gazzaniga (Eds.), *Methods in mind* (pp. 171–192). Cambridge, MA: MIT Press.

Henderson, J. M. (2007). Regarding scenes. *Current Directions in Psychological Science*, *16*(4), 219–222.

Henderson, J. M., & Hollingworth, A. (2003). Global transsaccadic change blindness during scene perception. *Psychological Science*, *14*(5), 493–497.

Hering, E. (1964). *Outlines of a theory of the light sense* (L. M. Hurvich & D. Jameson, Trans.). Cambridge, MA: Harvard University Press. (Original work published 1874)

Hershberger, W. (1970). Attached-shadow orientation perceived as depth by chickens reared in an environment illuminated from below. *Journal of Comparative and Physiological Psychology, 73*(3), 407–411.

Hess, E. H. (1950). Development of the chick's responses to light and shade cues of depth. *Journal of Comparative and Physiological Psychology, 43*(2), 112–122.

Hettinger, L. J. (2002). Illusory self-motion in virtual environments. In K. M. Stanney (Ed.), *Handbook of virtual environments: Design, implementation, and applications* (pp. 471–492). Mahway, NJ: Lawrence Erlbaum.

Hill, H., & Pollick, F. E. (2000). Exaggerating temporal differences enhances recognition of individuals from point light displays. *Psychological Science, 11*(3), 223–228.

Hillaire, S., Lécuyer, A., Cozot, R., & Casiez, G. (2008). Using an eye-tracking system to improve camera motions and depth-of-field blur effects in virtual environments. In *Proceedings IEEE Virtual Reality Conference* (pp. 47–50). Los Alamitos, CA: IEEE.

Hillstrom, A. P., & Yantis, S. (1994). Visual motion and attentional capture. *Perception & Psychophysics, 55*(4), 399–411.

Hinton, G. E., McClelland, J. L., & Rumelhart, D. E. (1986). Distributed representations: Vol. 1. Foundations. In D. E. Rumelhart, J. L. McClelland, & the PDF Research Group (Eds.), *Parallel distributed processing: Explorations in the microstructure of cognition* (pp. 77–109). Cambridge, MA: MIT Press.

Hiris, E., Humphrey, D., & Stout, A. (2005). Temporal properties in masking of biological motion. *Perception & Psychophysics, 67*(3), 435–443.

Ho, Y.-X., Landy, M. S., & Maloney, L. T. (2006). How direction of illumination affects visually perceived surface roughness. *Journal of Vision, 6*(5), 634–648.

Hochberg, C. B., & Hochberg, J. E. (1952). Familiar size and the perception of depth. *Journal of Psychology, 34*, 107–114.

Hochberg, J., & Brooks, V. (1962). Pictorial recognition as an unlearned ability: A study on one child's performance. *The American Journal of Psychology, 75*(4), 624–628.

Hodgins, J. K., O'Brien, J. F., & Tumblin, J. (1998). Perception of human motion with different geometrical models. *IEEE Transactions on Visualization and Computer Graphics, 4*(4), 307–317.

Hoffman, D. D., & Richards, W. A. (1984). Parts of recognition. *Cognition, 18*(1–3), 65–96.

Hoffman, D. M., Girshick, A. R., Akeley, K., & Banks, M. S. (2008). Vergence-accommodation conflicts hinder visual performance and cause visual fatigue. *Journal of Vision*, *8*(3), 1–30.

Hoiem, D., Efros, A. A., & Hebert, M. (2007). Recovering surface layout from an image. *International Journal of Computer Vision*, *75*(1), 151–172.

Hollingworth, A. (2003). Failures of retrieval and comparison constrain change detection in natural scenes. *Journal of Experimental Psychology: Human Perception and Performance*, *29*(2), 388–403.

Hollingworth, A. (2006). Visual memory for natural scenes: Evidence from change detection and visual search. *Visual Cognition*, *14*(4–8), 781–807.

Holmes, N. P., Crozier, G., & Spence, C. (2004). When mirrors lie: Visual capture of arm position impairs reaching performance. *Cognitive, Affective, & Behavioral Neuroscience*, *4*(2), 193–200.

Holmes, N. P., & Spence, C. (2006). Beyond the body schema: Visual, prosthetic, and technological contributions to bodily perception and awareness. In G. Knoblich, I. Thornton, M. Grosjean, & M. Shiffrar (Eds.), *Human body perception from the inside out* (pp. 15–64). Oxford, UK: Oxford University Press.

Holmes, O. W. (1859, June). The stereoscope and the stereograph. *The Atlantic Monthly*, *3*(20), 738–748.

Holway, A. H., & Boring, E. G. (1941). Determinants of apparent visual size with distance variant. *The American Journal of Psychology*, *54*(1), 21–37.

Hommel, B., Musseler, J., Aschersleben, G., & Prinz, W. (2001). The theory of event coding (TEC): A framework for perception and action planning. *Behavioral and Brain Sciences*, *24*(5), 849–878.

Hood, D. C., & Finkelstein, M. A. (1986). Sensitivity to light. In K. R. Boff, I. Kaufman, & J. P. Thomas (Eds.), *Handbook of perception and human performance: Vol. 1. Sensory processes and perception* (chap. 5). New York: Wiley.

Horn, B. K. P. (1974). Determining lightness from an image. *Computer Graphics and Image Processing*, *3*(4), 277–299.

Horn, B. K. P. (1977). Understanding image intensities. *Artificial Intelligence*, *8*(2), 201–231.

Horn, B. K. P., & Brooks, M. J. (1989). *Shape from shading*. Cambridge, MA: MIT Press.

Horn, B. K. P., & Schunck, B. (1981). Determining optical flow. *Artificial Intelligence*, *17*(1–3), 185–203.

Horn, B. K. P., & Sjoberg, R. W. (1979). Calculating the reflectance map. *Applied Optics*, *18*(11), 1770–1779.

Howard, I. P. (2002). *Seeing in depth: Vol. 1. Basic mechanisms*. Toronto, Ontario: I Porteous.

Howard, I. P., & Howard, A. (1994). Vection: The contributions of absolute and relative visual motion. *Perception*, *23*(7), 745–751.

Howard, I. P., & Rogers, B. J. (2002). *Seeing in depth: Vol. 2. Depth perception.* Toronto, Ontario: I Porteous.

Hubel, D. H., & Wiesel, T. N. (1959). Receptive fields of single neurons in the cat's striate cortex. *Journal of Psychology*, *148*(3), 574–591.

Hubel, D. H., & Wiesel, T. N. (1968). Receptive fields and functional architecture of monkey striate cortex. *Journal of Psychology*, *195*(1), 215–243.

Huffman, D. A. (1971). Impossible objects as nonsense sentences. *Machine Intelligence*, *6*, 295–323.

Hummel, J. E., & Biederman, I. (1992). Dynamic binding in a neural network for shape recognition. *Psychological Review*, *99*(3), 480–517.

Hummel, J. E., & Stankiewicz, B. (1996). Categorical relations in shape perception. *Spatial Vision*, *10*, 201–236.

Hurlbert, A. C. (1998). Computational models of color constancy. In V. Walsh & J. J. Kulikowski (Eds.), *Perceptual constancy: Why things look as they do* (pp. 283–322). Cambridge, UK: Cambridge University Press.

Hurvich, L. M., & Jameson, D. (1957). An opponent-process theory of color vision. *Psychological Review*, *64*(6), 384–404.

Hutchison, J. J., & Loomis, J. M. (2006). Does energy expenditure affect the perception of egocentric distance? A failure to replicate experiment 1 of Proffitt, Stefanucci, Banton, and Epstein (2003). *The Spanish Journal of Psychology*, *9*(2), 332–339.

Huttenlocher, D. P., & Ullman, S. (1990). Recognizing solid objects by alignment with an image. *International Journal of Computer Vision*, *5*(2), 195–212.

Interrante, V., Anderson, L., & Ries, B. (2006a). Distance perception in immersive virtual environments, revisited. In *Proceedings IEEE Virtual Reality* (pp. 3–10). Washington, DC: IEEE Computer Society.

Interrante, V., Anderson, L., & Ries, B. (2006b). Presence, rather than prior exposure, is the more strongly indicated factor in the accurate perception of egocentric distances in real world co-located immersive virtual environments. In *Proceedings Symposium on Applied Perception in Graphics and Visualization* (p. 157). New York: ACM.

Interrante, V., Ries, B., Lindquist, J., & Anderson, L. (2007). Elucidating the factors that can facilitate veridical spatial perception in immersive virtual environments. In *Proceedings IEEE Symposium on 3D User Interfaces* (pp. 11–18). Los Alamitos, CA: IEEE.

Intriligator, J., & Cavanagh, P. (2001). The spatial resolution of visual attention. *Cognitive Psychology*, *43*(3), 171–216.

Irani, M., & Anadan, P. (1998). A unified approach to moving object detection in 2D and 3D scenes. *IEEE Transactions on Pattern Analysis and Machine Intelligence, 20*(6), 577–589.

Ishikawa, T., & Montello, D. R. (2006). Spatial knowledge acquisition from direct experience in the environment: Individual differences in the development of metric knowledge and the integration of separately learned places. *Cognitive Psychology, 52*(2), 93–129.

Ittelson, W. H. (1951). Size as a cue to distance: Static localization. *The American Journal of Psychology, 64*(1), 54–67.

Itti, L., & Koch, C. (2001). Computational modelling of visual attention. *Nature Reviews Neuroscience, 2*(3), 194–203.

Izard, C. E. (1971). *The face of emotion.* New York: Appleton-Century-Crofts.

Izard, C. E. (1977). *Human emotions.* New York: Plenum.

Jacobs, A., Pinto, J., & Shiffrar, M. (2004). Experience, context, and the visual perception of human movement. *Journal of Experimental Psychology: Human Perception and Performance, 30*(5), 822–835.

Jacobs, A., & Shiffrar, M. (2005). Walking perception by walking observers. *Journal of Experimental Psychology: Human Perception and Performance, 31*, 157–169.

James, W. (1890). *The principles of psychology.* New York: Holt.

Jeannerod, M. (2001). Neural simulation of action: A unifying mechanism for motor cognition. *Neuroimage, 14*(1 Pt 2), S103–S109.

Jensen, H. W., & Buhler, J. (2002). A rapid hierarchical rendering technique for translucent materials. *Proc. SIGGRAPH '02, Transactions on Graphics, 21*(3), 576–581.

Johansson, G. (1950). *Configurations in event perception.* Uppsala: Almqvist & Wiksells.

Johansson, G. (1973). Visual perception of biological motion and a model for its analysis. *Perception & Psychophysics, 14*(2), 201–211.

Johnson, M. K., & Farid, H. (2007). Exposing digital forgeries in complex lighting environments. *IEEE Transactions on Information Forensics and Security, 3*(2), 450–461.

Johnson, S. H., & Grafton, S. T. (2003). From acting on to acting with: The functional anatomy of object-oriented action schemata. *Progress in Brain Research, 142*, 127–139.

Jolicouer, P. (1985). The time to name disoriented natural objects. *Memory & Cognition, 13*(4), 289–303.

Jones, A., McDowall, I., Yamada, H., Bolas, M., & Debevec, P. (2007). An interactive 360° light field display. In *SIGGRAPH Emerging Technologies* (p. 13). New York: ACM.

Jones, D. G., & Malik, J. (1992). A computational framework for determining stereo correspondence from a set of linear spatial filters. In *Proceedings European Conference on Computer Vision* (pp. 395–410). London: Springer-Verlag.

Jorke, H., Simon, A., & Fritz, M. (2008). Advanced stereo projection using interference filters. In *Proceedings 3DTV Conference* (pp. 177–180). Los Alamitos, CA: IEEE Press.

Joshi, P., Tien, W. C., Desbrun, M., & Pighin, F. (2003). Learning controls for blend shape based realistic facial animation. In *Proc. 2003 acm SIGGRAPH/Eurographics symposium on computer animation* (pp. 187–192). Aire-la-Ville, Switzerland: Eurographics Association.

Judd, D. B. (1940). Hue saturation and lightness of surface colors with chromatic illumination. *Journal of the Optical Society of America, 30*(1), 2–32.

Judd, T., Durand, F., & Adelson, E. H. (2007). Apparent ridges for line drawing. *ACM Transactions on Graphics, 26*(3), 19.

Julesz, B. (1971). *Foundations of cyclopean perception.* Chicago: University of Chicago Press.

Julesz, B. (1975). Experiments in the visual perception of texture. *Scientific American, 232*(4), 34–43.

Julesz, B. (1981). Textons, the elements of texture perception, and their interactions. *Nature, 290*, 91–97.

Just, M. A., & Carpenter, P. A. (1985). Cognitive coordinate systems: Accounts of mental rotation and individual differences in spatial ability. *Psychological Review, 92*(2), 137–172.

Kaiser, M. K., Proffitt, D. R., & Anderson, K. (1985). Judgments of natural and anomalous trajectories in the presence and absence of motion. *Journal of experimental psychology: Learning, memory, and cognition, 11*(4), 795–803.

Kane, M. J., Bleckley, M. K., Conway, A. R. A., & Engle, R. W. (2001). A controlled-attention view of working-memory capacity. *Journal of Experimental Psychology: General, 130*(2), 169–183.

Kanizsa, G. (1955). Condizioni ed effetti della transparenza fenomica. *Revista di Psicologia, 49*, 3–19.

Kanizsa, G. (1976). Subjective contours. *Scientific American, 234*(4), 48–52.

Kaplan, G. A. (1969). Kinetic disruption of optical texture: The perception of depth at an edge. *Perception & Psychophysics, 6*(4), 193–198.

Katz, D. (1925). *Der aufbau der tastwelt* [The world of touch]. Leipzig, Germany: Barth.

Keehner, M. (2008). Conflicting cues from vision and touch can impair spatial task performance: Speculations on the role of spatial ability in reconciling frames of reference. In C. Freksa, N. S. Newcombe, P. Gärdenfors, & S. Wölfl (Eds.), *In spatial cognition VI: Learning, reasoning, and talking about space* (pp. 188–201). Berlin, Germany: Springer.

Keehner, M., Hegarty, M., Cohen, C., Khooshabeh, P., & Montello, D. R. (2008). Spatial reasoning with external visualizations: What matters is what you see, not whether you interact. *Cognitive Science, 32*(7), 1099–1132.

Keehner, M., & Khooshabeh, P. (2005). Computerized representations of 3D structure: How spatial comprehension and patterns of interactivity differ among learners. In *Proceedings AAAI Spring Symposium Series, Reasoning with Mental and External Diagrams* (pp. 12–17). Menlo Park, CA: AAAI Press.

Keehner, M., Khooshabeh, P., & Hegarty, M. (2008). Individual differences among users: Implications for the design of 3D medical visualizations. In F. Dong, G. Ghinea, & S. Y. Chen (Eds.), *User centered design for medical visualization* (pp. 1–24). Hershey, PA: Idea Group.

Kelber, A., Vorobyev, M., & Osorio, D. (2003). Animal colour vision—behavioral tests and physiological concepts. *Biological Review, 78*(1), 81–118.

Kelly, D. H. (1979). Motion and vision. II. Stabilized spatio-temporal threshold surface. *Journal of the Optical Society of America, 69*(10), 1340–1349.

Kelly, J. W., Loomis, J. M., & Beall, A. C. (2005). The importance of perceived relative motion in the control of posture. *Experimental Brain Research, 161*(3), 285–292.

Kelly, J. W., & McNamara, T. P. (2008). Spatial memories of virtual environments: How egocentric experience, intrinsic structure, and extrinsic structure interact. *Psychonomic Bulletin & Review, 15*(2), 322–327.

Kennedy, J. M. (1988). Line endings and subjective contours. *Spatial Vision, 3*(3), 151–158.

Kenyon, R. V., Sandin, D., Smith, R. C., Pawlicki, R., & DeFanti, T. (2007). Size-constancy in the CAVE. *Presence: Teleoperations and Virtual Environments, 16*(2), 172–187.

Kerlow, I. (2009). *The art of 3D computer animation and effects* (4th ed.). Hoboken, NJ: Wiley.

Kersten, D., Knill, D., Mamassian, P., & Bülthoff, I. (1996). Illusory motion from shadows. *Nature, 379*, 31.

Kersten, D., Mamassian, P., & Knill, D. C. (1997). Moving cast shadows induce apparent motion in depth. *Perception, 26*(2), 171–192.

Kersten, D., Mamassian, P., & Yuille, A. (2004). Object perception and Bayesian inference. *Annual Review of Psychology, 55*, 271–304.

Khan, A., Mordatch, I., Fitzmaurice, G., Matejka, J., & Kurtenbach, G. (2008). Viewcube: A 3D orientation indicator and controller. In *Proceedings symposium on interactive 3D graphics and games* (pp. 17–25). New York: ACM.

Kilpatrick, F. P., & Ittelson, W. H. (1953). The size-distance invariance hypothesis. *The Psychological Review, 60*(4), 223–231.

Kim, S., Hagh-Shenas, H., & Interrante, V. (2004). Conveying shape with texture: Experimental investigations of texture's effects on shape categorization judgments. *IEEE Transactions on Visualization and Computer Graphics, 10*(4), 471–483.

Kimchi, R. (1992). Primacy of wholistic processing and global/local paradigm: A critical review. *Psychological Bulletin, 112*(1), 24–38.

King, M., Meyer, G. E., Tangney, J., & Biederman, I. (1976). Shape constancy and a perceptual bias towards symmetry. *Perception & Psychophysics, 19*(2), 129–136.

Kitchin, R. M. (1996). Methodological convergence in cognitive mapping research: Investigating configurational knowledge. *Journal of Environmental Psychology, 16*(3), 163–185.

Klatzky, R. L. (1998). Allocentric and egocentric spatial representations: definitions, distinctions, and interconnections. In C. Freksa, C. Habel, & K. F. Wender (Eds.), *Spatial cognition: An interdisciplinary approach to representation and processing of spatial knowledge* (Vol. 5, pp. 1–17). Berlin, Germany: Springer-Verlag.

Klatzky, R. L., Loomis, J. M., Beall, A. C., Chance, S. S., & Golledge, R. G. (1998). Spatial updating of self-position and orientation during real, imagined, and virtual locomotion. *Psychological Science, 9*(4), 293–298.

Klatzky, R. L., Loomis, J. M., Gollege, R. G., Cicinelli, J. G., Doherty, S., & Pelligrino, J. W. (1990). Acquisition of route and survey knowledge in the absence of vision. *Journal of Motor Behavior, 22*(1), 19–43.

Klatzky, R. L., Wu, B., Shelton, D., & Stetton, G. (2008). Effectiveness of augmented-reality visualization versus cognitive mediation for learning actions in near space. *ACM Transactions on Applied Perception, 5*(1), 1:1–1:23.

Knapp, J. M., & Loomis, J. M. (2004). Limited field of view of head-mounted displays is not the cause of distance underestimation in virtual environments. *Presence: Teleoperators and Virtual Environments, 13*(5), 572–577.

Knill, D. C. (1998a). Discriminating planar surface slant from texture: Human and ideal observers compared. *Vision Research, 38*(11), 1683–1711.

Knill, D. C. (1998b). Ideal observer perturbation analysis reveals human strategies for inferring surface orientation from texture. *Vision Research, 38*(11), 2635–2656.

Knill, D. C. (1998c). Surface orientation from texture: Ideal observers, generic observers and the information content of texture cues. *Vision Research*, *38*(11), 1655–1682.

Knoblich, G., & Flach, R. (2001). Predicting the effects of actions: Interactions of perception and action. *Psychological Science*, *12*(6), 467–472.

Knoblich, G., & Prinz, W. (2001). Recognition of self-generated actions from kinematic displays of drawing. *Journal of Experimental Psychology: Human Perception and Performance*, *27*(2), 456–465.

Knoblich, G., Thornton, I. M., Grosjean, M., & Shiffrar, M. (Eds.). (2006). *Human body perception from the inside out*. New York: Oxford University Press.

Knutsson, H., & Granlund, G. H. (1983). Texture analysis using two-dimensional quadrature filters. In *Proceedings IEEE Computer Society Workshop on Computer Architecture for Pattern Analysis and Image Database Management* (pp. 206–213). Los Alamitos, CA: IEEE.

Koenderink, J. J. (1998). Pictorial relief. *Philosophical Transactions of the Royal Society A*, *356*(1740), 1071–1086.

Koenderink, J. J., Pont, S. C., van Doorn, A. J., Kappers, A. M. L., & Todd, J. T. (2007). The visual light field. *Perception*, *36*(11), 1595–1610.

Koenderink, J. J., & van Doorn, A. J. (1976). The singularities of the visual mapping. *Biological Cybernetics*, *24*(1), 51–59.

Koenderink, J. J., & van Doorn, A. J. (1979). The internal representation of solid shape with respect to vision. *Biological Cybernetics*, *32*(4), 211–216.

Koenderink, J. J., & van Doorn, A. J. (1980). Photometric invariants related to solid shape. *Optica Acta*, *27*(7), 981–996.

Koenderink, J. J., & van Doorn, A. J. (2003). Shape and shading. In L. M. Chalupa & J. S. Werner (Eds.), *The visual neurosciences* (pp. 1090–1105). Cambridge, MA: MIT Press.

Koenderink, J. J., van Doorn, A. J., Christou, C., & Lappin, J. S. (1996a). Perturbation study of shading in pictures. *Perception*, *25*(9), 1009–1026.

Koenderink, J. J., van Doorn, A. J., Christou, C., & Lappin, J. S. (1996b). Shape constancy in pictorial relief. *Perception*, *25*(2), 155–164.

Koenderink, J. J., van Doorn, A. J., & Kappers, A. M. L. (1992). Surface perception in pictures. *Perception & Psychophysics*, *52*(5), 487–496.

Koenderink, J. J., van Doorn, A. J., & Kappers, A. M. L. (1994). On so-called paradoxical monocular stereoscopy. *Perception*, *23*(5), 583–594.

Koenderink, J. J., van Doorn, A. J., Kappers, A. M. L., te Pas, S. F., & Pont, S. C. (2003). Illumination direction from texture shading. *Journal of the Optical Society of America A*, *20*(6), 987–995.

Koffka, K. (1935). *Principles of gestalt psychology*. New York: Harcourt.

Kohler, I. (1962). Experiments with goggles. *Scientific American*, *206*(5), 62–86.

Kolers, P. A. (1972). *Aspects of apparent motion*. New York: Pergamon.

Korein, J., & Badler, N. (1983). Temporal anti-aliasing in computer generated animation. *Computer Graphics*, *17*(3), 377–388.

Kosslyn, S. M. (1994). *Image and brain: The resolution of the imagery debate*. Cambridge, MA: MIT Press.

Kosslyn, S. M., Ball, T. M., & Reiser, B. J. (1978). Visual images preserve metric spatial information: Evidence from studies of image scanning. *Journal of Experimental Psychology: Human Perception & Performance*, *4*(1), 47–60.

Kosslyn, S. M., Thompson, W. L., Wraga, M., & Alpert, N. M. (2001). Imagining rotation by endogenous versus exogenous forces: Distinct neural mechanisms. *Neuroreport*, *12*(11), 2519–2525.

Kowler, E. (1995). Eye movements. In S. M. Kosslyn & D. N. Osherson (Eds.), *An invitation to cognitive science: Vol. 2. Visual cognition* (pp. 215–265). Cambridge, MA: MIT Press.

Kozhevnikov, M., & Hegarty, M. (2001). A dissociation between object manipulation spatial ability and spatial orientation ability. *Memory & Cognition*, *29*(5), 745–756.

Kozlowski, L. T., & Cutting, J. E. (1977). Recognizing the sex of a walker from a dynamic point-light display. *Perception & Psychophysics*, *21*(6), 575–580.

Kraft, J. M., & Brainard, D. H. (1999). Mechanisms of color constancy under nearly natural viewing. *Proceedings of the National Academy of Sciences, USA*, *96*(1), 307–312.

Kröse, B. J. A. (1987). Local structure analyzers as determinants of preattentive pattern discrimination. *Biological Cybernetics*, *55*(7), 289–298.

Krukowski, A. E., Pirog, K. A., Beutter, B. R., Brooks, K. R., & Stone, L. S. (2003). Human discrimination of visual direction of motion with and without smooth pursuit eye movements. *Journal of Vision*, *3*(11), 831–840.

Kuhl, S. A., Creem-Regehr, S. H., & Thompson, W. B. (2008). Recalibration of rotational locomotion in immersive virtual environments. *ACM Transactions on Applied Perception*, *5*(3), 17:1–17:11.

Kuhl, S. A., Thompson, W. B., & Creem-Regehr, S. H. (2006). Minification influences spatial judgments in virtual environments. In *Proceedings Symposium on Applied Perception in Grapics and Visualization* (pp. 15–19). New York: ACM.

Kuhl, S. A., Thompson, W. B., & Creem-Regehr, S. H. (2009). HMD calibration and its effects on distance judgments. *ACM Transactions on Applied Perception*, *6*(3), 19:1–19:20.

Kunkel, T., & Reinhard, E. (2010). A reassessment of the simultaneous dynamic range of the human visual system. In *Proceedings 7th Symposium on Applied Perception in Grapics and Visualization* (pp. 17–24). New York: ACM.

Kunz, B. R., Wouters, L., Smith, D., Thompson, W. B., & Creem-Regehr, S. H. (2009). Revisiting the effect of quality of graphics on distance judgments in virtual environments: A comparison of verbal reports and blind walking. *Attention, Perception, & Psychophysics, 71*(6), 1284–1293.

Kurby, C. A., & Zacks, J. M. (2008). Segmentation in the perception and memory of events. *Trends in Cognitive Sciences, 12*(2), 72–9.

Lades, M., Vorbruggen, J. C., Buhmann, J., Lange, J., von der Malsburg, C., Wurtz, R. P., et al. (1993). Distortion invariant object recognition in the dynamic link architecture. *IEEE Transactions on Computers, 42*(3), 300–311.

Lakie, M., Caplan, N., & Loram, I. D. (2003). Human balancing of an inverted pendulum with a compliant linkage: Neural control by anticipatory intermittent bias. *The Journal of Physiology, 551*(1), 357–370.

Land, E. H. (1959a). Color vision and the natural image: Part I. *Proceedings of the National Academy of Sciences, USA, 45*(1), 115–129.

Land, E. H. (1959b). Color vision and the natural image: Part II. *Proceedings of the National Academy of Sciences, USA, 45*(4), 636–644.

Land, E. H. (1959c). Experiments in color vision. *Scientific American, 200*(5), 84–99.

Land, E. H. (1977). The retinex theory of color vision. *Scientific American, 237*(6), 108–128.

Land, E. H., & McCann, J. J. (1971). Lightness and retinex theory. *Journal of the Optical Society of America, 61*(1), 1–11.

Land, M. F., & Hayhoe, M. (2001). In what ways do eye movements contribute to everyday activities? *Vision Research, 41*(25–26), 3559–3565.

Landy, M. S., & Bergen, J. R. (1991). Texture segregation and orientation gradient. *Vision Research, 31*(4), 679–691.

Landy, M. S., & Graham, N. (2004). Visual perception of texture. In L. M. Chalupa & J. S. Werner (Eds.), *The visual neurosciences* (pp. 1106–1118). Cambridge, MA: MIT Press.

Lange, J., Georg, K., & Lappe, M. (2006). Visual perception of biological motion by form: A template-matching analysis. *Journal of Vision, 6*(8), 836–849.

Langer, M. S. (2000). Large-scale failures of $f^{-\alpha}$ scaling in natural image spectra. *Journal of the Optical Society of America A, 17*(1), 28–33.

Langer, M. S., & Bülthoff, H. H. (2000). Depth discrimination from shading under diffuse lighting. *Perception, 29*(6), 649–660.

Lappe, M., Bremmer, F., & van den Berg, A. V. (1999). Perception of self-motion from visual flow. *Trends in Cognitive Sciences*, *3*(9), 329–336.

Larson, G. W. (1998). Logluv encoding for full-gamut, high-dynamic range images. *Journal of Graphics Tools*, *3*(1), 15–31.

Larson, G. W., Rushmeier, H., & Piatko, C. (1997). A visibility matching tone reproduction operator for high dynamic range scenes. *IEEE Transactions on Visualization and Computer Graphics*, *3*(4), 291–306.

Larson, G. W., & Shakespeare, R. (2004). *Rendering with Radiance: The art and science of lighting visualization* (rev. ed.). Charleston, SC: Booksurge.

Lasseter, J. (2001). Tricks to animating characters with a computer. In E. Fiume (Ed.), *Proceedings of SIGGRAPH 2001, Computer Graphics Proceedings, Annual Conference Series* (pp. 45–47). Reading, MA: Addison Wesley.

Lavin, M. A. (1974). *An application of line labeling and other scene-analysis techniques to the problem of hidden-line removal* (Tech. Rep. No. Working Paper 66). Cambridge, MA: MIT Artificial Intelligence Lab.

Lavoué, G. (2009). A local roughness measure for 3D meshes and its application to visual masking. *ACM Transactions Applied Perception*, *5*(4), 21:1–21:23.

Lawton, C. A. (1994). Gender differences in way-finding strategies: Relationship to spatial ability and spatial anxiety. *Sex Roles*, *30*(11–12), 765–779.

Lederman, S. J. (1981). The perception of surface roughness by active and passive touch. *Bulletin of the Psychonomic Society*, *18*(5), 253–255.

Lederman, S. J. (1983). Tactual roughness perception: Spatial and temporal determinants. *Canadian Journal of Psychology*, *37*(4), 498–511.

Lederman, S. J., & Abbott, S. G. (1981). Texture perception: Studies of intersensory organization using a discrepancy paradigm and visual versus tactual psychophysics. *Journal of Experimental Psychology: Human Perception & Performance*, *7*(4), 902–915.

Lee, D. N. (1976). A theory of visual control of braking based on information about time-to-collision. *Perception*, *5*(4), 437–459.

Lee, D. N., & Aronson, E. (1974). Visual proprioceptive control of standing in human infants. *Perception & Psychophysics*, *15*(3), 529–532.

Lee, D. N., & Lishman, J. R. (1975). Visual and proprioceptive control of stance. *Journal of Human Movement Studies*, *1*(2), 87–95.

Lee, D. N., & Reddish, P. E. (1981). Plummeting gannets: A paradigm of ecological optics. *Nature*, *293*, 293–294.

Lee, H.-C. (1986). Method for computing the scene-illuminant chromaticity from specular highlights. *Journal of the Optical Society of America A*, *3*(10), 1694–1699.

Legge, G. E. (1980). A power law for contrast discrimination. *Vision Research*, *21*(4), 457–467.

Legge, G. E., & Foley, J. M. (1980). Contrast masking in human vision. *Journal of the Optical Society of America, 70*(12), 1458–1471.

Lenggenhager, B., Mouthon, M., & Blanke, O. (2009). Spatial aspects of bodily self-consciousness. *Consciousness and Cognition, 18*(1), 110–117.

Lenggenhager, B., Tadi, T., Metzinger, T., & Blanke, O. (2007). Video ergo sum: Manipulating body self-consciousness. *Science, 317*(5841), 1096–1099.

Lepecq, J. C., Jouen, F., & Dubon, D. (1993). The effect of linear vection on manual aiming at memorized directions of stationary targets. *Perception, 22*(1), 49–60.

Leslie, A. M. (1982). The perception of causality in infants. *Perception, 11*(2), 173–186.

Leslie, A. M., & Keeble, S. (1987). Do six-month-old infants perceive causality? *Cognition, 25*(3), 265–88.

Leung, T., & Malick, J. (2001). Representing and recognizing the visual appearance of materials using three-dimensional textons. *International Journal of Computer Vision, 43*(1), 29–44.

Leung, T., & Malik, J. (1997). On perpendicular texture: Why do we see more flowers in the distance? In *Proceedings IEEE Conference on Computer Vision and pattern recognition* (pp. 807–813). Los Alamitos, CA: IEEE.

Levin, D. R., & Simons, D. J. (1997). Failure to detect changes to attended objects in motion pictures. *Psychonomic Bulletin and Review, 4*(4), 501–506.

Lewis, J. W. (2006). Cortical networks related to human tool use. *The Neuroscientist, 12*(3), 211–231.

Leyton, M. (1992). *Symmetry, causality, mind.* Cambridge, MA: MIT Press.

Li, L., & Warren, W. H., Jr. (2000). Perception of heading during rotation: Sufficiency of dense motion parallax and reference objects. *Vision Research, 40*(28), 3873–3894.

Lipton, L. (1982). *Foundations of the stereoscopic cinema: A study in depth.* New York: Van Nostrand. (Available from `http://www.stereoscopic.org/library/`)

Liu, B., & Todd, J. T. (2004). Perceptual biases in the interpretation of 3d shape from shading. *Vision Research, 44*(18), 2135–2145.

Liu, S., Hua, H., & Cheng, D. (2010). A novel prototype for an optical see-through head-mounted display with addressable focus cues. *IEEE Transactions on Visualization and Computer Graphics, 16*(3), 381–393.

Liu, T., Abrams, J., & Carrasco, M. (2009). Voluntary attention enhances contrast appearance. *Psychological Science, 20*(3), 354–362.

Livingston, M. (2002). *Vision and art: The biology of seeing.* New York: Harry N. Abrams.

Livingstone, M. S., & Hubel, D. H. (1987). Psychophysical evidence for separate channels for the perception of form, color, movement, and depth. *Journal of Neuroscience*, *7*(11), 3416–3468.

Logvinenko, A., Petrini, K., & Maloney, L. T. (2008). A scaling analysis of the snake lightness illusion. *Perception & Psychophysics*, *70*(5), 828–840.

Logvinenko, A. D., & Maloney, L. T. (2006). The proximity structure of achromatic surface colors and the impossibility of asymmetric lightness matching. *Perception & Psychophysics*, *68*(1), 76–83.

Lohman, D. F. (1988). Spatial abilities as traits, processes, and knowledge. In R. J. Sternberg (Ed.), *Advances in the psychology of human intelligence* (Vol. 4, pp. 181–248). Hillsdale, NJ: Lawrence Erlbaum.

Longuet-Higgins, H. C. (1982). The role of the vertical dimension in stereoscopic vision. *Perception*, *11*(4), 377–386.

Longuet-Higgins, H. C., & Prazdny, K. (1980). The interpretation of a moving retinal image. *Proceedings Royal Society of London, B*, *208*(1173), 385–397.

Loomis, J. M., & Beall, A. C. (1998). Visually controlled locomotion: Its dependence on optic flow, three-dimensional space perception, and cognition. *Ecological Psychology*, *10*(3–4), 271–285.

Loomis, J. M., Beall, A. C., Macuga, K. L., Kelly, J. W., & Smith, R. S. (2006). Visual control of action without retinal optic flow. *Psychological Science*, *17*(3), 214–221.

Loomis, J. M., Klatzky, R. L., Golledge, R. G., & Philbeck, J. W. (1999). Human navigation by path integration. In R. G. Golledge (Ed.), *Wayfinding behavior: Cognitive mapping and other spatial processes* (pp. 125–151). Baltimore, MD: Johns Hopkins University Press.

Loomis, J. M., & Knapp, J. (2003). Visual perception of egocentric distance in real and virtual environments. In L. J. Hettinger & M. W. Haas (Eds.), *Virtual and adaptive environments: Applications, implications, and human performance issues* (chap. 2). Mahway, NJ: Lawrence Erlbaum.

Loomis, J. M., & Nakayama, K. (1973). A velocity analogue of brightness contrast. *Perception*, *2*(4), 425–428.

Loomis, J. M., & Philbeck, J. W. (2008). Measuring spatial perception with spatial updating and action. In R. L. Klatzky, B. MacWhinney, & M. Behrmann (Eds.), *Embodiment, ego-space, and action*. New York: Taylor & Francis.

Loomis, J. M., Silva, J. A. D., Fujita, N., & Fukusima, S. S. (1992). Visual space perception and visually directed action. *Journal of Experimental Psychology: Human Perception and Performance*, *18*(4), 906–921.

Lowe, D. G. (1985). *Perceptual organization and visual recognition*. Boston, MA: Kluwer.

Lu, C., & Fender, D. H. (1972). The interaction of color and luminance in stereoscopic vision. *Investigative Opthalmology, 11*(6), 482–490.

Lu, J., Georghiades, A. S., Rushmeier, H., Dorsey, J., & Xu, C. (2005). Synthesis of material drying history: Phenomenon modeling, transferring and rendering. In *Proccedings Eurographics Workshop on Natural Phenomena*. Aire-la-Ville, Switzerland: Eurogaraphics Association.

Lu, Z.-L., & Sperling, G. (1996). Three systems for visual motion perception. *Current Directions in Psychological Science, 5*(2), 44–53.

Lu, Z.-L., & Sperling, G. (2001). Three-systems theory of human visual motion perception: Review and update. *Journal of the Optical Society of America A, 18*(9), 2331–2370.

Lucretius. (1965). *On nature* (R. Geer, Trans.). Indianapolis, IN: Bobbs-Merrill. (Original work published 1st century BC)

Lumsden, E. A. (1980). Problems of magnification and minification: An explanation of the distortions of distance, slant, shape, and velocity. In M. A. Hagen (Ed.), *The perception of pictures I: Alberti's window: The projective model of pictures* (Vol. 1, pp. 91–135). New York: Academic Press.

Luo, X., Kenyon, R. V., Kamper, D., Santin, D., & DeFanti, T. (2007). The effects of scene complexity, stereovision, and motion parallax on size constancy in a mobile virtual environment. In *Proceedings IEEE Virtual Reality* (pp. 59–66). Los Alamitos, CA: IEEE.

Mack, A. (1986). Perceptual aspects of motion in the frontal plane. In K. R. Boff, I. Kaufman, & J. P. Thomas (Eds.), *Handbook of perception and human performance: Vol. 1: Sensory processes and perception* (chap. 17). New York: Wiley.

Mack, A., & Rock, I. (1998). *Inattentional blindness*. Cambridge, MA: MIT Press.

Maclean, N. (1976). *A river runs through it and other stories*. Chicago: University of Chicago Press.

Macuga, K. L., Loomis, J. M., Beall, A. C., & Kelly, J. W. (2006). Perception of heading without optic flow. *Perception & Psychophysics, 68*(5), 872–878.

Madison, C., Thompson, W. B., Kersten, D., Shirley, P., & Smits, B. (2001). Use of interreflection and shadow for surface contact. *Perception & Psychophysics, 63*(2), 187–194.

Malik, J. (1987). Interpreting line drawings of curved objects. *International Journal of Computer Vision, 1*(1), 73–103.

Malik, J., & Perona, P. (1990). Preattentive texture discrimination with early vision mechanisms. *Journal of the Optical Society of America A, 7*(5), 923–932.

Maloney, L. T. (1999). Physics-based approaches to modeling surface color perception. In K. R. Gegenfurtner & L. T. Sharpe (Eds.), *Color vision: From genes to perception* (pp. 387–422). Cambridge, UK: Cambridge University Press.

Maloney, L. T., Gerhard, H. E., Boyaci, H., & Doerschner, K. (2010). Surface color perception and light field estimation in 3D scenes. In L. R. Harris & M. Jenkin (Eds.), *Vision in 3D environments* (pp. 65–88). Cambridge, UK: Cambridge University Press.

Maloney, L. T., & Wandell, B. A. (1986). Color constancy: A method for recovering surface spectral reflectance. *Journal of the Optical Society of America A, 3*(1), 29–33.

von der Malsburg, C. (1987). Synaptic plasticity as basis of brain organization. In J. P. Changeux & M. Konishi (Eds.), *The neural and molecular bases of learning* (pp. 411–431). Chichester: John Wiley & Sons Ltd.

Mamassian, P., & Goutcher, R. (2001). Prior knowledge on the illumination position. *Cognition, 81*(1), B1–B9.

Mamassian, P., & Kersten, D. (1996). Illumination, shading and the perception of local orientation. *Vision Research, 36*(15), 2351–2367.

Mamassian, P., Landy, M., & Maloney, L. T. (2002). Bayesian modeling of visual perception. In R. P. N. Rao, B. A. Olshausen, & M. L. Lewicki (Eds.), *Probabilistic models of the brain: Perception and neural function* (pp. 13–36). Cambridge, MA: MIT Press.

Mann, S., & Picard, R. W. (1995). Being undigital with digital cameras: Extending dynamic range by combining differently exposed pictures. In *Proceedings IS&T 48th Annual Conference* (pp. 422–428). Springfield, VA: Society for Imaging Science and Technology.

Mao, J., & Jain, A. K. (1992). Texture classification and segmentation using multiresolution simultaneous autoregressive models. *Pattern Recognition, 25*(2), 173–188.

Marcos, S., Moreno, E., & Navarro, R. (1999). The depth-of-field of the human eye from objective and subjective measurements. *Vision Research, 39*(12), 2039–2049.

Mark, L. S. (1987). Eyeheight-scaled information about affordances: A study of sitting and stair climbing. *Journal of Experimental Psychology: Human Perception and Performance, 13*(3), 361–370.

Marr, D. (1982). *Vision.* San Francisco, CA: W. H. Freeman.

Marr, D., & Hildreth, E. (1980). Theory of edge detection. *Proceedings of the Royal Society of London, B, 207*(1167), 187–217.

Marr, D., & Nishihara, H. K. (1978). Representation and recognition of the spatial organization of three-dimensional shapes. *Proceedings of the Royal Society of London, B, 200*(1140), 269–294.

Marr, D., & Poggio, T. (1976). Cooperative computation of stereo disparity. *Science, 194*(4262), 283–287.

Marr, D., & Poggio, T. (1979). A computational theory of human stereo vision. *Proceedings of the Royal Society of London, B, 204*(1156), 301–328.

Marshall, J. A., Burbeck, C. A., Arely, D., Rolland, J. P., & Martin, K. E. (1996). Occlusion edge blur: A cue to relative visual depth. *Journal of the Optical Society of America A, 13*(4), 681–688.

Mather, G., Radford, K., & West, S. (1992). Low-level visual processing of biological motion. *Proceedings of the Royal Society of London, B, 258*(1325), 273–279.

Mather, G., & Smith, D. R. R. (2002). Blur discrimination and its relation to blur-mediated depth perception. *Perception, 31*(10), 1211–1219.

Mayhew, J. E. W., & Longuet-Higgins, H. C. (1982). A computational model of binocular depth perception. *Nature, 297*, 376–378.

McCarley, J. S., & He, Z. J. (2000). Asymmetry in 3-D perceptual organization: Ground-like surface superior to ceiling-like surface. *Perception & Psychophysics, 62*(3), 540–549.

McCloskey, M. (1983). Intuitive physics. *Scientific American, 248*(4), 122–130.

McCloskey, M., Caramazza, A., & Green, B. (1980). Curvilinear motion in the absence of external forces: Naïve beliefs about the motions of objects. *Science, 210*(4474), 1139–1141.

McCloud, S. (1993). *Understanding comics: The invisible art*. Northampton, MA: Kitchen Sink Press.

McDonnell, R., Jörg, S., Hodgins, J. K., Newell, F., & O'Sullivan, C. (2009). Evaluating the effect of motion and body shape on the perceived sex of virtual characters. *ACM Transactions on Applied Perception, 5*(4), 1–14.

McDonnell, R., Newell, F., & O'Sullivan, C. (2007). Smooth movers: Perceptually guided human motion simulation. In *Proceedings ACM SIG-GRAPH/Eurographics symposium on computer animation* (pp. 259–269). Aire-la-Ville, Switzerland: Eurogaraphics Association.

McNamara, T. P. (2003). How are the locations of objects in the environment represented in memory? In C. Freska, W. Brauer, C. Habel, & K. Wender (Eds.), *Spatial Cognition III: Routes and navigation, human memory and learning, spatial representation and spatial reasoning* (pp. 174–191). Berlin, Germany: Springer-Verlag.

Mendiburu, B. (2009). *3D movie making: Stereoscopic digital cinema from script to screen*. Burlington, MA: Elsevier.

Meng, J. C., & Sedgwick, H. A. (2001). Distance perception mediated through nested contact relations among surfaces. *Perception & Psychophysics, 63*(1), 1–15.

Meng, J. C., & Sedgwick, H. A. (2002). Distance perception across spatial discontinuities. *Perception & Psychophysics*, *64*(1), 1–14.

Messing, R., & Durgin, F. (2005). Distance perception and the visual horizon in head-mounted displays. *ACM Transactions on Applied Perception*, *2*(3), 234–250.

Metelli, F. (1974). The perception of transparency. *Scientific American*, *230*(4), 90–98.

Michotte, A. E. (1963). *The perception of causality* (T. R. Miles & E. Miles, Trans.). New York: Basic Books. (Original work published 1946)

Miller, R. J. (1973). Cross-cultural research in the perception of pictorial materials. *Psychological Bulletin*, *80*(2), 135–150.

Milner, A. D., & Goodale, M. A. (1995). *The visual brain in action*. Oxford, UK: Oxford University Press.

Milner, A. D., & Goodale, M. A. (2008). Two visual systems re-viewed. *Neuropsychologia*, *46*(3), 774–785.

Minnaert, M. (1954). *The nature of light & colour in the open air* (H. M. Kremer-Priest, Trans.). New York: Dover.

Mitroff, S. R., Simons, D. J., & Levin, D. T. (2004). Nothing compares 2 views: Change blindness results from failures to compared retained information. *Perception & Psychophysics*, *66*(8), 1268–1281.

Mittelstaedt, H., & Mittelstaedt, M. L. (1982). Homing by path integration. In F. Wallraff & H. G. Papi (Eds.), *Avian navigation* (pp. 290–297). Berlin, Germany: Springer.

Miyake, A., Rettinger, D. A., Friedman, N. P., Shaw, P., & Hegarty, M. (2001). Visuospatial working memory, executive functioning and spatial abilities. how are they related? *Journal of Experimental Psychology: General*, *130*(4), 621–640.

Mohler, B. J., Creem-Regehr, S. H., & Thompson, W. B. (2006). The influence of feedback on egocenteric distance judgments in real and virtual environments. In *Proceedings Symposium on Applied Perception in Grapics and Visualization* (pp. 9–14). New York: ACM.

Mohler, B. J., Thompson, W. B., Creem-Regehr, S. H., Willemsen, P., Pick, H. L., Jr., & Rieser, J. J. (2007). Calibration of locomotion resulting from visual motion in a treadmill-based virtual environment. *ACM Transactions on Applied Perception*, *4*(1), 4:1–4:15.

Mon-Williams, M., & Bingham, G. P. (2007). Calibrating reach distance to visual targets. *Journal of Experimental Psychology: Human Perception and Performance*, *33*(3), 645–656.

Mon-Williams, M., & Tresilian, J. R. (1999). Some recent studies on the extraretinal contribution to distance perception. *Perception*, *28*(2), 167–181.

Mon-Williams, M., & Tresilian, J. R. (2000). Ordinal depth information from accommodation? *Ergonomics*, *43*(3), 391–404.

Moon, P. H., & Spencer, D. E. (1981). *The photic field*. Cambridge, MA: MIT Press.

Moore, C. M., & Fulton, C. (2005). The spread of attention to hidden portions of occluded surfaces. *Psychonomic Bulletin & Review*, *2*(12), 301–306.

Mori, M. (1970). The valley of eeriness (K. F. MacDorman & T. Minato, Trans.). *Energy*, *7*(4), 33-35.

Morris, M. W., & Peng, K. (1994). Culture and cause: American and Chinese attributions for social and physical events. *Journal of Personality and Social Psychology*, *67*(6), 949–971.

Motoyoshi, I., Nishida, S., Sharan, L., & Adelson, E. H. (2007). Image statistics and the perception of surface qualities. *Nature*, *447*, 206–209.

Mou, W., & McNamara, T. P. (2002). Intrinsic frames of reference in spatial memory. *Journal of Experimental Psychology: Learning, Memory, and Cognition*, *28*(1), 162–170.

Mou, W., Zhao, M., & McNamara, T. P. (2007). Layout geometry in the selection of intrinsic frames of reference from multiple viewpoints. *Journal of Experimental Psychology: Learning, Memory, and Cognition*, *33*(1), 145–154.

Müller, G., Meseth, J., Sattler, M., Sarlette, R., & Klein, R. (2005). Acquisition, synthesis and rendering of bidirectional texture functions. *Computer Graphics Forum*, *24*(1), 83–109.

Munsell, A. H. (1905). *A color notation*. Baltimore, MD: Munsell Color.

Mury, A. A., Pont, S. C., & Koenderink, J. J. (2007). Light field constancy within natural scenes. *Applied Optics*, *46*(29), 7308–7316.

Musatti, C. L. (1924). Sui fenomeni stereocineti. *Archivio Italiano di Psicologia*, *3*, 105–120.

Mutch, K. M., & Thompson, W. B. (1985). Analysis of accretion and deletion at boundaries in dynamic scenes. *IEEE Transactions on Pattern Analysis and Machine Intelligence*, *7*(2), 133–138.

Myszkowski, K. (1998). The visible difference predictor: applications to global illumination problems. In *Proceedings 9th Eurographics Workshop on Rendering* (pp. 223–236). Aire-la-Ville, Switzerland: Eurogaraphics Association.

Nadel, L. (1999). Neural mechanisms of spatial orientation and wayfinding. In R. G. Golledge (Ed.), *Wayfinding behavior*. Baltimore, MD: Johns Hopkins University Press.

Nakayama, K., & Loomis, J. M. (1974). Optical velocity patterns, velocity sensitive neurons, and space perception: A hypothesis. *Perception*, *3*(1), 63–80.

Nakayama, K., & Shimojo, S. (1990). Da Vinci stereopsis: Depth and subjective occluding contours from unpaired image points. *Vision Research*, *30*(11), 1811–1825.

Navon, D. (1977). Forest before trees: The precedence of global features in visual perception. *Cognitive Psychology*, *9*(3), 353–383.

Neisser, U., & Becklen, R. (1975). Selective looking: Attending to visually specified events. *Cognitive Psychology*, *7*(4), 480–494.

Neri, P., Morrone, M. C., & Burr, D. C. (1998). Seeing biological motion. *Nature*, *395*, 894–896.

Newhall, S. M., Nickerson, D., & Judd, D. B. (1943). Final report of the O.S.A. subcommittee on the spacing of the Munsell colors. *Journal of the Optical Society of America*, *33*(7), 385–418.

Newton, I. (1704). *Opticks*. London: Smith and Walford.

Newtson, D. (1973). Attribution and the unit of perception of ongoing behavior. *Journal of Personality and Social Psychology*, *28*(1), 28–38.

Newtson, D., & Engquist, G. (1976). The perceptual organization of ongoing behavior. *Journal of Experimental Social Psychology*, *12*(5), 436–450.

Ngan, A., Durand, F., & Matusik, W. (2006). Image-driven navigation of analytical BRDF models. In *Proceedings Eurographics symposium on rendering* (pp. 399–408). Aire-la-Ville, Switzerland: Eurogaraphics Association.

Nicholls, A. L., & Kennedy, J. M. (1993). Angular subtense effects on perception of polar and parallel projections of cubes. *Perception & Psychophysics*, *54*(6), 763–772.

Niedenthal, P. M. (2007). Embodying emotion. *Science*, *316*(5827), 1002–1005.

Nishida, S., Motoyoshi, I., Nakano, L., Li, Y., Sharan, L., & Adelson, E. H. (2008). Do colored highlights look like highlights? (VSS abstract). *Journal of Vision*, *8*(6), no. 339.

Noh, J. Y., & Neumann, U. (1998). *A survey of facial modeling and animation techniques* (Tech. Rep. No. 99-705). University of Southern California.

Nothdurft, H. C. (1990). Texton segregation by associated differences in global and local luminance distribution. *Proceedings of the Royal Society of London, B*, *239*(1296), 295–320.

Nothdurft, H. C. (1991). Different effects from spatial frequency masking in texture segregation and texton detection tasks. *Vision Research*, *31*(2), 299–320.

Nusseck, M., Lagarde, J., Bardy, B., Fleming, R., & Bülthoff, H. H. (2007). Perception and prediction of simple object interactions. In *Proceedings 4th Symposium on Applied Perception in Grapics and Visualization* (pp. 27–34). New York: ACM.

O'Brien, V. (1958). Contour perception, illusion, and reality. *Journal of the Optical Society of America*, *48*(2), 112–119.

Oesker, M., Hecht, H., & Jung, B. (2000). Psychological evidence for unconscious processing of detail in real-time animation of multiple characters. *Journal of Visual Computation and Animation*, *11*(2), 105–112.

Ohmi, M., & Howard, I. P. (1988). Effect of stationary objects on illusory forward self-motion induced by a looming display. *Perception*, *17*(1), 5–12.

Ohmi, M., Howard, I. P., & Landolt, J. P. (1987). Circular vection as a function of foreground-background relationships. *Perception*, *16*(5), 17–22.

Okatani, T., & Deguchi, K. (2007). Estimating scale of a scene from a single image based on defocus blur and scene geometry. In *Proceedings IEEE Conference on Computer Vision and Pattern Recognition* (pp. 1–8). Los Alamitos, CA: IEEE.

Oliva, A., & Torralba, A. (2001). Modeling the shape of the scene: A holistic representation of the spatial envelope. *International Journal of Computer Vision*, *42*(3), 145–175.

Oliva, A., & Torralba, A. (2006). Building the gist of a scene: The role of global image features in recognition. In S. Martinez-Conde, S. Macknik, L. Martinez, J.-M. Alonso, & P. Tse (Eds.), *Progress in brain research: Visual perception, part 2* (Vol. 155, pp. 23–36). Amsterdam, Netherlands: Elsevier.

Oliva, A., & Torralba, A. (2007). The role of context in object recognition. *Trends in Cognitive Sciences*, *11*(12), 520–527.

Oliveira, M. M., Bishop, G., & McAllister, D. (2000). Relief texture mapping. In K. Akeley (Ed.), *Proceedings of SIGGRAPH 2000, Computer Graphics Proceedings, Annual Conference Series* (pp. 359–368). Reading, MA: Addison Wesley.

Ölveczky, B. P., Baccus, S. A., & Meister, M. (2003). Segregation of object and background motion in the retina. *Nature*, *423*, 401–408.

Olzak, L. A., & Thomas, J. P. (1986). Seeing spatial patterns. In K. R. Boff, I. Kaufman, & J. P. Thomas (Eds.), *Handbook of perception and human performance: Vol. 1. Sensory processes and perception* (chap. 7). New York: Wiley.

Ono, M. E., Rivest, J., & Ono, H. (1986). Depth perception as a function of motion parallax and absolute-distance information. *Journal of Experimental Psychology: Human Perception and Performance*, *12*(3), 331–337.

Ooi, T. L., Wu, B., & He, Z. J. (2001). Distance determination by the angular declination below the horizon. *Nature*, *414*, 197–200.

Ooi, T. L., Wu, B., & He, Z. J. (2006). Perceptual space in the dark affected by the intrinsic bias of the visual system. *Perception*, *35*(5), 605–624.

O'Regan, J. K., & Noë, A. (2001). A sensorimotor account of vision and visual consciousness. *Behavioral and Brain Sciences*, *24*(5), 939–1011.

Oren, M., & Nayar, S. (1995). Generalization of the lambertian model and implications for machine vision. *International Journal of Computer Vision*, *14*(3), 227–251.

Osterberg, G. (1935). Topography of the layer of rods and cones in the human retina (supplement). *Acta Ophthalmologica*, *6*(1), 11–97.

Ostrovsky, Y., Cavanagh, P., & Sinha, P. (2005). Perceiving illumination inconsistencies in scenes. *Perception*, *34*(11), 1301–1314.

O'Sullivan, C., & Dingliana, J. (2001). Collisions and perception. *ACM Transactions on Graphics*, *20*(3), 151–168.

O'Sullivan, C., Dingliana, J., Giang, T., & Kaiser, M. K. (2003). Evaluating the visual fidelity of physically based animations. *International Conference on Computer Graphics and Interactive Techniques*, *22*(3).

O'Sullivan, C., Howlett, S., Morvan, Y., McDonnell, R., & O'Conor, K. (2004). Perceptually adaptive graphics. In *Proceedings Eurographics (state-of-the-art reports)*. Aire-la-Ville, Switzerland: Eurogaraphics Association.

den Ouden, H. E. M., van Ee, R., & de Haan, E. H. F. (2005). Colour helps to solve the binocular matching problem. *Journal of Physiology*, *567*(2), 665–671.

Özgen, E., & Davies, I. R. L. (2002). Acquisition of categorical color perception: A perceptual learning approach to the linguistic relativity hypothesis. *Journal of Experimental Psychology: General*, *131*(4), 477–493.

Ozkan, K., & Braunstein, M. L. (2010). Background surface and horizon effects in the perception of relative size and distance. *Visual Cognition*, *18*(2), 229–254.

Padilla, S., Drbohlav, O., Green, P., Spence, A., & Chantler, M. (2008). Perceived roughness of $1/f^{\beta}$ noise surfaces. *Vision Research*, *48*(17), 1791–1797.

Pagano, C. C., & Bingham, G. P. (1998). Comparing measures of monocular distance perception: Verbal and reaching errors are not correlated. *Journal of Experimental Psychology: Human Perception and Performance*, *24*(4), 1037–1051.

Palmer, S. E. (1975). The effects of contextual scenes on the identification of objects. *Memory & Cognition*, *3*(5), 519–526.

Palmer, S. E. (1989). Reference frames in the perception of shape and orientation. In B. Shepp & S. Ballesteros (Eds.), *Object perception: Structure and process*. Hillsdale, NJ: Erlbaum.

Palmer, S. E. (1999). *Vision science—photons to phenomenology*. Cambridge, MA: MIT Press.

Palmer, S. E., Rosch, E., & Chase, P. (1981). Canonical perspective and the perception of objects. In J. Long & A. Baddeley (Eds.), *Attention and performance IX* (pp. 135–151). Hillsdale, NJ: Lawrence Erlbaum.

Palmisano, S., & Gillam, B. (1998). Stimulus eccentricity and spatial frequency interact to determine circular vection. *Perception, 27*(9), 1067–1077.

Pani, J. R., & Dupree, D. (1994). Spatial reference systems in the comprehension of rotational motion. *Perception, 23*(8), 929–946.

Paradiso, M. A., & Nakayama, K. (1991). Brightness perception and filling-in. *Vision Research, 31*(7–8), 1221–1236.

Parent, R. (2007). *Computer animation: Algorithms and techniques* (2nd ed.). San Francisco, CA: Morgan Kaufmann.

Parke, F. I. (1972). Computer generated animation of faces. In *Proceedings ACM Annual Conference* (pp. 451–457). New York: ACM.

Parke, F. I., & Waters, K. (1996). *Computer facial animation.* Natick, MA: A K Peters.

Parsons, L. M. (1987a). Imagined spatial transformation of one's body. *Journal of Experimental Psychology: General, 116*(2), 172–191.

Parsons, L. M. (1987b). Imagined spatial transformations of one's hands and feet. *Cognitive Psychology, 19*(4), 178–241.

Parsons, L. M. (1994). Temporal and kinematic properties of motor behavior reflected in mentally simulated action. *Journal of Experimental Psychology: Human Perception and Performance, 20*(4), 709–730.

Pashler, H. (1998). *The psychology of attention.* Cambridge, MA: MIT Press.

Pavlova, M., & Sokolov, A. (2000). Orientation specificity in biological motion perception. *Perception & Psychophysics, 62*(5), 889–899.

Peli, E. (1990). Contrast in complex images. *Journal of the Optical Society of America A, 7*(10), 2032–2040.

Pellacini, F., Ferwerda, J. A., & Greenberg, D. P. (2000). Toward a psychophysically-based light reflection model for image synthesis. In K. Akeley (Ed.), *Proceedings of SIGGRAPH 2000, Computer Graphics Proceedings, Annual Conference Series* (pp. 55–64). Reading, MA: Addison Wesley.

Pelli, D. G. (1987, May). Programming in postscript: Techniques and applications in vision research, plus a survey of postscript hardware and software. *Byte*, 185–202.

Petkova, V. I., & Ehrsson, H. H. (2008). If I were you: Perceptual illusion of body swapping. *PLoS ONE, 3*(12), e3832.

Philbeck, J. W., & Loomis, J. M. (1997). Comparison of two indicators of perceived egocentric distance under full-cue and reduced-cue conditions. *Journal of Experimental Psychology: Human Perception and Performance, 23*(1), 72–85.

Philbeck, J. W., O'Leary, S., & Lew, A. L. B. (2004). Large errors, but no depth compression, in walked indications of exocentric extent. *Perception & Psychophysics, 66*(3), 377–391.

Pick, H. L., Jr., Rieser, J. J., Wagner, D., & Garing, A. E. (1999). The recalibration of rotational locomotion. *Journal of Experimental Psychology*, *25*(5), 1179–1188.

Pinto, J. (2006). Developing body representations: A review of infants' responses to biological-motion displays. In G. Knoblich, I. M. Thornton, M. Grosjean, & M. Shiffrar (Eds.), *Human body perception from the inside out* (pp. 305–322). New York: Oxford University Press.

Pirenne, M. H. (1970). *Optics, painting & photography*. Cambridge, UK: Cambridge University Press.

Platt, S. M., & Badler, N. I. (1981). Animating facial expressions. *Proc. SIGGRAPH '81, Computer Graphics*, *15*(3), 245–252.

Polanyi, M. (1970). What is a painting? *The British Journal of Aesthetics*, *10*(3), 225–236.

Pollick, F. E., Paterson, H. M., Bruderlin, A., & Sanford, A. J. (2001). Perceiving affect from arm movement. *Cognition*, *82*(2), B51–B61.

Pont, S. C., & Koenderink, J. J. (2003). *The Utrecht oranges set*. (Technical Report and database)

Pont, S. C., & Koenderink, J. J. (2007). Matching illumination of solid objects. *Perception & Psychophysics*, *69*(3), 459–468.

Pont, S. C., Wijntjes, M. W. A., Oomes, S., van Doorn, A., de Ridder, H., & Koenderink, J. J. (2009). Cast shadows in perspective (ECVP abstract). *Perception*, *38*, 28.

Portilla, J., & Simoncelli, E. P. (2000). A parametric texture model based on joint statistics of complex wavelet coefficients. *International Journal of Computer Vision*, *40*(1), 49–71.

Posner, M. I., Nissen, M. J., & Ogden, W. C. (1978). Attended and unattended processing modes: The role of set for spatial locations. In H. L. Pick Jr. & B. J. Salzman (Eds.), *Modes of perceiving and processing information* (pp. 137–158). Hillsdale, NJ: Erlbaum.

Posner, M. I., & Raichle, M. E. (1994). *Images of mind*. Cambridge, MA: MIT Press.

Posner, M. I., Walker, J. A., Friedrich, F. J., & Rafal, R. D. (1984). Effects of parietal injury on covert orienting of attention. *Journal of Neuroscience*, *4*(7), 1863–1874.

Postle, B. R. (2006). Working memory as an emergent property of the mind and brain. *Neuroscience*, *139*(1), 23–38.

Potmesil, M., & Chakravarty, I. (1983). Modeling motion blur in computer-generated images. *Computer Graphics*, *17*(3), 389–399.

Potter, M. C. (1976). Short-term conceptual memory for pictures. *Journal of Experimental Psychology: Human Learning and Memory*, *2*(5), 509–522.

Pouli, T., Cunningham, D., & Reinhard, E. (2010). Image statistics and their applications in computer graphics. In *Proceedings Eurographics (state-of-the-art reports)*. Aire-la-Ville, Switzerland: Eurogaraphics Association.

Prazdny, K. (1985). Detection of binocular disparities. *Biological Cybernetics, 52*(2), 93–99.

Previc, F. H. (1998). The neuropsychology of 3-D space. *Psychological Bulletin, 124*(2), 123-164.

Prinz, W. (1990). A common-coding approach to perception and action. In O. Neurmann & W. Prinz (Eds.), *Relationships between perception and action: Current approaches* (pp. 167–201). New York: Springer-Verlag.

Proffitt, D. R. (2006). Embodied perception and the economy of action. *Perspectives on Psychological Science, 1*(2), 110–122.

Proffitt, D. R., Bhalla, M., Gosswiler, R., & Midgett, J. (1995). Perceiving geographical slant. *Psychonomic Bulletin and Review, 2*(4), 409–428.

Proffitt, D. R., & Gilden, D. L. (1989). Understanding natural dynamics. *Journal of Experimental Psychology: Human Perception and Performance, 15*(2), 384–393.

Proffitt, D. R., & Kaiser, M. K. (1995). Perceiving events. In W. Epstein & S. Rogers (Eds.), *Perception of space and motion* (pp. 227–261). New York: Academic Press.

Proffitt, D. R., Kaiser, M. K., & Whelan, S. M. (1990). Understanding wheel dynamics. *Cognitive Psychology, 22*(3), 342–373.

Proffitt, D. R., Rock, I., Hecht, H., & Schubert, J. (1992). Stereokinetic effect and its relation to the kinetic depth effect. *Journal of Experimental Psychology: Human Perception and Performance, 18*(1), 3–21.

Proffitt, D. R., Stefanucci, J., Banton, T., & Epstein, W. (2003). The role of effort in perceiving distance. *Psychological Science, 14*(2), 106–112.

Pylyshyn, Z. W. (1973). What the mind's eye tells the mind's brain: A critique of mental imagery. *Psychological Bulletin, 80*(1), 1–24.

Pylyshyn, Z. W. (2003). Return of the mental image: Are there really pictures in the brain? *Trends in Cognitive Sciences, 7*(3), 113–118.

Pylyshyn, Z. W., & Storm, R. W. (1988). Tracking multiple independent targets: Evidence for a parallel tracking mechanism. *Spatial Vision, 3*(3), 179–197.

Radvansky, G. A., & Copeland, D. E. (2006). Walking through doorways causes forgetting: Situation models and experienced space. *Memory & Cognition, 34*(5), 1150–1156.

Ramachandran, V. S. (1988). Perception of shape from shading. *Nature, 331*, 163–166.

Ramachandran, V. S., Cobb, S., & Rogers-Ramachandran, D. (1988). Perception of 3-D structure from motion: The role of velocity gradients and segmentation boundaries. *Perception & Psychophysics, 44*(4), 390–393.

Ramachandran, V. S., & Gregory, R. L. (1978). Does colour provide an input to human motion perception? *Nature, 275*, 55–56.

Ramachandran, V. S., & Rogers-Ramachandran, D. (1996). Synaesthesia in phantom limbs induced with mirrors. *Proceedings of the Royal Society of London, B, 263*(1369), 377–386.

Ramamoorthi, R., & Hanrahan, P. (2001a). An efficient representation for irradiance environment maps. In E. Fiume (Ed.), *Proceedings of SIGGRAPH 2001, Computer Graphics Proceedings, Annual Conference Series* (pp. 497–500). Reading, MA: Addison Wesley.

Ramamoorthi, R., & Hanrahan, P. (2001b). On the relationship between radiance and irradiance: Determining the illumination from images of a convex lambertian object. *Journal of the Optical Society of America A, 18*(10), 2448–2458.

Ramanarayanan, G., Ferwerda, J., Walter, B., & Bala, K. (2007). Visual equivalence: Towards a new standard for image fidelity. *ACM Transactions on Graphics, 26*(3), 3:1–3:12.

Randen, T., & Husøy, J. H. (1999). Filtering for texture classification: A comparative study. *IEEE Transactions on Pattern Analysis and Machine Intelligence, 21*(4), 291–310.

Rao, A. R., & Lohse, G. (1992). Identifying high level features of texture perception. In B. E. Rogowitz (Ed.), *Proceedings SPIE Conference on Human Vision, Visual Processing and Digital Display III* (pp. 424–435). Bellingham, WA: SPIE.

Rao, A. R., & Lohse, G. L. (1996). Towards a texture naming system: Identifying relevant dimensions of texture. *Vision Research, 36*(11), 1649–1669.

Raskar, R., & Cohen, M. (1999). Image precision silhouette edges. In *Proceedings symposium on interactive 3D graphics (I3D)* (pp. 135–140). New York: ACM.

Regolin, L., Tommasi, L., & Vallortigara, G. (2000). Visual perception of biological motion in newly hatched chicks as revealed by an imprinting procedure. *Animal Cognition, 3*(1), 53–60.

Reichardt, W. (1961). Autocorrelation, a principle for the evaluation of sensory information by the central nervous systems. In W. A. Rosenblith (Ed.), *Sensory communication.* New York: Wiley.

Reiger, J. H., & Lawton, D. T. (1983). Sensor motion and relative depth from difference fields of optic flows. In *Proceedings International Joint Conference on Artificial Intelligence* (pp. 1027–1031). New York: Morgan Kaufmann.

Reiger, J. H., & Lawton, D. T. (1985). Processing differential image motion. *Journal of the Optical Society of America A, 2*(2), 354–359.

Reinhard, E., Khan, E. A., Akyüz, A. O., & Johnson, G. M. (2008). *Color imaging: Fundamentals and applications.* Wellesley, MA: A K Peters.

Reinhard, E., Shirley, P., Ashikhmin, M., & Troscianko, T. (2004). Second order image statistics in computer graphics. In *Proceedings 1st Symposium on Applied Perception in graphics and visualization* (pp. 99–106). New York: ACM.

Reinhard, E., Ward, G., Pattanaik, S., & Debevec, P. (2006). *High dynamic range imaging.* San Francisco, CA: Morgan Kaufmann.

Reitsma, P. S. A., & O'Sullivan, C. (2009). Effect of scenario on perceptual sensitivity to errors in animation. *ACM Transactions on Applied Perception, 6*(3), 1–16.

Reitsma, P. S. A., & Pollard, N. S. (2003). Perceptual metrics for character animation: Sensitivity to errors in ballistic motion. *Proc. SIGGRAPH '03, Transactions on Graphics, 22*(3), 537–542.

Rensink, R. A. (2002). Change detection. *Annual Review of Psychology, 53,* 245–277.

Rensink, R. A., O'Regan, J. K., & Clark, J. J. (1997). To see or not to see: The need for attention to perceive changes in scenes. *Psychological Science, 8*(5), 368–373.

Richards, W. (1970). Stereopsis and stereoblindness. *Experimental Brain Research, 10*(4), 380–388.

Richards, W. (1971). Anomalous stereoscopic depth perception. *Journal of the Optical Society of America, 61*(3), 410–414.

Richardson, A. R., & Waller, D. (2005). The effect of feedback training on distance estimation in virtual environments. *Applied Cognitive Psychology, 19*(8), 1089–1108.

Richardson, A. R., & Waller, D. (2007). Interaction with an immersive virtual environment corrects users' distance estimates. *Human Factors, 49*(3), 507–517.

Riecke, B. E., Cunningham, D. W., & Büulthoff, H. H. (2006). Spatial updating in virtual reality: The sufficiency of visual information. *Psychological Research, 71*(3), 298–313.

Riecke, B. E., Feuereissen, D., & Rieser, J. J. (2009). Auditory self-motion simulation is facilitated by haptic and vibrational cues suggesting the possibility of actual motion. *ACM Transactions on Applied Perception, 6*(3), 1–22.

Rieser, J. J. (1989). Access to knowledge of spatial structure at novel points of observation. *Journal of Experimental Psychology: Learning, Memory, and Cognition, 15*(6), 1157–1165.

Rieser, J. J. (1999). Dynamic spatial orientation and the coupling of representation and action. In R. G. Golledge (Ed.), *Wayfinding behavior: Cognitive mapping and other spatial processes* (pp. 168–190). Baltimore, MD: Johns Hopkins University Press.

Rieser, J. J., Ashmead, D. H., Talor, C. R., & Youngquist, G. A. (1990). Visual perception and the guidance of locomotion without vision to previously seen targets. *Perception, 19*(5), 675–689.

Rieser, J. J., Pick, H. L., Jr., Ashmead, D. H., & Garing, A. E. (1995). Calibration of human locomotion and models of perceptual-motor organization. *Journal of Experimental Psychology: Human Perception and Performance, 21*(3), 480–497.

Ripamonti, C., Bloj, M., Hauck, R., Mitha, K., Greenwald, S., Maloney, S. I., et al. (2004). Measurements of the effect of surface slant on perceived lightness. *Journal of Vision, 4*(9), 747–763.

Rittenhouse, D. (1786). Explanation of an optical deception. *Transactions of the American Philosophical Society, 2*, 37–42.

Ritter, M. (1977). Effect of disparity and viewing distance on perceived depth. *Perception & Psychophysics, 22*(4), 400–407.

Rivlin, E., & Weiss, I. (1997). Deformation invariants in invariant object recognition. *Computer Vision and Image Understanding, 65*(1), 95–108.

Rizzolatti, G., & Craighero, L. (2004). The mirror neuron system. *Annual Reviews of Neuroscience, 27*, 169–192.

Roberts, L. G. (1965). Machine perception of three-dimensional solids. In J. T. Tippett et al. (Eds.), *Optical and electro-optical information processing.* Cambridge, MA: MIT Press.

Robilotto, R., Khang, B., & Zaidi, Q. (2002). Sensory and physical determinants of perceived achromatic transparency. *Journal of Vision, 2*(5), 388–403.

Robson, J. G. (1966). Spatial and temporal contrast-sensitivity functions of the visual system. *Journal of the Optical Society of America, 56*(8), 1141–1142.

Rock, I., & Brosgole, L. (1964). Grouping based on phenomenal proximity. *Journal of Experimental Psychology, 67*(6), 531–538.

Rock, I., Nijhawan, R., Palmer, S., & Tudor, L. (1992). Grouping based on phenomenal similarity of achromatic color. *Perception, 21*(6), 779–789.

Rogers, B., & Graham, M. (1979). Motion parallax as an independent cue for depth perception. *Perception, 8*(2), 125–134.

Rogers, B. J., & Bradshaw, B. F. (1995). Disparity scaling and the perception of frontoparallel surfaces. *Perception, 24*(2), 155–179.

Rogers, B. J., & Graham, M. E. (1983). Anisotropies in the perception of three-dimensional surfaces. *Science, 221*(4618), 1409–1411.

Rogers, S. (1995). Perceiving pictorial space. In W. Epstein & S. Rogers (Eds.), *Perception of space and motion* (pp. 119–163). San Diego, CA: Academic Press.

Rogers, S. (1996). The horizon-ratio relation as information for relative size in pictures. *Perception & Psychophysics, 58*(1), 142–152.

Rosch, E., Mervis, C. B., Gray, W. D., Johnson, D. M., & Boyes-Braem, P. (1976). Basic objects in natural categories. *Cognitive Psychology*, *8*(3), 382–439.

Rosenholtz, R., & Malik, J. (1997). Surface orientation from texture: Isotropy or homogeneity (or both)? *Vision Research*, *37*(16), 2283–2293.

Rosenholtz, R., Twarog, N. R., Schinkel-Bielefeld, N., & Wattenberg, M. (2009). An intuitive model of perceptual grouping for HCI design. In *Proceedings 27th International Conference on Human Factors in Computing Systems (SIGCHI)* (pp. 1331–1340). New York: ACM.

Rossignac, J. R., & Borrel, P. (1993). Multi-resolution 3D approximations for rendering complex scenes. In B. Falcidieno & T. L. Kunii (Eds.), *Geometric modeling in computer graphics*. New York: Springer Verlag.

Royden, C. S., Baker, J. F., & Allman, J. (1988). Perceptions of depth elicited by occluded and shearing motions of random dots. *Perception*, *17*(3), 289–296.

Royden, C. S., Crowell, J. A., & Banks, M. S. (1994). Estimating heading during eye movements. *Vision Research*, *34*(23), 3197–3214.

Royden, C. S., & Hildreth, E. C. (1996). Human heading judgments in the presence of moving objects. *Perception & Psychophysics*, *58*(6), 836–856.

Rubin, E. (2001). Figure and ground. In S. Yantis (Ed.), *Visual perception: Essential readings* (pp. 225–229). Philadelphia, PA: Psychology Press.

Rubin, G. S., West, S. K., Munoz, B., Bandeen-Roche, K., Zeger, S., Schein, O., et al. (1997). A comprehensive assessment of visual impairment in a population of older americans. The SEE study. *Investigative Opthalmology & Visual Science*, *38*(3), 557–568.

Rudd, M. E. (2001). Lightness computation by a neural filling-in mechanism. In B. E. Rogowitz & T. N. Pappas (Eds.), *Proceedings SPIE Conference on Human Vision and Electronic Imaging VI* (Vol. 4299, pp. 400–413). Bellingham, WA: SPIE.

Ruddle, R. A. (2001). Navigation: Am I really lost or virtually there? In D. Harris (Ed.), *Engineering psychology and cognitive ergonomics* (Vol. 6, pp. 135–142). Burlington, VT: Ashgate.

Ruddle, R. A. (2009). The benefits of using a walking interface to navigate virtual environments. *ACM Transactions on Computer-Human Interaction*, *16*(1), 1–18.

Ruddle, R. A., & Lessels, S. (2006). For efficient navigational search, humans require full physical movement but not a rich visual scene. *Psychological Science*, *17*(6), 460–465.

Ruddle, R. A., Payne, S. J., & Jones, D. M. (1999). Navigating large-scale virtual environments: What differences occur between helmet-mounted and desktop displays? *Presence: Teleoperators and Virtual Environments*, *8*(2), 157–168.

Ruddle, R. A., & Peruch, P. (2004). Effects of proprioceptive feedback and environmental characteristics on spatial learning in virtual environments. *International Journal of Human Computer Studies*, *60*(3), 299–326.

Rumelhart, D. E. (1980). Schemata: The building blocks of cognition. In R. J. Spiro, B. C. Bruce, & W. F. Brewer (Eds.), *Theoretical issues in reading comprehension: Perspectives from cognitive psychology, linguistics, artificial intelligence, and education* (pp. 33–58). Hillsdale, NJ: Erlbaum.

Runeson, S. (1977). *On visual perception of dynamic events*. Unpublished doctoral dissertation, University of Uppsala, Uppsala, Sweden.

Runeson, S. (1988). The distorted room illusion, equivalent configurations, and the specificity of static optic arrays. *Journal of Experimental Psychology: Human Perception and Performance*, *14*(2), 295–304.

Rushmeier, H. (2009). Computer graphics techniques for capturing and rendering the appearance of aging materials. In J. W. Martin, R. A. Ryntz, J. Chin, & R. Dickie (Eds.), *Service life prediction of polymeric materials: Global perspectives* (chap. 19). New York: Springer.

Rushton, S. K., Harris, J. M., Lloyd, M., & Wann, J. P. (1998). Guidance of locomotion on foot uses perceived target location rather than optic flow. *Current Biology*, *8*(21), 1191–1194.

Sagar, M. (2006). Facial performance capture and expressive translation for king kong. In *ACM SIGGRAPH sketches* (p. 26). New York: ACM.

Sagarin, G. J., Britt, M. A., & Heider, J. D. (2003). Bartering our attention: The distraction and persuasion effects of on-line advertisements. *Cognitive Technology*, *8*(2), 4–17.

Sahm, C. S., Creem-Regehr, S. H., Thompson, W. B., & Willemsen, P. (2005). Throwing versus walking as indicators of distance perception in real and virtual environments. *ACM Transactions on Applied Perception*, *1*(3), 35–45.

van Santen, J. P. H., & Sperling, G. (1985). Elaborated reichardt detectors. *Journal of the Optical Society of America A*, *2*(2), 300–320.

Saunders, J. A. (2003). The effect of texture relief on perception of slant from texture. *Perception*, *32*(2), 211–233.

Scharstein, D., & Szelisk, R. (2002). A taxonomy and evaluation of dense two-frame stereo correspondence algorithms. *International Journal of Computer Vision*, *47*(1–3).

Schiff, W., & Detwiler, M. L. (1979). Information used in judging impending collision. *Perception*, *8*(6), 647–658.

Schlosberg, H. (1941). Stereoscopic depth from single pictures. *American Journal of Psychology*, *54*(4), 601–605.

Schnapf, J. L., Kraft, T. W., & Baylor, D. A. (1987). Spectral sensitivity of human cone photoreceptors. *Nature*, *325*, 439–441.

Schneider, G. E. (1969). Two visual systems. *Science*, *163*(3870), 895–902.

Scholl, B. J. (2009). What have we learned about attention from multiple-object tracking (and vice versa)? In D. Dedrick & L. Trick (Eds.), *Computation, cognition, and Pylyshyn* (pp. 49–78). Cambridge, MA: MIT Press.

Scholl, B. J., & Nakayama, K. (2002). Causal capture: Contextual effects on the perception of collision events. *Psychological Science*, *13*(6), 493–498.

Scholl, B. J., Pylyshyn, Z. W., & Feldman, J. (2001). What is a visual object? Evidence from target merging in multiple-object tracking. *Cognition*, *80*(1/2), 159–177.

Scholl, B. J., & Tremoulet, P. D. (2000). Perceptual causality and animacy. *Trends in Cognitive Sciences*, *4*(8), 299–309.

Schor, C., Wood, I., & Ogawa, J. (1984). Binocular sensory fusion is limited by spatial resolution. *Vision Research*, *24*(7), 661–665.

Schroeder, W. J., Zarge, J. A., & Lorensen, W. E. (1992). Decimation of triangle meshes. *Proc. SIGGRAPH '95, Computer Graphics*, *26*(2), 65–70.

Schutz, M., & Lipscomb, S. (2007). Hearing gestures, seeing music: Vision influences perceived tone duration. *Perception*, *36*(6), 888–897.

Schweigart, G., Mergner, T., Evdokimidis, I., Morand, S., & Becker, W. (1997). Gaze stabilization by optokinetic reflex (OKR) and vestibulo-ocular reflex (VOR) during active head rotation in man. *Vision Research*, *37*(12), 1643–1652.

Schyns, P. G., & Oliva, A. (1994). From blobs to boundary edges: Evidence for time- and spatial-scale-dependent scene recognition. *Psychological Science*, *5*(4), 195–200.

Sedgwick, H. A. (1980). The geometry of spatial layout in pictorial representation. In *The perception of pictures i: Alberti's window: The projective model of pictures* (Vol. 1, pp. 33–90). New York: Academic Press.

Sedgwick, H. A. (1983). Environment-centered representation of spatial layout: Available information from texture and perspective. In J. Beck, B. Hope, & A. Rosenfeld (Eds.), *Human and machine vision* (pp. 425–458). Orlando, FL: Academic Press.

Sedgwick, H. A. (1986). Space perception. In K. Boff, L. Kaufman, & J. Thomas (Eds.), *Handbook of perception and human performance* (Vol. 1, pp. 21:1–21:57). New York: Wiley-Interscience.

Sedgwick, H. A. (1991). The effects of viewpoint on the virtual space of pictures. In S. R. Ellis, M. Kaiser, & A. J. Gurnwald (Eds.), *Pictorial communication in virtual and real environments* (2nd ed., pp. 460–479). London: Taylor & Francis.

Sekuler, A. B., Bennett, P. J., & Mamelak, M. (2000). Effects of aging on the useful field of view. *Experimental Aging Research*, *26*(2), 103–120.

Sekuler, R., Sekuler, A. B., & Lau, R. (1997). Sound alters visual motion perception. *Nature*, *385*, 308.

Sergent, J. (1984). An investigation into component and configural processes underlying face perception. *The British Journal of Psychology*, *75 pt 2*, 221–242.

Serre, T., Wolf, L., Bileschi, S., Riesenhuber, M., & Poggio, T. (2007). Robust object recognition with cortex-like mechanisms. *IEEE Transactions on Pattern Analysis and Machine Intelligence*, *29*(3), 411–426.

Shapiro, K. L., Raymond, J. E., & Arnell, K. M. (1997). The attentional blink. *Trends in Cognitive Sciences*, *1*(8), 291–296.

Shelton, A. L., & McNamara, T. P. (1997). Multiple views of spatial memory. *Psychonomic Bulletin & Review*, *4*(1), 102–106.

Shelton, A. L., & McNamara, T. P. (2001). Systems of spatial reference in human memory. *Cognitive Psychology*, *43*(4), 274–310.

Shelton, A. L., & McNamara, T. P. (2004). Orientation and perspective dependence in route and survey learning. *Journal of Experimental Psychology: Learning, Memory, and Cognition*, *30*(1), 158–170.

Shepard, R. N. (1981). Psychological complementarity. In M. Kubovy & J. R. Pomerantz (Eds.), *Perceptual organization* (pp. 279–342). Hillsdale, NJ: Lawrence Erlbaum.

Shepard, R. N., & Cooper, L. A. (1986). *Mental images and their transformations*. Cambridge, MA: MIT Press.

Shepard, R. N., & Metzler, J. (1971). Mental rotation of three-dimensional objects. *Science*, *171*(3972), 701–703.

Shiffrin, R. M., & Schneider, W. (1977). Controlled and automatic human information processing: II. perceptual learning, automatic attending and a general theory. *Psychological Review*, *84*(2), 127–190.

Shipley, T. F., & Zacks, J. M. (Eds.). (2008). *Understanding events: From perception to action*. New York: Oxford University Press.

Shirley, P., Marschner, S., Ashikhmim, M., Gleicher, M., Hoffman, N., Johnson, G., et al. (2009). *Fundamentals of computer graphics* (3rd ed.). Natick, MA: A K Peters.

Sholl, M. J. (1996). From visual information to cognitive maps. In J. Portugali (Ed.), *The construction of cognitive maps* (pp. 157–186). Dordrecht: Kluwer Academic.

Siegel, A. W., & White, S. H. (1975). The development of spatial representations of large-scale environments. In H. W. Reese (Ed.), *Advances in child development and behavior* (pp. 9–55). New York: Academic Press.

Simion, F., Regolin, L., & Bulf, H. (2008). A predisposition for biological motion in the newborn baby. *Proceedings of the National Academy of Sciences, USA*, *105*(2), 809–813.

Simons, D. J., & Chabris, C. F. (1999). Gorillas in our midst: Sustained inattentional blindness for dynamic events. *Perception*, *28*(9), 1059–1074.

Simons, D. J., & Levin, D. T. (1998). Failure to detect changes to people during a real-world interactions. *Psychonomic Bulletin and Review*, *5*(4), 644–649.

Simons, D. J., & Rensink, R. A. (2005). Change blindness: Past, present, and future. *TRENDS in Cognitive Sciences*, *9*(1), 16–20.

Simons, D. J., & Wang, R. F. (1998). Perceiving real-world viewpoint changes. *Psychological Science*, *9*(4), 315–320.

Sinai, M. J., Ooi, T. L., & He, Z. J. (1998). Terrain influences the accurate judgment of distance. *Nature*, *395*, 497–500.

Singh, M., & Anderson, B. L. (2002). Toward a perceptual theory of transparency. *Psychological Review*, *109*(3), 492–519.

Sinha, P. (1995). *Perceiving and recognizing three-dimensional forms*. Doctoral thesis, Department of Electrical Engineering and Computer Science, Massachusetts Institute of Technology, Cambridge, MA.

Skavenski, A. A., Hansen, R. M., Steinman, R. M., & Winterson, B. J. (1979). Quality of retinal image stabilization during small natural and artificial rotations in man. *Vision Research*, *19*(6), 678–683.

Slater, M., Perez-Marcos, D., Ehrsson, H. H., & Sanchez-Vives, M. V. (2008). Towards a digital body: The virtual arm illusion. *Frontiers in Human Neuroscience*, *2*(6), 1–8.

Smeets, J. B. J., & Brenner, E. (2006). 10 years of illusions. *Journal of Experimental Psychology: Human Perception and Performance*, *32*(6), 1501–1504.

Smith, A. R. (1978). Color gamut transform pairs. *Computer Graphics*, *12*(3), 12–19.

Snowden, R., Thompson, P., & Troscianko, T. (2006). *Basic vision: An introduction to visual perception*. Oxford, UK: Oxford University Press.

Snyder, J. L., Doerschner, K., & Maloney, L. T. (2005). Illumination estimation in three-dimensional scenes with and without specular cues. *Journal of Vision*, *5*(10), 863–877.

Speer, N. K., Swallow, K. M., & Zacks, J. M. (2003). Activation of human motion processing areas during event perception. *Cognitive, Affective, & Behavioral Neuroscience*, *3*(4), 335–345.

Spencer, G., Shirley, P., Zimmerman, K., & Greenberg, D. P. (1995). Physically-based glare effects for digital images. In R. Cook (Ed.), *Proceedings of SIGGRAPH 95, Computer Graphics Proceedings, Annual Conference Series* (pp. 325–334). Reading, MA: Addison Wesley.

Sperling, G. (1976). Movement perception in computer-driven visual displays. *Behavior Research Methods and Instrumentation*, *8*(2), 144–151.

Stappers, P. J., & Waller, P. E. (1993). Using the free fall of objects under gravity for visual depth estimation. *Bulletin of the Psychonomic Society*, *31*(2), 125–127.

Stefanucci, J. K., Proffitt, D. R., Clore, G., & Parekh, N. (2008). Skating down a steeper slope: Fear influences the perception of geographical slant. *Perception*, *37*(2), 321–333.

Stein, A. N., & Hebert, M. (2009). Local detection of occlusion boundaries in video. *Image and Vision Computing*, *27*(5), 514–522.

Stevens, K. A. (1981). The information content of texture gradients. *Biological Cybernetics*, *42*(2), 95–105.

Stockham, T. G., Jr. (1972). Image processing in the context of a visual model. *Proceedings of the IEEE*, *60*(7), 828–842.

Stockman, A., MacLeod, D. I. A., & Johnson, N. E. (1993). Spectral sensitivities of the human cones. *Journal of the Optical Society of America A*, *10*(12), 2491–2521.

Stoffregen, T. A., Smart, J. L., Bardy, B. G., & Pagulayan, R. J. (1999). Postural stabilization of looking. *Journal of Experimental Psychology: Human Perception and Performance*, *25*(6), 1641–1658.

Stone, M. C. (2003). *A field guide to digital color*. Natick, MA: A K Peters.

Stratton, G. (1897). Upright vision and the retinal image. *Psychological Review*, *4*(2), 182–187.

Stratton, G. M. (1896). Some preliminary experiments on vision without inversion of the retinal image. *The Psychological Review*, *3*(6), 611–617.

Strayer, D. L., & Drews, F. A. (2007). Attention. In F. T. Durso (Ed.), *Handbook of applied cognition* (pp. 30–54). West Sussex, England: John Riley & Sons.

Stuart, G. W., Edwards, M., & Cook, M. L. (1992). Colour inputs to random-dot stereopsis. *Perception*, *21*(6), 717–729.

Stull, A. T., Hegarty, M., & Mayer, R. E. (2009). Getting a handle on learning anatomy with interactive three-dimensional graphics. *Journal of Educational Psychology*, *101*(4), 803–816.

Sun, B., Sunkavalli, K., Ramamoorthi, R., Belhumeur, P., & Nayar, S. (2007). Time-varying BRDFs. *IEEE Transactions on Visualization and Computer Graphics*, *13*(3), 595–609.

Sundstedt, V., Debattista, K., Longhurst, P., Chalmers, A., & Troscianko, T. (2005). Visual attention for efficient high-fidelity graphics. In *Proceedings 21st Spring Conference on Computer Graphics* (pp. 169–175). New York: ACM.

Sutherland, I. E. (1965). The ultimate display. *International Federation of Information Processing*, *2*, 506–508.

Sutherland, I. E. (1968). A head-mounted three dimensional display. In *Proceedings Fall Joint Computer Conference* (pp. 757–764). New York: ACM.

Takeuchi, T., & Matsuoka, H. (2002). Material recognition under artificial illuminations. *Perception, 31*(ECVP abstract supplement).

Tanaka, J. W., & Farah, M. J. (1993). Parts and wholes in face recognition. *The Quarterly Journal of Experimental Psychology, 46A*(2), 225–245.

Tarr, M. J., & Bülthoff, H. H. (Eds.). (1999). *Object recognition in man, monkey, and machine*. Cambridge, MA: MIT Press.

Tarr, M. J., & Pinker, S. (1989). Mental rotation and orientation-dependence in shape recognition. *Cognitive Psychology, 21*(2), 233–282.

Taylor, H. A., Naylor, S. J., & Chechile, N. A. (1999). Goal-specific influences on the representation of spatial perspective. *Memory & Cognition, 27*(2), 309-319.

Thompson, E., Palacios, A., & Varela, F. J. (2002). Ways of coloring: Comparative color vision as a case study for cognitive science. In A. Noë & E. T. Thompson (Eds.), *Vision and mind: Selected readings in the philosophy of perception* (pp. 351–418). Cambridge, MA: MIT Press.

Thompson, P. (1980). Margaret Thatcher: A new illusion. *Perception, 9*(4), 483–484.

Thompson, W. B., Dilda, V., & Creem-Regehr, S. H. (2007). Absolute distance perception to locations off the ground plane. *Perception, 36*(11), 1559–1571.

Thompson, W. B., & Kearney, J. K. (1986). Inexact vision. In *Proceedings Workshop on Motion: Representation and Analysis* (pp. 15–21). Los Alamitos, CA: IEEE.

Thompson, W. B., Kersten, D., & Knecht, W. R. (1992). Structure-from-motion based on information at surface boundaries. *Biological Cybernetics, 66*(4), 327–333.

Thompson, W. B., Mutch, K. M., & Berzins, V. A. (1985). Dynamic occlusion analysis in optical flow fields. *IEEE Transactions on Pattern Analysis and Machine Intelligence, 7*(4), 374–383.

Thompson, W. B., & Pong, T. C. (1990). Detecting moving objects. *International Journal of Computer Vision, 4*(1), 39–57.

Thompson, W. B., Shirley, P., & Ferwerda, J. A. (2002). A spatial post-processing algorithm for images of night scenes. *Journal of Graphics Tools, 7*(1), 1–12.

Thompson, W. B., Shirley, P., Smits, B., Kersten, D. J., & Madison, C. (1998). *Visual glue* (Tech. Rep. No. UUCS-98-007). University of Utah Department of Computer Science.

Thompson, W. B., Willemsen, P., Gooch, A. A., Creem-Regehr, S. H., Loomis, J. M., & Beall, A. C. (2004). Does the quality of the computer graphics matter when judging distances in visually immersive environments? *Presence: Teleoperators and Virtual Environments, 13*(5), 560–571.

Thomson, J. A. (1983). Is continuous visual monitoring necessary in visually guided locomotion? *Journal of Experimental Psychology: Human Perception and Performance, 9*(3), 427–443.

Thorndyke, P. W., & Hayes-Roth, B. (1982). Differences in spatial knowledge acquired from maps and navigation. *Cognitive Psychology, 14*(4), 560–589.

Thornton, I. M. (2006a). Biological motion: Point light walkers and beyond. In G. Knoblich, I. M. Thornton, M. Grosjean, & M. Shiffrar (Eds.), *Human body perception from the inside out* (pp. 271–303). New York: Oxford University Press.

Thornton, I. M. (2006b). Of bodies, brains, and models: Studying the perception of biological motion. In G. Knoblich, I. M. Thornton, M. Grosjean, & M. Shiffrar (Eds.), *Human body perception from the inside out* (pp. 261–270). New York: Oxford University Press.

Thornton, I. M., Pinto, J., & Shiffrar, M. (1998). The visual perception of human locomotion. *Cognitive Neuropsychology, 15*(6–8), 535–552.

Thorpe, S., Fize, D., & Marlot, C. (1996). Speed of processing in the human visual system. *Nature, 381*, 520–522.

Todd, J. T. (1984). The perception of three-dimensional structure from rigid and nonrigid motion. *Perception & Psychophysics, 36*(2), 97–103.

Todd, J. T., & Mingolla, E. (1983). The perception of surface curvature and direction of illumination from patterns of shading. *Journal of Experimental Psychology: Human Perception and Performance, 9*(4), 583–595.

Todd, J. T., Norman, J. F., & Mingolla, E. (2004). Lightness constancy in the presence of specular highlights. *Psychological Science, 15*(1), 33–39.

Todd, J. T., Thaler, L., & Dijkstra, T. M. H. (2005). The effects of field of view on the perception of 3D slant from texture. *Vision Research, 45*(12), 1501–1517.

Todd, J. T., Tittle, J. S., & Norman, J. F. (1995). Distortions of three dimensional space in the perceptual analysis of motion and stereo. *Perception, 24*(1), 75–86.

Tokunaga, R., Logvinenko, A. D., & Maloney, L. T. (2008). Dissimilarity of yellow-blue surfaces under neutral light sources differing in intensity: Separate contributions of light intensity and chroma. *Visual Neuroscience, 25*(3), 395–398.

Tolman, E. C. (1948). Cognitive maps in rats and men. *Psychological Review, 55*(4), 189–208.

Torralba, A. (2003). Contextual priming for object detection. *International Journal of Computer Vision*, *53*(2), 169–191.

Torralba, A., & Oliva, A. (2002). Depth estimation from image structure. *IEEE Transactions on Pattern Analysis and Machine Intelligence*, *24*(9), 1–13.

Torralba, A., & Oliva, A. (2003). Statistics of natural image categories. *Network: Computation in Neural Systems*, *14*(3), 391–412.

Toye, R. C. (1986). The effect of viewing position on the perceived layout of space. *Perception & Psychophysics*, *40*(2), 85–92.

Treisman, A. (1960). Contextual cues in selective listening. *Quarterly Journal of Experimental Psychology*, *12*(4), 242–248.

Treisman, A. (1980). A feature-integration theory of attention. *Cognitive Psychology*, *12*(1), 97–136.

Treisman, A., & Sato, S. (1990). Conjunction search revisited. *Journal of Experimental Psychology: Human Perception and Performance*, *16*(3), 459–478.

Tresilian, J. R. (1991). Empirical and theoretical issues in the perception of time to contact. *Journal of Experimental Psychology: Human Perception and Performance*, *17*(3), 865–876.

Trevarthen, C. B. (1968). Two mechanisms of vision in primates. *Psychologische Forschung*, *31*(4), 299–337.

Troje, N. F. (2003). Reference frames for orientation anisotropies in face recognition and biological-motion perception. *Perception*, *32*(2), 201–210.

Troje, N. F., & Westhoff, C. (2006). The inversion effect in biological motion perception: Evidence for a life detector? *Current Biology*, *16*(8), 821–824.

Tucker, M., & Ellis, R. (1998). On the relations between seen objects and components of potential actions. *Journal of Experimental Psychology: Human Perception and Performance*, *24*(3), 830–846.

Tucker, M., & Ellis, R. (2001). The potentiation of grasp types during visual object categorization. *Visual Cognition*, *8*(6), 769–800.

Turano, K. A., & Heidenreich, S. M. (1999). Eye movements affect the perceived speed of visual motion. *Vision Research*, *39*(6), 1177–1187.

Turner, M. R., Gerstein, G. L., & Bajcsy, R. (1991). Underestimation of visual texture slant by human observers: A model. *Biological Cybernetics*, *65*(4), 215–226.

Tversky, B. (2003). Structures of mental spaces: How people think about space. *Environment and Behavior*, *35*(1), 66–90.

Uchikawa, K., & Boyntona, R. M. (1987). Categorical color perception of japanese observers: Comparison with that of americans. *Vision Research*, *27*(10), 1825–1833.

Ullman, S. (1979). *The interpretation of visual motion*. Cambridge, MA: MIT Press.

Ullman, S. (1989). Aligning pictorial descriptions: An approach to object recognition. *Cognition*, *32*(3), 193–254.

Ullman, S. (1996). *High-level vision: Object recognition and visual cognition.* Cambridge, MA: MIT Press.

Ullman, S. (1998). Three-dimensional object recognition based on the combination of views. *Cognition*, *67*(1–2), 21–44.

Ullman, S. (2007). Object recognition and segmentation by a fragment-based hierarchy. *Trends in Cognitive Sciences*, *11*(2), 58–64.

Ullman, S., & Basri, R. (1991). Recognition by linear combinations of models. *IEEE Transactions on Pattern Analysis and Machine Intelligence*, *13*(10), 992–1005.

Ullman, S., Vidal-Naquet, M., & Sali, E. (2002). Visual features of intermediate complexity and their use in classification. *Nature Neuroscience*, *5*(7), 682–687.

Ungerleider, L. G., & Mishkin, M. (1982). Two cortical visual systems. In D. J. Ingle, M. A. Goodale, & R. J. W. Mansfield (Eds.), *Analysis of visual behavior* (pp. 549–586). Cambridge, MA: MIT Press.

Vallacher, R. R., & Wegner, D. M. (1987). What do people think they're doing? Action identification and human behavior. *Psychological Review*, *94*(1), 3–15.

Van Nes, F. L., & Bouman, M. A. (1967). Spatial modulation transfer in the human eye. *Journal of the Optical Society of America*, *57*(3), 401–406.

Vandenberg, S. G., & Kuse, A. R. (1978). Mental rotations, a group test of three-dimensional spatial visualization. *Perceptual and Motor Skills*, *47*(2), 599–604.

vanMarle, K., & Scholl, B. J. (2003). Attentive tracking of objects vs. substances. *Psychological Science*, *14*(5), 498–504.

Varakin, D. A., Levin, D. T., & Fidler, R. (2004). Unseen and unaware: Implications of recent research on failures of visual awareness for human-computer interface design. *Human-computer Interaction*, *19*(4), 389–422.

Varma, M., & Zisserman, A. (2005). A statistical approach to texture classification from single images. *International Journal of Computer Vision*, *62*(1), 61–81.

Verfaillie, K., & Boutsen, L. (1995). A corpus of 714 full-color images of depth-rotated objects. *Perception & Psychophysics*, *57*(7), 925–961.

Vergne, R., Pacanowski, R., Barla, P., Granier, X., & Schlick, C. (2009). Light warping for enhanced surface depiction. *ACM Transactions on Graphics*, *28*(3), 1–8.

Viirre, E., Tweed, D., Milner, K., & Vilis, T. (1986). A reexamination of the gain of the vestibuloocular reflex. *Journal of Neurophysiology*, *56*(2), 439–450.

Vishwanath, D., Girshick, A. R., & Banks, M. S. (2005). Why pictures look right when viewed from the wrong place. *Nature Neuroscience, 8*(10), 1401–1410.

Voyer, D., Voyer, S., & Bryden, M. P. (1995). Magnitude of sex differences in spatial abilities: A meta-analysis and consideration of critical variables. *Psychological Bulletin, 117*(2), 250–270.

Wade, N. J., & Ono, H. (1985). The stereoscopic views of wheatstone and brewster. *Psychological Research, 45*(3), 125–133.

Wagner, M. (1985). The metric of visual space. *Perception & Psychophysics, 38*(6), 483–495.

Wallach, H. (1948). Brightness constancy and the nature of achromatic colors. *Journal of Experimental Psychology, 38*(3), 310–324.

Wallach, H., & Norris, C. M. (1963). Accommodation as a distance-cue. *The American Journal of Psychology, 76*(4), 659–664.

Wallach, H., & O'Connell, D. N. (1953). The kinetic depth effect. *Journal of Experimental Psychology, 45*(4), 205–217.

Wallach, H., & Slaughter, V. (1988). Viewing direction and pictorial representation. *Perception & Psychophysics, 43*(1), 79–82.

Waltz, D. (1975). Understanding line drawings of scenes with shadows. In P. H. Winston (Ed.), *The psychology of computer vision.* New York: McGraw-Hill.

Wandell, B. A. (1995). *Foundations of vision.* Sunderland, MA: Sinauer.

Wang, B., & Ciuffreda, K. J. (2004). Depth-of-focus of the human eye in the near retinal periphery. *Vision Research, 44*(11), 1115–1125.

Wang, Z., Bovik, A. C., Sheikh, H. R., & Simoncelli, E. P. (2004). Image quality assessment: From error visibility to structural similarity. *IEEE Transactions on Image Processing, 14*(4), 600–612.

Wann, J. P. (1996). Anticipating arrival: Is the tau margin a specious theory? *Journal of Experimental Psychology: Human Perception and Performance, 22*(4), 1031–1048.

Wann, J. P., & Mon-Williams, M. (1997). Health issues with virtual reality displays: What we do know and what we don't. In T. Whitted (Ed.), *Proceedings of SIGGRAPH 97, Computer Graphics Proceedings, Annual Conference Series* (pp. 53–57). Reading, MA: Addison Wesley.

Wann, J. P., Rushton, S., & Mon-Williams, M. (1995). Natural problems for stereoscopic depth perception in virtual environments. *Vision Research, 35*(19), 2731–2736.

Ward, G. J. (1992). Measuring and modeling anisotropic reflection. *Proc. SIGGRAPH '92, Computer Graphics, 26*(2), 265–272.

Ware, C. (2000). *Information visualization: Perception for design.* San Francisco, CA: Morgan Kaufmann.

Warren, W. H. (2004). Optic flow. In L. M. Chalupa & J. S. Werner (Eds.), *The visual neurosciences* (pp. 1247–1259). Cambridge, MA: MIT Press.

Warren, W. H. (2006). The dynamics of perception and action. *Psychological Review, 113*(2), 358–389.

Warren, W. H. (2008). Optic flow. In T. D. Albright & R. Masland (Eds.), *The senses: A comprehensive reference: Vol. 2. Vision II* (chap. 12). San Diego, CA: Academic Press.

Warren, W. H., Jr., & Hannon, D. J. (1988). Direction of self-motion is perceived from optical flow. *Nature, 336*, 162–163.

Warren, W. H., Jr., Kay, B. A., Zosh, W. D., Duchon, A. P., & Sahuc, S. (2001). Optic flow is used to control human walking. *Nature Neuroscience, 4*(2), 213–216.

Warren, W. H., Jr., Morris, M. W., & Kalish, M. (1988). Perception of translational heading from optical flow. *Journal of Experimental Psychology: Human Perception and Performance, 14*(4), 646–660.

Warren, W. H., Jr., & Whang, S. (1987). Visual guidance of walking through apertures: Body scaled information for affordances. *Journal of Experimental Psychology: Human Perception and Performance, 13*(3), 371–383.

Watanabe, K., & Shimojo, S. (2001). When sound affects vision: Effects of auditory grouping on visual motion perception. *Psychological Science, 12*(2), 109–116.

Waters, K. (1987). A muscle model for animation three-dimensional facial expression. *Proc. SIGGRAPH '87, Computer Graphics, 21*(4), 17–24.

Watson, A. B., & Ahumada, A. J., Jr. (1985). Model of human visual-motion sensing. *Journal of the Optical Society of America A, 2*(2), 322–342.

Watson, A. B., Ahumada, A. J., Jr., & Farrell, J. E. (1986). Window of visibility: A psychophysical theory of fidelity in time-sampled visual motion displays. *Journal of the Optical Society of America A, 3*(3), 300–307.

Watt, S. J., Akeley, K., Ernst, M. O., & Banks, M. S. (2005). Focus cues affect perceived depth. *Journal of Vision, 5*(10), 834–863.

Webster, M. A., & Mollon, J. D. (1995). Colour constancy influenced by contrast adaptation. *Nature, 373*, 694–698.

Welch, R. B. (1986). Adaptation of space perception. In K. R. Boff, L. Kaufman, & J. P. Thomas (Eds.), *Handbook of perception and human performance* (Vol. 1, pp. 24.1–24.41). New York: Wiley.

Westheimer, G. (2009). Hyperacuity. In L. R. Squire (Ed.), *Encyclopedia of neuroscience* (pp. 45–50). Oxford, UK: Academic Press.

Westheimer, G., & McKee, S. P. (1977). Spatial configurations for visual hyperacuity. *Vision Research, 17*(8), 941–947.

Weszka, J., Dyer, C. R., & Rosenfeld, A. (1980). A comparative study of texture measures for terrain classification. *IEEE Transactions on Systems, Man, and Cybernetics*, *6*(4), 269–286.

Wexler, M., Kosslyn, S. M., & Berthoz, A. (1998). Motor processes in mental rotation. *Cognition*, *68*(1), 77–94.

Wheatstone, C. (1838). Contributions to the physiology of vision. Part the first. On some remarkable, and hitherto unobserved, phenomena of binocular vision. *Philosophical Transactions of the Royal Society of London*, *128*, 371–394.

White, P. A., & Milne, A. (1997). Phenomenal causality: Impressions of pulling in the visual perception of objects in motion. *The American Journal of Psychology*, *110*(4), 573–602.

White, P. A., & Milne, A. (1999). Impressions of enforced disintegration and bursting in the visual perception of collision events. *Journal of Experimental Psychology: General*, *128*(4), 499–516.

Whitton, M. C. (2003). Making virtual environments compelling. *Communications of the ACM*, *46*(7), 40–47.

Wickelgren, D. S. M. E. A., & Bingham, G. P. (2000). Reaching measures of monocular distance perception: Forward versus side-to-side head movements and haptic feedback. *Perception and & Psychophysics*, *62*(5), 1051–1059.

Wickens, C. D., & Long, J. (1995). Object versus space-based models of visual attention: Implications for the design of head-up displays. *Journal of Experimental Psychology: Applied*, *1*(3), 179–193.

Wickens, C. D., Vincow, M., & Yeh, M. (2005). Design applications of visual spatial thinking. In P. Shah & A. Miyake (Eds.), *The Cambridge handbook of visuospatial thinking* (pp. 383–425). New York: Cambridge University Press.

Willems, B., & Wagemans, J. (2001). Matching multicomponent objects from different viewpoints: Mental rotation as normalization? *Journal of Experimental Psychology: Human Perception and Performance*, *27*(5), 1090–1115.

Willemsen, P., Colton, M. B., Creem-Regehr, S. H., & Thompson, W. B. (2009). The effects of head-mounted display mechanical properties and field-of-view on distance judgments in virtual environments. *ACM Transactions on Applied Perception*, *6*(2), 8:1–8:14.

Willemsen, P., Gooch, A. A., Thompson, W. B., & Creem-Regehr, S. H. (2008). Effects of stereo viewing conditions on distance perception in virtual environments. *Presence: Teleoperators and Virtual Environments*, *17*(11), 91–101.

Williams, L. (1990). Performance-driven facial animation. *Proc. SIGGRAPH '90, Computer Graphics*, *24*(4), 235–242.

Williams, N., Luebke, D., Cohen, J. D., Kelley, M., & Schubert, B. (2003). Perceptually guided simplification of lit, textured meshes. In *Proceedings symposium on interactive 3D graphics* (pp. 113–121). New York: ACM.

Wilson, M. (2002). Six views of embodied cognition. *Psychonomic Bulletin & Review*, *9*(4), 625–636.

Winston, P. H. (1992). *Artificial intelligence* (3rd ed.). Reading, MA: Addison Wesley.

Witkin, A. P. (1981). Recovering surface shape and orientation from texture. *Artificial Intelligence*, *17*(1–3), 17–45.

Witkin, H. A., & Wapner, S. (1950). Visual factors in the maintenance of upright posture. *The American Journal of Psychology*, *63*(1), 31–50.

Witmer, B. G., & Sadowski, W. J., Jr. (1998). Nonvisually guided locomotion to a previously viewed target in real and virtual environments. *Human Factors*, *40*(3), 478–488.

Witt, J. K., Proffitt, D. R., & Epstein, W. (2005). Tool use affects perceived distance, but only when you intend to use it. *Journal of Experimental Psychology: Human Perception and Performance*, *31*(5), 880–888.

Wohlschläger, A., & Wohlschläager, A. (1998). Mental and manual rotation. *Journal of Experimental Psychology: Human Perception and Performance*, *24*(2), 397–412.

Wolfe, J. M. (1994). Guided search 2.0: A revised model of visual search. *Psychonomic Bulletin and Review*, *1*(2), 202–238.

Wolfe, J. M. (1998). Visual memory: What do you know about what you saw? *Current Biology*, *8*(9), R303–R304.

Wolfe, J. M. (2003). Moving towards solutions to some enduring controversies in visual search. *Trends in Cognitive Sciences*, *7*(2), 70–76.

Wolfe, J. M., Kluender, K. R., Levi, D. M., Bartoshuk, L. M., Herz, R. S., Klatzky, R. L., et al. (2008). *Sensation & perception* (2nd ed.). Sunderland, MA: Sinauer.

Wolfson, S. S., & Landy, M. S. (1995). Discrimination of orientation-defined texture edges. *Vision Research*, *35*(20), 2863–2877.

Woodman, G. F., & Luck, S. J. (2004). Visual search is slowed when visuospatial working memory is occupied. *Psychonomic Bulletin & Review*, *11*(2), 269–274.

Woodman, G. F., Luck, S. J., & Schall, J. D. (2007). The role of working memory representations in the control of attention. *Cerebral Cortex*, *17*(Suppl. 1), i118–i124.

Woods, A. J., Philbeck, J. W., & Danoff, J. V. (2009). The various perceptions of distance: An alternative view of how effort affects distance judgments. *Journal of Experimental Psychology: Human Perception and Performance*, *35*(4), 1104–1117.

Wraga, M. (1999a). The role of eye height in perceiving affordances and object dimensions. *Perception & Psychophysics*, *61*(3), 490–507.

Wraga, M. (1999b). Using eye height in different postures to scale the heights of objects. *Journal of Experimental Psychology: Human Perception and Performance*, *25*(2), 518–530.

Wraga, M., Creem, S. H., & Proffitt, D. R. (1999). The influence of spatial reference frames on imagined object- and viewer rotations. *Acta Psychologica*, *102*(2–3), 247–264.

Wraga, M., Creem, S. H., & Proffitt, D. R. (2000). Updating displays after imagined object and viewer rotations. *Journal of Experimental Psychology: Learning, Memory and Cognition*, *26*(1), 151–168.

Wraga, M., Creem-Regehr, S. H., & Proffitt, D. R. (2004). Spatial updating of virtual displays during self- and display-rotation. *Memory & Cognition*, *32*(3), 399–415.

Wraga, M., Thompson, W. L., Alpert, N. M., & Kosslyn, S. M. (2003). Implicit transfer of motor strategies in mental rotation. *Brain and Cognition*, *52*(2), 135–143.

Wright, R. D., & Ward, L. M. (2008). *Orienting of attention*. New York: Oxford University Press.

Wright, W. D., & Pitt, F. H. G. (1934). Hue-discrimination in normal colour-vision. *Proceedings of the Physical Society*, *46*(3), 459–473.

Wu, B., Klatzky, R. L., Shelton, D., & Stetten, G. (2005). Psychophysical evaluation of in-situ ultrasound visualization. *IEEE Transactions on Visualization and Computer Graphics*, *11*(6), 684–699.

Wu, B., Klatzky, R. L., & Stetten, G. (2008). Learning to reach to locations encoded from imaging displays. *Spatial Cognition and Computation*, *8*(4), 333–356.

Wu, B., Ooi, T. L., & He, Z. J. (2004). Perceiving distance accurately by a directional process of integrating ground information. *Nature*, *428*, 73–77.

Wyszecki, G., & Stiles, W. S. (1982). *Color science: Concepts and methods, quantitative data and formulae* (2nd ed.). New York: John Wiley & Sons.

Yang, J. N., & Maloney, L. T. (2001). Illuminant cues in surface color perception: Tests of three candidate cues. *Vision Research*, *41*(20), 2581–2600.

Yang, T. L., Dixon, M. W., & Proffitt, D. R. (1999). Seeing big things: Overestimation of heights is greater for real objects than for objects in pictures. *Perception*, *28*(4), 445–467.

Yantis, S. (Ed.). (2001). *Visual perception: Essential readings*. Philadelphia, PA: Psychology Press.

Yantis, S., & Jonides, J. (1990). Abrupt visual onsets and selective attention: Voluntary versus automatic activation. *Journal of Experimental Psychology: Human Perception and Performance, 16*(1), 121–134.

Yim, R. K. (1969). Looking at upside-down faces. *Journal of Experimental Psychology, 81*(1), 141–145.

Yonas, A., Craton, L. G., & Thompson, W. B. (1987). Relative motion: Kinetic information for the order of depth at an edge. *Perception & Psychophysics, 41*(1), 53–59.

Yonas, A., Goldsmith, L. T., & Hallstrom, J. L. (1978). Development of sensitivity to information provided by cast shadows in pictures. *Perception, 7*(3), 333–341.

Yonas, A., Pettersen, L., & Granrud, C. E. (1982). Infants' sensitivity to familiar size as information for distance. *Child Development, 53*(5), 1285–1290.

Yoonessi, A., & Zaidi, Q. (2010). Roles of color & 3-D information in recognizing material changes (VSS abstract). *Journal of Vision, 10*(7).

Yuille, A. L. (1991). Deformable templates for face recognition. *Journal of Cognitive Neuroscience, 3*(1), 59–71.

Yuille, A. L., & Bülthoff, H. H. (1996). Bayesian decision theory and psychophysics. In D. C. Knill & W. Richards (Eds.), *Perception as Bayesian inference* (pp. 123–161). Cambridge University Press.

Yuille, A. L., & Kersten, D. (2006). Vision as Bayesian inference: Analysis by synthesis? *Trends in Cognitive Sciences, 10*(7), 301–308.

Zacks, J. M. (2004). Using movement and intentions to understand simple events. *Cognitive Science, 28*(6), 979–1008.

Zacks, J. M., Braver, T. S., Sheridan, M. A., Donaldson, D. I., Snyder, A. Z., Ollinger, J. M., et al. (2001). Human brain activity time-locked to perceptual event boundaries. *Nature Neuroscience, 4*(6), 651–5.

Zacks, J. M., & Michelon, P. (2005). Transformations of visuospatial images. *Behavioral and Cognitive Neuroscience Reviews, 4*(2), 96–118.

Zacks, J. M., Mires, J., Tversky, B., & Hazeltine, E. (2002). Mental spatial transformations of objects and perspective. *Spatial cognition and computation, 2*(4), 315–322.

Zacks, J. M., Rypma, B., Gabrieli, J. D. E., Tversky, B., & Glover, G. H. (1999). Imagined transformations of bodies: An fMRI investigation. *Neuropsychologia, 37*(9), 1029–1040.

Zacks, J. M., & Swallow, K. M. (2007). Event segmentation. *Current Directions in Psychological Science, 16*(2), 80–84.

Zacks, J. M., & Tversky, B. (2001). Event structure in perception and conception. *Psychological Bulletin, 127*(1), 3–21.

Zacks, J. M., & Tversky, B. (2003). Structuring information interfaces for procedural learning. *Journal of Experimental Psychology: Applied*, *9*(2), 88–100.

Zacks, J. M., Tversky, B., & Iyer, G. (2001). Perceiving, remembering, and communicating structure in events. *Journal of Experimental Psychology: General*, *130*(1), 29–58.

Zemel, R. S., Behrmann, M., Mozer, M. C., & Bavelier, D. (2002). Experience-dependent perceptual grouping and object-based attention. *Journal of Experimental Psychology: Human Perception and Performance*, *28*(1), 202–217.

Zhang, L., Snavely, N., Curless, B., & Seitz, S. M. (2004). Spacetime faces: High-resolution capture for modeling and animation. *Proc. SIGGRAPH '04, Transactions on Graphics*, *23*(3), 548–558.

Zickler, T., Mallick, S. P., Kriegman, D. J., & Belhumeur, P. N. (2008). Color subspaces as photometric invariants. *International Journal of Computer Vision*, *79*(1), 13–30.

Zone, R. (2007). *Stereoscopic cinema and the origins of 3-D film, 1838–1952*. Lexington, KY: University Press of Kentucky.

Index

T - #0160 - 111024 - C138 - 235/191/25 - PB - 9780367659288 - Gloss Lamination